UNDERSTANDING COMPUTERS
Today and Tomorrow

2000 EDITION

THE DRYDEN PRESS

A DIVISION OF
HARCOURT COLLEGE PUBLISHERS

FORT WORTH

PHILADELPHIA

SAN DIEGO

NEW YORK

AUSTIN

ORLANDO

SAN ANTONIO

TORONTO

MONTREAL

LONDON

SYDNEY

TOKYO

DEBORAH
MORLEY

EDITORIAL
CONSULTANT

UNDERSTANDING COMPUTERS

Today and Tomorrow

2000 EDITION

CHARLES S. PARKER

Enter 2000

Publisher	Mike Roche
Executive Editor	Christina A. Martin
Associate Editor	Elizabeth Hayes
Project Editor	Kathryn M. Stewart
Art Director	Scott Baker
Production Manager	Linda McMillan

Cover credit Lamberto Alvarez

ISBN: 0-03-025968-1

Library of Congress Catalog Card Number: 99-068140

Address for Domestic Orders
Harcourt, Inc., 6277 Sea Harbor Drive, Orlando, FL 32887-6777
800-782-4479

Address for International Orders
International Customer Service
Harcourt, Inc., 6277 Sea Harbor Drive, Orlando, FL 32887-6777
407-345-3800
(fax) 407-345-4060
(e-mail) hbintl@harcourtbrace.com

Address for Editorial Correspondence
Harcourt College Publishers, 301 Commerce Street, Suite 3700, Fort Worth, TX 76102

Web Site Address
http://www.hbcollege.com
THE DRYDEN PRESS, DRYDEN, and the DP LOGO are registered trademarks of Harcourt Brace & Company.

Printed in the United States of America

0 1 2 3 4 5 6 7 8 751 9 8 7 6 5 4 3 2

The Dryden Press
A Division of Harcourt College Publishers

To Chama

Adams
First Steps Series
Word 2000
Word 97
Excel 2000
Excel 97
Access 2000
Access 97
PowerPoint 2000
PowerPoint 97
Outlook 2000
Windows 98

Coorough
Getting Started with Multimedia

Fenrich
Practical Guidelines for Creating
Instructional Multimedia Applications

Fuller/Manning
Getting Started with the Internet

Fuller
Getting Started with E-Commerce

Gordon and Gordon
Information Systems: A Management
Approach
Second Edition

Gray, King, McLean, and Watson
Management of Information Systems
Second Edition

Harris
Systems Analysis and Design for the Small
Enterprise
Second Edition

Larsen/Marold
Using Microsoft Works 4.0 for Windows 95:
An Introduction to Computing

Laudon and Laudon
Information Systems and the Internet: A
Problem-Solving Approach

Licker
Management Information Systems: A Strategic Leadership Approach

Lorents and Morgan
Database Systems: Concepts, Management,
and Applications

Martin
Discovering Microsoft Office 2000
Discovering Microsoft Office 97

Martin/Parker
PC Concepts
Second Edition

Mason
Using Microsoft Excel 97 in Business

McKeown
Information Technology and the Networked
Economy

Millspaugh
Object-Oriented Programming with C++

Morley
Getting Started with Computers
Second Edition

Morley
Getting Started: Web Page Design with
Microsoft FrontPage 2000
Getting Started: Web Page Design with
Microsoft FrontPage 98
Getting Started: Web Page Design with
Microsoft FrontPage 97

Parker
Understanding Computers: Today and
Tomorrow
2000 Edition

Spear
Introduction to Computer Programming in
Visual Basic 6.0

Martin and Parker
Mastering Today's Software Series

**Texts available in any combination
of the following:**
Windows 98
Windows NT Workstation 4
Windows 95
Windows 3.1
Disk Operating System 6.0 (DOS 6.0)
Disk Operating System 5.0 (DOS 5.0)
Microsoft Office 2000
Microsoft Office 97 Professional Edition
Microsoft Office for Windows 95 Profes-
sional Edition
Word 2000
Word 97
Word 7.0 for Windows 95
Word 6.0 for Windows
Corel WordPerfect 7.0 for Windows 95
WordPerfect 6.1 for Windows
WordPerfect 6.0 for Windows
WordPerfect 5.1
Excel 2000
Excel 97
Excel 7.0 for Windows 95
Excel 5.0 for Windows
Lotus 1-2-3 97

Lotus 1-2-3 for Windows (5.0)
Lotus 1-2-3 for Windows (4.01)
Lotus 1-2-3 (2.4)
Lotus 1-2-3 (2.2/2.3)
Quattro Pro 4.0
Quattro Pro 6.0 for Windows
Access 2000
Access 97
Access 7.0 for Windows 95
Access 2.0 for Windows
Paradox 5.0 for Windows
Paradox 4.0
dBASE 5 for Windows
dBASE IV (1.5/2.0)
dBASE III PLUS
PowerPoint 2000
PowerPoint 97
PowerPoint 7.0 for Windows 95
Outlook 2000
A Beginner's Guide to QBASIC
A Beginner's Guide to BASIC
Netscape Navigator 4.0
Internet Explorer 2000
Internet Explorer 4.0

**The Dryden Online Series in
Information Technology**
Computers Online
Learning Office 2000
Learning Office 97
Learning Windows 98
Introduction to the Internet
Introduction to Multimedia
Introduction to Visual Basic 6.0
Systems Analysis and Design

PREFACE

We are living at a time when the key to success in virtually every profession depends on the skillful use of information. Whether one is a teacher, lawyer, doctor, secretary, manager, or corporate president, the main ingredient in the work involved is information—knowing how to get it, how to use it, how to manage it, and how to disseminate it to others.

At the root of information-based work activities are computers and the systems that support them. There are millions of computer systems in the world today, and collectively, they are capable of doing countless different tasks. Some of the tasks that computer systems can now handle—such as creating virtual worlds and beating a reigning world chess champion at his own game—were thought impossible not too long ago. Few professions remain untouched by computers today or will remain so in tomorrow's world. No matter who you are or what you do for a living, it is likely that computers will somehow impact both the way you work and your success at your work.

The importance of computers in virtually every profession brings us to the purpose of this book. *Understanding Computers: Today and Tomorrow,* 2000 *Edition,* has been written with the user of computers in mind. This nontechnical, introductory text explains in straightforward terms the importance of learning about computers, types of computer systems and their components, principles by which computer systems work, practical applications of computers and related technologies, and ways in which the world is being changed by computers. The goal of the text is to provide the reader both with a solid knowledge of computer basics and with a framework for using this knowledge effectively in the workplace.

The best way for students to learn about technology is to use it. In this exciting new edition, *Understanding Computers* provides a truly interactive approach to learning about computers with a text that is fully integrated with a completely updated, multimedia-enhanced Web site. Further, for instructors who want to progress to the next level, a full-content online course, *Computers Online,* is also available to be packaged with the text. *Understanding Computers* is but one component of a complete and flexible instructional package—one that can easily be adapted to virtually any teaching format.

THE TEXTBOOK

Understanding Computers: Today and Tomorrow, 2000 *Edition,* is designed for students taking a first course in computers. The text meets the requirements proposed for the first course in computing by both the Data Processing Management Association (DPMA) and the Association for Computing Machinery (ACM). Although it provides a comprehensive introduction to the world of computers, the text is not overly technical. Coverage is given to both commercial and personal applications of computers and both large and small computer systems.

KEY FEATURES

Like previous editions, *Understanding Computers: Today and Tomorrow, 2000 Edition* is current and comprehensive. It offers instructors a flexible teaching organization and students a presentation that is both edifying and engaging. Learning tools in each chapter help the reader master important concepts. Numerous icons lead students to highly interactive multimedia tutorials and review material. Boxed features on a variety of topics provide insight on current issues of interest. The thematic Windows, each of which highlights a major aspect of computer technology, bring the world of computers to life. A bottom-of-page running glossary and a glossary at the end of the book give concise definitions of important terms.

Flexible Organization   In order to make the 2000 edition as flexible as possible to meet a wide variety of classroom needs, this book is available in customized versions as well as a full sixteen-chapter text. As shown in the figure on page ix, the sixteen chapters are grouped into the following seven modules:

> Introduction (Chapter INT 1)
> Hardware (Chapters HW 1, HW 2, and HW 3)
> Software (Chapters SW 1 and SW 2)
> Computer Networks (Chapters NET 1, NET 2, and NET 3)
> Productivity Software (Chapters PS 1, PS 2, and PS 3)
> Information Systems (Chapters IS 1 and IS 2)
> Computers in Our Lives (Chapters LIV 1 and LIV 2)

Through the EXACT custom publishing program, the instructor has the option of eliminating any module or modules—or rearranging modules—to tailor the text to meet the needs of any specific course. In addition, *Understanding Computers* can be bound with a variety of software manuals. Contact your local Harcourt representative for further information concerning customization and the EXACT program.

Currency   Perhaps more than textbooks in any other field, computer texts must reflect the latest technologies, trends, and classroom needs. The state-of-the-art content of this book and its multimedia support package reflects these considerations. Before the 2000 edition was started, reviews were commissioned and meetings were held to identify key areas of change for the text and support package. Also, throughout the writing and production stages, enhancements were continually being made to ensure that the final product would be as current as possible throughout the life of the edition. A glance at the Windows, sidebars, and chapter outlines should illustrate why this text has been and will continue to remain a market leader.

Comprehensiveness and Depth   In planning for the 2000 edition of this book, the publisher conducted several extensive research studies to determine the selection of topics, degree of depth, and other features that instructors of introductory computer courses most want to see in their texts. As the manuscript evolved, instructors at a variety of schools around the country were asked for their comments. The resulting textbook accommodates a wide range of teaching preferences. It not only covers traditional topics comprehensively but also includes the facts every student should know about today's "hot" topics, such as the Internet, PCs, multimedia technology, wireless communications, electronic commerce, global computing issues, decision support and expert systems, data warehousing, object-oriented-language products, virtual reality, and user and programmer productivity tools.

Readability   We remember more about a subject if it is presented in a straightforward way and made interesting and exciting. This book is written

Modules   Chapters

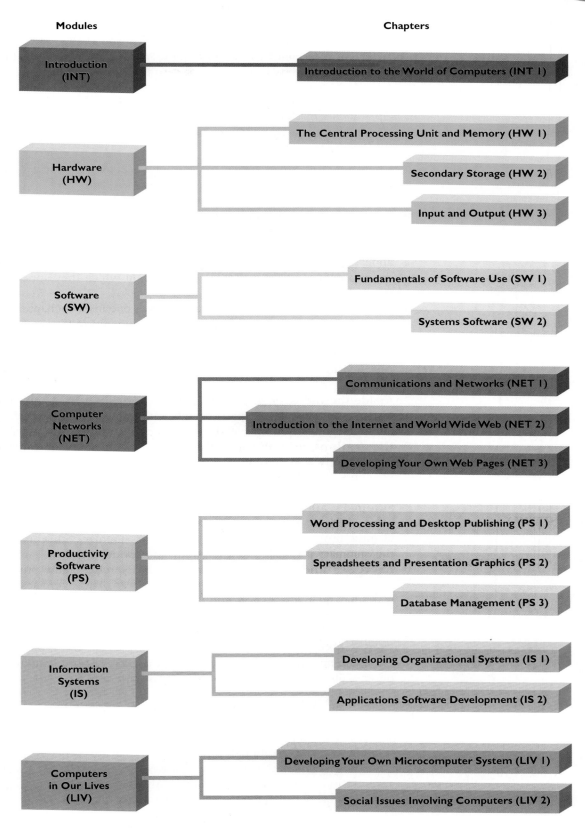

Introduction (INT)

Introduction to the World of Computers (INT 1)

Hardware (HW)

The Central Processing Unit and Memory (HW 1)

Secondary Storage (HW 2)

Input and Output (HW 3)

Software (SW)

Fundamentals of Software Use (SW 1)

Systems Software (SW 2)

Computer Networks (NET)

Communications and Networks (NET 1)

Introduction to the Internet and World Wide Web (NET 2)

Developing Your Own Web Pages (NET 3)

Productivity Software (PS)

Word Processing and Desktop Publishing (PS 1)

Spreadsheets and Presentation Graphics (PS 2)

Database Management (PS 3)

Information Systems (IS)

Developing Organizational Systems (IS 1)

Applications Software Development (IS 2)

Computers in Our Lives (LIV)

Developing Your Own Microcomputer System (LIV 1)

Social Issues Involving Computers (LIV 2)

Custom publishing options. *Understanding Computers* can be ordered as a complete text of seven modules or as an abbreviated text combination of modules bound in any order you like.

in a conversational, down-to-earth style—one designed to be accurate without being intimidating. Concepts are explained clearly and simply, without use of overly technical terminology. Where complex points are presented, they are made understandable with realistic examples from everyday life.

Chapter Learning Tools   Each chapter contains a number of learning tools to help students master the materials.

1. **Outline**   An Outline of the headings in the chapter shows the major topics to be covered.
2. **Learning Objectives**   A list of Learning Objectives is provided to serve as a guide while students read the chapter.
3. **Overview**   Each chapter starts with an Overview that puts the subject matter of the chapter in perspective and lets students know what they will be reading about.
4. **Boldfaced Key Terms and Running Glossary**   Important terms appear in boldface type as they are introduced in the chapter. These terms are also defined at the bottom of the page on which they appear and in the end-of-text Glossary.
5. **Tomorrow Boxes**   These special elements, one in each chapter, provide students with a look at possible future developments in the world of computers and serve as a focus for class discussion.
6. **Feature Boxes**   Each chapter contains one or more Feature boxes designed to stimulate interest and discussion about today's uses of technology.
7. **Inside the Industry Boxes**   These boxes, one to each chapter, provide insight into some of the personalities and practices that have made the computer industry unique and fascinating.
8. **Illustrations and Photographs**   Instructive, full-color figures and photographs appear throughout the book to help illustrate important concepts. Figures and screen dumps are carefully annotated to convey as much information as possible.
9. **Summary and Key Terms**   This is a concise, section-by-section summary of the main points in the chapter. Every boldfaced key term in the chapter also appears in boldface type in the summary. Students will find the Summary a valuable tool for study and review.
10. **Exercises and Projects**   End-of-chapter Exercises allow students to test themselves on what they have just read. The exercises include matching, fill-in, discussion, and true-false questions as well as problems in other formats. End-of-chapter Projects require students to extend their knowledge by doing research beyond merely reading the book. Special icons denote projects that are best done on the Internet, projects that are recommended for groups, and projects that require hands-on computer skills for productivity software applications.

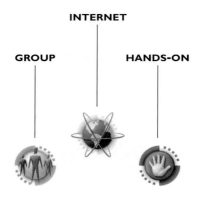

INTERNET

GROUP   HANDS-ON

Windows   The full, sixteen-chapter text contains four photoessays. Each of these Windows on the world of computers is organized around a major text theme and vividly illustrates state-of-the-art uses of computer technology. The new edition includes two brand new Windows—The "WebGuide" Window is a handy reference guide to over 100 useful Web sites for business, travel, computers, and more. The other new Window, "Multimedia Computing" explores the growing areas where multimedia is being used.

End-of-Text Glossary   The Glossary at the end of the book defines approximately 500 important computer terms mentioned in the text, including all boldfaced key terms. Each glossary item has a page reference indicating where it is boldfaced or where it first appears in the text.

NEW TO THIS EDITION

Although previous editions of this text have been highly successful, the relentless pace of technology has regularly necessitated a number of key changes in each new edition in order to keep content fresh. Among the noteworthy differences between the previous edition and the 2000 Edition of *Understanding Computers* are the following:

Web Tutor and Further Exploration Icons For an interactive experience in learning about computers, throughout the text students will find "Web Tutor" icons in the margins directing them to the Parker Web Site for multimedia-enhanced tutorials. "Further Exploration" icons point to Web sites with more in-depth information on a given topic.

Interactive Exercises At the end of selected modules students can complete a multimedia-rich "Interactive Exercise". This capstone exercise is described briefly in the text and then the student is directed to the Parker Web Site to complete the exercise. Students can practice putting together a computer, sending e-mail, creating a PowerPoint presentation, and more.

Additional Interactive Review Material At the end of each chapter, students can take advantage of more Web-related activities. Icons will direct students to the Online Glossary and Online Review, both at the Parker Web Site. The Online Reviews contain 50 study questions per chapter and provide immediate feedback. Also available at the site are new Interactive Crossword Puzzles and updated Internet Lab Assignments.

Emphasis on the Internet and World Wide Web Continuing the trend from earlier editions, this book presents an increased emphasis on the Internet and World Wide Web, PC-based processing, communications topics, and social issues regarding technology. This shift reflects the trend in applications as well as the reality of more and more people getting involved with technology in both their jobs and their personal lives.

New Topics Several topics have emerged in importance since the text was last published and receive greater attention here. Among these topics are the Internet and the World Wide Web, organizational intranets and extranets, electronic commerce, multimedia applications, client-server computing, mobile computing technologies, workgroup computing, DVD and new forms of secondary storage, new forms of computer crime and cyberterrorism, virtual reality, 64-bit and parallel processing systems, object-oriented and authoring languages, and global and international issues.

Art and Photo Program Both the art and photo programs have been extensively revised. Chapters include fully annotated illustrations integrated with the text material as well as numerous screen shots that showcase the latest applications. Many illustrations are rendered in a photorealistic style so that you can see the details of computer components close up. In addition, instructive, full-color photographs appear throughout to help illustrate important concepts.

Updated Boxed Features Most of these features—which include Tomorrow boxes, Feature boxes, and Inside the Industry boxes—are new to this edition and cover leading-edge or late-breaking computer topics. Topics held over from the previous edition have been updated to reflect the latest information. To keep the textbook at a reasonable length, the User Solution boxes have been dropped. New sidebars that would ordinarily have fallen into this feature category are now Feature boxes.

More Inside the Industry Boxes The well-received Inside the Industry boxes, first introduced in the 98 edition of the textbook, have been expanded to one per chapter. These boxes describe some of the colorful personalities and practices arising from PCs and related technologies.

STUDENT AND INSTRUCTOR SUPPORT MATERIALS

Understanding Computers: Today and Tomorrow 2000 Edition is available with a complete package of support materials for instructors and students. Included in the package are the comprehensive Parker Web Site, an Instructor's CD-ROM, a printed Instructor's Manual with transparency masters, a set of PowerPoint presentations, a set of Electronic Transparencies, a Test Bank in hard-copy and computerized forms, a full-content online course, and a variety of software manuals to meet lab needs.

THE PARKER WEB SITE

The Parker Web Site located at

http://www.harcourtcollege.com/infosys/parker2000

provides media-rich support for both instructors and students.

Students will find the following resources at the site:

Web Tutors The tutors are made up of a series of multimedia-enhanced tutorials that allow students to interact with the concepts discussed in the text.

Further Exploration This area provides links to Web sites with more in-depth information on a given topic from the text.

Interactive Exercises These multimedia-rich capstone exercises allow students to test their knowledge after completing a module.

Online Reviews Each review has fifty questions per chapter, some with graphics from the text, and provide immediate feedback.

Internet Lab Assignments Located here are updates for the end-of-chapter Internet projects as well as additional text-related projects and fun "Surfing on Your Own" activities.

Interactive Crossword Puzzles Students can review key terms by working these interactive puzzles.

Online Glossary The online glossary provides another venue for review of key concepts.

In the News These articles, which are updated monthly, will keep students informed of the latest happenings in the world of computers.

In the Instructor's section, teachers have access to the following:

Instructor's Manual Teachers can download an electronic version of the Instructor's Manual in Microsoft Word.

PowerPoint Presentation A PowerPoint presentation is available for each chapter in the text. Each presentation includes key points and illustrations from the text as well as embedded lecture notes from the Instructor's Manual.

Electronic Transparencies A set of over one hundred Electronic Transparencies for use in classroom presentations is available to help explain key points. The Electronic Transparencies cover key text figures, as well as illustrations not found in the text. The Teaching Outlines in the Instructor's Manual indicate when to show each of the Electronic Transparencies (as well as the Transparency Masters), and the Transparency Scripts in the Instructor's Manual list points to make about each.

INSTRUCTOR'S RESOURCE CD-ROM

The Instructor's Resource CD-ROM provides electronic versions of all the Parker supplements. Included on the CD-ROM is the Instructor's Manual, Computerized Test Bank, Electronic Transparencies, and PowerPoint presentations.

INSTRUCTOR'S MANUAL

In the Instructor's Manual I draw on my own teaching experiences to provide instructors with practical suggestions for enhancing classroom presentations. The Instructor's Manual contains suggestions for adapting this textbook to various course schedules, including one-quarter, two-quarter, one-semester, two-semester, and night courses. For each of the sixteen chapters of the text the Instructor's Manual provides:

1. A list of **Learning Objectives**.
2. **Summary,** oriented to the instructor, with teaching suggestions.
3. A list of the **Key Terms** in the chapter and their definitions.
4. A **Teaching Outline** that gives a detailed breakdown of the chapter, with all major headings and subheadings, as well as points to cover under each. References to the Electronic Transparencies and Transparency Masters are keyed in to this outline.
5. **Teaching Tips,** with recommended topics for class discussion, important points to cover on the transparencies, and mention of additional instructor resources.
6. **Lecture Anecdotes** providing additional stories, news items, and information specific to chapter content to liven up lectures.
7. **Transparency Scripts** for each Electronic Transparency and Transparency Master in the instructional package.
8. **Answers to Exercises** that appear at the end of the chapter.
9. **Suggestions for Projects** that appear at the end of the chapter.
10. **Transparency Masters** covering the chapter outline, chapter objectives, and other key topics for classroom discussion.

TEST BANK

The Test Bank contains over 3,200 test items in various formats, including true/false, multiple-choice, matching, fill-in, and short-answer questions. Answers are provided for all but the short-answer questions. The Test Bank is available in both hard-copy and electronic forms. The electronic versions—available for use with PC- and Macintosh-compatible computers—allow instructors to preview, edit, and delete questions as well as to add their own questions, print scrambled forms of tests, and print answer keys.

A key indicating the chapter section from which each question was taken is also provided as part of the Test Bank. Keys are included with each questions, except for the matching questions. Also provided is a ten-question, ready-to-copy-and-distribute multiple-choice quiz for every chapter, which tests students on a representative sample of important topics.

SOFTWARE MANUALS

Lab manuals, covering hands-on use of software products, are available from Harcourt for a number of widely used products. Using Harcourt's custom-publishing option, you can have virtually any combination of components bound together for your classes. Check with your Harcourt sales representative about the configuration options currently possible.

COMPUTERS ONLINE

For instructors who want to add a richer online component to their course, *Computers Online,* by Merrill Wells of Red Rocks Community College, is available for packaging with the text. This new full-content online course correlates with the text and can be used in a variety of ways: it can be used to supplement the text in a traditional classroom setting, or it can be used as a virtual classroom for distant learning students.   Students learn technology by interacting with the content in this rich, interactive multimedia environment. Each chapter of the course is filled with interactive activities, links, animations, demonstrations, collaborative classroom activities, critical thinking exercises, and self tests.

The *Computers Online* Course Homepage.

Computers Online has been designed using the WebCT course management system, one of the most popular tools used to provide virtual classroom environments. The WebCT environment provides instructors with such features as the ability to track student progress; timed, online quizzes; student management tools and the ability to customize course content. Student features include communication tools such as a bulletin board, electronic mail, and chat; student presentation areas which can be used for displaying course projects and other student work; student homepages, and much more. Visit www.drydenonline.com to see a demo.

Harcourt will provide complimentary supplements or supplement packages to those adopters qualified under our adoption policy. Please contact your sales representative to learn how you may qualify. If as an adopter or potential user you receive supplements you do not need, please return them to your sales representative or send them to:

Attn: Returns Department
Troy Warehouse
465 South Lincoln Drive
Troy, MO 63379

ACKNOWLEDGMENTS

I could never have completed a project of this scope alone. I owe a special word of thanks to the many people who reviewed the text—those whose extensive suggestions on past editions helped define the 2000 edition, those whose comments on drafts of the 2000 edition helped mold it into its final form, and those who reviewed the instructional package.

2000 EDITION

Beverly Amer, *Northern Arizona University*; Frederick W. Bounds, *Georgia Perimeter College*; Brenda K. Britt, *Fayetteville Technical Community College*; Janice Burke, *South Suburban College*; Jack W. Chandler, *San Joaquin Delta*

College; Edward W. Christensen, *Monmouth University;* Bennie Allen Dooley, *Pasadena City College*; Dwight Graham, *Prairie State College;* Wade Graves, *Grayson County College;* Ricci L. Heishman, *Northern Virginia Community College;* Mark W. Huber, *East Carolina University;* Richard Okezie, *Mesa Community College;* Mary T. Johnson, *Mt. San Antonio College;* Susan M. Jones, *Southwest State University;* Amardeep K. Kahlon, *Austin Community College;* Kathryn A. Marold, Ph.D., *Metropolitan State College of Denver;* Richard W. Manthei, *Joliet Junior College;* James W. McGuffee, *Austin Community College;* Carolyn H. Monroe, *Baylor University;* Robert F. Palank, *St. Louis Community College;* Gayla Jo Slauson, *Mesa State College;* and Patricia Joann Wykoff, *Western Michigan University.*

PREVIOUS EDITIONS

James Ambroise Jr., *Southern University—Louisiana;* Virginia Anderson, *University of North Dakota;* Robert Andree, *Indiana University Northwest*; Linda Armbruster, *Rancho Santiago College;* Michael Atherton, *Mankato State University*; Gary E. Baker, *Marshalltown Community College;* Richard Batt, *Saint Louis Community College at Meremec;* Luverne Bierle, *Iowa Central Community College*; Jerry Booher, *Scottsdale Community College;* James Bradley, *University of Calgary*; Curtis Bring, *Moorhead State University*; Cathy Brotherton, *Riverside Community College*; James Buxton, *Tidewater Community College, Virginia*; Gena Casas, *Florida Community College, Jacksonville*; Thomas Case, *Georgia Southern University*; John E. Castek, *University of Wisconsin—La Crosse*; Mario E. Cecchetti, *Westmoreland County Community College*; Jerry M. Chin, *Southwest Missouri State University*; Carl Clavadetscher, *California State Polytechnic University;* Vernon Clodfelter, *Rowan Technical College, North Carolina*; Laura Cooper, *College of the Mainland, Texas*; Cynthia Corritore, *University of Nebraska at Omaha*; Sandra Cunningham, *Ranger College*; Marvin Daugherty, *Indiana Vocational Technical College*; Donald L. Davis, *University of Mississippi*; Robert H. Dependahl Jr., *Santa Barbara College*, California; Donald Dershem, *Mountain View College*; John DiElsi, *Marcy College, New York*; Mark Dishaw, *Boston University*; Eugene T. Dolan, *University of the District of Columbia*; William Dorin, *Indiana University Northwest*; Jackie O. Duncan, *Hopkinsville Community College;* John W. Durham, *Fort Hays State University*; Hyun B. Eom, *Middle Tennessee State University*; Michael Feiler, *Merritt College*; J. Patrick Fenton, *West Valley Community College*; James H. Finger, *University of South Carolina at Columbia*; William C. Fink, *Lewis and Clark Community College, Illinois*; Ronald W. Fordonski, *College of Du Page*; Connie Morris Fox, *West Virginia Institute of Technology*; Paula S. Funkhouser, *Truckee Meadows Community College*; Gene Garza, *University of Montevallo*; Timothy Gottleber, *North Lake College*; Wade Graves, *Grayson County College*; Kay H. Gray, *Jacksonville State University;* David W. Green, *Nashville State Technical Institute, Tennessee*; George P. Grill, *University of North Carolina, Greensboro;* John Groh, *San Joaquin Delta College*; Rosemary C. Gross, *Creighton University*; Dennis Guster, *Saint Louis Community College at Meremec*; Joe Hagarty, *Raritan Valley Community College;* Donald Hall, *Manatee Community College*; Sallyann Z. Hanson, *Mercer County Community College*; L. D. Harber, *Volunteer State Community College, Tennessee*; Hank Hartman, *Iowa State University;* Richard Hatch, *San Diego State University*; Mary Lou Hawkins, *Del Mar College*; William Hightower, *Elon College, North Carolina*; Sharon A. Hill, *Prince George's Community College, Maryland*; Fred C. Homeyer, Angelo State University; Stanley P. Honacki, Moraine Valley Community College; L. Wayne Horn, *Pensacola Junior College*; J. William Howorth, *Seneca College, Ontario, Canada*; Peter L. Irwin, *Richland College, Texas*; Nicholas JohnRobak, *Saint Joseph's University*; Elizabeth Swoope Johnson, *Louisiana State University;* Jim Johnson, *Valencia*

Community College; Robert T. Keim, *Arizona State University*; Mary Louise Kelly, *Palm Beach Community College*; William R. Kenney, *San Diego Mesa College*; Richard Kerns, *East Carolina University, North Carolina*; Glenn Kersnick, *Sinclair Community College*, Ohio; Gordon C. Kimbell, *Everett Community College, Washington*; Robert Kirklin, Los Angeles Harbor Community College; Judith A. Knapp, *Indiana University Northwest*; Mary Veronica Kolesar, *Utah State University*; James G. Kriz, *Cuyahoga Community College, Ohio*; Joan Krone, *Denison University*; Fran Kubicek, *Kalamazoo Valley Community College*; Rose M. Laird, *Northern Virginia Community College*; Robert Landrum, *Jones Junior College*; Shelly Langman, *Bellevue Community College*; James F. LaSalle, *The University of Arizona*; Chang-Yang Lin, *Eastern Kentucky University*; Linda J. Lindaman, *Black Hawk College*; Alden Lorents, *Northern Arizona University*; Paul M. Lou, *Diablo Valley College*; Deborah R. Ludford, *Glendale Community College*; Barbara J. Maccarone, *North Shore Community College*; Wayne Madison, *Clemson University, South Carolina*; Donna L. Madsen, *Kirkwood Community College*; Richard W. Manthei, *Joliet Junior College*; Randy Marak, *Hill College*; Gary Marks, *Austin Community College, Texas*; Ed Martin, *Kingsborough Community College*; Vickie McCullough, *Palomar College*; James W. McGuffee, *Austin Community College*; James McMahon, *Community College of Rhode Island*; William A. McMillan, *Madonna University*; Don B. Medley, California State Polytechnic University; John Melrose, *University of Wisconsin—Eau Claire*; Mary Meredith, *University of Southwestern Louisiana*; Marilyn Meyer, *Fresno City College*; William J. Moon, *Palm Beach Community College*; Marilyn Moore, *Purdue University*; Marty Murray, *Portland Community College*; Don Nielsen, *Golden West College*; George Novotny, *Ferris State University*; Dennis J. Olsen, *Pikes Peak Community College*; Bob Palank, *Florissant Community College*; James Payne, *Kellogg Community College*; Robert Ralph, *Fayetteville Technical Institute, North Carolina*; Herbert F. Rebhun, *University of Houston—Downtown*; Arthur E. Rowland, *Shasta College*; Kenneth R. Ruhrup, *St. Petersburg Junior College*; John F. Sanford, *Philadelphia College of Textiles and Science*; Carol A. Schwab, *Webster University*; Larry Schwartzman, *Trident Technical College*; Benito R. Serenil, *South Seattle Community College*; Tom Seymour, *Minot State University*; John J. Shuler, *San Antonio College, Texas;* Harold Smith, *Brigham Young University*; Willard A. Smith, *Tennessee State University*; Alfred C. St. Onge, *Springfield Technical Community College, Massachusetts*; Timothy M. Stanford, *City University*; Michael L. Stratford, *Charles County Community College, Maryland*; Karen Studniarz, *Kishwaukee College*; Sandra Swanson, *Lewis & Clark Community College*; William H. Trueheart, *New Hampshire College*; Jane J. Thompson, *Solano Community College*; Sue Traynor, *Clarion University of Pennsylvania*; James D. Van Tassel, *Mission College*; James R. Walters, *Pikes Peak Community College*; Joyce V. Walton, *Seneca College, Ontario, Canada*; Diane B. Walz, *University of Texas at San Antonio*; Joseph Waters, *Santa Rosa Junior College, California*; Liang Chee Wee, *University of Arizona*; Fred J. Wilke, *Saint Louis Community College;* Charles M. Williams, *Georgia State University*; Roseanne Witkowski, *Orange County Community College*; James D. Woolever, *Cerritos College*; A. James Wynne, *Virginia Commonwealth University*; and Robert D. Yearout, *University of North Carolina at Asheville*.

I would also like to thank the following ancillary authors for their excellent work on the support package:

Beverly Amer, *Northern Arizona University*, Online Reviews
Robert H. Dependahl, Jr., *Santa Barbara City College*, Interactive Crossword Puzzles
Wade Graves, *Grayson County College*, Internet Lab Assignments

Deborah R. Ludford, *Glendale Community College*, PowerPoint Presentation

Deborah Morley, *College of the Sequoias*, co-author, Instructor's Manual, Test Bank

Merrill Wells, *Red Rocks Community College, Computers Online*

I would especially like to thank Deborah Morley in her role as Editorial Consultant in this edition. Deborah contributed numerous insights and suggestions as the manuscript was developed; her expertise during all phases of the project is greatly appreciated.

I am indebted to scores of people at dozens of organizations for the photographs they provided for this text. I would especially like to thank Jessie O. Kempter at IBM, Carol Parcels of Hewlett-Packard, the many helpful people at Waggner Edstrom, and computer artists Corinne Whitaker of The Digital Giraffe and Dan Younger of Dan Younger/Art Stuff.

At Harcourt, a special word of thanks to my publisher, Michael Roche, to my executive editor, Christina A. Martin, to Elizabeth Hayes, associate editor, and to Kathryn Stewart, project editor, for the suggestions and accommodations they made to produce a better manuscript. Also I would like to thank Scott Baker, Linda McMillan, Linda Blundell, Annette Coolidge, Mary Crouch and the many others who worked hard on behalf of this book.

Charles S. Parker

CONTENTS IN BRIEF

Note: This contents in brief shows entries for all 16 chapters of the text. You may have a customized version of the text that

CONTENTS

Note: This table of contents shows entries for all 16 chapters of the text. You may have a customized version of the text that does not contain all of the chapters indicated.

SW MODULE SOFTWARE   SW 1

BOXES

Chapter SW 2
Systems Software   SW 33

BOXES

NET MODULE COMPUTER NETWORKS
NET 1

Chapter NET 1
Communications and Networks   NET 3

Chapter NET 2
Introduction to the Internet and World Wide Web   NET 47

BOXES

PS MODULE PRODUCTIVITY SOFTWARE   PS 1

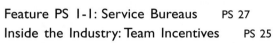

Chapter PS 2
Spreadsheets and Presentation Graphics   PS 35

Chapter PS 3
Database Management   PS 69

BOXES

IS MODULE INFORMATION SYSTEMS IS 1

Chapter IS 2
Applications Software Development   IS 35

MODULE

INT

INTRODUCTION

We live in an age of computers. Businesses, government agencies, and other organizations use computers and related technologies to handle tedious paperwork, provide better service to customers, and assist managers in making good decisions, to name just a few things. As computers continue to offer growing benefits, and as the costs of technology products continue to fall relative to the prices of everything else, computers will become even more widespread in our society. It is therefore essential to know something about them.

The chapter in this module introduces you to computers and some of their uses. It helps you understand what computer systems are, how they work, and how people use them. The chapter also presents some key terminology that you will encounter repeatedly throughout the text.

MODULE CONTENTS
Introduction

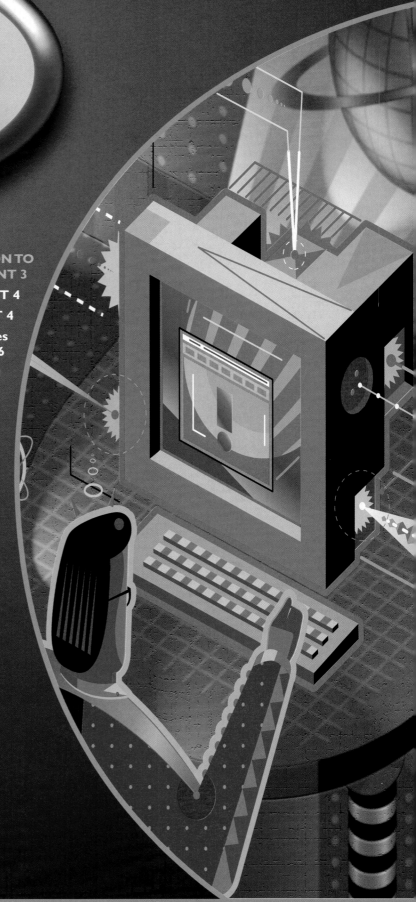

INT I

INTRODUCTION TO THE WORLD OF COMPUTERS

LEARNING OBJECTIVES

After completing this chapter, you will be able to:

1. Explain why it's especially important to learn about computers today.

2. Identify some of the major components in a computing environment and detail their relationships to one another.

3. Describe several applications for computers in business and other areas of society where they play important roles.

4. Define several terms that arise in reading about or discussing computers.

5. Describe the social impact of computers.

OVERVIEW

WebTutor

For a tutorial on uses of computers, go to www. harcourtcollege.com/infosys/ parker2000/student/tutor/ and click on **Chapter INT1.**

Unless you plan to live as a recluse in the wilderness, computers and other forms of technology will probably have a big impact on your life. Computer systems keep track of bank transactions and credit-card purchases. They are the cornerstones of the airlines' massive reservations systems. Computers perform the millions upon millions of computations needed to send equipment to distant places like Mars and to operate it once it's there. Computers also direct production in factories and provide business executives with up-to-date information that they need to make decisions. Computers are embedded in watches, television sets, phones, fax machines, kitchen appliances, and even the stationary workout bike at your local gym. In short, computers are used in virtually endless numbers of applications.

Fifty years ago, computers were part of an obscure technology that interested a handful of scientists. Today, they are part of almost everyone's daily life.

Computers share a characteristic with cars, in that you don't need to know everything about them to use them effectively. You can learn to drive a car without knowing much about internal combustion engines, and you can learn to use a computer without a complete understanding of technical details such as logic gates. Still, with both cars and computers, a little knowledge can give you a big advantage. Knowing something about cars can help you to make wise purchases and save money on repairs. Likewise, knowing something about computers can help you to use them for maximum benefit.

This book is a beginner's guide. If you're considering a career as a computer professional in business, it will give you a comprehensive introduction to the field. If not, it will give you the basic knowledge you need to understand and use computers in school and on the job. Today, many jobs depend heavily on computer-based information, and your success in the workplace is more likely to depend on your ability to manage that information and to use it to make effective decisions.

This chapter first examines what computers do and how they work. You'll learn about such concepts as input and output, memory, hardware and software, computer networks, and many others. A later section will look at the various sizes of computers that today's users encounter.

COMPUTERS IN THE WORKPLACE

Prior to 1980, it was not critical for the average person to know how to use a computer in his or her job. Computers were large and expensive, and few people in the working world had access to them. Furthermore, the use of computers generally required a lot of technical knowledge. Most computers used in organizations were equipped to do little but carry out high-volume paperwork processing, such as issuing bills and keeping track of customer and product balances. Not only were most ordinary working people afraid of computers, but there were few good reasons for getting familiar with them.

Then, suddenly, things began to change. Microcomputers—inexpensive personal computers (PCs) that you will read about later in this chapter—were created. Consequently, today there are thousands of times more computers and hundreds of times more people involved with computers than just a couple of decades or so ago. This transition has resulted in a flood of high-quality computer products in the marketplace. These products have changed the way many companies do business and the type of skills they seek in the people they hire.

Today we are living in the midst of a computer revolution, where most skill-based jobs heavily depend on the creation, collection, use, and dissemination of information. What's more, this revolution is showing no signs of slowing down; if anything, it's accelerating. Whether you become a teacher, lawyer, doctor, professional athlete, executive, or skilled tradesperson, your performance will largely depend on information and your use of it. Because computer systems can process facts at dizzying speeds, their value to you is equivalent to having both a skilled researcher and an army of clerks at your disposal.

Figure INT 1-1 provides several examples of how computers are being used in the workplace to enhance personal productivity.

FIGURE INT 1-1

Computers shaping the workplace.

MULTIPURPOSE WORKSTATION
Most business professionals today require their own desktop computer in the office or at home to prepare budgets and reports, exchange electronic mail, organize their work, and collect information from computer networks.

PRESENTATION TOOL
Increasingly, computers are being used to make presentations in front of an audience. The content of the presentation might be stored on a local disk drive or on a remote drive on a computer network.

NETWORKING
At many hotel chains, local desktop PCs at registration desks are hooked into a global communications network that keeps track of guest reservations and rooms.

DESIGN TOOL
The computer has become a vital creative tool in fields such as advertising art, architecture, and engineering. Affordable computers can quickly produce stunning photorealistic renderings that help designers sell ideas to clients.

WHAT'S A COMPUTER AND WHAT DOES IT DO?

Four words sum up the operation of a computer system: **input, processing, output,** and **storage.** To see what these words mean, look at a comparable device you probably have in your own home—a stereo system.

A simple stereo system might consist of a compact disk (CD) player, an amplifier, and a pair of speakers. To use the system, you place a CD in the CD player and turn on power to the system. The player converts the patterns in the CD's tracks into electronic signals and transmits them to the amplifier. The amplifier receives the signals, strengthens them, and transmits them to the speakers, which play music. In computer terms, the CD player sends signals as *input* to the amplifier. The amplifier *processes* the signals and sends them to the speakers, which produce a musical *output.* The CD player is an **input device,** the amplifier is a processing unit, and the speakers are **output devices.** The amplifier is the heart of the system, whereas the CD player and speakers are examples of **peripheral equipment.**

Most stereo systems include a variety of other peripheral equipment. An antenna, for example, is another kind of input device. Headphones are output devices. A tape deck functions as both an input device and an output device—you can use it to send signals to the amplifier or to receive signals from the amplifier. The tapes and CDs in your collection are, in computer terms, **storage media.** They *store* music in a **machine-readable form**—a form that the associated input device (tape deck or CD player) can recognize (that is, read) and convert into signals for the amplifier to process.

COMPUTER SYSTEMS

All of these elements in a stereo system have their counterparts in a computer system. At a minimum, a **computer system** consists of the computer itself and its peripheral equipment. It includes instructions and facts that the computer processes, as well as operating manuals, procedures, and the people who use the computer. In other words, all of the components that contribute to the computer's functioning as a useful tool can be said to be parts of a computer system (see Figure INT 1-2).

At the heart of any computer system is the **computer** itself, or the **central processing unit (CPU).** The CPU in a computer system is the equivalent of the stereo system's amplifier. Like its counterpart, the CPU can't do anything useful without both peripheral equipment for input, output, and storage functions, as well as storage media that hold the data it processes. Computer *input and output (I/O) devices* include, to name just a few, keyboards, display devices, and printers. *Storage devices* include the drives that hold disks and tapes—the storage media. The storage devices featured in Figure INT 1-2 are a hard-disk drive, a diskette drive, and a CD drive.

A computer system, of course, is not a stereo system, and a CPU is much more versatile than a stereo amplifier. For example, a computer system can

---

■ **Input.** What is supplied to a computer process. ■ **Processing.** The conversion of input to output. ■ **Output.** The results of a computer process. ■ **Storage.** An area that holds materials going to or coming from the computer. ■ **Input device.** Equipment that supplies materials to the computer. ■ **Output device.** Equipment that accepts materials from the computer. ■ **Peripheral equipment.** The devices that work with a computer. ■ **Storage media.** Objects that store computer-processed materials. ■ **Machine-readable form.** Any form that represents data so that computer equipment can read them. ■ **Computer system.** A collection of elements that includes the computer and components that contribute to making it a useful tool. ■ **Computer.** The piece of equipment, also known as the **central processing unit (CPU),** that interprets and executes program instructions and communicates with peripheral devices.

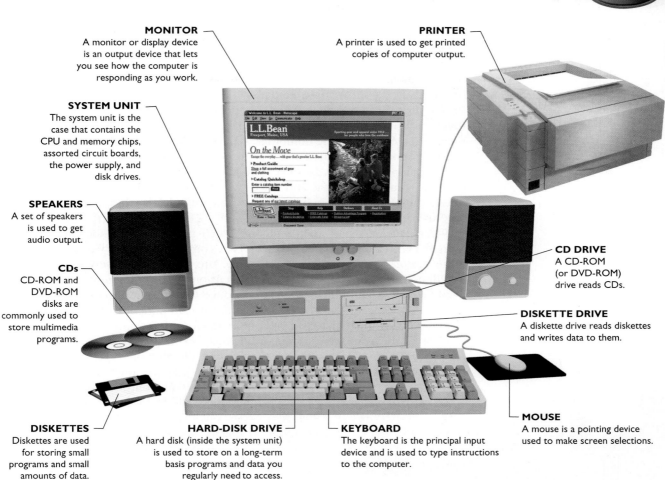

MONITOR
A monitor or display device is an output device that lets you see how the computer is responding as you work.

PRINTER
A printer is used to get printed copies of computer output.

SYSTEM UNIT
The system unit is the case that contains the CPU and memory chips, assorted circuit boards, the power supply, and disk drives.

SPEAKERS
A set of speakers is used to get audio output.

CDs
CD-ROM and DVD-ROM disks are commonly used to store multimedia programs.

CD DRIVE
A CD-ROM (or DVD-ROM) drive reads CDs.

DISKETTE DRIVE
A diskette drive reads diskettes and writes data to them.

DISKETTES
Diskettes are used for storing small programs and small amounts of data.

HARD-DISK DRIVE
A hard disk (inside the system unit) is used to store on a long-term basis programs and data you regularly need to access.

KEYBOARD
The keyboard is the principal input device and is used to type instructions to the computer.

MOUSE
A mouse is a pointing device used to make screen selections.

FIGURE INT 1-2

A computer system.

perform an enormous variety of processing tasks and a stereo system only a few. Also, a computer can support a much greater variety of input and output devices than can a stereo amplifier.

Two of the things that give a computer its flexibility are its memory and its ability to be programmed. The computer's *memory*, or "workspace," is an electronic storage area that allows the computer to retain the input it receives and both the intermediate and final results it produces. An ordinary home stereo system has no such memory; input from the compact disk player or tape recorder passes directly through the amplifier to the speakers. Because computers can hold materials in memory, they can rearrange or recombine *data* input in an amazing variety of ways under the direction of *program* input before sending them along as output.

DATA, INFORMATION, AND PROGRAMS

As already suggested, to produce results, a computer uses two kinds of materials as input: *data* and *programs*. The result—or output—of the subsequent processing is information.

Data   **Data** are essentially raw, unorganized facts. Almost any kind of fact or set of facts can become computer data: a letter to a friend, text and pictures for a 300-page book, a budget, a colorful graph, or a set of employee records.

■ **Data.** A collection of raw, unorganized facts.

Data can exist in many forms. Computer systems commonly handle four types of data: text, graphics, audio, and video data.

Text data have been around the longest of all. These data usually consist of standard alphabetic, numeric, and special characters—that is, the type of data one normally sees in a simple word-processed letter, a budget, or a printed report.

Graphics data consist of still pictures such as drawings, graphs, photographs, and illustrations. Graphics data often require more sophisticated representations inside the computer than those for text, because graphics are naturally more complicated, often with multiple colors.

An example of *audio* data is an ordinary telephone conversation. Any type of sound—including music and voice—is considered audio data. Modern computers can store sounds in machine-readable form, just as they store any other type of data.

Video data consist of motion pictures, such as a movie clip, a feature-length film, or live pictures of a conference. Two common types of video are *computer animation* and *full-motion video*. The former are a series of similar two-dimensional drawings or three-dimensional computer models that are displayed one right after another to produce the illusion of motion, like you see in TV cartoons, whereas the latter are usually a series of photographic frames such as those that comprise most motion pictures.

Most of the computer systems sold today are *multimedia computer systems* (see Figure INT 1-3). That is, they can handle multiple types of data. Multimedia systems display conventional text and graphics on a display screen, they play audio output over speakers, and they can run video clips stored on CDs, such as CD-ROM and its higher-capacity successor, DVD-ROM. CDs are covered in detail later in this book; *ROM*, which stands for *read-only memory*, means that users can read the disk but not write to it.

FIGURE INT 1-3

Multimedia computing. Most of the computers sold today have a multimedia capability, which means they can handle audio and video data in addition to conventional text and graphics.

Information When users input data into computer systems, they usually don't want to receive the same data back without changes. Instead, they want the system to process the data and give new, useful information. **Information,** in the language of computers, refers to data that have been processed into a meaningful form.

A computer user might want to know, for example, how many of a firm's employees earn more than $100,000, how many seats are available on a particular flight from Los Angeles to San Francisco, or what Mark McGwire's home-run total was during a particular baseball season. The difference between data and information lies in the word *meaningful*. Mark McGwire's home-run total may be meaningful to a baseball fan, because it could enhance the experience of watching baseball games. Someone who doesn't follow this sport, however, may regard Mark McGwire's home-run total as completely meaningless—just ordinary data, not information. Thus, information is a *relative* term; it identifies something that has significance to a specific person in a specific situation. Like beauty, the difference between data and information is strictly in the eye of the beholder.

 **Information.** Data that have been processed into a meaningful form.

Of course, you don't need a computer system to process a set of facts and produce information. Anyone can go through an employee file and make a list of people earning a certain salary. By hand, however, this work would take a lot of time, especially for a company with thousands of employees. Their high speeds allow computers to perform such tasks almost instantly. Conversion of data into information is called by a variety of terms, one of which is *information processing*.

Information processing has become an especially important activity in recent years, as the success of many businesses depends heavily on the wise use of information. Because better information often improves employee decisions and customer service, many companies today regard information as among their most important assets and consider the creative use of information to be a key competitive strategy.

Programs   A **program** is a set of instructions that tells the computer how to process data to produce the information that you, the user, want. Like many other machines, the amplifier in your home stereo system is a *special-purpose* device. It is designed to support only a few specific tasks—interacting with a CD player, playing music through speakers or headphones, and so forth. These functions are built into its circuitry. To say the same thing another way, the amplifier is "hardwired" to perform a very limited number of specific tasks.

Most computers, in contrast, are *general-purpose* devices. They can perform a large variety of tasks—for instance, preparing letters to clients, analyzing sales figures, and creating slide presentations, to name just a few. Because most computers must maintain flexible processing capabilities, they can't be hardwired to do all of these and hundreds of other tasks. Instead, they rely on programmed instructions for guidance. As a computer system processes each program, the user provides data for the program to respond to. The program and its data input then direct the circuits in the computer to open and close in the manner needed to do the desired task.

Computers cannot yet run programs written in ordinary English. Instead, specialists create programs in a **programming language**—a code that the computer system can read and translate into the electronic pulses that make it work. Programming languages come in many varieties—Visual BASIC, Pascal, C++, and Java are a few you may have heard about in the press. Millions of people now use computers without ever writing programs, leaving that task largely to computer professionals.

A LOOK AT COMPUTER STORAGE

So far, you've seen that you can get something done on a computer system only by supplying it with both facts (data) and instructions (a program) specifying how to process those facts. For example, if you want the system to write payroll checks, you must supply such data as employees' names, social security numbers, and salaries. The program instructions must indicate to the system how to compute taxes, how to take appropriate deductions, where and how to print checks, and so forth. Also, the computer relies on storage to retain all these details as it completes the work.

Actually, computer systems contain two types of storage. **Primary storage**—often called **memory**—temporarily holds the data and programs that the computer is currently processing. When the computer's memory captures data, it can rearrange or recombine them, as indicated by the instructions in

■ **Program.** A set of instructions that causes the computer system to perform specific actions. ■ **Programming language.** A set of rules used to write computer programs. ■ **Primary storage.** Also known as **memory**, this section of the computer system temporarily holds data and program instructions awaiting processing, intermediate results, and processed output.

the program. Memory is often contained within the system unit that houses the computer.

More often than not, the work that people create in a computer session needs to be used at a later time, say, tomorrow or next week. Because turning off the power to the computer destroys any data left in memory, another means of storage—called secondary storage—is needed for work to be saved, so it can be used multiple times.

The computer system stores data and programs that people need from session to session in **secondary storage**. In large computer systems, equipment separate from the system unit provides secondary storage. Smaller computer systems usually provide secondary storage through equipment that is factory installed inside the system unit. In either case, these pieces of equipment—such as disk drives—are called *secondary storage devices*. They enable users to conveniently save large quantities of data and programs in machine-readable form, avoiding the need to retype them into the system or reinstall them every time they're needed. Secondary storage devices can often store thousands of programs and billions of pieces of data.

When the CPU needs a certain program or set of data, it requests that input from a secondary storage device—much as you might request a particular song from a jukebox. It then reads the needed input into its memory for processing. Unlike a jukebox turntable, which puts the original CD or phonograph record in play, the CPU puts only a copy of the original program or data into memory for use. The original version remains on the secondary-storage medium—usually a disk—until you change it.

Figure INT 1-4 illustrates the relationships among input, processing, output, memory, and secondary storage.

FIGURE INT 1-4

Input, processing, output, and storage. These tasks require an interactive dialogue between the user and computer.

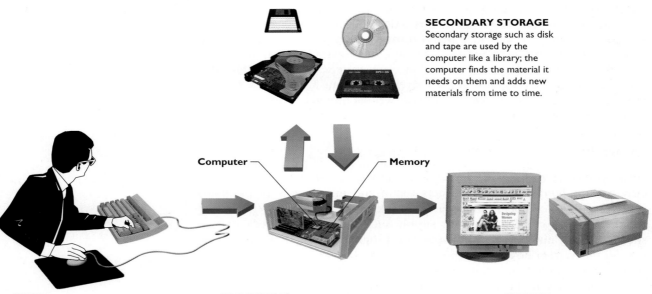

SECONDARY STORAGE
Secondary storage such as disk and tape are used by the computer like a library; the computer finds the material it needs on them and adds new materials from time to time.

Computer — Memory

INPUT
The user deploys a mouse and a keyboard to enter inputs to the computer.

PROCESSING
Every time the user inputs something, the computer must respond. For instance, when a program from secondary storage is requested, the computer must find it and load it into memory. Similarly, when a document is to be saved or output, the computer must transfer it from memory to secondary storage or to an output device.

OUTPUT
Output devices such as a monitor and a printer present computer results to the user.

■ **Secondary storage.** Storage on media such as disk and tape that supplements memory.

HARDWARE AND SOFTWARE

In the world of computers, a distinction is made between hardware and software.

Hardware The word **hardware** refers to the actual machinery that makes up a computer system—for example, the CPU, input and output devices, and storage devices. A good portion of this chapter has already focused on the hardware parts of a computer system, many of which were featured in Figure INT 1-2, so this section won't dwell on them.

Software The word **software** refers to computer programs. As already mentioned, programs direct the computer system to do specific tasks, just as your thoughts direct your body to speak or move in certain ways. Computers use two basic varieties of software: applications software and systems software.

Applications software is designed to assist with such tasks as computing bank-account interest, preparing bills, creating letters and book manuscripts, preparing and analyzing budgets, managing files and databases, playing games, scheduling airline flights, and diagnosing hospital patients' illnesses. In other words, applications software makes possible the types of work that most people have in mind when they acquire computer systems. **Productivity software** is the class of applications software designed to make workers more productive at their jobs. Some important types of productivity software are described in Figure INT 1-5.

Systems software consists of programs operating in the background that enable applications software to run on a computer system's hardware devices. One of the most important pieces of systems software is the *operating system*, a set of control programs that supervise the computer system's work. Without the operating system, none of the applications programs on your computer system can run.

When you buy software in a store or through the mail, you often receive it in some sort of a physical package (see Figure INT 1-6). Such a *software package* may consist of program disks, printed operating instructions and user manuals, instructional and help materials on disk, and a printed license to use the software, all or some of which are inside a shrink-wrapped box or plastic case. The programs on the disks have been written in some programming language, though, as a general rule, you will not have to learn a language to use the package. Increasingly, software is being distributed over the Internet. Such software may be available for free or you may have to pay a one-time fee or monthly subscription fee to use it.

The most widely used software products are revised every year or two to keep up with changes in technology, such as bigger disk drives, faster computer chips, larger memories, and the like. Each revision is commonly referred to as a *version* or *release* and is assigned a number—for instance, Windows 98, Office 2000, and WordPerfect 9.

ORGANIZING DATA AND PROGRAMS

Data, as mentioned earlier, are essentially facts, and programs are the instructions that process these facts into meaningful information. Unfortunately, you can't just randomly input a collection of facts and instructions into

---

■ **Hardware.** Physical equipment in a computing environment, such as the computer and its peripheral devices. ■ **Software.** Computer programs. ■ **Applications software.** Programs that help with the type of work that people acquire computer systems to do. ■ **Productivity software.** Computer programs, such as word processors and spreadsheets, designed to make workers more productive in their jobs. ■ **Systems software.** Background programs, such as the operating system, that enable applications programs to run on a computer system's hardware.

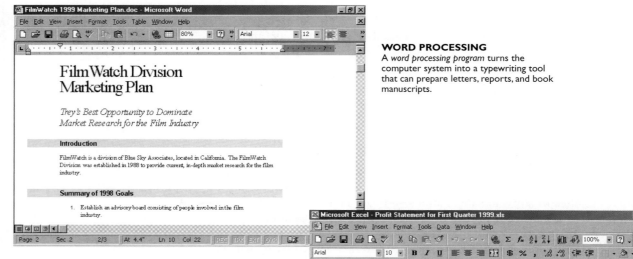

WORD PROCESSING
A *word processing program* turns the computer system into a typewriting tool that can prepare letters, reports, and book manuscripts.

SPREADSHEETS
A *spreadsheet program* turns the computer system into a sophisticated electronic calculator.

FIGURE INT 1-5

Productivity software. Productivity software is designed to help both ordinary users and computer professionals work more productively at their jobs.

PRESENTATION GRAPHICS
Presentation graphics programs turn the computer system into a tool that can be used to prepare slides, overheads, and other presentation materials for meetings.

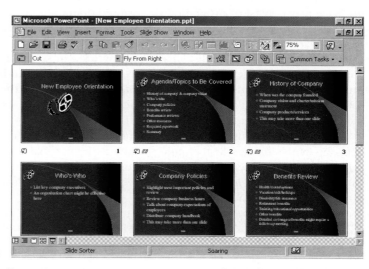

a computer system and expect to get the desired results. For a computer system to process them, data and programs must be organized in a systematic way (see Figure INT 1-7).

Documents and Folders One of the most fundamental ways that data and programs are organized is with documents and folders. For instance, when you are working with a word processing program, each memo, letter, or report that you create is stored as a separate electronic **document.** Related

---

■ **Document.** Any single piece of work that's created with software and then given a name by which it may be accessed.

DATABASE MANAGEMENT

A *database management system* turns the computer system into an electronic research assistant, capable of searching through mounds of data to prepare reports and answer queries.

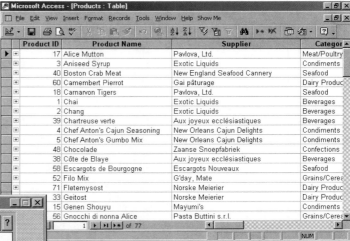

E-MAIL

An *electronic mail (e-mail) program* enables people to compose and send, receive, and manage electronic mail messages.

WEB BROWSER

Web browsers enable people to get to any of the thousands of sites on the Internet's World Wide Web and to output Web pages on a display screen.

documents are in turn stored in an electronic **folder.** For example, one folder might contain memos to business associates while another holds a set of budgets for a specific project. Related programs are stored in their own folders, too. Organizing data into documents and folders is natural for most office workers, a number of whom were using file folders to organize paperwork well before computers became a fixture on desktops.

In the documents-folders method of organization used by computers, you can also create *subfolders* within each folder. Consequently, you might create a letters folder that contains a subfolder with letters sent to friends and a second subfolder with letters sent to potential employers. A folder can contain a mixture of subfolders and independent documents.

■ **Folder.** A container for documents.

FIGURE INT 1-6

Software package. A typical software package consists of one or more program disks, a printed user's guide, and a printed user's license inside a shrink-wrapped box.

Web-Page Organization Many of you may have had the experience of looking at screen pages from the Internet's World Wide Web, or Web. A *Web page* is a document that is assigned a unique address on the computer on which it is stored. The *Disney.com* page in Figure INT 1-5 is such an example. By entering its address on your own, local computer, you can access such a page over ordinary phone lines if your computer is connected to the Internet. Usually Web pages are a little bigger than the size of a screen, and you will have to scroll the page up or down on your PC to see the parts of the page that are currently off the screen. When you click your mouse in special places on the page, the page is usually replaced with another that is linked to it.

Related Web pages are usually stored in the same folder on the remote computer, and the complete collection of such pages and folders is called a *Web site.* For instance, at the Disney Web site you will find pages about Disney movies (stored in a Movies folder), pages about Disney TV shows (stored in a TV folder), pages about Disney merchandise for sale (stored in a Shopping folder), and so on.

To gain access to a specific page at a Web site, type in the appropriate address or click your mouse on an appropriate descriptor. For instance, to get to pages about Disney movies, click on the word "Movies" on the Disney.com Web page. A detailed discussion of the Internet and Web is reserved for a later chapter.

Fields, Records, Files, and Databases Another common procedure—which is most widely used with data—is to organize the data into fields, records, files, and databases.

A **field** is a collection of characters (such as single digits, letters of the alphabet, or special symbols like a decimal point) that represents a single type of data. Two examples are a person's name and the price of a product. A **record** is a collection of related fields—say, the ID number, name, address, and phone number of John Q. Jones. A **file** is a collection of related records, and a **database** is a set of related files.

■ **Field.** A collection of related characters. ■ **Record.** A collection of related fields. ■ **File.** A collection of related records. ■ **Database.** A collection of related files.

DOCUMENTS AND FOLDERS

Documents and folders are handy for organizing such outputs as memos, letters, reports, budgets, and programs.

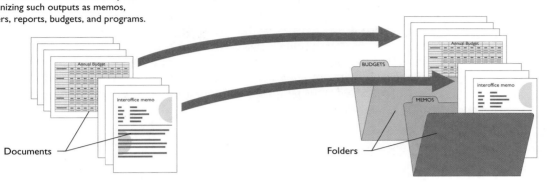

Documents

Folders

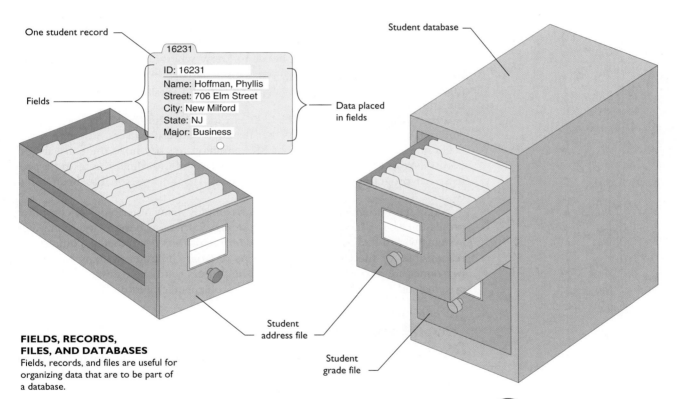

One student record

16231

ID: 16231
Name: Hoffman, Phyllis
Street: 706 Elm Street
City: New Milford
State: NJ
Major: Business

Fields

Data placed in fields

Student database

Student address file

Student grade file

FIELDS, RECORDS, FILES, AND DATABASES

Fields, records, and files are useful for organizing data that are to be part of a database.

 FIGURE INT 1-7

Organizing data and programs.

Your school, for example, probably has a *file*, stored on disk, of all students currently enrolled. The file contains a *record* for each student. Each record has several *fields* containing various types of data about a particular student: ID number, name, street, city and state of residence, major subject area, and the like. What's more, it probably even has a *database* that consists of several files—say, a student address file (such as the one in Figure INT 1-7), a student grade file (containing courses completed and grades earned by each student), and possibly other student-oriented files. Put another way, most of the information about students would be found in such a student database.

Documents, folders, fields, records, files, and databases usually have names or other unique ways of being identified. Both you and the computer system use such identifiers to find the entity when you wish to access, modify, or delete it.

Be aware that many of the terms you've learned about here can be used interchangeably or used in different contexts. For instance, a "word processed file" and a "word processed document" generally refer to the same thing—the output that a user creates with a word processing program and names. Also, the term "file," traditionally used to mean "group of records," is commonly extended to programs. Thus, the term "program file" is commonly used interchangeably with "program." As you learn more about computers, you'll get to see that it's not unusual for several terms to mean the same thing or for one term to mean several things.

USERS AND THE EXPERTS

In the early days of computing, a clear distinction separated the people who made computers work from those who used the results that computers produced. This distinction remains, but as computers become more available and easier to use, it is breaking down.

Users, or *end users*, are the people who need output from computer systems. They include the accountant who needs a report on a client's taxes, the secretary who needs a word processing program to create a letter, the engineer who needs to know whether a bridge design will be structurally sound, the shop-floor supervisor who needs to know whether workers have met the day's quotas, and the company president who needs a report on the firm's profitability over the past ten years. Even people playing computer games over the Internet are users.

Programmers, on the other hand, are people whose primary job responsibility is to write the programs that produce output for users. Although some users may do modest amounts of programming to customize the software on their desktop computers, the distinction between an ordinary user and a professional programmer is based on the work that the person has been hired to do.

Along with programmers, organizations employ many other types of computer professionals. For instance, they pay *systems analysts* to design large computer systems within their companies. *Computer operations personnel*, in contrast, are responsible for the day-to-day operations of large computer systems. Computer personnel are also often employed to help users with their desktop computer systems and to troubleshoot user-related problems (see Feature INT 1-1).

COMPUTER NETWORKS

Users often need to share hardware, software, and data. They meet this need by tying computer systems together into networks (see Figure INT 1-8). You will find *computer networks* in many sizes and types. For instance, a small office network might link together five or six desktop computers so that workers can share an expensive printer and a common bank of files on a very-high-capacity disk drive, both of which are also hooked up to the network. Far distant from such tiny networks on the size continuum is the *Internet*—a network that ties together thousands of other networks throughout the world. Millions of computers of all sizes, millions of people from all walks of life, and thousands of organizations worldwide are connected to the Internet.

Accessing Networks To access a computer network, you need at least two kinds of resources: a piece of hardware known as a *network adapter* and soft-

---

■ **User.** A person who needs the results that a computer produces. ■ **Programmer.** A person who writes computer programs.

Programs That Run Amok

More Embarrassing Evidence That Computers Do Only What They're Told

Computers sometimes do the craziest things. A litany of stories has been reported in the press throughout the years to remind us of this.

Heard the one about the company computer that sent reminders out to every customer—even if the total owed came to $0.00? This mishap resulted because a programmer failed to consider all of the possibilities and code them into the applicable program. Or how about the one where a borrower was paying on installment and tricked the computer by prematurely sending in the final coupon with the final monthly payment? The computer erroneously concluded that when a last coupon was successfully paid it should close the corresponding account. The programmer had failed to instruct it to first check for any unpaid balance.

In the early days of computing, it was the programmers who seemed to make all of the mistakes telling the computer what to do. Today, users are getting in on the action and catching up fast.

One interesting story surfaces from the Pacific Northwest. An office worker instructed his e-mail software—the program enabling him to correspond with colleagues via electronic mail—to generate an automatic "out of office" reply to every message he received while he was out traveling on business. Or so he thought. Instead, he had inadvertently instructed his e-mail program to

Help! My computer has gone insane. Computers precisely follow instructions laid out in programs. Not all programs contain "reality checks" to prevent users from doing something destructive.

send messages to all 2,000 people in his departmental address book for each message he received. And not only that; he also requested a return receipt for each message.

Within a few hours, the network was clogged with more than 150,000 messages. Trained computer personnel had to step in and temporarily pull the plug on the offender's system. But perhaps not before they had something to say to him in their own e-mail message.

ware that lets you connect to and use the facilities of the network. If you require the use of the Internet, you will also need an *access provider*—also called a *service provider*—an organization that will enable you to access the Internet as a user.

The most common type of adapter is a device called a *modem*. Through a modem, you can connect a computer system to virtually any public network—such as the Internet—that sends data over the phone lines.

The modem package or your operating system usually includes the communications software you will need to connect to a network. If it doesn't, you can also acquire this software separately. To use the Internet, you will also need software from your local access provider.

Most users gain access to networks like the Internet through their schools' or employers' computer systems or through other access providers. Providers commonly let users access, or *log on* to, the Internet via their systems after inputting an identification number or name (an ID) and a secret password.

Once you have an ID and a password and you set up your computer system to use a network, connecting is very simple. You might first use your keyboard or mouse to select the access provider's screen icon. At that point, the modem usually automatically dials a local access telephone number for you. Next, a screen appears on your display asking you to enter your ID and password. After you give the right input, you're on the network. From there,

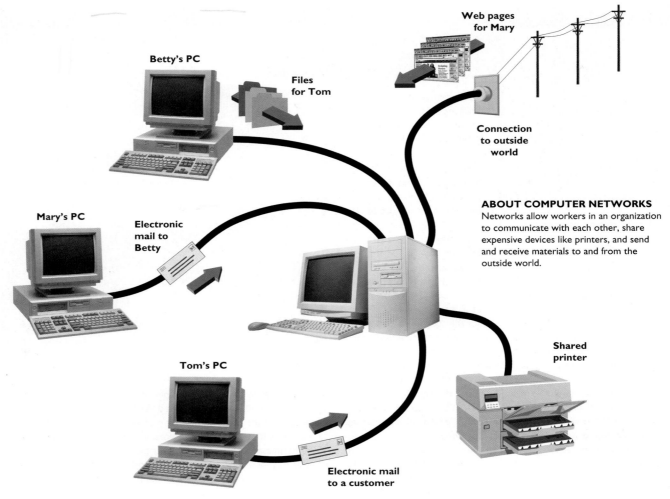

Web pages for Mary

Betty's PC

Files for Tom

Connection to outside world

Mary's PC

Electronic mail to Betty

ABOUT COMPUTER NETWORKS
Networks allow workers in an organization to communicate with each other, share expensive devices like printers, and send and receive materials to and from the outside world.

Tom's PC

Shared printer

Electronic mail to a customer

FIGURE INT 1-8

Computer networks. Computer systems meet users' need to share hardware, software, and data—as well as to communicate with each other—by tying devices together into networks.

you can select whatever type of application you want to run, just as you would with a regular software package.

Online and Offline   Computer users often hear the terms *online* and *offline* with reference to computer networks and in various other contexts. Any computer in a condition that allows it to send data to or receive data from a computer network or other device is said to be **online** to the network or device. If a device isn't online, it's **offline.**

For instance, one large retail chain keeps member stores throughout North America online to the central computer system at all times during business hours so that headquarters personnel can tightly control store prices. By keeping the stores online, the parent company also gains immediate access to the most recent sales information possible. Other companies may leave stores offline to headquarters computers most of the time, connecting to them only as needed to transmit and receive data.

Online and *offline* are terms that arise in a multitude of situations. For instance, when your printer is ready to receive signals from your computer system, it is online. Also, when people use their computers to perform a task over a network, the word *online* is commonly appended to the task name— such as "online banking" (see the Tomorrow box).

■ **Online.** A state that allows a device to send data to or receive data from other devices. ■ **Offline.** A state that *does not* allow a device to send data to or receive data from other devices.

Paying Bills over the Web

Possible Today. Widespread Tomorrow?

The Internet's World Wide Web has been widely embraced by users from all over the world. Many of them even trust it enough to regularly use it to buy goods from reputable firms by credit card. But relatively few people today are confident enough about security on the Web to do their banking online. A few wrong mouse clicks and one's hard-earned cash may get zapped forever. Strong safeguards are in the wind, however, and consumer reservations about online banking may soon change.

Today, banks and the companies that regularly bill consumers are aggressively teaming up. What they would like to offer is a one-stop solution for paying bills. It works like this: When you access your bank's Web site at the beginning of the month, online versions of all of your bills from last month can be pulled up (see the accompanying art). You can use your computer system to select underlined keywords and amounts in any of the bills. These highlighted entries are "hot links" that, when activated, deliver an appropriate Web page of new information to your screen. As you select links, you can do such things as get detailed questions answered, file an address change, or contest charges. If the bill is cor-

rect, you can then instruct the bank to pay it from your current balance.

Online banking, when it is fully developed, may prove to be a real convenience to the consumer. Besides the option of getting more information in your bill—and being able to respond to it—there's the following: no envelopes or stamps; no having to write checks; and having the ability to pay bills away from your home, such as while on vacation in a foreign country. What's more, the bill-paying process that can today consume an hour or two every month could be collapsed to a few minutes. The billions in savings realized by companies for handling less paper can also be passed back to you, the consumer.

Today, online banking has a long way to go to live up to the scenario described here. Only a tiny percentage of households in North America now bank by computer. Also, most online banking systems are still far too crude and too slow to draw wide appeal, and they lack widespread participation by the companies that bill consumers.

Online banking in its current state suffers from the chicken-or-the-egg effect. Companies don't want to commit to online banking until more consumers step forward to use it, and consumers will not step forward until more companies participate. What's more, a fight is brewing as to who will control the online banking business. The banks? The companies that bill? Your phone company? Microsoft or America Online? The stakes are high; winners will surely get a cut out of every bill paid.

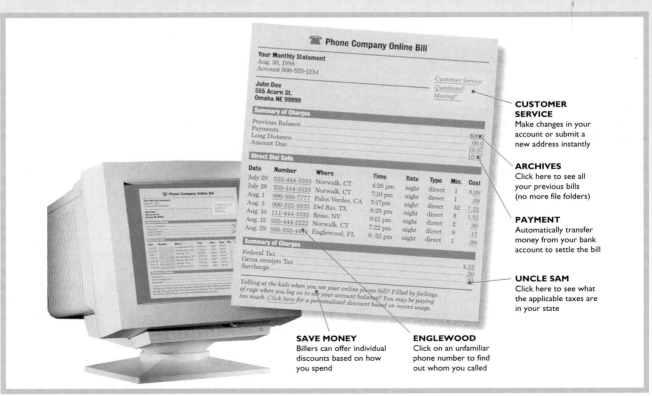

CUSTOMER SERVICE
Make changes in your account or submit a new address instantly

ARCHIVES
Click here to see all your previous bills (no more file folders)

PAYMENT
Automatically transfer money from your bank account to settle the bill

UNCLE SAM
Click here to see what the applicable taxes are in your state

SAVE MONEY
Billers can offer individual discounts based on how you spend

ENGLEWOOD
Click on an unfamiliar phone number to find out whom you called

The bill of the future? The Web provides a one-stop solution for receiving and paying bills and getting questions answered.

COMPUTER SYSTEMS TO FIT EVERY NEED AND POCKETBOOK

The computer market offers a great variety of systems to serve computer users' needs. This section will consider one important way in which computers differ from one another—size.

Computer systems are generally classified in one of four size categories: small, or microcomputers; medium-sized, or midrange computers; large, or mainframe computers; and superlarge, or supercomputers. In practice, the distinction among different sizes is not always clear-cut. Large midrange computers, for example, often are bigger than small mainframes.

In general, larger computers have greater processing power. For example, big computers can usually process data faster than small computers. Big computers can also accommodate larger and more powerful peripheral devices. Naturally, larger computers and peripheral equipment also have higher prices. A computer system can cost anywhere from a few hundred dollars to several million.

MICROCOMPUTERS

A technological breakthrough in the early 1970s allowed circuitry for an entire CPU to fit on a single silicon chip smaller than a dime. These computers-on-a-chip, or *microprocessors*, could be mass-produced at very low cost. Microprocessors were quickly integrated into all types of products, leading to powerful handheld calculators, digital watches, electronic toys, and sophisticated controls for household appliances such as microwave ovens and automatic coffeemakers.

Microprocessors also created the possibility of building inexpensive computer systems, such as those pictured in Figure INT 1-9, small enough to fit on a desktop or even in a shirt pocket. These small computer systems have informally come to be called **microcomputer systems** (or *microcomputers* or simply *micros*). Those that are designed to be used by one person at a time—at home or work—are commonly called **personal computers (PCs).**

Sizes of Microcomputer Systems   As illustrated in Figure INT 1-9 and explained below, most microcomputer systems currently available to individuals for business and home use can be classified as desktop or portable units.

DESKTOP UNITS   *Desktop computers* are most commonly found in schools, homes, and businesses. The names of these computer systems have become household words—IBM Aptiva, Apple Macintosh, Compaq Presario, and so on.

Desktop computers come in two models or styles. In the *desktop-case* style the system-unit case is designed specifically to rest on a desk. In the *tower-case* style, the system-unit case stands upright on either a desktop or floor. Tower cases have more room in which to mount secondary storage units, and they leave more work space on the desktop. Because the cases often sit at a distance further from users, however, tower-case models may not provide as convenient a way to insert and remove disks from drives.

WebTutor

For a tutorial on microcomputers and their various configurations, go to www.harcourtcollege.com/infosys/parker2000/student/tutor/ and click on Chapter INT1.

■ **Microcomputer system.** A computer system driven by a microprocessor chip. Also known as a **microcomputer,** or *micro.* ■ **Personal computer (PC).** A microcomputer system designed to be used by one person at a time. Also known as a *personal computer system.*

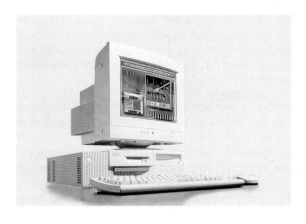

Most PCs sold today are equipped with disk drives and other types of secondary storage. Diskless desktop PCs called *network computers (NCs),* which are optimized for use in company networks, are also available. However, desktop PCs that now sell for less than $500 have all but killed off the consumer NC market.

PORTABLE UNITS   *Portable PCs* come in a variety of sizes, including (from largest to smallest) laptop, notebook, subnotebook, and palmtop.

Laptop computers, commonly weighing anywhere from 8 to 15 pounds, were designed for users who needed access to their microcomputers at remote sites. Today, most people prefer to carry lighter *notebook computers* (6 to 8 pounds) or *subnotebook computers* (2 to 6 pounds). The lighter units also bring smaller physical dimensions, allowing them to fit conveniently into users' briefcases. Although many notebooks and subnotebooks provide just about the same power as their desktop cousins, they tend to cost more, have smaller screens, and have denser keyboard arrangements. Such disadvantages notwithstanding, sales of notebooks and subnotebooks are currently among the fastest-growing segments of the microcomputer industry.

Palmtop (or *handheld*) *computers* look and work a lot like standard pocket calculators. Most palmtop computers perform relatively narrow, specialized tasks—keeping track of golf or bowling scores, translating words into foreign languages, checking word spellings, and scanning or recognizing bar codes on

FIGURE INT 1-9

PCs. (from left to right, top to bottom) Desktop PC with desktop-style case. Desktop PC with a tower-style case. Notebook computer. Handheld computer.

packages. Palmtop devices called *personal digital assistants*, or *PDAs*, are specifically geared to help users carry out such office-oriented tasks as maintaining addresses and phone numbers, scheduling events in an electronic calendar, manipulating numbers, filling in forms, and messaging, electronic mail, and other communications functions.

PC Compatible or Macintosh?   Most users choose between two major computer **platforms** when they buy desktop, laptop, notebook, or subnotebook computers—PC compatibles and Macintosh compatibles. The drift toward the two major standards started over a decade ago, when the IBM PC and the original Apple Macintosh were the two front-running microcomputer systems.

Most vendors followed IBM's lead, building their systems around Intel microprocessor chips and (later) catering to Microsoft Windows applications. Such computer systems are known as **PC compatibles**. Close to 90 percent of computers made today are PC-compatible devices. Among the largest vendors of these machines are Compaq, IBM, Dell, Hewlett-Packard, NEC/Packard Bell, and Gateway. Often, today, people refer to PC-compatible computers as the *Windows platform* or as *IBM-compatible PCs*.

Computers that instead follow Apple's design platform are known as Macintosh compatibles. *Macintosh compatibles,* because of their reputation for advanced graphics capabilities, are often the platform of choice for artists and designers. Today, Apple is virtually the only maker of Macintosh-compatible computers; the company has virtually driven all of its direct competitors out of business. Because there are so fewer Macintoshes being made than PC-compatibles, expect to pay more for comparable hardware.

Uses for Microcomputers   Microcomputers are widely used in both small and large businesses. A small business might use its PCs for all of its computing tasks, including tracking merchandise, preparing correspondence, billing customers, and completing routine accounting chores. A large business might use microcomputers as productivity tools for secretaries and as analysis tools for decision makers, to name just two important applications. Also, portable computers are popular with salespeople who need to make presentations at client sites and with managers who need computing resources as they travel.

PCs often connect to large communications systems to function as general-purpose workstations for individuals and as *network servers* that cater to the shared needs of groups of people. Network servers are computers—often powerful PCs or, in large networks, midrange or mainframe computers—that manage the storage devices that hold common banks of programs and data. For instance, servers are commonly used to store Web pages, some of which are accessed by millions of people daily.

Most PCs that function as network servers are based on the tower design, and they provide much more powerful capabilities than the "minitower" and desktop models that individuals buy for their own needs. Today, PC networks—that is, computer networks in which PC workstations and servers are prominent components—represent one of the hottest areas within the computer field.

The proliferation of microcomputing and networking products over the past quarter century has been fueled by entrepreneurs and venture capitalists. As the Inside the Industry box reveals, some have reaped enormous rewards for the risks they've taken.

Further Exploration

For links to further information about PCs, go to www. harcourtcollege.com/infosys/ parker2000/student/explore/ and click on Chapter INT1.

■ **Platform.** A foundation technology by which a computer system operates. ■ **PC compatible.** A personal computer based on Intel microprocessors or compatible chips.

Venture Capitalists

Often, behind the scenes of a newly formed technology company is a person known as a venture capitalist. He or she is the one who supplies the money to get the company started in earnest.

Perhaps the George Washington of venture capitalists in the short history of microcomputers is Mike Markkula—the man who got Apple Computer off to a sound financial beginning. Apple was founded in a California garage in 1976 by Steve Jobs and Steve Wozniak, two twentysomethings. Early on, the pair realized they would need a third partner, one with enough business knowledge and financial muscle to get their company off the ground. Through contacts in California's Silicon Valley, they were introduced to Markkula—then 33 and a recent, retired multimillionaire. At 26, he had been an Intel marketing director when the chipmaking giant went public, and his shares of the company had soared in price.

Jobs and Markkula couldn't have appeared more different on the surface to a casual onlooker in the mid-1970s. Jobs was a health fanatic who avoided meat and fats; he has sometimes been characterized as high-strung. Markkula, on the other hand, was laid back and often chain-smoked and drank whiskey. The men, however different, realized that a rare opportunity awaited them, and a great company was soon off to the races. Markkula helped Jobs and Wozniak prepare a business plan, threw in more than $90,000 of his own, and secured additional financing with Bank of America and two venture-capital firms. Within only a few years, each of the three men were hundreds of millions of dollars richer.

Following in Markkula's legendary footsteps in recent times is Michael Moritz, the venture capitalist who helped Yahoo!—the Internet search-engine company—get organized into a business. Moritz had originally heard raves about Yahoo! from an Internet-surfing friend, and decided to visit its two creators, Dave Filo and Jerry Yang. To his surprise, Moritz discovered the enterprise was being run as a hobby, not as a commercial venture, out of a disheveled trailer behind the Bill Gates building on the Stanford University campus. He offered the pair financial help. He also convinced them to keep their costs within line, to aggressively seek ad revenues, and to hold on to their interest in Yahoo! rather than selling out. Two years after the company went public in 1996, Moritz's $2 million stake was worth more than $1 billion.

MIDRANGE COMPUTERS

Midrange computers—sometimes called *minicomputers* or *minis*—are medium-sized computers (see Figure INT 1-10). Most of them fall between PCs and mainframes in processing power, although the very smallest midrange computers are virtually indistinguishable from the most powerful PCs, and the largest closely resemble small mainframes. Midrange computers usually cost far more than microcomputers, more than most individuals can afford.

Any of several factors might lead an organization to choose a midrange system over a PC or mainframe. A small or medium-sized company may simply find a microcomputer system too slow to handle its processing volume. Often, midrange buyers need computer systems that can interact with multiple users—perhaps hundreds—at the same time. Many microcomputer systems lack sufficient power to handle such complex applications. Mainframes, discussed in the next section of this chapter, can handle these applications with ease, but they are much larger and generally much more expensive than midrange computers.

■ **Midrange computer.** An intermediate-sized and medium-priced computer.

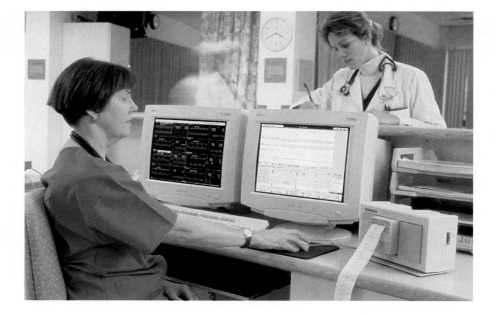

FIGURE INT 1-10

Midrange system. In a midrange system, several display workstations are connected to the same computer. A midrange computer is commonly used to run a small business, such as a healthcare facility, or a department within a larger company.

MAINFRAMES

The **mainframe computer** (see Figure INT 1-11) is a standard choice for almost any large organization. It often operates 24 hours a day, serving thousands of users interacting through display devices during regular business hours and processing large jobs late at night, such as payroll and billing. Many large organizations need several mainframes to complete their computing workloads. Typically these organizations own or lease a variety of computer types—mainframes, midrange computers, and micros—which collectively meet all of their processing needs. Increasingly, these organizations are linking together various sizes of computers into networks.

FIGURE INT 1-11

IBS ES/9000 mainframe. The ES/9000 series sets the performance standard for today's mainframes. IBM makes close to 75 percent of all mainframes sold.

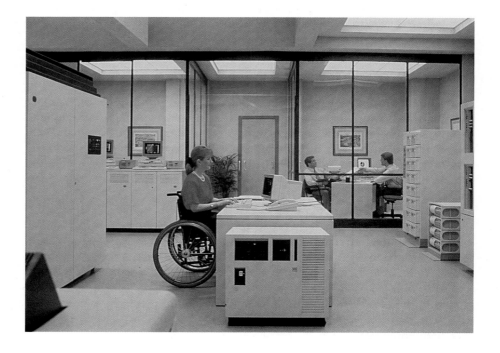

■ **Mainframe computer.** A large computer that performs extensive business transaction processing.

FIGURE INT 1-12

Supercomputers. Sandia Laboratories' ASCI Red, one of the world's fastest supercomputers at 1.8 trillion operations per second, consists of thousands of microprocessors linked together.

Most mainframes are assigned to handle high-volume processing of business transactions and routine paperwork. For a typical business, this workload includes tasks such as tracking customer purchases and payments, sending out bills and reminder notices, and paying employees. These operations were some of the earliest applications of computers in business and have been the responsibility of mainframes since the 1950s.

SUPERCOMPUTERS

Some organizations, such as large scientific and research laboratories, have extraordinary information processing needs. Applications such as sending astronauts into space, testing safety and aerodynamic features on cars and aircraft, and weather forecasting, for example, require extreme accuracy and extensive computations. To meet such needs, a few vendors offer very large, sophisticated machines called **supercomputers.**

Supercomputers can cost several million dollars each. During the past few years, innovators have tried to build less-expensive supercomputers by linking together hundreds or thousands of microprocessor chips. The resulting class of supercomputers—see Figure INT 1-12—is often referred to as *massively parallel processors (MPPs).*

COMPUTERS AND SOCIETY

The ability of computers to sort through massive amounts of data and quickly produce useful information for almost any kind of user—from payroll clerk to president—makes them indispensable tools in our modern society. Without computers, businesses could never function at the level they do today. Banks would be overwhelmed by the job of tracking all the transactions they must process. Familiar airline and telephone services would be impossible. Moon exploration and the space shuttle would still belong to science fiction.

■ **Supercomputer.** The fastest and most expensive type of computer.

But along with these benefits, computers have brought some troubling problems to society ranging from health concerns to personal security and privacy to ethics. Workers often spend many hours in front of their display screens. Do the radiation and glare emanating from the screens impair health? Banks store data about customers' accounts on multiuser storage devices. Can they prevent clever criminals from using their own computer systems to tie into a banking network and steal from those accounts? The government maintains confidential information about every American taxpayer. Can it protect that information from unauthorized use? Because commercial software and a lot of data exist in electronic form, they can be easily copied or stolen. What restrictions should limit access to software and data?

These are serious issues, and this chapter can only cover them briefly. Subsequent parts of this book will explore further both the social benefits and problems created by computers.

SUMMARY AND KEY TERMS

Go to the Online Glossary at www.harcourtcollege.com/infosys/parker2000/ student/ to review key terms.

Computers appear almost everywhere in today's world. They're embedded in consumer products, they help managers run businesses, and they direct production in factories, to name just a few applications.

Computers in the Workplace Computers abound in today's workplace largely because we are living in an era when most jobs heavily depend on the collection, use, creation, and dissemination of information.

What's a Computer and What Does It Do? Four words summarize the operation of a **computer system: input, processing, output,** and **storage.** The processing function is performed by the **computer** itself, which is sometimes called the **central processing unit,** or **CPU.**

The input and output functions are performed by **peripheral equipment,** such as **input devices** and **output devices.** Just as your stereo amplifier would play no music without speakers or headphones and turntable, tape deck, or CD player, the computer would be helpless without its peripheral devices.

Several of the peripheral equipment read from and write to **storage media.** Such media often store data and programs in **machine-readable form,** which the computer system can recognize and process.

A computer's input takes two forms: data and programs. **Data** are the raw, unorganized facts on which the computer carries out its processing; **programs** are sets of instructions that explain to the computer what to do with certain data. A program must be written in a **programming language** that the computer can understand. Data that the computer has processed into a useful form are called **information.**

Computer systems have two types of storage. **Primary storage** (sometimes called **memory**) is usually built into the unit that houses the computer itself; memory holds the programs and data that the system is currently processing. **Secondary storage** keeps programs and data indefinitely.

People who talk about computers commonly distinguish between hardware and software. **Hardware** refers to the actual machinery that makes up the computer system, such as the CPU, input and output devices, and secondary storage devices. **Software** refers to computer programs. Software comes in two basic forms: **applications software** and **systems software.** The class of applications software that helps people perform their jobs better is called **productivity software.**

One of the most fundamental ways that data and programs are organized is into **documents** and **folders.** On the Internet's World Wide Web, folders are used to store related *Web pages*, and the complete collection of pages and folders at a location is called a *Web site.* Another common procedure is to organize into fields, records, files, and databases. A **field** is a collection of characters that represents a single type of data. A **record** is a collection of related fields. A **file** is a collection of related records. A **database** is a collection of related files.

Users are the people who need the output that computer systems produce. Within a computing environment, many types of experts help users to meet their computing needs; for example, **programmers** are responsible for writing computer programs.

To allow users to share hardware, software, and data, networks tie together computers and related devices. To access many computer networks, you need a piece of hardware known as a *network adapter*, appropriate software, and the services of an *access provider*. Any device in a condition that allows it to send data to or receive data from a computer network is said to be **online** to the network. If a device isn't online, it's **offline.**

Computer Systems to Fit Every Need and Pocketbook Small computers are often called **microcomputers (microcomputer systems)** or **personal computers (PCs,** *personal computer systems*). Most microcomputer systems today are either desktop or portable computers, and they fall within either the **PC-compatible** or *Macintosh-compatible* **platform.**

Medium-sized computers are called **midrange computers,** and large computers are called **mainframe computers.** The very largest computers, which run applications that demand the most speed and power, are called **supercomputers.**

While categories of computers based on size can provide helpful distinctions, in practice it is sometimes difficult to classify computers that fall on the borders of these categories.

Computers and Society Although computer systems have become indispensable tools for modern life, their growing use has created troubling problems, ranging from health concerns to personal security and privacy to ethics.

EXERCISES

1. Match each term with the description that fits best:
   a. Midrange computer
   b. Input device
   c. Mainframe
   d. Palmtop computer
   e. Supercomputer
   f. Hardware
   g. Microcomputer
   h. Network computer

   _____ The equipment that makes up a computer system
   _____ Another name for personal computer
   _____ A medium-sized computer
   _____ A large computer used to process business transactions in high volume
   _____ A diskless desktop computer
   _____ Any piece of equipment that supplies programs and data to a computer
   _____ The most powerful type of computer
   _____ The smallest type of computer

2. For the following list of computer hardware, write the *principal* function of each device in the space provided. Choices include input device, output device, storage device, and processing device.
   a. CPU _____
   b. Mouse _____
   c. Monitor _____
   d. CD-ROM drive _____
   e. Keyboard _____
   f. Diskette drive _____
   g. System unit _____
   h. Printer _____
   i. Subnotebook computer _____

3. Define the following terms:
   a. Hardware
   b. Peripheral equipment
   c. Online
   d. Secondary storage
   e. Systems software

4. What is the difference between data and information? Provide an example not discussed in the chapter.

5. Order the following list of computer systems by size from the least powerful to the most powerful.
   a. Notebook computer
   b. Mainframe computer
   c. MPP
   d. PDA

   e. Desktop computer
   f. Midrange computer
   g. Laptop computer

6. What is the difference between a file and a database? Provide an example of each.

7. How does memory differ from secondary storage? Name the secondary storage media covered in this chapter.

8. Match each term with the best description.
   a. Word processing program
   b. Operating system
   c. Presentation graphics package
   d. Spreadsheet program
   e. Database management system
   f. Web browser

   _____ Helps search through a large bank of facts, such as airline flight schedules
   _____ Supervises the running of all other programs on the computer
   _____ Helps prepare documents like letters and reports
   _____ Turns the computer into a sophisticated electronic calculator and analysis tool
   _____ Displays resources on the Internet
   _____ Helps prepare slides and graphs for meetings

9. Name the four types of data covered in the chapter and answer the following questions:
   a. How are these types of data related to the term *multimedia*?
   b. You type a letter to a friend and include with it an electronic picture of your dog. What types of data does the letter include?

10. Identify at least three social problems created by computer systems.

11. Fill in the blanks.
    a. Memory is sometimes called _____ storage, whereas diskettes and CD-ROM disks are examples of _____ storage.
    b. Peripheral equipment fits in two categories: _____ devices, such as diskette and CD-ROM drives, and _____ devices, such as keyboards and printers.
    c. Another name for computer programs is _____.
    d. Programs are written using a programming _____.
    e. A desktop microcomputer without secondary storage is called a(n) _____ computer.

12. Each of the following definitions is not strictly true in some regard. In each definition, identify the flaw and correct it.
    a. Memory: Another name for computer storage
    b. Data: Information that has been processed into a meaningful form
    c. Computer: The CPU and all of the storage and input/output equipment that supports it
    d. Processing: The conversion of output to input
    e. Programmer: Anyone in an organization who writes computer programs

PROJECTS

1. The Internet The Internet and World Wide Web are both handy tools that can help you to research topics covered in this textbook and to complete many of the projects. Although a detailed explanation of the functions of the Internet and the Web is beyond the scope of this chapter—read Chapter NET 2 if you want to know more—it would be to your advantage to learn how to use these tools right from the outset. That's not a difficult task. It's just a matter of finding an Internet-enabled computer on your campus, logging on, typing in an address for a specific information site, and then choosing among the onscreen selections.

a. Find a computer at your school that has access to the Internet, then follow the directions provided by your instructor or lab aide to log on to the Internet.

b. What is the name of the software package running on your computer that helps you browse through Internet information?

c. Access the home page of your school. What is the *Web address* of this page—that is, the string of characters that anyone at any location can type into a computer to locate your school? (Somewhere on the screen, a box should display a long string of characters that starts with *http://*; right after this set of characters—often beginning with *www* and ending with *.edu*—is the address of your school's home page.)

d. What types of information did you find at your school's Web site? (To see information beyond the home page, select—with a mouse or keyboard—one of the highlighted pieces of text on the page. Each piece of highlighted text—usually distinguished by color and underlining—is called a *hyperlink*. By selecting hyperlinks, you can move to other pages.

e. Access the home pages of at least two other schools. You can find them by accessing an Internet *search site* such as any of the four listed here (with Web addresses in parentheses). Such sites let you type in keywords to find information or, alternatively, let you use a comprehensive menu system.

Yahoo! (www.yahoo.com)
Excite (www.excite.com)
Lycos (www.lycos.com)
Alta Vista (www.altavista.com)

When you reach the home page of the chosen search site, select the highlighted text that says *Colleges and Universities* or something like that. Then, keep on making selections on subsequent screens until you find the school you are seeking. What types of information or features did you find at these other college sites that were different from your own school's Web site?

f. What are the Web addresses of the two schools you looked up in part e?

g. Access the Parker Web site at

www.harcourtcollege.com/infosys/parker/

Here you will find updated information on the projects in this book as well as other items of interest. Make a preliminary exploration of the site by selecting hyperlinks.

h. Log off the Internet and shut off your computer.

2. Productivity Software Figure INT 1-5 lists several types of productivity software. For this project, find the names of two commercial programs that fit into each of the following categories. Also, identify the company that produces each of the programs you have chosen.
   a. Word processing program
   b. Spreadsheet program
   c. Database management program
   d. Presentation graphics program
   e. E-mail program

3. Computer Journals Go to your school library or a local bookstore and find five journals (magazines or newspapers) that focus on PCs. For each journal, list the following information:
   a. The name

b. The frequency of publication (e.g., weekly, monthly, bimonthly)

c. The target audience (for instance, word processing users, users of Macintosh computers, people who use the Internet)

d. For each of the five journals you named in part a, determine if a Web site exists with an online edition of the journal. If it does, provide the Web address. (You do not need Internet access to get this information.)

4. **Computer Advertisements** Look in a computer journal—such as *PC Magazine* or *MacWorld*—for an advertisement featuring a PC for sale. What are the principal hardware components of this system and their functions? What systems and applications software does the ad offer as part of the purchase price and what—specifically—does each of these programs do? Does the hardware and software system provide complete capabilities for performing simple chores like creating letters and writing term reports, or do you have to purchase additional hardware or software?

5. **Online Bookstores** Online bookstores are appearing on the World Wide Web with increasing frequency. Two popular ones are the Amazon Bookstore

www.amazon.com

which offers one of the largest collections of book titles you'll find in a single place, and Fatbrain.com

www.fatbrain.com

which has one of the largest collections of computer books and magazines available anywhere.

a. Get onto the Web and visit one of these bookstores (or perhaps another of your own choosing). Compare the online bookstore's prices on

two computer books with prices at a conventional bookstore in your area. Are the online bookstore's prices higher or lower? (*Hint*: You can search for other online bookstores through a search site such as Yahoo! or Lycos. Type "online bookstores"—including the quotation marks—into the space that offers the keyword search to see what is currently available.)

b. The software tools at many online bookstores let you search for books by typing in an author's name, a book's subject area, or a keyword from a book's title. Observe as many book-search tools as you can for at least one online bookstore and make a list of ways that you can locate books. Do you find the computer useful as a book-shopping tool?

c. The Amazon site currently lets visitors access book reviews and even write their own reviews for others to read. At the bookstore site you've chosen to visit, list as many features like this as you can—features that aren't typically available at conventional bookstores.

6. **Palmtop Computers** Hardware vendors today collectively sell a variety of palmtop computers, including personal digital assistants (PDAs). Choose a palmtop computer and report to your class about its features and price. Articles about palmtop computers appear regularly in computer journals such as *Computerworld* and *PC Magazine*; check your campus library or perform a search on the Internet.

7. **Online Shopping** The accompanying figure shows the Web site for L.L. Bean, a mail-order seller of outdoor clothing and equipment. The company is famous for its printed catalogs, which it still sends out annually to millions of people to supplement its Web site. For this project, visit the L.L. Bean Web site at

www.llbean.com

Report to the class about the contents of the site, how shoppers can electronically search for items of interest, and how shoppers can select a certain size or color of an apparel item. What are the advantages and disadvantages of an online catalog relative to a printed one?

8. **Computer Literacy**   The term *computer literacy*—knowing something about computers—is widely used today.

a. The following table lists some computer-oriented topics. For each one, declare whether or not you think it should be included among the basic skills that students should learn before they graduate from college. Briefly explain why you would or would not include each topic in the essential curriculum.

TOPIC	INCLUDE?	REASON
Using the Internet		
Programming in a specific computer language		
Understanding the technical details about how computers work		
Appreciating the dangers that computers pose to society		
Using a word processing package		
Learning the history of computers		
Understanding how businesses use computers		

b. A heated debate rages in many college computer departments over the emphasis placed on education versus training. *Training* prepares students to deal with situations they will likely encounter outside school, whereas *education* teaches students to deal with anything they might encounter. For instance, learning how to create reports with Microsoft Word is training; gaining an understanding of how to apply computers in the problem-solving process is education.

Many schools face a dilemma in this debate. Their mission is clearly education—they must teach students how to make tough decisions and to learn on their own. However, colleges also recognize a sad fact of life: Many companies won't hire graduates without a certain amount of training. Some people also argue that students need a certain amount of training to become educated; that is, you must complete several hands-on experiences with computers to become educated about them.

The list in part a addressed both matters that are related to training and matters that are re-lated to education. Which matters relate to training? To education? To both education and training?

c. Prepare a statement one or two pages long that summarizes your beliefs about the types of computer skills that students should pick up in college.

9. **Computer Case Study: Registering for Classes**   One of the ways computers have helped colleges and universities throughout the years is registering students for classes every semester.

a. On your own campus, how do computers help out in the registration process? Make a list of the individual tasks that computers perform that would otherwise be done manually.

b. News reports regularly feature stories about colleges using leading-edge technologies to help out in the registration process. For instance, some colleges let students register over the Internet or by Touch-Tone phone. Find one such story in a magazine or newspaper and report to your class about it.

10. **Benefits Provided by Computers**   Organizations acquire computers for many reasons. Most of them first flocked to computers because these awesome devices could do certain types of jobs much faster than humans and with far fewer errors. Such capabilities enabled computers to displace humans in many types of work at a great savings in labor costs. Eventually, computers gained capabilities to do far more than just faster, more accurate, and cheaper work. For instance, they could also be deployed to provide better information to decision makers, improve customer service, and create products that few dreamed possible before the age of computers. For this project, provide at least one real-world example from a computer journal or from your personal experience that illustrates how computers can help an organization achieve one of these latter types of benefits.

11. **Multimedia Titles**   Name at least three current multimedia CD products that fit into each of the following categories: computer games, educational products, and reference works. For each CD, describe its contents, name the company that publishes it, and write down its suggested list price. Several computer journals (including *PC Magazine*) and software stores regularly identify best-selling CDs.

12. **Weather Sites**   A veritable blizzard of weather sites exists on the World Wide Web. Besides getting forecasts for selected cities at home

and around the world, you can use your PC to track storms, inspect Doppler radar, and pore over historical weather data. And that's not all. At some sites you can get information about the best areas of the country to golf on a given day or delays at the nation's busiest airports.

Visit at least three weather sites and write a short report, not to exceed three pages, describing their principal features. Also explain which of the sites you liked the best. The accompanying list provides the addresses of some sites you may wish to visit.

Weather Sites

AccuWeather	www.accuweather.com
Intellicast	www.intellicast.com
National Weather Service	www.nws.noaa.gov
USA Today Weather	www.usatoday.com/weather
The Weather Channel	www.weather.com
Weather Underground	www.wunderground.com

ONLINE REVIEW

Go to the Online Review at www.harcourtcollege.com/infosys/parker2000/ student/ to test your understanding of this chapter's concepts.

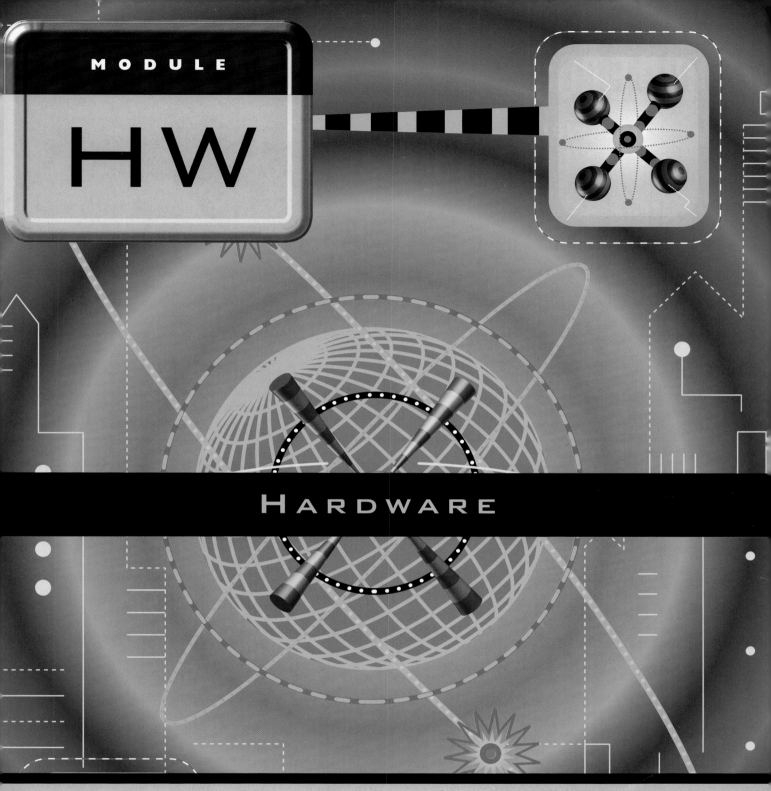

MODULE

HW

HARDWARE

When most people think of computer systems, images of hardware fill their minds. Hardware comprises the exciting pieces of equipment that you unpack from their boxes when you buy a computer system. This module explores the rich variety of computer hardware available in today's marketplace. But as you'll see later in this book, hardware needs guidance from software to perform any useful function. Hardware without software is like a human who cannot reason and think.

This module divides coverage of hardware into three subject areas. Chapter HW 1 describes the functions of the CPU—the computer itself—and memory. Chapter HW 2 discusses the class of hardware that provides an indispensable library of resources for the CPU—secondary storage devices. Chapter HW 3 delves into input and output equipment.

MODULE CONTENTS
Hardware

ISBN 0-03-025968-1

HW 1

THE CENTRAL PROCESSING UNIT AND MEMORY

OUTLINE

LEARNING OBJECTIVES

After completing this chapter, you will be able to:

1. Describe how the computer system's CPU and memory components process program instructions and data.

2. Identify several binary-based coding schemes used in computing environments.

3. Explain the functions of hardware components commonly found under the cover of a system unit.

4. Name several strategies for speeding the operations of computers.

OVERVIEW

So far, we've considered the system unit, which houses the central processing unit (CPU) and memory, to be a mysterious "black box." In this chapter, we'll demystify that notion by flipping the lid off the box and closely examining the functions of the parts inside. In doing so, the chapter will give you a feel for how the CPU, memory, and other devices commonly found in the system unit work together.

To start, we'll examine how a CPU is organized and how it interacts with memory to carry out processing tasks. Next, we'll discuss how a computer system represents data and program instructions. Here we'll talk about the codes through which computers translate back and forth from symbols the CPU can manipulate to symbols in which people find meaning. These topics lead into a discussion of how the CPU and its memory are packaged with other computing and storage components inside the system unit. Finally, we look at strategies to speed up CPU operations.

While most of you reading this chapter will be applying its principles to conventional systems—such as desktop and notebook PCs—keep in mind that the principles cover a broad range of computer products. Included are the computer chips increasingly being embedded into products like coffeemakers, VCRs, and cars. The Tomorrow box shows how some of the chips slated for future cars may make driving a completely different experience.

HOW THE CPU WORKS

Every computer's CPU is basically a collection of electronic circuits. Electronic impulses enter the CPU from an input device. Within the CPU, these impulses move under program control through circuits to create a series of new impulses. Eventually, a set of impulses leaves the CPU headed for an output device. What happens in those circuits? To begin to understand this process, you need to know first how the CPU is organized—what parts it includes—and then how electronic impulses move from one part to another to process data.

DIGITAL COMPUTERS

When we talk about computers today, most of us are referring to digital computers. **Digital computers** are devices that *count.* The types of microcomputers, midrange computers, mainframes, and supercomputers discussed in Chapter INT 1 are digital computers. As you will see in this chapter, digital computers do all of their counting by converting data and programs into strings of 0s and 1s, which they manipulate at lightning speed.

Analog computers are also widely found in practice. *Analog computers* are devices that *measure.* For example, a gasoline pump contains an analog computer that measures the amount of gas pumped and converts this reading into a gallon amount that appears on the pump's display. A car has an analog computer that measures rotation of a transmission shaft and converts this reading into speedometer output. Large systems call for analog computers, too; chemical processing companies use analog computers to measure such

---

■ **Digital computer.** A device that counts.

Vehicles That Think and Act

Tomorrow's Cars Will Be Smarter than Ever

Many people first noticed cars presumably getting smarter when antilock braking systems (ABSs) became a standard feature. When the people braked too hard, something strange happened. They would lose mechanical control of the brake as the intelligent ABS took over. Tomorrow's cars will want even more control of your wheel.

For a long time in their history, cars were strictly mechanical devices. When you turned the steering wheel or applied the brake, these movements directly turned your tires or slowed them down. This gave the driver full control over the vehicle. More recently, electrical systems have intervened in many cases to make such chores easier and less physical. In tomorrow's cars, computer chips will control mechanical and electrical systems. Like ABSs, they may even countervail some of the maneuvers you direct a car to make.

Take steering. In tomorrow's cars, when you turn the wheel, sensors will detect what you do and relay it to a computer chip. The computer chip will then take the appropriate action. Let's say the turn you are trying to make is too severe for the speed you are going. Yaw and pitch sensors in the car's computer system will detect an abnormal sideways force on the vehicle and cut its speed without your say so. Wet roads will work the same way; if your tires are not making sufficient contact with the road surface, sensors will detect this and take appropriate mechanical action.

Cruise controls will also be more advanced in the car of tomorrow. Instead of just moving your car at a preset constant speed, they will also slow your vehicle down as it begins to close in on a slower-moving car in the same lane. If the law dictates that you stay so many feet behind, your computer may enforce it. What's more, heat or vision sensors will be able to detect cars in your blind spot if you unsafely attempt to change lanes, and computer chips will take action to prevent an accident.

Seeing-eye vehicle. Cadillac's Night Vision system uses thermal sensors and a windshield display to help drivers detect objects in the road well before the car's headlights pick them up.

Such computerized controls as those mentioned here are in the testing stage now. They've enabled test drivers to go for many miles in moderate traffic without accelerating or braking.

Road rage may also become a thing of the past as smarts within the computerized part of a vehicle prevent a driver using a car as a weapon. If cars on a highway need to funnel into a single lane and other drivers won't let you in, relax; your car's computers and theirs will be communicating and controlling the situation. What's more, such problems as intoxication and drowsiness can also be caught by sensors, and a car can be programmed to not start when the driver is impaired.

In the future, when looking at buying a new car, you may instead choose to just get a software update. Dashboards will look more like computer systems, and to give your car new capabilities, it may just be a matter of reprogramming some of its features with a new disk.

To those who love the "feel" of a car, the smart car might seem regressive. Today, in fact, many complain about ABSs, and it's hard to predict how putting even less control in the hands of the driver will come off to the average consumer. Another possibility: in matters regarding public safety, the law may give you no choice.

data as temperature and time so that automatic systems can open and close valves on tanks.

People began counting and measuring long before they developed computers. One can count entities such as pages of a book, number of dollar bills in a wallet or purse, and elk on a wildlife reserve—all of which exist naturally in indivisible units. When we estimate that a car's gas tank contains 10 gallons of fuel, however, we are measuring. The tank may contain 9.99999 gallons or 10.00001 or some other number. Concepts such as volume and weight are *continuous* variables that can only be approximated, whereas concepts such as number of dollar bills or elk are *discrete* variables that can in many circumstances be determined exactly.

Digital computers can work with analog concepts by using rounded estimates. Henceforth in this textbook, all discussions will pertain to digital computers.

CONTROL UNIT
The control unit is the section of the CPU that directs the flow of electronic traffic.

ALU
The ALU is the section of the CPU that performs arithmetic and logical operations.

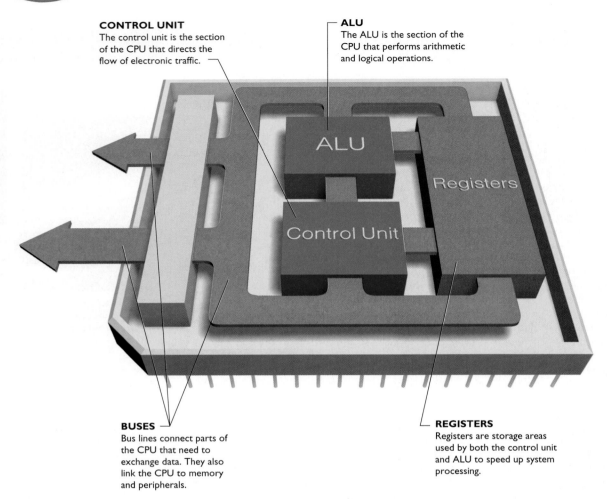

ALU

Control Unit

Registers

BUSES
Bus lines connect parts of the CPU that need to exchange data. They also link the CPU to memory and peripherals.

REGISTERS
Registers are storage areas used by both the control unit and ALU to speed up system processing.

 **FIGURE HW 1-1**

The CPU chip and its principal sections.

For a tutorial on CPUs and how they are made, go to www.harcourtcollege.com/infosys/parker2000/student/tutor/ and click on Chapter HW 1.

THE CPU AND MEMORY

The CPU works closely with memory to carry out processing inside the system unit. This relationship is described in the next few subsections.

The CPU   The CPU has two principal sections: an arithmetic/logic unit and a control unit (see Figure HW 1-1). It also contains several registers and a bus, which later subsections will describe.

The **arithmetic/logic unit (ALU)** is the section of the CPU that performs arithmetic and logical operations on data. In other words, it's the part of the computer that computes. *Arithmetic* operations include addition, subtraction, multiplication, and division. *Logical* operations compare pairs of data items to determine whether they are equal and, if not, which is larger. As later discussions will show, all data coming into the CPU—including letters of the alphabet and nonnumeric data such as voice, graphics, and video—are coded in digital (numeric) form. The ALU can perform logical operations on any type of data.

The computer can perform only the basic arithmetic and logical operations just described. That might not seem very impressive. But when combined in various ways at great speeds, these operations enable the computer to perform immensely complex and data-intensive tasks.

The **control unit** is the section of the CPU that directs the flow of electronic traffic between memory and the ALU and between the CPU and input

---

■ **Arithmetic/logic unit (ALU).** The part of the CPU that contains circuitry to perform arithmetic and logical operations.
■ **Control unit.** The part of the CPU that coordinates its operations.

and output devices. In other words, the control unit coordinates or manages the computer's operation, much like a traffic cop controls the flow of vehicles.

Memory   Memory—also called **primary storage**—holds the following:

- Programs and data passed to the computer system for processing
- Intermediate processing results
- Output ready for transmission to a secondary-storage or output device

Once the CPU stores programs, data, intermediate results, and output in memory, it must be able to find them again. Thus, each location in memory has an *address*. Whenever a block of data, instruction, program, or result of a calculation is stored in memory, it is assigned an address so that the CPU can find it again as needed. Computer systems automatically set up and maintain tables that provide the addresses of the first character of all stored programs and data blocks.

Memory size varies among computer systems anywhere from a few million characters to several hundred billion. Because memory circuitry is relatively expensive, computer systems limit its size and use it only for temporary storage. Once the computer has finished processing one program and set of data, it writes another program and data set over the same storage space. Thus, the contents of each memory location constantly change. The address of each location, however, never changes. This process can be roughly compared with handling of the mailboxes in a post office: The number on each box remains the same, but the contents change as patrons remove their mail and new mail arrives (see Figure HW 1-2).

Each location in memory has a unique address, just like mailboxes at the post office.

FIGURE HW I-2

Memory.

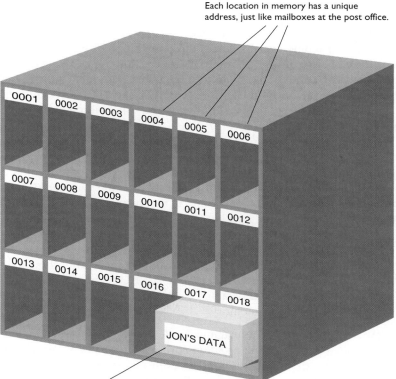

Programs and blocks of data are usually too big to fit in a single address. A directory keeps track of where the first character of each program and data block can be found and the number of addresses it spans.

■ **Memory.** The section of the computer system that holds data and program instructions awaiting processing, intermediate results, and processed output. Also called **primary storage**.

Sometimes the term *main memory* is used to distinguish conventional memory from storage products that have memory characteristics. These comparable products include *cache memory* and *read-only memory (ROM)*, both covered later in the chapter.

Registers   To enhance the computer's performance, the control unit and ALU access special storage locations (called **registers**) that act as high-speed staging areas. Registers play a crucial role in achieving extremely high computer speeds. Because registers are actually a part of the CPU, the CPU can access their contents much more rapidly than it can access memory. Program instructions and data are normally loaded (that is, staged) into the registers from memory just before CPU processing.

MACHINE CYCLES

The descriptions of the CPU, memory, and registers lead to questions about how these elements work together to process an instruction. Every instruction that you issue to a computer, either by typing a command or pointing to an icon with a mouse and clicking, is broken down into several smaller, machine-level instructions called **microcode.** Each piece of microcode corresponds directly to a set of the computer's circuits.

The computer system's built-in **system clock** synchronizes its operations, just as a metronome can synchronize the activities of an orchestra. During each clock tick, the CPU can execute a single piece of microcode, a single piece of data can move from one part of the computer system to another, and so on. Microcode instructions are a form of machine language, covered briefly later in the chapter.

As the CPU processes a single, machine-level instruction, it completes a **machine cycle.** A machine cycle has two parts: an *instruction cycle* (I-cycle) and an *execution cycle* (E-cycle). During the **I-cycle,** the control unit fetches a program instruction from memory and prepares for subsequent processing. During the **E-cycle,** the control unit locates data and the ALU carries out the instruction. Let's see how this works in more detail, using simple addition as an example.

I-Cycle

1. The control unit *fetches* from memory the next command to be executed.
2. The control unit *decodes* the command into an instruction that the ALU can process. In one register, it stores the identity of the instruction, and in another, it stores information about the location in memory of any required data.

E-Cycle

3. The control unit retrieves the needed data from memory and commands the ALU to *execute* the required instruction; the ALU complies. Registers temporarily store the retrieved data and final result.
4. The CPU *stores* the result in memory.

Figure HW 1-3 depicts how the machine cycle works.

These steps may seem to define a tedious process, especially when a computer must go through thousands, millions, or even billions of machine cycles

---

■ **Register.** A high-speed staging area within the CPU that temporarily stores data during processing. ■ **Microcode.** Instructions built into the CPU that control the operation of its circuitry. ■ **System clock.** The timing mechanism within the computer system that governs the transmission of instructions and data through the circuits. ■ **Machine cycle.** The series of operations involved in the execution of a single, machine-level instruction. ■ **I-cycle.** The part of the machine cycle in which the control unit fetches a program instruction from memory and prepares it for subsequent processing. ■ **E-cycle.** The part of the machine cycle in which the CPU locates data, carries out an instruction, and stores the results.

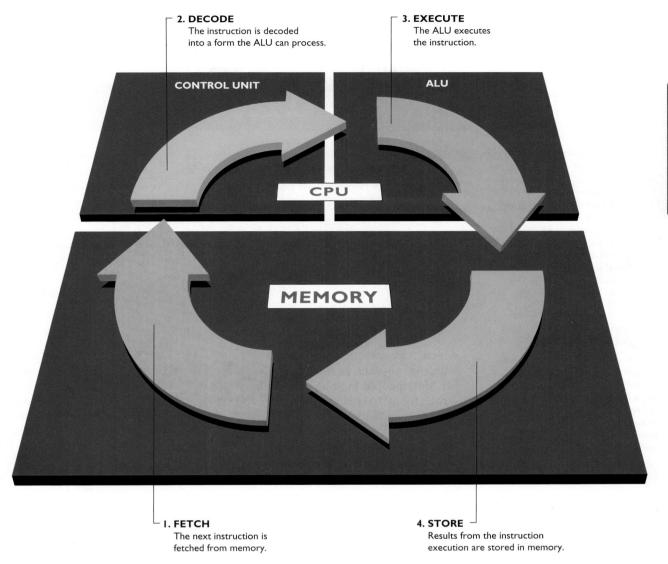

2. DECODE
The instruction is decoded
into a form the ALU can process.

3. EXECUTE
The ALU executes
the instruction.

CONTROL UNIT

ALU

CPU

MEMORY

I. FETCH
The next instruction is
fetched from memory.

4. STORE
Results from the instruction
execution are stored in memory.

to complete a single program's processing. But computer hardware works at almost unimaginably high speeds. The slowest hardware performs an operation in **milliseconds** (thousandths of a second) or **microseconds** (millionths of a second). In the fastest hardware, speeds are measured in **nanoseconds** (billionths of a second) or **picoseconds** (trillionths of a second). One of the fastest computers in the world operates at 3.9 trillion operations per second; put another way, it can do in a second what a person can accomplish by completing one arithmetic calculation per second for 123,000 years without a break.

Different terms describe speeds in different types of computers. Microcomputer speeds are most commonly rated in *megahertz (MHz).* Each 1 MHz represents 1 million clock ticks per second. While the original IBM PC of the early 1980s executed instructions at 4.77 MHz, many of today's personal computers run at 500 MHz or more.

Mainframe speeds are often rated in *mips* (millions of instructions per second); for supercomputers, it's most often *mflops* (millions of floating-point operations per second). Many of these speed measures can apply to any CPU;

FIGURE HW 1-3

Machine cycle. The processing of a single machine-level instruction is accomplished in a four-step machine cycle.

■ **Millisecond.** One one-thousandth of a second. ■ **Microsecond.** One one-millionth of a second. ■ **Nanosecond.** One one-billionth of a second. ■ **Picosecond.** One one-trillionth of a second.

for instance, today's microcomputers have become so fast that their speeds are often quoted in mips, and many mainframes handle some scientific work that calls for processing speeds measured in mflops.

DATA AND PROGRAM REPRESENTATION

For links to further information about binary and other types of data representation, go to www.harcourtcollege.com/infosys/parker2000/student/explore/ and click on Chapter HW 1.

FIGURE HW 1-4

The binary nature of electronics. Circuits are either open or closed, a current runs one way or the opposite way, a charge is either present or absent, and so forth. The two possible states of an electronic component define bits, represented by computer systems as 0s and 1s.

The electronic components of digital computer systems recognize two states. A circuit is either open or closed, a magnetic spot is either present or absent, and so on. This two-state, or **binary,** nature of electronic devices is illustrated in Figure HW 1-4. For convenience, think of these binary states as the *0-state* and the *1-state.* Computer people refer to such zeros and ones as **bits,** which is a contraction of the words *bi*nary dig*its.* With their electronic components, computers do all of their processing and communicating by representing programs and data in bit form. Binary, then, is the symbol set that forms the computer's "native tongue."

People, of course, don't speak binary language. You're not likely to go up to a friend and say,

0100100001001001

which translates in one binary coding system as "HI." People communicate with one another in *natural languages,* such as English, Chinese, and Spanish. Most people in your part of the world probably speak English. Also, they write with a 26-character alphabet and count with a number system that uses ten possible digits—0 through 9—rather than just two digits. Computers, however, understand only 0 and 1. So in order for us to interact with a computer,

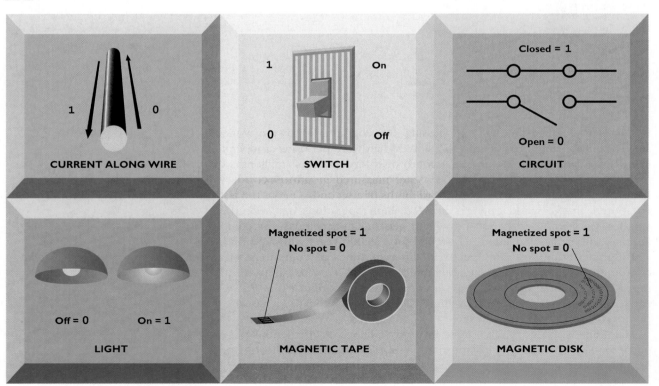

CURRENT ALONG WIRE   SWITCH   CIRCUIT

LIGHT   MAGNETIC TAPE   MAGNETIC DISK

■ **Binary.** The numbering system with two possible states. ■ **Bit.** A binary digit, such as 0 or 1.

our messages to it must be translated into binary form and its messages to us must be translated from binary into a natural language.

The languages through which most people interact with computer systems consist of a wide variety of natural-language symbols. When we type a message, the computer system translates all the natural-language symbols in the message into 0s and 1s. After it completes processing, the computer system translates the 0s and 1s that represent the program's results into natural language. This conversion process is illustrated in Figure HW 1-5.

Computer systems represent programs and data through a variety of binary-based coding schemes. For example, when data and programs are sent to or from the CPU (steps 2 and 4 in Figure HW 1-5), a fixed-length, binary-based code such as ASCII or EBCDIC is often used to represent each character transmitted. (The next subsection covers these two coding systems.)

Once data and programs enter the CPU (step 3 of Figure HW 1-5), they are represented by other types of binary codes. For example, a program instruction about to be executed is represented by a code known as *machine language*. Data, in contrast, may be represented by several different types of binary codes during manipulation by the computer. One such code stores numbers in *true binary representation*. The appendix at the end of this chapter reviews this code, as well as some fundamentals of numbering systems, in more detail. While the binary system is expected to be powering computers

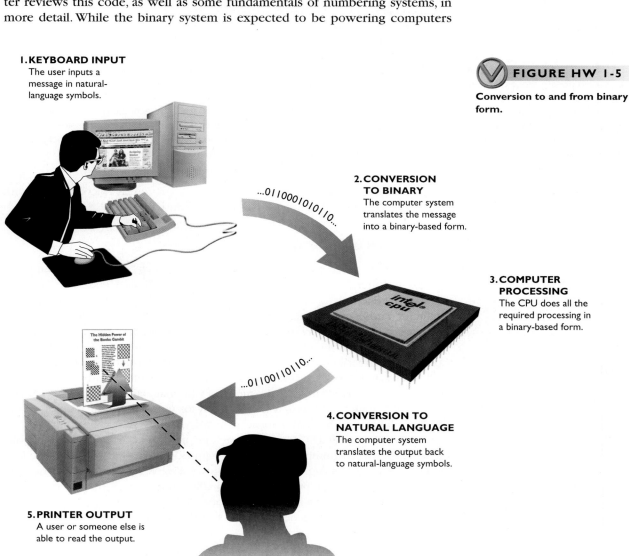

FIGURE HW 1-5

Conversion to and from binary form.

1. KEYBOARD INPUT
The user inputs a message in natural-language symbols.

...011000101011110...

2. CONVERSION TO BINARY
The computer system translates the message into a binary-based form.

3. COMPUTER PROCESSING
The CPU does all the required processing in a binary-based form.

...011001101110...

4. CONVERSION TO NATURAL LANGUAGE
The computer system translates the output back to natural-language symbols.

5. PRINTER OUTPUT
A user or someone else is able to read the output.

HW 1-1

Is Binary Showing Its Age?

Some Changes May Be in the Wind

For over half a century, computers have done their number crunching and storage with two binary digits—0 and 1. But things may be different in the future. Recently, chip giant Intel Corporation has started producing a new memory product called StrataFlash. It uses twice as many symbols as the binary system and therefore can store twice as much in roughly the same space used by a binary digit.

StrataFlash chips use a revolutionary technology that relies on multilevel cells. While binary technology recognizes whether a transistor on a chip is on or off (two states), multilevel cell technology applies a voltage to each transistor so that it can exist in any of four states—0, 1, 2, and 3. The breakthrough effectively doubles the amount of storage currently available in products using conventional components. As multilevel-cell technology is refined to accommodate more than four states, it offers the potential of exponential improvement in storage capability.

Currently, StrataFlash is being used in such battery-powered products as digital cameras, cellular phones, and memory cards for notebook computers. The breakthrough is not likely to have an impact anytime soon on the system boards of conventional com-

StrataFlash chips. Multilevel cell technology can store more data in the space used by a binary digit.

puter systems. Computer and memory chips on such systems currently rely on materials that do not easily accommodate multilevel cells. Furthermore, they require speeds hundreds or even thousands of times faster than multilevel cells can provide.

Yet, we all know how quickly technology changes. While it is speedy and simple, the binary system has been powering computer systems for an abnormally long time. It's been incredibly effective, but its future is anything but guaranteed.

for at least the foreseeable future, researchers are regularly coming up with new ways to store and process data (see Feature HW 1-1).

ASCII AND EBCDIC

As mentioned earlier, when data or programs are sent between the computer and its peripheral equipment, a *fixed-length,* binary-based code is commonly used. A fixed-length code allows communicating devices to tell where one character ends and another begins. Such codes represent *digits, alphabetic characters,* and *special characters* such as the dollar sign ($) and period (.).

Among the most widely used of these codes are **ASCII** (American Standard Code for Information Interchange) and **EBCDIC** (Extended Binary-Coded Decimal Interchange Code). Virtually all microcomputers employ ASCII, developed largely through the efforts of the American National Standards Institute (ANSI). ASCII is also widely adopted as the standard for data communications systems. EBCDIC, developed by IBM, is used primarily on IBM mainframes.

Both ASCII and EBCDIC represent each printable character as a unique combination of a fixed number of bits (see Figure HW 1-6). EBCDIC represents a character with 8 bits. A group of 8 bits allows 256 (2^8) different combinations; therefore, EBCDIC can represent up to 256 characters. This scheme leaves more than enough combinations to account for the 26 uppercase and 26 lowercase characters, the ten decimal digits, and several special characters.

■ **ASCII.** A fixed-length, binary coding system widely used to represent data for computer processing and communications.
■ **EBCDIC.** A fixed-length, binary coding system widely used to represent data on IBM mainframes.

ASCII originally was designed as a 7-bit code that could represent 128 (2^7) characters. Several 8-bit versions of ASCII have also been developed, because computers are designed to handle data in chunks of 8 bits. Many computer systems can accept data in either ASCII or EBCDIC and perform the necessary conversions to their native codes. The 8 bits that represent a character in ASCII or EBCDIC are collectively referred to as a *byte*.

A **byte** represents a single character of data. For this reason, many computer manufacturers define their machines' storage capacities in numbers of bytes. As you may have noticed, computer advertisements are filled with references to kilobytes, megabytes, gigabytes, and terabytes. In this terminology, 1 **kilobyte (KB)** equals a little over 1,000 bytes (1,024, to be precise); 1 **megabyte (MB** or *meg*) equals about 1 million bytes; 1 **gigabyte (GB)** equals about 1 billion bytes; and 1 **terabyte (TB)** equals about 1 trillion bytes.

The typical desktop computer sold today has a memory of about 64 to 128 megabytes and a hard disk that can store several gigabytes. For comparison, one of the fastest supercomputers in the world has a memory of 600 gigabytes and 2 terabytes of hard disk space. With computer storage capacities ever increasing, some vendors of software for large business and scientific applications have started to reach into the *petabyte (PB)* and *exabyte (EB)* ranges with their product offerings. A PB is about 1 quadrillion bytes; an EB about 1 quintillion.

Conversion from natural-language words and numbers to their ASCII (or EBCDIC) equivalents and back again usually takes place within an input or output device. When a user types a message, an encoder chip inside the keyboard usually translates this input into ASCII and sends it as a series of bytes to the CPU. The output that the CPU sends to the display screen or to some

FIGURE HW 1-6

ASCII and EBCDIC. These two common, fixed-length codes represent characters as unique strings of bits.

Character	ASCII Representation	EBCDIC Representation	Character	ASCII Representation	EBCDIC Representation
0	00110000	11110000	I	01001001	11001001
1	00110001	11110001	J	01001010	11010001
2	00110010	11110010	K	01001011	11010010
3	00110011	11110011	L	01001100	11010011
4	00110100	11110100	M	01001101	11010100
5	00110101	11110101	N	01001110	11010101
6	00110110	11110110	O	01001111	11010110
7	00110111	11110111	P	01010000	11010111
8	00111000	11111000	Q	01010001	11011000
9	00111001	11111001	R	01010010	11011001
A	01000001	11000001	S	01010011	11100010
B	01000010	11000010	T	01010100	11100011
C	01000011	11000011	U	01010101	11100100
D	01000100	11000100	V	01010110	11100101
E	01000101	11000101	W	01010111	11100110
F	01000110	11000110	X	01011000	11100111
G	01000111	11000111	Y	01011001	11101000
H	01001000	11001000	Z	01011010	11101001

■ **Byte.** A configuration of 8 bits that represents a single character of data. ■ **Kilobyte (KB).** Approximately 1,000 bytes (1,024, to be exact). ■ **Megabyte (MB).** Approximately 1 million bytes. ■ **Gigabyte (GB).** Approximately 1 billion bytes. ■ **Terabyte (TB).** Approximately 1 trillion bytes.

other output device is also coded in ASCII; the output device—with the aid of a decoder chip—translates this code into understandable words and numbers. Therefore, if the CPU were to send the ASCII message

010010000l001001

to your display device, the word *HI* would appear on your screen.

Computers usually handle data in byte multiples. For instance, a 32-bit computer is built to process data in chunks of 4 bytes; a (faster) 64-bit computer processes data in chunks of 8 bytes. These byte multiples are commonly called *words*. A later subsection of this chapter will look at words in more detail.

The Parity Bit   Suppose you press the *B* key on your computer's keyboard. If the keyboard encoder supports ASCII coding, it will transmit the byte 01000010 to the CPU. Sometimes, however, something happens during transmission and the CPU receives a garbled message. Interference on the line, for example, might cause the sixth bit to change from 0 to 1 so that the CPU receives the message 01000110. Unless something indicated the mistake to the CPU, it would wrongly interpret this byte as the letter *F.*

To enable the CPU to detect such transmission errors, an additional bit position is often appended to EBCDIC and ASCII bytes. This bit, called the **parity bit,** is automatically set to either 0 or 1 to force the sum of the 1 bits in a byte to either an even or an odd number. Computer systems support either even or odd parity. In an *odd-parity system,* the parity bit forces the 1 bits in a byte to add up to an odd number. In an *even-parity system,* it makes them add up to an even number. Figure HW 1-7 shows how the parity bit works for the ASCII representation of the word "HELLO" on an even-parity system.

FIGURE HW 1-7

The parity bit. If a system supports even parity, as shown here, the number of 1 bits in every byte must always be an even number. The parity bit is set to either 0 or 1 in each byte to force an even number of 1 bits.

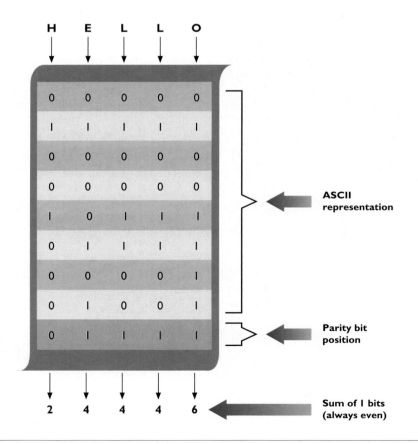

■ **Parity bit.** An extra bit added to the byte representations of characters to ensure there is always either an odd or even number of 1 bits transmitted with every character.

The parity bit is automatically generated by the keyboard's own circuitry. Thus, if you were to type the B character on an even-parity system, the keyboard would send 010000100 up the line to the CPU. If the message then became garbled so that the even-parity computer received 010001100 (an odd number of 1 bits), the CPU would immediately sense the error.

The parity check is not foolproof. For example, if 2 bits are incorrectly transmitted in a single byte, the errors will self-cancel. Such 2-bit errors rarely occur, though.

REPRESENTING NONTEXT DATA

So far, the discussion of data coding schemes has focused on *text* data, which consists of digits, letters, and special symbols such as the period and comma. Graphics, audio, and video data are also represented in binary form inside the computer system.

Graphics Data   Graphics data consist of still pictures. One of the most common methods for storing graphics data is in the form of a bitmap. *Bitmap* graphics assign each of the hundreds of thousands of display-screen dots—called pixels—some combination of 0s and 1s that represents a unique shade or color.

The simplest type of bitmap, a *monochrome* graphic, must differentiate between only a foreground color and a background color. Suppose that these colors are black and white, and the 1 bit represents white, while the 0 bit represents black. The system can then translate any picture into a black-and-white electronic bitmap, as shown in the top part of Figure HW 1-8.

Above monochrome graphics on the scale of realism are *grayscale* images, in which each pixel can be not only pure black or pure white but also any of 254 shades of gray in between. Thus, each dot could appear in any of 256 possible states. You may remember from an earlier discussion that a single byte can represent any of 256 states. So, 11111111 could represent a pure white pixel, 00000000 a pure black one, and any byte in between—such as 11001000 and 00001010—some shade of gray (see the middle part of Figure HW 1-8).

Color coding works similar to grayscale graphics—that is, each pixel is represented by some number of bytes. Computers often handle graphics with 16 colors, 256 colors, or 16,777,216 colors. A 16-color image assigns only one-half byte to each pixel (e.g., 0000, 1111, or a combination in between); a 256-color image assigns 1 byte for each pixel; and a 16.78-million-color (photographic-quality) image requires 3 bytes per pixel (see the bottom part of Figure HW 1-8).

It's sometimes difficult for the eye to tell much of a quality difference between low-end and high-end color images. Sixteen-color images, such as those you can see on the Internet, can actually be quite respectable looking. To save time in transmitting large graphics files over the phone lines, computers often reduce 256-color images to 16 colors by a process called *dithering.* Dithering produces colors not available on the limited palette by coloring neighboring pixels with two available colors that combine to make a new one. For instance, your eye will see a lime color on the screen when several yellow and green pixels are placed close together.

Audio Data   Computers often process audio data—such as the sound of someone speaking or a symphony playing—after digital encoding by a method called *waveform audio.* Waveform audio captures several thousand digital snapshots, called *samples,* of a real-life sound sequence every second. At the end of the sequence, the replayed collection of samples re-creates the voice or music.

Audio CDs sold in music stores, for instance, record sound sampled at a rate of 44,100 times per second. Each 2-byte sample corresponds to a unique

MONOCHROME GRAPHICS

With monochrome graphics, each pixel is represented by a single bit.

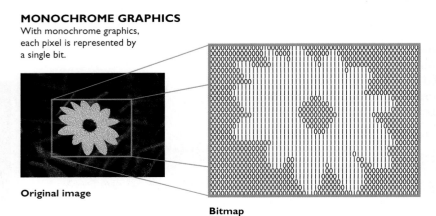

Original image

Bitmap

One sample pixel: 0

Displayed image

GRAYSCALE GRAPHICS

With 256-shade grayscale graphics, each pixel is represented by one byte. Different bytes represent different shades of gray.

One sample pixel:
01101110

One sample pixel:
1110

16-COLOR IMAGE

Each pixel is a half a byte and each half byte represents a different color.

COLOR GRAPHICS

Color images can be 16-color, 256-color, or photographic quality. The more colors used, the better the image quality.

One sample pixel:
01110110

256-COLOR IMAGE

Each pixel is one byte and each byte represents a different color.

One sample pixel:
101001100100110111001011

PHOTOGRAPHIC-QUALITY IMAGE
(16.7 million colors)
Each pixel is three bytes and each three-byte string represents a different color.

FIGURE HW 1-8

Bitmap graphics. Computer systems assign each of the hundreds of thousands of pixels on a display screen some combination of 0s and 1s that represents a unique shade or color.

sound. As you can imagine, when these sounds are played back at a rate of 44,100 per second, the human ear cannot distinguish them, and they collectively sound like real voice or music.

Video Data Films that you see at the movies or on TV are merely moving graphical data. Typically, films are projected at a rate of 30 frames per second;

each frame is a still graphic. The amount of data involved in showing a two-hour feature film can be quite substantial. For instance, just a single 256-color image shown on a 640-by-480-pixel display requires 307,200 bytes. When you multiply that figure by 30 times per second, 60 seconds per minute, and 120 minutes you get more than 66 gigabytes of information. Chapter SW 2 will describe methods for compressing video data so that computers can more readily handle them. In the next chapter we'll look at DVD, a technology for storing feature-length films on CDs.

That the human eye and ear cannot detect small alterations in images and sounds has led to a practice called *digital watermarking*. Digital watermarks protect digital creations, such as art and music, from theft or alteration (see Feature HW 1-2 on page HW 20).

MACHINE LANGUAGE

So far, this section has covered schemes for representing *data* by 0 and 1 bits. Computer circuitry must also store and process *programs*.

Every program contains instructions. Instructions can be used to read the next record in a file, move a block of data from one place to another, summon a new window to the screen, and so on. Before your computer can execute any program instruction, it must convert it into a binary code known as **machine language.** An example of a typical machine-language instruction appears below:

01011000011100000000000100000010

A machine-language instruction may look like a meaningless string of 0s and 1s, but it actually organizes bits into groups that represent specific operations and storage locations. The 32-bit instruction shown here, for instance, moves data between two specific memory locations. Similar instructions transfer data from memory to a register and vice versa, add or subtract values in registers, divide and multiply values, and so on. The set of microcoded machine-language instructions available to a computer is known as that computer's *instruction set.*

The earliest computers, and the first microcomputers, required users to write all their own programs in machine language. Today, of course, hardly anyone uses machine language, and most users don't even write their own programs. Instead, programming specialists rely on *language translators*—special systems programs that automatically convert instructions such as "Read the next record" or "Move the value in location A to location B" into machine language. The translation is so transparent that most people aren't even aware that it is taking place.

Each computer platform has its own machine language. Machine-level code for an IBM microcomputer will be totally foreign to an Apple Macintosh. This fact explains why you must buy a program, such as a word processor or spreadsheet, in a form intended for your specific type of computer system.

THE SYSTEM UNIT

Now that we've covered conceptually how the CPU and memory work, let's consider how they're realized in hardware and how they relate to other devices inside a system unit of a typical microcomputer system.

■ **Machine language.** A binary-based programming language that the computer can execute directly.

Almost all computers sold today follow a modular hardware design. For example, related circuitry is etched onto memory or processor chips, the chips are mounted onto carrier packages that are plugged into boards, and the boards are fitted into slots inside the system unit. The modules combine to make hardware components and define their capabilities.

The **system unit** often consists of at least one CPU chip, specialized processor chips, memory (RAM and ROM) chips, boards on which chips are mounted, ports that provide connections for external devices, a power supply, and internal circuitry to hook everything together (see Figure HW 1-9). Here we'll discuss these hardware elements. System units also often have built-in hard-disk drives and *bays*—open areas into which additional secondary-storage equipment can be mounted. Such devices as a diskette drive, a CD-ROM or DVD drive, a Zip or Jaz drive, a tape drive, and even a second hard-disk drive are among the most common candidates for mounting into empty bays. Disks and tapes will be covered in detail in Chapter HW 2.

The port on an add-in board extends through the back of the system unit's case.

PORTS
Ports located at the back of the system unit enable you to plug in peripherals that work with the add-in boards.

CPU CHIPS

Every microcomputer's system unit contains a specific microprocessor chip as its CPU (see Figure HW 1-10). This chip lies within a carrier package, and the carrier package is mounted onto a special board—called the **system board** or *motherboard*—inside the system unit. This board connects in one way or another to all other components of a microcomputer system and is usually located on the floor of the system unit, as shown in Figure HW 1-9.

Most microcomputer systems made today use CPU chips manufactured by either Intel or Motorola. Chips in the Intel line—such as the 80386, 80486, Pentium, Pentium Pro, Pentium II, Celeron, and Pentium III—appear in microcomputer systems made by IBM, Compaq, Dell, and scores of other makers of PC-compatible systems. Many of the older Intel chips are commonly known by the last three digits of their model numbers. For example, 486 refers to an 80486 chip. Many of the newer Pentium chips are MMX-enabled, meaning they are expressly configured for multimedia applications. In recent years, a number of *clone chips* have appeared on the market—made by companies such as Cyrix and Advanced Micro Devices—providing functionally compatible alternatives to Intel chips.

Chips in the Motorola line—including those in the 68xxx family—are found primarily in Apple Macintosh computers made before 1994. In recent years, Apple, Motorola, and IBM have teamed up to produce the PowerPC chip, which has become the standard CPU on Macintosh computers. This chip employs the RISC-based architecture (explained later in the chapter) that underlies many powerful engineering workstations. The PowerPC chip is smaller in size and generally less expensive than comparable Intel microprocessors. Some models in the PowerPC line are the 601, 603, 604, 620, and 750. Apple's Power Macintosh (or *Power Mac*) is one computer line based on PowerPC chips.

■ **System unit.** The hardware unit that houses the CPU and memory, as well as a number of other devices. ■ **System board.** The main circuit board of the computer to which all computer-system components connect. Also called a *motherboard*.

POWER SUPPLY
The power supply converts standard electrical power into a form the computer can use.

MEMORY (RAM)
Memory temporarily stores data while you are working on them.

SYSTEM BOARD
The system board is the main circuit board of the computer, and all components of the computer system connect to it.

HARD-DISK DRIVE
The hard-disk drive is the principal secondary storage medium.

STORAGE BAYS
Other secondary storage devices usually include a diskette drive and CD-ROM or DVD drive.

ADD-IN BOARDS
Add-in boards enable users to add new peripherals to expand the capabilities of a computer system.

CPU CHIP
The CPU chip does calculations and comparisons and controls other parts of the computer system.

EXPANSION SLOTS
Expansion slots exist so you can mount add-in boards in them.

 **FIGURE HW 1-9**

Inside a system unit. With the cover of a system unit removed, you can see the parts inside.

HW 1-2

A Watermark Runs through It

Embedded Digital Tags Could Foil Computer Thieves

With the advent of computer networks and CDs, copyrighted digital art, music, and movies have become ever more vulnerable to high-tech pirates. Take digital paintings and photographs. Anyone can relatively easily steal someone else's image off of the Internet, incorporate it into another work, and claim the finished product as his or her own.

That's where digital watermarking comes in. The process can randomly alter some pixel settings in an image ever so slightly. While the human eye cannot detect the changes, a computer prepared to read the underlying code can. Thus, the unique watermark pattern can identify the original creator of an image and enable him or her to establish legal claim. Many widely used graphics programs—such as CorelDraw! and Adobe Photoshop—can both embed and detect digital watermarks.

Digital watermarks are not only for computer graphics; they can protect audio data, too. This is important to the music industry, which is concerned that electronic thievery will become ever more rampant as online distribution of music takes off with consumers. Copyrighted music can be downloaded from the Internet as easily as art, then reprocessed and illegally grafted into new creations—advertisements, multimedia presentations, and even "original" music pieces, to name just a few.

With digital watermarking, a recording company protecting its work can encode such identifying information as the song title and artist during the original mastering process for the work. The watermark can be used to ensure that royalty and licensing agreements are upheld whenever decoder computers are monitoring

Digital watermarking. A few changed bits in a digital picture can identify its owner while not altering the image to the naked human eye.

any broadcast of the song, whether on the Internet or on the radio. Any time the song is sold by an authorized retailer, additional information—such as the purchaser's name and the time of the sale—can be added. Thus, anywhere a copy of the music is played, its origins can be traced.

Down the road, it is very possible that digital watermarking will be widely used in the production and distribution of movies. Lawyers for the movie industry and makers of digital versatile disks (DVDs) are jointly examining guidelines for watermarking movie CDs.

The type of CPU chip in a computer's system unit greatly affects what a person can do with the system. Software is optimized to work on a specific chip or chip family, and a program that works on one chip may not function on another unless modified. For instance, software does not transfer easily between Intel and PowerPC chip families, as these families employ somewhat dissimilar design standards. Also, a program designed for a speedy Intel Pentium III chip may not work well, or even at all, on the earlier and far less-capable 80486 chip.

Word Size CPU chips differ in many respects, one of the most important of which is word size. A computer **word** is a group of bits or bytes that a processor can manipulate as a unit. It is a critical concept, because the internal circuitry of virtually every computer system is designed around a certain word size. The Pentium chip, for instance, has an *internal bus* designed for 64-bit words, which means that data move within the CPU chip's microcircuitry in 64-bit chunks. The Pentium's data bus, or main bus, also accommodates 64-bit

---

■ **Word.** A group of bits that a computer system treats as a single unit.

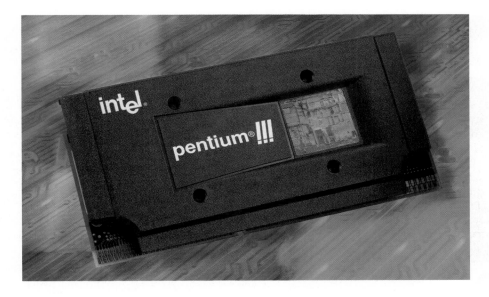

**FIGURE HW 1-10**

CPU chip. Shown here is an Intel Pentium III chip. It comes in a cartridge that also contains cache memory components.

words, meaning that a 64-bit-wide data path leads from the CPU to memory. Usually, a larger word size allows faster processing in a computer system.

Figure HW 1-11 shows changes in processing power for several important CPU-chip families over the years.

Specialized Processor Chips Working alongside the CPU chip in many system units are *specialized processor chips,* such as a numeric coprocessor chip, a graphics accelerator chip, and several DSP chips. These so-called "slave chips" are designed to perform specialized tasks for the CPU. By freeing it from certain processing burdens, they enhance overall system performance—often manyfold.

A *numeric coprocessor* chip helps the CPU with arithmetic. A *graphics accelerator* chip helps the CPU with the computationally intensive chore of creating complex screen displays. *DSP chips*—DSP is for *digital signal processor*—handle such chores as sending data to and from the hard disk as well as controlling the modem and sound card. For instance, a DSP chip is what converts the analog signals coming in over telephone lines into the digital bits the computer can understand, thereby enabling you to see Web pages on your PC.

For links to further information about CPU chips, go to www.harcourtcollege.com/ infosys/parker2000/student/ explore/ and click on Chapter HW I.

RAM

RAM (random access memory)—the computer system's *main memory*— stores the programs and data on which the computer is currently working. Like the microprocessor, a microcomputer system's RAM consists of circuits etched onto silicon-backed chips. These chips are mounted in carrier packages, just as the CPU is, and the packages are often arranged onto boards called *single in-line memory modules,* or *SIMMs.* These units plug into the system board.

Most desktop microcomputer systems sold today have enough RAM to store a few million to several million bytes of data. What's more, many computer systems allow memory expansion (within limits) to remedy insufficient amounts of RAM. RAM is *volatile,* meaning that the contents of memory are lost forever when the computer is shut off.

Ordinary RAM is often referred to as *DRAM* (for *d*ynamic *r*andom *a*ccess *m*emory) in the technical literature. This name refers to its need for regular

■ **Random access memory (RAM).** The computer system's main memory.

PC-COMPATIBLE COMPUTERS (Intel x86 chip family)

Year	Chip	Speeds	Internal Bus	Data Bus
1978	8086	4.77-10 MHz	16 bits	16 bits
1979	8088	4.77-8 MHz	16 bits	8 bits
1982	80286	6-12 MHz	16 bits	16 bits
1985	80386	16-33 MHz	32 bits	16 bits
1989	80486	16-100 MHz	32 bits	32 bits
1993	Pentium	60-233 MHz	64 bits	64 bits
1995	Pentium Pro	150-200 MHz	64 bits	64 bits
1997	Pentium II	233 MHz and higher	64 bits	64 bits
1998	Celeron	266–400 MHz	64 bits	64 bits
1999	Pentium III	450 MHz and higher	64 bits	64 bits

MACINTOSH COMPUTERS (Motorola 68x chip family and PowerPC chip family)

Year	Chip	Speeds	Internal Bus	Data Bus
1982	MC68000	8-12.5 MHz	32 bits	16 bits
1984	MC68020	16.7-33.3 MHz	32 bits	32 bits
1987	MC68030	20-50 MHz	32 bits	32 bits
1989	MC68040	25 MHz	32 bits	32 bits
1994	PowerPC 603	66-80 MHz	32 bits	64 bits
1994	PowerPC 604	120-133 MHz and higher	32 bits	64 bits
1994	PowerPC 620	133 MHz and higher	64 bits	64 bits
1997	PowerPC 750	233 MHz and higher	64 bits	64 bits
1999	PowerPC G4	400 MHz and higher	128 bits	64 bits

FIGURE HW 1-11

CPU-chip families.

recharging as processing takes place. During recharge, DRAM cannot be accessed by the CPU. A faster type of RAM—called *SRAM* (for *s*tatic *r*andom *a*ccess *m*emory)—does not need recharging. However, SRAM chips also offer less capacity at a higher cost than DRAM. Consequently, computer makers use it sparingly.

Cache Memory As you work at a desk, you naturally want to place the file folders or documents you most need within an arm's length. Other useful materials might rest in a nearby stack, somewhat farther away but still within easy reach.

The computer works in a similar way. Although it can access materials in main memory relatively quickly, it can work much faster if it places the most urgently needed materials into storage areas that allow even easier access. Such storage areas are known as **cache memory**. Every time the CPU requests data from RAM, it places a copy of them in cache memory. Thus, cache memory always contains the data most recently accessed by the CPU. Whenever the CPU needs data from RAM, it checks first to see if cache holds the needed input.

Two types of cache memory appear widely in computers. *Internal cache* is a form of cache memory that is built right into the CPU chip. *External (secondary) cache,* on the other hand, resides on SRAM chips located close to the CPU on the system board. Internal cache is the speedier of the two, but it also costs more than external cache and stores less data. As you might guess, the computer looks for data first in internal cache, then in external cache, and then in main memory. The relationship between cache memory and RAM is illustrated in Figure HW 1-12. Internal and external cache are sometimes respectively referred to as Level 1 (L1) and Level 2 (L2) cache.

■ **Cache memory.** A storage area, faster than RAM, where the computer stores data it has most recently accessed.

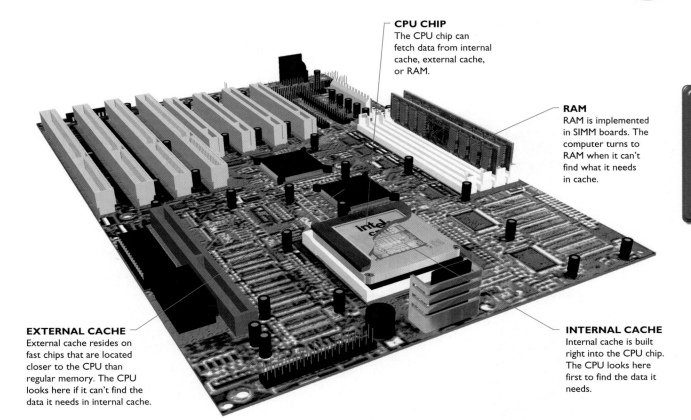

CPU CHIP
The CPU chip can fetch data from internal cache, external cache, or RAM.

RAM
RAM is implemented in SIMM boards. The computer turns to RAM when it can't find what it needs in cache.

EXTERNAL CACHE
External cache resides on fast chips that are located closer to the CPU than regular memory. The CPU looks here if it can't find the data it needs in internal cache.

INTERNAL CACHE
Internal cache is built right into the CPU chip. The CPU looks here first to find the data it needs.

FIGURE HW 1-12

Cache memory. Cache memory speeds processing by staging data in successive, fast-access storage areas.

ROM

Another kind of storage, **ROM** (for **read-only memory**), consists of non-erasable hardware modules that store program instructions. Like RAM, these software-in-hardware modules are mounted into carrier packages that, in turn, are plugged into one or more boards inside the system unit. You can neither write over these ROM programs (the reason they're called *read-only*) nor destroy their contents when you shut off the computer's power. (That is, they're nonvolatile.) The CPU can fetch a program from ROM more quickly than from disk, which is slower and located farther away.

Important pieces of systems software are often stored in ROM. For instance, one of the computer's first activities when you turn on the power is to perform a power-on self-test (POST). The POST program is stored in ROM, and it produces the beeps you hear as your computer system begins operation, or "boots up." POST takes an inventory of system components, checks each component for proper functioning, and initializes system settings.

PORTS

Most system units feature built-in, exterior sockets that enable you to plug in external hardware devices. These sockets are known as **ports** (see Figure HW 1-13).

Serial ports can transmit data only a single bit at a time. However, they require very inexpensive cables, and they can reliably send data over long distances. In contrast, *parallel ports* can transmit data one byte at a time—

For a tutorial on the various ports found on a PC, go to www.harcourtcollege.com/in fosys/parker2000/student/ tutor/ and click on Chapter HW 1.

■ **Read-only memory (ROM).** A software-in-hardware module from which the computer can read data, but to which it cannot write data. ■ **Port.** A socket on the exterior of a computer's system unit into which a peripheral device may be plugged.

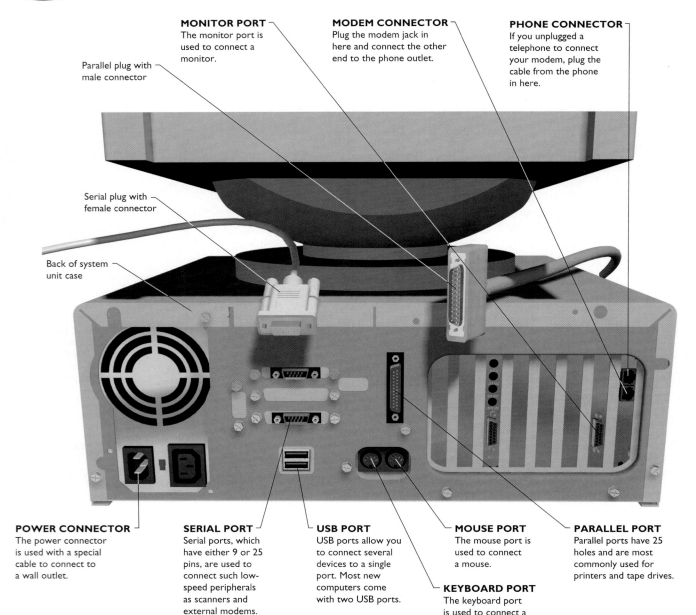

MONITOR PORT
The monitor port is used to connect a monitor.

MODEM CONNECTOR
Plug the modem jack in here and connect the other end to the phone outlet.

PHONE CONNECTOR
If you unplugged a telephone to connect your modem, plug the cable from the phone in here.

Parallel plug with male connector

Serial plug with female connector

Back of system unit case

POWER CONNECTOR
The power connector is used with a special cable to connect to a wall outlet.

SERIAL PORT
Serial ports, which have either 9 or 25 pins, are used to connect such low-speed peripherals as scanners and external modems.

USB PORT
USB ports allow you to connect several devices to a single port. Most new computers come with two USB ports.

MOUSE PORT
The mouse port is used to connect a mouse.

KEYBOARD PORT
The keyboard port is used to connect a keyboard.

PARALLEL PORT
Parallel ports have 25 holes and are most commonly used for printers and tape drives.

FIGURE HW 1-13

Ports.

making data transfers several times faster than those through serial ports—but they require more expensive cables and cannot reliably send data across distances greater than 50 feet. Parallel ports typically connect nearby printers and tape drives to a microcomputer system, whereas serial ports connect such devices as scanners and modems. Computers usually come with dedicated serial ports for keyboards and mice; they connect displays through dedicated parallel ports.

When you need to plug in an I/O device to a desktop system unit that has no built-in port for it, you normally must buy a special *add-in board* that has a port on it. When you install the board, the port typically extends through an opening in the back of the system unit so that you can plug the I/O device into it. For a notebook or handheld computer, a *PC card* provides add-in board functionality for external connections. The next section discusses add-in boards and PC cards in more detail.

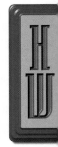

SYSTEM EXPANSION

Not everyone wants the same type of computer system. One person may be satisfied with 64 MB of RAM, while another may want 128 MB or 256 MB in the same model of computer. Similarly, while many people need only average sound capabilities from their computer systems, musicians and music buffs often desire top-of-the-line audio capabilities. To account for the wide variety of needs in the marketplace, most microcomputer-system vendors enable you to customize your system with either add-in boards or PC cards.

Add-In Boards **Add-in boards** expand the functions of desktop computers. These cardlike pieces of electronic circuitry plug into *expansion slots* within the computer's system unit (see Figure HW 1-14). Add-in boards enable users to add specific types of peripheral devices or otherwise expand the capabilities of their computer systems.

Computer systems accept many types of add-in boards. For example, displays usually connect to their own *video-adapter boards,* which both translate CPU instructions into a form the display can use and temporarily store information before it goes to the display screen. Similarly, your computer system can communicate with the Internet or with remote facsimile (fax) machines through a *fax/modem board.* To enhance your system's sound and graphics capabilities, you would respectively acquire a certain type of *sound board* and a certain type of *graphics board.* SIMMs are add-in boards, too. To add more memory to your system, you might plug in a SIMM with the extra storage you need—say, 64 more megabytes.

You can customize your computer by adding the right boards when you purchase it or, as new needs evolve, add boards at a later time. Because adding boards to a functioning computer system can be time consuming—and because many users dislike the idea of removing the covers from their system units and poking around inside—many vendors have drifted toward a plug-and-play strategy to ease the difficulties of installing new devices.

FIGURE HW 1-14

Add-in boards.

	Types of Add-In Boards	
	Board Type	**Purpose**
	Accelerator board	Uses specialized processor chips that speed up overall processing
	Disk controller card	Enables a particular type of disk drive to interface with the microcomputer system
	Video-adapter board	Enables a particular type of display to interface with the microcomputer system
	Emulator board	Allows the microcomputer system to function as a communications terminal
	Fax/modem board	Provides communications and facsimile capabilities
	Graphics adapter board	Enables the computer system to conform to a particular graphics standard
	Memory expansion board	Allows additional RAM to be put into the microcomputer system
	Sound board	Enables users to attach speakers to a microcomputer system
	TV-tuner card	Allows your PC to pick up television signals

■ **Add-in board.** A circuit board that may be inserted into a slot within a desktop computer's system unit to add one or more functions.

**FIGURE HW 1-15**

PC cards. PC cards allow notebook users to enhance their computing environments. The Type III card shown here has a built-in modem and separate ports for a phone jack and local-network connection.

Plug-and-play gives your computer system the ability to detect and automatically configure new hardware devices. Usage of the term sometimes optimistically implies that you can install new hardware simply by plugging a new device into the correct port and that, once the device is connected, the operating system will automatically recognize it the next time you turn on your computer. In reality, however, plug-and-play does not always work as smoothly as vendors or users would like.

PC Cards For many years, users of laptop and notebook computers could not expand their machines very much. Most portable computers lack room inside their system units to accommodate either the standard desktop bus or its big internal boards. Then came PCMCIA. *PCMCIA*—which stands for *Personal Computer Memory Card International Association*—refers to a standard way to connect peripheral devices to notebook computers.

The mainstay of the PCMCIA standard is a credit-card-sized adapter card known as the *PCMCIA card,* or more commonly, the **PC card** (see Figure HW 1-15). PC cards typically plug into slots in the edge of a notebook computer's case. Cards come in three basic thicknesses. A Type I card, the thinnest of the lot, is often used to add memory. A Type II card typically adds networking capabilities or sound. Type III cards, the thickest type, often contain a removable hard drive, or perhaps several communication functions. A notebook computer may provide a multipurpose slot that can accommodate two Type I cards, two Type II cards, or a single Type III card. Because the cards plug in externally to the computers, you can take them out as easily as unplugging a table lamp when you don't need them.

Hardware considerations impose a practical limit on the number of peripheral devices a CPU can handle. Generally, each new device interfaced through a port, an add-in board, or a PC card adds to the CPU's processing burden, possibly degrading system performance.

BUSES

A **bus** is an electronic path within a computer system along which bits are transmitted (see Figure HW 1-16). Earlier we touched on the *internal bus,*

■ **Plug-and-play.** The ability of a computer to detect and configure new hardware components. ■ **PC card.** A small card that fits into a slot on the exterior of a portable computer to provide new functions. ■ **Bus.** An electronic path within a computer system along which bits are transmitted.

which moves data around the CPU chip. Here we'll cover buses that extend off of the CPU chip and show how the CPU connects to RAM as well as to peripheral devices.

Data and Expansion Buses   A computer system's *data bus* links its CPU to RAM. From RAM, an expansion bus extends the data bus to establish links with peripherals. Today's computer systems implement a number of expansion bus standards. The most widely used, *ISA* (for *Industry Standard Architecture*), has been around since 1984. Three newer standards—*EISA* (for *Enhanced Industry Standard Architecture*), IBM's *Micro Channel Architecture,* and Apple's *NuBus*—define wider buses. Just a few years ago, many people in the computer industry figured that these newer bus designs would eclipse the ISA standard, but the large base of ISA boards in use and the recent popularity of local buses—which have diminished the demands placed on the standard expansion bus—have given ISA new life.

Local Buses   Early microcomputers suffered from the drawback that a single expansion bus had to carry all of data and program traffic between RAM and peripheral devices. That arrangement created no problem in the days when monitors displayed text only, and data could creep along at a snail's pace. But times have changed. Graphical user interfaces (GUIs) have come to dominate computer software, and they demand fast speeds to generate their complex screens. Multimedia applications—with their video clips and other

FIGURE HW 1-16

Buses. Buses transport bits and bytes from one computer-system component to another.

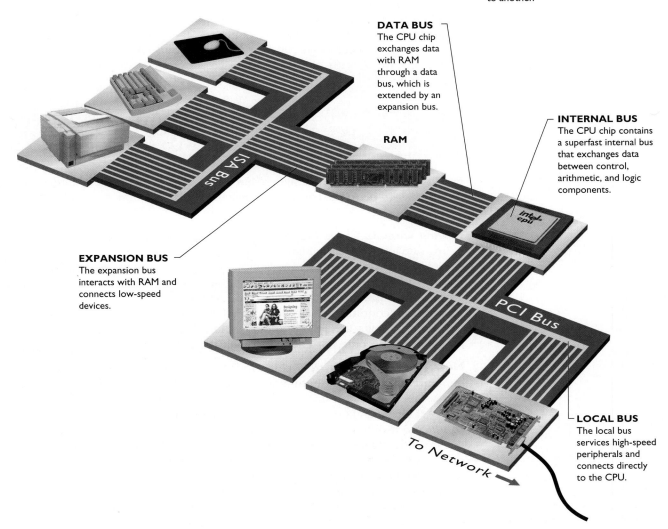

DATA BUS
The CPU chip exchanges data with RAM through a data bus, which is extended by an expansion bus.

RAM

INTERNAL BUS
The CPU chip contains a superfast internal bus that exchanges data between control, arithmetic, and logic components.

EXPANSION BUS
The expansion bus interacts with RAM and connects low-speed devices.

LOCAL BUS
The local bus services high-speed peripherals and connects directly to the CPU.

data-intensive needs—also require lightning quickness. Adding fuel to the fire, many more devices are around these days competing for expansion-bus space: mice, scanners, backup tape devices, sound boards, graphics boards—you name it.

To provide faster system response times, hardware producers have connected peripherals that need extremely fast response times—such as the display, disk drives, and boards connecting to high-speed local networks—to their own bus. This special bus is called a *local bus,* and it links directly to the CPU. All other (slower) devices—such as the system's mouse, modem, and sound board—work off the traditional expansion bus. The local bus carries data in larger chunks and at faster clock speeds than the regular expansion bus. The local bus standard most commonly seen today on desktops is *PCI,* for *Peripheral Component Interconnect.*

The Universal Serial Bus (USB)   The most recent advances in bus architectures have brought the *universal serial bus (USB).* USBs enable up to 128 devices—all of which use the same type of plug—to connect to a computer through a single port. You can link peripherals to a port by chaining them together—say, by plugging the printer into the port and then plugging a modem or a scanner into the printer, and so on.

USB makes devices *hot swappable.* This means that you can add or unplug devices with the system power on. Also, the computer system will immediately recognize the change, so you don't have to reboot in order to have the system acknowledge and work with new devices.

While users can connect their old peripheral devices to a USB-enabled computer, maximum performance requires USB-enabled peripherals. Ideally, a USB-enabled system can produce speeds about 100 times higher than those of systems with older buses. Newer operating systems support the USB standard.

MAKING COMPUTERS SPEEDIER

Over the years, computer designers have developed a number of strategies to achieve faster performance in their machines. This section discusses five of these methods.

Moving Circuits Close Together   As complex as computers seem, all must follow one intuitive natural law: Shorter circuits require less time to move bits. During the past several decades, computer-chip makers have packed circuitry progressively closer together. Today, they fit several million circuits on a single, fingernail-sized chip. This remarkable achievement doesn't mean that chip makers can continue to shrink circuitry without constraint. Unfortunately, when the circuits are in use, they generate heat; circuits placed too close together can become hot enough to melt the chip.

New Materials   Most CPU chips today carry out processing through aluminum circuitry etched onto a silicon backing. Silicon is used for a number of reasons. First, as the main ingredient in beach sand, it is one of the most plentiful elements known. Second, it is lightweight. Third, it is a natural *semiconductor.* It differs from metal, which conducts electricity, and wood, which doesn't; silicon falls somewhere in between. The significance of this is that its properties may be altered to let electricity pass or prevent it from passing. Silicon-backed chips have been in wide use since the 1970s, when manufacturing techniques for microminiature circuitry became widely available.

Today, because designers are quickly reaching limits on the number of circuits that they can pack onto a silicon chip without heat damage, several other

alternative technologies are attracting considerable attention. One of these is *optical processing*, which uses light waves to do the work of a silicon-backed chip's electrons. Optical chips emit less heat and can move data faster; however, the technology is still in its infancy and optical chips are currently limited to few applications. *Biotechnology* and *superconductive materials* are two other alternative approaches. Biotechnology enables circuits to be grown and shaped as tiny molecules, whereas superconductive materials—which resist heat buildup—can be used to pack a chip's circuitry closer together.

Some new approaches to chip design are far less radical. In 1997, for instance, IBM discovered a way to replace the aluminum on silicon chips with copper. Copper is a far better electrical conductor, and it can produce chips with denser circuitry at a lower price (see Figure HW 1-17). Aluminum has been used on chips for more than 30 years; until IBM's breakthrough, copper would bleed into the chip's silicon backing. IBM's new chips are already starting to show up in its mainframe line; Intel has announced it may go with copper chips as soon as 2002.

 **FIGURE HW 1-17**

New materials. Newly introduced copper chips conduct electricity far better than traditional aluminum-circuited ones and require less power. The portion of the fingernail-sized chip pictured here has six circuit layers, and each of the millions of circuits is 500 times thinner than a human hair.

Reduced Instruction Set Computing (RISC) An earlier discussion in this chapter mentioned that each computer has its own *instruction set*. Each instruction of this set corresponds to microcode.

Traditionally, computers have been built under a design principle called *complex instruction set computing (CISC)*. A computer chip with CISC design contains a relatively rich and sophisticated set of instructions by which to process data. Such complexity comes at a cost, however—CISC computers often need several clock cycles to execute each instruction.

Starting in the mid-1970s, processors with limited instruction sets became available. These devices follow a principle called **reduced instruction set computing (RISC).** Experience has shown that computers with only a fraction of the traditional instructions actually process work faster. RISC processing is faster than CISC processing because most of the instructions that a computer processes are relatively simple operations. Thus, computers can maximize speed when they are designed to carry out this large body of simple instructions most rapidly. While RISC computers can execute simple instructions much faster than their CISC counterparts, they run more slowly when doing work that involves executing an unusually large number of complex instructions. RISC chips must rely on software routines to break the latter into sequences of smaller instructions before processing can take place.

Today, RISC devices define performance standards in high-speed, graphically oriented environments—such as engineering and movie making. RISC also represents the resident architecture of the PowerPC chip, and even Intel—a proponent of CISC architecture—is adding RISC components to many of its future CPU chips. One of the downsides to RISC-based computers is that conventional software needs modification to work on them. The Inside the Industry box on page HW 31 features one of the companies that specializes in RISC-based computing—Sun Microsystems.

Pipelining In older microcomputer systems, the CPU had to completely finish processing one microcoded instruction before starting another. Later computer systems, however, practice a method called **pipelining,** which starts a new instruction as soon as the previous one reaches the next stage of the machine cycle. Figure HW 1-18 illustrates this process. Note that by the time

---

■ **Reduced instruction set computer (RISC).** A processor design architecture that incorporates fewer instructions in CPU circuitry than do conventional computer systems. ■ **Pipelining.** A CPU feature designed to begin processing a new instruction as soon as the previous instruction reaches the next stage of the machine cycle.

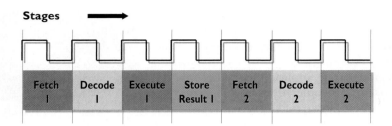

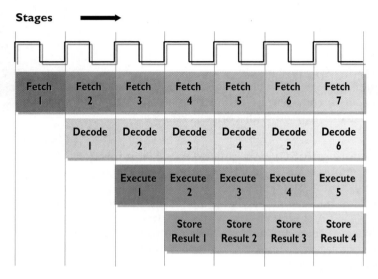

WITHOUT PIPELINING
Without pipelining, an instruction finishes an entire machine cycle before another instruction is started.

WITH PIPELINING
With pipelining, a new instruction is begun when the preceding instruction moves to the next stage of the machine cycle.

"1" means instruction 1, "2" means instruction 2, and so on.

FIGURE HW 1-18

Pipelining. Pipelining streamlines the machine cycle by staging instructions.

a pipelined CPU finishes processing the first instruction in a sequence, the second, third, and fourth instructions have entered the processing "pipeline" and are at various stages of completion. A nonpipelined CPU would not even have begun processing for any of these later instructions. CPUs are commonly built today with multiple pipelines.

Parallel Processing Despite the astounding evolution of computer technology over the past half century, the vast majority of them are still driven by single CPUs. A single CPU executes instructions serially, or one at a time, whether it works exclusively on one program or juggles several concurrently.

In the race to develop tomorrow's ever-faster computer systems, scientists have developed ways for two or more sets of CPU and memory components to perform tasks in parallel. Instead of relying on one processor to perform a lengthy task, a computer system using **parallel processing** assigns portions of the problem to several CPUs operating simultaneously (see Figure HW 1-19).

The marketplace offers examples of two principal approaches to parallel-processing computer systems. One common approach that began several years ago is represented by the Cray-2, a supercomputer that carries a price tag of several million dollars. This computer's parallel design philosophy hooks up a small number of expensive, state-of-the-art CPUs. The Cray-2 uses four such processors, all of which carry out both parallel and serial processing.

The second method of parallel processing involves building computers from hundreds or thousands of relatively inexpensive, off-the-shelf microprocessors. Such computers are known as *massively parallel processors (MPPs)*. The Cray T3E supercomputer—which uses 256 450-MHz microprocessors—is an example of such a machine. Today's trend emphasizes MPP

■ **Parallel processing.** A computing system in which two or more CPUs share work, simultaneously processing separate parts of it.

The Mistake That Launched Sun Microsystems

One of the largest producers of workstations based on RISC microprocessors, and also the company that created the Java programming language, is Sun Microsystems. Like a few other billion-dollar giants in the computer industry, Sun got its start because of mistakes made by other companies.

Xerox made the first mistake. Several years ago, the Advanced Research Projects Agency (ARPA) of the U.S. Department of Defense wanted to buy a standard workstation for its employees. ARPA initially went to Xerox, but that company's price on its newly developed Alto workstation was too high even for the government. ARPA's search led next to nearby Stanford University, where it saw an attractive, generic workstation called *S.U.N.* (for *Stanford University Network*).

Stanford University is not a commercial enterprise, so the designer of the S.U.N., graduate student Andy Bechtolsheim, had to approach several private companies himself in order to get the product manufactured. For one reason or another, all of the firms he contacted turned down the offer. One was IBM. According to legend, Bechtolsheim, hearing about IBM's formal standards for dress and behavior, made his presentation wearing a tuxedo borrowed from Stanford's drama department along with white tennis shoes. When IBM balked at the deal, Bechtolsheim finally formed his own company, Sun Microsystems, in partnership with several other graduate students. One of those students was Scott McNealy, the company's current president.

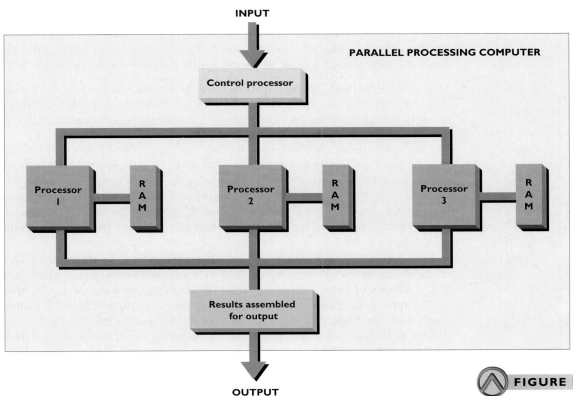

INPUT

PARALLEL PROCESSING COMPUTER

Control processor

Processor 1 — RAM

Processor 2 — RAM

Processor 3 — RAM

Results assembled for output

OUTPUT

FIGURE HW 1-19

Parallel processing. A computer system using parallel processing divides up a computing problem and assigns portions of it to several processors operating simultaneously.

and the possibilities it provides for scalable design; manufacturers can use the same chips in all sizes of computers and make any computer system more powerful at any time simply by adding more chips to it.

SUMMARY AND KEY TERMS

Go to the Online Glossary at www.harcourtcollege.com/infosys/parker2000/ student/ to review key terms.

In Chapter HW 1 we flipped the lid off of a typical microcomputer's system unit and examined the functions of the parts inside.

How the CPU Works   When we talk about computers today, most of us are referring to digital computers. **Digital computers** are devices that *count.*

A digital computer's CPU has two major sections. The **arithmetic/logic unit (ALU)** performs arithmetic and logical operations on data. The **control unit** directs the flow of electronic traffic between memory and the ALU and also between the CPU and input and output devices. Both of these units work closely with memory to carry out processing tasks inside the system unit.

Memory—also called **primary storage**—holds the programs and data that pass on to the CPU, the results of intermediate processing, and output ready for transmission to secondary storage or an output device. **Registers** are high-speed staging areas within the CPU that hold program instructions and data immediately before processing.

The CPU processes a single, machine-level instruction in a sequence called a **machine cycle.** Each machine-language instruction is broken down into subinstructions called **microcode,** and each piece of microcode corresponds directly to a set of the computer's processing circuits. The computer system has a built-in **system clock** that synchronizes the processing of microcode.

A machine cycle has two parts. During the **I-cycle** (instruction cycle), the control unit fetches and examines an instruction; during the **E-cycle** (execution cycle), the ALU executes the instruction under control-unit supervision. Processing times on computer hardware generally are measured in **milliseconds** (thousandths of a second), **microseconds** (millionths of a second), **nanoseconds** (billionths of a second), or **picoseconds** (trillionths of a second).

Data and Program Representation   The electronic components of a digital computer work in a two-state, or **binary,** fashion. It is convenient to think of these binary states as the 0 state and the 1 state. Computer people refer to such 0s and 1s as **bits.**

Computers represent and process text data according to several binary-based codes. Two popular coding schemes are **ASCII** and **EBCDIC.** These systems assign fixed-length codes to represent single characters of data—a digit, alphabetic character, or special symbol—as strings of seven or eight bits. Each string of bits is called a **byte.** Computer systems allow for an additional bit position, called a **parity bit,** in each byte to reveal transmission errors.

The storage capacity of computers often is expressed in **kilobytes (KB),** or thousands of bytes; **megabytes (MB** or *meg),* millions of bytes; **gigabytes (GB),** billions of bytes; and **terabytes (TB),** trillions of bytes.

The binary system can represent not only text but also graphics, audio, and video data. **Machine language** is the binary-based code through which computers represent program instructions. A program must be translated into machine language before the computer can execute it.

The System Unit   Almost all computer systems sold today combine modular hardware components to create functional units. For instance, related circuitry is etched onto processor chips or memory chips, and the chips are mounted onto carrier packages. These carriers are then fitted into boards, and the boards are positioned in slots inside the **system unit.**

Every microcomputer's system unit contains a specific microprocessor chip

as its CPU. Within its carrier package, this chip is mounted onto a special board, called the **system board**, that fits inside the system unit. CPU chips differ in many respects; one difference is word size. A computer **word** is a group of bits or bytes that the processor can manipulate as a unit. A larger word size usually implies a more powerful processor.

Working alongside the CPU chip in many system units are specialized processor chips such as *numeric coprocessors* and *graphics coprocessors*.

The main memory chips on a microcomputer system are commonly referred to as **RAM,** for **random access memory.** Every time the CPU accesses data from RAM, it places a copy of them in a special place known as **cache memory,** from which it can retrieve them more quickly than from RAM. Memory chips that store nonerasable programs comprise the computer's **ROM,** for **read-only memory.**

Many system units have external input/output **ports** through which peripheral devices connect to the computer. Also, many desktop system units contain limited numbers of internal expansion slots, into which users can mount **add-in boards.** The **plug-and-play** standard provides a computer with the ability to detect and configure new hardware as a user adds it to the system. Owners of notebook computers normally expand their systems by adding **PC cards**.

The CPU connects to RAM, ROM, and peripherals over circuitry called a **bus.** The most widely used *expansion bus* architecture is ISA, and the most widely used local bus architecture is PCI.

Making Computers Speedier   Over the years, computer designers have developed a number of strategies to make their machines work faster. The chapter text discussed five of these: packing circuits close together, building components out of new materials, **reduced instruction set computing (RISC), pipelining** instructions, and **parallel processing.**

EXERCISES

1. Match each term with the description that fits best.
   a. ALU
   b. binary
   c. bit
   d. EBCDIC
   e. ASCII
   f. word
   g. PC card
   h. parity bit

   _____ The numbering system that consists of 0s and 1s
   _____ The fixed-length code most often associated with IBM mainframes
   _____ A device that provides extra capability for a laptop computer
   _____ A fixed-length code developed by the American National Standards Institute
   _____ Used to check for transmission errors
   _____ The section of the CPU that performs computations
   _____ A group of bits or bytes that a processor can manipulate as a unit
   _____ A binary digit

2. What does each of the following acronyms stand for?
   a. RAM _____
   b. ROM _____
   c. USB _____
   d. RISC _____
   e. SIMM _____
   f. DSP _____

3. Answer the following questions about byte representations of data:
   a. Given the following ASCII character representations and the specified parity settings, indicate whether a 0 or 1 should be added to the end of the character:

BYTE REPRESENTATION	PARITY	0 OR 1?
00110101	even	_____
01011010	odd	_____
01001001	odd	_____
00110000	odd	_____
01000001	even	_____

   b. What five characters do the bytes in the table above represent?
   c. You receive the following stream of bits in ASCII. Is odd or even parity in use? What does the message say?

   0101011101001111010101111

4. Calculate the following speeds and times:
   a. How many milliseconds are in a minute?
   b. How much faster is 5 microseconds than 200 milliseconds?

5. Fill in the blanks:
   a. A(n) _____ computer is one that counts.
   b. Most CPU chips today consist of metallic circuitry etched onto a(n) _____ backing.
   c. Through a method called _____, as soon as an instruction reaches the next stage of the machine cycle, the processor begins a new instruction.
   d. Processing shared by two or more computers working together is known as _____ processing.
   e. Two _____ bus standards are PCI and VESA.
   f. The term _____ refers to the ability of the computer system to automatically recognize and configure newly added hardware.
   g. _____ language is a binary-based dialect that the computer can execute directly.
   h. Another name for the system unit's motherboard is the _____.
   i. _____ memory is a storage area, faster than RAM, where the computer system stores data it has most recently accessed.
   j. A(n) _____ is a socket on the back of a computer's system unit into which a peripheral device may be plugged.

6. Define the following terms:
   a. PC card
   b. External cache memory
   c. POST
   d. Parallel processing
   e. Nonvolatile
   f. Expansion slots
   g. System clock

7. Identify each of the following statements as true or false:

   _____ Logical computer operations include such things as addition, subtraction, multiplication, and division.
   _____ A millisecond is one one-millionth of a second.
   _____ The computer's machine cycle consists of two parts: the I-cycle and the E-cycle.
   _____ "Megahertz" refers to a measure of a computer's speed.

_____ The 8 bits that represent a character in ASCII or EBCDIC are collectively referred to as a megabyte.

_____ CISC refers to a processor design architecture that incorporates fewer instructions in CPU circuitry than conventional computer systems.

_____ "MMX enabled" specifically refers to RAM chips that are especially configured for multimedia computing.

_____ A word is a group of bits that a computer system treats as a single unit.

_____ PC Cards are devices designed to be fit into expansion slots within a desktop PC's system unit.

_____ A computer's expansion bus extends its data bus.

8. Name at least eight devices located under the cover of a microcomputer's system unit. What functions do these devices perform?

9. What roles do the hardware units listed below play in a computer system?
   a. Control unit
   b. ROM
   c. Main memory
   d. Registers
   e. Internal cache memory

10. From smallest to largest, place the following terms in the correct order: petabyte, kilobyte, gigabyte, exabyte, byte, terabyte, bit, megabyte.

11. DRAM and SRAM, although related, differ in a number of respects.
   a. What is the technical difference between the two?
   b. Which is used for external cache memory?
   c. Which gives faster access to data?
   d. Which is more expensive?
   e. Which provides more storage capacity?

12. Match the PC component shown in each of the following pictures with the appropriate term.
   _____ RAM SIMM board
   _____ Plug for a parallel port
   _____ PC card
   _____ Plug for a serial port
   _____ Add-in board

a.

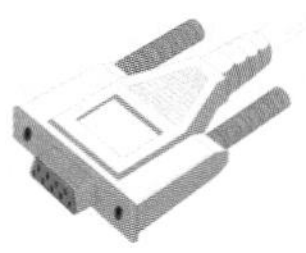

b.

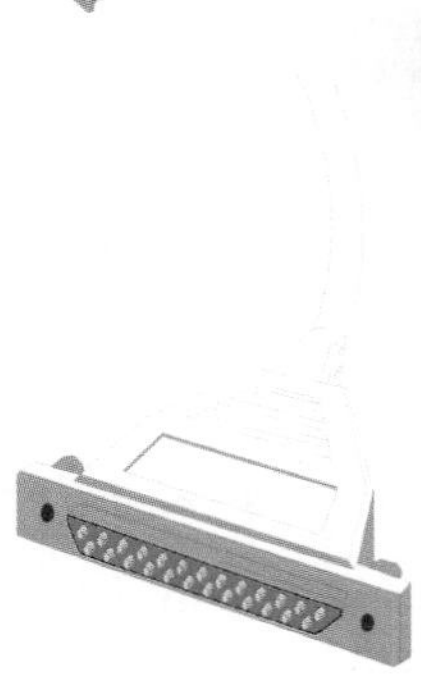

c.

d.

e.

PROJECTS

1. **Intel Corp.** Intel is the world's largest producer of CPU chips and also the leading chip vendor for PC-compatible computers.

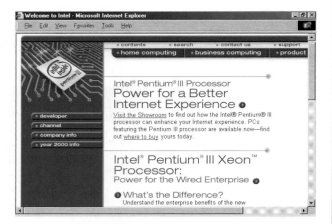

Consult either computer periodicals in a library available to you or Intel's Web site (www.intel.com) to answer the following questions:

a. What is the name of the fastest Intel CPU chip currently being sold with PCs?

b. At what speed does this chip run? State the answer in MHz.

c. What is the size of this chip's internal cache?

d. What products besides CPU chips does Intel produce?

2. **PC Makers** Virtually all of the leading PC makers maintain Web sites and regularly run advertisements in computer journals. For any three of the PC makers listed in the following figure, answer the questions that follow. Feel free to do this project using either Web-based information or information found in computer journals. You can do

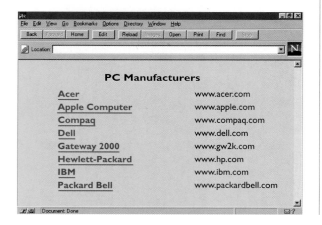

the project in groups of three students each, if your instructor permits.

a. What is the model name or number of a current desktop computer sold by each vendor? A current notebook computer?

b. What top processing speeds do these computers achieve? Give your answer in MHz.

c. What type of CPU powers each of these computers—for instance, a Pentium III or PowerPC 750?

d. How many megabytes of RAM does each computer include as a maximum?

e. How large is the hard disk (measured in bytes)?

3. **Desktop Mainframes** The chapter mentions the continuing quest for faster computers. What difference might ordinary users experience if their microcomputers could match the power of today's supercomputers—processing, say, hundreds or thousands of times faster than current microcomputers? Write a small paper, not to exceed three pages, with your response.

4. **New Key Terms** A textbook chapter of this sort cannot possibly cover every important technology or term regarding the technical aspects of how computers work. Several important terms are listed next that are not covered in the chapter. Through library or Internet research, determine the meanings of any three of these terms, and write out a one-to-three sentence explanation describing each of the three terms in your own words.

a. VRAM   d. CMOS RAM

b. Flash memory   e. Fault tolerance

c. BIOS

Hint: If you are going to research this topic through the Internet, you might want to consult some available online computer dictionaries and glossaries. For starters, access a search site such as Yahoo! or Excite and select the hyperlink for reference materials. By making successive choices, you should easily access a computing dictionary.

5. Soapbox Department Comment on this statement: "Computers are now so easy to work with that it's no longer necessary for the average user to know any of the technical details about how they work." In making your comments, be sure to state how much technical knowledge about computers you think the average student needs.

6. Inspecting a System Unit Open up a system unit and look at the parts inside. Make one or two diagrams labeling components that you recognize. Be sure to include the following components: CPU chip, RAM SIMMs, expansion slots, add-in boards, hard-disk drive, diskette drive(s), CD drive (if present), power supply, and ports.

7. Microprocessor History Microprocessors improved dramatically between the 2,300-transistor Intel 4004 chip introduced in 1971 and the multi-million-transistor Intel Pentium III that came out in 1999. For this project, determine the number of transistors, or circuit elements, in use on each of the ten Intel chips named in Figure HW 1-11.

Hint: If you are going to research this topic through the Internet, you might want to start with the Intel Web site at www.intel.com

8. Future Chips Companies such as Intel and Motorola often announce to the press plans for their future CPU chips well before these chips are available to the public. Using articles from such news-oriented computer periodicals as *Computerworld, PC Week, InfoWeek,* or *MacWeek,* write a paper (one or two pages) about a next-generation CPU chip—say, the one that either Intel or Motorola has on the drawing board to replace its current top-of-the-line model. Describe in the paper how much faster and more capable the newer chip is expected to be as compared to the current model.

9. Extra Memory Virtually all desktop and notebook computers made today let you expand memory within certain limits. Pick out a desktop or notebook model and answer the following questions:

a. What is the name of the computer? How much memory does it come with?

b. How much would you have to spend to expand the base level of memory sold with the computer? Make sure that your answer includes the memory increments you could choose as well as the costs of those increments—for example, each 32 MB expansion often costs less than $100.

c. Up to what maximum can you expand the memory?

 10. Audio Data on the Web Several Web sites cater to users who want their Web pages talking or playing music. Three major categories of audio sites are those that let you download audio software for your Web browser; those that let you listen to radio stations over the Internet; and those that let you download such audio products as books, courses, and music singles. For this project, pick one of these three categories and write a paper (3 to 5 pages) describing specific audio resources that Web sites in the category collectively provide. The accompanying figure lists several sites, any of which might be a good starting point for your research.

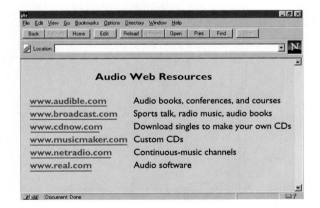

ONLINE REVIEW

 Go to the Online Review at www.harcourtcollege.com/infosys/parker2000/ student/ to test your understanding of this chapter's concepts.

APPENDIX

NUMBERING SYSTEMS

LEARNING OBJECTIVES

After completing this chapter you will be able to:

1. Describe how the decimal, binary, and hexadecimal numbering systems work.

2. Convert values from one numbering system to another.

3. Add and subtract within the binary and hexadecimal numbering systems.

In Chapter HW 1, you learned that fixed-length coding schemes such as ASCII and EBCDIC are often used to represent numbers, letters of the alphabet, and special characters. Although these codes are handy for storing data and transporting them around a computer system, the codes are not designed to do arithmetic operations. For this task, numbers must be stored in a true-binary form that can be manipulated quickly by the computer.

This appendix covers several fundamental characteristics of numbering systems. The two primary systems discussed are the decimal numbering system (used by people) and the binary numbering system (used by computers). Also discussed is the hexadecimal numbering system, which is a shorthand way of representing long strings of binary numbers so that they are more understandable to people. The appendix also covers conversions between numbering systems and principles of computer arithmetic. Instructions for using the Microsoft Windows scientific calculator to perform conversions are also provided, in Figure HW 1-28 on page HW 46.

WHAT IS A NUMBERING SYSTEM?

A *numbering system* is a way of representing numbers. The system we most commonly use is called the decimal, or base 10, system. (The word *decimal* comes from the Latin word for *ten.*) It is called base *10* because it uses ten symbols—the digits 0, 1, 2, 3, 4, 5, 6, 7, 8, and 9—to represent all possible numbers. Numbers greater than nine, such as 21 and 683, are represented by combinations of these symbols.

Because we are so familiar with the decimal system, it may never have occurred to most of us that we could represent numbers in any other way. However, nothing says that a numbering system has to have ten possible symbols. Many other numbers would do as a base.

We saw in Chapter HW 1 that the *binary,* or *base 2,* system is used extensively by computers to represent numbers and other characters. Computer systems can perform computations and transmit data thousands of times faster in binary form than they can using decimal representations. Thus, it's important for anyone studying computers to know how the binary system works. Anyone contemplating a professional career in computers should also understand the hexadecimal (base 16) system. Before we examine some of the numbering systems used in computing—and learn how to convert numbers from one system into another—let's look more closely at the decimal numbering system. Insight into how the decimal system works will help us understand more about the other numbering systems.

THE DECIMAL NUMBERING SYSTEM

All numbering systems, including the decimal system with which people work in everyday life, represent numbers as combinations of ordered symbols. As stated earlier, the **decimal** (or base 10) system has ten acceptable symbols—

■ **Decimal.** A numbering system with ten symbols—0, 1, 2, 3, 4, 5, 6, 7, 8, and 9.

Consider the decimal number

7216

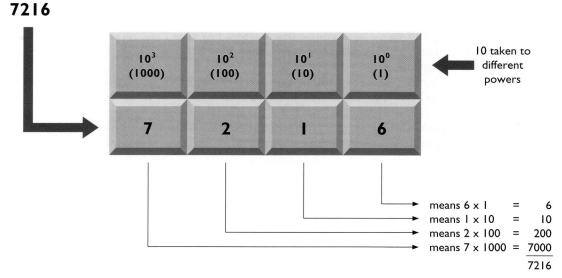

10 taken to different powers

means 6 x 1 = 6
means 1 x 10 = 10
means 2 x 100 = 200
means 7 x 1000 = 7000
7216

FIGURE HW 1-20

How the decimal (base 10) system works. Each digit in a decimal number represents 10 taken to a different power.

the digits 0, 1, 2, ..., 9. The positioning of the symbols in a decimal number is important. For example, 891 is a different number than 918 (with the same symbols occupying different positions).

The position of each symbol in any decimal number represents the number 10 (the base number) raised to a power, or exponent, determined by that position. Going from right to left, the first position represents 10^0, or 1; the second position represents 10^1, or 10; the third position represents 10^2, or 100; and so forth. Thus, as Figure HW 1-20 shows, a decimal number such as 7,216 is understood as $7 \times 10^3 + 2 \times 10^2 + 1 \times 10^1 + 6 \times 10^0$.

THE BINARY NUMBERING SYSTEM

The **binary**, or base 2, system works in a manner similar to the decimal system. One major difference is that the binary system has only two symbols—0 and 1—instead of ten. A second major difference is that the position of each digit in a binary number represents the number 2 (the base number) raised to an exponent based on that position. Thus, the binary number 11100 represents

$$1 \times 2^4 + 1 \times 2^3 + 1 \times 2^2 + 0 \times 2^1 + 0 \times 2^0$$

which, translated into the decimal system, is 28. Another example of a binary-to-decimal conversion is provided in Figure HW 1-21.

Converting in the reverse direction—from decimal to binary—is also rather easy. A popular approach for doing this is the remainder method. This procedure employs successive divisions by the base number of the system to which we are converting. Use of the remainder method to convert a decimal to a binary number is illustrated in Figure HW 1-22.

To avoid confusion between different number bases, it is common to use the base as a subscript. So, referring to Figures HW 1-21 and HW 1-22, for example, we could write

$$89_{10} = 1011001_2$$

■ **Binary.** A numbering system with two possible states—0 and 1.

Consider the
binary number
1011001

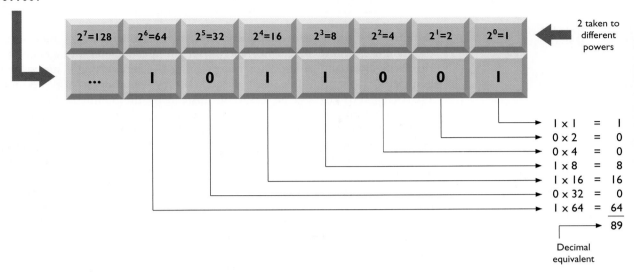

2 taken to
different
powers

1 × 1	= 1
0 × 2	= 0
0 × 4	= 0
1 × 8	= 8
1 × 16	= 16
0 × 32	= 0
1 × 64	= 64
	89

Decimal
equivalent

In addition, when we are using numbering systems other than the decimal system, it is customary to pronounce each symbol individually. For example, 101 is pronounced "one-zero-one" rather than "one hundred one." This convention also applies to other nondecimal systems.

The binary system described here is sometimes referred to as *true-binary representation*. True-binary representation does not designate a fixed number of bits, as do ASCII and EBCDIC, nor is it used to represent letters or special characters.

FIGURE HW 1-21

Binary-to-decimal conversion. To convert any binary number to its decimal counterpart, take the rightmost digit and multiply it by 2^0 (or 1), take the next digit to the left and multiply it by 2^1 (or 2), and so on, as illustrated here. Then add up all the products so formed.

Consider the
decimal number
89

Dividends   Remainders

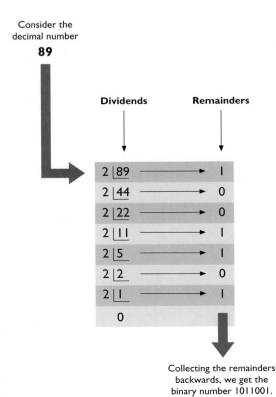

Collecting the remainders
backwards, we get the
binary number 1011001.

FIGURE HW 1-22

Decimal-to-binary conversion using the remainder method. This approach starts by using the decimal number to be converted (89) as the initial dividend. Each successive dividend is the quotient of the previous division. Keep dividing until you reach a zero quotient, whereupon the converted number is formed by the remainders taken in reverse order.

THE HEXADECIMAL NUMBERING SYSTEM

Computers often output diagnostic and memory-management messages to programmers and technically oriented users in hexadecimal (or *hex*) notation. Hex is a shorthand method for representing the binary digits stored in the computer system. Because large binary numbers—for example, 1101010001001101_2—can easily be misread by programmers, binary digits are grouped into units of four that, in turn, are represented by other symbols.

Hexadecimal means base 16, implying that there are 16 different symbols in this numbering system. With only 10 possible digits, hex uses letters instead of numbers for the extra 6 symbols. The 16 hexadecimal symbols and their decimal and binary counterparts are shown in Figure HW 1-23.

Hexadecimal is not itself a code that the computer uses to perform computations or to communicate with other machines. This numbering system does, however, have a special relationship to the 8-bit bytes of ASCII and EBCDIC that makes it ideal for displaying messages quickly. As you can see in Figure HW 1-23, each hex character has a 4-binary-bit counterpart, so any combination of 8 bits can be represented by exactly 2 hexadecimal characters. Thus, the letter A (represented in EBCDIC by 11000001) has a hex representation of C1.

Let's look at an example to see how to convert from hex to decimal. Suppose you receive the following message on your display screen:

PROGRAM LOADED AT LOCATION 4F6A

This message tells you the precise location in memory of the first byte in your program. To determine the decimal equivalent of a hexadecimal number such as 4F6A, you can use a procedure similar to the binary-to-decimal conversion shown in Figure HW 1-21 (refer to Figure HW 1-24).

FIGURE HW 1-23

Hexadecimal characters and their decimal and binary equivalents.

Hexadecimal Character	Decimal Equivalent	Binary Equivalent
0	0	0000
1	1	0001
2	2	0010
3	3	0011
4	4	0100
5	5	0101
6	6	0110
7	7	0111
8	8	1000
9	9	1001
A	10	1010
B	11	1011
C	12	1100
D	13	1101
E	14	1110
F	15	1111

■ **Hexadecimal.** Pertaining to the numbering system with 16 symbols: 0, 1, 2, 3, 4, 5, 6, 7, 8, 9, A, B, C, D, E, and F.

Consider the
hexadecimal number

4F6A

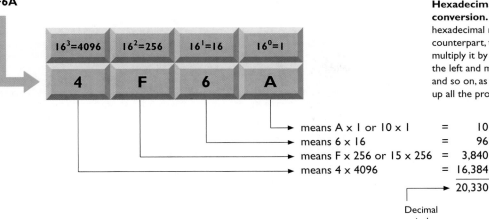

FIGURE HW 1-24

Hexadecimal-to-decimal conversion. To convert any hexadecimal number to its decimal counterpart, take the rightmost digit and multiply it by 16^0 (or 1), the next digit to the left and multiply it by 16^1 (or 16) and so on, as illustrated here. Then add up all the products so formed.

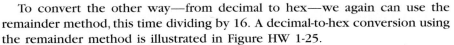

means A x 1 or 10 x 1	=	10
means 6 x 16	=	96
means F x 256 or 15 x 256	=	3,840
means 4 x 4096	=	16,384
		20,330

Decimal
equivalent

To convert the other way—from decimal to hex—we again can use the remainder method, this time dividing by 16. A decimal-to-hex conversion using the remainder method is illustrated in Figure HW 1-25.

To convert from base 16 to base 2, we convert each hex digit separately to 4 binary digits (using the table in Figure HW 1-23). For example, to convert F6A9 to base 2, we get

$$\begin{array}{cccc} F & 6 & A & 9 \\ 1111 & 0110 & 1010 & 1001 \end{array}$$

or 1111011010101001_2. To convert from base 2 to base 16, we go through the reverse process. If the number of digits in the binary number is not divisible by 4, we add leading zeros to the binary number to force an even division. For example, to convert 1101101010011_2 to base 16, we get

$$\begin{array}{cccc} 0001 & 1011 & 0101 & 0011 \\ 1 & B & 5 & 3 \end{array}$$

or $1B53_{16}$. Note that three leading zeros were added to make this conversion. A table summarizing all of the conversions covered in this appendix is provided in Figure HW 1-26.

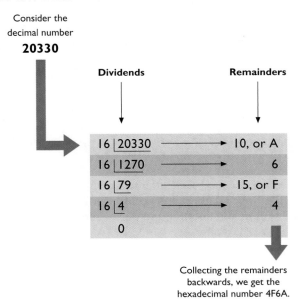

FIGURE HW 1-25

Decimal-to-hexadecimal conversion using the remainder method. To convert $20,330_{10}$ to a hexadecimal number, start successive divisions by 16 using 20,330 as the initial dividend. Each successive dividend is the quotient of the previous division. As in Figure HW 1-22, divide until you reach a zero quotient and form the converted number by taking the remainders in reverse order.

FIGURE HW 1-26

Summary of conversions.

From Base	To Base		
	2	**10**	**16**
2		Starting at right-most digit, multiply binary digits by 2^0, 2^1, 2^2, etc., respectively. Then add products.	Starting at right-most digit, convert each group of four binary digits to a hex digit.
10	Divide repeatedly by 2; then collect remainders in reverse order.		Divide repeatedly by 16; then collect remainders in reverse order.
16	Convert each hex digit to four binary digits.	Starting at rightmost digit, multiply hex digits by 16^0, 16^1, 16^2, etc., respectively. Then add products.	

COMPUTER ARITHMETIC

To most people, decimal arithmetic is second nature. Addition and subtraction have been part of Western education since kindergarten or first grade. Addition and subtraction using binary and hexadecimal numbers are not much harder than the same operations with decimal numbers. Practically the only difference is in the number of symbols used in each system.

Figure HW 1-27 provides an example of addition and subtraction with decimal, binary, and hexadecimal numbers. Note that with binary and hexadecimal, as in decimal arithmetic, you carry to and borrow from adjacent positions as you move from right to left. Instead of carrying or borrowing 10, however—as you would in the decimal system—you carry or borrow 2 (binary) or 16 (hexadecimal).

FIGURE HW 1-27

Adding and subtracting with the decimal, binary, and hexadecimal numbering systems.

		Decimal	Binary	Hexadecimal
Addition		142	10001110	8E
		+47	+101111	+2F
		189	10111101	BD
Subtraction		142	10001110	8E
		−47	−101111	−2F
		95	1011111	5F

SUMMARY AND KEY TERMS

This appendix covers several fundamentals of numbering systems, including examples showing how numbering systems work, converting values between one numbering system and another, and performing simple types of computer arithmetic.

Numbering Systems A *numbering system* is a way of representing numbers.

The Decimal Numbering System The numbering system that people most commonly use is called the **decimal,** or base 10, system. It is called base 10 because it uses ten symbols—the digits 0, 1, 2, 3, 4, 5, 6, 7, 8, and 9—to

represent all possible numbers. The position of each symbol in any decimal number represents the number 10 (the base number) raised to a power, or exponent, determined by that position.

Because we are so familiar with the decimal system, it may never have occurred to many of us that we could represent numbers in any other way. However, nothing says that a numbering system has to have ten possible symbols. Many other numbers would do as a base.

The Binary Numbering System   The **binary**, or base 2, system works in a manner similar to the decimal system. One major difference is that the binary system has only two symbols—0 and 1—instead of ten. A second major difference is that the position of each digit in a binary number represents the number 2 (the base number) raised to an exponent determined by that position.

The binary system described in this appendix is sometimes referred to as *true-binary representation*. True-binary representation does not set a fixed number of bits, as do ASCII and EBCDIC, nor is it used to represent letters or special characters.

The Hexadecimal Numbering System   Because large binary numbers can easily be misread by programmers, binary digits often are grouped and represented by other symbols. The **hexadecimal**, or base 16, system represents groups of four binary digits. With only ten possible digits, the letters A–F are used instead of numbers for the extra six symbols. The position of each digit in a hexadecimal number represents the number 16 raised to an exponent determined by that position.

Computer Arithmetic   It is a relatively straightforward process to convert any value in one numbering system into a value in another system and to perform computer arithmetic on these values.

EXERCISES

1. Convert the following binary numbers to decimal numbers:
   a. 1011_2
   b. 101110_2
   c. 1010011_2

2. Convert the following decimal numbers to binary numbers:
   a. 51_{10}
   b. 260_{10}
   c. 500_{10}

3. Convert the following binary numbers to hexadecimal numbers:
   a. 101_2
   b. 11010_2
   c. 11110100010_2

4. Convert the following hexadecimal numbers to binary numbers:
   a. $F2_{16}$
   b. $1A8_{16}$
   c. $39EB_{16}$

5. Convert the following hexadecimal numbers to decimal numbers:
   a. $B6_{16}$
   b. $5E9_{16}$
   c. $CAFF_{16}$

6. Drawing on techniques you've learned in this appendix, provide an expression to convert the base 6 (yes, six) number 451_6 to a decimal number.

7. Adding the binary numbers 11011001 and 1011101 yields _____.

8. Adding the hexadecimal numbers 8E and 5D yields _____.

9. Subtracting the binary number 1011 from 101110 yields _____.

10. Subtracting the hexadecimal number B6 from F2 yields _____.

Hint: You can use the Windows scientific calculator (see Figure HW 1-28 on the next page) to check exercise results.

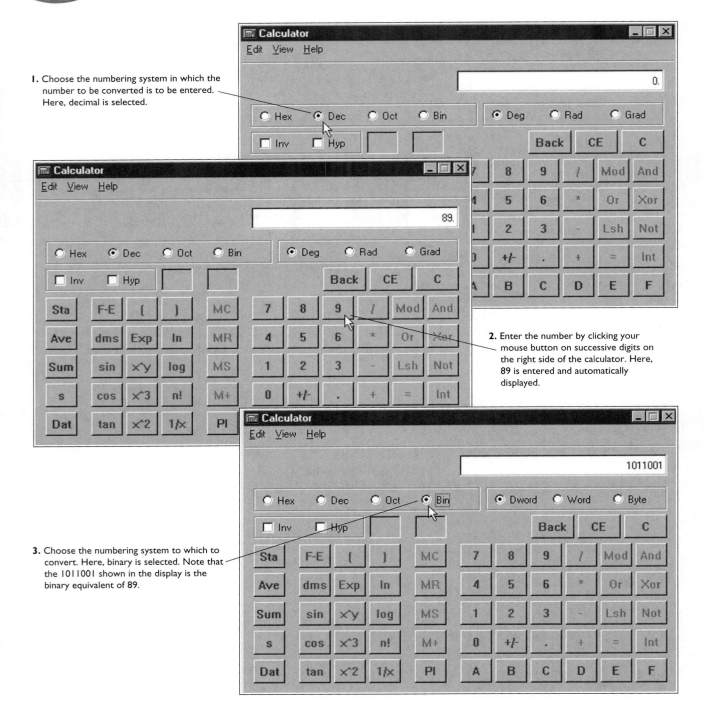

1. Choose the numbering system in which the number to be converted is to be entered. Here, decimal is selected.

2. Enter the number by clicking your mouse button on successive digits on the right side of the calculator. Here, 89 is entered and automatically displayed.

3. Choose the numbering system to which to convert. Here, binary is selected. Note that the 1011001 shown in the display is the binary equivalent of 89.

 FIGURE HW 1-28

Checking results. Microsoft Windows contains a scientific calculator that lets you check conversions between the decimal, binary, and hexadecimal numbering systems. The Calculator program is located under Accessories on the Start menu; select the scientific calculator using Calculator's View menu.

SECONDARY STORAGE

LEARNING OBJECTIVES

After completing this chapter, you will be able to:

1. Name several general properties of secondary storage systems.

2. Identify a number of storage systems based on magnetic disks and describe how they work and where they are particularly useful.

3. Detail the roles of optical-disk and magnetic-tape storage media and equipment.

4. Demonstrate the significance of several emerging secondary storage alternatives.

5. Name several types of data access and organization strategies and cite processing situations appropriate for each.

OVERVIEW

In Chapter HW 1, we discussed the role of memory. Memory circuitry is designed to provide immediate access to stored data and programs. It temporarily holds program instructions, input data, intermediate results, and output as the computer works on them. However, as soon as the computer finishes with programs and their data, it writes new ones over them. Thus, if programs, data, and processing results are to be preserved for repeated use, a computer system needs additional storage beyond memory. Secondary (external) storage fills this role. Although it provides slower access than memory, secondary storage has a much greater storage capacity and is far less expensive.

We will begin this chapter with a discussion of certain common characteristics of secondary storage systems. Then we'll cover the most important kinds of secondary storage systems in use today—those based on magnetic disks. While this part of the chapter is mostly about diskettes and hard disks, we will also look at some other common storage devices, such as Zip and Jaz drives. From there we will study optical-disk and tape storage systems. Following this is a summary and comparison of the secondary storage devices we've covered in the chapter. Chapter HW 2 closes with a discussion of data organization strategies—methods of maintaining data in secondary storage for efficient access.

PROPERTIES OF SECONDARY STORAGE SYSTEMS

Web Tutor

For a tutorial on various types of secondary storage systems, go to www. harcourt college.com/ infosys/parker2000/student/ tutor/ and click on Chapter HW 2.

Several important properties characterize secondary storage systems. Here, we will consider several of them, including the two physical parts of a secondary storage system, the nonvolatility property of secondary storage, the ability to remove storage media from a secondary storage device, and methods of accessing data.

Physical Parts Any secondary storage system involves two physical parts: a *peripheral device* and an *input/output medium*. A disk drive and a tape drive are examples of peripheral devices; diskettes and magnetic tape cartridges are types of media. The drives write data and programs onto, and read them from, the storage media. A medium must be situated on or inserted into a peripheral device for the CPU to process its contents.

Peripheral storage devices can be internal or external. *Internal devices—* such as diskette, hard-disk, and CD drives—typically come installed and configured within the system unit when you buy a computer system. These devices can also be installed in empty bays in the system unit when necessary. *External devices* are stand-alone pieces of hardware that connect via cables to ports on the system unit. Internal devices bring the advantage of requiring no additional desk space, but external devices can more easily be shared between two or more computer systems.

The computer system keeps track of disk drives and other storage devices in an unambiguous way by assigning letters of the alphabet or names to each of them. Letter designations, which are common in the PC-compatible world, are illustrated in Figure HW 2-1. Thus, if you declare you want to save a document to the A drive, the computer system encounters no confusion about where you want the document to be stored.

In most secondary storage systems, media must pass by **read/write heads** inside the peripheral devices for programs and data to be read from or writ-

---

■ **Read/write head.** The component of a disk access mechanism or tape drive that retrieves or inscribes data.

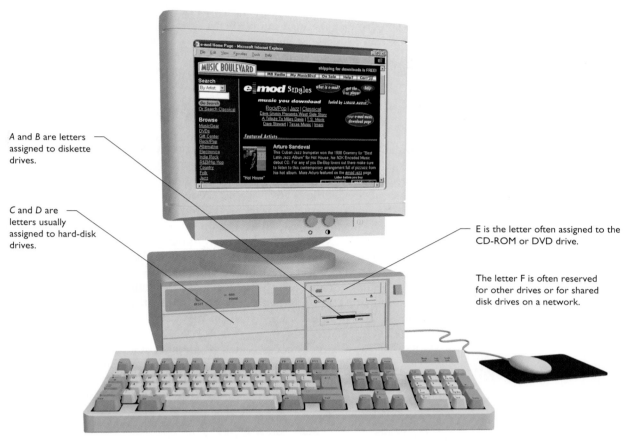

A and B are letters assigned to diskette drives.

C and D are letters usually assigned to hard-disk drives.

E is the letter often assigned to the CD-ROM or DVD drive.

The letter F is often reserved for other drives or for shared disk drives on a network.

FIGURE HW 2-1

Disk-device identifiers. To keep track of disk drives in an unambiguous way, the computer system assigns letters of the alphabet or names to each of them.

ten to the media. For instance, when you listen to music on a cassette or record it on your home stereo system, the tape passes by a head on the tape deck, which either plays or records music. Tapes and disks on computer systems work by similar principles.

Nonvolatility Property Secondary storage media are **nonvolatile.** This means that when you shut off power to the peripheral device, the data stored on the medium remain there. This feature contrasts with many types of memory (including RAM), which are **volatile.** Data held in volatile storage disappear once you shut off the computer system's power.

Removable versus Nonremovable Media In many secondary storage systems, although the peripheral device is online to the computer, the associated medium must be loaded into the device before the computer can read from it or write to it. These are called *removable-media* secondary storage systems. Diskettes, CDs, and magnetic-tape cartridges are examples of removable media. On the other hand, *fixed-media* secondary storage systems, such as most hard-disk systems, encase the media in sealed units from which users cannot easily remove them.

Fixed-media devices generally provide higher speed and better reliability at lower cost than removable-media alternatives. Removability has its advantages too, however, including the following:

■ UNLIMITED STORAGE CAPACITY You can replace the medium on the storage device when it becomes full.

■ **Nonvolatile storage.** Storage that retains its contents when the power is shut off. ■ **Volatile storage.** Storage that loses its contents when the power is shut off.

- TRANSPORTABILITY   You can swap media between computers and people.
- BACKUP   You can write a duplicate set of valuable data or programs onto the removable medium and store the copy away from the computer, for use if the originals are destroyed.
- SECURITY   Sensitive programs or data can be placed offline in a secured area.

Virtually all computer systems have both removable-media and fixed-media storage components.

Accessing Data   When the computer system receives an instruction pertaining to data or programs in secondary storage, it must first find the materials. The process of retrieving data and programs in storage is called *access*.

Two basic access methods are available: sequential and direct access. **Sequential access** means that you can retrieve the records in a file only in the same order in which they are physically stored on the medium. **Direct access,** also called **random access,** means that you can retrieve records in any order.

Computer systems' tape drives allow only sequential access to data. Computer tapes work like a cassette tape on your stereo system—to get to some spot in the middle of the tape, you must pass through all of the preceding ones. Computer disks, in contrast, allow both sequential and direct access to data. They work like music CDs—you can play selections in sequence or go directly to a particular one.

Media that allow direct access—such as memory and disks—are *addressable*. This means that the storage system can locate each stored data record or program at a unique *address,* which is automatically determined by the computer system. Tape systems, in contrast, are generally not addressable.

MAGNETIC DISK SYSTEMS

Speedy access to data and relatively low cost make **magnetic disks** the most widely used secondary storage media on today's computer systems. With magnetic storage systems, data are written by read/write heads magnetizing particles a certain way on a medium's surface. The particles retain their magnetic orientation when they are later read, and the orientation can be changed by rewriting to the medium. Storing data on a magnetic disk is illustrated in Figure HW 2-2; magnetic tape works in a similar way.

Without disk storage, many of the familiar computer applications we see around us would be impossible. In this section we cover the most common types of magnetic disks: hard disks and diskettes.

DISKETTES

Diskettes, or *floppy disks,* store data on small, round platters made of tough plastic. Because they are removable and very inexpensive, diskettes are handy for such tasks as backing up small programs and small amounts of data, sending programs and data to others, storing rarely used files, and sharing data between two computers—such as a computer at home and one at school. The latter use of diskettes in our age of increasing networking, incidentally, is sometimes condescendingly referred to as a *sneakernet* (see the Inside the Industry box on page HW 52).

- **Sequential access.** Fetching stored records in the same order in which they are physically arranged on the medium.
- **Direct access.** Reading or writing data in storage so that the access time is independent of the physical location of the data. Also known as **random access.** ■ **Magnetic disk.** A secondary storage medium that records data through magnetic spots on platters made of rigid metal or flexible plastic. ■ **Diskette.** A low-capacity, removable disk made of a tough, flexible plastic and coated with a magnetizable substance.

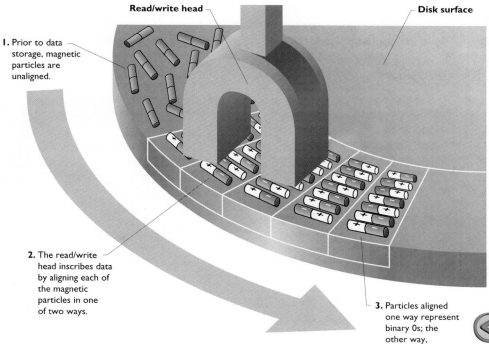

Read/write head

Disk surface

1. Prior to data storage, magnetic particles are unaligned.

2. The read/write head inscribes data by aligning each of the magnetic particles in one of two ways.

3. Particles aligned one way represent binary 0s; the other way, binary 1s.

FIGURE HW 2-2

Storing data on magnetic disks.

Diskette Sizes   Most diskettes in use today measure 3½ inches in diameter. The actual, circular-shaped storage medium is contained in a square, rugged plastic case that can fit into a shirt pocket.

Despite its small dimensions, a 3½-inch diskette can store a respectable amount of data. The most common capacity is 1.44 megabytes. The 1.44-megabyte diskettes are often called *high-density* diskettes; older 720-kilobyte diskettes are called *double-density* or *low-density* diskettes. Density, incidentally, refers to how tightly bits of data are packed onto the diskette. A diskette with a capacity of 1.44 megabytes has enough room to store the text of a book about 400 pages long.

Strange as it may seem, 3½-inch diskettes are faster and store more data than the 5¼-inch diskettes that were prevalent only a few years ago and have all but disappeared from the marketplace.

Physical Properties   The physical properties of a diskette are illustrated in Figure HW 2-3. The plastic surfaces of a diskette's storage medium are coated with a magnetizable substance. The jacket is lined with a soft material that wipes the disk clean as it spins. The diskette's write-protect square can block writing operations to prevent users from accidentally destroying data. To prevent the drive from writing to a diskette, slide the small piece of plastic to expose this square opening. Inside a drive, a diskette rotates when the drive mechanism engages its hub and begins to spin.

Diskette Addresses   Each side of a diskette platter contains a specific number of concentric **tracks,** which the read/write head encodes with 0 and 1 bits when it writes data and programs to the diskette. In order to work on a particular computer system, disks must be *formatted.* Formatting divides the disk surface into pie-shaped **sectors,** and thereby prepares it for use with a particular operating system. On many microcomputer systems, the part of any track crossed by a fixed number of contiguous sectors—anywhere from two to eight sectors is typical—forms a unit called a **cluster.** A cluster represents

---

■ **Track.** A path on an input/output medium where data are recorded. ■ **Sector.** A pie-shaped area on a disk surface.
■ **Cluster.** An area formed where a fixed number of contiguous sectors intersect a track.

A Technobabble Miniglossary

A Combat Guide to Talking Technology

Many years ago, computer jargon was spoken with confidence only at staff meetings of technical specialists. But now that computers have entered the mainstream, everyone seems to want to belong to their growing subculture. One key to membership is technobabble—a dialect for digital conversations that splices computer and networking terminology into everyday speech. Here's a smattering of technobabble terms to use or avoid at your pleasure:

Alpha Geek The person in a group who is most respected for his or her technical proficiency. *Sample technobabble:* "The one with the pointy head must be their alpha geek."

Bandwidth Brain power. *Sample technobabble:* "She's a high-bandwidth woman."

Betazoid A person who lives to test prereleases, termed *beta copies*, of software. *Sample technobabble:* "The betazoids will go wild when they see this new screen menu."

Big Iron Mainframe computer. *Sample technobabble:* "We replaced the big iron with a client-server network."

Digerati Computer professionals. *Sample technobabble:* "The digerati says the server's going down at 3 P.M."

E To send someone electronic mail, or e-mail. *Sample technobabble:* "E me on that, would you?"

Flame Mail Electronic mail that is critical or abusive. *Sample technobabble:* "I got some flame mail from my supervisor this morning about my handling of that situation."

Meatspace The "real" or physical world, as opposed to the Internet. *Sample technobabble:* "We've just met through e-mail; meatspace is still months away."

Net Surfing Casually browsing a computer network to see what is there. *Sample technobabble:* "You won't believe what I found net surfing last night."

Newbie A new user to an online computer group. *Sample technobabble:* "Those know-nothing newbies are really slowing the system down today."

Random Illogical or nutty. *Sample technobabble:* "His ideas on that subject are totally random."

Rumorazzi The people who write industry-insider columns for the computer journals. *Sample technobabble:* "The rumorazzi tells us that Company XYZ is going to miss its shipping deadline."

Scud Memo A misguided or poorly conceptualized e-mail message, memo, or letter. *Sample technobabble:* "He sent me his usual scud memo on it."

Shovelware Extra, poorly integrated software or documentation that is hastily dumped by a software publisher onto a CD-ROM to fill any space on the disk left over from the main application. *Sample technobabble:* "Ninety percent of this disk is pure shovelware."

Sneakernet Transferring electronic information by manually carrying disks or tapes from one machine to another. *Sample technobabble:* "Not only does that company rely on snail mail (the Post Office), they're a sneakernet outfit, too."

Spam Junk e-mail. *Sample technobabble:* "Don't go with that access provider unless you like getting spammed."

Speeds and Feeds The technical specifications of a product. *Sample technobabble:* "Give me the speeds and feeds of that new system, will ya?"

Taking It Offline Resolving an issue after a meeting. *Sample technobabble:* "I'll get back to you on that offline."

WADR In an online computer-chat session, a shorthand way of saying "with all due respect." *Sample technobabble:* "WADR and IMHO (in my humble opinion), I think you're not telling me the truth."

Zorch Raw power. *Sample technobabble:* "Does this machine have plenty of zorch, or what?"

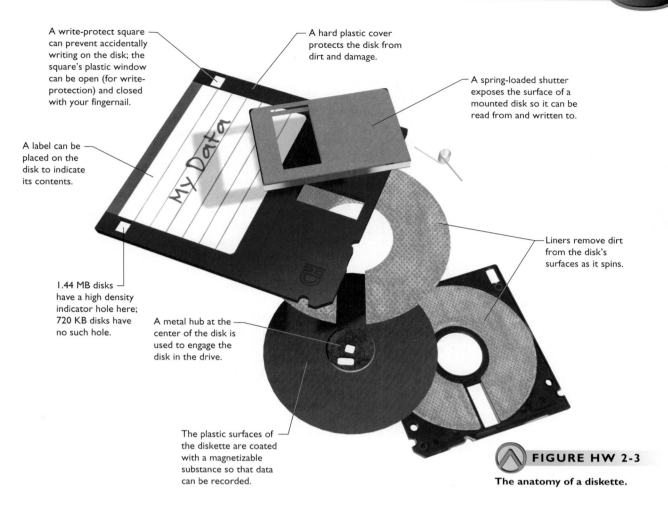

A write-protect square can prevent accidentally writing on the disk; the square's plastic window can be open (for write-protection) and closed with your fingernail.

A hard plastic cover protects the disk from dirt and damage.

A spring-loaded shutter exposes the surface of a mounted disk so it can be read from and written to.

A label can be placed on the disk to indicate its contents.

Liners remove dirt from the disk's surfaces as it spins.

1.44 MB disks have a high density indicator hole here; 720 KB disks have no such hole.

A metal hub at the center of the disk is used to engage the disk in the drive.

The plastic surfaces of the diskette are coated with a magnetizable substance so that data can be recorded.

FIGURE HW 2-3

The anatomy of a diskette.

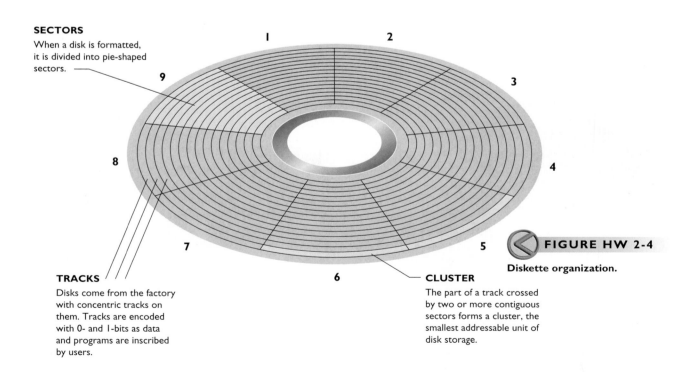

SECTORS
When a disk is formatted, it is divided into pie-shaped sectors.

FIGURE HW 2-4

Diskette organization.

TRACKS
Disks come from the factory with concentric tracks on them. Tracks are encoded with 0- and 1-bits as data and programs are inscribed by users.

CLUSTER
The part of a track crossed by two or more contiguous sectors forms a cluster, the smallest addressable unit of disk storage.

a single disk address (see Figure HW 2-4). You can buy preformatted diskettes, and you can also use your computer's operating system to format diskettes for you. A diskette cannot store data unless it has been formatted.

The computer system automatically maintains a diskette's **file directory,** which keeps track of the diskette's contents. This directory shows the name of each diskette file, its size, and the cluster at which it begins.

FIGURE HW 2-5

Inserting a diskette into a drive. Diskettes go into a drive only one way—label side up, with the disk shutter facing the drive door.

Using Diskettes To use a diskette, you insert it into a device called a **disk drive,** or *disk unit* (see Figure HW 2-5). There is only one correct way to insert the diskette into a drive—with the disk label facing up and the end with the metallic shutter mechanism going in first. Disk doors on 3½ inch drives automatically accept a disk that has been inserted properly—you'll hear a click when this happens.

While the diskette platter rotates, the read/write heads access tracks through the shutter's recording window. If the drive's *indicator light* is on, meaning that the read/write heads are accessing the tracks, you must not try to remove the diskette. After the light goes off, you generally press an *eject button* to remove the disk.

Superdiskettes A drawback to diskettes is their storage capacity. Not long ago, computer users considered 1.44 megabytes a reasonable amount of storage. Now, however, multimedia applications are rapidly increasing storage demands, and 1.44 MB is looking smaller and smaller with each passing year. Consequently, a number of other storage products have emerged in recent years, either as replacements for standard diskettes or as supplemental storage solutions (see Figure HW 2-6).

FIGURE HW 2-6

Superdiskette drives with cartridges. Disk-cartridge products with capacities of 100 megabytes or more are commonly sold either as replacements for standard diskettes or as supplemental storage solutions. (left: 250 MB Iomega Zip drive and cartridge; right: 120 MB Imation SuperDisk drive and cartridges.)

ZIP DRIVES Introduced by Iomega Corporation in 1995, *Zip drives* are magnetic-disk drives that accept removable 3½-inch disk cartridges with a capacity of 100 megabytes or more; the newer Zip 250 drives can use both 100 and 250 megabtye cartridges. The drives and disks are incompatible with standard diskettes, but they provide a very affordable storage alternative. Drives typically run $100 or so and disks cost about $15 each. Zip drives are ideal for users who need to store large files offline or transfer large files between systems or other users.

■ **File directory.** A listing on a storage medium that provides such data such as name, length, and starting address for each stored file. ■ **Disk drive.** A direct-access secondary storage device that uses a magnetic or optical disk as the principal medium.

LASER-SERVO DRIVES   *Laser-servo (LS) drives* resemble Zip drives in that they accept disk cartridges with larger capacities (120 megabytes) than standard diskettes. While LS drives give slower access than Zip drives, however, they can also read from and write to standard diskettes. LS drives work through a combination of magnetic and optical technology—storing data magnetically, but optically locating tracks and positioning read/write heads. Because optical positioning locates heads much more precisely than magnetic positioning, LS technology can place tracks closer together than conventional diskette drives can manage. In 1996, some computer makers began installing internal LS drives on some of their desktop computer systems.

HIFD DRIVES   More recent to the market than Zip and LS drives is Sony's *HiFD* technology. HiFD cartridges have a capacity of 200 MB, enough to store 100,000 pages of text or the contents of approximately 140 diskettes. HiFD drives are faster than Zip and LS drives and can also read conventional diskettes. Whether HiFD will overtake Zip and LS technology in the fierce fight to be the prevailing low-end-disk standard of the future remains to be seen.

HARD DISKS

Virtually every computer system today stores data and programs on some type of hard disk. A typical **hard disk** consists of one or more rigid metal platters mounted onto a shaft and sealed along with an access mechanism inside a case (see Figure HW 2-7). In PC systems, the terms *hard disk* and *hard-disk*

   **FIGURE HW 2-7**

A hard-disk drive. Hard-disk systems for microcomputers commonly have capacities in the gigabyte range. Featured here is an *internal* hard-disk system.

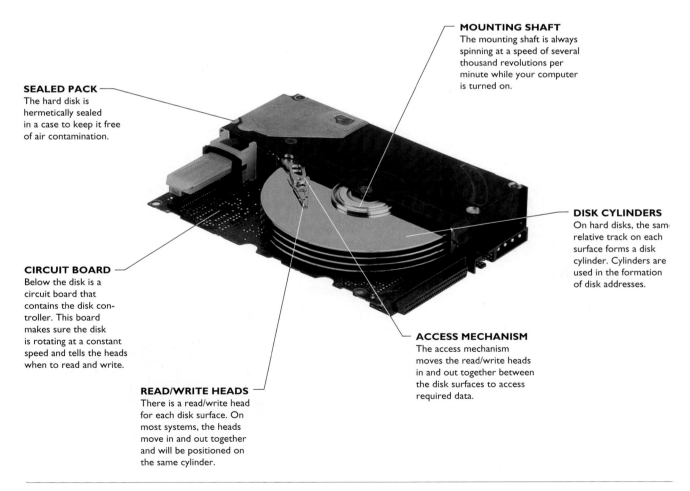

MOUNTING SHAFT
The mounting shaft is always spinning at a speed of several thousand revolutions per minute while your computer is turned on.

SEALED PACK
The hard disk is hermetically sealed in a case to keep it free of air contamination.

DISK CYLINDERS
On hard disks, the same relative track on each surface forms a disk cylinder. Cylinders are used in the formation of disk addresses.

CIRCUIT BOARD
Below the disk is a circuit board that contains the disk controller. This board makes sure the disk is rotating at a constant speed and tells the heads when to read and write.

ACCESS MECHANISM
The access mechanism moves the read/write heads in and out together between the disk surfaces to access required data.

READ/WRITE HEADS
There is a read/write head for each disk surface. On most systems, the heads move in and out together and will be positioned on the same cylinder.

■ **Hard disk.** A system consisting of one or more rigid platters and an access mechanism.

For links to further information about nonremovable storage devices and media, go to www.harcourtcollege. com/infosys/parker2000/ student/explore/ and click on Chapter HW 2.

drive commonly refer to the same thing—a single *pack* of disks as well as accompanying read/write heads, circuit board, and case.

Most PC hard disks are hermetically sealed units. This precaution keeps the disk surfaces completely free of air contamination, enabling the disks to spin faster and limiting causes of operational problems. While a standard diskette spins at about 300 revolutions per minute (rpm), hard disks typically spin anywhere from 3,600 to 9,600 rpm.

Hard disks provide greater amounts of online storage and significantly faster access to programs and data than diskettes. New PC hard disks most commonly offer capacities in the gigabyte range. Thus, if you have a 20-gigabyte hard disk, you have the online storage equivalent of more than 13,800 3½-inch diskettes the minute you turn on the system's power. Also, you don't have to constantly shuffle diskettes into and out of drives. Speed improves as well; hard disks can access data at least ten times faster than diskette drives. The difference results both from faster spinning and the fact that the hard disk is constantly rotating whenever your computer is turned on—eliminating the waiting time for the drive to come up to the correct speed. A diskette, in contrast, does not start spinning until you try to access it.

PCs can include internal or external hard disks (or both). An *internal* hard-disk system, such as the one in Figure HW 2-7, is by far the most common type. It is standard equipment on virtually all PCs sold. An *external* hard-disk system is a detached device that can supplement the storage built into the computer system. External disks are often slightly slower and more expensive than their internal counterparts, but they provide flexibility by allowing two or more computers to share their contents.

While most hard disks are *fixed,* meaning that you cannot separate them from their drives, systems that use *removable* hard-disk cartridges are gaining popularity (see Figure HW 2-8). One of the most widely used systems is Iomega's Jaz drive. A Jaz cartridge, which can store one or two gigabytes, takes slightly longer to access than a conventional, fixed hard disk. Jaz drives exist in both an internal and external version, each available for less than $400.

Like diskettes, hard-disk surfaces are divided into tracks and sectors—but many more of both. A new hard disk is typically formatted for use at the factory before it is sold.

On most desktop PCs and powerful network file servers, hard-disk platters measure 3½ inches in diameter; most notebook computers have 2½-inch hard disks. Even smaller-diameter disks are forthcoming in the marketplace. Feature HW 2-1 provides some interesting facts that show how far hard-disk technology has advanced within the past half century.

FIGURE HW 2-8

Removable hard disk. Iomega's Jaz drives work with removable, gigabyte-range cartridges to deliver performance close to a computer system's native fixed hard disk. The Jaz drive is available in external and internal models.

HW 2-1

The Evolution of the Hard Disk

How Far We've Come

The world's first hard disk—the Ramac 305—was unveiled in 1956. It consisted of a pack of 50 platters, each two feet in diameter. The entire pack stored the equivalent of about 2.4 million characters. In other words, between two and three megabytes.

By contrast, today's state-of-the-art hard disk improves on this standard several millionfold. Some disks can store about 12 billion bits per square inch. That's more than 725,000 typewritten pages in a space slightly larger than a thumbprint.

The latest hard disks going into electronic products are about the size of a large coin. The photo to the right features quarter-sized hard disk. Its 340 MB capacity stores the equivalent of 230 diskettes.

Reading and Writing Data Most hard-disk systems have at least one read/write head for each recording surface. These heads are mounted on a device called an **access mechanism** (refer back to Figure HW 2-7). The rotating mounting shaft spins at high speeds—thousands of revolutions per minute—and the access mechanism moves the heads in and out *together* between the disk surfaces to access the required data. Such a *movable access mechanism* as described here is by far the most popular type of access mechanism for hard disks.

A read/write head never touches the surface of a hard disk platter at any time, even during reading and writing. The heads approach the disk very closely, however—often within millionths of an inch above the recording surfaces. The presence of a human hair or even a smoke particle (about 2,500 and 100 millionths of an inch, respectively) on a hard-disk surface will damage the disks and heads—an event known as a *head crash*. As Figure HW 2-9 shows, the results are like placing a huge boulder on a road and then trying to drive over it with your car. One never knows when a hard disk will crash—there may be no warning whatsoever—and this is a good reason for keeping the disk regularly backed up (see also Feature HW 2-2 on page HW 59).

Disk Cylinders An important principle for understanding disk storage and access strategies in hard-disk systems is the concept of **disk cylinders.** The four-disk pack in Figure HW 2-7 contains eight possible recording surfaces. Suppose that each surface carries 800 tracks. You might envision the disk pack as a collection of 800 imaginary, concentric cylinders, each consisting of eight vertically aligned tracks. For instance, one cylinder would represent track 357 on Surface 1, track 357 on Surface 2, and so on, all the way up to track 357 of Surface 8. Outer cylinders fit over the inner ones like sleeves. Hard disks are commonly organized into anywhere from a few hundred to a couple of thousand cylinders.

■ **Access mechanism.** A mechanical device in a disk drive that positions the read/write heads on the proper tracks. ■ **Disk cylinder.** On a disk pack, a collection of tracks that align vertically in the same relative position on different disk surfaces.

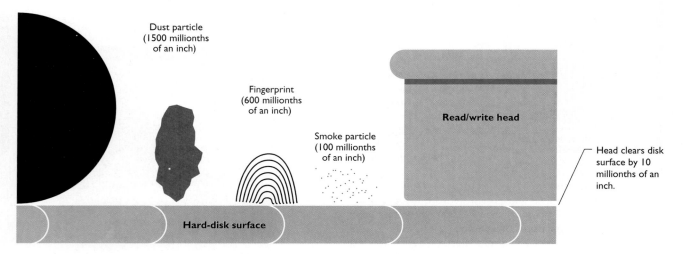

Human hair
(2500 millionths
of an inch)

Dust particle
(1500 millionths
of an inch)

Fingerprint
(600 millionths
of an inch)

Smoke particle
(100 millionths
of an inch)

Read/write head

Head clears disk
surface by 10
millionths of an
inch.

Hard-disk surface

 **FIGURE HW 2-9**

Obstacles on a hard-disk surface. A human hair or even a smoke particle on a fast-spinning hard-disk surface can damage both the surface and the read/write head.

Disk Access Time   A hard disk with a movable access mechanism shifts the read/write heads in and out among the tracks in concert. It positions all the heads on the same cylinder when data are read from or written to any of the tracks on that cylinder. A disk system with a movable access mechanism must carry out three events in order to read or write data.

First, the read/write heads must move to the cylinder that stores (or will store) the desired data. Suppose, for example, that the read/write head is on Cylinder 5, and it needs to retrieve data from Cylinder 36. To do this, the mechanism must move inward to Cylinder 36. The time required for this task is referred to as *seek time.*

When a read or write order is issued, the correct head is usually not aligned over the desired position on the track. Hence, some delay occurs while the mounting shaft rotates the disks into the proper position. (The disks are always spinning, whether or not reading or writing is taking place.) The time needed to complete this alignment is called *rotational delay.*

Third, once the access mechanism positions the read/write head over the correct data, the system must read the data from disk and transfer them to the RAM. (To write data, the reverse happens—the system must transfer them from RAM onto the moving disk.) This last step is known as *data movement time.* The sum of these three components—seek time, rotational delay, and data movement time—is known as **disk access time.**

Hard-disk access times often run from 10 to 20 milliseconds. To minimize disk access time on a system with a movable access mechanism such as the one depicted in Figure HW 2-7, drives store related data on the same cylinder. This strategy sharply reduces the seek-time component.

Disk Cache   Disk caching refers to a strategy for speeding up system performance. Here's how it works: During any disk access, the computer system also fetches program or data contents in neighboring disk areas and transports them to a dedicated part of RAM known as a **disk cache** (see Figure HW 2-10). For instance, if a particular command calls for only a single data record, a disk-caching feature may direct the drive to read the entire track on which the

■ **Disk access time.** The time taken to locate and read (or position and write) data on a disk device. ■ **Disk cache.** A disk-management scheme that directs a drive to read more data than necessary for an immediate processing task during each disk fetch; a part of RAM stores the extra data to minimize the number of disk fetches.

HW 2-2

Professional Data Detectives

Specialists in Hard-Disk Disasters

It happens far more often than most people imagine. Files can't be accessed or recovered from a local hard disk and there's no backup.

Here's how the trouble begins. Your hard disk, which worked like a charm last night, is suddenly unresponsive. In fact, it's dead. You think you backed it up, but that was a long time ago. And now you're not even sure whether you did it correctly. You begin to sweat. There's a lot of valuable data you can't afford to lose on the disk.

If you find yourself in such a situation, it may be time to seek out a professional data detective. This is a company that specializes in disassembling defective hard disks and recovering the data on them.

For many types of hard-disk problems, the standard file-recovery programs that come with your operating system or with program packages such as the Norton Utilities will work just fine. Files you've erased and lost clusters on the disk can be easily relocated. Where such programs begin to falter is when the directories showing where files are stored have been corrupted. At this point, you'll probably need a higher level of help.

Disk recovery done by companies specializing in this area often involves two stages. In the first stage, the company trying to repair your disk will often try to do it remotely—that is, by modem, over the phone lines—with their own diagnostic software. If it fails at this effort, you advance to stage 2. Here, you or a qualified professional must remove the hard disk and ship it to a disk-recovery center. At the center, your disk is opened by technicians wearing space suits in a "clean room," in which dust particles in

Maybe more than just broken hardware. A hard disk may or may not be repairable once it goes bad, so regularly back up valuable programs and data.

the air are regularly removed. The technicians will check for defective parts and try to get the drive working again. If this doesn't succeed, many shops will resort to more extreme approaches to try to read data on the disk.

Disk repair is expensive. It could cost anywhere from $500 to a few thousand dollars to get a hard disk back in working order. The amount you will have to pay is usually far more than if the original hard disk had been properly backed up.

There are, of course, some types of disk problems that no repair shop can fix. For example, once data on the disk are overwritten, it is impossible to retrieve the original contents. If this happens, forget data recovery; you're out of luck.

---

record is located. The theory behind disk caching assumes that neighboring data will likely have to be read soon anyway, so the computer system can save disk accesses by bringing such data into RAM—an area from which they can be more quickly retrieved—early. When it's time for the next disk fetch, the computer system checks the disk-cache area first, to see if the data it needs are there. If they are, the data are transferred to main memory for processing; if they aren't, the computer makes another disk fetch.

Caching saves not only time but also wear and tear on the disk. In portable computers, it can also extend battery life. Disk caching is frequently implemented through circuitry on the disk controller board—the circuit board that manages the hard disk.

Disk Standards Buying a hard disk for a microcomputer system can lead to confusing chatter from vendors spiced with such acronyms as RLL, ESDI, IDE, EIDE, and SCSI. These acronyms generally refer to performance characteristics like the density with which data can be packed onto the disk, the speed of disk access, and the way the disk drive interfaces with other hardware.

Today, two standards dominate the market: *EIDE,* for *e*nhanced *i*ntegrated *d*rive *e*lectronics, and *SCSI,* for *s*mall *c*omputer *s*ystem *i*nterface. EIDE is less expensive and often easier to configure, but SCSI provides faster access,

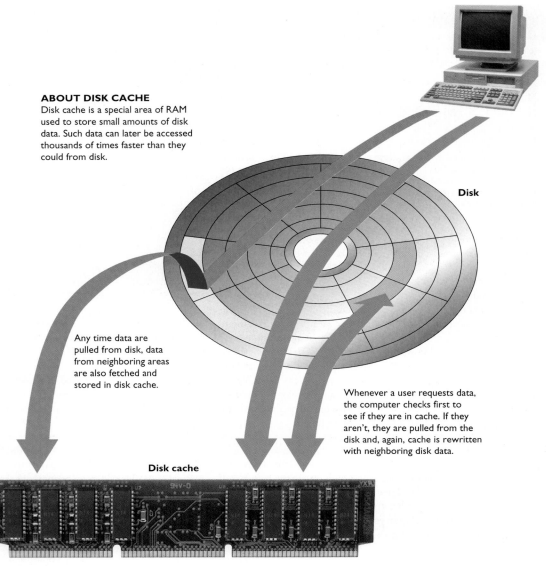

ABOUT DISK CACHE
Disk cache is a special area of RAM used to store small amounts of disk data. Such data can later be accessed thousands of times faster than they could from disk.

Disk

Any time data are pulled from disk, data from neighboring areas are also fetched and stored in disk cache.

Whenever a user requests data, the computer checks first to see if they are in cache. If they aren't, they are pulled from the disk and, again, cache is rewritten with neighboring disk data.

Disk cache

FIGURE HW 2-10

Disk cache.

enables you to connect more devices from a single board, and allows longer cable lengths. SCSI (pronounced "scuzzy") comes in several varieties, including SCSI-1, SCSI-2, SCSI-3, and UltraSCSI. When buying any new peripheral, it's important to check out which standards the device supports and to make sure your computer system is equipped to deal with them.

Partitioning Partitioning a hard disk enables you to divide its capacity into separate areas—or *partitions*. You can then treat each of the partitions as an independent disk drive, such as a C drive and a D drive. You can change the number and sizes of the partitions at any time, although this action will destroy any data in those partitions. Consequently, you should transfer any affected data onto another disk or tape first and then load the data back onto the repartitioned hard disk.

Partitioning a hard disk also enables you to assign different operating systems—say, Windows and UNIX—to parts of your disk. Each operating system has its own method of formatting and managing disk space. By assigning each operating system to a different partition, you gain a more flexible computer system while you avoid the problem of an operating system encountering data stored in a manner that is foreign to it.

DISK STORAGE FOR LARGE COMPUTER SYSTEMS

Hard-disk systems on large computers implement many of the same principles as microcomputer-based hard disks. Instead of finding a single disk pack sealed inside a case installed within a system unit, however, you are most likely to find several removable disk packs that are placed into a refrigerator-sized unit that is separate from the system unit (see Figure HW 2-11). Storage capacities on such disk systems can run from a few dozen gigabytes up into the terabyte range.

Not too long ago, disk systems on large computers stored data on very-large-diameter disks—say, 14 inches or so across. This design created several problems. Large disks cannot rotate at the high speeds that smaller ones can manage. What's more, larger disks require greater seek time. Also, as the diameter of a disk increases, so does the potential for wobble at its outer edge as it spins. Larger wobble forces the read/write heads to ride farther away from the disk surface to prevent a head crash. This also detracts from performance.

Today's large-system drives employ smaller disks. Even though they may need more platters to store the same amount of data, several smaller disks have even another critical advantage over a single, larger disk—they provide better support for parallel processing. For instance, if eight smaller disks replace a single, larger one, the system can read from all eight disk surfaces at the same time. Particularly in the computer-networking market, a small-disk storage procedure called RAID has been catching on fast.

RAID   RAID (for *r*edundant *a*rrays of *i*nexpensive *d*isks) hooks up several arrays of relatively small disks in parallel to do the job of a larger disk. The disks are separated from the system unit in a cabinet that, because it comprises a sophisticated system within the computer system, is often referred to as the *disk subsystem* (refer again to Figure HW 2-11). The subsystem is set up to record redundant copies of information so that, in the event of a system crash, the redundant data can be used to reconstruct the lost data.

Computer systems define several different *levels* of RAID. In the most expensive—known as RAID Level 1—a backup disk pack corresponds to each production disk pack (see the top part of Figure HW 2-12). If any production pack fails, its backup immediately takes over. Level-1 RAID is *hot swappable*,

FIGURE HW 2-11

Hard-disk subsystem for a midrange computer. Hard-disk subsystems on larger computers often contain arrays of hard-disk packs, each array occupying its own drawer in a disk cabinet.

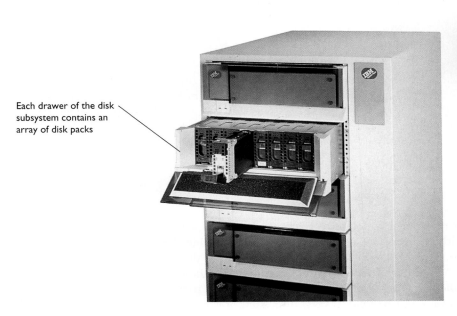

Each drawer of the disk subsystem contains an array of disk packs

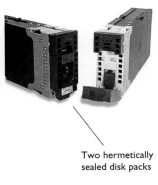

Two hermetically sealed disk packs

■ **RAID.** A storage method that hooks up several small disks in parallel to do the job of a larger disk, but with better performance.

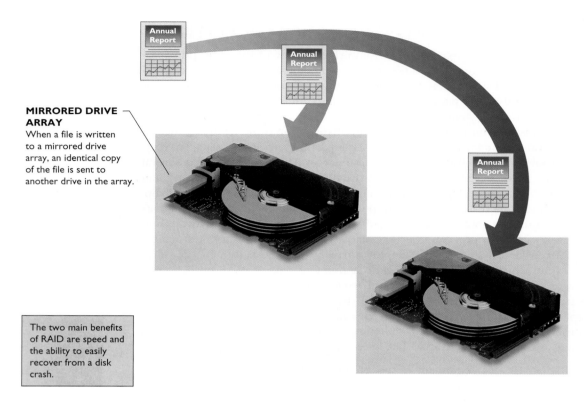

MIRRORED DRIVE ARRAY
When a file is written to a mirrored drive array, an identical copy of the file is sent to another drive in the array.

The two main benefits of RAID are speed and the ability to easily recover from a disk crash.

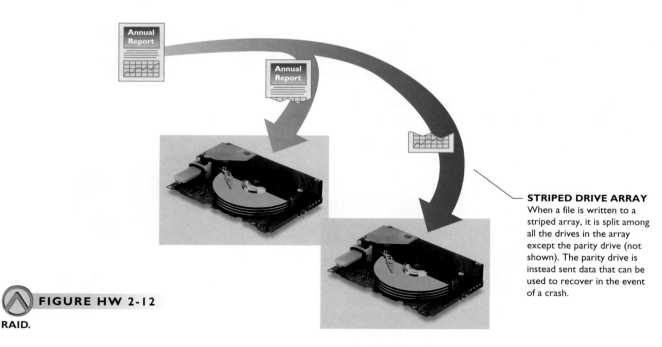

STRIPED DRIVE ARRAY
When a file is written to a striped array, it is split among all the drives in the array except the parity drive (not shown). The parity drive is instead sent data that can be used to recover in the event of a crash.

FIGURE HW 2-12

RAID.

meaning that a defective pack can be taken offline for repair and replaced without even turning the power off. Duplicating the entire contents of a disk on another disk in this manner is sometimes described as *disk mirroring*.

When performance can be sacrificed to gain a cost advantage, a procedure called *striping* is often used (see the bottom part of Figure HW 2-12). All levels of RAID beyond Level 1 use some form of striping, which spreads files over several packs. These systems protect data by duplicating them on additional disk packs called *parity disks* or *check disks*. If the disk system crashes, any lost data can be reconstructed from the contents of the parity disks.

OPTICAL DISK SYSTEMS

Optical disks are often referred to as *CDs*. CD technology employs laser beams to write and read data—which can consist of text, graphics, audio clips, or video images—at densities many times finer than those of a typical magnetic disk. Although hard disks offer faster access, CDs have caught on in a big way both in the business and consumer markets.

Today's optical disk can store anywhere from several hundred megabytes of data to several gigabytes on a single platter. So-called *optical jukeboxes* and *towers* are also available and offer online access to scores of optical disks. Like old phonograph-record jukeboxes, these optical data warehouses "play" selected platters from collections that can reach thousands of online CDs.

TYPES OF OPTICAL DISKS

Optical-disk systems are widely used on computer systems of all sizes. The most common types of systems are CD-ROMs, WORM CDs, rewritable CDs, and DVDs (see Figure HW 2-13). DVD is an emerging CD technology that many people expect to shortly inherit the roles of both CD-ROM technology and videocassette recorders connected to television sets.

CD-ROM By far, most optical disk drives sold today are of the **CD-ROM** (*compact disk, read-only memory*) type. Specialized equipment stores data on CD-ROMs at the factory by burning tiny holes into the disks' surfaces with high-intensity laser beams. Then, your CD drive's lower-intensity laser beam reads the data so inscribed (see Figure HW 2-14). Because the storage process permanently etches the surface of the CD-ROM, you cannot write new data to the disk in any way.

Internal CD-ROM drives costing less than $100 are standard components of PCs today. CD-ROM functionality is generally acquired as part of a multimedia kit when buying a new PC. Such a kit often includes a CD-ROM drive, several CD-ROM disks, speakers, a sound board, and a video board.

Most CD-ROM disk drives available on the market today are touted as 24×, 32×, 36×, and so on. These labels convey the speeds of the drives. For instance, 36× indicates 36 times the speed of the baseline unit that was originally manufactured.

Only one side of a CD-ROM contains data—the side opposite the printed label. When you mount a CD-ROM on a drive tray, you place it with the printed side up. Be careful not to get dirt, fingerprints, or anything else that might hinder light reflectivity on the CD's surface.

While many computer-industry forecasters have for years been predicting that the CD-ROM would be replaced by new CD technologies, it is instead still going strong. Integration with the Internet has been able to extend the power of CD-ROMs, and the millions of new owners of sub-$1,000 PCs have also swelled the ranks of potential CD-ROM buyers.

WORM Optical-disk systems are available that will let you write once to a disk; once written, the data cannot be erased. These are called **WORM** (*write once, read many*) CD systems. The most widely used WORM standard is *CD-R*, the *R* standing for "recordable." CD-R lets users create their own CD-ROM master disks, which can be used to create inexpensive CD-ROMs for distribution

---

■ **Optical disk.** A disk read by reflecting pulses of laser beams. ■ **CD-ROM.** A low-end optical disk that allows a drive to read data but not write it. ■ **WORM.** An optical disk that allows the user's drive to write data only once and then read it an unlimited number of times.

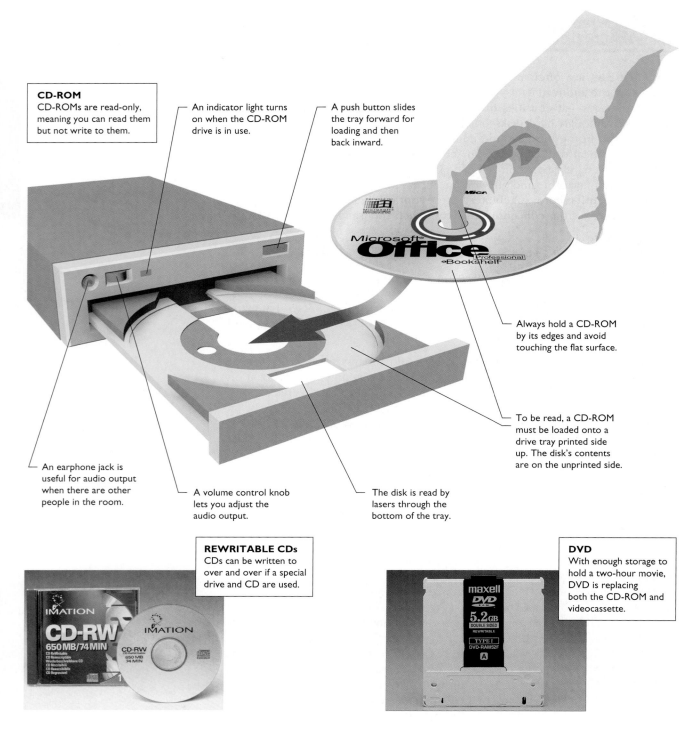

CD-ROM
CD-ROMs are read-only, meaning you can read them but not write to them.

An indicator light turns on when the CD-ROM drive is in use.

A push button slides the tray forward for loading and then back inward.

Always hold a CD-ROM by its edges and avoid touching the flat surface.

To be read, a CD-ROM must be loaded onto a drive tray printed side up. The disk's contents are on the unprinted side.

An earphone jack is useful for audio output when there are other people in the room.

A volume control knob lets you adjust the audio output.

The disk is read by lasers through the bottom of the tray.

REWRITABLE CDs
CDs can be written to over and over if a special drive and CD are used.

DVD
With enough storage to hold a two-hour movie, DVD is replacing both the CD-ROM and videocassette.

FIGURE HW 2-13

Optical-disk drives and their storage media.

purposes. WORM disks have a built-in security measure; because others can't rewrite to the disk, you know that what you put on it can't be accidentally erased or altered in any way. In recent years, with drives selling for less than $400 and blank CDs going for about $3 or $4 apiece, CD-R has seen a new application—home users making high-quality music CDs on their own.

Rewritable CDs Optical-disk systems that allow you to both write and erase data—possibly hundreds of thousands of time—have also recently become

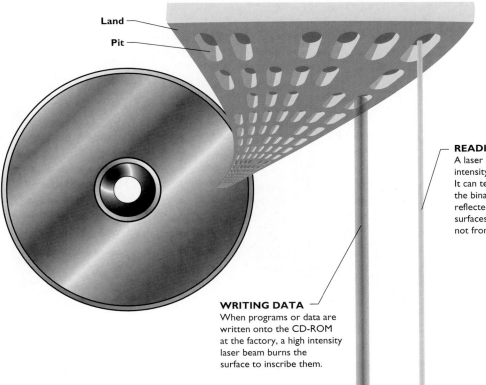

Land

Pit

READING DATA
A laser beam of lower intensity reads the CD-ROM. It can tell the binary 1s from the binary 0s because light is reflected from nonburned surfaces—called *lands*—but not from the darkened *pits*.

WRITING DATA
When programs or data are written onto the CD-ROM at the factory, a high intensity laser beam burns the surface to inscribe them.

FIGURE HW 2-14

How CD-ROMs work.

available. **Rewritable CDs** use either *MO* (for magneto-optical) or *phase-change* technology. Phase-change drives are generally faster than MO drives and, unlike MO drives, can sometimes also read CD-ROMs. However, the various MO drives in the marketplace are more compatible with one another, making it easier for users to exchange information. CD PD (the *PD* is for *power drive)* and CD-RW (the *RW* is for *rewritable)* are the two prevailing phase-change standards. CD PD's cartridge technology enables CDs to be read far more often before the disk degrades, but CD-RW disks and drives are more compatible with other cartridge-less CD standards—such as CD-ROM, CD-R, and DVD.

DVDs The acronym **DVD** (for *digital versatile disk*) refers to a relatively new high-capacity CD storage format that was initially developed to store the full contents of a standard two-hour movie. The acronym DVD originally stood for *digital video disk*. Proponents of the technology later felt that the word *video* was too limiting—the disks can also store text, graphics, and audio data—so the longer name is often dropped or, alternatively, the word *versatile* substituted for *video*.

DVD-ROM technology is seen by many as the successor to music CDs, computer CD-ROMs, and prerecorded VHS videotapes that people buy or rent for home viewing—in other words, read-only products. As consumers begin to appreciate the extra value that 4.7, 9.4, and 18.8 GB DVD-ROM can offer, expect to see rewritable DVDs—*DVD-RAM*—following into the market. In a few years, it is likely that many people will be recording television programs at home on blank DVDs, just as they do today on blank VHS tapes.

DVDs require DVD-enabled disk drives. DVD is backward compatible, which means that you can play CD-ROMs on DVD drives. You can also play audio CDs on DVD drives.

■ **Rewritable CD.** An optical disk that allows users to repeatedly read from and write to its surface. ■ **DVD.** An optical-disk standard that enables very high capacities.

FIGURE HW 2-15

Magnetic tape. Three tape cartridges sit in front of a detachable tape reel.

MAGNETIC TAPE SYSTEMS

Magnetic tape has provided a prominent secondary storage alternative for computer systems over several decades. It is far less popular than disk storage, because its sequential-access property makes it unsuitable for direct access. It does provide an extremely low cost per byte stored, however, so magnetic tape is still widely used both to back up the contents of other storage systems and to support low-speed, sequential-processing operations.

TYPES OF TAPE SYSTEMS

Virtually all magnetic-tape systems store data on either detachable-reel or cartridge tapes (see Figure HW 2-15). The tapes are made of plastic coated with a magnetizable substance that can be polarized to represent the bit patterns of digital data. Computer tapes differ in a number of respects, including the sizes of the reels or cartridges, tape width, and the formats and densities with which they record data.

The device that reads magnetic tapes is called a **tape drive,** or *tape unit.* It may be an internal or external piece of hardware. The tape drives for microcomputers are small enough for a person to hold in one hand, while the refrigerator-sized drives connected to large mainframes often occupy several square feet of floor space. Whatever its size or type, every tape drive contains one or more read/write heads over which the tape passes to allow the drive to read or write data.

Tapes for PCs   **Cartridge tapes** are the predominant form of magnetic-tape storage medium for PCs (see Figure HW 2-16). Within its plastic casing, such a tape typically functions as a backup for the contents of a hard disk. You can

---

■ **Magnetic tape.** A plastic ribbon with a magnetizable surface that stores data as a series of magnetic spots. ■ **Tape drive.** A secondary storage device that reads from and writes to mounted magnetic tapes. ■ **Cartridge tape.** Magnetic tape in which the supply and take-up reels are contained in a small plastic case.

TAPE DRIVES
Cartridge tape drives are available as both internal and external devices.

CARTRIDGE TAPES
There are a very large number of tape formats in use—QIC-80, TR-1, DAT, and so on. When buying tapes, be sure that they conform to the format specified by the drive's manufacturer.

As a tape is being processed, it spools from one reel onto another and then back again.

FIGURE HW 2-16

Microcomputer cartridge tape system. Microcomputer systems often back up the contents of hard disks on tape cartridges.

copy onto a tape the entire contents of a hard disk—on many PCs, an hour or longer is not unusual for such a task—or just selected files. Because of their extremely long access times and other considerations, backup tapes are not usually used for day-to-day data storage and retrieval. When data on a backup tape is needed, that data is first copied to a hard disk.

Both internal and external tape drives are widely found in practice. While internal drives are faster, you can share an external drive between two or more computers. A drive may cost as little as $150; cartridges, $10 to $20 apiece.

Cartridges for backing up desktop computers come in several sizes and formats. Today's systems commonly employ quarter-inch-wide *QIC-80* tapes and minicartridges that use one of the Travan formats, such as T-1 or T-4. A single tape can hold anywhere from a few hundred megabytes of data to a few gigabytes, and twice as much if you compress the data. Data compression is covered in Chapter SW 2.

PC networks commonly include tape drives for higher-capacity, 4-millimeter-wide *DAT* (for *digital audio tape).* DAT can typically store several gigabytes of data each.

Tape Systems for Larger Computer Systems   Larger computer systems—say, those powered by midrange or mainframe computers—often store data on either detachable-reel or cartridge tapes. The tape systems are always external devices, and they may perform either backup or processing duties.

Detachable-reel tapes, which commonly measure one-half inch wide, have been around the longest. When the tape drive is first started, a *supply reel* contains the data to be processed; an empty *take-up reel* winds tape with records that have finished processing. When processing is complete, the drive rewinds the tape back onto the supply reel. Such tape typically stores data at densities up to several thousand bits per inch (bpi). Because cartridges are easier to handle and provide far larger capacities than they offered only a few years ago, detachable-reel tape drives are rapidly losing popularity.

Many midrange and mainframe computers today store data on cartridge tape systems, such as the IBM 3590 tape storage system (see Figure HW 2-17). An automatic loader mounts the cartridges, eliminating the need for human intervention during processing. The tapes used in such systems have at least twice as many tracks as traditional, detachable-reel tapes, boosting their storage capacities into the multigigabyte range. A new format called *digital linear tape (DLT)* now enables anywhere from 100 GB to almost 1 TB of information to be stored on a single cartridge tape.

FIGURE HW 2-17

Mainframe cartridge tape. Automatic loaders are used to mount the cartridges, so that no human intervention is necessary during processing.

USING TAPES

Figure HW 2-18 shows how data are often stored on tape. Some tape systems record data perpendicular to the edge of the tape, some (like QIC-80) parallel, and some (like DAT) at an angle. Data may be coded in eight-bit bytes of either the EBCDIC or ASCII systems. Magnetized (polarized) spots of iron oxide represent 1 bits; nonmagnetized (depolarized) areas represent 0s.

COMPARING SECONDARY STORAGE ALTERNATIVES

Secondary storage alternatives are often compared by weighing a number of product characteristics and cost factors. Some of these product characteristics include internal versus external installation, access time (speed), types of access available, storage capacity, and ability to remove the storage media (see Figure HW 2-19).

Keep in mind that each storage alternative normally involves trade-offs. For instance, you usually must sacrifice access speed to gain the convenience of removability. Also, although virtually everyone wants the fastest possible secondary storage, higher speeds generally come at greater expense.

Today, most users need at least a fixed hard disk, a CD drive, and a diskette drive. Fixed hard disks have become the workhorses among secondary storage choices because they provide, at a reasonable cost, the fastest data access.

■ **Detachable-reel tape.** Magnetic tape wound onto a single reel, which in turn is mounted next to an empty take-up reel onto a tape drive.

PARALLEL TRACKS
Tapes such as QIC-80 often use 20 or 32 parallel tracks.
Each track organizes data into blocks of 512 or 1,024 bytes.

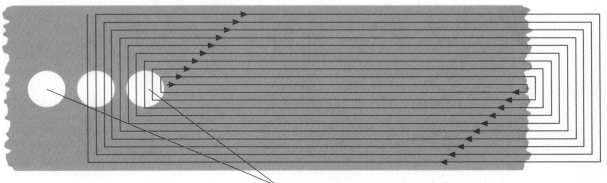

When the tape reaches either end of the spool, holes
on the tape signal the drive to reverse direction, and
the read/write head shifts up to the next outside track.
The head loops through the tracks in the spiral fashion
shown above.

DIAGONAL TRACKS
DATs store data diagonally to the edge of the tape.
Fine storage densities can be achieved because data can
be stored in crisscrossing tracks, each of which can be
several times longer than the width of the tape. Data
aren't misread, because the drive uses two sets of
read/write heads, each of which reads or writes at a
different polarity.

FIGURE HW 2-18

Storing data on magnetic tape.
Data are stored either parallel or at an
angle to the tape.

CD-ROM disks are the most popular storage choices today for multimedia
applications and for installing new software. Diskettes, on the other hand, are
widely used for transferring small amounts of data between computer systems
and for small backup jobs.

To transfer data between systems or to back up greater amounts of data,
users need to step up to either superdiskettes, WORM or rewritable optical
disks, or magnetic tape. Recently, the Internet has begun to function in yet
another role—as a backup alternative. Companies offering online backup
often charge a few dollars or more per month, depending on storage needs.

In addition, when comparing media with respect to their ability to back up
your data, you may also want to look at how long each medium can reliably
store information. The chapter Tomorrow box on page HW 71 examines this
consideration in depth.

DATA ORGANIZATION

When a computer system receives an instruction calling for data or programs
from secondary storage, it must first find those materials. The process of

Peripheral Device	Internal/ External	Speed	Media Capacity	Media Removable?	Type of Access Available	Cost
Diskette	Both	Slow	Very low	Yes	Direct	Low
Zip/LS/HiFD	Both	Medium	Low to Medium	Yes	Direct	Low
Fixed hard disk	Both	Fast	Very high	No	Direct	Medium
Removable hard disk	Both	Medium to fast	Medium to high	Yes	Direct	Medium
CD-ROM	Both	Medium	High	Yes	Direct	Low
CD-R	External	Slow	High	Yes	Direct	Medium
CD-MO	External	Medium	High	Yes	Direct	High
Phase-change CD	External	Medium	High	Yes	Direct	Medium
DVD-ROM	Both	Medium	High	Yes	Direct	Medium
DVD-RAM	Both	Medium	Very High	Yes	Direct	High
Tape	Both	Very slow	High	Yes	Sequential	Medium

FIGURE HW 2-19

Secondary storage alternatives compared.

retrieving data and programs in storage is called **data access.** Arranging data for efficient retrieval is called **data organization.**

Recall that a major difference between devices, say tape and disk, is that data on tape can be *accessed* only sequentially, whereas data on disk can be retrieved both sequentially and in a direct (random) fashion. With sequential access, the records in a file can be retrieved only in the same sequence in which they are physically stored. With direct, or random, access, the time needed to fetch a record is independent of its storage location.

The speed with which data must be retrieved necessarily dictates the choice of ways to *organize* data files. Consider a practical example. Most libraries organize their books in indexed systems ordered by title, author, and subject, so you can retrieve them directly from their places on the shelves. To locate a particular book, you simply look under the book's title in the index, find its call number, and go directly to the appropriate shelf. Books on the same subject matter are physically grouped together on the shelves because people often like to browse at titles once they've reached a particular subject area.

However, suppose that the librarians maintained no indexes and instead physically organized books alphabetically by title on shelves. With this sequential organization scheme, it would take you a long time to retrieve several books on a related subject—although you would get a lot of exercise.

People organize data on computers in a similar fashion. First, they decide on the type of access users need—direct, sequential, or both. Then they organize the data in a way that will minimize the time needed to retrieve them with the chosen access method.

Data may be organized in many ways. This section describes three: sequential, indexed, and direct organization. For any method of organization, typically one or more **key fields** must be declared so that records can be identified

■ **Data access.** The process of fetching data either sequentially or directly from a storage device. ■ **Data organization.** The process of setting up data so that they may subsequently be accessed in some desired way. ■ **Key field.** A field that helps identify a record.

How Many Tomorrows Will Today's Data Last?

The Answer May Shock You

As the computer age began to mature and high-capacity archival media became available to store information recorded on paper, many people saw these things as the answer to preserving information forever. Paper degrades over time and eventually turns to dust. Many types of electronic media, by contrast, were far more durable—at least that's what the experts were saying.

Today, a far less rosy picture is emerging.

The problem is that digital tapes and CD-ROMs are degrading far more quickly than anyone thought possible. Many experts are now warning that tapes can begin losing data in as little as five years, and CD-ROMs can start producing reading errors within the same time span. Tape breaks down with exposure to air, heat, and humidity, and contact with stray magnetic fields can rearrange the magnetized particles that store data on them. The surface of a CD-ROM can erode with exposure to ordinary light, causing the loss of data on the disk's surface.

The results of media degradation are already beginning to be felt. Close to 20 percent of the information collected on tapes made during NASA's 1976 Viking mission to Mars has been lost due to deterioration. Thus, part of our nation's heritage is gone forever. Also, some drug companies have been getting reading errors when moving product-testing data from one computer system to another, due to degraded bits on the original storage medium. How sympathetic would a jury be if these companies try to claim in court that tests showed their products to be safe and effective, but their computers destroyed data? Not very, probably. It sounds too much like the I-did-my-homework-but-my-dog-ate-it excuse.

Unfortunately, tapes and disks—unlike paper—usually do not show signs of degradation until it's too late.

And that's not the end of the bad news. A potentially more serious problem: the software needed to read a lot of archival data has long ago been tossed out and is no longer supported by anyone. Critical satellite data collected in the Amazon forest in the 1970s—data needed to establish deforestation trends—are

Perishable commodities. Tapes and disks degrade over time, making unusable the programs and data stored on them.

trapped on magnetic tapes that no one can read. Also no longer accessible because of missing or outmoded software are some POW and MIA records from the Vietnam War as well as many records at one large eastern university.

Close to three quarters of the data created today is in digital form. Much of this never makes it into paper. Electronic data are accumulated so easily and quickly that many people don't think about holding on to it for the long run. At best, an incomplete legacy of the world today may be left for future generations; at worst, a disaster looms if critical pieces of information are lost.

Today, many organizations are taking steps to be more cautious with information maintenance. For instance, the National Archives now requires the submission of technical information about how documents or records provided to them are created. The Securities and Exchange Commission has gone one step further; it makes companies filing electronic reports submit them in certain file formats only.

Digital media manufacturers are trying to help by developing new products that will be able to withstand the test of time. At this writing, however, if you want something to last at least 100 years or more, the top choice in media has been around before "computers" became a household word: paper.

and processed. For instance, if the social-security-number field serves as a key field in an employee file, you can search employee records to find data about a unique employee or sort the entire file by social security numbers.

Sequential Organization In a file with **sequential organization,** records follow one another on the storage medium in a predetermined sequence. Sequentially organized files generally are ordered by the contents of some key field, such as an account number. Thus, if a four-digit account number serves as a file's key field, the

---

■ **Sequential organization.** Arranging data on a physical medium in either ascending or descending order by the contents of some key field.

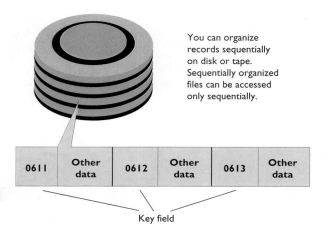

You can organize records sequentially on disk or tape. Sequentially organized files can be accessed only sequentially.

| 0611 | Other data | 0612 | Other data | 0613 | Other data |

Key field

▶ FIGURE HW 2-20

Sequential organization.

record belonging to, say, Account 0612 will be stored after the record for Account 0611 but before the record for Account 0613 (see Figure HW 2-20).

Now that you have an idea of what sequential organization is, let's see how it might be used. Companies involved with billing often update customer balances at the end of each month. Such an activity is an example of **batch processing**—so named because transactions are batched together and processed on the computer all at one time. Processing often takes place at night, when computing demands are unlikely to disrupt other uses of the computer.

Two data files are often used in batch processing: a master file and a transaction file. The *master file* normally contains relatively permanent information such as a customer's account number, name, address, and phone number. For sake of example, let's say it also contains data about any outstanding balance the customer owes. The master file is often sorted by a key field, such as customer account number, and records are arranged in ascending sequence, from the lowest number to the highest. The *transaction file* contains data about all transactions during the month (or some other period) by old customers, whose records already appear in the master file, and by new customers, for whom the master file holds no current records. Transactions include purchases and payments. Like the master file, the transaction file can be ordered in ascending sequence by customer ID number.

A sequential batch updating operation processes the two files together in the manner shown in Figure HW 2-21. The update program reads a record from each file. If the key fields match, it performs the operation specified in the transaction file. Note from Figure HW 2-21 that the key fields of the first records in each file match. Thus, the program updates Record 101 to produce the new version of the customer master file. For example, if the transaction file shows that Customer 101 bought a toaster, the program adds the amount of this purchase to the outstanding balance in the master file.

Next, the program "rolls forward" both files to the next record. It observes that Customer 102 is not in the master file, because the next master file record after 101 is 103. Therefore, the record must relate to a new customer, and the program creates a new record for Customer 102 in the updated master file. At this point, it rolls forward only the transaction file, reaching a record for Customer 103. The program observes that this record matches the one to which it is currently pointing in the master file. However, the transaction file indicates that 103 is a new customer. The comparison appears to reveal an inconsistency, because the master file contains records only for old customers. The program makes no entry in the updated master file but sends information about this transaction to the error report. The processing continues in this manner until the program exhausts available records in both files.

Indexed Organization **Indexed organization** provides a way of arranging data for both sequential and direct access. This type of organization

---

■ **Batch processing.** Processing transactions or other data in groups, at periodic intervals. ■ **Indexed organization.** A method of organizing data on a direct-access storage medium so that they can be accessed directly (through an index) or sequentially.

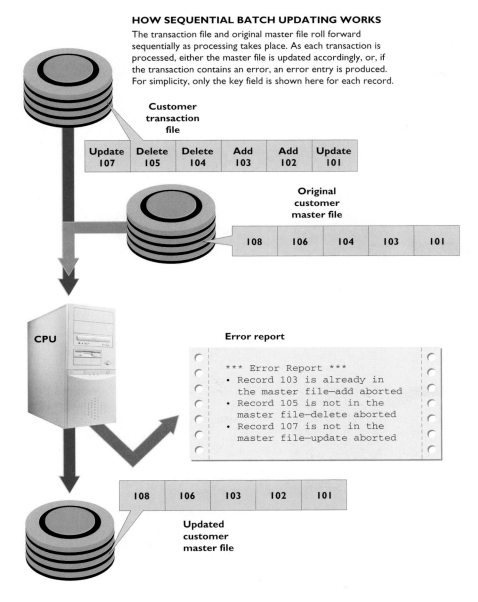

HOW SEQUENTIAL BATCH UPDATING WORKS
The transaction file and original master file roll forward sequentially as processing takes place. As each transaction is processed, either the master file is updated accordingly, or, if the transaction contains an error, an error entry is produced. For simplicity, only the key field is shown here for each record.

FIGURE HW 2-21

A sequential batch update.

requires disk storage, because tapes cannot provide direct access. It orders records on the disk by key field. Also, several indexes indicate the locations of these records for later access. These indexes work similarly to the pages and columns of data in a phone book. For example, if the top of a phone book page reads "Alexander–Ashton," you know to look for the phone number of Amazon Sewer Service on that page. When implemented on a computer, as Figure HW 2-22 shows, such indexes permit rapid access to records.

Both indexed and direct organization, covered in the next section, permit **transaction processing**—updating transaction data in random order. For instance, a teller in a bank's lobby may need to find out how much money is in Sandy Patz's checking account. Seconds later, a customer named Merlene Jones may call up someone working in a back room to find out her current balance. Then, a question comes up on Lee Shin's account. In each case, the

■ **Transaction processing.** Processing transaction data in a random sequence, as the transactions normally occur in real life.

HOW INDEXED ORGANIZATION WORKS

Records are ordered on disk by key, and all record addresses are entered in an index. To process a request to find a record—say, record 200—the computer system first searches a cylinder index and then a track index for the record's address. In the cylinder index, it learns that the record is on cylinder 009. The computer system then consults the track index for cylinder 009, where it observes that the record is on track 2 of that cylinder. The access mechanism then proceeds to this track to locate the record.

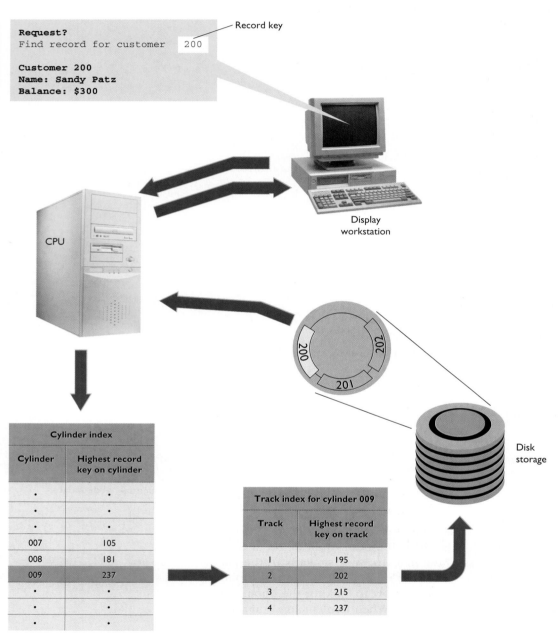

Request?
Find record for customer 200 ── Record key

Customer 200
Name: Sandy Patz
Balance: $300

Display workstation

CPU

Disk storage

Cylinder index	
Cylinder	**Highest record key on cylinder**
•	•
•	•
•	•
007	105
008	181
009	237
•	•
•	•
•	•

Track index for cylinder 009	
Track	**Highest record key on track**
1	195
2	202
3	215
4	237

 **FIGURE HW 2-22**

Indexed organization.

computer must move back and forth randomly through the checking-account records to obtain information.

Processing of such transactions as bank withdrawals often takes place in real time. **Realtime processing** implies that transactions are processed quickly enough so that people can immediately act on the results. For example, banks need to prevent overwithdrawals, so they must inspect computer records of balances in checking accounts as soon as customers attempt to take

■ **Realtime processing.** Processing that takes place quickly enough so that results can guide current and future actions.

out money. If a withdrawal is subsequently permitted, the computer updates the customer's balance on the spot. Not all banking transactions take place in real time; the recording of customer deposits, for instance, is usually batched and processed at day's end.

Systems software is available to help programmers set up indexes and index-organized files. As records are added to or deleted from a file, the software automatically updates the index. Because records remain organized sequentially on the disk, indexed files can be processed sequentially at any time.

Direct Organization   Although indexed files are suitable for many applications, they demand a potentially time-consuming process of finding disk addresses through index searches. Direct-organization schemes have been developed to provide faster direct access.

Direct organization eliminates the need for an index by translating each record's key field directly into a disk address. The computer does this by applying mathematical formulas called *hashing algorithms.* Several hashing procedures have been developed. One of the simplest involves dividing the key field by the prime number closest to, but not greater than, the number of records to be stored. (A prime number can be divided evenly by itself and 1 but not by any other number.) The remainder of this division procedure (not the quotient) becomes the relative address at which the record will be stored.

Consider a reasonably straightforward example. Suppose that a company has 1,000 employees and therefore 1,000 active employee numbers. Suppose also that all employee identification numbers (the key field) are four digits long. Therefore, the possible range of ID numbers is from 0000 to 9999.

Assume that this company wants to store the record of Employee 8742 on disk. The hashing procedure defines a disk address as follows: The computer determines the prime number closest to 1,000 (the number of records to be stored) to be 997. Figure HW 2-23 shows that the hashed disk address for Employee 8742's record computes to 766. After placing the record at an address corresponding to this number, the computer can retrieve it as needed by applying the hashing procedure to its key field again. The computer can usually calculate an address in this manner in much less time than it would take to search through one or more indexes.

Hashing procedures are difficult to develop, and they pose certain problems. For example, it is possible for two or more records to be hashed to the same relative disk location. This, of course, means they will "collide" at their

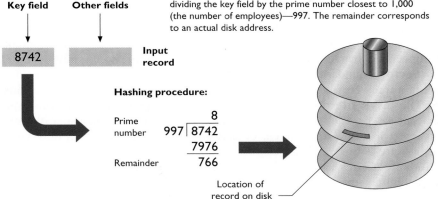

HOW DIRECT ORGANIZATION WORKS
The CPU follows a hashing procedure to assign a record to a disk address. In this case, the hashing procedure involves dividing the key field by the prime number closest to 1,000 (the number of employees)—997. The remainder corresponds to an actual disk address.

FIGURE HW 2-23

Direct organization.

■ **Direct organization.** A method of arranging data on a storage device so they can be accessed directly (randomly).

common disk address. When this happens, one record is placed in the computed location and assigned a "pointer" that chains it to the other, which often goes in the closest-available location to the hashed address. Good hashing procedures result in few collisions.

While direct organization speeds access, it has another disadvantage. Because records are not stored in sequence on the medium, programs usually cannot practically process them sequentially.

SUMMARY AND KEY TERMS

Go to the Online Glossary at www.harcourtcollege.com/infosys/parker2000/ student/ to review key terms.

Secondary storage technologies make it economically feasible to keep many programs and sets of data online to the CPU for repeated use. The most common types of secondary storage media are magnetic disk, optical disk, and magnetic tape.

Properties of Secondary Storage Systems   Any secondary storage system involves two physical parts: a peripheral device and an input/output medium. In most systems, media must pass by **read/write heads** in the peripheral devices so the systems can access or record data.

Secondary storage media provide **nonvolatile storage**—when the power to an associated peripheral device is shut off, the data stored on its medium remain intact. This trait contrasts with most types of memory, which provide **volatile storage.** Secondary storage devices can record data on *removable media,* which provide access only when mounted on the devices, or *fixed media,* which remain permanently mounted. Removable media provide the advantages of unlimited storage capacity, transportability, safer backup capability, and security. Fixed media have the advantages of higher speed, lower cost, and greater reliability.

Two basic *access* methods characterize secondary storage systems: sequential and direct access. **Sequential access** allows a computer system to retrieve the records in a file only in the same order in which they are physically stored. **Direct access** (or **random access**) allows the system to retrieve records in any order. Disk systems provide flexible storage in that they allow both random and sequential access to data. Tape systems provide sequential access only.

Magnetic Disk Systems   **Magnetic disk** storage is most widely available in the form of hard disks and diskettes.

Computer systems commonly store data on **diskettes** because they provide removable storage at low cost. Each side of a diskette holds data and programs in concentric **tracks** encoded with magnetized spots representing 0 and 1 bits. **Sector** boundaries divide a diskette surface into pie-shaped pieces. The part of a track crossed by a fixed number of contiguous sectors forms a **cluster.** The disk's **file directory,** which the computer system maintains automatically, keeps track of the contents at each disk address. To use a diskette, you insert it into a **disk drive,** or *disk unit.* A disk drive works only when the diskette is inserted correctly.

Today, diskettes are facing challenges from other removable media with much higher storage capacities. Products that can supplement or replace diskette drives include Zip drives, HiFD drives, and LS-120 drives.

Hard disks offer faster access than diskettes and greater data-carrying capacity. A hard-disk system encases one or more rigid disk platters in a permanently enclosed case along with an **access mechanism.** A separate

read/write head corresponds to each recordable disk surface, and the access mechanism moves the heads in and out among the concentric tracks to fetch data. All tracks in the same position on the tiered platters of a disk pack form a **disk cylinder.**

Three events determine the time needed to read from or write to most disks. *Seek time* is the time required for the access mechanism to reach a particular track. The time needed for the disk to spin to a specific area of a track is known as *rotational delay.* Once the drive locates desired data, the time required to transfer them to or from the disk is known as *data movement time.* The sum of these three time components is called **disk access time.** A **disk cache** strategy increases speed by expanding the limits of any hard-disk access; the computer fetches program or data contents in neighboring disk areas and transports them to RAM.

Disk drives on larger computers implement many of the same principles as microcomputer-based hard disks. Instead of finding a single pack of hard disks inside a small box permanently installed within a system unit, however, a refrigerator-sized cabinet separate from the system unit often encloses several removable packs of disk platters. Recently, **RAID** technology (for *r*edundant *a*rrays of *i*nexpensive *d*isks) has infiltrated the disk market for larger computers.

Optical-Disk Systems   **Optical disks,** which work with laser read/write devices, are a relatively recent secondary storage technology. Most optical-disk systems available today are **CD-ROM, WORM, rewritable CD,** or **DVD** systems. CD-ROM (*c*ompact *d*isk *r*ead-*o*nly *m*emory) systems enable an optical drive to read from a disk an unlimited number of times but cannot write to these disks. A WORM (*w*rite *o*nce, *r*ead *m*any) system allows you to write only once to the disk, but you can read it an unlimited number of times. Rewritable systems, which allow repeated reading and writing, often rely on *MO* and *phase-change* technology. DVD-ROM systems are similar to CD-ROM systems, but with a much greater storage capacity. DVD-RAM systems can store, erase, and rewrite data to DVD disks.

Magnetic Tape Systems   **Magnetic tape** stores data on a plastic strip coated with a magnetizable substance and wound onto a reel. A computer can access such a tape only if it is mounted on a hardware device called a **tape drive.** The drive spins the tape past a read/write head, which either reads from or writes to the tape.

Virtually all tape systems use either **cartridge tapes** or **detachable-reel tapes.** Computer tapes differ in a number of respects, including the sizes of the reels or cartridges, the width of the tape, and the format and density with which data are recorded.

Each character of data is represented in byte form across the tracks in the tape, either perpendicular, parallel, or at an angle to the edge of the tape. Often records are systematically organized on a tape by means of a key field, such as customer ID number.

Comparing Secondary Storage Alternatives   Computer users often compare secondary storage alternatives by weighing a number of product characteristics relative to cost factors.

Data Organization   The process of retrieving stored data and programs on disk or tape is called **data access.** Systematically arranging data for efficient retrieval is called **data organization.**

The three major methods of arranging files in secondary storage are sequential, indexed, and direct organization. **Sequential organization** often suits the data requirements of **batch processing** operations by ordering records with respect to a **key field. Indexed organization** also arranges records in order by key field on disk to facilitate sequential access; one or more indexes list storage addresses for specific records to permit direct access to them. **Direct**

organization facilitates even faster direct access. Both indexed and direct organization support the data needs of **transaction processing** and **realtime processing** applications.

EXERCISES

1. Match each term with the description that fits best.
   a. diskette
   b. disk cache
   c. cartridge tape
   d. hard disk
   e. optical disk
   f. phase change

   _____ A storage technology with media read by a laser beam

   _____ A storage alternative, often under 2 megabytes in capacity, available in low-density and high-density formats

   _____ A high-capacity storage alternative used on PCs mostly for backing up a hard disk

   _____ A specialized CD technology

   _____ The most indispensable of secondary-storage medium

   _____ A method of accelerating storage access by fetching more data from disk on each read than the immediate processing task requires

2. Assume, for simplicity's sake, that a kilobyte is 1,000 bytes, a megabyte is 1,000 × 1,000 bytes, and a gigabyte is 1,000 × 1,000 × 1,000 bytes. You have a 10-gigabyte hard disk with the following usage characteristics:

APPLICATIONS	BYTES
Operating system	7,600,453
Other systems software	2,184,605
Office suite	83,701,460
Other software	479,842,809
Documents	27,904,668

   What percentage of the hard disk is used up?

3. What term does each of the following acronyms stand for?
   a. SCSI
   b. MO
   c. RAID
   d. WORM
   e. DAT

4. Define the following terms:
   a. Nonvolatile storage
   b. Random access
   c. Cluster
   d. Transaction processing
   e. RAID

5. Name a microcomputer-oriented storage medium discussed in the chapter that meets each of the following criteria:
   a. A sequentially organized medium with a low cost per byte of information stored
   b. A CD that allows both reading and one-time writing
   c. A medium that works like a standard diskette but provides 120 MB or more storage capacity instead of just 1.44 MB; you can use standard diskettes on the drive that reads this medium.

6. Match the PC component shown in each of the following pictures with the appropriate term.

   _____ Removable hard disk and drive

   _____ Cartridge tape

   _____ Diskette

   _____ CD-ROM

   _____ RAID

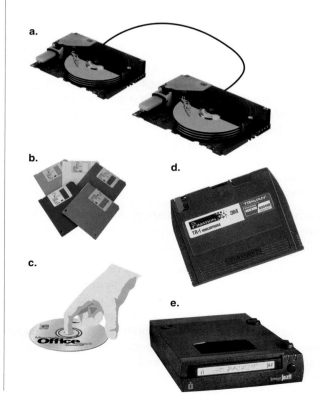

a.

b.

c.

d.

e.

7. On PC-compatible storage systems, what type of storage device is normally assigned to the various letters?

   a. A: _____

   b. B: _____

   c. C: _____

   d. D: _____

   e. E: _____

   f. F: _____

8. Fill in the blanks:

   a. A storage medium is _____ if it loses its contents when the power is shut off.

   b. For rapid access, related data often are stored on the same _____, a collection of disk tracks that are in the same relative position on different surfaces of a disk pack.

   c. MO and CD-ROM refer to types of _____ disks.

   d. TR-1, QIC-80, and DAT are types of magnetic _____ storage.

   e. Iomega's _____ drive resembles a diskette drive, only it reads 100 or 250 MB cartridges.

9. What is the difference between sequential access and direct access?

   a. Which of the two would support faster processing of 25 records at random from a file of 100,000 records?

   b. Which of the two would be most appropriate in realtime applications?

10. Each of the following definitions is not strictly true in some regard. In each case, identify and correct the error.

    a. Realtime processing: Recording transactions on the computer as soon as they take place.

    b. Data movement time: The interval between the time a user types in a command to fetch disk data and the time the data appear on the display.

    c. Cluster: The intersection of a sector and a track on disk.

    d. Optical disk: A CD-ROM disk.

    e. Sequential organization: Arranging data in either ascending or descending order on a key field; used only with tape.

11. Identify each of the following statements as true or false.

    _____ Superdiskette drives typically work with nonremovable media.

    _____ 1.44 MB diskettes are called high-density diskettes.

    _____ Exposing a diskette's write-protection square prevents writing anything to it.

    _____ A disk cluster is typically larger than a disk track.

    _____ Disk access time is greater than seek time.

    _____ EIDE commonly refers to a tape format.

    _____ A computer system with a C and D drive may have only one physical disk drive, which is partitioned.

    _____ DVD refers to a hard-disk standard.

    _____ You cannot write to a CD-RW disk an unlimited number of times.

    _____ Even on a microcomputer system, it can take over an hour to back up a hard disk onto tape.

12. Compare and contrast the three types of data organization discussed in the chapter: sequential, indexed, and direct organization.

PROJECTS

1. Secondary Storage Companies The following figure lists the Web sites of several companies that make secondary storage products. Choose any company on the list and determine the types of products it makes.

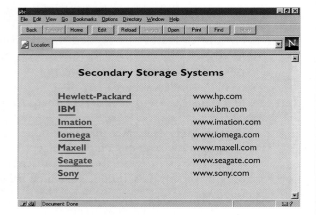

Hint: Many companies also have toll-free phone numbers, which you can get by dialing Directory Assistance. If you can't get the product information you need over the Internet, you may be able to get it though the mail or have it faxed to you.

2. The Computer in Your Backyard Inspect the computer you regularly use in your lab, dorm room, or home and answer the following questions about it:

a. What devices are assigned to the drive letters A, B, C, D, and E? Does the system include other active drive letters or drive names? If so, what device is assigned to each of them?

b. What is the capacity of the hard disk?

c. What percentage of the hard disk is used up?

d. Is the hard disk on the system partitioned?

3. Magnetic Tape Tape systems are widely used on microcomputer systems for hard-disk backup. For this project, choose a particular tape drive and answer the following questions about it. Feel free to consult Internet resources in your research, as well as journal articles and product brochures.

a. What is the name of the drive and who makes it? Is it an internal or external device?

b. What is the approximate price of the drive?

c. What tape formats does the drive support—for instance, T-1, QIC-80, and so on?

d. What is the most capacious tape cartridge that the drive will accept? How much time will it take to back up a half-full 10 GB hard disk on such a tape?

e. What do tape cartridges cost?

4. Rewritable CD Choose a rewritable-CD storage device and answer the following questions. Feel free to consult Internet resources in your research, as well as journal articles and product brochures.

a. What is the name of the device? Who makes it?

b. Does the device use MO technology, phase-change technology, or something else?

c. What is the price of the device?

d. What storage capacities do the device's rewritable CDs provide? What are the unit prices of these CDs?

e. What is the device's average access time? How does this access time compare with that of a hard disk, which is also a read/write technology?

f. Can standard CD-ROMs be used in any way on the device?

5. **CD Product Review** Thousands of CD titles compete for attention in today's commercial marketplace. Some, such as *Flight Simulator* and *Myst* have become runaway bestsellers, while some others are arguably not worth the plastic needed to publish them. For this project, choose any CD title and write a short review about it, not exceeding three pages. In the review, cover both good and bad points that you see in the product. Also, make sure that your critique has a "bottom line;" in other words, after you weigh the pros and cons, would you recommend the CD to others or suggest that people stay away?

6. **Holographic Storage** Holographic storage technology has received a lot of attention in the news lately as a possible replacement for conventional storage methods. As hard as it is to believe, the entire holdings of the Library of Congress could fit within a three-dimensional holographic cube smaller than the size of your PC's display device. Research this technology and answer these questions:
    a. What is holographic storage?
    b. What potential lies in holographic storage?
    c. Is holographic storage targeted as a replacement for memory, hard disk, both memory and hard disk, or some other system component entirely?
    d. How far advanced is holographic storage? In other words, how soon can people expect to use it on desktop PCs or in other applications?

7. **"Dumb" Questions Project** While the chapter mentions a number of useful facts about secondary storage technologies, it does not always provide reasons why certain things work the way they do. In some cases, the answers are self-evident; in others, the underlying reasons are more complicated and will demand a little research on your part. With that background, answer the following questions:
    a. Why do hard disks continue to spin while the computer is turned on, even when you do not access them?
    b. Since RAM is so much faster than hard disks and costs less than a hundred dollars for every 16 megabytes, why not just put more RAM into every computer and completely eliminate the hard disk?

8. **Removable Hard Disks** Search the Internet, journal articles, or product brochures to find a state-of-the-art *removable-media* hard-disk system for a microcomputer. Answer the following questions about it.
    a. Who makes the hard-disk drive? What is the name of the drive?
    b. What is the capacity of the cartridges the drive can accept?
    c. What is the speed of the drive relative to a conventional, fixed hard disk?

    d. How much does the drive cost? How much do cartridges cost?

9. **Making Your Own CD-ROMs** Technology is now available so that you can download music over the Internet, directly onto your hard disk, and from there, burn the music onto a local CD. Do the necessary research so that you can describe to your classmates exactly how homemade CDs can be produced on an ordinary computer system and what sorts of special equipment you need to do it. Make sure that the procedure you come up with is legal; remember that most music is copyrighted.

10. **CD-ROM Books** In recent years, many books have been published not only in traditional print format, but also as CD-ROMs. Electronic books have certain advantages and disadvantages over printed ones. Identify as many as you can of these.

11. **Information Overload** Perhaps no type of hardware is more responsible for the amount of information we have at our disposal today than the electronic disk. However, it is often said that today's managers are deluged with too much information rather than having too little. Some critics even believe that computer systems are primarily to blame for this information overload. How do you feel? Can having too many facts to mull over possibly be a bad thing or is there something else causing the problem here?

12. **Internet Backup** In addition to the many types of backup devices mentioned in the chapter—tape drives, Zip and Jaz drives, CD-RW drives, and so on—there is also the Internet as a backup possibility. Increasingly, Web sites are becoming available that, for a fee, will let users store data remotely through their home modem and an Internet connection. For this project, find a Web site that provides Internet backup and answer the questions on the following page.

a. What is the Web address of the site?
b. How much does it cost to back up data?
c. What advantages and disadvantages are there to backing up data on the Internet?

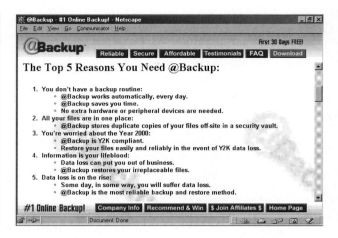

ONLINE REVIEW

Go to the Online Review at www.harcourtcollege.com/infosys/parker2000/ student/ to test your understanding of this chapter's concepts.

INPUT AND OUTPUT

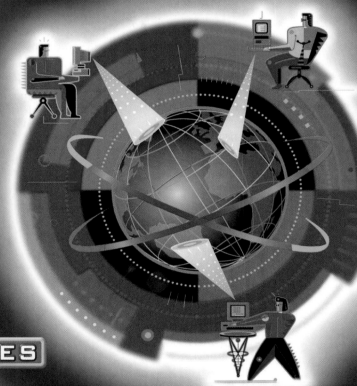

LEARNING OBJECTIVES

After completing this chapter, you will be able to:

1. Identify several types of input and output devices and explain their functions.

2. Describe the characteristics of input equipment that most users encounter regularly—namely, keyboards and pointing devices.

3. Explain what source data automation means and discuss several ways to accomplish it.

4. Describe the characteristics of output equipment that most users encounter regularly—namely, display devices and printers.

5. Discuss several other types of output equipment.

OVERVIEW

In Chapter HW 2, we covered secondary storage devices. Although those devices perform both input and output operations for the computer, storage is their main function. In this chapter, we turn to equipment designed primarily for inputting programs and data into a form the computer can use, outputting results to users, or both. Many of these devices possess limited amounts of storage capacity, as well.

We'll begin the chapter with a look at input. First up are keyboards and then pointing devices such as mice and trackballs. Most users at home and in offices require these types of devices to enter commands, programs, or data into their computer systems.

From there, we'll cover hardware designed for source data automation. This equipment provides fast, relatively error-free input for certain kinds of applications.

Then we'll explore output, starting with display devices. Here, we'll highlight some of the qualities that distinguish one display device from another.

Next, we will turn to printers. In this section, you will learn about the wide variety of devices that place computer output on paper.

The chapter then discusses other types of output equipment. Included among these devices are speakers, machines that record computer output onto microfilm, voice-output hardware, plotters, and film recorders.

Keep in mind that this chapter describes only a small sample of the input/output equipment available today. In fact, the marketplace offers thousands of hardware products, and they can work together in so many ways that you can create a computer system to fit almost any conceivable need.

FIGURE HW 3-1

Keyboard. This keyboard typifies those sold with many PCs. For operator convenience, the keyboard features duplicates of many keys.

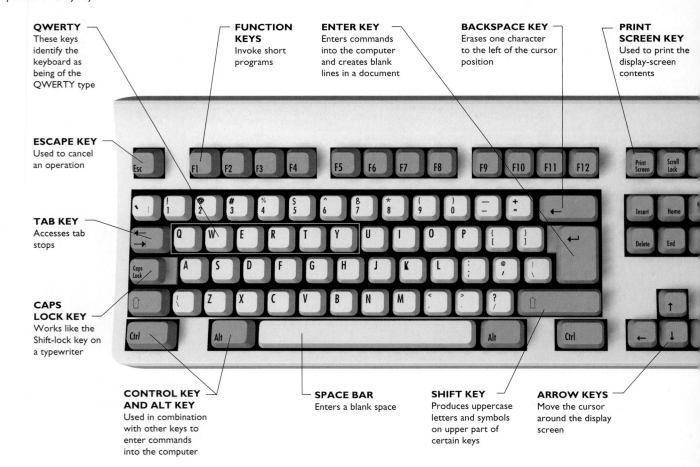

QWERTY
These keys identify the keyboard as being of the QWERTY type

FUNCTION KEYS
Invoke short programs

ENTER KEY
Enters commands into the computer and creates blank lines in a document

BACKSPACE KEY
Erases one character to the left of the cursor position

PRINT SCREEN KEY
Used to print the display-screen contents

ESCAPE KEY
Used to cancel an operation

TAB KEY
Accesses tab stops

CAPS LOCK KEY
Works like the Shift-lock key on a typewriter

CONTROL KEY AND ALT KEY
Used in combination with other keys to enter commands into the computer

SPACE BAR
Enters a blank space

SHIFT KEY
Produces uppercase letters and symbols on upper part of certain keys

ARROW KEYS
Move the cursor around the display screen

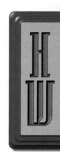

INPUT AND OUTPUT

Input and output equipment allow people to communicate with computers. An **input device** converts data and programs that humans can understand into a form the computer can process. Such a device translates the letters, numbers, and other natural-language symbols that humans conventionally use in reading and writing into the configurations of 0 and 1 bits that the computer processes. **Output devices,** on the other hand, convert strings of computer bits back into natural-language form to make them understandable to humans. These devices present output on screen displays, on paper or film, and in other forms.

Much of a computer system's peripheral equipment performs input or output functions. Keyboards, pointing devices, and optical character recognition devices are designed primarily for input. Printers and monitors specialize in output. Output devices produce results in either hard-copy or soft-copy form. The term **hard copy** generally refers to output permanently recorded onto an easily portable medium such as paper or film. Printed reports and output put into slide or transparency form are common examples. The term **soft copy** generally refers to display output—output that appears temporarily in a form with limited portability, such as on a computer screen.

KEYBOARDS

Most computers would be useless without **keyboards** (see Figure HW 3-1). Keyboards are the main devices through which computers receive user input. The large majority of keyboards follow a standard arrangement for letter keys called *QWERTY* (named for the first six letter keys at the top left of most typewriter keyboards).

Figure HW 3-1 shows a typical PC keyboard layout and describes the purposes of several keys. A Delete (Del) key, for example, removes characters from the screen, and an Insert (Ins) key enables the user to add characters between those on the current display. Keyboards also feature several *function keys,* which are labeled F1, F2, F3, and so on (see the top of Figure HW 3-1). When the user taps one of these keys, the keystroke initiates a special command or even an entire computer program. Each software program defines the actions of function keys in its own way. For example, tapping the F2 key in your word processing program may enable you to indent text, but the same keystroke in your spreadsheet program may let you edit cells. Most keyboards also have a *numeric keypad;* activate it by pressing the NumLock key, and you can easily and quickly enter numbers.

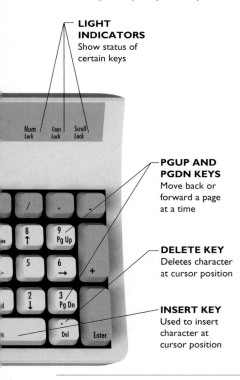

LIGHT INDICATORS Show status of certain keys

PGUP AND PGDN KEYS Move back or forward a page at a time

DELETE KEY Deletes character at cursor position

INSERT KEY Used to insert character at cursor position

Web Tutor

For a tutorial on the various parts of a keyboard, go to www.harcourtcollege.com/ infosys/parker2000/student/ tutor/ and click on **Chapter HW 3.**

■ **Input device.** Equipment that supplies data and programs to the computer. ■ **Output device.** Equipment that accepts data and programs from the computer. ■ **Hard copy.** A permanent form of computer system output—for example, information printed on paper or film. ■ **Soft copy.** A nonpermanent form of computer system output—for example, a screen display. ■ **Keyboard.** An input device composed of numerous keys, arranged in a configuration similar to that of a typewriter, that generate letters, numbers, and other symbols when depressed.

The number of special keys, as well as their capabilities and placement, varies among manufacturers. When buying a computer system, look carefully at the keyboard's key selection and the placement of keys. Also, when buying a portable computer, pay special attention to spacing between the keys, and make sure that the keyboard allows comfortable typing.

POINTING DEVICES

For a tutorial on the mouse and other types of input devices, go to www. harcourtcollege.com/infosys/ parker2000/student/tutor/ and click on Chapter HW 3.

Pointing devices refer to input hardware that moves an onscreen pointer such as an arrow, cursor, or insertion point. As the pointing device is moved along a surface or, alternatively, as it remains stationary while a finger or hand operates it, the pointing device determines position, distance, or speed and repositions the onscreen pointer accordingly.

Some common types of pointing devices are the mouse, light pen, touch screen, joystick, trackball, and graphics tablet.

Mouse   Many people supplement keyboard input with a **mouse** (see Figure HW 3-2). When you move the mouse along a flat surface, the onscreen pointer—often referred to as a *mouse pointer*—moves correspondingly. Mice provide capabilities to move rapidly from one location to another on a display screen, to make screen selections, to move and resize screen images, and to draw on the screen. A mouse often accomplishes such tasks much faster or far more effectively than you could complete them by pressing combinations of keys on the keyboard.

Mice are especially handy tools for working with *icons* on the screen—small graphics symbols that represent commands or program options. When you use the mouse to *select* an icon, you point to it on the screen and press—or click—the left mouse button once or twice. To *move* an icon from one part of the screen to another, you position the mouse pointer on the icon, hold down the button while moving the mouse to drag the icon to its new position, and release the mouse button. This operation is commonly known as *dragging and dropping.* Many mice today come with a wheel on top of them, which enables you to more easily *scroll* the display-screen contents.

While most mice sold with computer systems connect via serial cables to a computer's system unit, cordless mice are also available. These mice, powered by batteries, send wireless signals to which the computer responds.

Light Pen   A **light pen** senses marks or other indicators through a light-sensitive cell in its tip. When the tip of the pen is placed close to the screen, the display device can identify its position (see Figure HW 3-3). Some pens are equipped with buttons that users press to flip stored pages forward or backward on the screen, and many come with their own command sets. Potential users of portable computers equipped with light pens include inspectors, factory workers, sales representatives, real-estate agents, police officers, doctors and nurses, insurance adjusters, store clerks, and truck drivers—in other words, anybody that regularly carries around a clipboard and has forms to fill out.

Touch Screen   Some display devices are designed to allow a finger rather than a light pen to activate onscreen commands. They are commonly called

---

■ **Pointing device.** A piece of input hardware that moves an onscreen pointer such as an arrow, cursor, or insertion point.
■ **Mouse.** A common pointing device that you slide along a flat surface to move a pointer around a display screen and make selections. ■ **Light pen.** An electrical device, resembling an ordinary pen, used to enter computer input.

touch screen displays (see Figure HW 3-4). Touch screens are widely employed today in information *kiosks,* which are often used by people who are not necessarily computer literate. Touch screens are also useful for factory applications and fieldwork, where users wear gloves or cannot operate keypads for other reasons.

Joystick A **joystick** (see Figure HW 3-5) provides input through a grip that looks like a car's gearshift. This input device often supports computer games and computer-aided design (CAD) work. The speed at which the joystick is manipulated and the distance it travels determine the screen pointer's movement. Today, some electronic games replace joysticks with gloves containing built-in sensors, enabling the computer to detect hand movements directly.

Trackball A **trackball** (see Figure HW 3-5) consists of a sphere with its top exposed through a case. The onscreen pointer travels in the same direction as

FIGURE HW 3-2

Using a mouse.

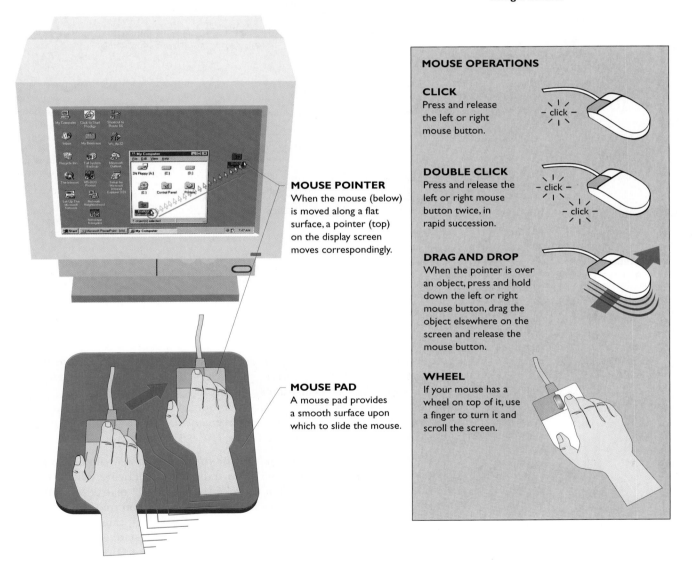

MOUSE POINTER
When the mouse (below) is moved along a flat surface, a pointer (top) on the display screen moves correspondingly.

MOUSE PAD
A mouse pad provides a smooth surface upon which to slide the mouse.

MOUSE OPERATIONS

CLICK
Press and release the left or right mouse button.

– click –

DOUBLE CLICK
Press and release the left or right mouse button twice, in rapid succession.

– click –
– click –

DRAG AND DROP
When the pointer is over an object, press and hold down the left or right mouse button, drag the object elsewhere on the screen and release the mouse button.

WHEEL
If your mouse has a wheel on top of it, use a finger to turn it and scroll the screen.

■ **Touch-screen display.** A display device that generates input when you touch a finger to the screen. ■ **Joystick.** An input device that resembles a car's gear shift. ■ **Trackball.** An input device that exposes the top of a sphere, which the user moves to control an onscreen pointer.

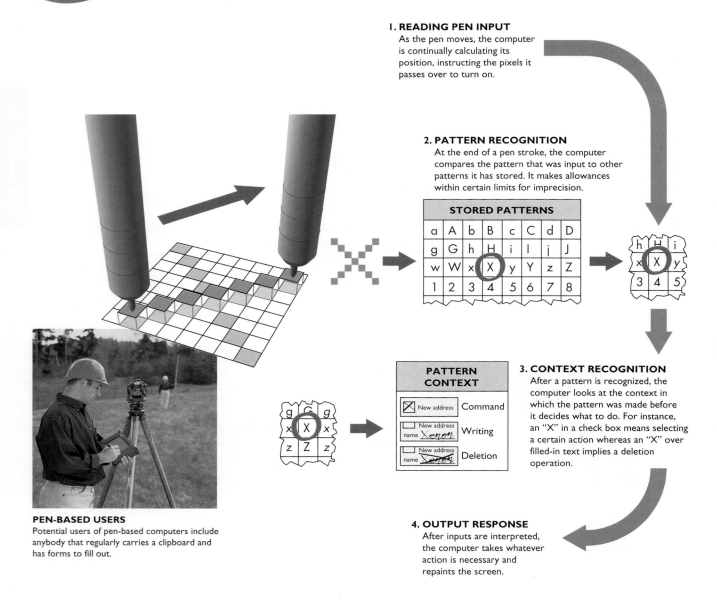

1. READING PEN INPUT
As the pen moves, the computer is continually calculating its position, instructing the pixels it passes over to turn on.

2. PATTERN RECOGNITION
At the end of a pen stroke, the computer compares the pattern that was input to other patterns it has stored. It makes allowances within certain limits for imprecision.

STORED PATTERNS

a	A	b	B	c	C	d	D
g	G	h	H	i	I	j	J
w	W	x	X	y	Y	z	Z
1	2	3	4	5	6	7	8

3. CONTEXT RECOGNITION
After a pattern is recognized, the computer looks at the context in which the pattern was made before it decides what to do. For instance, an "X" in a check box means selecting a certain action whereas an "X" over filled-in text implies a deletion operation.

PATTERN CONTEXT

☒ New address	Command
New address name *Xenon*	Writing
New address name *Xenon*	Deletion

4. OUTPUT RESPONSE
After inputs are interpreted, the computer takes whatever action is necessary and repaints the screen.

PEN-BASED USERS
Potential users of pen-based computers include anybody that regularly carries a clipboard and has forms to fill out.

FIGURE HW 3-3

Pen-based computing.

the operator spins the sphere. In fact, a trackball is merely a mouse turned upside down. Recently, a number of devices have come on the market to compete with the traditional trackball and mouse. The *pointing stick,* which appears on the keyboard of many notebook computers, is ideal when a pointing device is needed and it's inconvenient to carry around or use a conventional mouse or trackball (see Figure HW 3-5).

Graphics Tablet   A **graphics tablet,** or *digitizing tablet,* often employs a penlike stylus (see Figure HW 3-5). You trace over a drawing placed on the flat, touch-sensitive tablet. You can think of the tablet as a matrix of thousands of tiny dots, each with its own machine address. When you trace a line on the tablet, the stylus or cursor passes over some of the dots, causing their status in computer memory to change from a 0 state to a 1 state. When the drawing is complete, it is stored in digital form as a large matrix of 0s and 1s; you can then recall it at any time.

■ **Graphics tablet.** An input device that consists of a flat board and a pointing mechanism that traces over it, storing the traced pattern in computer memory.

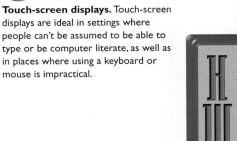

Touch-screen displays. Touch-screen displays are ideal in settings where people can't be assumed to be able to type or be computer literate, as well as in places where using a keyboard or mouse is impractical.

SOURCE DATA AUTOMATION

Applications often require translation of handwritten data into digital form that allows electronic processing. This procedure sometimes consumes thousands of hours of wasteful, duplicated effort, and it can result in many mistakes and delays. Data originally recorded by hand onto source documents or forms must then be keyed into digital form on some input device, verified, and read into the computer. Usually, several people must cooperate in such a process, complicating matters further.

Source data automation eliminates much of this duplicated effort, delay, extra handling, and potential for error by initially collecting data in digital form. The people who collect ready-to-process transaction data are those who know most about the events that the data represent. Thus, such people can instantly check for accuracy during the data entry process. Its many benefits have made source data automation a compelling choice for many types of commercial data entry today.

Source data automation has transformed a number of information-handling tasks. For example, workers who take orders over the phone today usually enter needed input directly at display workstations, so they don't have to

■ **Source data automation.** The process of collecting data at their point of origin in digital form.

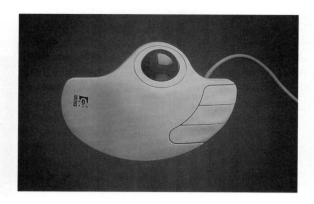

TRACKBALL
A trackball consists of a sphere in a case, with only the top of the sphere exposed. A trackball requires less desk space to use than a mouse.

POINTING STICK
Many notebook computers have a small keyboard stick that you push in different directions to move the onscreen pointer.

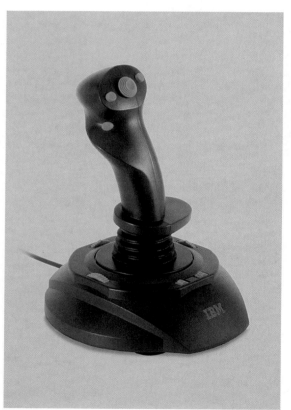

GRAPHICS TABLET
A graphics tablet is used to draw or trace on and thereby create data the computer can read.

JOYSTICK
A joystick looks like a car's stick shift and is most often used for

FIGURE HW 3-5

Pointing devices.

record the same data twice. Source data automation also speeds up checkout lines and inventory taking at supermarkets, quality control operations in factories, and check processing by banks. This section discusses several technologies and devices that contribute to source data automation.

OPTICAL CHARACTER RECOGNITION (OCR)

Optical character recognition (OCR) technology encompasses a wide range of optical-scanning procedures and equipment designed for machine

■ **Optical character recognition (OCR).** The use of reflected light to input marks, characters, or codes.

recognition of marks, characters, and codes. OCR devices transform symbols into digital data for storage in the computer.

Optical Marks   One of the oldest applications of OCR focuses on processing tests and questionnaires completed on special forms using *optical marks.* For example, a student darkens the bubbles on an answer sheet to indicate the answers to multiple-choice test questions. A hardware device called an optical document reader scans the answer sheets by passing a light beam across the spaces corresponding to the sets of possible responses to the questions. Filled-in responses reflect the light, and the machine tallies that choice. Results are usually then printed on the test form and can also be processed by a computer system if the reader is attached to a computer or allows the data to be stored on a disk or tape cartridge.

Optical Characters   *Optical characters* are characters specially designed to be identifiable by humans as well as by some type of OCR reader. Optical characters conform to a certain font design, such as the one shown in Figure HW 3-6. The optical reader shines light on the characters and converts the reflections into electronic patterns for machine recognition. The reader can identify a character only if it is familiar with the font standard used. Today, most machines are designed to read several standard OCR fonts, even when these fonts are mixed in a single document.

Optical characters are widely used in processing *turnaround documents,* such as the credit-card slips used for customer transactions in stores and restaurants. They also speed processing of the monthly bills that are typically sent by credit-card, utility, and cable-TV companies to their customers. Such documents are imprinted in certain places with optical characters that aid processing when consumers send them back with payment—or "turn them around." Sometimes, as in the case of the restaurant bill in Figure HW 3-6, it's easy to spot the optical characters (see the top row of numbers). Today, however, many OCR fonts look so much like normal text that it's hard for an ordinary person to tell what parts the digital systems can read.

FIGURE HW 3-6

Optical characters.

OPTICAL FONTS

Optical fonts have the advantage of being readable by both computers and human beings.

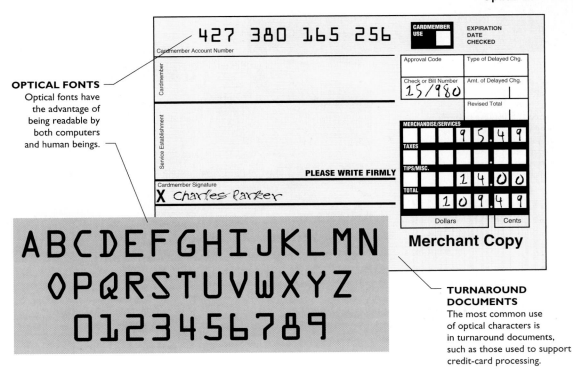

TURNAROUND DOCUMENTS

The most common use of optical characters is in turnaround documents, such as those used to support credit-card processing.

Optical Codes The most widely used type of *optical code* is the **bar code**, which records data by arranging several vertical bars of varying widths. The code supplies data on a product or transaction when the system reads it, either by the operator passing a scanning *wand* or *gun* over the coded label or moving the item past a *fixed scanning station* (see Figure HW 3-7).

▲ **FIGURE HW 3-7**

Bar coding.

BAR-CODE READER
Most bar-code readers employ either a gun, wand, or scanning station.

GUN
A gun is used with a display device in many types of product-checkout environments

WAND
A wand is lightweight and particularly handy when the operator has to do scanning while on the move.

BAR CODE
The most widely known bar code is the universal product code (UPC), used on supermarket products. The numbers below the bars identify the manufacturer and product.

SCANNING STATION
A scanning station is the type of reader found most in supermarkets

■ **Bar code.** A machine-readable code that stores data as sets of bars of varying widths.

The most familiar bar code is the *universal product code (UPC)* commonly found on packaged goods in supermarkets and in use since the early 1970s. Each code describes a product and identifies its manufacturer. The checkout system's bar-code reader gathers data that allows computers to identify the item, look up the current price, and print the information on a receipt. While many customers are still suspicious of the accuracy of bar-coded-pricing systems, a recent study by the Federal Trade Commission reported that such systems are far more accurate than manual data entry and that customers are more likely to be undercharged than overcharged.

While supermarket packaging probably represents the most common use of bar codes, codes similar to the UPC support a variety of other applications. For instance, shippers such as Federal Express and United Parcel Service use their own bar codes to mark and track packages, hospitals use bar codes to identify patient samples, and the police use bar codes to mark evidence.

Retail-based bar-coding systems that use special terminals to verify customer credit, compute sales taxes on transactions, and record transaction data—such as product descriptions and sales amounts—are examples of **point-of-sale (POS) systems.** When the store clerk reads the label attached to each purchased item with a wand or gun connected to the sales register, a computer within the register performs all of the necessary arithmetic, prepares a customer receipt, and accumulates input for subsequent management analysis. Not all POS systems use bar codes; for example, those at restaurants and hotels often work exclusively with the magnetic strips on credit cards, supplemented with keyboard input.

IMAGE SCANNERS

Image scanners convert flat images—such as photographs, drawings, and documents—into digital data. After storing the images in the computer system, you can manipulate them as you like and then drop them into slides, a desktop-published document, a Web page, or another type of output.

Scanners work in a variety of ways (see Figure HW 3-8). A *flatbed scanner* inputs one page at a time and works a lot like a photocopier. Many models scan color documents, and some even have attachments for capturing image data from 35 mm slides. A *drum (sheetfed) scanner* functions in ways similar to a flatbed scanner, with a few important differences. For instance, it accepts source materials differently; a roller mechanism grasps and carries inputs fed through a narrow slot. This design cuts the scanner's cost, the amount of desk space required, and makes automatic sheet feeding possible. However, the feature also prevents the device from scanning bound-book pages. *Handheld scanners* are useful for inputting small amounts of data and cost less than other types of scanners, but they also provide the most limited capabilities.

Many image scanners that work with PCs scan at resolution rates of 300, 600, or 1,200 dpi (dots per inch). As you might expect, a higher number of dots generates better resolution when the image is finally output. Keep in mind that image resolution is ultimately determined by an output device, however, so it may not make sense to buy a 1,200 dpi scanner if your printer can't produce hard copy sharper than 600 dpi.

Image scanners labeled "dumb" devices can't recognize any of the text they read. So-called intelligent image scanners, on the other hand, are accompanied by optical character recognition (OCR) software, which enables them to recognize as well as read most standard text characters. Thus, an OCR-capable image scanner can produce text that can later be edited through a standard word processing program.

■ **Point-of-sale (POS) system.** A computer system, commonly found in department stores and supermarkets, that uses electronic cash register terminals to collect, process, and store data about sales transactions. ■ **Image scanner.** A device that can read into computer memory a hard-copy image such as a text page, photograph, map or drawing.

FLATBED SCANNER
A flatbed scanner looks and works a lot like a photocopier, except that it produces a computer file instead of paper output.

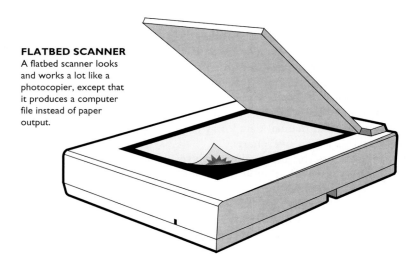

RESOLUTION
Many scanners let you specify the resolution (in dpi) at which you wish to scan. High-resolution images look sharper but take more time to input and require more bytes to store.

DRUM SCANNER
Drum scanners, such as this one that attaches to an ordinary keyboard, use a roller as opposed to a flatbed mechanism to input images.

HANDHELD SCANNER
Handheld scanners are useful for inputting small amounts of information and work by sliding over images.

FIGURE HW 3-8

Image scanning.

Scanners can cost anywhere from one hundred to a few thousand dollars, and professional-level models can cost tens of thousands of dollars.

DIGITAL CAMERAS

Digital cameras are much like regular cameras, but instead of recording images on print or slide film they record onto removable memory cards like those used in notebook computers (see Figure HW 3-9). As snapshots are taken, the cards are loaded with the digital data that form the picture image.

Digital cameras targeted for consumers use storage media that hold from a half dozen or so to 100 or more images. The number held depends both on the capacity of the medium and the image resolution you select. Many cameras will let you preview an image after you take it so that you can immediately erase it if it's not suitable. Once the card is full, you often connect the camera via a special cable to a port on your PC. The software that comes with the camera then allows you to transfer images to the PC's RAM. The software also clears the card's memory so that you can take more pictures at a later time. After storing the images on your PC's hard disk, you

■ **Digital camera.** A camera that records pictures as digital data instead of as film images.

can retouch them with image-enhancement software, adjusting contrast, brightness, color, and focus—or adding special effects such as sepia tones or psychedelic colors.

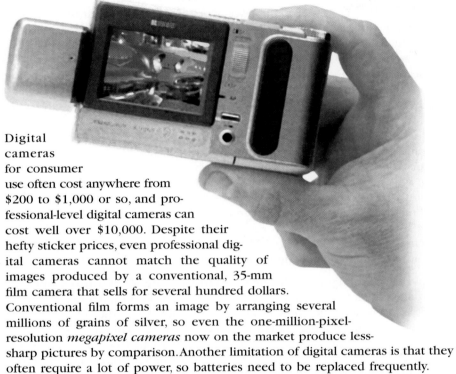

Digital cameras for consumer use often cost anywhere from $200 to $1,000 or so, and professional-level digital cameras can cost well over $10,000. Despite their hefty sticker prices, even professional digital cameras cannot match the quality of images produced by a conventional, 35-mm film camera that sells for several hundred dollars. Conventional film forms an image by arranging several millions of grains of silver, so even the one-million-pixel-resolution *megapixel cameras* now on the market produce less-sharp pictures by comparison. Another limitation of digital cameras is that they often require a lot of power, so batteries need to be replaced frequently.

Disadvantages notwithstanding, digital cameras can produce respectable images that make them useful for many types of business and recreational applications. For instance, an insurance adjuster may need a no-fuss picture of accident damage that can be quickly inserted into an electronic database. A home or business user may require a simple snapshot for a newsletter or a Web page. A news photographer often needs to capture an image immediately and send it over phone wires to an anxious editor. Two compelling advantages to digital cameras are that you need not develop film and you don't need a scanner to get images into the computer.

You don't, incidentally, need to go out and buy a digital camera or even an image scanner to get digital photographs that you can use on Web pages or in greeting cards or letters. Kodak and a number of other image-processing companies will let you send them conventional film; they'll develop it for you in a digital format and give you a password to pick your photos up on the Internet. On the other hand, if you need something with more capability than a digital camera, there are also *digital camcorders* that can be used to make videos for multimedia presentations, as well as *digital video cameras* for holding realtime videoconferences over the Internet.

FIGURE HW 3-9

Digital camera. Unlike their conventional counterparts, digital cameras store images on reusable cartridges. Most cameras let you display and erase images while shooting, and come with a cable that lets you transfer images to your computer.

OTHER TECHNOLOGIES

Many other technologies in addition to the ones we've already covered exist for source data automation. Four we'll briefly cover here are voice-input systems, handwriting-recognition devices, smart cards, and magnetic ink character recognition (MICR).

Voice-Input Systems   A hardware-and-software combination that can convert spoken words into digital data is known as a **voice-input system.** If you

---

■ **Voice-input system.** A system that enables a computer to recognize the human voice.

For links to further information about input devices, go to www.harcourtcollege.com/infosys/parker2000/student/explore/ and click on Chapter HW 3.

stop to think about the complex work that humans do in interpreting speech, you can appreciate the challenge of designing technology to do the same thing. Two people may pronounce the same word differently because of accents, personal styles of speech, and the unique quality of each person's voice. A single person may pronounce words differently at various times—when eating, for example, or when suffering from a cold. Moreover, in listening to others, humans not only ignore background noises but also decode sentence fragments.

Researchers have tried a number of tricks to overcome the obstacles for which humans naturally compensate. Many voice-input systems are designed to screen out background noises and to accept "training" from users, who repeat words until the system recognizes the patterns in their voices. The training often only requires a few minutes of time, though some systems have the option of longer training for increased accuracy. Some voice-input systems can recognize only limited numbers of isolated words, while others attempt to recognize whole sentences composed of continuous speech. This latter type is commonly referred to as a *continuous-speech recognition system*.

Continuous-speech-recognition products have dramatically increased in quality and dropped in price in recent years. You can pay less than $200 for a system that can recognize over 250,000 words. Today's principal application for continuous-speech recognition is dictation.

Handwriting Recognition Devices   **Handwriting recognition devices** often collect data through a flat-screen display tablet and a penlike stylus. In theory, as users write words and numbers on the tablet, the devices recognize this input. In practice, however, handwriting recognition is still in the pioneering stage, and most systems available today can recognize only hand-printed characters. That computer systems have difficulty recognizing characters should not strike you as surprising. After all, if humans have difficulty reading each others' handwriting, how can computers be programmed to fare much better?

Smart Cards   A **smart card** is a credit-card-sized piece of plastic that contains, at a minimum, a microprocessor chip and memory circuits. The memory capacity may be as small as a few thousand characters or as large as a few million. Smart cards serve most often as electronic payment systems for retail purchases and to transfer funds between bank accounts.

Although they remain largely in the pioneering stage, uses for smart cards abound. A university might issue such cards to allow students access to their own grade or financial data. Smart cards also could be useful for making phone calls; a cardholder would have an electronic record of all phone calls made—useful for tax and billing purposes—right on the card. In security applications, such a card could carry a digitized version of a fingerprint or voice and serve as an electronic passkey, allowing an authorized user access to restricted areas or a sensitive computer network. The use of smart-card technology at sporting events and also for reducing highway traffic and pollution is described in Features HW 3-1 and HW 3-2.

Magnetic Ink Character Recognition (MICR)   **Magnetic ink character recognition (MICR)** is a technology confined almost exclusively to the banking industry, where it supports high-volume processing of checks. Figure HW 3-10 illustrates a check encoded with MICR characters and a reader/sorter that processes such checks. The standard font adopted by the industry contains only 14 characters—the ten decimal digits (0 through 9)

■ **Handwriting recognition device.** A device that can identify handwritten characters. ■ **Smart card.** A credit-card-sized piece of plastic with storage and microprocessor. ■ **Magnetic ink character recognition (MICR).** A banking-industry technology that processes checks by sensing special characters inscribed in a magnetic ink.

Smart Cards and Salted Peanuts

The San Diego Padres Go "High Tech"

The San Diego Padres recently tried a high-tech experiment. In concert with a local bank, the major-league baseball team put its support behind smart cards and made them available to fans.

The Padres plastic cards—each of which contains a magnetic reading strip on its back and a microprocessor inside—are in essence *virtual wallets*. Each contains authorization to spend a specific amount of money—$5, $10, $25, or even more. As vendors at stadium concession stands swipe the cards through enabled reading terminals to record fan purchases, the card's microprocessor subtracts the amount of the purchase from the card's balance. The terminal then prepares a receipt for the fan and transfers electronic money to the Padres bank. Information about the purchase—for example, whether a hot dog or a bag of salted peanuts was bought—is also recorded by the system.

Currently, the Padres have several dozen terminals located in their ballpark, Qualcomm Stadium, to handle the cards during the pilot program for the new technology. For promotion purposes, the ball club has given away free $5 cards to season ticketholders, and the bank has kicked in complementary $25 cards to anyone opening a new account of $600 or more.

A major benefit to both fans and the Padres is that there's no fumbling around for change. For the fan, this means waiting is minimized at concession stands. Coins do not have to be counted and verified, and because the cards are preloaded with money, there's no authorization process to go through. The club is also spared the hassle of having to count physical money at the end of the day—a laborious and often error-ridden process.

Virtual wallets are being used by other organizations for other purposes as well. In some cities, for instance, they give people an easier way to pay for metered parking. They can also be used at tollbooths on bridges or parkways.

Whether wallet-type smart cards will muscle their way into general usage in the future is anyone's guess. While they do have a clear benefit for some types of applications, a fact of life today is that every commercial enterprise seems to be looking for a way to sneak another card into your regular wallet.

MICR-ENCODED CHECK
MICR characters on the bottom of the check respectively identify bank, account number, and check amount. The first two (left bottom) are put on when checks are preprinted; the latter (right bottom) is added when a check is cashed.

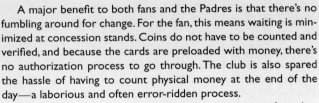
FIGURE HW 3-10
MICR.

MICR READER/SORTER
The high-speed IBM device shown here is capable of processing 2,400 checks a minute.

HW 3-2

Road Pricing

Controlling Traffic and Pollution with Smart Cards

Many cities around the world are running out of space to build new roads. And they quickly need to do something about increasing traffic. Current thoroughfares cannot adequately accommodate the number of vehicles that flow in and out each day during rush hour.

That's why a number of urban planners are turning to smart cards to solve their car woes. In Amsterdam and Rotterdam, two large cities in the Netherlands, drivers will soon have to start carrying smart cards if they want to gain entrance. The cards will come loaded with a preset amount of electronic money and will allow several different types of transactions. The cost of a highway toll—which will be set very high during the busiest hours—will be subtracted automatically from each dashboard-mounted card that passes a toll station. At off-peak hours, the toll will be lowered considerably.

Variable road pricing and charging cars to enter cities is a matter not without controversy. It generally doesn't sit well with people to have to pay for something they've always received free.

Vehicle Control. Are smart cards and variable pricing a solution?

What's more, it's easy for a pricing system to discriminate against the less economically fortunate. One thing is for sure, however: if the price to drive is set high enough, traffic will surely decrease and air will be easier to breathe. Research has shown that cars stuck in traffic jams pollute the environment at a rate three times greater than moving cars.

and four special symbols. MICR characters are inscribed on checks with magnetic ink by a special machine. As people write and cash checks, the recipients deposit them in the banking system. At banks, reader/sorter machines magnetically sense and identify MICR-encoded characters. Such a system sorts and records checks so that they can be routed to the proper banks for payment.

DISPLAY DEVICES

A **display device** presents computer system output on some kind of viewing screen, often resembling a television set. Most display devices fall into one of two categories: monitors and display terminals. A **monitor,** which is the type of display most people have on their PCs, is an output device limited to a viewing screen. The keyboard is a separate device, with its own port on the system unit. A *display terminal*—which is found on some large business networks—is a communications workstation that includes a screen (for output) and an attached keyboard (for input).

On all display devices, as each key on a keyboard is tapped, the corresponding character representation of the key appears on a display screen at the *cursor* position. The cursor—or *insertion point* as it is called in some

■ **Display device.** An output device that contains a viewing screen. ■ **Monitor.** A display device without a keyboard.

contexts—is a highlighted symbol on the screen that indicates where the operator input will be placed. Alternatively, the cursor may point to an option that the user can select.

Display devices are handy when the user requires only small amounts of output and has to see what is being sent as input to the computer system. A student word processing a paper for a class, an airline clerk making inquiries to a flight information database, a stockbroker analyzing a security, and a bank teller checking the status of a customer account would each employ a display device. However, displays are useful only up to a point. If, for example, the student writing the paper wanted to take a copy of it home, he or she would have to direct the output to a printer.

Most monitors sold for desktop computers come with screens of 14, 15, 17, 19, 20, or 21 inches—measured diagonally along the screen surface. Many features other than screen size differentiate the hundreds of display devices currently in the market. The following sections discuss some noteworthy features.

RESOLUTION

A key characteristic of any display device is its *resolution,* or sharpness of the screen image. Most displays form images by lighting up tiny dots on their screens called **pixels** (a contraction of the phrase "picture elements"). Resolution is measured by the density of these pixels, or dot pitch. A display's *dot pitch* indicates the distance between pixels in millimeters. Many displays in use today have a dot pitch of .26 or .28. A smaller dot pitch produces better resolution—that is, a crisper picture.

Resolution is often also specified as a matrix of pixels. A display resolution of 640 by 480 means that the screen consists of 640 columns by 480 rows of pixels—that is, 640 × 480, or 307,200 pixels.

Display devices form text characters and graphics and video images alike by lighting appropriate configurations of pixels (see Figure HW 3-11). Because pixels are so finely packed, when viewed from a distance they appear to blend together to form continuous images.

Each pixel on a screen is individually assigned a color to form the screen image. The higher the pixel density, or resolution, the crisper the screen image.

FIGURE HW 3-11

Pixels.

■ **Pixel.** A single dot on a display screen.

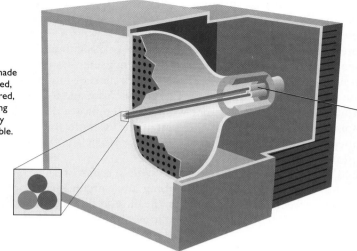

ONE COLOR PIXEL
Each pixel on the screen is made up of some combination of red, green, and blue light. When red, green, and blue light of varying intensities are blended, a very wide range of colors is possible.

Pixels on a typical desktop display screen are refreshed—that is, recharged with built-in electron guns so they will remain bright—at a rate of 60 times each second.

FIGURE HW 3-12

Color display on an RGB monitor.

A typical desktop display electronically manipulates and refreshes (redraws) pixels at lightning-fast speeds by firing an electron gun. Pixels on the screen are refreshed—that is, redrawn with the gun so they will remain bright—at a typical rate of 60 times each second.

COLOR DISPLAYS

By far, most monitors sold with desktop PCs today produce *color* output and are of the *red-green-blue (RGB)* type (see Figure HW 3-12). An RGB monitor forms all colors available on the screen by mixing combinations of only these three colors. Three colors may not sound like much of a base, but when a monitor blends red, green, and blue light of varying intensities—for each of the hundreds of thousands of pixels on the screen—it can produce an enormous spectrum of colors.

Most monitors sold today with desktop PCs produce *noninterlaced* images (see Figure HW 3-13). This term means that a monitor draws every screen line each time it refreshes the screen in order to provide a stable image. *Interlaced displays*—including most television sets—instead redraw every other line of the image each time the screen is refreshed and fill in the alternate lines on the next refresh. While interlaced monitors cost less than noninterlaced ones,

FIGURE HW 3-13

Interlaced and noninterlaced monitors.

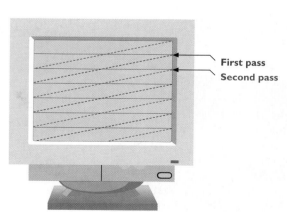

First pass
Second pass

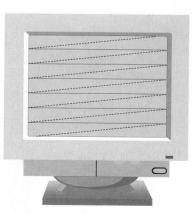

INTERLACED MONITOR
Every other line of the image is drawn on a refresh and alternate lines are filled in on the next pass.

NONINTERLACED MONITOR
Every screen line is redrawn on each screen refresh.

HDTV Is Here

Well, Almost

When the first sets went on sale in San Diego in August 1998, high-definition television (HDTV) was officially launched in the United States. $5,499 could get you a 56-inch-screen television set that could receive high-resolution, digital broadcast signals and produce a picture both bigger and four times clearer than today's top-of-the-line analog TV.

But, there are some catches.

One is receiving a high-resolution digital broadcast. The U.S. government has mandated that the major broadcast networks—CBS, NBC, ABC, and Fox—phase into digital programming over the next few years. By 2002, all commercial stations carrying these networks are required to be digital, with public ones following suit within a year. By 2006, if consumers embrace HDTV, all analog broadcasting ceases. To date, the phase-in has been slow, with only a handful of major cities offering a very limited number of HDTV programs.

Another problem is standards. What, really, is meant by "high resolution"? Technically speaking, it is several things. For instance, high resolution can mean 720 scan lines broadcast to your TV screen or as many as 1,080. While 720 scan lines is double the resolution most people are getting today on their screens, 1,080 lines yield greater picture clarity but take up more bandwidth, or transmission capacity. Many of the HDTV sets being sold today support more than a dozen digital formats as well as analog TV.

Cable broadcasters favor the lower-resolution pictures because more channels can fit through the "pipe" going into your home. The computer industry likes higher resolutions because they are more compatible with the computer-interactive data services that they want to deliver to television. The major networks are divided on the issue. Consequently, what consumers are left with is a product that's still up in the air.

HDTV. High prices and few programs will initially hurt its acceptance with consumers.

Still another problem is price. Most families balk at the idea of forking over a few thousand dollars for a new TV. Many will even be upset over the fact that if they want their old TV to work in the coming high-resolution digital world, they'll have to spend a few hundred bucks on a converter box for it—or *them;* many families have multiple TVs.

Implementation problems aside, HDTV is a compelling product. It's like having a movie theater in your home. Grass shows up as individual blades, not just a blurry swatch of green. When people talk, you can see the lines on their faces or their veins pop out. Six channels of Dolby sound make it possible to set up left, right, and center speakers in the front of a room, two surround-sound speakers in the back, and a woofer under your couch.

Is HDTV a sure bet? Probably, but not right away. There's no question that prices on sets will fall, as they have for other new consumer technologies. But one can't forget that some years ago it took color TVs well over a decade to outsell black-and-white sets, and that transition was far less complicated.

they can produce some screen flicker. That's why it's easier to read small text on a computer monitor than on a television set. Recently, the television industry is attempting with HDTV to support both screen-refreshing standards, moving television and Internet technology closer together (see the Tomorrow box).

Most monitors for desktop PCs present images with a **landscape** orientation, which means that their screens are more wide than high. Some monitors reverse these measurements to provide a **portrait** orientation. Portrait screens are more high than wide. Figure HW 3-14 shows a monitor that can tilt to change between the portrait and landscape modes.

Many color monitors can also produce grayscale and monochrome output. *Grayscale* output resembles the pictures on old black-and-white television sets.

■ **Landscape.** An output mode with images more wide than high. ■ **Portrait.** An output mode with images more high than wide.

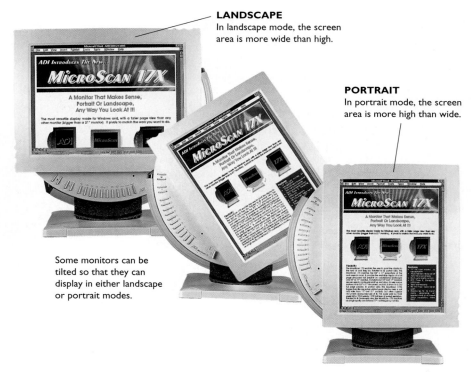

LANDSCAPE
In landscape mode, the screen area is more wide than high.

PORTRAIT
In portrait mode, the screen area is more high than wide.

Some monitors can be tilted so that they can display in either landscape or portrait modes.

FIGURE HW 3-14

Portrait and landscape modes.

These images include not only black and white, but also many shades of gray in between. A *monochrome* image, on the other hand, features a single foreground color and single background color; the contrast reveals images on the screen.

Displays that produce only monochrome output are also widely available. Because they cost slightly less than color displays, they often perform basic output tasks in factories and field work that do not require color. Organizations may settle on these simple displays when they must acquire hundreds or thousands of devices at a time, creating very price-sensitive purchase decisions. Many mainframe, midrange, and palmtop computers utilize monochrome displays.

CRT AND FLAT-PANEL DISPLAY DEVICES

Monitors for most desktop systems project images on large picture-tube elements similar to those inside standard TV sets. This type of monitor (illustrated in Figure HW 3-12) is commonly called a **CRT (cathode-ray tube)** display. CRT technology is relatively mature, and over the years, CRTs have become very inexpensive and have gained capabilities for excellent color output. These features notwithstanding, CRTs are bulky and fragile, and they consume a great deal of power.

Another class of display devices form images by manipulating charged chemicals or gases sandwiched between panes of glass instead of firing a bulky electron gun. These much slimmer alternatives to CRTs are called **flat-panel displays.** Flat-panel displays take up little space, are lightweight, and require less power than CRT monitors. Because of these features, they are commonly found on notebook computers and in a variety of other products (see Figure HW 3-15). Most flat-panel displays on ordinary computer systems use *liquid*

For links to further information about display devices, go to www.harcourtcollege.com/infosys/parker2000/student/explore/ and click on Chapter HW 3.

■ **Cathode-ray tube (CRT).** A display device that projects images on a long-necked display tube similar to that in a television set. ■ **Flat-panel display.** A slim-profile display device.

DESKTOP MONITOR
Flat-panel displays provide sharper images and take up less desk space than conventional desktop CRTs, and they are now becoming cost competitive.

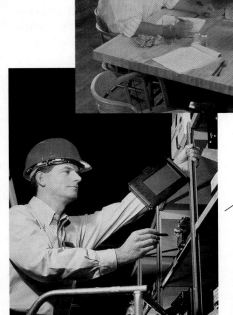

MOBILE WORKERS
People who have to move around with a computer to do their work need a display that is both lightweight and easy to carry.

TIGHT SPACES
In automobiles and forklifts, there is absolutely no room for a monitor that requires lots of space.

FIGURE HW 3-15

Flat-panel displays. These compact, lightweight, low-power-consumption displays suit a wide range of applications.

crystal display (LCD) technology. LCD displays light up charged liquid crystals, and special color filters manipulate this light to paint the screen. Until recently, LCD screens for desktop computers have been too costly compared to CRTs. The price gap is getting smaller, however, and it is largely expected that LCDs will overtake CRTs on the desktop in the not-too-distant future. In addition to the size and portability advantages already named, desktop LCDs provide a sharper picture than CRTs and emit less radiation.

A new development that may someday be mass marketed is the organic light-emitting diode, or OLED. Ultrathin, ultralight, and durable LEDs can be inexpensively "painted" onto flexible surfaces such as plastic and cloth. Also, no backlighting is required to charge liquid crystals. OLEDs could be used by people to send video-bearing digital postcards through the mail and used to make a fashion statement on apparel like T-shirts and caps.

Many flat-panel displays use either *active-matrix* or *passive-matrix* color-display technology. Active-matrix displays provide much sharper screen images than passive-matrix screens, but they provide this benefit at a higher cost.

GRAPHICS STANDARDS

The earliest display devices were strictly *character addressable;* that is, they could display only certain text characters in limited sizes as output. As demand grew for devices with graphics capabilities, manufacturers developed displays capable of more complex output.

Almost all monitors sold with PCs today generate screen images through a technique called **bit mapping.** Bit mapping allows software to control each pixel on the screen as an individual element. Thus, the computer can create virtually any type of image on the screen. Monitors sold today can output text in a variety of sizes, complex graphics images, and moving video sequences. All of the complex art images shown in the Window at the end of this chapter, "The Electronic Canvas," were made possible by computers being able to address individual screen pixels.

Computer graphics standards specify several modes in which a display device can operate. For example, a VGA display (for *v*ideo *g*raphics *a*rray)—the standard for many of the older 386 and 486 computers with 14-inch and 15-inch displays—uses a resolution of 640 by 480 pixels. VGA allows a screen to display at most 256 colors.

The SVGA standard (for *s*uper VGA) took over when Pentium computers and 17-inch monitors became popular. It allows even larger pixel matrices. SVGA monitors often display at resolutions of either 800 by 600 pixels or 1,024 by 768 pixels and feature up to 16,777,216 colors (see Figure HW 3-16). An SVGA monitor can display 2½ times as much information as a VGA monitor of the same size, though the information appears smaller. A major drawback to displaying at fine resolutions is that characters are minimally readable on a 14- or 15-inch display and often unreadable on a laptop screen. Two other drawbacks are speed—because there is more information to paint on a high-resolution screen, the screen takes longer to rewrite every time it is changed—and the greater memory required.

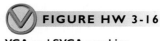

FIGURE HW 3-16

VGA and SVGA graphics standards.

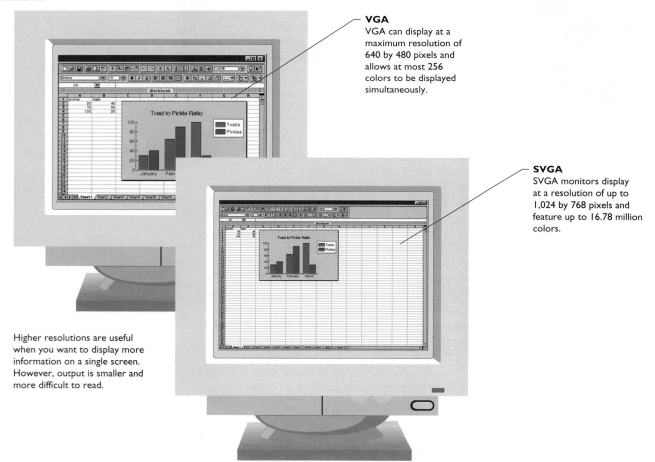

VGA
VGA can display at a maximum resolution of 640 by 480 pixels and allows at most 256 colors to be displayed simultaneously.

SVGA
SVGA monitors display at a resolution of up to 1,024 by 768 pixels and feature up to 16.78 million colors.

Higher resolutions are useful when you want to display more information on a single screen. However, output is smaller and more difficult to read.

■ **Bit mapping.** A graphical output technique in which software individually controls each pixel in a screen image.

In response to the large number of currently active graphics standards and display modes—VGA and SVGA are only two of well over a dozen standards widely seen in practice—many manufacturers have developed *multisync* monitors. These devices accommodate a wide variety of graphics standards and—supported by matching video-adapter boards—they can display images at various resolutions. Software controls a multisync monitor's screen resolution. By making the appropriate screen-menu choice, for instance, you can operate an SVGA monitor in VGA mode.

PRINTERS

Displays have two major limitations as output devices: (1) Only a small amount of data can appear on the screen at one time, and (2) their soft-copy output lacks portability. To obtain portable output, you must either take notes or direct the output to a device that captures it on paper. **Printers** overcome these limitations by producing hard copy—a permanent record of computer system output.

TYPES OF PRINTERS

Printers differ in a number of important respects. One involves the technology through which they output images. Another is size; you can hold some computer printers in your hand, while others—like those that serve high-speed mainframe systems—can fill your living room. Here, we consider such differences.

Dot-Matrix Characters Most printing technologies today form characters as matrices of dots. In contrast, if you look at the printing mechanism of an old typewriter, you'll notice a selection of embossed, solid characters on spokes. Many of the earliest computer printers used similar print heads to stamp output onto paper—and some printers still do. However, most of today's printers form not only characters but also graphics images too, by placing dots on paper in some way. Print resolution has become so good in recent years that the characters on paper look like smooth, continuous strokes rather than collections of dots—even under close inspection (see Figure HW 3-17).

Impact versus Nonimpact Printing Printers produce images through either impact or nonimpact technologies. **Impact printing** is the older method of the two, mimicking the operation of typewriters, which were invented over a century ago. A typewriter key activates a metal hammer embossed with a character, which strikes a print ribbon and presses the character's image onto paper.

An **impact dot-matrix printer** for a desktop computer system works in a similar fashion—a print head produces characters by repeatedly activating one or more vertical columns of pins, as illustrated in Figure HW 3-18. The pins press into a ribbon and force it to strike the paper. Before 1995, most computer printers sold for personal use employed impact dot-matrix technology. In recent years, however, the popularity of these printers has been eclipsed by sales of ink-jet and laser printers. Ink-jet and laser printers often sell at slightly higher prices than impact dot-matrix printers but operate more

---

■ **Printer.** A device that records computer output on paper. ■ **Impact printing.** A technology that forms characters by striking a pin or hammer against an inked ribbon, which presses the desired shape onto paper. ■ **Impact dot-matrix printer.** A device with a print head holding multiple pins, which strike an inked ribbon in various combinations to form characters on paper.

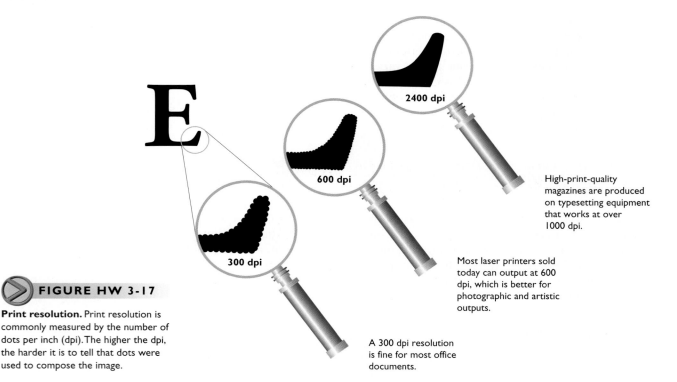

High-print-quality magazines are produced on typesetting equipment that works at over 1000 dpi.

2400 dpi

600 dpi

Most laser printers sold today can output at 600 dpi, which is better for photographic and artistic outputs.

300 dpi

A 300 dpi resolution is fine for most office documents.

FIGURE HW 3-17

Print resolution. Print resolution is commonly measured by the number of dots per inch (dpi). The higher the dpi, the harder it is to tell that dots were used to compose the image.

quietly and produce better-looking output. Today, impact dot-matrix printers, with many models selling for under $200, are favored mostly for producing multipart forms like those for invoices and credit-card receipts.

Nonimpact printing does not depend on the impact of a print head on paper. In fact, the printing mechanism makes no physical contact at all with the paper. This, of course, makes for a quieter operation. Also, because nonimpact printers contain fewer moving parts than impact-based alternatives, they generally work much faster and more reliably with fewer breakdowns. They are cost competitive, too. Today, the printer market is inclined clearly toward nonimpact printers, and the large majority of the printers sold today are nonimpact machines.

PRINTERS FOR SMALL COMPUTER SYSTEMS

Most printers found in small computer systems today are geared to either personal use or to shared, specialized needs (such as those of a team of artists or compositors). These printers often create images through either laser, ink-jet, thermal-transfer, solid-ink, or electrothermal technology, all of which are nonimpact methods. Here, we'll discuss each of these technologies in turn.

Laser Printers   Many microcomputer systems rely on relatively inexpensive personal **laser printers** costing between $300 and $1,500 and printing 4 to 12 pages per minute (ppm). Most of these generate resolutions of at least 600 dpi. At 600 dpi, every square inch of the output image is broken down into a 600-by-600 matrix of dots. That's 360,000 dots packed into every square inch. Laser devices are especially popular in business, in fact, they are the most common type of printer sold to that market segment.

Laser printers form images much as photocopying machines do—by charging thousands of dots on a drum with a very-high-intensity laser beam.

For links to further information about printers, go to www.harcourtcollege.com/ infosys/parker2000/student/ explore/ and click on Chapter HW 3.

■ **Nonimpact printing.** A technology that forms characters and other images on a surface by means of heat, lasers, photography, or ink jets. ■ **Laser printer.** A printer that works on a principle similar to that of a photocopier.

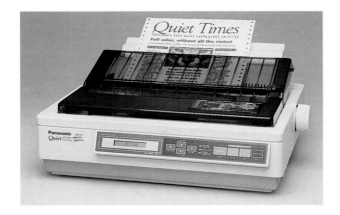

IMPACT DOT-MATRIX PRINTING
Because of the force of the print head on paper, impact dot-matrix printers are ideal for printing multipart forms. Many impact dot-matrix printers cost less than $200 and cost about a penny a page to operate.

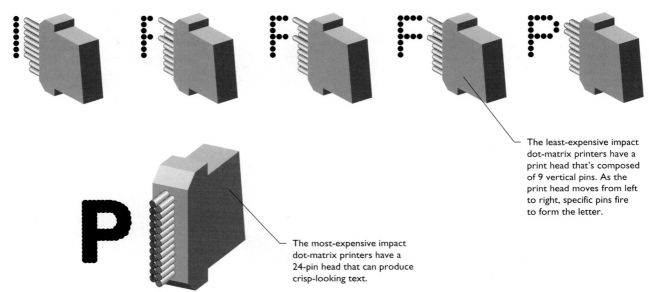

The least-expensive impact dot-matrix printers have a print head that's composed of 9 vertical pins. As the print head moves from left to right, specific pins fire to form the letter.

The most-expensive impact dot-matrix printers have a 24-pin head that can produce crisp-looking text.

FIGURE HW 3-18

Impact dot-matrix printing.

The charged positions attract oppositely charged particles of toner from a cartridge. When paper contacts the drum, it picks up the toner that forms an image. A heating unit fuses the image permanently onto the paper (see Figure HW 3-19).

While most laser printers—like the one featured in Figure HW 3-19—produce only monochrome and grayscale outputs, some color laser printer models now cost only a few thousand dollars. While they do not generate output of photographic quality, color laser printers work faster than many other types of color printers, and the output quality is quite acceptable for a rather simple page image. For magazine-quality images, these printers often produce pages sharp enough to accommodate proofing purposes.

Ink-Jet Printers **Ink-jet printers** produce images by spraying thousands of droplets of electrically charged ink onto a page (see Figure HW 3-20). For the last several years, ink-jet printing has been the technology of choice for home users who want to produce affordable, hard-copy color output from their personal desktop systems. Most ink-jet printers sold today can produce black-and-white, grayscale, and color outputs.

The principal advantage to ink-jet printing is its low cost. While some commercial-level ink-jet printers cost thousands of dollars, you can buy a respectable color ink-jet printer for your desktop PC for as little as $100 or

■ **Ink-jet printer.** A printer that forms images by spraying droplets of charged ink onto a page.

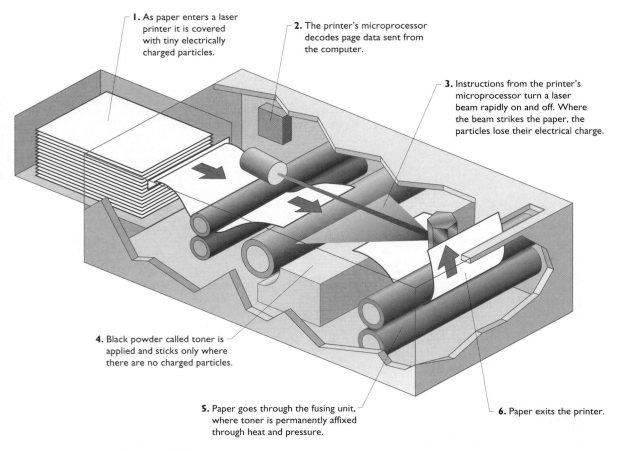

1. As paper enters a laser printer it is covered with tiny electrically charged particles.

2. The printer's microprocessor decodes page data sent from the computer.

3. Instructions from the printer's microprocessor turn a laser beam rapidly on and off. Where the beam strikes the paper, the particles lose their electrical charge.

4. Black powder called toner is applied and sticks only where there are no charged particles.

5. Paper goes through the fusing unit, where toner is permanently affixed through heat and pressure.

6. Paper exits the printer.

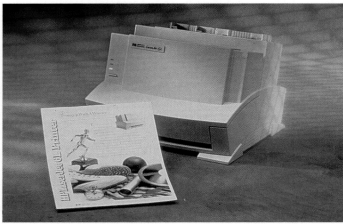

ABOUT LASER PRINTERS

Because of their speed and output quality, laser printers are by far the most popular type of printer for business applications.

Common speeds for personal laser printers are 4, 6, 8, and 12 pages per minute (ppm).

Many personal printers come with at least 1 MB RAM. While this is fine for text, 4 MB is better for intensive graphics work.

 **FIGURE HW 3-19**

Laser printing. Costing less than $500, personal laser printers are useful for routine business reports, correspondence, and also for graphics outputs.

so. Color printers using other technologies generally carry higher prices on low-end models. Ink-jet printers bring some disadvantages, however. They often take longer to output text than laser printers require, and the hard copy may not look as crisp. What's more, ink-jet printers draw ink from replaceable color cartridges, and the cost of new cartridges can mount up over time if you print documents with a lot of color.

Thermal-Transfer Printers Thermal-transfer printers place color images on paper by heating ink from a wax-based ribbon or by heating dye. Users buy these types of printers almost exclusively for their color-printing capabilities, although they can produce crisp-looking text output as well.

Thermal-wax-transfer printers often cost $2,000 or more. They produce output that's similar in quality to comparatively priced, high-end ink-jet printers.

INK-JET PRINTING

Ink-jet printers create colors by mixing different combinations of ink. Devices targeted to personal use output text at a rate of one-to-five pages per minute but are far slower for color output.

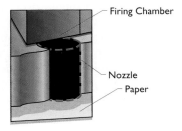

Print head

Nozzles

HOW INK-JET PRINTING WORKS

The print head in an ink-jet printer contains four ink cartridges—one each for magenta, cyan, yellow and black. Each cartridge is made up of some 50 ink-filled firing chambers, each attached to a nozzle smaller than a human hair. When output is to be formed, certain cartridges and nozzles are activated.

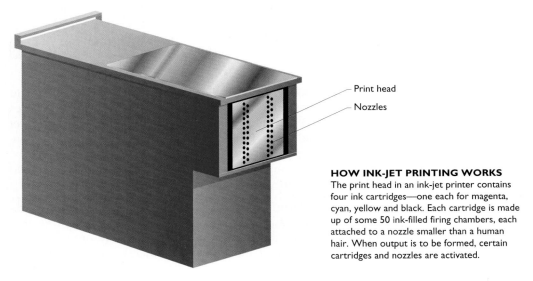

Firing Chamber

Nozzle

Paper

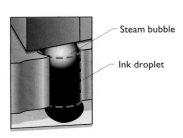

Steam bubble

Ink droplet

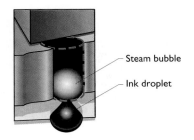

Steam bubble

Ink droplet

1. An electric current flows along the bottom of a firing chamber. This makes the ink boil and a steam bubble forms.

2. As a bubble expands, it pushes ink through the nozzle. The pressure of the bubble forces an ink droplet to be ejected onto the paper (see Step 3).

3. The volume of ink deposited is about one millionth that of a drop of water from an eyedropper. A typical character is formed by a 20-by-20 array of drops.

Thermal-wax-transfer printers achieve their best performance producing color transparencies and proofs of complex color images. If you want color images with a magazine-cover look, you'll have to step up to a thermal-dye-transfer printer.

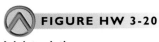

FIGURE HW 3-20

Ink-jet printing.

 FIGURE HW 3-21

Thermal-transfer printing. Thermal-transfer printers that use a dye-sublimation technology are capable of producing photographic-quality outputs, like the images you see on slick magazine covers.

Thermal-dye-transfer printers, often called *dye-sublimation printers,* yield photographic-quality color output (see Figure HW 3-21). The printers themselves are expensive—$3,000 to $5,000 is a typical price range for a commercial-level device—and you can spend about $4.50 per page in color ink and other consumable supplies to operate one of them. New to the consumer market since 1997 are *snapshot printers*—small dye-sublimation printers costing about $500 that are targeted to photographers.

Solid-Ink Printers   *Solid-ink printers*—also known as *solid-wax, phase-change,* and *wax-jet printers*—apply color supplied by wax sticks. A heating device in the printer melts the differently colored sticks before printing starts, and a print head sprays the color out of small nozzles. However, instead of shooting the colors directly onto paper as an ink-jet printer does, the nozzles apply the droplets to a rapidly rotating drum. Then, as in laser and offset printing, the drum transfers the color image to paper. An advantage over ink-jet printing is that the ink dries faster.

Compared to color laser printers, solid-ink printers are less picky about the type of paper or transparency film they handle. Solid-ink printers also work at faster speeds for color output and often cost less per page of output produced. On the downside, output is not as crisp.

Electrothermal Printers   In *electrothermal printing,* a device burns characters onto a special paper by heating rods on a print head. Electrothermal printers carry low price tags, but they often suffer from serious disadvantages: poor output quality, a need for special paper (which may feel slippery), and an inability to produce color output. Electrothermal printing is most commonly found in low-end fax machines and portable printers.

PRINTERS FOR LARGE COMPUTER SYSTEMS

In a networked computer system, a printer is often shared by several people. The people may be located in the same office, floor, building, or site. High-end printers targeted to shared usage generally are too big to fit on a desktop. They begin their speed ranges where those of printers meant for personal use top

out. High-end printers may work from twice as fast to 100 or more times as fast as their personal-system counterparts and cost anywhere from a few thousand dollars to more than $100,000.

Line Printers **Line printers** get their name because they print a line of text at a time. Not long ago, virtually all printers in midrange and mainframe computer systems were line printers, but now such devices are less common than those using other technologies. In one of their common uses today, line printers function as shared devices on office networks (see Figure HW 3-22).

Most line printers produce images through impact printing. *Band printers,* which form lines of text by impact of character-embossed metal print ribbons, are currently the most common type of line printer. Speeds typically range from a few hundred to a few thousand lines per minute (lpm).

FIGURE HW 3-22

Line printer. Line printers can produce hard-copy output at speeds ranging from a few hundred to a few thousand lines per minute.

Page Printers As the name suggests, a **page printer** produces a full page of output at a time. On office networks, the most common type of page printer is the *network laser printer.* Typically, these printers are bigger versions of personal laser printers, with several additional paper trays (see Figure HW 3-23). Network laser printers work much faster than their personal counterparts, producing output at a rate of anywhere from 12 to 40 ppm. Many of the high-end models can collate and staple as well. A typical 24-ppm office printer is designed to handle workloads of up to 150,000 pages of output per month.

FIGURE HW 3-23

Network laser printer. Network laser printers usually output anywhere from 12 to 40 ppm.

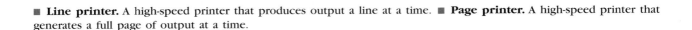

■ **Line printer.** A high-speed printer that produces output a line at a time. ■ **Page printer.** A high-speed printer that generates a full page of output at a time.

Page printer. Operating at peak capacity over a weekend, some page printers can produce well over 1 million pages of output.

Page printers for midrange and mainframe computer systems can print up to a few hundred pages of output per minute (see Figure HW 3-24). Such printers may cost $100,000 or even more. An organization that produces several hundred thousand or more pages of output per month may find one of these machines an extremely cost-effective alternative.

Page printers offer an advantage over line printers in their ability to output digital images of forms and letterheads. They can even print on both sides of the paper. Thus, page printers can offer considerable savings over line printers, which require human intervention to switch paper and printing elements when a change in output dictates a new form or format.

OTHER OUTPUT EQUIPMENT

In addition to display devices and printers, computer systems often need hardware to generate several other kinds of output. In this section, we will consider speakers, plotters, voice-output devices, film recorders, and computer-output microfilm (COM)—all of which are output devices appropriate for specialized uses.

Speakers   Most computer systems sold today, especially for home use, come with a set of **speakers.** Speakers provide audio output for such consumer-oriented multimedia applications as playing computer games, listening to audio or video clips on the Internet, listening to background music on CD, and watching television in an onscreen window. Common business applications include video demonstrations and presentations, as well as videoconferencing. As more and more computer systems include sound capabilities, increasing numbers of applications are integrating sound components.

Computer speaker systems resemble their stereo-system counterparts. You can pay well under $100 for a set, or you can spend over a thousand dollars. While an inexpensive speaker outputs the full frequency range through a single cone, a costlier model might include a special bass unit and separate output cones for different sound frequencies; collectively, these components may

---

■ **Speakers.** Output devices that produce sound.

Stock Options

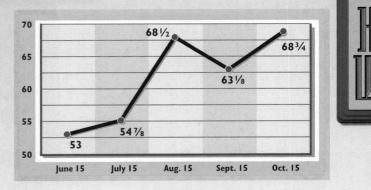

Because many high-tech companies are growing by leaps and bounds, they are regularly in need of money. One effective way for them to get extra cash in the short term is by making stock options available to employees.

Stock options, if your employer offers them, give you the future right to buy up to a fixed number of shares of its stock at a reduced price—for instance, 100 shares at $3 per share. If, later, each share is worth $12 and you decide to exercise your option, you pay $300 for the shares and sell them for $1,200—making a profit of 300 percent. Multiply this scenario by many thousands of shares, and you can see why it can be so attractive.

For many workers willing to take risks, forget the steady salary. It's far more alluring to dream of becoming an instant millionaire. What if your company decides to go public—offering its stock for sale on the open market—and your options are suddenly worth 100 times the issue price?

It's happened before. At Microsoft, CEO and founder Bill Gates became legendary for offering new employees attractive options packages when they hired on. In the early 1990s, about 2,200 employees—about a quarter of all of those who worked at Microsoft at the time—became millionaires through their options.

For a company with great prospects, an option plan works well because many employees will readily accept options in lieu of some of their regular pay. Also, employees holding options are more likely to be dedicated—their financial well-being depends upon the continuing health of the company's stock price. What's more, for the company, options get favorable tax treatment.

According to recent industry data, stock options are most popular at cash-poor startup companies in the high-tech area. Options are increasingly being used by the industry giants too, including Compaq, Dell, and Hewlett-Packard, to name just a few. According to one recent study, about five years ago only 10 percent of large companies in the United States had option plans. Today, that number is over 50 percent.

The terms of an option plan can vary, so you need to ask plenty of questions before you sign on to one. Are all employees eligible for options or just some? Is there a time limit on exercising the options? Are options a mandatory part of the compensation package or is there a choice? Can you change your mind later on if you initially make a wrong decision? Note also that there are different types of options. For instance, executives may have a clause that requires the stock price to advance by so many percentage points in order for options to be exercised.

Whatever you do, remember that options entail risk. If the organization you work for goes belly up, its options become worthless. While many companies try to make their option plans attractive to employees, sometimes there's no substitute for good, old, plain-and-boring cash.

---

even provide near-theater-quality audio. Cases on speakers are often shielded to prevent magnetic interference with nearby storage devices. Also, speakers may come with brackets, stands, or other mounting devices to provide you flexibility in arranging them on your desk or wall.

Just as important as the purchase of the speaker system itself is the selection of a sound card. A *sound card* is an add-in board that fits in an expansion slot inside a desktop system unit. It lets your computer system play sound through speakers or headphones. On the input side, the sound card also supports recording through a microphone or music keyboard. Many of the sound cards sold today provide audio compatible with the Sound Blaster standard. Sound Blaster was one of the first computer sound boards to win a large following among users and computer-game makers. Notebook computers can gain sound-card capabilities through added PC cards.

The whirlwind success of such products as Sound Blaster brings up an interesting side point about the computer industry. When new products take off, often so does a company's fortunes. This has led many employees to demand—and a number of companies to offer—stock option plans that tie compensation to success (see the Inside the Industry box).

Plotter. Ink-jet plotters, by far the most prevalent type today, are useful for wide-format graphics that are too big for a standard ink-jet printer.

Plotters   A **plotter** is an output device that is designed primarily to produce charts, drawings, maps, three-dimensional illustrations, and other forms of hard copy. Plotters work by a variety of technologies. The two most common types of plotters in use today are ink-jet plotters and electrostatic plotters (see Figure HW 3-25).

At the low-cost end of the plotter market are *ink-jet plotters.* Ink-jet technology has dropped dramatically in price in recent years, and the popularity of these plotters has surged as a result. Many of them roll out paper over a space-saving drumlike mechanism, while others use cut sheets stored in a feeder tray. While virtually all ink-jet printers can also double as plotters, users with specialized graphics needs—say, an engineer who produces oversized drawings—may want to consider ink-jet devices targeted principally to commercial plotting rather than general-purpose desktop applications. By far, most plotters are of the ink-jet type today.

Electrostatic plotters define the faster and more expensive end of the plotter market. These widely used devices create images with a toner bed similar to that of a photocopying machine, but instead of light pulses, they use a matrix of tiny wires to charge the paper with electricity. When the charged paper passes over the toner bed, the toner adheres to it and produces an image.

Voice-Output Systems   For a number of years, computers have been able to communicate with users, after a fashion, by imitating human speech. How often have you dialed a phone number only to hear, "We're sorry, the number you are trying to reach, 555-0202, is no longer in service," or "The time is 6:15. . . . The downtown temperature is 75 degrees?" **Voice-output systems,** the hardware and software responsible for such messages, convert stored digital data into spoken messages.

Computerized voice output systems operate extensively at airline terminals to broadcast information about flight departures and arrivals. In the securities business, they quote the prices of stocks and bonds; in supermarkets, they announce descriptions and prices of items that pass over the scanner; in electronic-mail systems, they greet users and tell them about any waiting electronic

■ **Plotter.** An output device that prints graphs and diagrams. ■ **Voice-output system.** A system that enables a computer to play back or imitate human speech.

mail. In business, voice output has great potential in any company with employees who do little other than, say, verbally provide account balances, prices, and status reports. This technology also adds value to applications—such as electronic mail—that have not had voice components until recently.

There are two types of voice-output systems. The first type digitizes voice messages, stores them electronically, and then converts them back to voice messages when the user triggers a playback command—sort of the digital version of the traditional tape recorder. Probably the most common examples of this type of voice output are the phone-menu-message systems that answer calls at many businesses. The second type of system produces synthetic speech by storing digital patterns of word sounds and then creating sentences extemporaneously. Many of the systems that rely on synthetic speech have vocabularies of about several hundred words and limited abilities to combine words dynamically to form intelligible sentences. As a result, these devices perform best in creating short messages—a telephone number, stock price, and so on.

Film Recorders **Film recorders** convert high-resolution, computer-generated images directly into slides, transparencies, and other film media. Just a few years ago film recorders served only large computer systems, through such applications as art, medical imaging, and scientific work. Today, they connect to PCs and are used for such applications as making slides for meetings and client presentations. Today, computer-generated slides account for a large percentage of all business slides made.

Film recorders, like cameras, are "dumb" devices that do not recognize images in order to record them. Film recorders can transfer onto film virtually any image that can be captured on a display screen.

Computer Output Microfilm A **computer output microfilm (COM)** system places computer output on microfilm media, typically either a *microfilm reel* or *microfiche card.* Microfilming can result in tremendous savings in paper costs, storage space, mailing, and handling. A four-by-six-inch microfiche card can store the equivalent of 270 printed pages. COM technology is useful for organizations that must keep massive files of information that they need not update. It's also useful for organizations that need to manipulate large amounts of data but find online access to a computer system impractical or too costly. In recent years, as optical disks have gained in popularity, COM systems have faced serious challenges to the near monopoly they once held on archival document storage and retrieval.

SUMMARY AND KEY TERMS

Go to the Online Glossary at www.harcourtcollege.com/infosys/parker2000/ student/ to review key terms.

Today's computer marketplace offers a wide and expanding variety of input and output devices.

Input and Output Input and output devices enable people and computers to communicate. **Input devices** convert data and program instructions into a form that the CPU can process. **Output devices** convert computer-processed information into a form that people comprehend.

Output devices produce results in either hard-copy or soft-copy form. The term **hard copy** generally refers to output that has been recorded in

---

■ **Film recorder.** A device that converts computer output to film. ■ **Computer output microfilm (COM).** A system for reducing computer output to microscopic form and storing it on photosensitive film.

a *permanent* form onto a medium such as paper or microfilm. The term **soft copy,** in contrast, generally refers to display output, which appears only *temporarily.* Hard-copy output is the more portable of the two, but it costs more to produce and creates waste.

Keyboards Most people could not interact with a computer system without a **keyboard,** which is often the main source of system input. The large majority of keyboards lay out keys in the QWERTY arrangement.

Pointing Devices **Pointing devices** include input hardware that moves an onscreen pointer. The most widely used pointing device is the **mouse.** Some other common pointing devices are the **light pen, joystick, trackball,** and **graphics tablet.** Display devices that are designed to allow a finger rather than a light pen to activate onscreen commands are called **touch-screen displays.**

Source Data Automation **Source data automation** deploys technologies to collect digital data at their point of origin. Many input technologies fall within this description.

Optical character recognition (OCR) refers to a wide range of optical-scanning procedures and equipment designed for machine recognition of marks, characters, and codes—such as **bar codes.** Among the best-known uses of OCR are the **point-of-sale (POS) systems** installed at checkout counters in stores.

An **image scanner** allows users to input such images as photographs, drawings, and documents into a computer system. Many scanners are of the *flatbed, drum,* or *handheld* type. Scanners are often accompanied by OCR software that enables computer systems to recognize scanned text characters.

Digital cameras work much like regular cameras, but instead of capturing images on print or slide film, they record digital data onto memory cards like those found in notebook computers. When you take a snapshot, the camera loads its memory card with digital data that enable a desktop PC to later process the image.

Voice-input systems enable computer systems to recognize spoken words. Voice-input technologies offer tremendous work-saving potential, but they are only slowly reaching market acceptance.

Practical **handwriting recognition devices** are still in the pioneering stage, and virtually all systems commercially available today can recognize only hand-printed characters.

Smart cards are credit-card-sized pieces of plastic that contain microprocessor chips and memory circuitry. They, too, remain largely in the pioneering stage.

Magnetic ink character recognition (MICR) is an input technology confined almost exclusively to the banking industry; it enables automated systems to rapidly sort, process, and route checks to the proper banks.

Display Devices **Display devices** are peripheral hardware that contain television-like viewing screens. Most display devices fall into one of two categories: **monitors** and display terminals. A key characteristic of any display is its *resolution,* or the sharpness of its screen image. On many displays, users measure resolution by the number of dots, or **pixels,** that make up the screen.

By far the largest number of displays sold with computer systems today produce color output and are *noninterlaced.* Most also present images with a **landscape** orientation; that is, more width than height. Some displays reverse this arrangement for a **portrait** orientation.

Most desktop displays on the market today project images on large, picture-tube elements similar to those found inside standard TV sets. These devices are called **CRTs (cathode-ray tubes).** Slim-profile devices called **flat-panel**

displays also are in wide use, especially on portable computers. Most flat-panel devices use *LCD (liquid crystal display)* technology.

Bit mapping allows software to control the placement of each pixel on the screen. Most displays implement either the VGA or SVGA graphics standard.

Printers **Printers** produce hard-copy output through either impact or non-impact printing technology. In **impact printing,** the older of the two, metal pins or embossed characters strike paper or ribbons to form characters. The most common type of impact printer is the **impact dot-matrix printer. Nonimpact printing,** which is quieter and more reliable, is by far the most prevalent type of printing technology today. Nonimpact printing creates printed images through any of a wide variety of techniques.

The most popular printers today for microcomputer systems are **laser printers** and **ink-jet printers.** Both employ nonimpact methods. Other relatively common nonimpact devices are thermal-transfer, solid-ink, and electrothermal printers.

Most of the printing done on large computer systems is accomplished by line or page printers. **Line printers** produce a line of output at a time, and **page printers** produce a full page of output at a time.

Other Output Equipment   A large number of other output devices accommodate a variety of applications. Among these are speakers, plotters, voice-output devices, film recorders, and computer output microfilm (COM) equipment.

Most computer systems sold today come with **speakers** for audio output. Just as important as the speaker system itself is the selection of a *sound card.*

A **plotter** is an output device designed primarily to produce graphics output such as charts, maps, and engineering drawings. *Ink-jet plotters* squirt jets of ink on the paper surface, and *electrostatic plotters* create images by adhering toner to electrostatic charges.

Voice-output systems enable computer systems to play back or compose spoken messages from digitally stored words, phrases, and sounds. One of the main shortcomings of this technology is the limited number of messages that the computer can extemporaneously create.

Film recorders convert computer-generated images to 35-mm slides, transparencies, and other film media. They can output onto film virtually any image that can be captured on a display screen.

Computer output microfilm (COM) systems place computer output on microscopically read media such as microfilm reels or microfiche cards. COM can cut document costs for paper, storage space, mailing, and handling.

EXERCISES

1. Fill in the blanks:
   a. The term _____ generally refers to output that has been recorded onto a medium such as paper or film.
   b. Resolution on a display screen is measured by the number of dots, or _____ .
   c. A display device that outputs images in a single foreground color is known as a(n) _____ display.
   d. A(n) _____ printer heats ink from a dye-based or wax-based ribbon and deposits it onto paper.
   e. A(n) _____ is a device that converts computer-generated images directly onto 35-mm slides.
   f. _____ is a term that refers to the process of collecting data, at their point of origin, in digital form.
   g. A display device that generates input when you touch a finger to the screen is called a(n) _____ device.
   h. A(n) _____ system, commonly found in department stores and supermarkets, uses

electronic cash register terminals to collect, process, and store data.

2. Match each term with the description that fits best.
   a. memory card
   b. OCR
   c. noninterlaced
   d. UPC
   e. LCD
   f. SVGA
   g. plotter
   h. trackball

   _____ Used to make flat-panel display devices but not CRTs

   _____ A graphics standard for displays

   _____ A collection of different technologies devoted to optical recognition of marks, characters, and codes

   _____ A code that appears prominently on the packaging of most supermarket goods

   _____ A type of output device designed especially to produce graphics images on paper

   _____ A device that stores images within a digital camera

   _____ A device that moves a pointer rapidly around the display screen

   _____ A characteristic of some CRTs that controls how they refresh screen images

3. Review the list of input and output devices that follows, and state whether each device provides input to the computer, provides output to the user, or both.
   a. Plotter
   b. Joystick
   c. Graphics tablet
   d. Image scanner
   e. Digital camera
   f. Film recorder
   g. Handwriting recognition device
   h. Trackball
   i. Light pen
   j. Flat-panel display

4. Identify each of the following statements as true or false.

   _____ Digital cameras are known as film recorders.

   _____ The human finger can serve as a pointer-movement device in some computer systems.

   _____ QWERTY refers to the way some keyboards are arranged.

   _____ Many voice-output systems need to be trained before they are put into operation.

   _____ Interlaced monitors are superior to noninterlaced ones.

   _____ Relative to such input devices as image scanners, handwriting recognition devices are still in the pioneering stage.

   _____ Pages that are output in a portrait mode are output in a wider format than if they had been specified as landscape.

   _____ Touch screens are useful in factory applications and fieldwork, where users wear gloves.

   _____ Many notebook computers employ a pointing stick that the user can push in different directions to move an onscreen pointer.

   _____ The most widely known bar code is POS.

5. Describe the following characteristics of display devices:
   a. Active-matrix
   b. LCD
   c. Noninterlaced
   d. VGA
   e. Multisync
   f. CRT
   g. RGB
   h. Resolution

6. Identify at least six pointing devices designed for entering data into the computer system.

7. What type of microcomputer printer would you prefer for each of the following applications?
   a. To get very inexpensive color outputs
   b. To get photographic-quality color output
   c. To generate both daily business correspondence and weekly drafts of a book you are writing in your spare time
   d. To generate multipart forms

8. Answer the following questions about source data automation.
   a. What is source data automation and what are its benefits?
   b. Name as many technologies as you can that can fall under the heading of source data automation.
   c. Why isn't voice output considered part of source data automation?

9. Match the pictures on the following page with the terms below. Note that each term can match one or two pictures or none at all.

   _____ VGA

   _____ MICR

   _____ SVGA

   _____ Joystick

   _____ Image scanner

   _____ POS

   _____ Thermal-wax printer

   _____ Digital camera

   _____ Trackball

a.

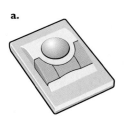

b.

c.

d.

e.

10. Define the following terms:
    a. Soft copy
    b. Solid-ink printer
    c. Bar code
    d. Nonimpact printing
    e. Smart card
    f. Dot pitch
    g. Point-of-sale system
    h. Universal product code

11. Digital cameras have become increasingly popular with both business and home users in recent years.
    a. How does a digital camera take pictures?
    b. How do you transfer the pictures the camera takes into a desktop computer's storage?
    c. What can you do if the pictures you take turn out too light?
    d. For what types of applications is a digital camera suitable and unsuitable?

12. Describe what each of the following units measure, and identify a hardware device to which the measurement applies.
    a. dpi
    b. ppm
    c. lpm

13. What are the purposes of the following keyboard keys?
    a. Escape (Esc) key
    b. Function keys
    c. Control (Ctrl) key
    d. Backspace key
    e. Arrow keys
    f. Delete (Del) key
    g. Numeric keypad keys

14. Each of the following definitions is not strictly true in some regard. In each case, identify and correct the error.
    a. Dot pitch (dpi): The amount of space, measured in millimeters, between pixels on a display screen.
    b. Monochrome monitor: A monitor that can output in only a single color.
    c. Voice-output system: A system designed to create sentences extemporaneously from digitally stored words.
    d. Display device: Peripheral equipment that outputs computer-processed results on a screen; also known as a *display terminal*.
    e. Dot-matrix printer: A printer that uses hammers to produce output onto paper as configurations of dots.

15. Match each term with the description that fits best.
    a. pixel
    b. MICR
    c. impact
    d. bit mapping
    e. COM
    f. light indicator
    g. landscape
    h. thermal transfer

    _____ A term that refers to the placement of output on microfilm.

    _____ A banking-industry technology that processes checks by sensing special characters inscribed in magnetic ink.

    _____ A technology that places color images on paper by heating ink from a wax-based ribbon or by heating dye.

    _____ Found on most keyboards, it can tell the user whether or not the Caps Lock is activated.

    _____ Resolution on a display screen is specified by the density of these.

    _____ An output mode with images more wide than high.

    _____ A graphical output technique in which software individually controls each pixel in a screen image.

    _____ A technology, used in printing, that forms characters by striking a pin or hammer against an inked ribbon.

PROJECTS

1. **Keyboards** One interesting story claims that the QWERTY keyboard, which became a typewriter standard more than a century ago, was actually created to slow down typists, so that they wouldn't get their fingers stuck between the keys. Despite the QWERTY keyboard's somewhat controversial design, it has managed to survive through the years, becoming the standard keyboard arrangement for computer systems, as well. For this project, answer the following questions. Feel free to consult Internet resources in your research as well as journal articles and books.

   a. Why has QWERTY prevailed over other, more highly praised keyboard designs?

   b. Many people prefer the Dvorak keyboard over QWERTY. How does the Dvorak keyboard differ, and why do many people prefer it?

   c. What is the least-expensive way to implement a Dvorak keyboard?

2. **I/O Products** Find a currently available product within each of the following technologies. For each product, identify the manufacturer, model name, and model number. Additionally, write a short paragraph on each product telling of its capabilities, such as its speed or resolution. Feel free to consult Internet resources in your research as well as journal articles and product brochures.

   a. Laser printer

   b. Ink-jet printer

   c. Thermal-dye-transfer printer

   d. Flat-panel monitor

   e. Color flatbed scanner

3. **Bit-Picking Project** A page of text typed and saved with a word processing program takes up a different amount of storage than a copy of that same page read by a scanner. Why do you think this is so? Which would take up more space? Support your argument by presenting some calculations.

4. **Ink-Jet Printers** Ink-jet printers have become very popular in recent years. Three important characteristics have contributed to their acceptance: low cost, low noise level, and color capabilities. For this project, choose a vendor of ink-jet printers and answer the following questions about the products in its current line. Feel free to consult Internet resources in your research, as well as journal articles and product brochures.

   a. What are the names or model numbers of the ink-jet printers produced by the manufacturer you have chosen?

   b. Provide as many of the following statistics as you can about each of these printers: list or street price, rated speed for text pages, rated speed for color pages, number of ink cartridges used, colors of ink cartridges used, and maximum resolution possible.

   Hint: Three of the biggest makers of ink-jet printers are Canon, Epson, and Hewlett-Packard. These companies provide product information at the following Web addresses:

COMPANY	WEB ADDRESS
Canon	www.canon.com
Epson	www.epson.com
Hewlett-Packard	www.hp.com

   Also note that *PC Magazine* publishes an annual printer issue, usually in November, that contains a lot of useful information for this project.

5. **Laser Printers** Laser printers that produce black-and-white and grayscale outputs define today's standard for business use. For this project, choose a vendor of such laser printers and answer the following questions about the products in its current line. Feel free to consult Internet resources in your research as well as journal articles and product brochures.

   a. What are the names or model numbers of the laser printers produced by the manufacturer you have chosen?

b. Provide as many of the following statistics as you can about each of these printers: list or street price, maximum speed, and maximum text resolution.

c. Which of these printers qualify as *personal* laser printers? Which are *network* laser printers?

Hint: Two of the biggest makers of laser printers are Hewlett-Packard and NEC. These companies provide product information at the following Web addresses:

COMPANY	WEB SITE
Hewlett-Packard	www.hp.com
NEC	www.nec.com

Also note that *PC Magazine* publishes an annual printer issue, usually in November, that contains a lot of useful information for this project.

 6. Color Scanners Color scanners have become very popular peripheral devices in recent years for home and office use. Scanners convert flat images—such as a page of text or a photograph—into digital files that you can manipulate on your computer. For this project, choose a recent color personal scanner model and answer the following questions about it. Feel free to consult Internet resources in your research as well as journal articles and product brochures.

a. What is the name or model number of the scanner you have chosen? Who manufactures the product?

b. How does the scanner handle documents— through a flatbed or drum mechanism, or by moving a handheld unit over the documents, or in some other way?

c. Does any software come with the scanner? If it does, describe the types of capabilities the software provides.

d. At what color depths does the scanner work— 16-bit color, 24-bit, or something else?

e. At what maximum resolution (stated in dpi) does the scanner accept inputs?

f. What is the list or street price of the scanner?

7. Digital Cameras Digital cameras are beginning to appear more often for various types of applications. For this project, choose a digital camera that costs less than $1,000 and answer the following questions about it. Feel free to consult Internet resources in your research as well as journal articles and product brochures.

a. What is the name or model number of the camera you have chosen? Who manufactures the product?

b. Describe the storage medium the camera substitutes for conventional film.

c. At what maximum resolution can the camera take pictures? At what minimum resolution? Also determine the number of pictures that can be taken at each resolution.

d. What is the street or list price of the camera?

e. Some people classify the digital camera as a type of scanner. In what ways are the two devices similar?

Hint: Among the companies currently making digital cameras are Kodak, Sony, Epson, Canon, and Casio. Each of these companies maintains Web sites, any of which you can easily get to by typing the company name in between the "www." and ".com" in the Web address (for instance, www.kodak.com). Most of these companies also maintain toll-free phone numbers for product information, which you can obtain for free from Directory Assistance.

8. Computer Math SVGA displays can produce up to 16,777,216 colors.

a. How do manufacturers arrive at such a number?

b. How many bits would the computer need to color a pixel in any of 16,777,216 colors?

9. Flat-Panel Screens Flat-panel displays have become extremely popular during the past several years for a variety of applications. Several uses are illustrated in Figure HW 3-15 in the chapter. Can you come up with at least three others?

10. Special-Purpose Devices Some input and output devices are designed to carry out a single, specialized task. For instance, the purpose of the printer shown in the picture on page HW 122 is to produce bar-coded labels. For this project, find an example of another special-purpose device currently on the market and report the following to the class.

a. The name of the device and its maker.

b. The suggested retail price of the device.

c. The specialized task the device is designed to do.

a. The name of the device and its maker.

b. The suggested retail price of the device.

c. The capabilities of the device.

11. **Multifunction Devices**   Some printers today are marketed as *multifunction devices*. Such printers not only print, but they also perform a number of other duties as well—for instance, copying documents, faxing, or scanning. For this project, find an example of a multifunction device currently on the market and report the following to the class.

12. **Virtual Wallets**   Feature HW 3-1, on the San Diego Padres, introduces the use of virtual wallets—smart cards that are preloaded with money. Today, virtual wallets are being used in a wide variety of applications. In some cities, they give people an easier way to pay for metered parking. They can also be used at tollbooths on bridges or parkways. Identify at least two more uses for virtual wallets. What business advantage is gained by the issuer of such cards?

INTERACTIVE EXERCISE

PUTTING TOGETHER YOUR NEW PC

You've just gotten your brand new PC and it is time to get it up and running. Go to the Interactive Exercise at www.harcourtcollege.com/infosys/parker2000/student/exercise/ to complete this exercise.

ONLINE REVIEW

Go to the Online Review at www.harcourtcollege.com/infosys/parker2000/student/ to test your understanding of this chapter's concepts.

WINDOW

THE ELECTRONIC CANVAS

A PEEK AT THE LEADING EDGE IN COMPUTER ART

Probably no field exemplifies the rapid changes made in computer output over the years more vividly than the field of computer art. Early computer artists were scientists who worked on supercomputers. As demand grew for electronic art in such fields as advertising, publishing, and movie making, hardware and software for non-computer professionals began to emerge. Many of today's computer artists work at home from PCs and use a variety of input and output devices that specialize in handling byte-hungry color images.

1. Poster art is often output on large-format ink-jet plotters. Other common output devices for computer art are display devices, film recorders, and thermal-dye-transfer printers.

2

2–5. Corel's annual World Design contest draws entries from around the globe. The diversity of images shown here from a recent show illustrate how computer systems can create a wide range of image types—pure art, technical drawings, corporate logos, and book and cover illustrations.

3

4

5

6–9. Intergraph Corporation's annual art show features images produced on superfast graphics workstations. Many of the images submitted are by technically oriented people who work in such areas as architecture and engineering. Fast processor speeds are necessary for three-dimensional modeling and realistic lighting effects.

6

7

8

9

10–12. The images of Dan Younger, an assistant professor of art at the University of Missouri-St. Louis, evoke thoughts of the 1950s and the sci-fi craze. Professor Younger often uses a scanner to input hard-copy photos taken decades ago and then uses art and illustration software on a Macintosh platform to produce the stunning visual effects.

13–15. Corinne Whitaker—who began working with computers after a successful career as a photographer—has achieved national acclaim for her abstract art. Ms. Whitaker uses both Windows and Macintosh platforms to create her art.

16. Robert Silvers is known for his photomosaics, which have appeared on many national magazine covers and in corporate advertisements. To create each photomosaic, he uses a fast computer and a program that selects—based on coloring and an ability to trace outlines of the shapes in the larger picture—hundreds of images from a large picture database.

16

MODULE

SW

SOFTWARE

In this module, we look at the software concepts with which you should be familiar in order to get up and running on a computer system. The module serves as a springboard for working with applications programs—the reason you usually acquire a computer system.

Chapter SW 1 offers an overall introduction to the world of software. Here, you will learn about the principal categories of software, as well as many of the graphical tools that make today's software products easy to use.

Systems software, the subject of Chapter SW 2, encompasses the programs that enable hardware devices to run applications software. Every computer user must in some way interact with systems software.

MODULE CONTENTS
Software

SW I

FUNDAMENTALS OF SOFTWARE USE

LEARNING OBJECTIVES

After completing this chapter, you will be able to:

1. Describe the major classes of software available in the marketplace.

2. Demonstrate how users gain access to software and the restrictions that sometimes limit their activities.

3. Explain the differences among user interfaces.

4. Identify common elements of a graphical user interface (GUI) and their functions.

5. List the types of online help available.

6. Describe what virtual reality is and discuss its applications.

OVERVIEW

Today's computer users choose among thousands of different software products that perform a wide range of different tasks. Users can buy software to write and produce books, keep track of their finances, send electronic mail and schedule meetings, learn foreign languages, entertain themselves, create music and movies, manage entire businesses, create greeting cards and flyers, and compress files; the complete list of uses is far too long to enumerate. Despite many differences, software products share some striking similarities. These similarities—which include the tools that most users require to perform basic types of work—are the subject of this chapter.

To begin, we will review the difference between systems software and applications software. We will also explore the benefits of software suites and document-centered computing and consider such topics as proprietary software, shareware, and freeware.

Next, we turn to the user interface. Not too long ago, most computer users had to write their own applications in programming languages to get computers to perform needed work. This situation has radically changed over the past decade or two. Desktop systems with sophisticated graphics capabilities and graphical user interfaces have emerged to set the standard for computers, making it easy for even novice users to take advantage of technology.

Chapter SW 1 deals chiefly with the components of graphical user interfaces. It covers the wide variety of menus, windows, and icons you are likely to encounter, and it indicates where to turn when you need online help. The chapter also looks briefly at trends that will lead toward the interfaces of the future—including social and virtual-reality interfaces that are beginning to pop up in software packages.

ABOUT SOFTWARE

For a tutorial on various types of software, go to www.harcourtcollege.com/ infosys/parker2000/student/ tutor/ and click on Chapter SW 1.

In this section we'll address a variety of general topics related to software, including systems software and applications software, software suites, software ownership, and software updates.

SYSTEMS SOFTWARE AND APPLICATIONS SOFTWARE

Computers run two general classes of software: systems software and applications software (see Figure SW 1-1).

Systems Software   **Systems software** consists of "background" programs that enable applications software to work with a computer system's hardware devices. This class of software enables you to perform important jobs like transferring files from one storage medium to another, configuring your computer system to work with a specific brand of printer or display device, managing files on your hard disk, and protecting your computer system from unauthorized use.

Three types of systems software are the operating system, language translators, and utility programs. The next chapter will cover these types of programs.

■ **Systems software**. Computer programs, such as the operating system, that enable applications programs to work with a computer system's hardware.

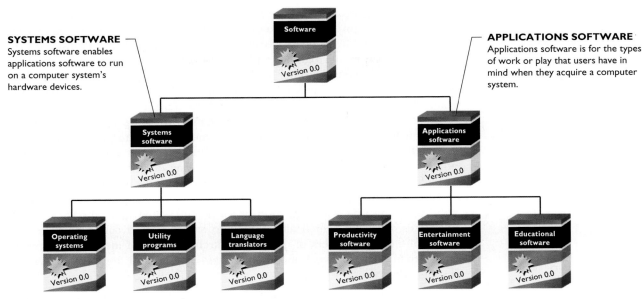

SYSTEMS SOFTWARE
Systems software enables applications software to run on a computer system's hardware devices.

APPLICATIONS SOFTWARE
Applications software is for the types of work or play that users have in mind when they acquire a computer system.

FIGURE SW 1-1

Systems and applications software.

Applications Software **Applications software** provides tools to carry out the types of computer work for which users buy computer systems. When you write a letter within a word processing program or when your bank uses a program to produce your monthly checking account statement, applications software performs the job. Applications programs are often referred to as *applications*.

The largest body of applications software is *productivity software,* which is designed to improve workers' job performance. The principal types of productivity software—word processing programs, spreadsheet programs, presentation graphics programs, and database managers—are covered in depth in versions of this book that contain a PS module. Other types of applications software include computer games, educational software, software geared to scientific research, and programs to make gadgets such as exercise bikes and television sets more capable.

The difference between systems and applications software is not always so clear-cut in practice. Systems programs often contain applications-software components. For example, Microsoft's Windows operating system contains such productivity-software enhancements as a Web browser, calendar, and notepad. A program's classification as systems or applications software usually depends on the principal task the program does.

For links to further information about applications software, go to www. harcourtcollege.com/ infosys/parker2000/student/ explore/ and click on Chapter SW 1.

SOFTWARE SUITES AND DOCUMENT-CENTERED COMPUTING

Only just a few years ago, most computer users who wanted to write letters bought stand-alone word-processing programs. Those who wanted to create business worksheets and charts acquired separate spreadsheet programs. All of that has now changed.

Software Suites Today, most office-oriented programs such as word processors and spreadsheets are sold bundled together with other related applications software in **software suites.** The dominant leader in suite sales for office

---

■ **Applications software.** Programs that provide tools for performing the type of work that people buy computer systems to do; commonly called *applications programs*, or simply, *applications*. ■ **Software suite.** A collection of software products bundled together into a single package and sold at a price that is less than the sum of the prices of the individual components.

applications is Microsoft Office. The high-end edition of this package bundles Word (for word processing), Excel (for spreadsheet work), PowerPoint (for presentation graphics), Access (for database management), and FrontPage (for Web site development) together with several other programs. You can also buy suites that are targeted to other applications—such as desktop illustration and Web-site development—as well as *minisuites* that bundle together fewer programs. Minisuites, as you might guess, cost less than full software suites.

Closely related to suites are *integrated software programs*—such as Microsoft Works—which compress suite functionality. Thus, instead of a full-featured word processor or spreadsheet, an integrated software package incorporates watered-down versions of each, providing only their main features in a single package. Users in the home market usually do not miss the omitted capabilities; most people who buy full-featured software for their own use wind up using only a tiny fraction of the features anyway. Companies prefer full suites, however, which allow them to satisfy with a single package the needs of a large numbers of users. The purchase price of integrated software is less than suite software and requires less storage and fewer other system resources to run.

Document-Centered Computing   A software suite handles its core applications—word processing and spreadsheets, for instance—through shell programs. Each shell contains all of the needed code used to perform its work except for instructions to do tasks that are common to other shells in the suite. Shells request instructions from a shared *task library* for this latter set of duties. Thus, if you want to create a diagram in a document you are writing within your word processing shell, you summon a drawing program by clicking an icon on the word processor's toolbar or selecting the appropriate item from one of the word processor's other menus. The word processor in turn calls for an art-tools routine from the task library. If you later want to draw something while in your spreadsheeting shell, the spreadsheet program requests the same art-tools routine.

Since the core applications of the suite need not include redundant code for shared functions, the task library both lowers storage requirements for the user and simplifies the development of new programs for the software maker. What's more, a suite presents users with a single interface for handling tasks.

Suites also allow users to easily nest applications and to jump back and forth between applications. For instance, let's say you are writing a letter in your word processing program, and you want to insert a spreadsheet table. You can launch (start or open) your spreadsheet program, locate the particular table you want in a stored worksheet, and then copy and paste the table back into your letter—all without ever closing the word processing program (see Figure SW 1-2).

Software suites and their nesting capabilities have moved computer users toward a work routine called **document-centered computing.** The term implies that a user can call on a variety of applications programs at any time as needed to help create a document. Such phrases as "word processing application" and "spreadsheet application" are of limited use in the context of document-centered computing; they are certainly not as pivotal as the document itself.

WHO OWNS SOFTWARE?

Sensitive questions sometimes arise about ownership and user rights regarding software products. Typically, a software maker or publisher develops a program, secures a copyright on it, and then retains ownership of all rights to it.

■ **Document-centered computing.** A view of computing in which the document itself is more central than the applications program or programs in which the document was created.

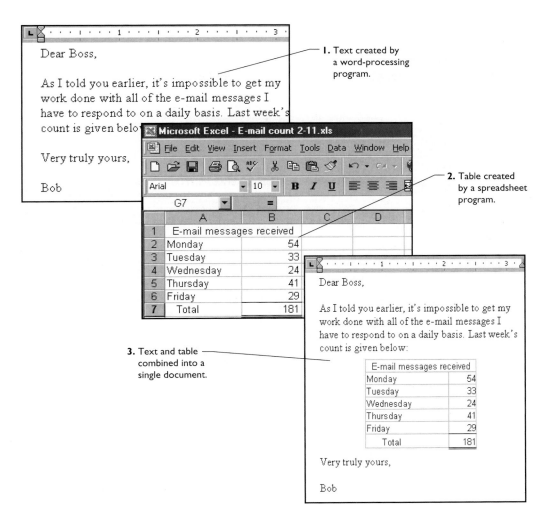

1. Text created by a word-processing program.

2. Table created by a spreadsheet program.

3. Text and table combined into a single document.

FIGURE SW 1-2

Document-centered computing. With a software suite, you can create a single document that contains information developed with two or more program-suite components.

The publisher then dictates who can use, copy, or distribute the program. Next we discuss various classes of ownership and use.

Proprietary Software Many of the systems and applications programs used today are **proprietary software.** This means that someone owns the rights to the program, and the owner expects users to buy their own copies.

Microsoft Office is a typical example. If you want to acquire this software to write letters or produce graphics, you must purchase a registered copy in a store, through a mail-order house, or over the Internet. In buying the software, you pay not to own it, but to acquire a *license* that makes you an authorized user (see Figure SW 1-3). Organizations such as businesses and schools, which may need software for use by several people, generally acquire **site licenses** that allow access by multiple users.

If you buy a copy of Microsoft Office (or similar proprietary software) for your own use, you cannot legally make copies of it for your friends, nor can you reproduce parts of the package's code to build your own suite program. You cannot even rent or lease the software to others. You have bought only the right to operate the software yourself and for its intended use—creating documents. Part of the price that you pay for the program becomes profit for the software publisher—Microsoft Corporation—for its efforts in bringing the product to the marketplace.

■ **Proprietary software.** A software product to which someone owns the rights. ■ **Site license.** An agreement that allows access by several people in an organization to a proprietary software product.

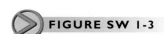

LIMITED WARRANTY. Microsoft warrants that (a) the SOFTWARE PRODUCT will perform substantially in accordance with the accompanying written materials for a period of ninety (90) days from the date of receipt, and (b) any Support Services provided by Microsoft shall be substantially as described in applicable written materials provided to you by Microsoft, and Microsoft support engineers will make commercially reasonable efforts to solve any problem issues. Some states and jurisdictions do not allow limitations on duration of an implied warranty, so the above... PRODUCT, if any, are...

CUSTOMER REMED... (a) return of the price p... Warranty and which is... PRODUCT has resulte... remainder of the origin... product support service...

NO OTHER WA... MICROSOFT A... EITHER EXPRE... OF MERCHAN... INFRINGEMEN... FAILURE TO P... LEGAL RIGHTS... STATE/JURISDI...

LIMITATION O... IN NO EVENT S... INCIDENTAL, I... WITHOUT LIMI... INTERRUPTION... ARISING OUT C... PROVISION OF... BEEN ADVISED... ENTIRE LIABIL... GREATER OF T... U.S.$5.00; PROV... SERVICES AGR... SHALL BE GOV... JURISDICTIONS... ABOVE LIMITA...

MISCELLANEOUS

If you acquired this produ... If you acquired this produ... irrevocably attorns to the j... hereunder in the courts lo... If this product was acquir... Should you have any ques... subsidiary serving your co...

- **Rental.** You may not rent, lease, or lend the SOFTWARE PRODUCT.
- **Support Services.** Microsoft may provide you with support services related to the SOFTWARE PRODUCT ("Support Services"). Use of Support Services is governed by the Microsoft policies and programs described in the user manual, in "online" documentation, and/or in other Microsoft-provided materials. Any supplemental software code provided to you as part of the Support Services shall be considered part of the SOFTWARE PRODUCT and subject to the terms and conditions of this EULA. With respect to technical information you provide to Microsoft as part of the Support Services, Microsoft may use such information for its business purposes, including for product... you.
- **Software Transfer.** ...the SOFTWARE PR... applicable, the Certifi... upgrade, any transfer...
- **Termination.** Witho... conditions of this EU...

3. UPGRADES. If the SO... Microsoft as being eligi... replaces and/or supplem... product only in accorda... software programs that... single product package...

4. COPYRIGHT. All title... animations, video, audio... and any copies of the S... copyright laws and inte... material except that you... archival purposes. You...

5. DUAL-MEDIA SOFT... medium you receive, yo... medium on another con... permanent transfer (as p...

6. U.S. GOVERNMENT... RIGHTS. Use, duplicat... Technical Data and Co... Software—Restricted R... WA 98052-6399.

END-USER LICENSE AGREEMENT FOR MICROSOFT SOFTWARE

IMPORTANT—READ CAREFULLY: This Microsoft End-User License Agreement ("EULA") is a legal agreement between you (either an individual or a single entity) and Microsoft Corporation for the Microsoft software product identified above, which includes computer software and may include associated media, printed materials, and "online" or electronic documentation ("SOFTWARE PRODUCT"). By installing, copying, or otherwise using the SOFTWARE PRODUCT, you agree to be bound by the terms of this EULA. If you do not agree to the terms of this EULA, do not install or use the SOFTWARE PRODUCT; you may, however, return it to your place of purchase for a full refund.

SOFTWARE PRODUCT LICENSE

The SOFTWARE PRODUCT is protected by copyright laws and international copyright treaties, as well as other intellectual property laws and treaties. The SOFTWARE PRODUCT is licensed, not sold.

1. GRANT OF LICENSE. This EULA grants you the following rights:

- **Applications Software.** You may install and use one copy of the SOFTWARE PRODUCT, or any prior version for the same operating system, on a single computer. The primary user of the computer on which the SOFTWARE PRODUCT is installed may make a second copy for his or her exclusive use on a portable computer.
- **Storage/Network Use.** You may also store or install a copy of the SOFTWARE PRODUCT on a storage device, such as a network server, used only to install or run the SOFTWARE PRODUCT on your other computers over an internal network; however, you must acquire and dedicate a license for each separate computer on which the SOFTWARE PRODUCT is installed or run from the storage device. A license for the SOFTWARE PRODUCT may not be shared or used concurrently on different computers.
- **License Pak.** If you have acquired this EULA in a Microsoft License Pak, you may make the number of additional copies of the computer software portion of the SOFTWARE PRODUCT authorized on the printed copy of this EULA, and you may use each copy in the manner specified above. You are also entitled to make a corresponding number of secondary copies for portable computer use as specified above.

2. DESCRIPTION OF OTHER RIGHTS AND LIMITATIONS.

- **Academic Edition Software.** If the SOFTWARE PRODUCT is identified as "Academic Edition" or "AE," you must be a "Qualified Educational User" to use the SOFTWARE PRODUCT. If you are not a Qualified Educational User, you have no rights under this EULA. To determine whether you are a Qualified Educational User, please contact the Microsoft Sales Information Center/One Microsoft Way/Redmond, WA 98052-6399 or the Microsoft subsidiary serving your country.
- **Not for Resale Software.** If the SOFTWARE PRODUCT is labeled "Not for Resale" or "NFR," then, notwithstanding other sections of this EULA, you may not resell, or otherwise transfer for value, the SOFTWARE PRODUCT.
- **Limitations on Reverse Engineering, Decompilation, and Disassembly.** You may not reverse engineer, decompile, or disassemble the SOFTWARE PRODUCT, except and only to the extent that such activity is expressly permitted by applicable law notwithstanding this limitation.
- **Separation of Components.** The SOFTWARE PRODUCT is licensed as a single product. Its component parts may not be separated for use on more than one computer.

(Continued)

Microsoft

FIGURE SW 1-3

User license for a proprietary software product. Shown here is the English-language portion of the standard Microsoft license.

For links to further information about shareware, go to www.harcourtcollege.com/ infosys/parker2000/student/ explore/ and click on Chapter SW 1.

Along with its restrictions, licensed proprietary software generally brings many benefits, including quality, ongoing product support, and a large base of users. If, for instance, you buy a product from a well-known software maker such as Microsoft, Corel, or Lotus Development, you generally know that millions of dollars supported its creation, that the product will likely remain in use for several years, and that many sources will be available to offer help.

Shareware Some software is available as **shareware.** While you don't have to pay to use shareware, you must pay for support of any type. The software publisher expects you to pay a nominal contribution or "registration fee" to receive written or online documentation, software updates, or technical help and advice. The amount charged typically ranges anywhere from $5 to $75. Many shareware creators also ask that you register their software if you continue to use it for a certain period of time—say, a month or longer.

The shareware creator normally doesn't mind if you make copies of the program for your friends. That's because even though you may choose not to register or continue to use the program, your friends may love it more than you do and decide to pay the creator for support items. After all, support is how this type of software publisher makes money, so the more exposure its programs get, the better.

Keep in mind that many shareware products are copyrighted, so someone owns their rights. Thus, you cannot copy code from such a program to make

---

■ **Shareware.** Software that people can copy and use in exchange for a nominal fee.

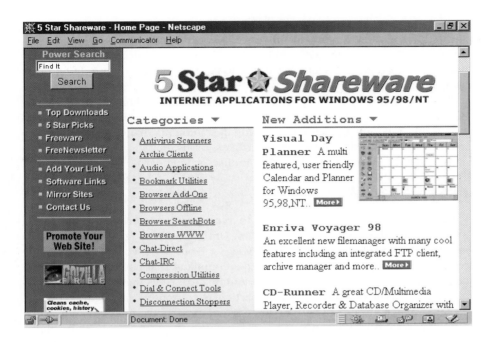

Shareware. Shareware and freeware are plentiful on the Internet.

your own competing program. Internet sites provide access to many shareware and freeware programs (see Figure SW 1-4).

Freeware   Freeware, or *public-domain software*, refers to programs that you can use free of charge, with no strings attached. Who, you may ask, would want to give away software and not make so much as a dime off of it? Plenty of people, it so happens. College and university professors, and also graduate students, are motivated to develop freeware because they are doing something academic institutions promote—advancing the state of the art of computer science and making new breakthroughs available as soon as possible to the public. Others may want to develop freeware just because it can be fun or because it provides excellent practice in honing one's programming skills. Still others may want to encourage as many people as possible to test their software's marketability. If the freeware turns out to be popular, the developer may polish it up a bit and include documentation and support—and then turn around and sell the program for profit.

In recent years, even established software publishers have started embracing the freeware concept, giving it greater respectability with mainstream users. For instance, Netscape and Microsoft both give away their browser software for free on the Internet. Also, users of office suites can often find several free applications that enhance working with suite components at their software publisher's Web site. And for users of Linux—a freeware version of the Unix operating system—Corel and Oracle have many applications available for free. With freeware like Linux, support is often available through a loose confederation of software developers, Internet newsgroups, and Web sites.

THE USER INTERFACE

Users interact with software in a variety of ways. Those whose computers still run Microsoft's now-discontinued MS-DOS operating system, for instance, often perform work by typing DOS-language commands at a prompting character.

■ **Freeware.** Software offered for use without charge.

Users of Microsoft's Windows, on the other hand, choose options from menus and point and click icons with mice to perform similar operations. The manner in which a program makes its resources available to users is known as its **user interface.** In this section, we will look at elements commonly found in user interfaces.

The backbone of most software programs is their command set. It is by issuing commands that you get a program to perform any desired action. Commands are often invoked either by typing in statements that conform to a command syntax, by using shortcut keystrokes, or by making selections from a graphical user interface (GUI) with a mouse or keyboard.

COMMAND SYNTAX

Early user interfaces required users to type precise instructions indicating exactly what the computers should do. Until the 1980s, this command-line interface was pretty much the only way to work with computers. At some type of system **prompt,** the user typed a command that conformed to a strict command syntax. **Syntax** refers to the grammatical rules that govern the structure and content of statements in a particular computer language.

For instance, the MS-DOS operating system accepts typed commands at the operating-system prompt. If you are currently in the DOS directory on the C drive and want to erase a file named FRED from the A drive, then at the prompt:

```
C:\DOS>
```

you must type

```
ERASE A:FRED
```

If you were to type

```
ERASE FRED FROM A
```

an error message would display on the screen, indicating that the command does not conform to the official syntax of the MS-DOS language.

Unfortunately, using a command syntax effectively is often beyond the patience and capabilities of most users. Syntax can impose exacting demands, and the average person tends to treat such formal rules rather casually and to make typing mistakes. For instance, imagine having to regularly create DOS statements such as the following:

```
DEVICE=C:\DOS\DRIVER.SYS /D:0 /F:1
```

Not only do you have to be very careful in making sure each of the characters in the statement is correct—including blank spaces appearing where they should be—but also, if you can't remember the syntax, you have to look it up.

To make software available to the widest audience possible, software publishers have added features such as shortcut keystrokes and GUIs to simplify the work of entering commands. However, such developments have not completely eliminated command syntax. Although shortcut keystrokes and graphical user interfaces have certainly helped more people than ever to interact easily with computers, many applications still require painstakingly typing in commands. Examples include creating one's own computer programs and customizing software packages to work in nonstandard ways. Also, many users still prefer working with command syntax, because it frees the computer from the processing necessary to handle graphical screens. Therefore, it requires fewer system resources than GUIs, speeding up the computer's work.

■ **User interface.** The manner in which a computer program makes its resources available to users. ■ **Prompt.** Displayed text or symbols indicating the computer system's readiness to receive user input. ■ **Syntax.** The grammatical rules that govern a language.

Indenting a paragraph

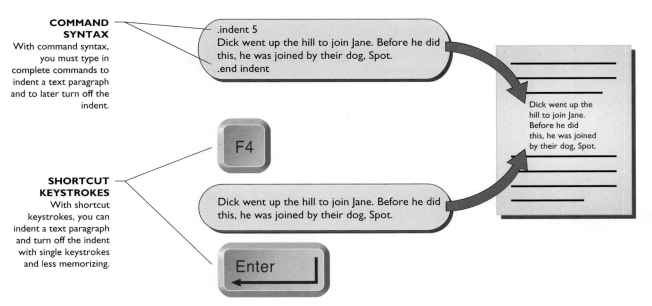

COMMAND SYNTAX
With command syntax, you must type in complete commands to indent a text paragraph and to later turn off the indent.

```
.indent 5
Dick went up the hill to join Jane. Before he did
this, he was joined by their dog, Spot.
.end indent
```

F4

SHORTCUT KEYSTROKES
With shortcut keystrokes, you can indent a text paragraph and turn off the indent with single keystrokes and less memorizing.

Dick went up the hill to join Jane. Before he did this, he was joined by their dog, Spot.

Enter

Dick went up the hill to join Jane. Before he did this, he was joined by their dog, Spot.

SHORTCUT KEYSTROKES

Shortcut keystrokes enable you to invoke commands with a minimal number of keystrokes. For instance, when you want to indent text with many versions of the WordPerfect word processing program, you strike the F4 function key. Next, you type the text you want indented. To turn off the indent, you tap the Enter key. To perform the same type of task with a command syntax—something people had to do during the early days of word processing—would take much greater effort (see Figure SW 1-5).

In Microsoft Word, you can change from single-spacing to double-spacing in a document just as easily—just hold down the Control key and press 2 (Ctrl+2).

Shortcut keystrokes save a great deal of time when compared to conventional command syntax. However, they can also tax the user's memory. Someone who can't remember the shortcut keystrokes for seldom-used commands will have to spend time looking them up in a printed manual or an online help system.

GRAPHICAL USER INTERFACES (GUIS)

Graphical user interfaces (GUIs) have become popular in recent years with the availability of high-resolution display screens, faster CPUs, and larger capacity RAM and hard disks. Before these types of hardware improvements, computer designers could not practically implement GUIs. The systems of the day could not adequately deliver *WYSIWYG* displays (for *w*hat *y*ou *s*ee *i*s *w*hat *y*ou *g*et)—screen images that resemble printed documents—since the output looked far too crude. And later, when screen outputs started to look acceptable, the systems just took too long to generate the graphics on the computer. These days, of course, most computers can rapidly display desktop graphics, and the most constraining factor is when byte-hungry data have to travel at slow modem speeds to reach one's desktop from afar.

Today's most widely used GUIs are Microsoft Windows and the Apple Macintosh interface. Virtually all modern PC software follows at least one of these

FIGURE SW 1-5

Shortcut keystrokes. Key combinations help users issue commands—such as indenting a paragraph—with minimal input from the keyboard.

■ **Shortcut keystrokes.** Keystrokes that make it possible for commands to be entered with minimal keystroking. ■ **Graphical user interface (GUI).** A term that refers to the graphics screens that make it easier for users to interact with software.

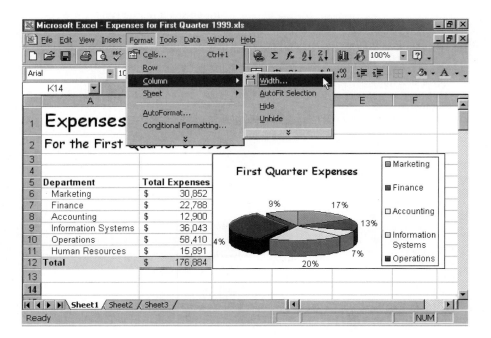

FIGURE SW 1-6

Graphical user interfaces. GUIs, which contain menu choices that you can select with a mouse, have become the standard desktop user interface as graphics displays evolved.

standards. Thus, if you are comfortable with the applicable standard, a conforming software package will have an immediate familiarity to it when you first use it. A growing trend is for each of the standards to borrow from one another, increasingly giving all software the same look and feel.

GUIs employ such devices as pull-down menus, windows and icons, hyperlinks, and toolbars to make it easier than ever for users to navigate successfully through software packages (see Figure SW 1-6). Each of these devices will be explained shortly. Instead of having to remember a complicated command syntax or shortcut-keystroke sequence, all the GUI user has to do is look for the command on a menu, point to it using a mouse or keyboard, and select it. A variety of online tools are available to assist users who cannot recall instantly the command necessary to perform a specific operation.

GUIs also provide a means of customizing screens to suit each user's personal work style. Menus and toolbars can often be personalized with favorite commands and then moved anywhere on the screen. Also, screens can be altered in a variety of ways to suit individual tastes. For instance, with a couple of mouse actions, users can temporarily get rid of the Windows' bottom-of-screen taskbar (containing the Start button and time) and other screen clutter to make more room for documents.

Despite the usefulness of GUIs, some users may not want to rely on them exclusively. For example, longtime users of a particular program complete tasks faster by typing familiar shortcut keystrokes than by selecting comparable commands from menus. Also, longtime users of MS-DOS often prefer to copy files using its command syntax rather than performing the same operation through a sequence of selections from Windows menus. GUIs are particularly helpful, however, in jogging your memory when you need to issue seldom-used commands. Today, most software packages combine command syntax, shortcut keystrokes, and GUIs, enabling users to switch among these alternatives as desired.

OTHER INTERFACES

Although using a keyboard or a mouse with a standard GUI is by far the most common way for people to interact with computer systems today, several other methods are in wide use. Among these are pen-based user interfaces, touch screens, and voice input and output—all of which were covered in

Continuous-Speech Recognition

How Far Away Are Mainstream Applications?

If you've ever thought about the future of technology, you've probably wondered when the day will come when people will be conversing with their PCs as though the computers were human. That day may not be as close as Hollywood science-fiction movies would lead you to believe. Even though computer systems can decipher what people *say* with 95 percent accuracy, continuous-speech-recognition technology still has a long way to go to figure out what people really *mean* when they speak.

A top strategist at Microsoft—the world's largest software company—even recently conceded that continuous-speech-recognition technology isn't yet ready for prime time and that it's difficult to predict when it will be. Microsoft is vigorously preparing for the day when computers and users will communicate largely in spoken, natural language. More than $100 million and close to a hundred employees have been set aside for speech development at Microsoft.

Microsoft's main competitors in the office-suite area, Lotus and Corel, have been far more aggressive in pushing continuous-speech recognition on the desktop PC. Lotus' SmartSuite includes IBM's ViaVoice Gold and Corel offers its WordPerfect Suite with Dragon's NaturallySpeaking. Both products are used mostly for dictation, and you have to enunciate words distinctively for them to work. Also, both have their limits as tools to communicate at a deeper level with your computer system.

Continuous-speech recognition, if it is ever to match the capability of humans to deal with language, will have to go well beyond recognizing individual, spoken words. For computers to comprehend human language, they need to be programmed with a lot of information about how the world works too. In other words, they have to understand the context of what is being said and be able to fill in things that humans understand but never directly put into words.

Techniques of artificial intelligence (AI) have been widely used over the past several years in helping computers process speech.

Continuous-speech recognition. Still far from being a prime-time technology.

Recognizing what people mean when they speak is an inherently difficult challenge, and progress has been slow.

A sure-bet early application in almost every continuous-speech user interface when the technology reaches maturity will be voice-actuated file retrieval. If you say something like "Get the letter I sent to Betty last week," or "Pull up the five most recent files that mention XYZ Company," your computer should be able to know what you mean and hop to it. Even if you should have said "XYZ *Corporation*" instead.

Another common application that will likely be overhauled is today's familiar phone-menu interface—the tedious, voice system found on so many automated lines. Instead of having to listen to 10 or 12 choices before going to the next menu, you will hear a pleasant voice starting off with "How can I help you?" If you respond "What's the weather going to be like in Cairo tomorrow?" the computer should be able carry the ball from there. "Illinois or Egypt?" it may ask back. If you respond with "Illinois," it should be able to check its database and answer you so quickly you'd swear a human was on the line.

Chapter HW 3 (see also the Tomorrow box). A recent development that is rapidly gaining favor is the social interface.

Social Interfaces　Social interfaces often borrow techniques from 3-D graphics to immerse users into environments that simulate those in real life (see Figure SW 1-7).

The interest in social interfaces is spurred by the realization that today's familiar GUIs take time to master and, also, by advances in techniques to create three-dimensional desktop graphics. Users of today's Windows and Macintosh GUIs often take months to get reasonably comfortable with the icons, folders, and shortcut keystrokes involved. What's more, users often limit themselves to working with only a small percentage of the features in these massive programs—they don't bother to learn the rest. A more intuitive

Net2Phone's dialing interface looks just like a real phone.

A ticket counter makes visitors to the Southwest Airlines Web site immediately familiar with where to go for specific information.

FIGURE SW 1-7

Social interfaces. Social interfaces immerse program users into environments that simulate real life.

social interface could not only cut learning time dramatically but also make it simple for users to find useful features they would not otherwise know about. Later in the chapter we will look at *virtual reality,* a hardware-and-software technology that extends the social-interface concept with sensory phenomena such as sound, movement, and feeling.

A word of caution: You should not expect some upstart social interface to displace such well-entrenched GUIs as Microsoft Windows and the Macintosh interface in the foreseeable future, although the possibility exists. Nor should you presume that your mouse and keyboard will suddenly give way to a continuous-speech-enabled GUI. The computer industry has matured to the point where *evolution* is a more likely scenario than *revolution.* The many billions of dollars that organizations are spending on technology favor gradual change. Thus, a better bet is that the Windows and the Macintosh interfaces will evolve by incorporating the best features from social-interface and voice research.

ELEMENTS OF A GRAPHICAL USER INTERFACE

Most software packages today interact with users through graphical user interfaces of some type. Consequently, virtually everyone learning about computers should know how the basic elements incorporated into GUIs work.

MENUS

A **menu** is a set of options from which the user can choose to take a desired action in a program. Several types of menus are used, including those that follow.

Menu Bars   At the top of many GUI screens or windows is a **menu bar** showing the governing command set (see Figure SW 1-8). Generally, commands can be selected with a mouse or by some simple shortcut-keystroke procedure. For instance, to select the View command off the menu bar in Figure SW 1-8, you can either click on it with a mouse or depress the Alt key while tapping the V key on the keyboard. Generally, the key that is to be struck in combination with the Alt key (or another control key) is underlined or highlighted on the menu, thereby putting less of a strain on your memory. Such special keys are called *access keys.*

■ **Menu.** A set of options from which the user chooses to take a desired action. ■ **Menu bar.** A horizontal list of choices that appears on a highlighted line, usually below the window title. Often called the *main menu.*

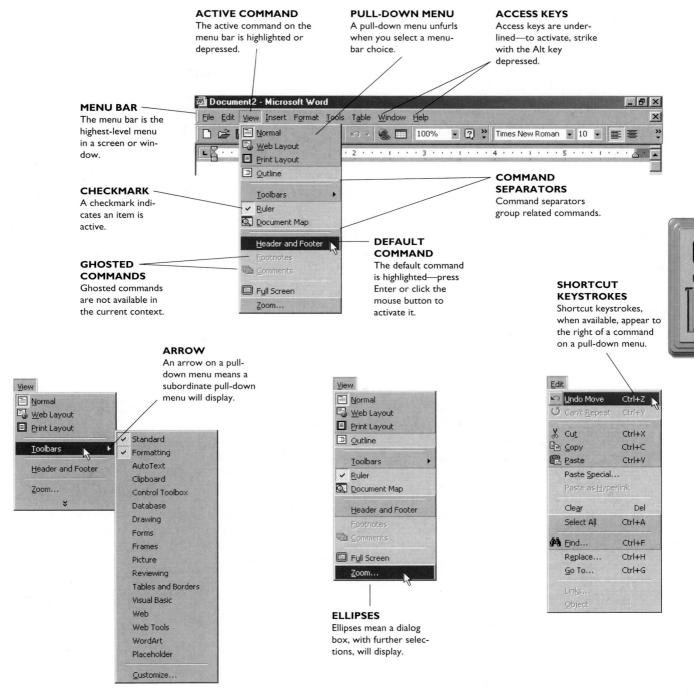

ACTIVE COMMAND
The active command on the menu bar is highlighted or depressed.

PULL-DOWN MENU
A pull-down menu unfurls when you select a menu-bar choice.

ACCESS KEYS
Access keys are under-lined—to activate, strike with the Alt key depressed.

MENU BAR
The menu bar is the highest-level menu in a screen or window.

CHECKMARK
A checkmark indi-cates an item is active.

GHOSTED COMMANDS
Ghosted commands are not available in the current context.

COMMAND SEPARATORS
Command separators group related commands.

DEFAULT COMMAND
The default command is highlighted—press Enter or click the mouse button to activate it.

SHORTCUT KEYSTROKES
Shortcut keystrokes, when available, appear to the right of a command on a pull-down menu.

ARROW
An arrow on a pull-down menu means a subordinate pull-down menu will display.

ELLIPSES
Ellipses mean a dialog box, with further selec-tions, will display.

**FIGURE SW 1-8**

Menu-bar and pull-down menu elements.

Pull-Down Menus **Pull-down menus** (or *drop-down menus*) display on the screen when the user makes a choice on a menu bar. Subcommand options on pull-down menus prompt the user for finer levels of detail. Pull-down menus typically conform to certain conventions:

ACTIVE AND DEFAULT CHOICES The active and default commands are respec-tively highlighted on the menu bar and pull-down menu. The *active* command (View, in the top screen of Figure SW 1-8, which is highlighted by having a depressed appearance) is the command that you have already selected, while

■ **Pull-down menu.** A menu of subcommands that drops down vertically from a horizontal menu bar or appears along-side another pull-down menu. Also called a *drop-down menu.*

the *default* command (Header and Footer, in the top screen of Figure SW 1-8) is a command that can be activated merely by striking the Enter key or by clicking the mouse button.

You can often escape from an active command by striking the Escape key or merely by pointing to another command on the menu bar. As you slide the mouse sideways, you'll see other pull-down menus unfurl as the *mouse pointer* passes over corresponding menu-bar commands. There are several ways to select a choice other than a default—you can position the mouse pointer on it and click the mouse button, invoke its access key, or move to it with the appropriate arrow key on the keyboard and then strike the Enter key.

GHOSTED TYPE   On the View pull-down menu in the top screen of Figure SW 1-8, the Footnotes and Comments subcommands are shown in *ghosted* or faded type. This means that these particular choices are unavailable in the context of what you're currently doing. For instance, if you haven't created any footnotes in a document, viewing any is impossible. Ghosted type extends beyond pull-down menus to other GUI elements, such as menu tabs and command buttons.

CHECKMARKS   An item with a *checkmark* to the left of it means that the associated option is "active" or "selected." For instance, the check by Ruler in the top screen of Figure SW 1-8 means that this element will appear on the screen display. Software programs also have ways of letting you deselect checkmarked options. One widely used procedure is allowing you to point to the option and then selecting it again with a mouse or by striking the Enter key. So, for instance, by selecting Ruler after it had already been checked, both the onscreen ruler and its checkmark on the pull-down menu would disappear.

COMMAND SEPARATORS   A command separator is used to group related commands. In the top screen in Figure SW 1-8, Normal, Web Layout, Print Layout, and Outline all pertain to ways to view an onscreen document. Normal view is used for everyday typing and editing, for instance, whereas Print Layout shows how elements such as graphics and page numbering will be put on a page.

ARROWS   An *arrow* to the right of a pull-down menu option (▶)—such as Toolbars in the bottom left screen in Figure SW 1-8—means that the choice leads to another, subordinate pull-down menu. When you position the mouse pointer over the Toolbars choice, the pull-down menu showing the available toolbars automatically appears.

ELLIPSES   On pull-down menus, *ellipses* (. . .) often display to the right of a command—such as Zoom in the bottom center screen in Figure SW 1-8. Ellipses mean that by selecting the command, you will call up a dialog box. As discussed shortly, a dialog box contains further available selections.

SHORTCUT KEYSTROKES   Many GUI menus show shortcut keystrokes next to command options, such as Ctrl+Z for Undo and Ctrl+C for Copy on the Edit menu shown at the bottom right of Figure SW 1-8. While you can execute such command options with the mouse button or the appropriate access keys (such as the *U* key for Undo) when a menu is open, you use a shortcut-keystroke sequence (such as holding down the Ctrl key while tapping the Z key) when a menu is not open.

Icon Menus   Often, menus are in the form of a set of **icons.** An icon can represent a computer program or a group of computer programs, a command or a group of commands, a document—such as a letter or fax transmission— or a group of documents, and the like. As you can see, virtually anything that can go into a computer file or a collection of files can be represented onscreen

---

■ **Icon.** A graphical image on a display screen that invokes some action when selected.

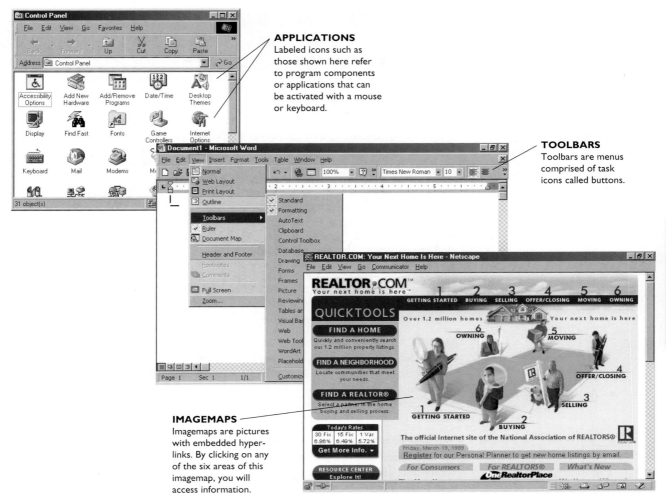

APPLICATIONS
Labeled icons such as those shown here refer to program components or applications that can be activated with a mouse or keyboard.

TOOLBARS
Toolbars are menus comprised of task icons called buttons.

IMAGEMAPS
Imagemaps are pictures with embedded hyperlinks. By clicking on any of the six areas of this imagemap, you will access information.

as an icon. When you select an icon from the displayed arrangement, software takes the corresponding action.

Figure SW 1-9 shows a variety of icon menus. Several types of elements found in icon menus are described next.

PROGRAMS AND APPLICATIONS   Program components or applications are commonly represented as icons. If such icons are not built into a software package you wish to use, no problem. Many packages allow you to prepare a set of commands to perform a job you frequently want done and, then, enable you to create a customized icon to represent the job. The icon can be placed either in a conventional icon menu like the one at the top of Figure SW 1-9 or turned into a toolbar button like those you see in the middle part of the same figure.

TOOLBARS   A **toolbar** is an icon menu comprised of small graphics called *toolbar buttons* that stretches either horizontally or vertically across the screen. Each button has a name, which displays if you point to the button (see Figure SW 1-10). In a software suite, toolbar buttons often invoke tasks that are common across applications—for instance, saving documents, printing documents, changing and sizing typefaces, and so on.

IMAGEMAPS   *Imagemaps* are pictures with embedded links or icons that can take you to other programs or features. When you click on any of the links,

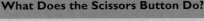

FIGURE SW 1-9

Icon menus.

What Does the Scissors Button Do?

Each toolbar button has a name that describes what it does. The name will display if you point to the button on the screen.

FIGURE SW 1-10

Toolbar buttons.

■ **Toolbar.** An icon menu comprised of small graphics called *buttons* that stretches either horizontally or vertically across the screen.

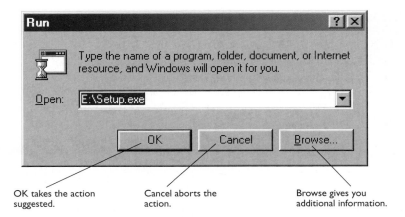

FIGURE SW 1-11

Command buttons. Shown here are three command buttons: OK, Cancel, and Browse.

OK takes the action suggested.

Cancel aborts the action.

Browse gives you additional information.

you are launched somewhere else—such as to a new Web page or to a particular feature in the program you are using.

COMMAND BUTTONS   A *command button* is an icon that represents a simple program command (see Figure SW 1-11). For instance, command buttons labeled *OK* and *Cancel* allow users to approve or abort program actions. A ghosted command button represents an action that is unavailable for current operation.

NAVIGATION BARS   On the Internet, World Wide Web users often have to deal with *navigation bars*. A navigation bar is typically comprised of closely grouped text, buttons, or icons, each of which takes you to a different location at a Web site (see Figure SW 1-12). By activating one of these items, the Web page on your screen is replaced by a page whose contents are described in the icon.

Users of Windows and Macintosh programs can often customize icon menus to meet their application needs. For instance, you may be able to choose the icons that are to appear on a menu, sequence the icons in any desired order, and move the icon menu to the most convenient place on the screen—say, to the top or right. As already hinted, you can usually also create your own icons to place on menus. Most Web sites currently do not support customization of menus, but tailoring sites to individual users is a growing trend on the Web and who knows what changes time may bring.

FIGURE SW 1-12

A navigation bar.

Navigation bar

Hypertext Menus Textual **hyperlinks**—referred to as *hypertext*—add another common control option in GUIs, especially on the Internet's World Wide Web. Hypertext is commonly boldfaced or underlined to make it stand out and is often in a different color than regular text. When you move the mouse pointer over hypertext, the pointer's shape often changes to a pointing hand (see Figure SW 1-13). Clicking then selects the link, generally retrieving a new Web page to your screen. Sometimes, in the context of the Internet, the term *hypermedia* is used to include not only hypertext but also other items such as feature-launching graphical icons and imagemaps.

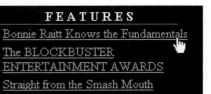

Palettes A **palette** is a menu that enables you to choose among colors, textures, and other art-oriented items. Generally, the palette is arranged in a grid—as in Figure SW 1-14—and you choose a selection either by clicking with the mouse or by tapping the arrow keys to highlight it and striking the Enter key.

Tab Menus A common fixture in GUIs is the *tab menu*, such as the one shown in Figure SW 1-15. Tab menus organize a screen into natural-looking file-folder tabs. By clicking on any of the tabs, the information within the folder corresponding to the tab can be accessed. Tab menus are functionally equivalent to the more conventional bar and pull-down menus.

Dialog Boxes Menu items also often appear in *dialog* boxes that pop onto the screen. These items—which include radio buttons, check boxes, and list boxes—will be discussed shortly.

FIGURE SW 1-13

Hypertext. Hypertext changes the mouse pointer to a pointing hand when the pointer passes over it. By selecting hypertext, you are launched to a new screen, feature, or application.

FIGURE SW 1-14

Palettes. A palette is a menu that allows users to specify colors, textures, and other attributes for art-oriented output.

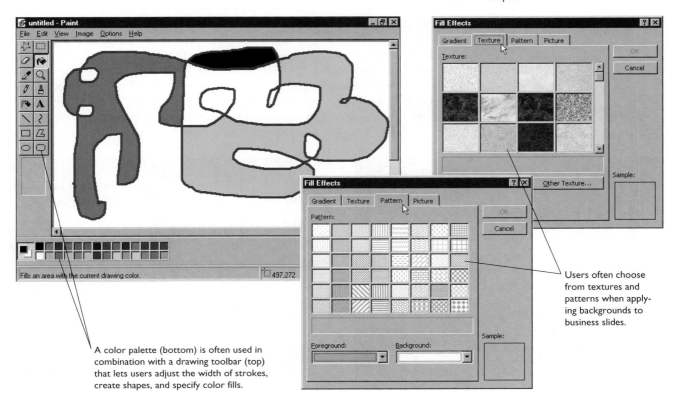

A color palette (bottom) is often used in combination with a drawing toolbar (top) that lets users adjust the width of strokes, create shapes, and specify color fills.

Users often choose from textures and patterns when applying backgrounds to business slides.

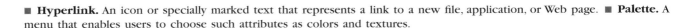

■ **Hyperlink.** An icon or specially marked text that represents a link to a new file, application, or Web page. ■ **Palette.** A menu that enables users to choose such attributes as colors and textures.

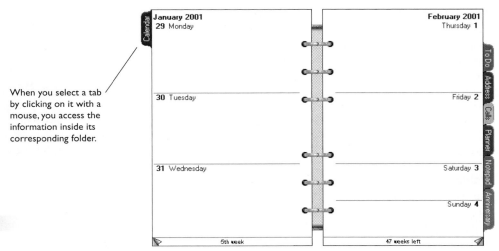

When you select a tab by clicking on it with a mouse, you access the information inside its corresponding folder.

FIGURE SW 1-15

Tab menu.

Web Tutor

For a tutorial on the various parts of a window, go to www.harcourtcollege.com/ infosys/parker2000/student/ tutor/ and click on Chapter SW 1.

WINDOWS

The staple of the GUI is the window. A **window** is a box of information that is overlaid on the display screen. A window can contain programs and documents, as well as menu items, instructions, and a variety of other types of data.

Customizing Windows Often, windows can be tailored to meet an application's needs. Several of the ways this can be done are described next.

CASCADING VERSUS TILING WINDOWS As shown in Figure SW 1-16, a user can quickly arrange windows onscreen in either of two ways: by *cascading* them one on top of another (left part of Figure SW 1-16) or by *tiling* them side by side (right part of Figure SW 1-16). Tiling enables you to see information in several windows at the same time, while cascading lets you see as much information as possible in the foreground window but only the titles of the windows underneath.

Whatever arrangement you choose for your windows, only one window can be active at a time. To make any onscreen window active, click the mouse pointer on the window. When you are cascading, the foreground window is

FIGURE SW 1-16

Cascaded and tiled windows.

CASCADED WINDOWS
Cascading overlaps windows. It lets you see as much information as possible in the foreground window but only the titles of the windows underneath.

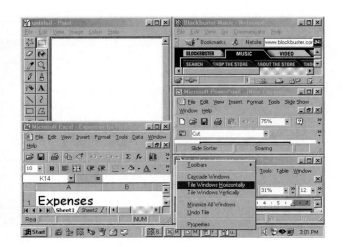

TILED WINDOWS
Tiling places windows side by side and enables you to see information in two or more windows at the same time.

■ **Window.** A box of related information that appears overlaid on a display screen.

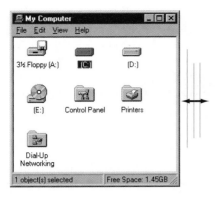

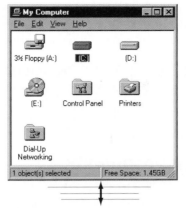

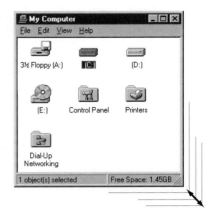

WIDTH
You change the width of a window by dragging its left or right border edge.

HEIGHT
You change the height of a window by dragging its top or bottom border edge.

WIDTH AND HEIGHT
You change both width and height together by dragging a corner sizing handle.

FIGURE SW 1-17

Resizing a window.

active; when you are tiling, a darkened title bar indicates the active window. (The *title bar* shows the name of the file displayed in the window.)

RESIZING AND MOVING WINDOWS   Resizing windows, making them larger or smaller, allows more detailed control of a screen display. Many software products let you resize the active window by selecting a window border (the frame enclosing the window) with a mouse. When the mouse pointer is moved over a window border, it looks like a double-pointed arrow. You can make the window wider or taller by moving the pointer inward or outward with the mouse button depressed. Alternatively, to adjust the window width and height at the same time, point the mouse at a *sizing handle* at the window's corner; then hold down the button and drag the mouse. (See Figure SW 1-17).

You can often customize your display further by moving any window from one part of the screen to another. Typically, this requires you to select the window's title bar with a mouse, hold down the mouse button, and then drag the window to the desired location and release the mouse to drop it there.

MINIMIZING VERSUS MAXIMIZING WINDOWS   Windows can be minimized to icon size or maximized to fill the entire screen. In the Windows 95 and 98 environments, buttons to do either of these tasks are at the top right of most windows (such as those in Figure SW 1-17). By clicking on the *minimize button* (), the window is reduced to an icon on the taskbar. A program that has been minimized is still actively running in the background and you can pull it up on the screen again by clicking its button on the taskbar. By clicking on the *maximize button* ( ), the window fills the screen. When a window is maximized, in the space where you would normally see the maximize button, a *restore button* ( ) is displayed instead. Restore simply reduces a maximized window to its previous size. To close a window and thereby leave the application for good, you must click on the *close button* () at the far upper-right corner of the window.

CHANGING A WINDOW'S LOOK   Operating systems such as Windows 98 take the customization process further by letting you change the look of a window. You can add a picture or pattern as a background to a window or have file-folder names display as Web pages (see Figure SW 1-18). What's more, icons can appear in a large or small format, you can display details about each icon, and some windows can be accompanied with sound effects.

As you perform work within screen windows, the mouse pointer often visibly changes in a **context-sensitive** way. In other words, the shape of the

■ **Context sensitive.** A characteristic of a user interface that adjusts program actions to accommodate the type of operation the user is currently performing.

pointer is automatically altered with respect to the operation you are performing. Figure SW 1-19 shows some of the shapes that you may see on the screen. For instance, when you are resizing a window (refer back to Figure SW 1-17), the pointer will often resemble a double-pointed arrow. Also, as discussed earlier, when you are moving the pointer over hypertext, the pointer often changes to a pointing hand.

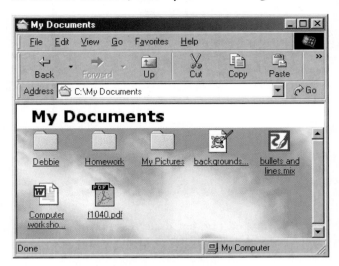

Scroll Bars Often, a screen window is not big enough to display all of the information required for a particular file. When this happens, **scroll bars** appear at the bottom and/or right edge of the window (see Figure SW 1-20). By manipulating elements in these bars, you can display the rest of the information.

Scrolling moves information up, down, and even sideways through the window or screen. When you are scrolling down, for example, as lines successfully disappear from the top of the window or screen, new ones appear at the bottom.

By activating a *scroll arrow* on any scroll bar, you move the window a small amount, in the direction of the arrow, to see offscreen information. The principle resembles slowly moving a magnifying glass (the window) over a map (the information).

Between its two scroll arrows, each scroll bar contains a *scroll box*. By clicking and dragging with the mouse, you can move this box up or down (or left to right) in the direction of the desired information. For instance, if you move the scroll box from the top of the scroll bar to the middle, the display will immediately move halfway through the information. By instead clicking before or after a scroll box, you move the screen one page at a time.

FIGURE SW 1-18

Changing the "look" of a window. You can customize a window by adding a background picture or by having folder names display as hypertext.

FIGURE SW 1-19

Context-sensitive pointer shapes. Most software programs cause the mouse pointer to be context sensitive, changing its shape with respect to the operation the user is performing.

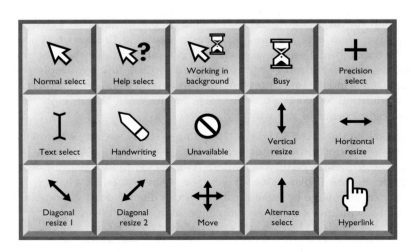

■ **Scroll bar.** A horizontal or vertical bar along an edge of a window that allows the user to view information that will not fit within the window.

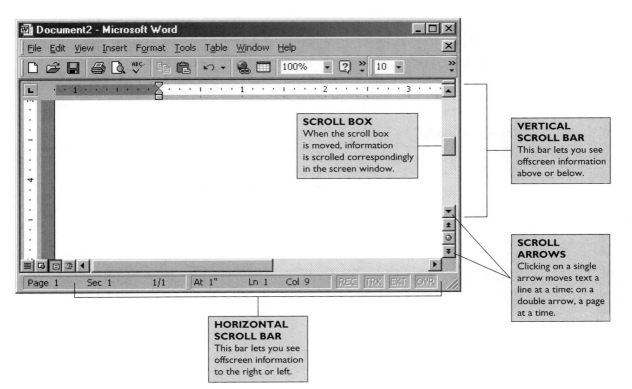

SCROLL BOX
When the scroll box is moved, information is scrolled correspondingly in the screen window.

VERTICAL SCROLL BAR
This bar lets you see offscreen information above or below.

SCROLL ARROWS
Clicking on a single arrow moves text a line at a time; on a double arrow, a page at a time.

HORIZONTAL SCROLL BAR
This bar lets you see offscreen information to the right or left.

FIGURE SW 1-20

Scroll bars.

In Windows 3.1, scroll boxes are always square; in Windows 95 and later, they are sized in proportion to the percentage of information currently displayed. Instead of the scroll bars, you can often use the keyboard's cursor-movement keys—such as PageUp (PgUp), PageDown (PgDn), and Tab—to scroll up, down, left, or right.

DIALOG BOXES

Dialog boxes are special windows that prompt the GUI user to provide further information. Such information can be supplied by a variety of means, several of which are covered in the following subsections and illustrated in Figure SW 1-21.

Radio Buttons   *Radio buttons*, also known as *option buttons*, are rounded buttons that work like the push buttons on old radios—only one choice in the panel can be active at any one time. You activate a radio button by clicking on it.

Check Boxes   To make any of the choices in a panel of *check boxes* active, you place a check in the appropriate box by clicking it with a mouse. Check boxes differ from radio buttons in that you can activate more than one option in the panel or no options at all. To deactivate any check box, click on its check mark.

Text Boxes   *Text boxes* provide spaces where you can type information into the computer—such as a number, or the name of a particular document or folder. After you type the information into the text box, striking the Tab key generally moves the cursor forward to the next section of the dialog box.

List Boxes   Several kinds of list boxes appear in Figure SW 1-21. Like a pull-down menu, a *simple list box* presents a list of options, allowing you to choose any one. Often, the list exceeds the size of its window, and a vertical

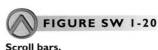

For a tutorial on using menus and dialog boxes, go to www.harcourtcollege. com/infosys/parker2000/ student/tutor/ and click on Chapter SW 1.

■ **Dialog box.** A box that requires the user to supply information to the computer system about the task being performed.

RADIO BUTTONS

Radio buttons work like the push buttons on old radios in that only one button in a panel can be active at one time.

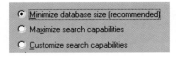

SIMPLE LIST BOXES

In a list box, you make a choice by clicking on it with a mouse or by reaching it through the arrow keys and striking Enter. A vertical scroll bar lets you access choices not currently onscreen.

CHECK BOXES

When a check is placed in a check box, the associated action is selected. Several, none, or all boxes in a check-box panel can be active at one time.

DROP-DOWN LIST BOXES

A drop-down list box has a down-facing arrow to the right of the first choice in the list. When you click on the arrow, other choices appear.

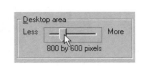

TEXT BOXES

Text boxes require you to type information into the computer— such as a page number.

SPIN BOXES

A spin box controls a fixed set of numeric values. You click on an up or down arrow to the right of a value to make the value higher or lower.

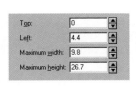

MESSAGE BOXES

A message box pops up on the screen when a potential problem is unfolding.

SLIDERS

A slider lets you select a value from a range.

FIGURE SW 1-21

Dialog-box elements.

scroll bar or similar mechanism allows you to see parts of the list currently off the screen.

To save even more space, a dialog box sometimes includes a *drop-down list box*, which displays only one selection initially, allowing you to see the others by activating the drop-down arrow to the right. A *spin box* lets you tweak a numeric value up or down by clicking on an up-arrow or down-arrow icon.

A *slider,* when you drag it with a mouse, lets you select a value from a range. Sliders are commonly used for adjusting audio volume, changing the pixel resolution on a display, and setting a difficulty level at which you want to play a computer game.

Message Boxes A *message box* pops on the screen when the program needs to provide status information or when a potential problem is unfolding. You may see such a message when you attempt to execute an improper command or try to take an action for which a mistake could have grave consequences. In any type of message box, the user must acknowledge the message by choosing one of the supplied command buttons—Retry or Cancel in Figure SW 1-21—before proceeding further.

For a tutorial on using a help system, go to www. harcourtcollege.com/ infosys/parker2000/student/ tutor/ and click on Chapter SW 1.

ONLINE HELP

Most people run into problems or think of questions as they work with a software program. To provide help without forcing you to leave your computer screen, many GUIs have an *online help feature*. Programs employ a variety of tools to provide online assistance, as Figure SW 1-22 and the following paragraphs explain.

Each book in the list corresponds to a finer breakdown of choices.

As you select books, they open, revealing the contents inside.

By selecting question-mark icons, you get to the actual help information.

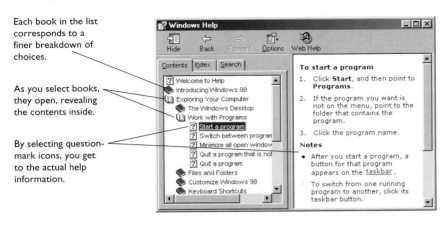

TABLE OF CONTENTS
A table-of-contents feature groups related information into books.

INDEXING
An indexing feature lets you select a help topic from a large alphabetical list.

As you begin typing in a topic name, the window displaying the list of topics changes correspondingly with each keystroke you press. When you see the topic you want in the window, highlight and select it.

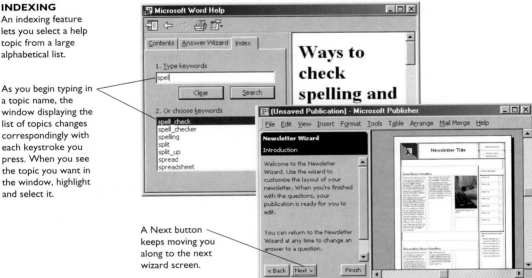

A Next button keeps moving you along to the next wizard screen.

WIZARDS
Wizards provide you with simple, step-by-step guidance for performing difficult or time-consuming tasks.

FIGURE SW 1-22

Online help.

Help Table of Contents A highly useful online support tool is a help table of contents (TOC), which works similar to the TOCs found in many books. The TOC shown in Figure SW 1-22 features a selection of book icons related to help files on some general topics. Selecting a book opens the associated information to reveal either another set of books or a set of question marks. The question marks represent the specific information that you ultimately want; they link you to screenfuls of facts about topics. Some such screens contain hyperlinks to further levels of support information.

Indexing Many help routines sport an *indexing feature* that lets you choose from a lengthy list of help topics. The topics are displayed in a list box, and you can scroll to the topic you wish to find in the standard fashion. The topic list may be huge, however, and there is a way that lets you search even faster. As illustrated in Figure SW 1-22, you can position the screen cursor in a typing area, and then begin to type in the word you want to look up in the index. As you key in each letter, the list-box display changes accordingly. As soon as the topic you want to look up appears in the display window, you can point to it with the mouse or keyboard and select it.

Wizards Many programs provide automated tools to assist users by quickly performing repetitive or complicated tasks. Different software publishers call these tools **wizards,** *coaches, assistants, tutors, experts, advisors,* or similar names. By any name, such a tool guides you through a step-by-step procedure for completing standard tasks, such as preparing letters, invoices, reports, and the like. They do this either by providing directed tutorials or by performing the difficult phases of a task automatically, through choices you make. Figure SW 1-22 shows how a wizard might help you to prepare a newsletter.

Natural-Language Help Many programs today supply a limited form of *natural-language help* to users—that is, help in which you type in a question and the software package tries to recognize the topic on which assistance is required. For instance, in Microsoft Office 2000, clicking on the question-mark icon that's located on the standard toolbar makes a text box pop up for you to type in a query. Office 2000 then looks for keywords in the sentence you've entered and tries to provide help on what it believes to be the suggested topic.

Online Tutorials Many software publishers provide online tutorials with their software. The tutorials may be accessed from your hard drive, CD, or through a Web site, depending on the program used. These tutorials enable you to do such things as learn how to use the package, as well as observe examples and demonstrations.

Many of the screens in this section follow the Microsoft Windows GUI. Both programmers and designers of user interfaces at high-tech companies like Microsoft often enjoy engaging in occasional on-the-job antics to let off stress, as the Inside the Industry box explains.

VIRTUAL REALITY

Virtual reality, or *VR*, is a hardware-and-software technology that refers to using computer systems to create illusion. Here's an example of a possible VR scenario: A VR user with special goggles for viewing an artificial, comic-book world makes a movement with a special glove. As the movement is made, the display in the goggles changes instantly to reflect new information that is presented from the user's point of view.

Although we are still far from the virtual reality that science fiction writers tell us about, many industry experts believe that standard user-and-computer interfaces will someday seem like real-life experiences. Several VR applications are highly visible in the world of today, and new applications are regularly being reported by the press. Below is a small sample.

Architecture Through VR, it is possible to take "tours" of buildings whose foundations are yet to be poured. A computer model of the building is first made in three dimensions. Later, a client taking a computer "tour" on a desktop can move from room to room in the order in which he or she chooses, inspecting the premises close up or far away and from different views. Routines are also available that can show how natural light falls in the building on a sunny or rainy day and how artificial light changes a room. Does the client hate the look and size of the lounge? No problem. With a remodeling software package, it can be reshaped, repainted, relighted, refurnished, and ready for reinspection—in seconds.

Entertainment VR applications have arrived at full force in the entertainment industry, where illusion is the principal product. In many cities, amusement

---

■ **Wizard.** A program feature that assists users in completing tasks. ■ **Virtual reality.** A hardware-and-software technology that allows computer systems to create illusions of real-life experiences.

Lake BillG

Microsoft Corporation's headquarters is a campus of more than two dozen buildings located within easy reach of Seattle. On that campus is a small body of water that goes by the name of Lake BillG (pronounced "bilge"). Weird moniker? Not really. BillG is the e-mail address of chairman and founder Bill Gates. We've got lakes named after presidents, animals and birds, and even a bunch of pioneers who ate each other in the Sierra Nevada back in the 1840s. So why not a slot on a mail server?

As you may have guessed, being surrounded by a lot of creative people who are regularly under deadline pressures, Lake BillG has occasionally been the site of manic merriment. A few years ago, a manager in the Windows NT group bet another manager that his team would finish coding on time. If he lost, he promised to swim Lake BillG in a woman's swimsuit. While he did lose, he raised the ante by promising that his whole team would swim if a later date was missed. Fortunately for both the manager and his team, they finished the work on time.

If you think swimming Lake BillG is an activity confined to low-level personnel, think again. Several years back, Steve Ballmer—then a vice president and now president of Microsoft—made a bet with another vice president that would have the loser swimming the lake. Both lost, so both had to swim. On the chilly day the two arrived at the lake, they discovered a bunch of thoughtful programmers had stocked it with large chunks of dry ice. Just so they wouldn't overheat going across, right?

arcades feature virtual reality games in which players can battle demons on realistic computer-generated landscapes. In many cases, the VR participant must don special goggles, which project computer-generated images directly toward the eye, and wear gloves with built-in sensors, which change the goggle images when the hands are moved. Feature-length movies and computer-game software also increasingly employ virtual-reality technology.

Investments   Investment analysts apply VR techniques to the study of securities. One of the problems inherent in conventional analysis is the complexities of tracking a group of securities relative to changes in the market as a whole. A virtual reality system can color-code stocks belonging to a certain group—say, technology stocks. A 3-D animation of general stock movements over time can help the analyst to clearly visualize how a particular group behaves within the overall market.

World Wide Web   Virtual reality applications on the Internet are usually built in VRML (Virtual Reality Modeling Language)—a way of adding 3D objects and virtual worlds to a Web page. VRML can allow shoppers to view cars and other products from all angles, allow home buyers to "walk" through homes for sale before visiting them in person, and enable "virtual tourists" to tour art museums and make-believe Internet communities.

Other Applications   In addition to the applications already mentioned, press reports regularly highlight a variety of other VR applications. For instance, medical students use VR techniques to simulate injections and medical operations before needles or scalpels ever touch patients (see Feature SW 1-1). In sports, researchers using VR techniques can model subtle body movements in order to figure out what makes certain athletes fantastically successful.

Further Exploration

For links to further information about virtual reality, go to www.harcourtcollege.com/ infosys/parker2000/student/ explore/ and click on Chapter SW 1.

Virtual Surgery

Interfaces with Feeling

If you think that 3-D user interfaces go about as far as computers can reach to simulate reality, guess again. The latest computer-game and medical-visualization software allows you to actually *feel* the effects of computer-generated events.

Take medical visualization. First-generation computerized virtual reality models enabled medical students to view a human body in three dimensions and practice operating on it with software tools rather than real scalpels. These days, to make such experiences even more realistic, a hypodermic-needle device teaches students to give injections using feedback that approximates the sensation of skin popping back as the needle pierces it. As another example, as a student practices removing a liver, a software-hardware interface can detect and feed back to the student the collision of scalpel with organ.

Many computer games now feature similar interfaces. A special joystick lets users feel the bumps in simulated roads, the recoils of a piston, or the jar of a crash landing.

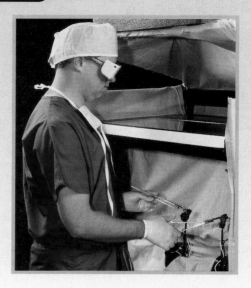

Virtual reality goes to med school. Medical students get a true feel for the operating table with this Boston Dynamics surgical simulator. Holding surgical instruments, trainees receive a physical response as they simulate the cutting and suturing of tissue.

SUMMARY AND KEY TERMS

Go to the Online Glossary at www.harcourtcollege.com/infosys/parker2000/ student/ to review key terms.

In Chapter SW 1 we explore several fundamental properties of computer software.

About Software The computer world generally divides software into two distinct classes: **systems software** and **applications software.** Within each of these classes are several subdivisions.

Software publishers often bundle together programs such as word processors and spreadsheets along with other software into **software suites.** An *integrated software program* compresses the functionality of a suite into a smaller package. The success of bundling has supported **document-centered computing.**

Many of the applications and systems software products on the market today are examples of **proprietary software.** Individual users purchase licenses authorizing them to use such software, while businesses often seek **site licenses.** Some software is also available as **shareware.** The shareware creator normally does not charge for use of the software, but users will have to pay for any support. Still another class of software is **freeware**—programs that are available without restrictions of any sort.

The User Interface The manner in which a program makes its resources available to users is known as its **user interface.**

The three most widely used user interfaces are command syntax, shortcut keystrokes, and graphical user interfaces. Command **syntax** relies on users typing in, at some sort of software **prompt,** statements that conform to strict grammatical rules and structure. **Shortcut keystrokes,** which represent commands, are designed to be both easier and faster than using a command syntax. **Graphical user interfaces (GUIs)** employ such screen-oriented recall devices as pull-down menus, windows, and icons to make it easy for users to execute commands.

Elements of a Graphical User Interface   Most users today work with programs that have graphical user interfaces.

Menus are often one of several principal types. At the top of many GUI screens or windows is a **menu bar** showing the governing command set. **Pull-down menus** unfurl on the screen when the user makes a choice from a menu bar or another pull-down menu. Menus also exist in the form of a set of **icons;** names such as **toolbars,** command buttons, and navigation bars refer to *icon menus.* **Hyperlinks**—text that displays other documents when they are clicked—are commonly used on the World Wide Web. Additionally, tab menus, **palettes,** and dialog boxes are other types of menus.

The staple of the GUI is the **window—**a box of related information that is overlaid on the display screen. A *title bar* at the top of a window normally names the document or program displayed inside. Windows can be customized onscreen to meet applications needs in a variety of ways. The mouse pointer is **context sensitive** and changes with respect to the operation the user is performing onscreen. When the information available to a window cannot fit on the screen at one time, **scroll bars** can be used to get to other parts of it.

Dialog boxes are special windows that prompt the user for further information. They employ a variety of tools, including radio buttons, check boxes, text boxes, list boxes, message boxes, and the like.

Many GUIs have an *online help* feature to make it easy for users to get help when they are sitting at their display screens. Some examples of online help are a table-of-contents feature, an indexing feature, **wizards,** a natural-language help feature, and tutorials.

Virtual Reality   Virtual reality, or *VR*, is a hardware-and-software technology through which computer systems create illusions of real-life experiences.

EXERCISES

1. Fill in the blanks.
   a. Software that doesn't cost users anything—either to use or for support—is referred to as _____.
   b. A group of related, fully featured programs bundled together for sale is called a(n) _____.
   c. Software that you must purchase a license to use is known as _____.
   d. The manner in which a program package makes its resources available to the user is known as its _____.
   e. The grammatical rules that govern a computer language are called the language's _____.
   f. A(n) _____ lets you control the computer by entering keystrokes such as Alt+F1 or Del instead of typing in a command.
   g. GUI is an acronym for _____.
   h. A command _____ is a horizontal line that groups related commands.

2. Describe the purpose of each of the GUI elements at the top of the next page.

a. Ghosted type
b. Imagemap
c. Command buttons
d. Ellipses
e. Spin box
f. Checkmark

3. In your own words, define the following terms:
   a. Hypertext
   b. Context sensitive
   c. Toolbar
   d. Palette
   e. Site license
   f. Virtual reality

4. Match each term with the description that fits best.
   a. Menu bar
   b. Pull-down menu
   c. Cascading
   d. Tiling
   e. Toolbar
   f. Scroll bar
   g. Radio button
   h. Text box
   _____ A method of arranging windows side by side
   _____ A dialog-box feature that provides a set of options preceded by round symbols, only one of which can be darkened
   _____ A dialog box that requires you type some input
   _____ A horizontally arranged menu that appears at the top of the screen
   _____ A method of arranging windows so that they overlap
   _____ A feature that lets you move offscreen information into a window
   _____ A type of icon menu
   _____ A menu that drops vertically below a choice made on a menu bar

5. Describe and compare the three basic ways in which software designers enable users to enter commands into computers.

6. In your own words, define the following terms and describe their similarities and differences:
   a. Software suite
   b. Software minisuite
   c. Integrated software package
   d. Document-centered computing

7. Describe in a sentence each of the following types of online help:
   a. Table of contents
   b. Indexes
   c. Wizards
   d. Natural-language help
   e. Tutorials

8. Match the terms with the pictured dialog-box elements.
   _____ Radio buttons
   _____ Simple list box
   _____ Check box
   _____ Command buttons
   _____ Message box
   _____ Drop-down list box

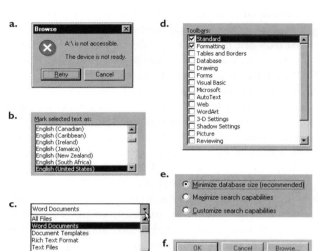

9. Match the phrases with the pictured GUI elements.
   _____ Options aren't available in the current context
   _____ A toolbar
   _____ Restores the previous screen size
   _____ Closes an application
   _____ Lets you see offscreen information
   _____ Expands an application to fill the entire screen

10. Explain the differences, if any, between the following pairs:
    a. Shareware and freeware
    b. Pull-down menu and menu bar
    c. Radio button and option button
    d. Maximizing and minimizing a window
    e. Scroll arrow and scroll box
    f. Simple list box and drop-down list box
    g. Ellipses and arrow (on a pull-down menu)
    h. Access key and shortcut keystroke

PROJECTS

1. **Microsoft Office**   Microsoft Office is by far the best-selling software suite, with over an 80 percent share of the office-suite market. If you have Microsoft Office at your school, answer the following questions:
   a. What version number does your school run?
   b. What are the names and functions of the main-component programs in the suite?
   c. How many toolbars can you summon through the Toolbars command in one of the suite's programs? What are the names and purposes of these toolbars? Where, exactly, is the Toolbars command located? How do you get rid of one toolbar and summon another?
   d. Identify the name and purpose of each toolbar button pictured below. Also, identify the toolbar on which each of the following buttons appears.

   i.   iii.   v.

   ii.   iv.

2. **Office-Suite Comparison**   The three major office-software suites in the marketplace are Microsoft Office, Lotus SmartSuite, and Corel WordPerfect Suite. Pick any one of these suites. Identify the main program components in the suite and the principal function of each component. If there are different versions available of the suite you have chosen, describe the differences.

3. **Software Licenses**   Virtually every proprietary software package that you buy in a store includes a usage license tucked inside the shrink-wrapped box. For this project, your instructor might decide to distribute a typical license to everyone in the class or ask you to find a license on your own. In either case, answer the following questions about the sample license:
   a. How does the license state the passage that prohibits you from copying the software and distributing it to others?
   b. How does the license state the passage that prohibits you renting the software to others?
   c. Does the license allow you to copy the software onto both a desktop computer and a portable computer? If so, where does it say so?

   d. Suppose that you don't like the software and want to sell it for half price to a friend (removing it from your own computer in the process). Does the license prohibit such a sale?

4. **Shareware and Freeware I**   Find the names of at least five products that are either shareware or freeware. For each product, write down the following:
   a. The name of the product and the publisher
   b. The program's intended application
   c. For shareware, the suggested registration fee

   Hint: For this project, you may wish to search the Internet for any of the many sites that offer shareware and freeware for downloading. If you are using a search engine, type "Shareware" or "Freeware" into the text box provided for the search string.

5. **Shareware and Freeware II**   Using computer magazines and newspapers, or the Internet, find a shareware or freeware product that falls into each of the following categories. Describe each product briefly, providing its name, facts about what it does, and the company or individual that publishes it.

CATEGORY	PRODUCT NAME/ FUNCTION/PUBLISHER
Computer game	_____
Educational software	_____
Productivity software	_____
Systems software	_____
Internet software	_____

6. **Sliders**   Many programs use sliders, which let users choose a setting within a range. Describe at least three different uses for sliders, and for each one, identify a program that provides its use. Your descriptions should be detailed enough so that anyone reading them has a good idea of not only what the slider is used for but also what types of choices the slider provides.

7. **Online Help**   Choose any current applications program—such as a word processor or a spreadsheet—and research its online help feature. For the software you have chosen, report the characteristics below and on the following page to your class.
   a. The types of online help available within the program
   b. A description of how you would access each of the types of help described in part a

c. The names and descriptions of the wizards available within the program

8. **Online Documentation**   Increasingly, software publishers are putting the documentation telling how their products work—documentation such as tutorials and reference manuals—on the installation CD-ROMs that come with those products. When you install the programs, you can then reference this documentation online. While this practice saves the cost of printing hard-copy documentation and supports online searches, many users have objected. Some feel that online help cannot effectively replace a well-written, hardcopy manual for learning about and using a software package.

For this project, list the advantages and disadvantages of online documentation relative to hardcopy documentation from your own perspective as a user. What kind of documentation provides the most valuable help to you in learning or using a software package?

9. **Command Syntax**   Many longtime computer professionals who have become familiar with command syntax complain that GUIs interfere with their work and slow down the computer. Do you feel any sympathy for this position, or do you feel that these people just don't like change? Defend your position in a paragraph or two.

10. **Properties of Good User Interfaces**   Effective user interfaces should be transparent, attractive, forgiving, unburdensome, and customizable. *Transparent* interfaces make software function in a way that seems natural to users. *Attractive* interfaces inspire more use than ugly ones. *Forgiving* interfaces help users to recover easily from mistakes. *Unburdensome* interfaces make the software accommodate users rather than users compensating

for the program's quirks. *Customizable* interfaces allow users to tweak settings to fit personal work habits. For this project, choose a suite product—such as Microsoft Office or Lotus SmartSuite—and provide one example of a well-designed feature for each of the five properties.

 11. **Social Interfaces**   Much research has focused on creating social interfaces within the past few years. The interest in social interfaces is spurred by the realization that even today's popular GUIs can take a long time to master and by the recent emergence of techniques for three-dimensional desktop graphics. For this project, choose a program with a social interface and write a paper two or three pages long about it. Make sure you cover the following points:
a. The name of the interface or the environment in which it operates
b. The name of the company owning the interface
c. The principal tactic for simulating something from everyday life

Hint: Many World Wide Web sites employ social interfaces. You may wish to base this project on one of those sites.

12. **Virtual Reality**   Virtual reality elements are becoming increasingly common in applications environments. The chapter text mentioned several such environments—architecture, entertainment, investments, medicine, and sports. For this project, find a specific application of virtual reality and report to the class about it. In addition to naming the product and the company that created it, explain what type of virtual world or space the product creates, who makes up the audience for the product, how users gain access to the product, and whether or not the product requires any special hardware.

ONLINE REVIEW

Go to the Online Review at www.harcourtcollege.com/infosys/parker2000/ student/ to test your understanding of this chapter's concepts.

SYSTEMS SOFTWARE

OUTLINE

LEARNING OBJECTIVES

After completing this chapter, you will be able to:

1. Describe the types of systems software.

2. Explain the activities of an operating system and cite some similarities and differences between operating systems.

3. List several ways in which computer systems interleave operations to enhance processing efficiency.

4. Name today's most widely used operating systems and highlight the strengths and weaknesses of each.

5. Detail the role of a utility program and outline several duties that these programs perform.

6. Explain the role of a language translator and describe several types of language translators.

OVERVIEW

Systems software consists of programs that coordinate the various parts of the computer system to make it run efficiently. These programs perform such tasks as translating your commands into a form that the computer can understand, managing your program and data files, and getting your applications software and hardware to work together, among many other things.

Most users aren't aware of all the tasks that systems software is doing for them. On a microcomputer system, for example, issuing a Save command to store a document on disk requires that systems software look for adequate space on the disk, write the document onto this space, and update the disk's directory so both you and the computer system can find the document again. As users run their systems to communicate with databases on remote mainframes, they may not realize that systems software busily checks the validity of their ID numbers or passwords and translates their database commands into machine language.

Systems software is available in three basic types: operating systems, utility programs, and language translators. In this chapter, we'll first look closely at the *operating system,* which is the main piece of systems software. Here we'll discuss what operating systems do and examine various similarities and differences among them. Next, we will cover *utility programs,* or utilities. Utilities typically perform support functions for the operating system—less-critical types of functions such as allowing you to install new types of hardware or to recover inadvertently erased disk files. Finally, we look at *language translators.* Such programs translate sets of instructions coded in BASIC, COBOL, or any other programming language into machine language.

THE OPERATING SYSTEM

A computer's **operating system** is the main collection of programs that manage its activities. The primary chores of an operating system are management and control. The operating system ensures that all actions requested by a user are valid and processed in an orderly fashion. It also manages the computer system's resources to perform those operations with efficiency and consistency.

Most tasks that you do on the computer involve some work by the operating system. For example, when you want to finish the letter you started typing yesterday, the operating system fetches the appropriate word processing program and document from disk and loads them into memory. It also prepares the CPU and printer. As the word processor carries out its processing tasks, the operating system acts as a watchdog, monitoring every step of the application to make sure it doesn't perform illegal operations that would corrupt other computer-system resources. Typically, the operating system does all of these things and much more as you issue commands. When you finish, it saves your updated document onto disk and, often, logs you off the computer system too.

In effect, the operating system is the go-between that meshes you and your application's needs with the computer's hardware (see Figure SW 2-1). Because of its central role in coordinating all of the computer's work, many consider the operating system to be the most critical piece of software in the computer system. Without an operating system, no other program can run.

■ **Systems software.** Computer programs that enable application programs to run on a given set of hardware.
■ **Operating system.** The main collection of systems software that enables the computer system to manage the resources under its control.

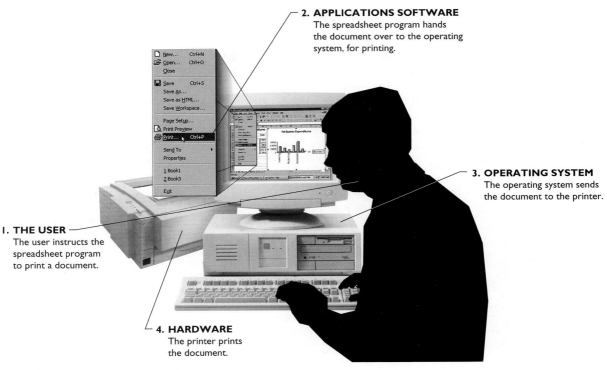

2. APPLICATIONS SOFTWARE
The spreadsheet program hands the document over to the operating system, for printing.

3. OPERATING SYSTEM
The operating system sends the document to the printer.

1. THE USER
The user instructs the spreadsheet program to print a document.

4. HARDWARE
The printer prints the document.

DIFFERENCES AMONG OPERATING SYSTEMS

The marketplace offers a wide selection of operating systems (see Figure SW 2-2). Because the needs of people differ, there are often major differences among operating systems. As Figure SW 2-2 hints, less clear-cut differences also distinguish these products.

A major distinction between operating systems is whether they are targeted to personal or network-administration needs. About a decade or so ago, when PCs were far less powerful than today's machines, most operating systems accommodated either single users or multiple users, not both. Single-user products such as MS-DOS served people working alone on their PCs in their homes or on company desks. Multiple-user products such as Unix and IBM's MVS—now known as OS/390—served those working on larger computer systems, who needed links to shared resources and other users. This product distinction still persists, but it is breaking down around the edges. Many operating systems designed for single users also come in versions that can control small networks, and some versions of operating systems intended mainly for network applications can also meet needs at the user-desktop (workstation) level.

FUNCTIONS OF AN OPERATING SYSTEM

Now that you have a general idea of what operating systems do and what some of the differences among them are, we can discuss their properties in greater detail. As we examine these properties, keep in mind that not all of them will apply to the operating system on your own computer.

Interacting with Users One of the principal roles of every operating system, as Figure SW 2-1 suggests, is to translate user intentions into a form the computer understands. In the other direction, it translates any feedback from the hardware—such as a signal that the printer has run out of paper or the CPU is busy with a processing task—into a form the user understands. In the previous chapter we saw that there were several ways that users can command a computer to take an action. Two of these—*typing* instructions that

FIGURE SW 2-1

The gateway role of the operating system. The operating system is the gateway between user applications and the computer system's hardware.

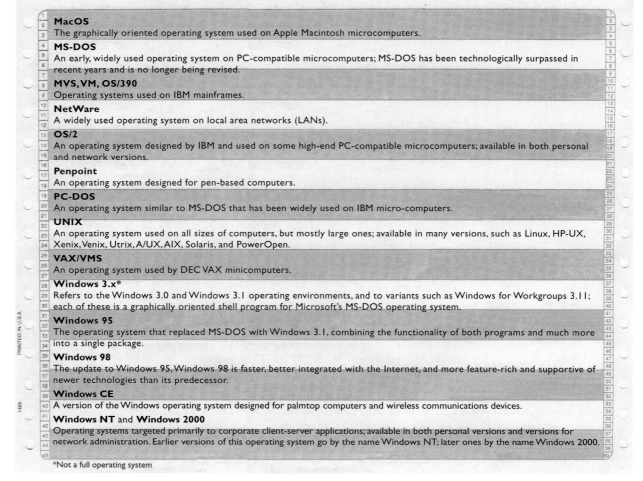

MacOS
The graphically oriented operating system used on Apple Macintosh microcomputers.

MS-DOS
An early, widely used operating system on PC-compatible microcomputers; MS-DOS has been technologically surpassed in recent years and is no longer being revised.

MVS, VM, OS/390
Operating systems used on IBM mainframes.

NetWare
A widely used operating system on local area networks (LANs).

OS/2
An operating system designed by IBM and used on some high-end PC-compatible microcomputers; available in both personal and network versions.

Penpoint
An operating system designed for pen-based computers.

PC-DOS
An operating system similar to MS-DOS that has been widely used on IBM micro-computers.

UNIX
An operating system used on all sizes of computers, but mostly large ones; available in many versions, such as Linux, HP-UX, Xenix, Venix, Utrix, A/UX, AIX, Solaris, and PowerOpen.

VAX/VMS
An operating system used by DEC VAX minicomputers.

Windows 3.x*
Refers to the Windows 3.0 and Windows 3.1 operating environments, and to variants such as Windows for Workgroups 3.11; each of these is a graphically oriented shell program for Microsoft's MS-DOS operating system.

Windows 95
The operating system that replaced MS-DOS with Windows 3.1, combining the functionality of both programs and much more into a single package.

Windows 98
The update to Windows 95, Windows 98 is faster, better integrated with the Internet, and more feature-rich and supportive of newer technologies than its predecessor.

Windows CE
A version of the Windows operating system designed for palmtop computers and wireless communications devices.

Windows NT and **Windows 2000**
Operating systems targeted primarily to corporate client-server applications; available in both personal versions and versions for network administration. Earlier versions of this operating system go by the name Windows NT; later ones by the name Windows 2000.

*Not a full operating system

PRINTED IN U.S.A. 1485

FIGURE SW 2-2

Some popular operating systems. Operating systems can differ substantially with respect to ease of use, speed, features, portability, and cost. Each operating system is targeted to one or more specific types of computers.

conform to a command syntax and *selecting* instructions from a graphical user interface—are the ways that most people will interact with operating systems.

As soon as the user enters keystrokes or clicks a mouse, the operating system summons a translator to convert what the user wants done into machine language. It then passes these digitally coded instructions to the CPU for processing. In the absence of instructions from the user, the operating system makes some standard assumptions about appropriate activities. Such assumptions are called **defaults,** and you can often override any of them if you wish. For instance, you can change the standard default of one printed copy of a document by asking for two, or you can change the way characters and graphics appear on the screen by asking for a higher or lower resolution.

To work effectively with your operating system, you must observe certain conventions. For instance, every operating system sets rules for naming files (or documents) and the directories (or folders) that group them together. Also, many operating systems supplement filenames with sets of characters called **file extensions** that carry special meanings. Usually, a file extension identifies the type of file in use, such as a Word document or a specific type of graphics file. Figure SW 2-3 shows how filenames and extensions work on many PC-compatible systems.

A systematic naming of files and extensions is useful when working with computers. For instance, by naming the 25 chapters of a book on your hard

■ **Default.** The assumption that a computer program makes when the user indicates no specific choice. ■ **File extension.** A group of characters appended to the main part of a filename to qualify it or to identify a specific type of file.

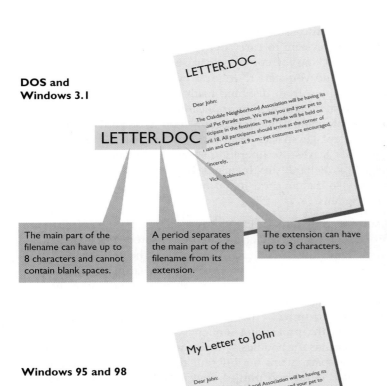

DOS and Windows 3.1

LETTER.DOC

The main part of the filename can have up to 8 characters and cannot contain blank spaces.

A period separates the main part of the filename from its extension.

The extension can have up to 3 characters.

Windows 95 and 98

My Letter to John.Monday.edited

Filenames can have up to 255 characters, including blank spaces and multiple extensions.

WIDELY USED EXTENSIONS			
DOCUMENTS			
.doc	.txt	.htm	.html
PROGRAMS			
.bat	.com	.exe	
GRAPHICS			
.bmp	.pict	.jpg	.eps
.gif	.png	.cdr	.pcx
AUDIO			
.wav	.au		
VIDEO			
.mpg	.mov	.avi	
COMPRESSED FILES			
.arc	.arj	.bin	.zip
.lhz	.pak	.seq	.sit

FIGURE SW 2-3

Filenames and extensions. Every operating system has its own rules for naming and adding extensions.

disk Chap01, Chap02, and so on, to Chap25, a single command such as

```
COPY Chap* A:
```

would allow you to transfer the entire book manuscript from hard disk to diskette. Similarly, a command such as

```
COPY *.DOC A:
```

would transfer between the same two disks all files with DOC extensions. Many operating systems allow you to specify **wildcard characters** like the asterisk (*) in these two examples to signify that a command or search condition should apply to filenames with any characters in the wildcard location.

Making Resources Available When you first turn on power to the computer system, the operating system **boots** up or is *bootstrapped*.

During the booting procedure, parts of the operating system are loaded into memory. Before control is passed to the user, the operating system determines what hardware devices are online, makes sure that its own files tell it how to deal with those devices, and reads an opening batch of directives.

■ **Wildcard character.** A character that substitutes for other characters in a filename. ■ **Boot.** The process of loading the operating system into the computer system's RAM.

These directives—which the user can customize to his or her tastes—assign chores for the operating system to carry out before the current user session begins; for instance, checking for computer viruses.

As a session begins and you start to request programs and data, the operating system retrieves them from disk and loads them into RAM as needed. Once the operating system activates an applications program, it relinquishes some control to that program. While a program such as a word processor or spreadsheet might accept keystrokes from users or conduct a spelling check on its own, it generally leaves the operating system to ensure proper use of storage and availability of hardware. In managing storage, the operating system protects memory so that an error in a program will not corrupt vital data created in other programs.

Scheduling Resources and Jobs   Along with assigning system resources to user jobs, the operating system performs a closely related process: scheduling those resources and jobs. Scheduling routines in the operating system determine the order in which jobs are processed on hardware devices. An operating system serving multiple users does not necessarily assign jobs on a first-come, first-served basis. Some users may have higher priority than others, the devices needed to process the next job in line may not be free, or other factors may affect the processing sequence.

The operating system also schedules operations throughout the computer system so that different parts work on different portions of the same jobs at the same time. Because input and output devices work much more slowly than the CPU itself, the CPU may complete billions of calculations for several programs while the contents of a single program are being printed or displayed. Using a number of techniques, the operating system juggles the computer's work in order to employ system devices as efficiently as possible. A later section will discuss some of the methods that allow a computer to process a number of jobs at more or less the same time. These procedures—such as multitasking and multiprogramming—are known collectively as *interleaved processing techniques*.

Monitoring Activities   Another major function of operating systems is overseeing activities while processing is under way. For instance, the operating system terminates programs that contain errors or exceed their maximum storage allocations. In doing so, it sends an appropriate message to the user or system operator. Similarly, the operating system informs the user of any equipment abnormalities that arise.

Besides apprising users when problems occur, many operating systems also monitor routine computer system performance and report on its status. Users and system administrators need to know information such as how much hard-disk space is used up, how fast the hard disk accesses data, and how response time changes as more and more users try to access the same resources. Programs called *performance monitors* keep track of such activities.

Housekeeping   One of the most important tasks of the operating system is housekeeping, and one of the most important housekeeping tasks is organizing the hard disk and making users aware of its contents.

To simplify access to hard disks, operating systems commonly organize files hierarchically into **directories.** As Figure SW 2-4 shows, at the top of the hierarchy is a "master" directory called the *root directory*. The root directory contains, among other elements, several lower-level directories, or *subdirectories*. You can organize your operating-system files in one directory, your applications programs in several other directories, and the files you create with those applications programs in still others. As shown in Figure SW 2-4, for instance,

---

■ **Directory.** A collection of files grouped under a name of its own. Also commonly called a *folder.*

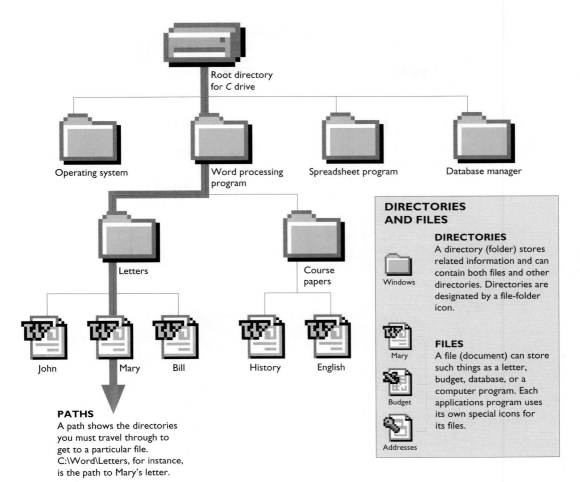

PATHS

A path shows the directories you must travel through to get to a particular file. C:\Word\Letters, for instance, is the path to Mary's letter.

DIRECTORIES AND FILES

DIRECTORIES

A directory (folder) stores related information and can contain both files and other directories. Directories are designated by a file-folder icon.

FILES

A file (document) can store such things as a letter, budget, database, or a computer program. Each applications program uses its own special icons for its files.

you can organize your word-processed files by putting letters and course papers into their own directories. In many GUI-oriented operating systems, files, directories, and subdirectories are respectively referred to as *documents, folders,* and *subfolders*.

When you want to access a file in any directory, you must specify the **path** through the directories to reach it. For example, as Figure SW 2-4 shows, the path

`C:\Word\Letters`

leads through the C, Word, and Letters directories to a file named Mary. The same path can also be used to access the files John and Bill.

Most operating systems with graphical user interfaces provide special programs to display the contents of hard disks and other storage devices (see Figure SW 2-5). Such programs can also provide screen listings that detail the sizes of files and directories, in bytes, along with the dates and times that the files and directories were created or last accessed—and by whom.

The housekeeping functions of the operating system extend well beyond file and directory status. Many operating systems compile records of user log-on and log-off times, programs' running times, programs that each user has run, and other useful information. In some environments, such records enable organizations to bill users. They also assist with security.

Security A computer's operating system can protect against unauthorized access by collecting system-usage statistics for those in charge of the computer

FIGURE SW 2-4

Organizing files (documents) into directories (folders).

■ **Path.** An ordered list of directories that lead to a particular file or directory.

DISK CONTENTS
The Explorer window contains two panes. On the left are all of the top-level disk directories (folders), while on the right are the contents of the active directory.

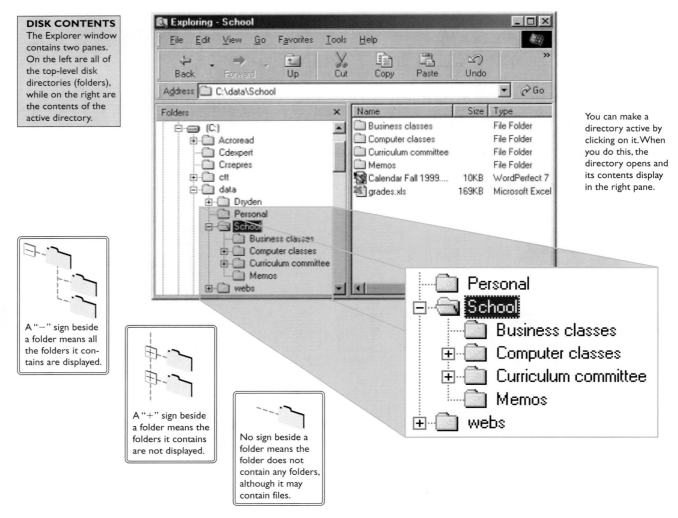

You can make a directory active by clicking on it. When you do this, the directory opens and its contents display in the right pane.

A "−" sign beside a folder means all the folders it contains are displayed.

A "+" sign beside a folder means the folders it contains are not displayed.

No sign beside a folder means the folder does not contain any folders, although it may contain files.

FIGURE SW 2-5

Using Windows Explorer to view disk contents.

system and by reporting any attempts to breach system security. To further ensure the security of computer systems, many operating systems contain *password* procedures to prevent outsiders from accessing system resources not open to them. Many also provide encryption procedures that disguise valuable programs and data when they are transmitted to other computers. The subject of security is a lengthy one, and we will be considering it in depth in a later chapter.

Other Tasks The tasks already described in this section should give you a pretty good idea of the types of work that operating systems do. In addition, each operating system usually has a variety of standard utility programs available to it that perform such chores as formatting disks, copying files from one storage medium onto another, sorting records, and so on. A number of third-party, or aftermarket, vendors produce software that performs additional utility functions or improves on the standard functions of an operating system. A later section of this chapter covers utility programs.

INTERLEAVED PROCESSING TECHNIQUES

Computers often take advantage of *interleaved processing techniques* to operate more efficiently. These techniques enable computers to process many programs at almost the same time, so, consequently, they increase system throughput—the number of jobs the computer system can handle in any given period.

Multiprogramming **Multiprogramming,** a term that typically refers to multiuser operating systems, is somewhat similar to the operation of a busy dentist's office. The dentist *concurrently* attends to several patients in different rooms within a given time period. The dentist may pull a tooth in Room 1, move to Room 2 to prepare a cavity for filling, move back to Room 1 to treat the hole left by the pulled tooth, and so forth. As the dentist moves from patient to patient, assistants carry out minor tasks.

A computer operating system with multiprogramming capabilities can manipulate several applications programs stored in memory at the same time. The CPU, like the dentist, works on only one program at a time. When it reaches a point at which peripheral devices or other elements of the computer system can take over some of the work, the CPU interrupts processing to move on to another program, returning to the first one when the situation allows further processing. While the computer waits for a disk drive to read data on one program, for example, it can perform calculations for another program. The systems software for the disk unit, like a dental assistant, does background work; in this case, it retrieves the data stored on disk.

Multiprogramming speeds processing because computers can perform thousands of computations in the time a disk drive can load a single piece of data. Such disk I/O operations run much more slowly than computations because the computer must interact with an external device to obtain needed data. Also, secondary storage speeds cannot keep pace with CPU speeds.

Multitasking **Multitasking** most commonly refers to a multiprogramming capability on a single-user operating system. It's the ability of an operating system to enable two or more programs or program tasks, from a single user, to execute concurrently on one computer. This feature allows a user to perform such work as editing a file in one program while the computer performs calculations in another program or printing a document while the user is editing another document at the same time. Remember, one processor, like one dentist, can attend to only one task at a time. But today's CPUs work so fast that users often perceive two things happening at once.

Users can fully appreciate multitasking when they need continuing access to their computers while performing operations that require exceptionally long processing times. For example, suppose that you want to search through a large database for all people between the ages of 25 and 35 with six years of service and some experience with computers. On a small computer with an extremely large personnel database, such a search may take several minutes; multitasking allows you to use your computer to perform another task, in the same or a different program, while the search continues in the background.

Several types of multitasking are found in practice. *Preemptive multitasking,* or *true multitasking,* works without annoying delays; for instance, you need not wait to type text for a document because another program is being output by the printer. By contrast, *cooperative multitasking* is fraught with delays; one task (say, typing) may have to yield to another task (say, printing) when the two tasks are concurrently active. Preemptive multitasking also allows the operating system to seize control of the computer system to serve the user if an application causes conflicts. This results in fewer system crashes. In cooperative multitasking, one task may freeze the computer system, and the user can regain control only by turning the system off.

The difference between the two types of multitasking described here is a process called *multithreading.* A thread is a set of processing activities smaller than a task; that is, many threads make up a single task. Preemptive multitasking schedules operations thread by thread, making the computer more

■ **Multiprogramming.** Concurrent execution of two or more programs on a single, multiuser computer. ■ **Multitasking.** A capability of an operating system to execute for a single user two or more programs or program tasks concurrently.

responsive to the user, whereas cooperative multitasking completes operations only in full tasks.

Time-Sharing Time-sharing is an interleaved processing technique that allows a single computer system—usually a mainframe—to support numerous users at separate workstations. The operating system cycles through all the active programs in the system that need processing and gives each one a small time slice during each cycle.

For example, say that users have loaded 20 programs into the system, which allocates a time slice of 1 second for each one. (Time-sharing systems usually slice processing time in pieces much smaller than this, and all pieces are not necessarily equal.) The computer works on Program 1 for 1 second, then on Program 2 for 1 second, and so forth. When it finishes working on Program 20 for 1 second, it returns to Program 1 for another second, Program 2 for another second, and so on. Thus, if 20 programs run concurrently on the system, each program will get a total of 3 seconds of processing during each minute of actual clock time, or 1 second in every 20-second period. As you can see, in a time-sharing system it is difficult for a single program to dominate the CPU's attention, thereby holding up the processing of shorter programs.

Both time-sharing and multiprogramming work on many programs concurrently by allotting short, uninterrupted time periods to each. They differ in the way they allot time, however. A time-sharing computer spends a fixed amount of time on each program and then goes on to another. A multiprogrammed computer works on a program until it encounters a logical stopping point, such as a need to read more data, before going on to another program.

Virtual Memory In the early days of computing, users faced numerous problems loading large programs into memory. Often they had to split programs into pieces so that only small portions of them resided in the limited memory at any one time. In the early 1970s, operating systems responded to this problem by offering a virtual-memory feature. This development permitted users to write extremely long programs, leaving the operating systems to automatically split up and manage them. Today, even personal operating systems like Windows 95 and Windows 98 use virtual memory.

Virtual memory uses disk storage to extend conventional memory, or RAM. It usually works in a sequence like this: The operating system delivers programs for processing to the virtual-memory area on disk. Here the programs generally are divided into either fixed-length *pages* or variable-length *segments*. (Whether the programs are subdivided into pages or segments depends on the operating system's capabilities.)

A virtual-memory system based on paging might break a program 400 kilobytes long into ten pages of 40 kilobytes each. As the computer works on the program, it stores only a few pages at a time in RAM. As it requires other pages during program execution, it selects them from virtual memory and writes over the pages in RAM that it no longer needs. All the original pages, or modified ones, remain intact in virtual memory as the computer processes the program. If the computer again needs a page previously in RAM but now written over, it can readily fetch the needed instructions. This process continues until the program finishes executing.

Segmentation works like paging except that the lengths of segments vary. Each segment normally consists of a contiguous block of logically interrelated program instructions. Some systems combine segmentation and paging.

■ **Time-sharing.** An interleaved processing technique for a multiuser environment in which the computer handles users' jobs in repeated cycles. ■ **Virtual memory.** An area on disk where the operating system stores programs divided into manageable pieces for processing.

Not all operating systems offer virtual memory. Although this technique permits a computer system to get by with limited RAM, it can chew up a lot of processing time swapping pages or segments in and out of RAM.

Multiprocessing **Multiprocessing** links together two or more computers to perform work at the same time. Of course, the operating system must acknowledge multiple processors and assign processing tasks to them as efficiently as possible. In contrast with multiprogramming, in which a single computer processes several programs or tasks *concurrently* (taking turns during the same time interval), multiprocessing carries out multiple programs or tasks *simultaneously* (at precisely the same instant) on separate processors. Computer systems often implement multiprocessing through either coprocessing or parallel processing.

Coprocessing, mentioned briefly in Chapter HW 1, coordinates the functions of a native central processor (CPU) with those of "slave" processors that perform specialized chores, such as high-speed calculations for screen graphics. At any point in time, two or more processors may be performing work simultaneously, but the single CPU still largely determines the time taken to perform an entire job.

In *parallel processing,* the most sophisticated and fastest method of multiprocessing, there are several processors, each of which constitutes a full-fledged general-purpose CPU that operates at roughly the same level as the others. These tightly integrated computers work together on a job at the same time by sharing memory. This concept may sound simple, but many practical problems complicate its implementation, and parallel processing often requires special software. Symmetric multiprocessing is a form of parallel processing that appears commonly in today's networks. *Symmetric multiprocessing* splits up tasks so that multiple processors can work simultaneously on separate threads; however, the processors must all run the same operating system.

Symmetric multiprocessing is closely related to *fault-tolerant computing,* in which a computer system includes duplicates of important circuitry. The duplicate components may or may not function together. In one example of fault-tolerant computing, if one critical component fails, its identical backup component can take over. In another example, both components may be working side-by-side on the same task, comparing results at checkpoints.

Spooling Software Some input and output devices work at extremely low speeds. Tape drives and printers, for example, work at a snail's pace compared to the CPU. If the CPU had to wait for these slower devices to finish their work, the computer system would face a horrendous bottleneck. For example, suppose that the computer has just completed a five-second job that generated 100 pages of hard copy for the printer. A printer might output 8 pages per minute, requiring over 12 minutes to finish the job. If the CPU had to deal directly with the printer, memory would be tied up waiting for the printer to complete the job. As a result, other programs would have to sit unattended while this output was sent from memory to paper.

To avoid such a delay, many computer systems set up *output spooling* areas in disk storage to store output destined for the printer (see Figure SW 2-6). When the computer receives a Print command, a **spooling program** rapidly transfers, or spools, the output from memory to the disk spooling area. The computer is then free to process another program in this memory area, leaving it to the spooling program to transfer the output of the first program from disk to printer.

■ **Multiprocessing.** A technique for simultaneous execution of two or more program sequences by multiple processors operating under common control. ■ **Spooling program.** A program that manages input or output by temporarily holding it in secondary storage to expedite processing.

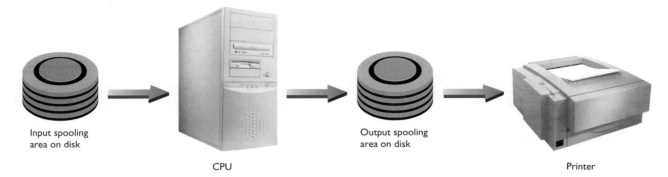

Input spooling
area on disk

CPU

Output spooling
area on disk

Printer

FIGURE SW 2-6

Spooling. On busy computer systems, input is spooled before it is processed and output is spooled before it is sent to the printer.

As Figure SW 2-6 shows, spooling can also be used to hold, or stage, input on its way to the computer. As programs enter the computer system, they are stored in an *input spooling area,* or *queue.* When the operating system is ready to deliver the next program to the CPU, it checks the queue to see which one to process next. On many computer systems, priorities can be assigned to programs. If this is possible, the computer will attend to high-priority jobs before it processes jobs that may have been waiting longer but have a lower priority.

PERSONAL OPERATING SYSTEMS

Here, we briefly cover several of the most widely used operating systems employed by individuals for *personal use* on their own PCs, including MS-DOS and PC-DOS, Windows, and Mac OS. We will also cover the Windows 3.1 operating environment.

MS-DOS AND PC-DOS

During the 1980s and early 1990s, DOS* (for Disk Operating System) was the dominant operating system for microcomputers. Millions of copies of DOS have been sold to date, making it one of the most widely used software packages ever developed. Even though it has been made technologically obsolete by newer products, many of today's microcomputer users still work with DOS.

DOS is available in two forms: PC-DOS and MS-DOS. Both were originally developed by Microsoft Corporation of Redmond, Washington (see Feature SW 2-1). Only minor differences separate these virtually identical operating systems. **PC-DOS** was created originally for IBM microcomputers, whereas **MS-DOS** was devised to operate on PC-compatibles. PC-DOS is now owned by IBM, which still updates the program. The latest version, PC-DOS 2000, works on both IBM microcomputers as well as PCs made by other manufacturers. Microsoft still owns MS-DOS, but the firm no longer updates the program; Version 6 was the last Microsoft update.

Both the MS-DOS and PC-DOS operating systems have passed through many revisions since they were first developed. All versions starting with the number 1 (such as 1.0 and 1.1) were designed for the original IBM PC and other early PCs, which used only floppy disks and cassette tapes for secondary storage. Some

*For simplicity, this text limits the acronym *DOS* to MS-DOS and PC-DOS. DOS is not a proprietary name, however, and many less-well-known operating systems also include DOS in their product titles.

■ **PC-DOS.** The operating system designed for and widely used on early IBM microcomputers. ■ **MS-DOS.** An operating system widely used on early PC-compatible microcomputer systems.

Bill Gates

The First and Most Famous High-Tech Billionaire

In the late 1970s, few people would have predicted that a systems-software programmer—a "techie"—would become the richest person in the United States. But that's exactly what happened.

Today, William H. Gates III has a net worth of about $100 billion. As founder and chairman of the board of Microsoft Corporation, the largest microcomputer-software company in the world, Gates became the first American ever to reach billionaire status—and he's not even 50 years old! Bill Gates has made scores of other people rich too. Had you bought $1,000 worth of Microsoft stock when the company went public in 1986, those shares would be worth close to a quarter of a million dollars.

Before he graduated from high school, Bill Gates was already an accomplished computer programmer. He wrote a class-scheduling program for his high school and a traffic-logging program for the city of Bellevue, Washington. What's more, he also worked as a programmer for TRW, a large computer-services firm—reportedly the only time he has ever worked for someone else.

After high school, Gates continued on to Harvard. He never finished, dropping out instead in the mid-1970s to work on a BASIC language translator for the Altair 8800 computer, the world's first microcomputer system. The Altair was a commercial flop. (Available only in kit form, it would only work if a diligent and talented buyer assembled it correctly.) Despite this market failure, the microcomputer industry continued to grow, and Gates started creating language translators for others.

Bill Gates. America's $100-billion man (standing) in one of his lighter moments

His biggest break came around 1980, when IBM was looking for a company to deliver an operating system for the IBM PC, its first foray into microcomputers. At that time, Microsoft employed only 50 people writing mostly BASIC, COBOL, and FORTRAN language translators. IBM first contacted a California company called Digital Research, which produced CP/M, then the most widely used operating system for personal computers. According to industry legend, however, Digital Research founder Gary Kildall, a PC pioneer who was already rich beyond most people's wildest dreams, was off flying his plane in the Santa Cruz mountains when the IBM people came calling. Put off, the IBMers left for the state of Washington to meet with Bill Gates.

The rest, as they say, is history. Microsoft is now the largest software company in the world and employs over 30,000 people.

---

of today's computers run DOS Version 7 and later, with capabilities for managing hard disks and working on networks. Yet its original design based on 16-bit CPU chips—which supported only 1 megabyte of RAM—prevents DOS from taking full advantage of the power of newer Intel chips. Feature SW 2-2 on page SW 46 takes a look at how the capabilities of operating systems are in large measure a function of the computer chips around which they are designed.

A sample of DOS commands is provided in Figure SW 2-7.

DOS WITH WINDOWS 3.X

Microsoft created **Windows 3.x** in an effort to meet the needs of users frustrated by issuing DOS commands. Windows 3.x—the x stands for the version number of the software—is an interconnected series of programs that supplies a graphical user interface for microcomputer systems that use DOS. By replacing the DOS command line with a system of menus, windows, and icons, Windows 3.x eliminates the need to remember a command syntax.

■ **Windows 3.x.** A graphical operating environment created by Microsoft Corporation to run in conjunction with DOS. Two widely used versions are Windows 3.1 and Windows 3.11.

64-Bit Operating Systems

Coming Soon to Your Desktop

The power of a personal computer has always been defined by its microprocessor. The more powerful the CPU chip, the more powerful the operating system and the set of applications programs it can support.

The first PCs, in the late 1970s, used 8-bit chips. These microprocessors ran the Radio Shack TRS-80, Commodore Pet, Apple II, and other computer systems whose names are now familiar only to trivia buffs and longtime PC users. These computers mostly did text processing, and getting colors, graphs, and fancy fonts on the display was a challenge and not always possible. The operating systems that ran on these machines—CP/M, Radio Shack TRSDOS, and Apple ProDos—are long gone.

With the 1980s came 16-bit chips and the IBM PC, the most successful microcomputer system of its time. The 16-bit chips could only cleanly support about a megabyte of RAM, and throughout their useful lives they tended mostly to DOS-based

applications. When Windows 3.x and its graphical user interface (GUI) arrived in the early 1990s, it stretched this chip almost beyond its limits.

The 32-bit microprocessors ushered us full bore into the age of graphics and true multitasking. With machines like the Apple Macintosh and with the modern Windows platforms that use the Intel Pentium processor, point-and-click software became standard. It also became possible to have several applications running at the same time, and computers crashed far less often.

The 64-bit chips, deployed on server computers such as those that manage Web pages on the Internet, are now beginning to gravitate to the user desktop. With them come another wave of powerful features. Among these are a wider bus, the ability to move data along in bigger chunks and at faster speeds, an improved instruction set that better supports complex applications, and the capability of addressing more storage.

To use advanced features optimally requires the use of new, 64-bit operating systems—like the personal versions of Windows that are now in development at Microsoft. PCs using such operating systems are able to run realistic virtual-reality and 3-D graphics applications, use voice processing in new ways, and manipulate moving images just as smoothly as a television set does.

All versions of Windows 3.x—such as 3.1 (for single-user environments) and 3.11 (for small-network environments)—are not full-fledged operating systems. Instead, they merely define *operating environments* that form a graphical shell around DOS, allowing users to point and click the mouse instead of typing long command strings—thereby making DOS easier to use. Windows 3.x also allows DOS to address more than 1 megabyte of RAM, perform cooperative multitasking, and run several built-in utility applications—such as a card file, calendar, and paint program. Still, the shortcomings of DOS limit the effectiveness of Windows 3.x.

The basic elements of a Windows 3.1 desktop are shown in Figure SW 2-8.

FIGURE SW 2-7

DOS. Even though DOS has become technologically obsolete, many PCs still use it. This table lists some of the most common DOS commands.

WINDOWS 95 AND WINDOWS 98

Although Windows 3.1 and 3.11 continue in use, they are only graphical shells and not entire operating systems. In 1994, Microsoft announced that all soon-

Command	Description	Example	Explanation
COPY	Copies individual files	COPY BOSS A:WORKER	Makes a copy of BOSS and stores it, on the A drive, in WORKER
DIR	Displays the names of files on a disk	DIR A:	Displays names of files on the A drive
ERASE (DEL)	Erases individual files	ERASE A:DOLLAR	Erases DOLLAR from the A drive
REN	Renames individual files	REN SAM BILL	Renames SAM to BILL
DISKCOPY	Copies the contents of one disk to another disk	DISKCOPY A: B:	Copies the contents of the disk in drive A to the disk in drive B
FORMAT	Prepares a disk for use, erasing what was there before	FORMAT A:	Formats the disk in the A drive

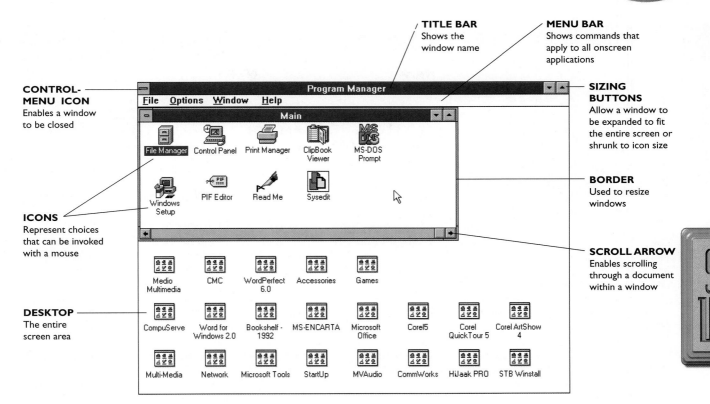

TITLE BAR
Shows the window name

MENU BAR
Shows commands that apply to all onscreen applications

CONTROL-MENU ICON
Enables a window to be closed

SIZING BUTTONS
Allow a window to be expanded to fit the entire screen or shrunk to icon size

BORDER
Used to resize windows

ICONS
Represent choices that can be invoked with a mouse

DESKTOP
The entire screen area

SCROLL ARROW
Enables scrolling through a document within a window

FIGURE SW 2-8

Microsoft Windows 3.1. Microsoft Windows 3.1 provides computers running MS-DOS with a graphical user interface. Annotated in the figure are some of the principal elements of the Windows 3.1 electronic desktop.

to-be-released versions of Windows after 3.11 would bundle language commands (including those in DOS) and a graphical user interface into a single product. It also announced a new numbering system. Instead of calling the next upgrade Windows 4.0—as many had anticipated about the new operating system that Microsoft had been code-naming "Chicago" (see the Inside the Industry box on page SW 48)—it would number new versions of Windows with respect to the year of release. So, for instance, **Windows 95** refers to the 1995 version of Windows and **Windows 98** refers to the 1998 version.

Both Windows 95 and 98 employ a similar but easier-to-learn-and-use GUI than the one in Windows 3.x. Along with this improved interface and faster system response—the latter due to the fact that they are predominantly 32-bit operating systems—Windows 95 and 98 permit preemptive multitasking, longer filenames than Windows 3.x, and plug-and-play support. Windows 98 (see Figure SW 2-9) differs from Windows 95 in that it adds new Web-browsing capabilities, more options for customizing the desktop user interface, the ability to turn a computer on and off automatically, improved support for large hard disks, and support for the digital versatile disk (DVD) and the universal serial bus (USB) standards. The Web-browsing features are part of Microsoft's *Active Desktop* technology, which lets users add active Web content to the Windows electronic desktop and enables file folders to be treated like Web pages. The launch of Windows 98 was enveloped in controversy, as the Tomorrow box on page SW 50 explains. The next personal version of Windows, a product based on Windows 2000 and targeted to consumers, is due shortly.

Windows CE *Windows CE* is a compact version of Windows that is targeted to palmtop computers and wireless communications devices. It has the "look and feel" of the larger desktop versions of Windows, can preemptively multitask, and supports such Internet components as e-mail and

For a tutorial on using Windows, go to www.harcourtcollege.com/infosys/parker2000/student/tutor/ and click on Chapter SW 2.

■ **Windows 95.** The operating system that succeeded the combination of DOS with Windows. ■ **Windows 98.** The upgrade to Windows 95.

Project Code Names

When computer companies are developing new hardware and software products, they typically assign internal code names to the projects. For instance, Microsoft assigned the code names Chicago and Memphis, respectively, to the prerelease versions of Windows 95 and Windows 98. Less well-known code names for Windows products are Champaign (Windows NT 3.5), Cairo (Windows NT 4.0), Sparta (Windows for Workgroups), and Cleveland (Windows 4, which was never released).

Often companies stick with standard themes for code names on related products. For Windows, Microsoft has gone with midwestern city names. Development of IBM's OS/2 operating system featured project names with a *Star Trek* theme, such as Warp, Borg, Q, and Ferengi. Other popular themes include beer, sushi, boats, Shakespeare, celebrities, animals, and mythical gods. Some code names stick—for instance, Macintosh and OS/2 Warp.

KLAMATH MEMPHIS Copeland Cairo
Nashville Pandora ROAD PIZZA Harpo
Bladerunner Tsunami Rolling Rock
Kitty Hawk Jaws Zappa Calimari
Wombat Ali Baba Snow White
Sweet Pea KRYPTONITE ROSEBUD
Zone V Expresso Visine Dr. Pepper

Some of the most interesting code names are Road Pizza (Apple's QuickTime software), Bladerunner (Borland's dBASE for Windows), Rolling Rock (Go Corporation's PenPoint for Hobbit), Shamu (the GUI for CompuServe), CyberDog (Apple browser), Dr. Pepper (an AppleTalk protocol), Mothra (Borland's Paradox for DOS 4.0), Big Foot (Borland's 32-bit DOS extender), and Bogart (Apple's Applesearch). One of the least interesting code names is P5 (Intel's Pentium chip).

the World Wide Web. Because Windows CE is intended to be used on portable devices, it is very memory efficient. Windows CE is far less dominant in the marketplace than are the desktop versions of Windows. Many popular palmtop devices, such as those from Palm Computing, use their own operating systems.

MAC OS

Mac OS—until recently called *Macintosh Operating System*—is the proprietary icon-oriented operating system for Apple's Macintosh line of computers. The Apple Macintosh, introduced in 1984, set the standard for graphical user interfaces. Many of today's new operating systems follow the trend that the Mac started.

Mac OS has grown with the times, keeping pace with increases in power brought by each new CPU chip and Macintosh model. The latest version of the operating system is Version 8.6. Mac OS works almost exclusively on Macintosh-compatible computers. An example of its graphical user interface appears in Figure SW 2-10. Macintosh computers that help manage networks often run Unix.

NETWORK OPERATING SYSTEMS

Many new operating systems come in two versions—one that can help network administrators run networks, often called a *network operating system (NOS)*, and a second version that can serve the applications needs of ordinary

■ **Mac OS.** The operating system for Apple's Macintosh line of computer systems.

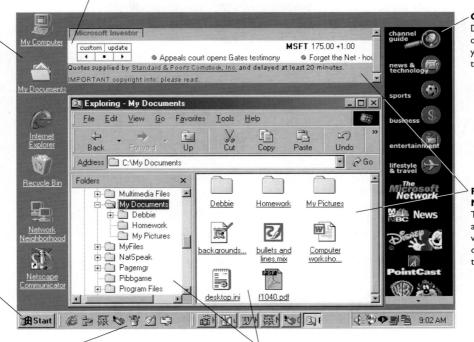

ACTIVE DESKTOP
Lets you add active Web content—such as weather, sports, or stock-market news—to your desktop. It also enables file folders to be treated like Web pages.

EASY-TO-USE INTERFACE
Most operations are a single mouse-click or mouse-movement away.

CHANNEL BAR
Displays the names of Web sites that you can access with the click of a mouse.

START BUTTON
Click for access to programs and documents.

PREEMPTIVE MULTITASKING
There are no annoying delays when you need to do several tasks at the same time.

TASKBAR
Shows applications running on your computer. You can use these buttons to switch between programs.

EXPLORER
A two-pane window displays hierarchically and pictorially a list of all your documents and programs.

FIGURE SW 2-9

Windows 98. Windows 98—the update to Windows 95—is faster, better integrated with the Internet, and more feature-rich and supportive of new technologies than its predecessor.

desktop users. This section will cover some widely used NOSs found in PC-network environments: Unix, NetWare, Windows NT, and Windows 2000. All except NetWare come also in personal versions.

UNIX

Unix was originally developed about three decades ago at Bell Laboratories as an operating system for midrange computers. Many properties of Unix make it a compelling choice for high-end 32-bit PCs and graphics workstations as well.

First, Unix has established a long and relatively successful track record as a multiuser, multitasking operating system. During the quarter-century since its introduction, Unix has attracted a large and loyal following. Today, Unix is the most frequent choice on server computers that store information carried over the Internet.

Second, Unix is flexibly built, so it can be used on a wide variety of machines. Unlike other operating systems—such as Windows 95 and 98, which are based on Intel chips, or Mac OS, which is based on PowerPC chips—Unix is not built around a single family of processors. Computer systems from micros to mainframes can run Unix, and it can easily integrate a variety of devices from different manufacturers through network connections. This flexibility gives Unix a big advantage over competing operating systems for many types of applications.

■ **Unix.** A long-standing operating system for midrange computers, microcomputer networks, graphics workstations, and the Internet.

Will the Government Begin Regulating Software Design?

Many in the Industry Are Worried

When Windows 98 was months away from its launch date, the U.S. Justice Department began to get tough with Microsoft Corporation. At issue was whether the software giant would be allowed to bundle its Internet Explorer browser into Windows 98, thereby making the former a sort of "free" product. Competitor Netscape Communications (now part of America Online) complained that if Microsoft got its way, few people would want to buy Netscape's own browser, Navigator, which then sold for about $50.

Many people sympathized with Netscape. It was the "little guy" with the market-leading browser. And here was the industry giant, late to the party, swooping down and attempting to change the ground rules for competition. Unfairly, cried many. Netscape supporters feared that if Microsoft and other software giants continued to have free rein regarding what goes into their products, creativity would be stifled. Who wants to play a game where the big guys always walk away with all of the marbles? Also, once all the little guys are gone, what's to keep the big guys from gradually raising prices?

Those at Microsoft felt they did what they had to do to protect their core business—systems and applications software for the desktop. The Web was threatening to establish itself everywhere, and the desktop PC was right in the middle of the action. Would it not have been foolish for Microsoft to ignore these facts? There's a fine line, sometimes, between being smart in business and engaging in anticompetitive practices. People have been divided on which of these categories the browser issue falls into.

Beyond the browser war, however, perhaps a bigger and more general issue has also been at stake here: Will consumers ultimately benefit if curbs are imposed on the content of a software publisher's products? Put another way, is it wise for the government to establish regulations on what goes into programs? The courts are mulling the matter—and probably will for a long time, even after they move beyond Microsoft.

Getting lawyers involved in deciding software features is indeed a scary thought to many in the technology community. Would we have built-in fonts in word processors today if lawyers had gone to bat for the font industry back in the 1980s? Would modern spreadsheet packages have built-in graphics if lawyers for

Microsoft Corporation. Government controls to reign in the software giant could wind up having a huge effect on the entire U.S. software industry.

independent graphics companies had been on top of the situation early on? Will Windows and other software packages be allowed to have native voice capabilities in the future or will those be mandated to be separately acquired pieces?

Let's say the lawyers decide that you can't freely bundle products together. Most programmers and experienced users will tell you that when a single vendor assembles code into one, seamless package, it works better and faster than a hodgepodge of plug-ins, all of which come from different vendors. It's probably going to be cheaper and easier to use too. The value of bundling products into a working whole can be considerable to users, the great majority of whom are not software engineers, and arguably more productive in a world dominated by a single interface. What's more, computer technology is so unpredictable and so fast-moving that by the time laws are drafted, they could be useless and perhaps even counterproductive.

The U.S. software industry is the envy of the world and some may even say it's widening the productivity gap it enjoys over other nations. Will the federal government be so bold as to put at risk the industry's domestic growth at a time when it's becoming ever more obvious that technology will be a key to world leadership in the 21st century? Should the playing field be leveled by forces other than the marketplace so that weaker companies continue to survive? Or is government policing of the competitive practices of technology companies long overdue and, in the long run, healthy for both the industry and consumers? Stay tuned.

But certain disadvantages also plague Unix. Many people complain that it isn't very easy to use. What's more, the same features that give Unix its flexibility make it run more slowly than operating systems tailored around a particular family of microprocessors. This characteristic limits the benefits of applying Unix in an environment dominated by, say, Intel CPUs. Perhaps the greatest disadvantage of Unix is that several "brands" of it are now available, many of them incompatible with each other.

MENU BAR
Shows commands that
apply to all selections

TITLE BAR
Displays window, program,
or document names

APPLICATION ICON
Displays a menu of open
applications that you can
immediately launch

SCROLL ARROWS
Enable scrolling through
a document window

SIZING HANDLES
Can be mouse-dragged
to make a window larger
or smaller

ICONS
Represent choices
that can be invoked
with a mouse

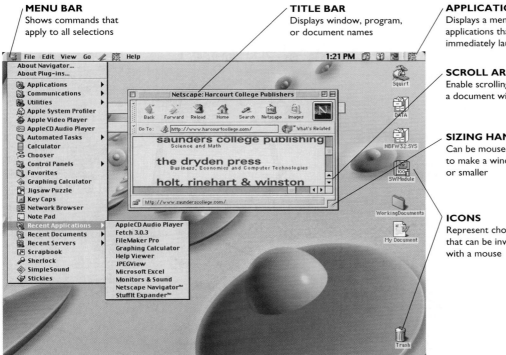

Linux A version of Unix that has achieved a loyal band of followers over the past few years is *Linux*. Originally created in 1991, Linux is available without charge over the Internet and is largely being improved by volunteers submitting new programming code over that same medium. While successful in many regards—some estimates show more than 10 million users—most companies are leery about using Linux in anything other than small applications. The main reservation: if something goes wrong, who do you go to for reliable help? With the increasing support of mainstream companies, such as Corel (see Figure SW 2-11) and Lotus, however, and the introduction of graphical interfaces for Linux to make it more user-friendly, this operating system will likely continue to grow in acceptance and popularity in the near future.

FIGURE SW 2-10

Mac OS. Mac OS remains very popular many years after emerging as the first commercially successful operating system with a graphical user interface.

FIGURE SW 2-11

Linux. As Linux gains acceptance as an operating system, mainstream companies—such as Corel and Lotus—have begun supporting Linux. At this Corel site, you can download a free Linux version of WordPerfect and access newsgroups and links to other Linux resources and information.

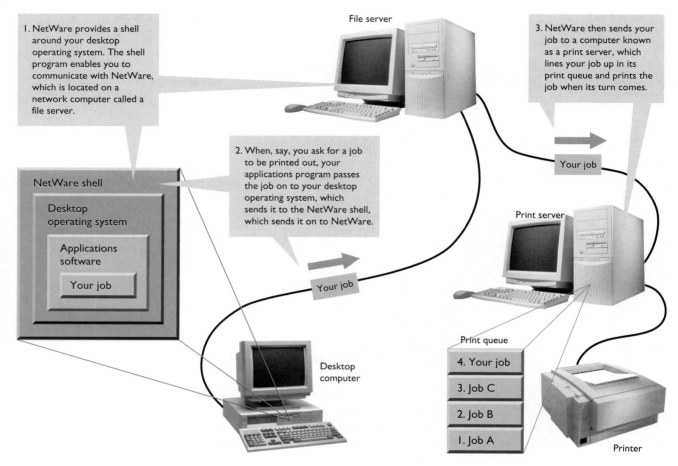

1. NetWare provides a shell around your desktop operating system. The shell program enables you to communicate with NetWare, which is located on a network computer called a file server.

2. When, say, you ask for a job to be printed out, your applications program passes the job on to your desktop operating system, which sends it to the NetWare shell, which sends it on to NetWare.

3. NetWare then sends your job to a computer known as a print server, which lines your job up in its print queue and prints the job when its turn comes.

File server

Print server

Your job

Your job

NetWare shell

Desktop operating system

Applications software

Your job

Desktop computer

Print queue

4. Your job

3. Job C

2. Job B

1. Job A

Printer

FIGURE SW 2-12

Working with a NOS. The diagram shows how you would interact with a NetWare-controlled computer network. Many other network operating systems work in similar ways.

NETWARE

NetWare—developed by Novell, Inc., during the mid-1980s—is today the most widely used operating system on microcomputer-based local area networks (LANs). Most users of NetWare interact with it when they log on to a network or when they deal with a network print server or a file server. NetWare provides a shell around your personal, desktop operating system through which you can retrieve files from or save them on a shared hard disk and also print them on a shared printer (see Figure SW 2-12). The shell routine enables you to communicate with NetWare, which is located on the shared disk.

Here's how a typical NetWare session might unfold on a PC network: When you turn on a connected workstation, the network sends a prompt—such as F>—to your display or displays a log-on dialog box. At this point, you can decide to work on or off the network. If you wish to work on the network, you type the appropriate log-on message or user name. For instance, if the network recognizes you as KJOHNSON, you might have to type in KJOHNSON.

When the operating system accepts your input, it gives you access rights to the network, and you are free to do any network operation within those assigned access rights. They include such operations as reading or writing to files, executing programs, and creating or deleting files. When you are working with a shared hard disk on the network, you generally treat it simply as another disk drive on your own computer system.

■ **NetWare.** The most widely used operating system on local area networks (LANs).

If you choose not to work on the network, you simply do not log onto the network. You then work just as you would on an independent computer system. Keep in mind, however, you can gain access to a program on the shared hard disk, save a program to the shared hard disk, or output to a shared printer only after you reestablish network access. Many other NOSs work similarly to NetWare as regards to basic operations.

WINDOWS NT AND WINDOWS 2000

Windows NT (for *New Technology*)—which now goes by the name **Windows 2000**—is a full 32-bit operating system developed by Microsoft Corporation for organizational computer systems. Several principal forms of this program exist. The *Workstation* or *Professional* edition is targeted to ordinary users working at powerful desktop computers, while the *Server* family of products is aimed at network administrators and network-management tasks. All versions of both Windows NT and Windows 2000 use more or less the same graphical user interface employed in Windows 95 and 98. An important feature of Windows NT/2000 is its ability to be run on a variety of computer systems, not just those using conventional Intel chips. Thus, applications written for Windows NT/2000 can be developed on a PC that uses a Pentium chip and can be run on a workstation that uses another chip, such as the PowerPC. Another key feature of NT/2000 is its multiple versions. This flexibility gives it an advantage in some environments over NetWare, which offers no personal version.

Although Windows NT/2000 has had a later start than both Unix and NetWare, many industry experts consider it to be the front-running NOS in the race to capture the lead in corporate networking. One of the major disadvantages of Windows NT/2000 relative to Windows 95 or 98 as a personal operating system is its large storage requirements. This limitation may be somewhat alleviated by the introduction of a consumer version of Windows 2000 expected in the near future.

UTILITY PROGRAMS

Computer users must perform some tasks repeatedly in the course of routine processing, including sorting records, checking spelling and grammar, and copying programs from one medium to another. Programmers prefer to avoid the extremely inefficient practice of including code for these tasks in every program. General-purpose software tools called **utility programs** help to eliminate this waste by performing standard processing routines for all applications that require them. Computer systems normally include large libraries of utility programs to perform common functions.

Utility programs are packaged in a variety of ways. Some are bundled into operating systems. For instance, standard utilities for copying disk files accompany the Windows 95 and 98 operating systems. In other cases, utilities are independent programs that can be acquired from third-party vendors and made to run with a given operating system. This latter class of programs can perform chores your operating system is incapable of doing as well as do some types of operating-system tasks better.

Two widely used types of utility programs that we will cover in depth here are disk utilities and device drivers. Figure SW 2-13 briefly describes these and other types of utilities.

■ **Windows NT.** An operating system designed by Microsoft Corporation for both workstation and network applications within organizations. Beginning in 1999, Microsoft started naming versions of this operating system **Windows 2000.** ■ **Utility program.** A general-purpose program that performs some frequently encountered operations in a computer system.

Control Panel

Antivirus programs
Protect your system from virus attack

Backup utilities
Quickly and easily back up the contents of a hard disk

Data compressions utilities
Enable files to be compressed

Desktop enhancers
Let you customize your graphical user interface—say, by changing the way in which menus are presented

Device drivers
Enable applications software to work on a specific configuration of hardware

Diagnostic software
Enables problems to be more easily rooted out of your computer system

Disk optimizers
Better utilize space on disk; for instance, disk defragmenters rearrange files for faster access

Disk toolkits
Recover and repair damaged or lost files

Document managers
Enable you to find a lost file on your system by typing in part of its name or by typing in short strings of text known to be contained in the file

Extenders
Let you add new fonts, commands, or programs to your system

File viewers
Make it easy to view files without opening the applications in which they were created

Internet utilities
Enable you to more easily locate and keep track of resources on the Internet, censor downloaded content, keep track of connect time, and so forth

Keyboard utilities
Let you construct keyboard macros (small programs that execute when you press a certain key) or let you reconfigure your keyboard

Memory managers
Enable you to increase available memory and/or speed up system performance

Performance monitors
Tell you how efficiently your computer system is performing its work

Screen-capture programs
Enable you to download any screen image onto a storage or output device, as well as to edit and view images

Screen savers
Show random patterns on the display to prevent the phosphor coating on the screen from burning

Uninstallers
Remove applications programs, including all files and directories and any references to them

22 object(s)

FIGURE SW 2-13

Utility programs. Utility programs extend the capabilities of a computer's systems software.

DISK UTILITIES

A **disk utility** is a program that performs useful operations for controlling a hard disk. Four types of disk utilities are disk toolkits, data compression programs, disk optimizers, and backup utilities.

Disk Toolkits *Disk toolkits* help users to recover from accidental data destruction. Such a program allows you to recover damaged or erased files, repair damaged format markings and directories, and recover from a disk crash (a crippling failure of the disk itself). At one time, virtually all disk toolkits came from third-party vendors, but operating systems are increasingly including very adequate disk toolkits. Still, vendors of disk toolkits seem to supply a continuing stream of useful disk-management routines beyond those of operating-system software.

Data Compression Programs **Data compression** programs enable files to be stored in a smaller space. This helps to free up disk space and to speed

■ **Disk utility.** A program that assists users with such disk-related tasks as backup, data compression, space allocation, and the like. ■ **Data compression.** A utility function that squeezes data into a smaller storage space than it would normally require.

transmissions of files over networks. Data compression programs are frequently used when sending files over the Internet. Sending compressed files over a network requires the receiver to run the proper decompression program. Data compression is also commonly a space-saving strategy in file backup.

Data compression has become a relatively hot topic in recent years, largely because of two trends: the spread of multimedia applications and the ever-increasing popularity of the Internet. Color graphics, sound, and video all consume a great deal of storage space. Even text sent in volume over the telephone lines can cause bottlenecks unless it is compressed. Both Figure SW 2-14 and Feature SW 2-3 show how data compression works.

Disk Optimizers   *Disk optimizers* enable programs on disk to be accessed faster. They perform such tasks as allocating certain files to outer disk cylinders (where the read/write heads can reach them quickly), consolidating fragmented files (that is, rewriting related blocks of programs and data in contiguous sectors on the disk surface for fast access), and sorting file-folder names for fast access.

Disk fragmentation has certainly become a major problem as multimedia resources and large applications programs have imposed growing demands. A file becomes fragmented when it's too large to be stored in contiguous locations (clusters) on disk. When this happens, the file is split and stored in noncontiguous locations. A defragmentation utility speeds disk access by rearranging files and free space on your disk, so files are stored in contiguous locations and free space is consolidated into a single block. Figure SW 2-15 shows how such a utility consolidates fragmented files. Many operating systems have their own defragmentation utilities.

Backup Utilities   *Backup utilities* are programs designed to back up a hard-disk's contents (see Figure SW 2-16). You can back up an entire disk or merely selected directories and files. Most serious backup systems store copies on magnetic tape, rewritable optical disk, or some other such high-capacity medium. Many users rely on the backup utilities supplied by their disk- or tape-drive makers. Using the Internet for backup is becoming another popular option for storing duplicates of important files.

DEVICE DRIVERS

When a computer system's hardware must communicate with input or output hardware such as a display device, printer, or scanner, the operating system commonly works through a utility program known as a *device driver*.

FIGURE SW 2-14

Text compression. Using the characters &, @, and # to substitute for repeating strings, a phrase is reduced from 40 to 20 characters—half its original size.

1. Original (uncompressed) phrase (40 characters)

s h e ☐ s e l l s ☐ s e a s h e l l s ☐ d o w n ☐ b y ☐ t h e ☐ s e a s h o r e

2. Pattern substitution for repeating character strings

h e ☐   **e l l s ☐**   **s e a s h**
&   @   #

☐ = blank space

3. Final (compressed) phrase (20 characters)

s & s @ # @ down ☐ by ☐ t & # ore

SW 2-3

Data Compression

How to Squeeze More Data into Less Space

Even though storage capacities of ordinary desktop systems are now in the multi-gigabyte range—an unimaginable threshold until very recently—software developers continue to feel pinched by limitations on storage space. Some might even say that user expectations have increased so much that the space problem has actually intensified.

Blame the increasing demand for photographic-quality screen displays and full-motion desktop video, both of which put acute strains on storage. A modest photographic-quality image that you see in a book can easily consume 20 megabytes or so. That's the capacity of about 14 high-density diskettes. Now think of simultaneously storing several such images on your hard disk and running full-motion video at about 30 frames per second, and you can see why software developers are crying the blues.

Developers have found one way out of the storage crunch by compressing data. The following paragraphs discuss a few of many compression methods.

Stacking Algorithms   Some software packages apply stacking algorithms, or formulas, to perform modest data compression. The stacker program included with most tape drives, for instance, enables you to double the space on your tape. Similar stacker programs let you double hard-disk space.

When you turn on the stacker, it compresses anything written to the storage medium or, alternatively, decompresses data as you read it. Generally you can choose which applications you want compressed. Compression and decompression eat up computer time, so that decision requires some thought.

Zipping Files   Zipping refers to a particular method of compressing files onto a diskette or hard disk using software programs such as WinZip—a shareware utility program. Compressing data is known as *zipping* a file and decompressing is known as *unzipping*. WinZip can perform only modest amounts of file compression, and it works best for text and Windows BMP files. When a file is zipped and unzipped, no quality or contents of the file is lost.

JPEG and MPEG   The JPEG and MPEG standards define compression routines in the world of computer graphics. JPEG (named for the Joint Photographic Experts Group that developed it) implements an algorithm to compress still images. It can reduce the size of a picture file to take up 100 times less space than the original version (referred to as a 100:1 compression ratio), though quality is lost in the compression process. JPEG works by looking for redundant information in a picture. For instance, an image half filled with blue sky has a lot of redundancy. The JPEG algorithm reproduces this image by describing the color blue to the computer and telling the computer how many adjacent pixels to paint that shade of blue.

WinZip (Unregistered) - elizxx.zip						
Name	Date	Time	Size	Ratio	Packed	Path
S0060.bmp	10/19/96	13:12	311,486	95%	16,346	
Scn0049.bmp	10/19/96	11:36	311,486	96%	12,406	
Scn0048.bmp	10/19/96	11:35	311,486	89%	35,159	
Scn0047.bmp	10/19/96	11:33	311,486	89%	32,821	
Scn0046.bmp	10/19/96	11:30	311,486	86%	44,859	
Scn0045.bmp	10/19/96	11:28	311,486	89%	34,763	
Scn0044.bmp	10/19/96	11:18	311,486	75%	79,097	
Scn0043.bmp	10/19/96	11:16	311,486	97%	8,567	
Scn0042.bmp	10/19/96	11:03	311,486	97%	8,112	
Scn0041.bmp	10/19/96	10:49	311,486	89%	34,752	
Scn0040.bmp	10/19/96	10:39	311,486	97%	9,970	
Scn0039.bmp	10/19/96	10:36	311,486	82%	55,517	
Scn0038.bmp	10/19/96	10:27	311,486	90%	29,748	
Scn0037.bmp	10/19/96	10:25	311,486	93%	20,818	

Selected 0 files, 0 bytes   Total 131 files, 40,443KB

Zipped files. Zipping is a common practice for compressing BMP files (note the rate of compression in the ratio column).

MPEG (named for the Moving Pictures Expert Group) defines a standard for compressing video data that works a lot like JPEG, except that it also removes redundancy from image to image. Adjacent frames on a piece of film look very similar; the illusion of movement comes from small differences between them. MPEG attempts to remove the redundant information in such a sequence of images, producing a 200:1 or greater compression ratio. MPEG also cheats a bit, removing some information that is never restored on decompression. It does this because humans cannot process 30 frames per second and still perceive every detail. A newer version of MPEG—called MP3—is used to compress audio files. The standard compresses files to less than one-tenth of their original size, and is commonly used to download music from the Internet.

Fractals   Some of the highest compression ratios result from fractal algorithms. Fractal algorithms generate random numbers and formulas to produce patterns "on the fly," leaving hardly any data to store. For instance, a program sequence might describe to a computer what a single leaf of a tree looks like and how the leaf can vary in texture, shape, and color. The computer can then generate a realistic-looking tree with thousands of leaves in almost no time, using hardly any stored data. Fractal algorithms have also successfully produced images of erosion patterns on mountains.

Data compression utilities provide valuable benefits beyond conserving disk or tape space. Compression of many data transmissions sent over the Internet, for instance, saves line capacity.

FRAGMENTATION
As a hard disk fills, it gets harder to store new files in adjacent clusters. Large files must be broken up and stored in nonadjacent clusters. Such fragmented files take longer to retrieve.

File A
File B
File C
Unused

DEFRAGMENTATION
When a utility program is used to defragment the hard disk, files are rewritten into adjacent clusters.

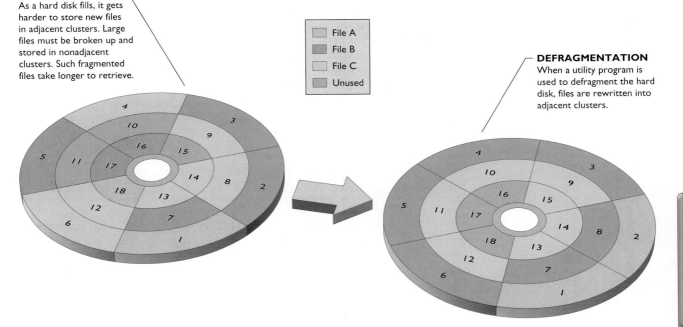

Device drivers make it possible for specific hardware devices to function with software.

Most hardware you buy will include one or two diskettes with device drivers that enable the equipment to be installed on your specific type of computer system. You can tell when you buy the hardware which types of drivers are included; for instance, if the outside package says "for Windows 98" or "for Mac OS 8.6," then you know that drivers for those systems are inside. Generally, the major PC hardware vendors create drivers to support a large variety of computer systems.

Driver installation requires some relatively easy steps. Typically, you insert the diskette into the computer's A drive and run the programs on it, following

FIGURE SW 2-15

Defragmenting a hard disk.

FIGURE SW 2-16

Backing up a hard disk on tape.
Most tape backup utilities, like the Colorado Backup program shown here, allow you to back up either the full or partial contents of a hard disk.

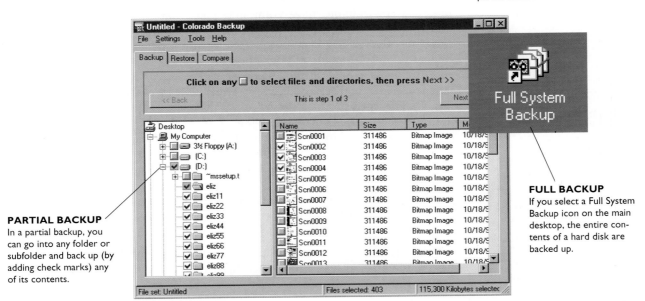

PARTIAL BACKUP
In a partial backup, you can go into any folder or subfolder and back up (by adding check marks) any of its contents.

FULL BACKUP
If you select a Full System Backup icon on the main desktop, the entire contents of a hard disk are backed up.

■ **Device driver.** A utility program that enables an operating system to communicate with a specific hardware device.

For links to further information about utility programs, go to www.harcourtcollege.com/infosys/parker2000/student/explore/ and click on Chapter SW 2.

the instructions printed on the disk label and on the screen. After all the questions are satisfactorily answered, the necessary driver files will be stored on your hard disk, and the equipment will be ready to use.

Newer operating systems are coming equipped with drivers to handle widely used hardware, and both computers and peripheral hardware are now supporting the universal serial bus (USB) standard to make installation even easier. With a true *plug-and-play* operating system, a computer system is able to automatically recognize and work with any device plugged into it. However, installing devices on many computer systems is far from this ideal.

LANGUAGE TRANSLATORS

As mentioned in an earlier chapter, computers can execute programs only in the form of instructions stated in machine language. Programmers write instructions in other, easier-to-code languages, however, so something must translate the programmer's statements into machine language. A **language translator** is a systems software program that converts the programmer's applications program into machine language. For example, if you create a program in the BASIC or COBOL programming languages, you cannot run it on a computer until you summon the proper translator to restate your commands in machine language.

Three common types of language translators are compilers, interpreters, and assemblers. Each one performs translations in its own way.

Compilers   A **compiler** translates an entire program into machine language before executing it. Every compiler-oriented language requires its own special compiler. For instance, a COBOL program needs a COBOL compiler; it cannot run using a BASIC compiler.

The collection of program statements that you write and enter in the computer is called a *source module*. The compiler then produces a machine-level equivalent of your program called an *object module*.

Normally, before the object module actually begins execution, it combines with other object modules that the CPU may need in order to process the program. For example, most computers can't compute square roots directly. To do so, they rely on small object modules held in secondary storage. If your program calls for a square root calculation, the operating system temporarily binds the object module of your program together with a copy of the square root routine. The binding process is referred to as *linkage editing,* or the *link-edit stage;* this activity produces an executable package called a *load module*. Systems software includes a special program called a *linkage editor* that automatically carries out this binding.

The computer actually executes or runs the load module. When your program is ready to run, it has reached the *Go (execution) stage*. Figure SW 2-17 shows the complete process from compiling to linkage editing to execution. You can save both object and load modules on disk for later use to avoid repeating the compilation and linkage editing every time you want to execute the program. Filenames for object and load modules often carry the extensions .obj and .exe, respectively.

Interpreters   An **interpreter** translates programming language statements in a different way than a compiler. Rather than creating a complete object

---

■ **Language translator.** Systems software that converts applications programs into machine language. ■ **Compiler.** A language translator that converts an entire program into machine language before executing it. ■ **Interpreter.** A language translator that converts program statements line by line into machine language, immediately executing each one.

module for a program, an interpreter reads, translates, and executes the source program one line at a time. It performs the translation into machine language while the program runs.

Interpreters offer both advantages and disadvantages compared with compilers. Two major advantages are that interpreters are easier to use, and—because the execution usually stops at the point where an error is encountered—they help programmers to discover errors in programs easily. The interpreter program itself requires relatively little storage space, and it does not generate an object module to occupy still more storage space. For these reasons, interpreters provide ideal tools for beginning programmers and nonprogrammers.

The major disadvantage of interpreters is that they work less efficiently than compilers do, so interpreted programs run more slowly than compiled programs. Because an interpreter translates each program statement into machine language just before executing it, it can chew up a lot of time—especially when the program must repeatedly execute the same statements thousands of times, reinterpreting each one every time. In contrast, a compiler translates each program statement only once—before program execution begins. In addition, by storing the object module of a compiled program on disk, the programmer can avoid the need to retranslate the source program every time the program runs.

Some programming-language packages include both interpreter and compiler software, giving the programmer the best of both worlds. He or she can work with the interpreter to root out program errors and then compile the error-free program, saving and running it in object-module form.

Assemblers The third type of language translator, an **assembler,** converts only assembly language statements into machine language. *Assembly languages* are used almost exclusively by professional programmers to write efficient programming code. An assembler works like a compiler, producing a stored object module. A computer system typically operates only one assembly language; thus, only one assembler is required.

Users of any language-translator program should recognize the difference between it and the programming language it translates. A programming language is a set of rules for coding program commands, whereas a language translator is a systems software program that translates code written under the rules into the bits and bytes that the computer understands.

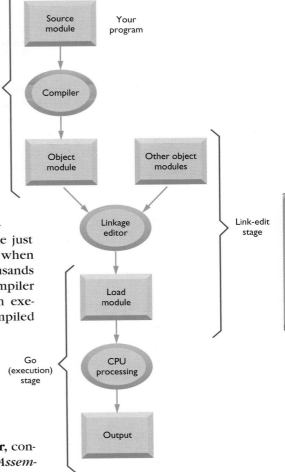

FIGURE SW 2-17

Compile, link edit, go. A compiler and linkage editor convert a source module into a load module for processing by the CPU.

SUMMARY AND KEY TERMS

Go to the Online Glossary at www.harcourtcollege.com/infosys/parker2000/ student/ to review key terms.

Systems software consists of the programs that coordinate the activities in various parts of the computer system to promote rapid and efficient operation. The basic role of systems software is to act as a mediator between applications programs and the computer system's hardware.

■ **Assembler.** A language translator that converts assembly language instructions into machine language.

The Operating System A computer's **operating system** is the main collection of systems-software programs that manage the computer system's resources. The functions of the operating system include communicating with the user, making computer-system resources available for use, scheduling jobs for processing, monitoring activities, housekeeping, and security.

As soon as the user enters keystrokes or clicks a mouse, the operating system summons a translator to convert this input into machine-language commands. In the absence of instructions from the user, the operating system implements assumptions called **defaults.**

To interact effectively with your operating system, you must recognize certain conventions. Every operating system maintains its own rules for naming files, adding **file extensions,** and grouping files into directories or folders, among other things. Systematic naming of filenames and extensions help computer users to keep track of a file's contents. **Wildcard characters** help users to perform copying, moving, and deleting operations.

When you turn on power to the computer, the operating system **boots** up. During the boot procedure, the operating system checks for hardware devices online, verifies the presence of files that tell it how to deal with those hardware devices, and does a number of other setup chores before the user begins the current session.

To manage the enormous collection of files on a hard disk, the operating system commonly allows the user to organize files hierarchically into **directories.** To access a file in any directory, the user must specify the **path** that leads through intervening directories to the file. In many desktop operating systems, *files* and *directories* are respectively referred to as *documents* and *folders*.

Computers often enhance efficiency by implementing interleaved processing techniques. **Multiprogramming** allows a multiuser computer system to work concurrently on several programs from several users. **Multitasking** allows concurrent execution of two or more programs from any single user as well as concurrent execution of two or more tasks performed by a single program. **Time-sharing** is a technique in which the operating system cycles through all active programs currently running in the system that need processing, giving a small slice of time on each cycle to each one. **Virtual memory** employs disk storage to extend conventional memory. **Multiprocessing** links together two or more computers to perform work at the same time. **Spooling programs** free the CPU from time-consuming interaction with I/O devices such as printers.

Personal Operating Systems Some of today's most widely used personal operating systems include MS-DOS and PC-DOS (with or without Windows 3.x), Windows 95 and Windows 98, and Mac OS.

MS-DOS and **PC-DOS** are commonly found on older PC-compatible microcomputers and similar devices. DOS—the abbreviated name for these operating systems—is one of the most widely used software packages ever developed. Today, many DOS users of past years prefer the Windows user interface. Rather than a separate operating system, **Windows 3.x** adds a GUI shell to DOS that replaces its command line with a system of menus, icons, and screen boxes called *windows*. **Windows 95** and **Windows 98,** both successors to Windows 3.x, are 32-bit operating systems that free the user from the limitations of working with DOS. *Windows CE* is a compact version of Windows that runs on portable devices.

Mac OS is the operating system native to the Apple Macintosh line of computers.

Network Operating Systems Network operating systems (NOSs) are so named because their main purpose is serving several users working over a computer network. **Unix** is a flexible, general-purpose operating system that works on mainframes, midrange computers, PCs that act as network servers, graphics workstations, and even the desktop PCs of ordinary users. **NetWare** is an operating system specifically designed to manage the activities of server computers on local area networks (LANs). **Windows NT**—the most recent versions of which go by the name **Windows 2000**—is a general-purpose operating system widely found in the corporate world. It runs mostly on desktop computers in local area networks.

Utility Programs   A **utility program** is a type of systems software program written to perform repetitive processing tasks. There are many types of utility programs. **Disk utility** routines extend the operating system's disk-management capabilities, enabling users to recover erased files, perform **data compression**, reorganize disk data for fast access, and back up data, among other things. **Device drivers** act as interfaces between operating systems and specific hardware devices.

Language Translators   A **language translator** is a systems software program that converts into machine language an applications program written in a higher-level language. There are three common types of language translators: compilers, interpreters, and assemblers.

   A **compiler** translates a program entirely into machine language before preparing it for execution. An **interpreter** reads, translates, and executes source programs one line at a time. The translation into machine language occurs while the program runs. The third type of translator, an **assembler**, works like a compiler, but it converts only assembly language programs.

EXERCISES

1. Fill in the blanks:
   a. In a multiuser computer system with _____, the computer works on several users' programs concurrently, leaving one idle at some logical stopping point to begin work on another.
   b. _____ is a technique with cooperative and preemptive varieties.
   c. A(n) _____ is an assumption that a computer program makes when the user has indicated no specific choice.
   d. _____ programs are systems software written to perform standard processing tasks, such as sorting and copying data.
   e. Loading the operating system into RAM is known as _____ up the operating system.

2. Define the following terms in your own words:
   a. Data compression
   b. Multitasking
   c. Time-sharing
   d. Virtual memory
   e. Multiprocessing

3. Identify the operating system or operating environment, covered in the chapter, that is described in each sentence:
   a. Windows 3.x provides a graphical user interface for it.
   b. Microsoft designed it to run in organizations, on both office-desktop machines and the network administrator's workstation.
   c. It was originally developed at Bell Labs about 30 years ago.
   d. This product by Novell is designed to manage local area networks (LANs).
   e. While this Microsoft product cannot provide multithreading, it does allow cooperative multitasking.

4. Define the following terms in your own words:
   a. Path
   b. Directory
   c. File extension
   d. Fault-tolerant computing
   e. Wildcard character

5. Match each term with the description that fits best:
   a. Device driver
   b. Compiler
   c. Disk utility
   d. Spooling software
   e. Interpreter
   f. Operating system

   _____ A language translator that reads, translates, and executes source programs a line at a time

   _____ A program that temporarily saves output on disk and then sends it on to the printer as needed

   _____ A program that enables an operating system to work with a specific hardware device

   _____ A data-compression program is an example

   _____ A collection of systems software without which a computer cannot function

   _____ A language translator that creates an object module

6. Describe, in your own words, the differences between the following terms:
   a. Multiprogramming and multiprocessing
   b. Cooperative multitasking and preemptive multitasking
   c. Compiler and interpreter
   d. Segmentation and paging
   e. Coprocessing and parallel processing

7. Explain what happens to a disk when it becomes fragmented. Also, describe what happens when a fragmented disk is defragmented.

8. In what ways does Windows 98 improve on Windows 95?

9. Which of these files would be copied from one disk to another in response to a COPY command with each set of wildcard characters?

MARY	CH01	CH05	FILE3
MAX	CH02	WAV	MMX
MARTY	CH03	TAXES	X23.WAV

   a. MA* c. AX.* e. CH* g. *.WAV
   b. M*   d. *.*   f. *3   h. *X

10. Fill in the blanks:
   a. _____ is a simplified form of parallel processing that splits up tasks on multiple processors running the same operating system.
   b. Windows NT/2000 comes in two principal versions: a(n) _____ or Professional edition, for ordinary users, and a(n) _____ family, for network administrators.
   c. An input spooling area is sometimes called a(n) _____.
   d. Microsoft's operating system for handheld computers is called _____.
   e. In network operating systems, a user's _____ specify the types of tasks that the user is authorized to carry out.

PROJECTS

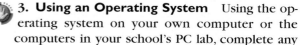

1. **Windows**   Two up-to-date forms of Windows enjoy large user bases today: Windows 98 and Windows 2000 Professional. Research these two operating systems and answer the following questions:
   a. In what major ways are these two operating systems alike? In what major ways are they different?
   b. What is the street or list price of Windows 98? Windows 2000 Professional?
   c. How much RAM does a PC need to run Windows 98? Windows 2000 Professional?

2. **The Operating System at Your School**   Gather the following information about the operating system that runs your school's PC lab:
   a. Find out the name of the operating system, the name of the company that makes it, and the version your class uses. You should be able to find out the version number from the operating system itself by clicking on a menu choice or typing a command.

   b. Which of the following capabilities does the operating system support?
      Multithreading
      Symmetric multiprocessing
      Virtual memory
      Spooling
      Preemptive multitasking
      Multiple users
   c. How much disk storage does the operating system use up?

3. **Using an Operating System**   Using the operating system on your own computer or the computers in your school's PC lab, complete any ten of the following tasks:
   a. Open a file.
   b. Close a file.
   c. Format a diskette.
   d. Copy a file from the hard disk to a diskette.
   e. Make a duplicate copy of a diskette.

f. Rename a file.
g. Create a new folder.
h. Delete a document.
i. Restore a deleted document.
j. View the contents of the hard disk.
k. Access the online help feature.
l. Find all files with a certain extension.

4. **Compression Problems**   Answer the following questions about compression ratios, which were covered in Feature SW 2-3. For simplicity, assume that a megabyte is exactly 1,000 KB.
   a. A software package offers a compression ratio of 150:1. How much space will a 50-MB file consume after compression?
   b. If a 10-MB file compresses to 100 KB, what's the compression ratio?
   c. A software package offers compression ratios that range from 10:1 to 200:1. What's the smallest compressed size of a 5-MB file?

5. **Utility Software**   Look through computer journals or consult the Internet to identify at least one independent software product in each of the listed categories. Besides giving the name of each product, also name the company that sells it, and state its list or street price. In addition, write a sentence or two describing the capabilities of the product.
   a. Desktop enhancer
   b. Uninstaller
   c. Antivirus
   d. File viewer
   e. Memory manager

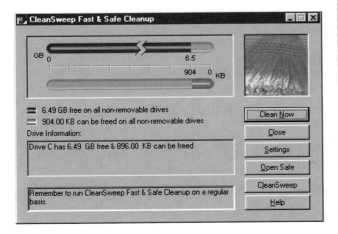

6. **Backup**   Many operating systems include built-in routines for backing up hard disks. For any one of the following—DOS, Windows 3.1, Windows 95, Windows 98, Windows NT/2000, or Mac OS— answer the following questions:
   a. How can you access the backup feature?
   b. How does the backup feature work?
   c. On what types of storage media can you store backup copies? Does the operating system impose any limitations on the amount of hard-disk storage you can back up?
   d. Identify at least one utility software product sold by a third-party vendor with backup capabilities comparable to or better than those of your operating system. Provide the name of the product's vendor and the product's approximate street price.

7. **Microsoft Corporation I**   Microsoft Corporation—like IBM and many other prominent companies in the history of business—has stirred strong opinions among many people about its practices. Write position statements a paragraph or two in length on each of the following:
   a. Some observers have suggested that Microsoft can determine the future direction of desktop PC software better than any other company, because it easily leads the market in sales of both applications and systems PC software. Comment on this statement.
   b. Some people have criticized Microsoft's dominance in systems software as an unfair advantage in the market for applications software. Comment on this statement from three separate viewpoints: as a competitor to Microsoft, as a consumer and user of desktop software, and as a representative of the federal government charged with protecting the public interest. As you take the government's viewpoint, be sure to define your notion of the public interest.

8. **Microsoft Corporation II**   In 1998, the U.S. Department of Justice began proceedings against Microsoft Corporation for unfair business practices. Included among the issues being looked into by the Feds was integrating the Internet Explorer Web browser into the Windows operating system.
   a. Identify the core issues at the heart of this Justice Department's objection.
   b. Take a stand. Who do you side with—Microsoft or the Justice Department—and why?

9. **Microsoft Corporation III**   Microsoft Corporation began in a humble fashion in the 1970s, as a small company making language compilers for PCs. In the early 1980s it produced DOS—its flagship product for many years—and success snowballed from there. Microsoft branched from systems software into application software, and soon thereafter into a variety of other ventures—communications, travel, auto sales, and television broadcasting, to name just a few. Microsoft spends more than $2.5 billion a year on product development, which is more than the combined annual profits of several of its closest competitors.

For this project, write a five-to-eight-page paper describing the many business activities in which Microsoft is involved. Try to be as specific as possible. In other words, break down each category of business as closely as you can and provide examples—for instance, operating systems (Windows 98 and Windows 2000), productivity software (Office 2000), and so on.

10. Researching an Operating System Information about major operating systems is widely available on the Internet and can be collected by visiting the sites of software publishers, user groups, and people who have an interest in this type of systems software. You easily can find such sites if you know the name of an operating system's publisher or if you type the name of the operating system into a Web-based search engine like Yahoo! or Alta Vista. For this project, choose an operating system—say, one from the list in Figure SW 2-2. Then, prepare a short report (not exceeding five pages) describing such important matters as the operating system's origin or history, user base, main features, hardware requirements, future direction, and the like. Your report should go well beyond the coverage of the operating system in the chapter. Be sure to state the sources of your information and be sure to double-check any facts coming from online sources that you think may be unreliable.

11. Apple Computer: What Could Have Been Not too many years ago, before the world even heard of Microsoft Windows, close to one out of every five computers sold was made by Apple. Throughout most of the 1980s, the Apple Macintosh graphical user interface (GUI) was virtually without peer. It won a loyal following of users, while those using PC-compatibles were stuck with non-GUI DOS. By the late 1990s, however, Apple's share of the PC market was down to less than 5 percent and close to 90 percent of all PCs used Windows. What went wrong for Apple? Since 1998, Apple has been staging a comeback. Do you think it will ever be able to recapture the market share it lost?

12. Linux In recent years, enthusiasm has been mounting for Linux, a version of the Unix operating system available as freeware on the Web or on CD-ROM from a number of vendors for about $50. Linux was created in the early 1990s by Linus Torvalds, a Finnish developer who released the program to the public domain. There, it continues to be upgraded by volunteers worldwide. Use your local library or the Internet to determine the following:

a. Why has Linux been gathering such a faithful following?

b. Does Linux pose a threat to mainstream proprietary operating systems like Windows?

c. Name at least three free useful software programs available for Linux.

INTERACTIVE EXERCISE

USING YOUR NEW PC

Your new PC is up and running—now it's time to try it out. Go to the Interactive Exercise at www.harcourtcollege.com/infosys/parker2000/student/exercise/ to complete this exercise.

ONLINE REVIEW

Go to the Online Review at www.harcourtcollege.com/infosys/parker2000/student/ to test your understanding of this chapter's concepts.

Computer networks play a critical role in society and business today. Without computer networks, it would be impossible for us to enjoy many of the modern conveniences upon which we have come to depend or for most businesses to compete effectively.

Chapter NET 1 introduces principles of telecommunications and networks. Here you will learn about many of the hardware, software, and communications-media products used to build networks as well as common types of networks and transmission methods.

The Internet and its World Wide Web are covered in Chapter NET 2. We will look in turn at the components that comprise the Internet, how addresses on the Internet work, Web browsers and their support tools, and choosing among the alternatives available for getting online.

In Chapter NET 3 you will be introduced to some of the principles behind creating Web pages. Advances in software are making it easier and easier for ordinary people to develop their own presence on the Internet. It is conceivable that someday in the not-too-distant future creating a personal Web site will be a task expected of most business professionals.

MODULE CONTENTS
Computer Networks

NET I

COMMUNICATIONS AND NETWORKS

LEARNING OBJECTIVES

After completing this chapter, you will be able to:

1. Describe several uses of telecommunications technology.

2. Appreciate the changing nature of the telecommunications industry and the effects of government legislation.

3. Name various types of communications media and explain how they carry messages.

4. Identify the hardware, software, and procedural components that link telecommunications systems.

5. Describe several types of local networks and how they work.

6. Explain how users transmit data over wide area networks.

7. Identify some of the dangers posed by computer networks.

OVERVIEW

Telecommunications, or *telecom,* refers to communications over a distance—over long-distance phone lines, privately owned cables, or satellites, for instance. Telecommunications has both extended the usefulness of the computer in the workplace and boosted its popularity as a fixture in the home.

In business, telecommunications has become an integral part of operations through the years. Businesspeople throughout the world regularly use electronic mail and messaging systems to communicate with fellow employees and distant associates. Documents that companies once maintained in dog-eared file folders and hand delivered from person to person now zip along at electronic speeds from one desktop computer to another at the press of a button. Ordering and shipping systems depend on computers that regularly touch base with other computers miles away, thereby ensuring on-time deliveries and keeping customers informed. The list of applications is virtually endless.

In the home, the biggest telecom happening in recent years has been the whirlwind popularity of the Internet and World Wide Web. Almost overnight, the desktop computer has evolved into a vehicle through which people communicate with faraway friends and seek useful facts at online sites. Information on virtually any topic, stored on computers located almost anywhere on the globe, can be retrieved within seconds. With telecom companies scrambling to bring faster transmissions into the home and with the Internet evolving to deliver new forms of business services and entertainment, many industry experts predict that the best is yet to come.

In Chapter NET 1, we look first at several critical business applications of telecommunications. Next, we profile the telecommunications industry and discuss how government legislation has shaped its growth. Then, we touch on a number of technical issues, including the various ways in which computers transmit data and how networked devices connect to one another. From there, we proceed to the two major types of networks: local networks and wide area networks. The chapter closes with coverage of some of the dangers posed by computer networks. The Internet is treated in depth in Chapters NET 2 and NET 3.

TELECOMMUNICATIONS APPLICATIONS

Today, a wide variety of important business applications involve telecommunications, and the roster of uses is growing rapidly.

ELECTRONIC MAIL AND MESSAGING

One of the biggest applications for telecommunications today is electronic mail and messaging. Several technologies play key roles.

Electronic Mail   **Electronic mail,** or **e-mail,** is an application in which users employ software known as *e-mail programs* to exchange electronic messages. The user often composes a message within such a program at a desktop PC and then sends it over long-distance wires or interoffice cables by clicking a Send button. The software deposits the message in an electronic mailbox maintained by the receiver's network, where it can be retrieved and read at a convenient

For a tutorial on the uses of telecommunications and networks, go to www. harcourtcollege.com/infosys/ parker2000/student/tutor/ and click on Chapter NET 1.

■ **Telecommunications.** Transmission of data over a distance. ■ **Electronic mail.** The computer-to-computer counterpart for interoffice mail or the postal service. Also called **e-mail.**

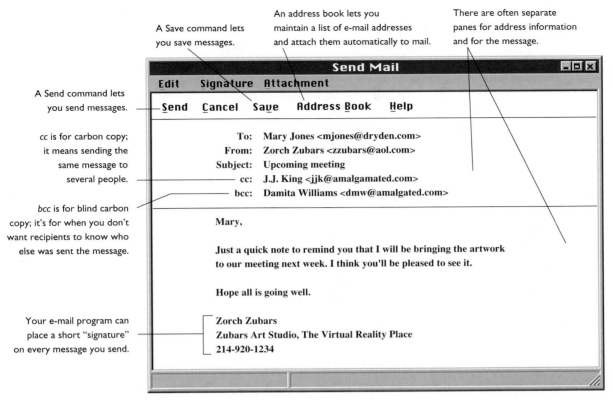

A Save command lets you save messages.

An address book lets you maintain a list of e-mail addresses and attach them automatically to mail.

There are often separate panes for address information and for the message.

A Send command lets you send messages.

cc is for carbon copy; it means sending the same message to several people.

bcc is for blind carbon copy; it's for when you don't want recipients to know who else was sent the message.

Your e-mail program can place a short "signature" on every message you send.

Send Mail

Edit   Signature   Attachment

Send   Cancel   Save   Address Book   Help

To: Mary Jones <mjones@dryden.com>
From: Zorch Zubars <zzubars@aol.com>
Subject: Upcoming meeting
cc: J.J. King <jjk@amalgamated.com>
bcc: Damita Williams <dmw@amalgated.com>

Mary,

Just a quick note to remind you that I will be bringing the artwork to our meeting next week. I think you'll be pleased to see it.

Hope all is going well.

Zorch Zubars
Zubars Art Studio, The Virtual Reality Place
214-920-1234

FIGURE NET 1-1

Electronic mail.

time. **Electronic mailboxes** are the computer equivalents of traditional mailboxes. They represent space on some computer's hard disk set aside to store e-mail messages. Figure NET 1-1 shows briefly how using e-mail software works. E-mail will be covered in greater depth in the next chapter, NET 2.

Voice Mail   **Voice mail** is a telecommunications technology that takes electronic mailboxes one step further. A voice-mail system digitizes the sender's spoken message and stores it in bit form on an answering device at the receiver's location. When the receiver presses a Listen key, the digitized message is reconverted to voice data.

Bulletin Boards   Unlike an electronic mailbox, which restricts access to an area on disk to only a single individual, an electronic **bulletin board system (BBS)** sets up an area to which several people have access. Functionally, BBSs work like the bulletin boards at supermarkets or health-foods stores—people post notices that may interest others, any of whom may respond. Typically, a single computer bulletin board focuses on a particular interest area. For instance, a company may set up one bulletin board for employees to post computer-related questions and another for customers to ask questions about particular products, while a bulletin board set up by a college professor may encourage members of a class to share ideas about projects or assignments. Bulletin boards are also commonly called *newsgroups* or *discussion groups.*

Facsimile   **Facsimile,** or **fax,** technology resembles e-mail, except it employs different methods and it can be more convenient or less convenient for certain types of uses (see Figure NET 1-2).

■ **Electronic mailbox.** A storage area on a hard disk that holds messages, memos, and other documents for the receiver. ■ **Voice mail.** An electronic mail system that digitally records spoken phone messages and stores them in an electronic mailbox. ■ **Bulletin board system (BBS).** A computer file shared by several people that enables them to post or broadcast messages. ■ **Facsimile.** A method for transmitting text documents, pictures, maps, diagrams, and the like over the phone lines. Abbreviated as **fax.**

FAX MACHINES
Facsimile (fax) machines make it possible for hard-copy images of documents to be sent from one location to another over ordinary phone lines.

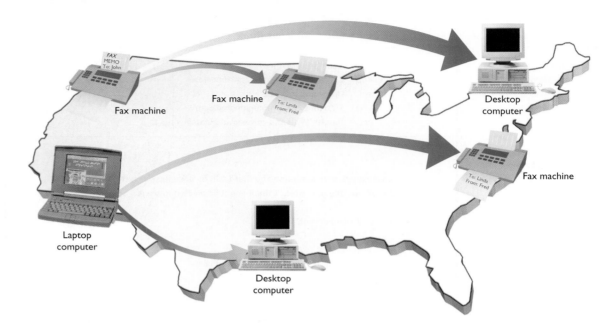

Fax machine

Fax machine

To: Linda From: Fred

Desktop computer

Fax machine

To: Linda From: Fred

Laptop computer

Desktop computer

FIGURE NET 1-2

Faxing.

FAX MODEMS
Fax modems and fax software make it possible for PCs to communicate with both fax machines and other PCs with faxing capabilities.

FIGURE NET 1-3

Paging. Pagers are carried by people on the move. Close to 50 million people use pagers in the United States alone.

Facsimile (fax) machines allow users to send images of hard-copy documents from one location to another over ordinary phone lines. For example, a secretary in Seattle may place a short document containing both text and pictures into a fax machine like the one in Figure NET 1-2. The fax machine digitizes the page images and transmits the resulting data over the phone lines to Chicago and Boston. In Chicago, another fax machine receives the electronic page images and reproduces them in hard-copy form. In Boston, a PC's hard disk picks up the fax image in soft-copy form for later viewing on a display screen. All of this data exchange may take place in less than a minute.

PCs need *fax modems* and *fax software* to communicate with both fax machines and other computers with faxing capabilities (return to Figure NET 1-2). Computer-to-computer faxing brings certain advantages, including saving paper, preventing time lost waiting in line for the office fax machine, and allowing recipients to electronically save and modify faxed documents and to route them elsewhere.

Faxing capabilities are often integrated with other mail and messaging technologies. For instance, e-mail-to-fax software lets users turn their e-mail messages into faxes, and free *e-faxing* services are available on the Internet to allow a person to receive faxes as e-mail messages.

Paging Through a pocket-sized, wireless device called a *pager,* someone can send short messages to another person who is on the move, even across the world (see Figure NET 1-3). Pagers provide either send-only or send-and-receive capabilities, and they often communicate over special wireless networks. Many newer pagers will also let users exchange e-mail messages with anyone having an e-mail connection—including other pager users. About 50 million people use pagers in the United States alone, and that number is growing.

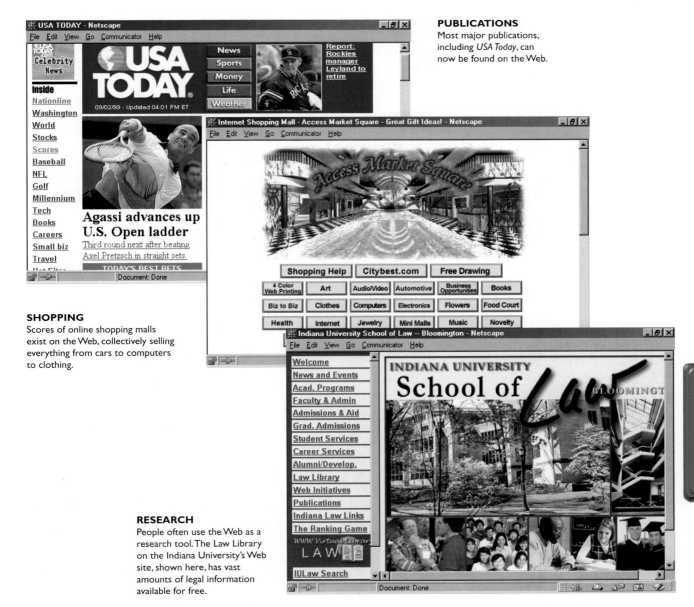

PUBLICATIONS
Most major publications, including *USA Today*, can now be found on the Web.

SHOPPING
Scores of online shopping malls exist on the Web, collectively selling everything from cars to computers to clothing.

RESEARCH
People often use the Web as a research tool. The Law Library on the Indiana University's Web site, shown here, has vast amounts of legal information available for free.

INFORMATION RETRIEVAL AND THE WEB

FIGURE NET I-4

The Internet's World Wide Web. One of the most popular features of the Internet is the World Wide Web, which brings virtually any sort of information anyone could imagine to a computer's display screen in the form of easy-to-read pages.

The assortment of information you can get over ordinary phone lines today is, in a word, amazing. Thousands of public and private databases are currently available for online *information retrieval,* many over the Internet's World Wide Web.

The **Internet** (named as a contraction of the two words *inter*connected *net*works) is a global "network of networks." It links thousands of networks and millions of individual users, businesses, schools, government agencies, and other organizations. It is a favorite source of information today because its resources include a vast storehouse of facts that people can easily obtain. The Internet's *World Wide Web*, or "Web," is widely used by individuals to access news and weather, financial, travel, entertainment, and shopping information (see Figure NET 1-4). The Internet is also used for e-mail and for a variety of other applications.

■ **The Internet.** A global network linking thousands of networks and millions of individual users, schools, businesses, and government agencies.

Individuals access the Internet through a company known as an *Internet service provider (ISP),* sometimes also called a *service provider* or an *access provider* for short. Today's most widely used ISP is America Online (AOL), featured in Figure NET 1-5. Other ISPs with a strong national following are the Microsoft Network (MSN), CompuServe (owned by AOL), Prodigy, EarthLink, and MCI WorldCom. In addition, there are thousands of small local ISPs located in cities and towns throughout the United States, serving local audiences with local or toll-free telephone numbers and possibly faster lines or better service than the bigger providers.

Most ISPs charge individuals between $15 and $25 per month for Internet access. People can bypass signing up with their own service provider by getting access to the Internet through their school, employer, or local library.

We will be covering the Internet in depth in Chapter NET 2.

COLLABORATIVE COMPUTING

In addition to ordinary electronic mail and messaging, modern communications technology and the Internet enable geographically scattered workers to collaborate in their work tasks in other, more sophisticated ways. Three such uses of technology are briefly covered here: workgroup computing, teleconferencing, and telecommuting (see Figure NET 1-6).

Workgroup Computing   **Workgroup computing** allows several people to use their desktop workstations to collaborate in their job tasks, without ever leaving their offices. The insurance industry provides a good example. Years ago, clerks would have processed an accident claim by filling out forms by hand and manually walking file folders around from desk to desk for approvals and signatures. Today, such claims are processed electronically with special *workgroup-computing software,* or *groupware* as it is more commonly

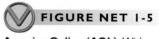

FIGURE NET 1-5

America Online (AOL). With millions of subscribers, AOL is the world's biggest Internet service provider.

■ **Workgroup computing.** Several people using desktop workstations to collaborate in their job tasks.

OFFICE AT WORK
At a company work site, employees can meet with coworkers without ever leaving their offices by teleconferencing, by using e-mail, or by using workgroup software that lets them share documents.

HOME OFFICE
Through the Internet, you can complete many tasks at home as easily as you could in the office. What's more, with no commute, you have the freedom to live almost anywhere you would like.

MOBILE OFFICE
Telecommunications hardware and software is near the point where workers can keep in touch by satellite almost anywhere on the globe.

FIGURE NET 1-6

Collaborative computing in the twenty-first century. Computer networks enable people to work where they wish and to collaborate on tasks without having to get together physically in a single place, at the same time.

known. The software generates electronic forms and displays them as necessary so workers can fill them in with data, review their work, and approve payment at desktop computer workstations. The software can automatically route and monitor the progress of forms as well. Consequently, insurers can process claims more rapidly and reliably and with far fewer errors than they could before groupware was available. Better service is often provided too, since an adjuster can give claimants progress reports after pressing only a few keystrokes. Alternatively, claimants can get reports themselves over the Internet.

Groupware is getting attention wherever people need to collaborate on their jobs. Engineers and architects commonly use groupware to collaborate on designs, newspapers use it to circulate pieces among writers and editors, and so on.

Teleconferencing   **Teleconferencing** refers to the use of computer and communications technology to conduct meetings between people in different locations. Such meetings may take place via sophisticated computer-messaging techniques, through video technology that lets people see and hear each other, and by a number of other means. For instance, using relatively inexpensive *videoconferencing* software and hardware, people in contact by computer can see and hear each other on their PCs. Or workers can engage in a virtual conference at their PC workstations by using *conferencing software* that organizes comments typed during online discussions.

Telecommuting   **Telecommuting** refers to people working at home and being connected to their employers through such means as the Internet and a modem, fax machines, personal computers, and pagers. With such tools, the employee can tap into e-mail at work, access database information and presentation materials when making on-site pitches to clients, and get in touch with callers almost immediately while on the road. Telecommuting enables a company to save on office and parking space and offers an employee considerable freedom in choosing to work when, and where, he or she wishes to work.

Both telecommuting and teleconferencing are covered in greater depth in versions of this book with an IS module.

TRANSACTION PROCESSING

Transaction-processing operations such as entering orders and handling accounts receivable are the lifeblood of most companies. Pull the plug on the computers doing these tasks, and the companies go out of business.

At one time, transaction-processing operations were totally centralized. As communications systems allowed firms to distribute workloads to multiple sites, many organizations modified their transaction-processing systems accordingly.

The airlines' passenger reservation systems offer a noteworthy example; thousands of ticketing agents located across the globe use display workstations to tap into distant computerized databases full of flight, hotel, and rental-car information. While a computer in, say, Chicago is gathering flight information for an agent in Cerritos, California, that same agent may be completing local processing of a ticket for another client. Credit-card systems, such as the one for VISA illustrated in Figure NET 1-7, are also good examples of distributed transaction processing. Once a store clerk inserts a credit card into a verification terminal, computers thousands of miles away approve or deny the purchase. Today with the Internet, transaction-processing systems are more distributed than ever, as ordinary people can book flights and pay by credit card from their home PCs and bypass "middleman" companies entirely.

Virtually every large organization today maintains several types of distributed transaction-processing systems. For instance, chain stores often collect and process data locally and then transmit these data to headquarters sites for timely analysis. Mail-order firms frequently process orders at central sites and then transmit transaction data to warehouse sites to initiate packing and delivery. The applications are countless.

Interorganizational Systems   Many companies have extended their distributed transaction-processing systems a step further by creating *interorganizational systems (IOSs),* which strategically link their computers to the computers of key customers or suppliers. For instance, the major automakers

---

■ **Teleconferencing.** Using computer and communications technology to carry on a meeting between people in different locations. ■ **Telecommuting.** Working through one's home and being connected by means of electronic devices to co-workers at remote locations.

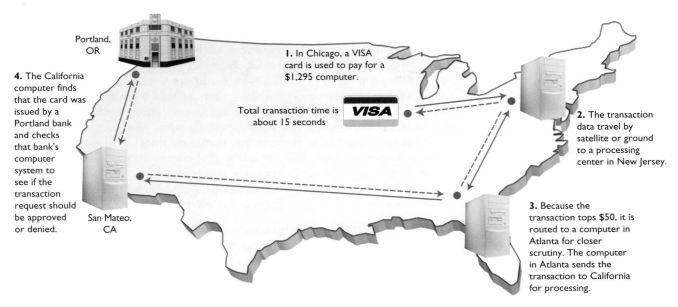

Portland, OR

1. In Chicago, a VISA card is used to pay for a $1,295 computer.

4. The California computer finds that the card was issued by a Portland bank and checks that bank's computer system to see if the transaction request should be approved or denied.

Total transaction time is about 15 seconds

2. The transaction data travel by satellite or ground to a processing center in New Jersey.

3. Because the transaction tops $50, it is routed to a computer in Atlanta for closer scrutiny. The computer in Atlanta sends the transaction to California for processing.

San Mateo, CA

FIGURE NET 1-7

Trailing a VISA transaction. In a routine transaction, the response retraces the same path as the query back to the originating store. Total elapsed time for a typical transaction is approximately 15 seconds.

constantly monitor their suppliers' computer systems via internal computers to ensure proper inventory levels for critical parts. They also use the IOSs to shop electronically for the best prices.

Another common type of interorganizational system, **electronic data interchange (EDI),** facilitates the exchange of standard business documents—such as purchase orders and invoices—from one company's computer system to the system of another company. What's more, the company doing the purchasing often uses EDI to electronically track its order's progress on the seller's computer system. Many large companies today order sizable percentages of their supplies or raw materials through EDI.

Some firms use modern communications technology to take EDI a step further. At such giant companies as General Motors and DuPont, large suppliers of key items no longer even have to wait for purchase orders. When the suppliers see low stocks of materials on General Motors' or DuPont's computers, they automatically ship the goods and send electronic invoices.

THE TELECOMMUNICATIONS INDUSTRY

Here, we look at the types of firms that make up the telecommunications industry. We also consider the role government plays in shaping that industry's future.

THE MAJOR PLAYERS

At one time, the telecommunications industry was synonymous with the phone company. While phone companies are still a major part of the telecommunications scene, these days many more players participate as well.

Phone Companies The phone companies own the mammoth telephone network that can connect virtually any two points on the globe. These companies not only provide regular phone service, but they also transmit data

---

■ **Electronic data interchange (EDI).** A computer procedure that enables firms to electronically exchange standard business documents such as purchase orders and invoices.

between businesses and handle most of the traffic on the Internet. Traditional —or "regular"—phone companies are of two types—long-distance carriers and regional Bell operating companies (RBOCs) or "Baby Bells." Two of the biggest long-distance service providers are AT&T and MCI WorldCom; the Baby Bells include such firms as PacTel, Nynex, and Ameritech.

Many of the big phone companies—such as MCI WorldCom, and GTE— provide and maintain the extremely fast, high-capacity, fiber-optic lines that are called *Internet backbones*. The lines are designed to carry data at very high speeds between regions of the country. Backbone lines are used by Internet service providers to route Internet traffic that comes in over ordinary phone lines or special cables from home users and businesses.

In addition to the regular phone companies, many firms—such as AirTouch Cellular—operate cellular-phone networks for people using cellular phones.

Cable-TV and Satellite Companies   At one time this industry sector operated almost exclusively to transmit television broadcasts to homes. The situation is dramatically changing. With cable now reaching into most major cities and towns, and with satellite dishes serving outlying areas, companies in this sector—such as TCI and Time Warner—are well positioned to use their communications infrastructures to disseminate new information products such as electronic shopping and banking, on-demand television, and Internet services. While cable-TV and satellite firms have powerful transmission capabilities, however, most of their systems are designed for one-way broadcasting, and major overhaul is needed to handle interactive exchanges.

Service and Content Providers   The types of companies discussed thus far collectively own and operate the infrastructure over which information travels. Many of these companies also provide services along this infrastructure— such as phone, Internet, and television services—and are therefore also service providers. But you don't have to own part of the infrastructure to operate a service business. Service providers like America Online, for instance, rent capacity over a communications infrastructure and sell it to users.

America Online also supplies information content to the Internet, such as its own Web site and celebrity forums, so it is therefore also a content provider. The Internet has countless content providers—ranging from such familiar companies as Disney (entertainment content) and CNN (news content) down to ordinary people who post personal information at their own Web sites.

Other Companies   This group includes software companies—like Microsoft, IBM, and Oracle—whose main strength centers on building the necessary computer capabilities into the information products of the future. Will people use a Windows-like interface to control the television sets of tomorrow? Some people think so. Also included in this industry-support group are firms like Cisco Systems and Lucent Technologies, both of which have expertise in the area of supplying communications hardware to the marketplace.

Throughout the entire telecom industry, the current wave of mergers and acquisitions, partnering arrangements, and shakeouts will determine within the next few years who will win and who will lose. Firms that have traditionally operated in one sector are quickly expanding into other sectors to position themselves for success. For instance, a communications infrastructure needs content to deliver, and a content provider needs infrastructure to carry its product. Furthermore, all of this activity requires the development of new software and the construction of new networks. To deliver the information products of the future, companies will have to think beyond their traditional markets and boundaries. Microsoft is one familiar company that's seriously taken a plunge into this uncertain future, for instance, rapidly transforming itself from strictly a software company to also a provider of both Internet access and online content.

GOVERNMENT LEGISLATION

Not too long ago, AT&T was "the" phone company in the United States. It owned essentially all of the phone lines, as well as all of the phones on its lines. The federal government believed that the survival of the phone system depended on protecting the interests of a single provider. The government also tightly regulated both AT&T and practices within its industry.

The wheels of change began to turn in 1968, when the Federal Communications Commission (FCC) produced the *Carterfone Decision,* allowing a small company to connect its own two-way radios to the phone lines. This ruling opened the doors for anyone to buy a non-AT&T phone and hook it up to the AT&T system. Later federal-government rulings forced AT&T to divest its regional phone services—today's Baby Bells—and enabled companies like MCI and Sprint to compete with AT&T for long-distance phone business.

Despite the injection of competition, however, industry regulation was still relatively tight at the end of the 1980s. A license to operate in one sector of the industry often prohibited a company from entering another. Critics of government policy argued that this regulatory model would not serve the public well in the upcoming age of fast-paced technological change. They felt that if government were to tear down barriers to competition, so that companies were free to operate wherever they wanted, consumers would ultimately get better products at lower prices.

Further Exploration

For links to further information about government legislation regarding telecommunications, go to www.harcourtcollege.com/infosys/parker2000/student/explore/ and click on Chapter **NET 1**.

SENDER

As complicated as telecommunications systems may seem, at their simplest level they allow one device to communicate effectively with another.

MESSAGE

The Telecommunications Act of 1996 essentially deregulated the entire telecommunications industry. Consequently, telephone companies, cable-TV and satellite operators, and firms in other segments of the industry are now free to enter each other's markets. If telephone companies can compete unrestricted with cable-TV operators, so the thinking goes, then perhaps the final result will be better television programming and service at lower prices. Similarly unconstrained cable-TV operators might also be able to produce better results with phone service.

Conventional wisdom may or may not prove correct, and you should expect turbulence in the future regulatory environment of the telecommunications industry. Of course, it is not out of the realm of possibility that the government could reverse itself back into a regulatory mode. A change in policy would be most likely if deregulation served to produce monopolistic giants who kept prices high while thwarting industry progress.

RECEIVER

FIGURE NET 1-8

A simple telecommunications system.

TELECOMMUNICATIONS MEDIA

Figure NET 1-8 shows a simple telecommunications system, in which two distant hardware units transfer messages over some type of **communications medium.** The hardware units may be two desktop computers, a desktop computer and a mainframe, or some other combination of two devices. The

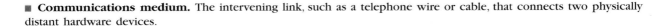

■ **Communications medium.** The intervening link, such as a telephone wire or cable, that connects two physically distant hardware devices.

medium may be a privately operated set of cables or it may consist of public phone lines, microwaves, or some other alternative. When a message is transmitted, one of the hardware units is designated as the *sender* and the other as the *receiver.* The message may be sent over the medium in several ways, as this section will demonstrate.

Communications media fall into one of two classes: wire and wireless media.

For a tutorial on the different types of cabling and other telecommunications media, go to www. harcourtcollege.com/infosys/ parker2000/student/tutor/ and click on Chapter NET 1.

WIRE MEDIA

Telecommunications systems commonly carry messages over three types of wiring: twisted-pair wires, coaxial cable, and fiber optic cable (see Figure NET 1-9).

Twisted-Pair Wires   Twisted-pair wires, in which thin strands of wire are twisted together in sets of two, is the communications medium that has been in use the longest. The telephone system still carries most of the data transmitted in this country and abroad primarily over inexpensive twisted-pair wires. In some cases, several thousand pairs may be bound together into single cables to connect switching stations within a city. By contrast, only a few pairs are needed to connect a home phone to the closest telephone pole.

Coaxial Cable   Coaxial cable, the medium pioneered by the cable television industry, was originally developed to carry high-speed, interference-free video transmissions. Coaxial cable is now also widely used in other types of communication applications, such as linking computers in office networks. Additionally, phone companies rely heavily on coaxial cable.

FIGURE NET 1-9

Wire media. Three types of wiring are commonly used today in telecommunications systems: coaxial cable, twisted-pair wire, and fiber-optic cable.

Fiber-Optic Cable   One of the most successful developments in transmission media in recent years has been fiber optics. **Fiber-optic cables often consist of hundreds of clear glass or plastic fiber strands, each approximately the thickness of a human hair. Transmission requires the transformation of data

COAXIAL CABLE

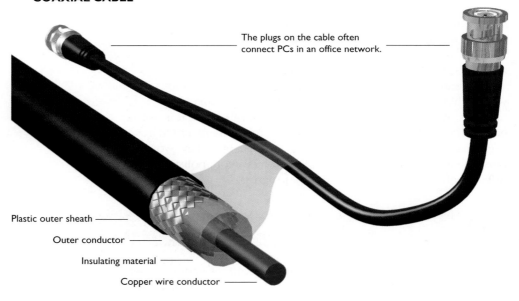

The plugs on the cable often connect PCs in an office network.

Plastic outer sheath

Outer conductor

Insulating material

Copper wire conductor

■ **Twisted-pair wire.** A communications medium consisting of wire strands twisted in sets of two and bound into a cable. ■ **Coaxial cable.** A transmission medium, consisting of a center wire inside a grounded, cylindrical shield, capable of sending data at high speeds. ■ **Fiber-optic cable.** A transmission medium composed of hundreds of hair-thin, transparent fibers along which lasers carry data as light waves.

TWISTED-PAIR WIRES

The plastic connector at this end fits into a standard phone outlet.

Plastic outer sheath

Four twisted-pair wires, with each wire in a plastic insulator

The plastic connector at this end plugs into the back of a PC.

FIBER-OPTIC CABLE

A plastic outer sheath holds the fibers together.

A metal wire gives support to the cable, so the glass or plastic fibers can't bend and break.

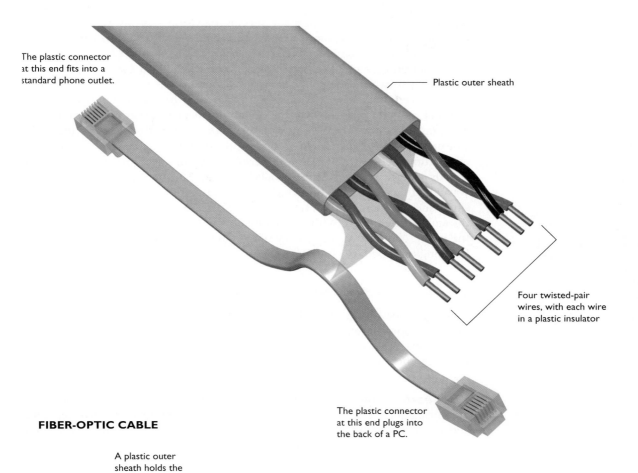

A single fiber

An outer plastic coating protects the fiber inside.

A reflective shield helps channel the light through the fiber.

A fiber consists of a single glass or plastic tube.

into light beams, which are sent through the cable by a laser device at speeds on the order of billions or even trillions of bits per second. Each hairlike fiber has the capacity to carry data for several television stations or thousands of two-way voice conversations. Cables that link big cities often carry several hundred fibers in a single cable.

The advantages of fiber optics over other wire media include speed, size, weight, security, and longevity. In particular, enormous speed differences separate conventional wire and fiber-optic cable. In the few seconds it takes to transmit a single page of Webster's unabridged dictionary over conventional wire, more than a dozen copies of the entire 2,000-plus pages of the work can be transmitted over a single fiber-optic strand.

A stunning new advance in fiber-optic technology may someday yield speeds far greater than those available today. Through a technology called wavelength division multiplexing (WDM), laser devices exist that can now simultaneously transmit multiple color beams—perhaps a hundred or more—through a single fiber. With speeds of up to 200 trillions of bits per second, the entire contents of the Library of Congress can pass through a single fiber in a single second.

WIRELESS MEDIA

Wireless transmission media have become especially popular in recent years. They support communications in situations in which physical wiring is impractical. What's more, the lack of wiring can serve to make devices highly portable. Three widely used media for wireless communications are microwave technology, cellular technology, and infrared technology.

Microwave Technology **Microwaves** are high-frequency radio signals. Text, graphics, audio, and video data can all be converted to microwave impulses and transmitted through the air. Microwave signals can be sent in two ways: via terrestrial stations or by way of satellites (see Figure NET 1-10). Both can transmit data in large quantities and at high speeds.

Terrestrial microwave stations can communicate with each other directly over distances of no more than about 30 miles or so. The stations need not be within actual sight of each other; however, they should have a clear path along which to communicate. To avoid obstacles like mountains and the curvature of the earth, the stations often are placed on tall buildings and mountaintops. When one station receives a message from another, it amplifies it and passes it on to the next station.

Communications satellites were developed to reduce the cost of long-distance transmission via terrestrial microwave repeater stations and to provide a cheaper and better overseas communications medium than undersea cable. Many older satellites maintain *geosynchronous orbits* 22,300 miles above the earth. "Geosynchronous" means that, because the satellites travel at the same speed as the earth's rotation, they appear to remain stationary over a given spot on the globe. Such satellites are so far above the surface of the earth that it takes only three of them to blanket the planet with signals.

Not all satellites travel thousands of miles above the earth. Two relatively new satellite projects that use a low-earth-orbit (LEO) strategy are IRIDIUM and Teledesic. LEO satellites circle the globe at an altitude of less than 500 feet. They are cheaper to build, and, because of their lower orbits, they provide faster message transmission than traditional satellites.

Further Exploration

For links to further information about wire and wireless telecommunications media, go to www.harcourtcollege.com/infosys/parker2000/student/explore/ and click on Chapter NET 1.

■ **Microwave.** An electromagnetic wave in the high-frequency range. ■ **Terrestrial microwave station.** A ground station that receives microwave signals, amplifies them, and passes them on to another station. ■ **Communications satellite.** An earth-orbiting device that relays communications signals over long distances.

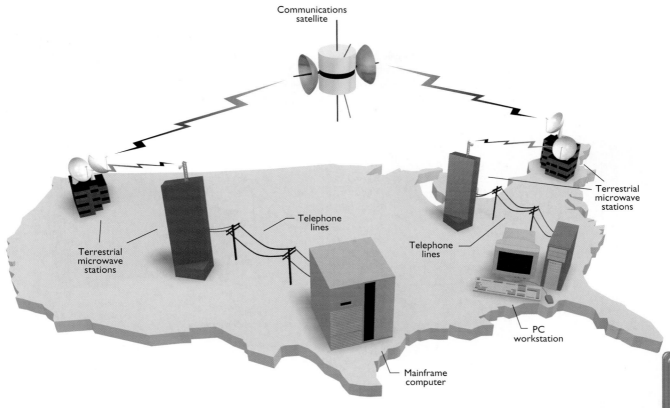

Communications satellite

Terrestrial microwave stations

Telephone lines

Telephone lines

Terrestrial microwave stations

PC workstation

Mainframe computer

FIGURE NET 1-10

Microwave transmission. Microwave signals can move in two ways: via terrestrial stations or satellites.

The *IRIDIUM* project, spearheaded by Motorola, uses about 60 satellites and provides global wireless communications service for phoning, faxing, paging, and low-speed data transmission. The creation of Craig McCaw, a cellular-phone pioneer, *Teledesic* will become operational in 2003 with 288 satellites and data will be able to travel at screamingly fast, fiber-optic-cable-caliber speeds. Both IRIDIUM and Teledesic are designed to provide contact between any two points on the globe.

Both communications satellites and terrestrial microwave stations work best when they transmit large amounts of data one way at a time. Thus, they are ideal for applications such as television and radio broadcasting and getting information from the Internet.

Cellular Technology **Cellular phones** are special mobile telephones that do not need hookups to standard phone outlets in order to work. They can put two people into communication with each other almost anywhere, even if the parties are in motion.

Cellular phones, which use radio waves, operate by keeping in contact with cellular antennae (see Figure NET 1-11). These antennae, which resemble tall, metal telephone poles, are strategically placed throughout a calling area. Calling areas are divided into zones measuring ten miles wide or so, called *cells*, each with its own antenna. The antennae perform two essential functions: (1) they enable a moving cellular phone to transmit and receive signals without interruption by passing signals off to antennae in contiguous cells into which the phones are moving, and (2) they provide an interface with the regular public phone network via a switching office.

■ **Cellular phone.** A mobile phone that transmits calls through special ground stations that cover areas called *cells* to communicate with the regular phone system.

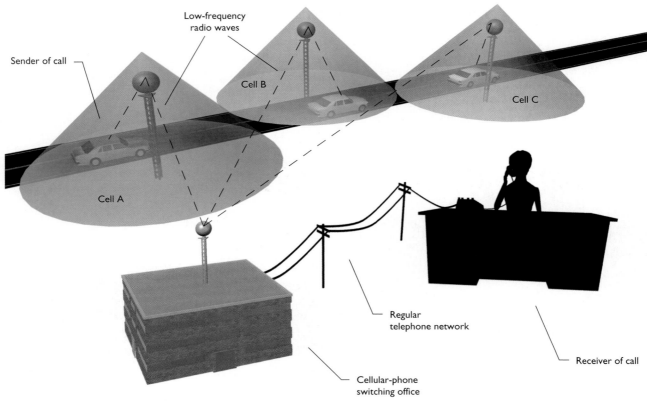

Low-frequency
radio waves

Sender of call

Cell B

Cell C

Cell A

Regular
telephone network

Cellular-phone
switching office

Receiver of call

ABOUT CELLULAR CALLS

When you make a cellular call from your car, it is
picked up by the antenna in the cell from which
you are calling. As you move from one cell to another,
the call is switched seamlessly to the new cell's antenna—
which broadcasts at a different frequency.

FIGURE NET 1-11

Cellular phones.

Cellular phone use has increased from 1.6 million users to 66.5 million users in the last decade and is expected to reach over 100 million users by the year 2002.

Currently, those who most benefit from the cellular phone boom are people who need to maintain constant contact with the office or clients but must be on the move as well—such as a busy executive, salesperson, truck driver, or real-estate agent. Farmers, refinery workers, and others who work outdoors are reaping the benefits of cellular technology to stay in contact with others when they cannot afford the time it would take to get to a regular phone. Cellular phones that enable busy families and teenagers to keep in touch are also becoming more popular.

The latest generation of cellular phones has adopted several functions found in handheld computers and pagers. The transmission networks that support cellular phones are also useful for sending business data. Through a laptop computer with a cellular modem, you can gain access to huge databases of information and the Internet while you are far from an office or a regular phone. Cellular networks are a hit internationally too, especially in less-developed countries such as Poland and China. In places like these, communication systems are crude by North American standards, and it is much easier to build new cellular networks than to fix current facilities or to install wired systems.

Infrared Technology   *Infrared technology* has gained popularity in recent years as a way to set up wireless links between office PCs. As opposed to microwave and cellular technologies, which use *radio* waves, infrared technology sends data as *light* rays. One system, for instance, places a device on each computer through which it can send and receive messages via a transmitter located on the office ceiling. This setup provides an unobstructed, line-of-sight path to and from the computers. Recently, a beaming device has become available that hooks up with a PC card and cable to a laptop's infrared port. The device beams print commands to a desktop computer's display screen, which wires the message to its attached laser printer.

ADAPTING COMPUTERS TO TELECOMMUNICATIONS MEDIA

A computer needs special equipment to send messages over a communications medium. The type of equipment depends on such factors as the medium itself and how data are sent over it.

SENDING DATA OVER MEDIA

Data travel over communications media in various ways. The following paragraphs describe several of them.

Analog or Digital?   One of the most fundamental distinctions in data communications is the difference between analog and digital transmissions (see Figure NET 1-12).

The regular phone system, established many years ago to handle voice traffic, carries **analog** signals—that is, *continuous* waves over a certain frequency range. Changes in the continuous wave reflect the myriad variations in the pitch of the human voice. Transmissions for cable TV and large satellite dishes also use analog signals, as do many wireless networks.

Most business computing equipment, in contrast, transmits **digital** signals, which handle data coded in two *discrete* states: 0 and 1 bits. Your desktop computer is a digital device; so, too, are midrange and mainframe computers. Also, networks often carry digitally encoded data transmissions within office buildings. Whenever communications require an interface between digital computers and analog networks, an adaptive device called a *modem* (covered in more detail shortly) is needed to translate between the two.

Bandwidth and Speed   Over an analog medium, data travel at various frequencies. The difference between the highest and lowest frequencies available on such a medium is known as the medium's **bandwidth.** For example, many telephone lines have a bandwidth of 3,000 hertz (Hz), which is the difference between the highest (3,300 Hz) and lowest (300 Hz) frequencies at which it can send data. Transmissions of text data require the least amount of bandwidth and video data need the most.

Just as a wide fire hose permits more water to pass through it per unit of time than a narrow garden hose, a medium with great bandwidth allows more data to pass through it per unit of time than a medium or small bandwidth. Put another way, greater bandwidth allows data to travel at higher speeds. The speed at which data travel over both analog and digital media is often given in **bits per second (bps),** kbps (thousands of bits per second), or mbps (millions of bits per second).

Analog mode

Digital mode

FIGURE NET 1-12

Analog and digital transmissions.

■ **Analog.** Transmission of data as continuous-wave patterns. ■ **Digital.** Transmission of data as 0 and 1 bits.
■ **Bandwidth.** The difference between the highest and lowest frequencies that a transmission medium can accommodate.
■ **Bits per second (bps).** A measure of a transmission medium's speed.

Speed Comparison

	Type	Speed
Wire Media	Twisted-pair wire (dial-up lines)	300 bps to 56 kbps
	Twisted-pair wire (dedicated lines)	1 to 10 mbps
	Coaxial cable	1 to 20 mbps
	Fiber-optic cable	up to 200 mbps
Wireless Media	Radio wave	4.8 to 19.2 kbps
	Satellite	64 to 512 kbps
	Terrestrial microwave	1.544 mbps
	Infrared (laptop ports)	115 kbps to 4 mbps

FIGURE NET 1-13

Speed. A wider bandwidth allows a medium to carry more data per unit of time and to support more powerful communications applications.

Figure NET 1-13 compares the speeds of several media. As the figure shows, twisted-pair wire has the lowest speed, with increasingly better rates for coaxial cable, radio waves, and fiber-optic cable. Twisted-pair wire is often called a "low-bandwidth" medium; fiber-optic cable, a "high-bandwidth" medium. Increasingly, high-bandwidth media are being installed in many homes and businesses to accommodate the growing number of byte-hungry, information-related products coming into the marketplace.

Parallel versus Serial Transmission   In most communications networks, and especially where long distances are involved, data travel serially. In **serial transmission,** all of the bits in a message are sent one after another along a single path. On the other hand, **parallel transmission** sends each set of 8 bits needed to convey each byte in a message at one time over eight separate paths. Figure NET 1-14 illustrates the difference between the two.

As the figure suggests, parallel transmission is much faster than serial transmission. However, because it requires a cable with eight tracks rather than one, it is also much more expensive. Thus, parallel transmission usually is limited to short distances, such as computer-to-printer communications.

NETWORK INTERFACE CARDS AND MODEMS

Workstations such as PCs and display terminals are usually connected to a network with either a network interface card or a modem. The type of connection required often depends on whether the workstation accesses the network through a *dedicated line* that is set up for private use (which plugs into a network interface card) or through a conventional *dial-up line* (which plugs into a modem).

For a tutorial on connecting computers to telecommunications media, go to www.harcourtcollege.com/infosys/parker2000/student/tutor/ and click on Chapter NET 1.

■ **Serial transmission.** Data transmission in which every bit in a byte must travel down the same path in succession.
■ **Parallel transmission.** Data transmission in which each bit in a byte follows its own path simultaneously with all other bits.

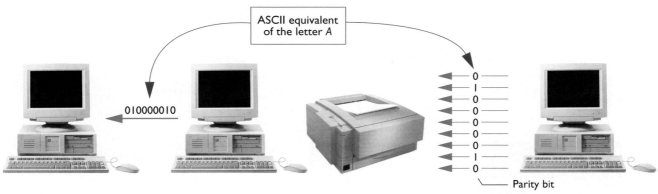

ASCII equivalent
of the letter A

010000010

Parity bit

SERIAL TRANSMISSION
In serial transmission, all of the bits of a byte follow one
another over a single path.

PARALLEL TRANSMISSION
In parallel transmission, the bits of a byte are split into separate paths
and transmitted along the paths at the same time.

Dial-up lines—the type of telephone connections found in most homes and many small businesses—let you call anywhere in the world. They are sometimes called "switched lines" because switching stations within the phone network route your call to the desired destination. A dedicated line, on the other hand, provides a permanent connection between two points. Although dial-up lines are much cheaper, they are slower, and busy signals often prevent connections.

FIGURE NET 1-14

Serial and parallel transmissions.
The figure illustrates a transmission of
the ASCII representation of
the letter A.

Network Interface Cards A **network interface card (NIC)** is an add-in board that plugs into an expansion slot within the system unit (see Figure NET 1-15). These cards often connect to coaxial cables between the workstations in *local networks,* which span small areas like an office building or college campus. NICs pass on to the network any outgoing data from workstations, and they also collect incoming data to the workstations.

FIGURE NET 1-15

Network interface cards (NICs).
NICs are often used to connect
workstations via coaxial cable to
networks that span small areas, like
office buildings or college campuses.

Modems Because digital impulses—such as those sent by desktop workstations—cannot be transmitted over analog phone lines, communications

Rear view of workstation, with case removed

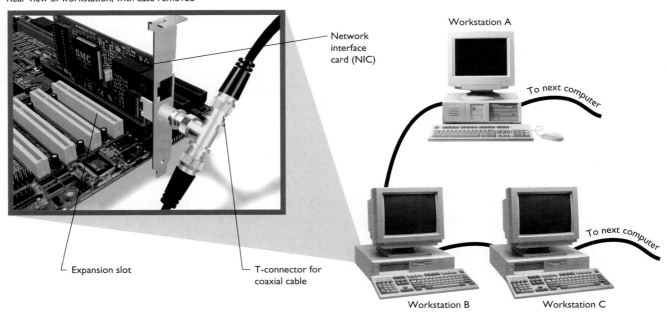

Network
interface
card (NIC)

Workstation A

To next computer

Expansion slot

T-connector for
coaxial cable

Workstation B

Workstation C

To next computer

■ **Network interface card (NIC).** An add-in board through which a workstation connects to a local network.

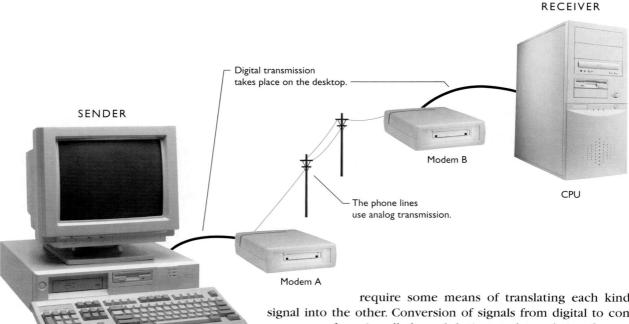

RECEIVER

SENDER

Digital transmission
takes place on the desktop.

Modem B

CPU

The phone lines
use analog transmission.

Modem A

PC workstation

FIGURE NET 1-16

How modems work. An operator of a PC workstation types in data that become digitally encoded. Modem A converts these digital data to analog form and sends them over the phone lines to Modem B. Modem B reconverts the data to digital form and delivers them to the receiving CPU. This latter CPU transmits back to the workstation by reversing these steps.

require some means of translating each kind of signal into the other. Conversion of signals from digital to continuous-wave form is called *modulation,* and translation from continuous waves back to digital impulses is termed *demodulation.* A **modem** (coined from the terms *mo*dulation and *dem*odulation) takes care of both operations.

Modems are most often used to connect desktop computers to *wide area networks,* such as the Internet. Wide area networks join devices spread much farther apart than just a few miles. As Figure NET 1-16 shows, when a workstation sends a message to a remote CPU over an analog line, a modem at the sending end converts from digital to analog, and another at the receiving end converts from analog to digital.

Modems are most commonly available as add-in boards, which are designed to be inserted into an expansion slot within a desktop computer's system unit, and as stand-alone hardware devices (see Figure NET 1-17). The former type, called *internal modems,* are popular because they don't take up extra desk space and are generally cheaper. Some prefer the latter type, called *external modems,* because they can be moved from one computer to another and because they have display panels that can provide useful diagnostics. PC-card modems for laptop computers are also available. Common transmission rates found on modems are 14.4, 28.8, 33.6, and 56 kbps. Modems capable of higher speeds can also function at the lower rates as well.

A few words of caution about modems: Your Internet service provider may not support your calling area with the highest possible speeds, even though your modem is capable of them. Also, your phone company may not be able to deliver data at your modem's top speed because of line loads. What's more, data compression can slow down considerably the rate at which information is handled.

Modems can now deliver data as fast as the present phone system can carry it. To achieve more speed, you need either an ISDN line or some other faster alternative.

MODEM SOFTWARE The programs that work with modems to enable your PC to communicate with the Internet and remote databases are commonly referred to in the PC world as *modem software.* When you buy a new PC

■ **Modem.** A communications device that enables digital computers and their support devices to communicate over analog media.

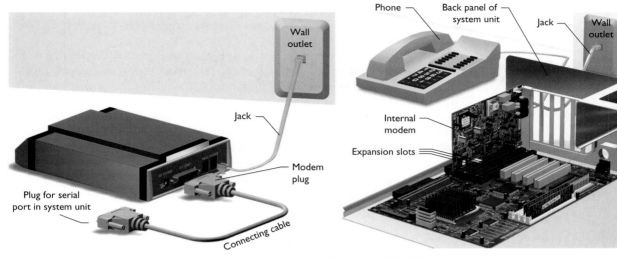

EXTERNAL MODEM
External modems are detached from the system unit and can be moved from computer to computer.

INTERNAL MODEM
Internal modems are boards that fit in an expansion slot within the system unit and are the type of modem recommended for most personal uses.

with a modem, you will usually get modem software as part of the bundle. Although products in the modem-software marketplace provide different features, most of them let you access the Internet and service providers, receive and send electronic mail and faxes, and exchange files with other computers.

In addition, many modem programs will automatically place and answer calls for you, interface with voice machines, provide security for your files, and simplify a number of routine, phone-related tasks (such as accessing phone directories and keying in IDs and passwords to online service providers or newsgroups).

FIGURE NET 1-17

Types of modems. Modems are either external or internal.

ISDN AND BEYOND

If you need more speed than you can squeeze out of a modem, your best bet is an ISDN line or something even faster.

ISDN (for *Integrated Services Digital Network)* is a digital phone service that operates over ordinary dial-up phone lines or over dedicated lines leased for private use. ISDN gives access to one or two 64 kbps channels. With two channels, you can use each separately—say, one to talk to a friend about a homework assignment while you watch as a Web page downloads from the Internet over the other. You can also combine the two lines into one for a full 128 kbps of bandwidth. To use ISDN, a special *ISDN adapter*—the ISDN counterpart of a modem—must be connected to your computer. The adapter allows you to communicate with other ISDN devices, such as the ISDN adapter owned by your Internet service provider.

ISDN is more expensive than modem transmission. An adapter can easily cost more than $300, and the installation charge on an ISDN line—if you don't live too far out in the country—can run another couple of hundred dollars or so. Also, you must often pay a per-minute connect charge for your time on the line, even for a local call.

DirecPC works with a small $200 satellite dish that is similar to the one used with digital television's DirecTV service. DirecPC can provide up to 400 kbps speeds when data are downloaded but only modem-fast speeds when data are sent the other way, up to the satellite. Fortunately, most applications

■ **ISDN.** A digital phone service that offers high-speed transmissions over ordinary phone lines.

require far more data sent down than up. Typical monthly costs, which include an Internet connection and an e-mail account, are $30 for 25 hours of access per week or $50 for 100 hours.

Businesses often require faster speeds than any of the alternatives mentioned so far. Such options offer more speed than ISDN and DirecPC, but—no surprise—they also bring higher prices. With a *T1 dedicated line* or a *frame-relay service,* for instance, a company can get speeds up to a few mbps over coaxial cable. Companies often lease these lines and then split the bandwidth among several users. *T3 fiber optic dedicated lines* are even faster and can reach 45 mbps and upward. Also, lines that follow the *asynchronous transfer mode (ATM)* standard can deliver speeds of 155 mbps over fiber optic lines—and perhaps over 600 mbps in the near future. T3 and ATM are most often used by communications companies for network *backbones*—those parts of a network that carry the most traffic.

The Tomorrow box covers two promising alternatives for the future of mass communication in the home—cable modems and ADSL. These two technologies are the ones most mentioned with regard to the coming of Internet-enabled television.

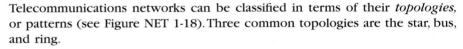

NETWORK TOPOLOGIES

For a tutorial on the various types of network topologies, go to www.harcourtcollege. com/infosys/parker2000/ student/tutor/ and click on Chapter NET 1.

Telecommunications networks can be classified in terms of their *topologies,* or patterns (see Figure NET 1-18). Three common topologies are the star, bus, and ring.

Star Networks   The **star network**—the oldest topology for computer networks—often consists of a large computer hierarchically connected to several workstations through point-to-point links. Star networks are common in traditional mainframe environments. The mainframe serves as the *host computer,* and it hooks up to several PC workstations or to several display terminals. The display terminals are sometimes referred to as *dumb terminals* because they are workstations that can do little more than send and receive data; the mainframe does virtually everything else.

Bus Networks   A **bus network** operates a lot like ordinary city buses in a ground transportation system. The hardware devices are like bus stops, and the data move like passengers. For example, the bus network labeled in Figure NET 1-18 contains four workstations (bus stops) at which the system picks up or lets off data (passengers). The bus line commonly consists of a high-speed cable with inexpensive twisted-pair wires dropped off each workstation. A bus network contains no host computer.

Ring Networks   A less common and more expensive alternative to the star and bus is the **ring network,** which lacks any host computer; instead, a number of computers or other devices are connected by a loop. A ring network is also shown in Figure NET 1-18.

Networks often combine topologies, in effect turning several smaller networks into one larger one. Figure NET 1-18 shows two star networks *daisy chained* together with a bus. In the figure, cluster stations—or *hubs*—coordinate the traffic of sent and received messages on workstations that are hooked up to them. Figure NET 1-18 also shows three star networks linked

---

■ **Star network.** A telecommunications network consisting of a host device connected directly to several other devices.
■ **Bus network.** A telecommunications network consisting of a transmission line with lines dropped off for several devices.
■ **Ring network.** A telecommunications network that connects machines serially in a closed loop.

The Battle for the "Last Mile"

Who Will Win the Race to Deliver High-Bandwidth Products?

Companies in the telecommunications industry are struggling to solve a huge problem. They know that twenty-first-century, Internet multimedia products are ready for prime time, and interactive TV and HDTV are waiting in the wings. But how can they get such products to work over computer networks when most homes—located within the so-called "last mile" of each network terminus—connect only through ordinary telephone lines, which transmit at comparatively snail-paced speeds?

The answer, many feel, is to build a new communications infrastructure. Unfortunately, conventional modems have pretty much peaked and cannot support further large speed increases, so observers see little likelihood of big advancements on that front. What's more, today's television infrastructure is mostly geared for one-way broadcasting—a huge limitation for a system that will incorporate computers and the Internet.

A technology that many industry analysts see as a front-runner to become the medium of choice in the early twenty-first-century home is two-way cable. Two-way cable—a hybrid system based on coaxial and fiber-optic technology—replaces or augments the one-way cable that currently serves most of today's cable-TV customers. It connects devices through an interfacing device called a *cable modem*.

How fast is two-way cable? It can reach 10 and maybe up to 30 mbps, say the cable companies—hundreds of times faster than today's top-of-the-line conventional modems. Put another way, it would take 23 minutes to transmit a 10 MB file by 56 kbps modem and only 8 seconds by 10 mbps cable modem.

The complete upgrade of existing cable networks is expected to cost the cable companies billions of dollars, and the investment will probably pay off only over a long time. Only a few million U.S. homes are currently using the new cable service.

The principal rival to two-way cable—a technology called *ADSL* (for Asymmetric Digital Subscriber Line)—is being served up by the phone companies. ADSL, the successor to ISDN, uses a digital-filtering method to turn twisted-pair copper wires into digital lines with megabit-per-second speeds.

ADSL lines now in the test stage provide speeds of about 8 mbps for transmissions downstream (from the service provider to the user) and 1 mbps upstream (from the user to the provider). This rate is more than adequate to provide high-speed

The cable and phone companies square off. The winner—and early bets favor cable—could wind up providing TV, Internet, and phone service to most homes.

television and Internet service, as well as phone service. Recently, a brand of ADSL dubbed *ADSL Lite* (1.5 mbps downstream, 512 kbps upstream) is getting a lot of attention; it is easier and less expensive to install.

Both cable modem and ADSL put the cable and phone companies on a collision course, since it will be possible to get phone service over cable modem and TV service over ADSL. The eventual winner of the just-begun battle between the cable and phone companies is at this point in time anyone's guess. Cable modems are off to a big lead, but they cost far more to implement than ADSL. What's more, the cash-strapped cable companies are fending off additional assaults on their mainstream business—cable television service—by digital satellite services such as DirecTV and digital wireless cable. And future satellite services such as Teledesic threaten both phone and cable companies.

The battle to network the last mile has enormous stakes. Most consumers prefer to receive all of their communications—TV, Internet, and telephone service—from a single company. Consequently, firms that bet on the right technology may wind up winning the lion's share of the communications business.

---

together in a ring by a high-speed *fiber-optic backbone.* Additionally, network topologies can contain redundant links, as the Internet does, so that they conform to no well-known, geometric pattern.

Workstations send and receive messages according to some predefined method or *protocol.* The topic of protocols is discussed later in the chapter.

BASIC TOPOLOGIES

Most network topologies follow a simple star, bus, or ring pattern.

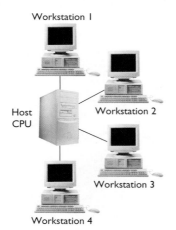

Workstation 1

Host
CPU

Workstation 2

Workstation 3

Workstation 4

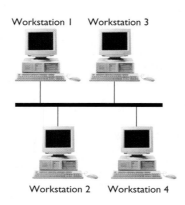

Workstation 1   Workstation 3

Workstation 2   Workstation 4

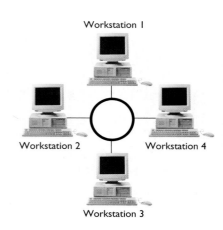

Workstation 1

Workstation 2   Workstation 4

Workstation 3

STAR NETWORK

A star network often consists of a mainframe host that's connected to several workstations in a point-to-point fashion.

BUS NETWORK

A bus network uses a high-speed cable that workstations tap into—in the manner shown—to pick up and drop off messages.

RING NETWORK

In a ring network, computers and other devices are connected in a loop.

COMBINATION TOPOLOGIES

Many networks are formed by combining topologies—such as the bus and star.

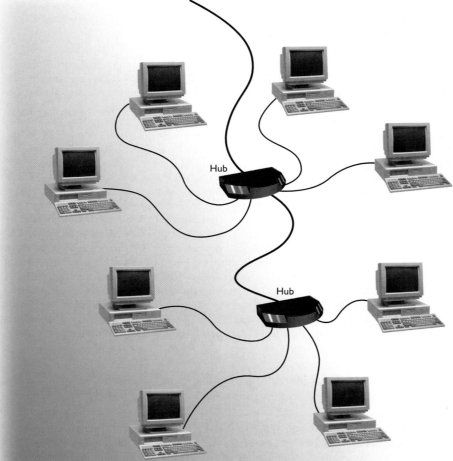

Hub

Hub

DAISY CHAINING

Daisy chaining refers to connecting devices serially with a bus line. Here, two hubs (cluster stations that manage workstations) coordinate the sending and receiving of messages from two star networks.

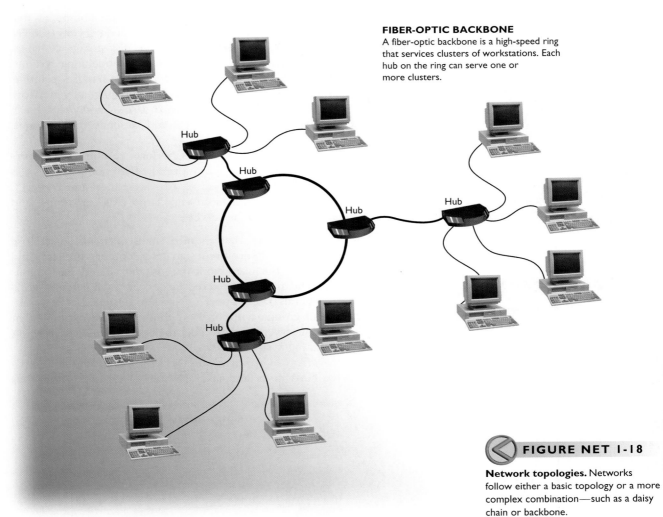

FIBER-OPTIC BACKBONE
A fiber-optic backbone is a high-speed ring that services clusters of workstations. Each hub on the ring can serve one or more clusters.

FIGURE NET 1-18

Network topologies. Networks follow either a basic topology or a more complex combination—such as a daisy chain or backbone.

LOCAL NETWORKS

Organizations need communications facilities that connect geographically close resources, such as PCs located in the same college campus or classroom or workstations located in the same office. Such networks are known as **local networks.** Three common types of local networks are host-independent local area networks (LANs), hierarchical local networks, and private branch exchanges (PBXs).

LOCAL AREA NETWORKS (LANS)

The term **local area networks (LANs)** typically refers to local networks without any host computer as such. Instead, most LANs use either a bus or ring topology, and computers within the network itself manage workstations' demands for shared facilities. LANs are available principally in the client-server and peer-to-peer varieties.

■ **Local network.** A privately run communications network of several machines located within a few miles or so of one another. ■ **Local area network (LAN).** A local network without a host computer, usually comprised of microcomputer workstations and shared peripherals.

Client-Server LANs Client-server LANs are so named because each workstation that receives network service is called a **client,** while the computers that manage the requests for facilities within the network are called **servers** (see Figure NET 1-19). For example, a *file server* might manage disk-storage activities, enabling workstation users to access any of several available operating systems, applications programs, or data files. Similarly, a *print server* handles printing-related activities, such as managing user outputs on a high-quality network printer. LANs also incorporate such devices as *mail servers* and *fax servers,* which are dedicated to managing electronic mail and facsimile transmissions, respectively.

Because servers often manage large databases, perform certain types of processing chores for clients, and interact with several other computers, LANs often include powerful PCs like those based on the latest Intel and PowerPC processor chips to perform server duties. In very large LANs, midrange and mainframe computers often function as servers.

Peer-to-Peer LANs Applications that require small networks often use **peer-to-peer LANs.** These LANs do not predesignate computers as clients and servers per se. Instead, all of the user workstations and shared peripherals work on the same level, and users have direct access to each other's workstations and shared peripherals. Peer-to-peer LANs were designed as a way to bring networking to small groups without the complexity and expense that normally accompany client-server systems. Peer-to-peer capabilities are built into many personal operating systems.

LANs are used for a variety of applications, the simplest of which involve just sharing expensive hard disks and laser printers. LAN technology has

FIGURE NET 1-19

Client-server LAN. In a client-server LAN, each workstation that receives network service is called a *client,* while the computers that manage requests for network services are called *servers*.

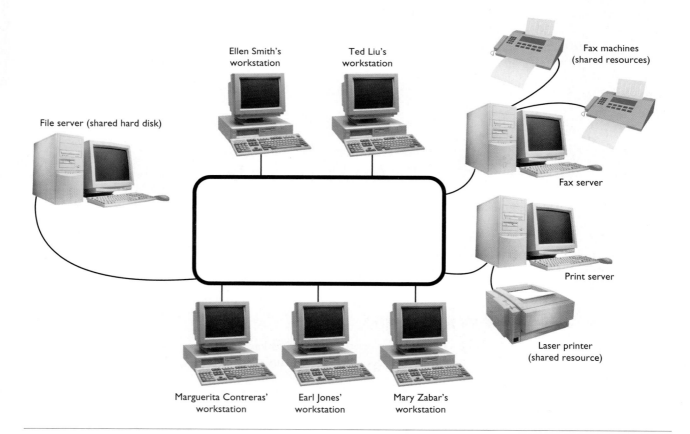

■ **Client-server LAN.** A LAN composed of *client* devices, which receive network services, and *server* devices, which provide the services. ■ **Client.** A device designed to receive service in a client-server network. ■ **Server.** A computer that manages shared devices, such as laser printers or high-capacity hard disks, on a client-server network. ■ **Peer-to-peer LAN.** A LAN in which all of the user workstations and shared peripheral devices operate on the same level.

Uses for LANs

Sharing expensive devices like network printers among several users

Handling certain types of applications better than mainframes

Performing electronic mail operations

Implementing an intranet

FIGURE NET 1-20

Uses for LANs.

evolved beyond these initial applications to include numerous other uses (see Figure NET 1-20). One of the newest functions is the so-called *intranet.*

An **intranet** is a private LAN—set up by a company for its employees—that implements the infrastructure and standards of the Internet and its World Wide Web. Intranets today serve a variety of purposes, such as making company phone books and procedure manuals available to employees, disseminating forms, and enabling employees to communicate and work together on projects (see Figure NET 1-21). Because many company sites are fitted with high-bandwidth cable media, intranets make possible much richer multimedia displays than the Internet as it is seen in most homes.

In many ways, intranets provide the logical framework with which to build a company LAN. Many employees are already familiar with the Internet and its World Wide Web, so the similar-looking intranets minimize training requirements. Also, Internet technology (and therefore intranets) can function on almost any computer platform, and many companies have diverse mixtures of computers that need to communicate with one another. What's more, development costs are relatively small—no highly unique, proprietary system has to be designed.

Much newer to the scene than intranets are *extranets,* extensions of intranets out onto the Internet itself. Extranets provide such people as mobile workers and selected customers and suppliers access to a company's internal data and applications via the Web. Because they generally cover long distances, extranets are often wide-area networks (WANs). WANs are covered later in the chapter.

Feature NET 1-1 covers one of the most recent applications of LAN technology—setting up a LAN in your home.

Microcomputer-based LANs have a big advantage over host-based hierarchical systems, which we'll be looking at next: Organizations can inexpensively add small increments of extra computing power to their LANs as needs grow. For instance, companies can add extra workstations or more servers at any time. Also, expandable machines called *scalable superserver computers,* which cater to LANs, have designs expressly intended for easy additions of processing power and memory. On the disadvantage side, security on LANs still lags behind that on mainframe-based host systems, and LANs often run up higher costs for development and support.

FIGURE NET 1-21

Uses for intranets. Companies can get an intranet up and running on a local-area network by following the standards and guidelines of the Internet and World Wide Web. Any or all of the applications listed here can become part of a company intranet.

USES FOR INTRANETS

Facilitating electronic mail

Maintaining internal phone books

Storing procedure manuals

Posting training materials

Disseminating employee forms

Posting internal job listings

Providing electronic catalogs for ordering supplies

Facilitating workgroup computing

Scheduling meetings and appointments

Making available critical expertise

Disseminating newsletters

Posting reports and other types of information

OTHER TYPES OF LOCAL NETWORKS

Two other common types of local networks are hierarchical local networks and PBXs.

■ **Intranet.** A private network—often one set up by a company for employees—that implements the infrastructure and standards of the Internet and World Wide Web.

NET 1-1

Home LANs

More Popular Today Than the Backyard Pool

Up until the past few years, one prominent northern California housing developer could easily predict the types of options new homebuyers wanted most—wall-to-wall carpeting or perhaps a swimming pool in the backyard. Then, something interesting happened. Almost out of the blue, LANs popped up on the list. Now, they are the most requested option.

Home LANs are not just for computer professionals. Barry Bonds, the San Francisco Giants three-time Most Valuable Player, likes the idea too (see photo). As his $2.5 million house was recently being built in northern California, Bonds announced that he was "prewiring . . . for the twenty-first century" as well as planning for PC plugability in every major room.

A home LAN provides many sorts of useful benefits. For one, it allows computers and other devices in your house to communicate directly with each other. Thus, no more manually carting floppy disks around from room to room to transfer files between systems or to print files. What's more, people in the house can play games together—on their own machines, in their own rooms—at dazzling speeds, and they can teleconference too. The computers can also share the Internet connection to your home.

There's more. You can check on the dog in the backyard or see who's at the front door while never taking your eyes off your computer's display screen—via electronic eyes that are also connected to the LAN. You can use the LAN to program your VCR, to automatically turn on your coffee every morning, to run the lighting or sprinkler system, and to check—remotely—that your home is in a safe state when a trip takes you out of town.

Eventually, of course, standards will be established for devices that can be plugged into home-based LANs. Consequently, any type of device that is LAN-compatible will be operable through a single, familiar interface—such as Windows or something like it. This would enable you to do such things as use your computer to regulate your water heater and diagnose plumbing problems online. The LAN plumbing system could even have your water pump automatically shut down if pipes spring a leak.

Installing a home LAN can be done in several ways. Many new homes, like Barry Bonds' for instance, are being built with LAN cabling so that virtually anywhere a device is plugged in it can access the LAN and handle data at high speeds. But those living in homes built when hardly anyone knew what a LAN was have several options too.

Baseball slugger Bonds. It's not just computer wizards who are buying into home LANs.

One option, of course, is retrofitting the home with new cable. This can be expensive as well as an aesthetic challenge. A second and cheaper option is to buy LAN equipment that enables PCs to communicate along temporary cables you set up in your home. A popular choice is going with 10BaseT Ethernet NICs for each PC, a multiport 10BaseT hub that lets PCs be shared, and 5 UTP cables to connect each PC to the hub in the form of a star network. A third option is a wireless LAN. But beware. Some wireless media—such as infrared—do not penetrate walls. Two other options: LAN products that use the existing telephone or electrical wiring in your home, and a hybrid approach that combines any of the choices already mentioned.

Hierarchical Local Networks **Hierarchical local networks** are the oldest type of local computer network. They follow a star topology. At the top of the hierarchy is a host computer such as a mainframe or midrange computer

---

■ **Hierarchical local network.** A local network in which a relatively powerful host CPU at the top of the hierarchy interacts with workstations at the bottom.

that controls virtually all of the processing. At the bottom are display workstations. Between the top and bottom, devices such as communications controllers manage exchanges between the host and workstations.

Workstations in hierarchical local networks can either download files from the host or upload files to it. **Downloading** means that copies of existing files move from the host to the PC workstations. **Uploading** means that new data created at the PC workstations move to the host system.

Both downloading and uploading usually require stringent organizational control. Downloading presents the danger of unauthorized access to data, whereas uploading entails the risk of garbage data corrupting other applications. Uploading and downloading are also common operations in client-server LANs, where clients download files off of a server or upload files to it.

A major difference between a hierarchical local network and a host-independent client-server LAN is *where* the processing takes place. In the client-server LAN, a lot of the processing can be done at the client or desktop level. Except for database retrievals, possibly very little other processing is done at the server end. In the hierarchical local network, by contrast, the processing is typically concentrated at the host or "server" level. In many such systems, the "client" is a dumb terminal that has very little processing capability beyond sending and receiving data.

Private Branch Exchanges (PBXs) The telephone system consists of numerous switching stations that essentially are public branch exchanges. When a company leases or purchases a switching station for its own use, such a facility becomes a **private branch exchange (PBX).** Most PBXs are commonly referred to as "company switchboards"—you call a company's number and a private operator routes you to the proper extension. A PBX is essentially a hierarchical local network dedicated to intracompany phoning.

In today's world of computers and Touch-Tone phones, modern PBXs minimize the workloads on human operators by putting technology to work for most incoming calls. Callers hear a voice recording of menu options and make selections from their Touch-Tone phones. Host computers control the PBXs, routing machine-to-machine calls automatically and letting the human operator deal with interpersonal communications as exceptions. Sometimes these computer-based private branch exchanges are referred to as *CBXs (computerized branch exchanges)* or *PABXs (private automatic branch exchanges).*

WIDE AREA NETWORKS (WANS)

Wide area networks (WANs) are communications networks that encompass relatively wide geographical areas. Many WANs link together geographically dispersed LANs or LAN clusters. The mix also often includes hundreds or thousands—or, in the case of the Internet, millions—of independent user workstations that connect from remote locations. WANs may be publicly accessible, like the Internet, or privately owned and operated.

HANDLING WAN TRAFFIC

Two big issues with WANs are interconnectivity and network management. Because these networks tie together so many devices across such long distances,

---

■ **Downloading.** The process of transferring a file from a remote computer to a requesting computer over a network.
■ **Uploading.** The process of transferring a file from a local computer to a remote computer over a network. ■ **Private branch exchange (PBX).** A call-switching station dedicated to a single organization. ■ **Wide area network (WAN).** A network that spans a large geographic area.

Internet Traffic Cops

Sending information through the Internet is not only about hardware and software. People figure in prominently too. Just as airport control systems have human beings working alongside computers in order to make difficult decisions, so, too, does the Internet have men and women manually taking care of many of the problems that arise in computer-equipped control rooms.

One such installation is UUNet's Network Operation Center (NOC) in Fairfax, Virginia. UUNet, owned by MCI/WorldCom, provides and maintains many of the fiber-optic pipelines that make up the heavily trafficked backbone of the Internet. Other big backbone providers include GTE and Sprint, and these companies work in concert with each other and with UUNet to create what looks like a single, seamless network to those outside the telecom industry. Such data pipelines are used by thousands of ISPs, from America Online down to community bulletin boards in rural Wyoming.

UUNet's NOC is operated 24 hours a day, and the human "traffic cops" that respond to transmission problems work in shifts. Many cops sit in a darkened, amphitheater-like control room, working at desktop display devices and looking at wall-mounted projection screens that contain text and visual information about patterns in network traffic. One of the first things a cop does when starting a shift is check the displays to find out which parts of the Internet are down or currently experiencing flow bottlenecks and what is being done to fix the problems. During the day, a cop may receive messages from ISPs that are experiencing slowdowns and send messages to technicians at communications companies to get specific problems resolved.

On many days, UUNet's computer systems can automatically resolve the traffic problems that come up. However, things often happen that even a computer is not programmed to deal with. For instance, a connection between Denver and London may suddenly go down. If the computer reroutes packets through a preset alternate route—say, Dallas—and the Dallas-to-London connection is already overloaded due to another problem, a ripple effect can occur. Eventually, a computer can be faced with possibilities that even the most thorough programmer could never have imagined—and then do something crazy. Thus, some human intervention is necessary to ensure that catastrophes do not occur.

At places like UUNet, cops are often empowered to do whatever it takes to get a problem resolved. This may mean jumping in one's car at 3 a.m. and finding a router that's sitting in a warehouse, then driving it to a distant city so that a local technician can install it before people are out of bed for the day.

they need a number of special pieces of equipment. Such devices will be discussed in the paragraphs that follow. The Inside the Industry box describes in brief the work of the men and women who keep the equipment and connections on a large WAN running smoothly.

Repeaters *Repeaters* are devices that amplify signals along a network. WANs need them because signals often have to travel farther than the wires or cables that carry them are designed to support. Repeaters are also commonly used on LANs when longer distances are involved.

Routers **Routers** work in large switched networks—like the Internet—to pass messages along to their destinations. Each router along the path to the destination passes any message it receives along to the next router, and the routers work together to share information about the network. If one part of the network is congested or out of service, a router can choose to send a message by an alternate route. Routers are to networks like the Internet what

---

■ **Router.** A device used on WAN's to decide the paths along which to send messages.

switching stations are to the phone system, with one important exception: The phone network predetermines the message path whereas routers on the Internet make their own decisions and one never knows ahead of time the path a message will take.

Gateways and Bridges   Local networks often must communicate with outside resources, such as those on wide area networks and other local networks. Messages sent between two distinct networks reach their destinations via gateways and bridges.

A **gateway** is a collection of hardware and software resources that enables devices on one network to communicate with those on another, *dissimilar* network. Workstations on a LAN, for instance, require a gateway to access the Internet. Suppose an executive working at an office workstation on a LAN wishes to access the Internet through America Online; a gateway is necessary to link the two kinds of networks.

Two networks based on similar technology—such as a LAN in one city and a LAN in another—communicate via a device called a bridge. A **bridge** is a collection of hardware and software resources that enables devices on one network to communicate with devices on another, *similar* network. Bridges can also partition a large LAN into two smaller ones and connect two LANs that are nearby each other.

Multiplexers   Communications lines almost always have far greater capacity than a single workstation can use. Because communications lines are expensive, networks can run efficiently if several low-speed devices share the same line. A special device called a **multiplexer** makes this possible by interleaving the messages of several low-speed devices and sending them along a single high-speed path.

Concentrators   A **concentrator** is a multiplexer with a store-and-forward capability. Messages from slow devices accumulate at the concentrator until it collects enough characters to make a message worth forwarding to another device. In airline reservation systems, for instance, concentrators placed at such key sites as New York and Los Angeles allow travel agents to share communications lines economically. Messages initiated by agents are sent to the concentrator, stored, multiplexed with messages from other agents, and transmitted at very high speeds over long-distance lines to central processing sites. In the world of LANs, concentrators are known as *hubs*.

COMMUNICATIONS PROTOCOLS

Because manufacturers have long produced devices that use a variety of transmission techniques, the telecommunications industry has adopted standards called *protocols* to rectify the problem of conflicting procedures.

The term *protocol* comes from the areas of diplomacy and etiquette. For instance, at a dinner party in the elegant home of a family on the Social Register, the protocol in effect may be formal attire, impeccable table manners, and remaining at the table until beckoned to the parlor by the host or hostess. At a casual backyard barbecue, a different protocol will probably exist. In the communications field, protocols have comparable roles.

For a tutorial on the various types of communications protocols, go to www. harcourtcollege.com/ infosys/parker2000/student/ tutor/ and click on Chapter NET I.

■ **Gateway.** An interface that enables two dissimilar networks to communicate. ■ **Bridge.** An interface that enables two similar networks to communicate. ■ **Multiplexer.** A communications device that interleaves the messages of several low-speed devices and sends them along a single, high-speed path. ■ **Concentrator.** A communications device that combines control and multiplexing functions.

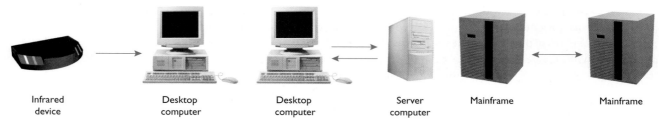

SIMPLEX
Messages can only go in a single, prespecified direction.

HALF DUPLEX
Messages can go both ways, but only one way at a time.

FULL DUPLEX
Messages can go both ways, simultaneously.

 **FIGURE NET 1-22**

Simplex, half-duplex, and full-duplex transmissions.

A communications **protocol** is a collection of procedures to establish, maintain, and terminate transmissions between devices. Protocols specify how devices will physically connect to a network, how data will be packaged for transmission, how receiver devices will acknowledge signals from sender devices (a process called *handshaking*), how errors will be handled, and so on. Just as people need an agreed-upon set of rules to communicate effectively, machines also need a common set of rules to help them get along with one another.

Protocols are found in all types of networks. How many protocols are there? Thousands. The following paragraphs discuss a few of the most common ones. As you will shortly see, each protocol addresses a highly specific type of situation.

Simplex, Half Duplex, or Full Duplex?   One level of protocol found in virtually all types of telecommunications addresses the direction in which transmitted data move (see Figure NET 1-22).

Simplex transmission allows data to travel only in a single, prespecified direction. An example from everyday life is a doorbell—the signal can go only from the button to the chime. Two other examples are television and radio broadcasting. The simplex standard is relatively uncommon for most types of computer-based telecommunications applications; even devices that are designed primarily to receive information, such as printers, must be able to communicate acknowledgment signals back to the sender devices.

In **half-duplex transmission,** messages can move in either direction, but only one way at a time. The press-to-talk radio phones used in police cars employ the half-duplex standard; only one person can talk at a time. Often the line between a desktop workstation and a remote CPU conforms to the half-duplex pattern as well. If another computer is transmitting to a workstation, the operator cannot send new messages until the other computer finishes its message or pauses to acknowledge an interruption.

Full-duplex transmission works like traffic on a busy two-way street—the flow moves in two directions at the same time. Full-duplexing is ideal for hardware units that need to pass large amounts of data between each other, as in mainframe-to-mainframe communications.

Asynchronous versus Synchronous Transmission   Another level of protocol commonly encountered by PC owners addresses packaging of data for serial transmission. As mentioned earlier, most data are transmitted serially in communications networks.

■ **Protocol.** A set of conventions by which machines establish communication with one another in a telecommunications environment. ■ **Simplex transmission.** Any type of transmission in which a message can move along a path in only a single, prespecified direction. ■ **Half-duplex transmission.** Any type of transmission in which messages may move in two directions—but only one way at a time—along a communications path. ■ **Full-duplex transmission.** A type of transmission in which messages may travel in two directions simultaneously along a communications path.

In **asynchronous transmission,** one character at a time is sent over a line. When the operator strikes a key on a keyboard, the character's byte representation moves up the line to the computer. Striking a second key sends the byte for a second character, and so forth. But because even the fastest typist can generate only a very small amount of data relative to what the line can accept, the line sits idle a lot of the time. Furthermore, each character sent must be packaged with a "start bit" and "stop bit," resulting in substantial transmission overhead.

When large blocks of data have to be sent, asynchronous transmission is too slow. **Synchronous transmission** increases speed on a line by dispatching data in blocks of characters rather than one at a time. Each block can consist of thousands of characters. The blocks are timed so that the receiving device knows that it will be getting them at regular intervals. Because no idle time occurs between transmission of individual characters in the block—and because less transmission overhead is required—this method allows more efficient utilization of the line. Synchronous transmission is made possible by a *buffer* at the workstation, a storage area large enough to hold a block of characters. As soon as the buffer is filled, all the characters in it are sent up the line to the destination computer.

Figure NET 1-23 shows the difference between asynchronous and synchronous transmission. Synchronous transmission is available on most high-speed modems.

LAN Protocols In the LAN world, the protocols in effect depend on the particular type of network architecture used. *Network architecture* refers to both the particular topology the network follows—say, bus or ring—as well

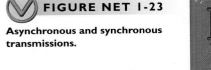

FIGURE NET 1-23

Asynchronous and synchronous transmissions.

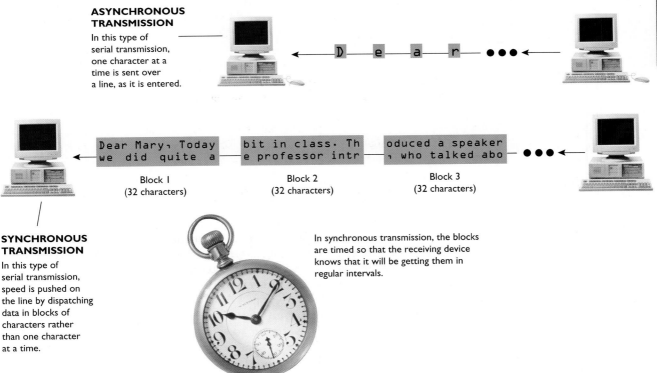

ASYNCHRONOUS TRANSMISSION

In this type of serial transmission, one character at a time is sent over a line, as it is entered.

D e a r ●●●

Dear Mary, Today we did quite a

Block 1
(32 characters)

bit in class. The professor intr

Block 2
(32 characters)

oduced a speaker , who talked abo

Block 3
(32 characters)

●●●

SYNCHRONOUS TRANSMISSION

In this type of serial transmission, speed is pushed on the line by dispatching data in blocks of characters rather than one character at a time.

In synchronous transmission, the blocks are timed so that the receiving device knows that it will be getting them in regular intervals.

■ **Asynchronous transmission.** The transmission of data over a line one character at a time, with variable time intervals between characters. ■ **Synchronous transmission.** The timed transmission of data over a line one block of characters at a time.

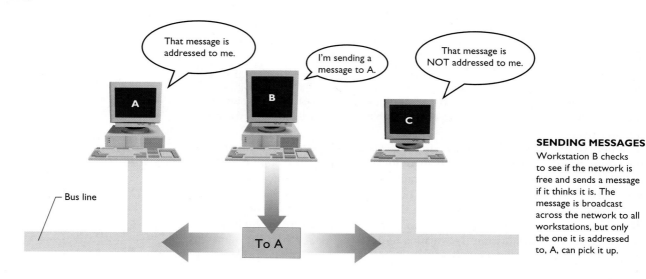

SENDING MESSAGES

Workstation B checks to see if the network is free and sends a message if it thinks it is. The message is broadcast across the network to all workstations, but only the one it is addressed to, A, can pick it up.

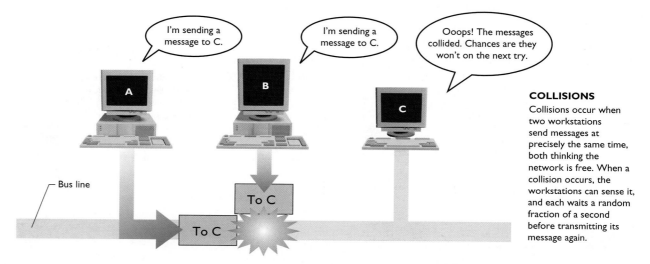

COLLISIONS

Collisions occur when two workstations send messages at precisely the same time, both thinking the network is free. When a collision occurs, the workstations can sense it, and each waits a random fraction of a second before transmitting its message again.

FIGURE NET 1-24

Ethernet's CSMA/CD protocol.

as scores of little details, only a few of which we'll talk about here. By far, the two most common LAN architectures are Ethernet and token ring.

ETHERNET **Ethernet** refers to a collection of protocols that specify a standard way of setting up a LAN in a bus network. It specifies the types and lengths of cables, how the cables connect, how devices communicate data, how the system detects and corrects problems, and so on.

Data communications and problem checking in an Ethernet network require a set of procedures collectively called *CSMA/CD,* which stands for *carrier sense multiple access with collision detection* (see Figure NET 1-24). *Carrier sense* means that when a workstation has to send a message, it first "listens" for other messages on the line. If it senses no messages, it sends one. *Multiple access* means that two workstations might want to send a message at the same time. *Collision detection* means that when a workstation initiates a message, it listens to see if the message might have collided with one from another workstation.

A collision takes place when two messages are sent at exactly the same time, so they temporarily jam the network. When they suspect a collision, the

■ **Ethernet.** A collection of protocols that specify a standard way of setting up a bus-based LAN.

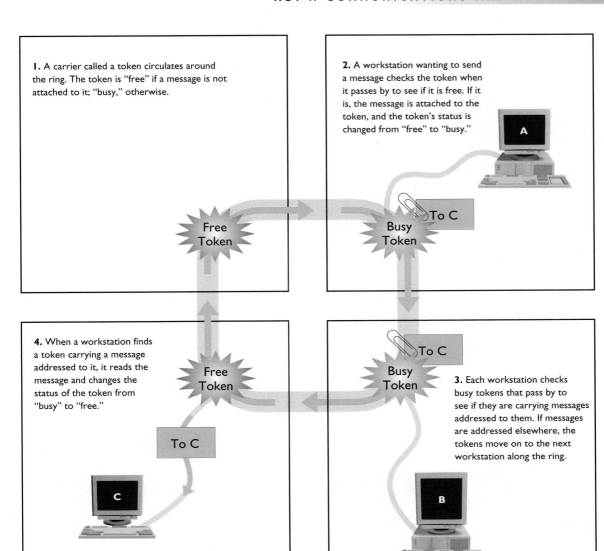

1. A carrier called a token circulates around the ring. The token is "free" if a message is not attached to it; "busy," otherwise.

2. A workstation wanting to send a message checks the token when it passes by to see if it is free. If it is, the message is attached to the token, and the token's status is changed from "free" to "busy."

Free Token

Busy Token — To C

4. When a workstation finds a token carrying a message addressed to it, it reads the message and changes the status of the token from "busy" to "free."

Free Token

To C — Busy Token

3. Each workstation checks busy tokens that pass by to see if they are carrying messages addressed to them. If messages are addressed elsewhere, the tokens move on to the next workstation along the ring.

To C

▲ **FIGURE NET 1-25**

Token ring and the token-passing protocol.

two sending workstations wait for short, random periods of time and send their messages again. The chance of the messages colliding a second time is extremely small.

A standard Ethernet system can send data at a rate of up to 10 mbps, and newer versions can transmit even faster. *Fast Ethernet,* for instance, runs at 100 mbps and *gigabit Ethernet* is even faster.

TOKEN RING Like Ethernet, **token ring** is a network architecture. It is used with a ring network topology and employs a *token-passing* protocol.

Here's how a token-ring network works (see also Figure NET 1-25): A small packet called a *token*—which has room for messages and addresses—is sent around the ring. As the token circulates, workstations either check to see if the token is addressed to them or try to seize it so that they can assign messages to it. A token contains a control area, which specifies whether the token is free or carries a message. When a sender device captures a free token, it changes the status of the token from free to busy, adds an addressed message, and releases the token. The message then travels around the ring to the receiver location. The receiver copies the message and changes the status of the token back to free. Then it releases the token.

■ **Token ring.** A ring-based LAN that uses token passing to control transmission of messages.

I. Each message is split into packets.

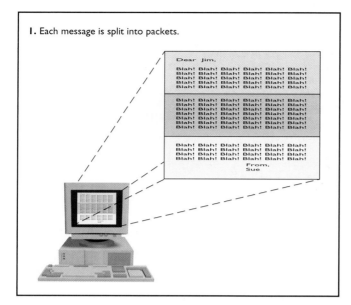

2. The packets are addressed to the same destination.

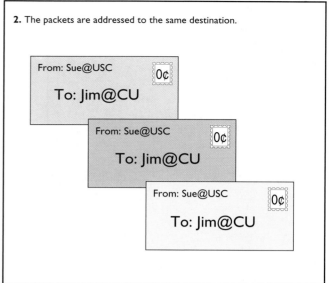

3. The packets may travel the same or different routes to the destination.

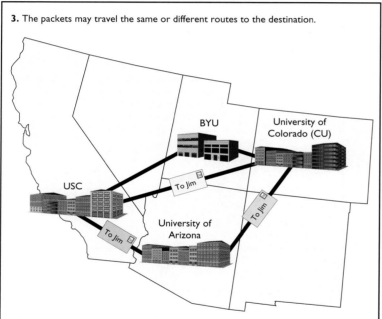

4. The packets are reassembled into the message at the destination.

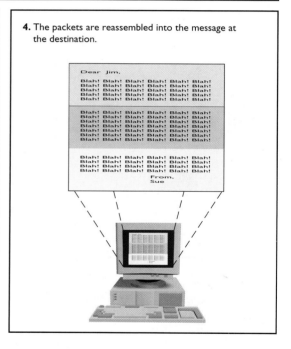

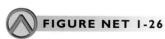

FIGURE NET 1-26

Packet switching.

Although the token ring architecture maintains more order than Ethernet in that it allows no collisions, sometimes a computer with a defective network interface card will swallow a token. If the token is gone for too long, the LAN assumes it's vanished and generates another. Several versions of the token ring architecture exist, the newer ones being faster and allowing more than a single token. Typical speeds run from a few mbps to several mbps.

WAN Protocols Like LANs, WANs also conform to particular network architectures. One rather common architecture, *Systems Network Architecture (SNA),* has operated for years in the IBM mainframe world. SNA is most commonly used for private networks—such as airlines' reservation systems and large banking networks—that have tens of thousands of workstations. Instead of CSMA/CD or token passing, SNA often runs a *polling* protocol to transmit data. With polling, devices are asked—one by one and over and over again—if they have messages to send.

Another widely used architecture, *Fiber Distributed Data Interface (FDDI),* is commonly used to set up the fiber-optic backbones that connect dispersed campus LANs at large universities. These backbones use a ring topology and a token-passing protocol similar to token-ring networks to span over a hundred miles or more and run at speeds of over 100 mbps (refer back to Figure NET 1-18).

The Internet, too, relies on many protocols. One, called *transmission control protocol/Internet protocol (TCP/IP),* specifies how to package and send messages for the hundreds of different types of computers that hook up to the Internet. TCP/IP relies on a procedure known as packet switching to do this. **Packet switching** (see Figure NET 1-26) divides messages into smaller units called *packets.* Packets may travel along the Internet to their destination by the shortest path, but sometimes links along this path are heavily congested or broken due to the weather or an accident. Consequently, packets can be routed through any feasible link—and not necessarily all together—to reach their destination. They are reassembled when they arrive. A typical router can handle about 10,000 packets per second, and some routers are rated at 200,000 or more packets per second.

Note that just because a network divides data into packets, it does not necessarily mean that packet switching is in effect. Strictly speaking, any block of data—from a single asynchronous bit to several thousand bytes—can be referred to as a packet. The use of packet switching in tomorrow's phone systems is covered in Feature NET 1-2 on page NET 40.

DANGERS POSED BY COMPUTER NETWORKS

So far in this chapter we've looked at the opportunities that computer networks have made possible. Unfortunately, there is also a dark side to this rosy picture. Because computers and networks are so pervasive today—and the social controls needed to harness them have lagged well behind the torrid pace set by technological change—there is unprecedented opportunity for criminals and other individuals to commit acts that are not in the public interest. Such acts run the gamut from stealing money to intentionally destroying corporate data to stalking children over the Internet.

Figure NET 1-27 lists many of the dangers that computer networks pose to society. Some of these dangers—such as those associated with the risk of using

FIGURE NET 1-27

Dangers posed by computer networks.

DANGERS POSED BY COMPUTER NETWORKS
Stealing and/or distributing information that individuals or organizations consider confidential or private, such as corporate secrets, credit-card numbers, tastes and habits, and the like
Stealing money, software, phone time, and other assets
Intentionally destroying or corrupting the data and programs of others, say, by implanting computer viruses on their computer systems or by altering materials in storage
Distributing pornographic materials, hate literature, and other objectionable items
Distributing, without express permission, materials that are owned and merchandised by someone else
Sending nuisance electronic mail, or "spam"
Snooping around computer systems that are considered off limits
Stalking people through the Internet
Using communications technology to misrepresent a situation, for purposes of committing a crime

■ **Packet switching.** A transmission technique that breaks messages into smaller units that travel to a destination along possibly different paths.

NET 1-2

The Phone System of the Future

Packet Switching Is Making Calling Cheaper

Qwest Communications and MCI WorldCom are two companies betting on digital networks and packet switching for the phone system of the future.

Qwest was one of the pioneers. In the late 1990s, it began laying its own fiber-optic cable and using the Internet to offer voice subscribers in selected cities a faster, cheaper, system than the traditional phone network. Customers may pay 5 cents a minute or less for calls. Today, voice quality over the Internet isn't as seamless as the regular phone system—there's an annoying split-second delay between voice transmissions—but it is nonetheless respectable and is catching up fast in quality.

Qwest's network and those of its closest competitors deploy packet-switching, a technology made famous by the Internet. All messages traveling through the network—whether they consist of voice, text, graphics, or video data—are subdivided into units called *packets*. Packets travel independently across long distances and are assembled at the destination.

MCI WorldCom—the telecom giant—recently acquired Sprint Corporation, which began building its own packet system, Ion Network, in the late 1990s. Ion enables a half dozen people to simultaneously talk on the phone, send faxes, or get data over the Internet—using a single phone line and all at a fraction of today's cost. While packets can blast through the backbone parts of MCI WorldCom's network at extremely high speeds, the main bottleneck is the slow copper wiring that feeds into most homes—the socalled "last mile" addressed in the chapter Tomorrow box on page NET 25. Here, Ion uses compression technology and fast processors to compensate for sparse bandwidth.

None of this is to say that packet switching and compression technology will be the definitive answer to current bandwidth

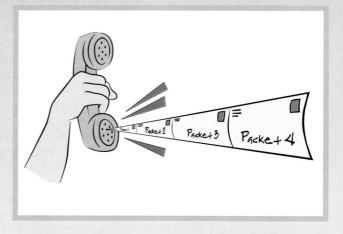

Packet calling. It will result in lower phone charges and changes in the way people are billed.

woes. Even a direct T1 line can have trouble delivering a video-rich multimedia presentation over the Internet. More likely, such new technologies as ADSL, cable modem, and satellite will figure in to the overall picture.

The world's largest phone company, AT&T, has also joined Quest and MCI WorldCom in the race to provide inexpensive packet calls. While the Internet now accounts for only 1 or 2 percent of all voice traffic, it could grow to as much as 15 percent by the year 2002. By 2005, close to 95 percent of all telecom traffic is expected to be data as opposed to voice. Consequently, it's no surprise many futurists believe that digital Internet telephony and its packet-switching technology will eventually take over conventional phone networks.

At some point in the future, even your phone bill may change, looking more like the one from the electric company. Instead of being charged for the distance a call travels, you may be metered for the amount of time you are connected.

credit cards over the Internet—are explored in Chapter NET 3. In versions of this textbook that contain the LIV module, we cover in greater detail many of the problems created by technology in general.

SUMMARY AND KEY TERMS

Go to the Online Glossary at www.harcourtcollege.com/infosys/parker2000/ student/ to review key terms.

Telecommunications, or *telecom,* refers to communications over a distance—over long-distance phone lines, via privately owned cables, or by satellite, for instance.

Telecommunications Applications A wide variety of important business applications involve telecommunications. Among these are **electronic mail** or

e-mail (exchanging messages through **electronic mailboxes**), **voice mail, bulletin board systems (BBSs), facsimile** or **fax,** paging, information retrieval (including **Internet** access), **workgroup computing, teleconferencing, telecommuting,** transaction processing, and interorganizational systems such as **electronic data interchange (EDI).**

The Telecommunications Industry The key players in the telecommunications industry include phone companies, cable-TV and satellite companies, service and content providers, and a wide variety of supporting hardware and software companies. Current deregulation is creating a telecom industry characterized by mergers and acquisitions, partnering arrangements, and shakeouts that will determine the winners and losers in the early part of the twenty-first century.

Telecommunications Media Messages sent in a telecommunications system are transmitted over some type of **communications medium.** Wiring, such as **twisted-pair wires, coaxial cable,** and **fiber-optic cable,** constitutes one major class of media. Messages also are commonly sent through the air in the form of **microwave** signals or over cellular or infrared networks. **Terrestrial microwave stations** accommodate microwave transmissions when either the sender or the receiver is on the ground. **Communications satellites** reduce the cost of long-distance transmissions via terrestrial microwave stations and provide overseas communications. **Cellular phones** use special ground stations that cover areas called *cells* to enable users to communicate with others. *Infrared technology* relies on infrared light beams to transmit data.

Adapting Computers to Communications Media Signals sent along a phone line travel in an **analog** fashion—that is, as continuous waves. Computers and their support equipment, however, are **digital** devices that handle data coded into 0s and 1s.

The difference between the highest and lowest frequencies on an analog medium is known as the medium's **bandwidth.** A higher bandwidth allows a medium to support more powerful communications applications. Media speed is often measured in **bits per second (bps),** kbps (thousands of bits per second), or mbps (millions of bits per second).

Messages move between machines either in **parallel transmissions,** in which each bit of a byte follows a different path, or in **serial transmissions,** in which bits of a byte follow one another in series along a single path.

Workstations are usually connected to a network through either a **network interface card (NIC)** or a **modem.** Typically, NICs connect workstations to local networks with dedicated lines, whereas modems connect workstations to wide-area networks with dial-up lines. If you need more bandwidth than you can squeeze out of a modem, your best bet is an **ISDN** line or something beyond.

Network Topologies Telecommunications networks can be classified in terms of their *topologies,* or geometrical patterns. Three common topologies are the **star network,** the **bus network,** and the **ring network.** Network topologies are often combined to aggregate smaller networks into larger ones.

Local Networks Many organizations build their own **local networks,** which connect devices in a single building or at a single site. Three common types of local networks are local area networks, hierarchical networks, and private branch exchanges.

Local area networks (LANs) fall into two categories. The first, **client-server LANs,** consist of **server** devices that provide network services to **client** workstations. Services often include access to expensive printers and vast secondary storage, database access, and computing power. In the second

type of LANs, **peer-to-peer LANs,** the user workstations and shared peripherals in the network operate at the same level. The term **intranet** refers to a private LAN that implements the infrastructure and standards of the Internet and World Wide Web.

A **hierarchical local network** consists of a powerful *host* CPU at the top level of the hierarchy and microcomputer workstations or display terminals at lower levels. The workstations or terminals can either **download** data from the host or **upload** data to it.

A **private branch exchange (PBX)** consists of a central, private switchboard that links internal devices to switched lines.

Wide Area Networks **Wide area networks (WANs)** are communications networks that span relatively wide geographical areas. Because they tie together so many devices over such long distances, they require a number of special pieces of equipment.

Repeaters amplify signals along a network. **Routers** work in large switched networks like the Internet to pass messages along to their destinations. Devices on two dissimilar networks can communicate with each other if the networks are connected by a **gateway.** Devices on two similar networks can communicate with each other if they are connected by a **bridge.** A **multiplexer** enables two or more low-speed devices to share a high-speed line. A **concentrator** is a multiplexer with a store-and-forward capability.

Protocols A communications **protocol** is a collection of procedures to establish, maintain, and terminate transmissions between devices. Because devices transmit data in so many ways, they collectively employ scores of different protocols.

One type of protocol classifies transmissions in the **simplex, half-duplex,** or **full-duplex** modes.

Serially transmitted data are packaged either **asynchronously** (one byte to a package) or **synchronously** (several bytes to a package). Synchronous transmissions use a timing mechanism to coordinate exchanges of data packets between senders and receivers.

Two major LAN architectures are **Ethernet** and **token ring.** Each of these architectures is specified in a detailed set of protocols. Ethernet LANs commonly use a protocol called *CSMA/CD* to exchange messages, whereas token ring LANs use a protocol called *token passing.*

Like LANs, WANs also conform to particular network architectures. Three such architectures are *SNA, FDDI,* and *TCP/IP.* TCP/IP relies on a procedure known as **packet switching.**

Dangers Posed by Computer Networks Because computers and networks are so widespread, there is unprecedented opportunity for criminals and other individuals to commit acts that are not in the public interest. Such acts run the gamut from stealing money to intentionally destroying corporate data to stalking children over the Internet.

EXERCISES

1. Define the following terms and answer the questions that follow:
   a. E-mail
   b. Voice mail
   c. Fax
   d. Paging

   Which of the four would most effectively transmit a 15-page business report that has several handwritten comments by the boss? Which of the four would most effectively remind a person walking in a park of an important phone call that must be made this afternoon?

2. Fill in the blanks:
   a. Two types of modems are _____ modems and _____ modems.
   b. _____ is the process of transferring a file from a host or server computer to a requesting workstation over a network.
   c. A(n) _____ is a private LAN that uses the standards of the Internet and World Wide Web.
   d. All the bits in a byte follow each other in succession over a single path in _____ transmission.
   e. In _____-duplex transmission, messages may travel in two directions simultaneously.

3. Name at least one company in each of the following segments of the telecommunications industry:
   a. Phone company
   b. Cable-TV company
   c. Content provider
   d. Computer-software company
   e. Communications-hardware company

   Why is it getting increasingly difficult to put many large companies into any one segment?

4. List the types of telecommunications media covered in the chapter. Which is the most appropriate for each of the following situations?
   a. Getting output from a hard disk on a laptop computer onto a nearby desktop printer without the use of wire
   b. Transmitting data as quickly as possible, regardless of the cost
   c. Establishing contact between two people on the move
   d. Connecting a modem to a wall in the cheapest way possible
   e. Connecting workstations in a LAN

5. Many types of communications software will tell you how long you will spend downloading a particular file. Answer the following questions, assuming that a ten-page document occupies about 35 kilobytes (35,000 bytes) of storage space. Assume also 8 bits in a byte, and each byte is transmitted with an extra parity bit for error checking—in other words, a byte actually takes up 9 bits.
   a. How long will a 56 kbps modem take to download 100 pages of information? A 28.8 kbps modem?
   b. How much faster could you complete the transfer in part a over an ISDN line that runs at 128 kbps? Over a 1.54 mbps T1 connection? Over a fiber-optic backbone that runs at 100 mbps?
   c. All of the calculations you have made so far reflect maximum speeds. What real-world conditions would slow the rate of transfer?

6. Identify the three most basic network topologies and answer the following questions:
   a. Which is most appropriate to link a host mainframe computer with dumb terminals?
   b. Which most commonly uses a token-passing protocol?
   c. On which does Ethernet most commonly run?

7. What terms do the following acronyms represent?
   a. bps
   b. LAN
   c. PBX
   d. EDI
   e. NIC

8. Describe in your own words the functions of each of the following types of equipment:
   a. Router
   b. Repeater
   c. Gateway
   d. Bridge
   e. Concentrator

9. How does CSMA/CD work? How does it differ from token passing?

10. Identify several dangers posed by computer networks.

11. Determine whether the following statements are true or false.

   a. Most modems plug into dedicated lines.

   b. Infrared transmission is a wireless transmission technique that works with radio waves.

   c. A ring network connects devices serially in a closed loop.

   d. An intranet is a private LAN.

   e. A bridge is an interface that enables two dissimilar networks to communicate.

   f. *Internet* is a contraction of two words: *internal* and *network.*

   g. The "Baby Bells" include such firms as America Online and CompuServe.

   h. Coaxial cable consists of a center wire inside a grounded, cylindrical shield.

   i. Microwaves are radio signals.

   j. Peer-to-peer LANs are often smaller networks than client-server LANs.

12. Match each term with the description that fits best:

   a. NIC   d. Bps
   b. Analog   e. ISDN
   c. Token passing f. Uploading

   _____ A protocol used in a type of LAN.

   _____ The process of transferring a file from a local computer to a remote computer over a network.

   _____ A digital phone service that offers high-speed transmission over ordinary phone lines.

   _____ An add-in board through which a workstation connects to a local network.

   _____ A measure of a transmission medium's speed.

   _____ The transmission of data as continuous wave patterns.

PROJECTS

1. **The Telecommunications Industry** The telecommunications industry has evolved in the past quarter of a century to encompass many organizations, not just a single phone company. Among today's key players are content providers, communications-hardware companies, communications-software companies, and companies that provide the infrastructure over which communications services are offered. For this project, write a small report not to exceed ten pages that discusses some aspect of the telecommunications industry. You can choose any of the topics that follow or choose one of your own. Your report should go well beyond the information presented in the text.

   ■ A History of AT&T

   ■ Cisco Systems: A Closer Look at One of the Internet's Most Successful Hardware Firms

   ■ The Evolution of Satellite Products: What's Around the Corner?

   ■ How the Need for Bandwidth Is Shaping the Telecommunications Industry

   ■ The Battle for the Last Mile: What's the Latest News?

   ■ Blockbuster Communications Products for the Twenty-First Century: Some Predictions

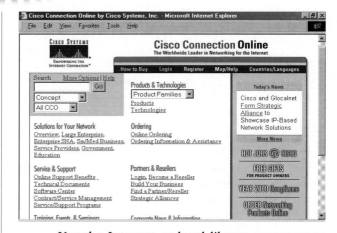

Use the Internet or local library resources to help you with your research. If your report is on a particular company, note that all of the major players in the telecommunications industry maintain Web sites containing useful information about their products and services (see accompanying figure). You can easily reach any of these sites by typing the company's name into the search box of any widely used, Web-based search engine. A list of search engines and information on how to reach them is given in Project 6 on page NET 89.

 2. Research on the Internet The Internet contains lots of information on communications-related topics. Use the Internet and a search site such as Yahoo! or Excite to find information about any three of the following topics:

a. Cable Modems

b. Ethernet

c. Fiber-optic cable

d. Client-server LANs

e. Cellular phones

f. The World Wide Web

g. Teledisc

Report to the class about the sites you visited and the contents of each one.

3. Digital Satellites Some exciting new digital satellite services are being pioneered by technologies such as DirecTV (18-inch rooftop dishes that can accept a few hundred television channels with sharp resolution) and DirecPC (digital information downloads from satellite to your PC). What potential do you foresee for these relatively new telecommunications technologies as television and computing technologies merge together? Can you buy one system that will cater to both TV and PC needs?

4. If You Think PBXs Can Be Obnoxious, Please Raise Your Hand Here's a project in human engineering. Many people dislike dealing with PBX phone-menu systems because they often involve long waits as recorded voices rattle off choices. Also, you can often spend a couple of minutes making choices on early menus and then wind up at a final menu without satisfaction. As your project, look into a PBX-menu system of your choice or your instructor's choice and evaluate its good points and weak points. A large government site—such as the one for the Internal Revenue Service—will work well here if you can't find another example. A number of such menus can be reached by local dialing or toll-free numbers (with 800 and 888 area codes), so you won't get stuck paying long-distance charges.

5. Wireless LANs LANs often use cellular and other types of wireless technologies to link stations. Name three types of applications that work best through wireless LANs and identify in each case the benefits that result.

6. Becoming a High Roller Online A rapidly growing application on the Internet is personal investing. Users can look up stock prices by computer, maintain lists of their favorite stocks or mutual funds for automatic price quotes, buy and sell stocks and mutual funds online, communicate with other investors about specific companies, access research reports and filings at the Securities and Exchange Commission (SEC), and so on. For this exercise:

a. Write a 3- to 5-page paper about resources available on the Web that cater to ordinary people who want to invest money. Some of the sites listed in the accompanying table will help get you started.

b. What, in your opinion, are the three biggest advantages of the Internet for the small investor?

7. LANs Evaluate a client-server LAN on your campus or at a local business and answer the following questions:

a. Does the LAN use Ethernet, token ring, or some other LAN architecture?

b. How many workstations are connected to the LAN?

c. Identify the servers on the network and tell what each one does.

d. How fast can data travel through the LAN?

8. **Research Revisited** A textbook of this sort cannot possibly cover every emerging communications technology. The following list identifies several technologies that have received a lot of attention in the computer press in recent years. For any three of these, explain what the technologies do and their significance.

a. PCS (personal communications services)

b. GPS (global positioning system)

c. ARCnet

d. Thin clients

e. Baud rate

f. Http (hypertext transfer protocol)

9. **Extranets** Find an example of an extranet reported in a magazine or newspaper and report to the class about it. Be sure to cover such details as the name of the company that runs the extranet, the types of users and applications involved, and the method by which unauthorized users are blocked out.

10. **Global Positioning Systems** Global positioning systems (GPSs) involve the use of small computing devices combined with special satellites—24 of them that orbit the earth at a height of 10,900 miles. With such a device tucked into a backpack, a hiker can retrieve satellite data that tells him or her their position on earth within a few feet. GPS devices can also be used by drivers of rental cars in conjunction with maps to tell them exactly where they are at any given moment. Using the Internet or other research tools, determine as many uses as you can for GPSs.

INTERACTIVE EXERCISE

CONNECTING YOUR PC TO A NETWORK

Your work PC is to be connected to the company network. Go to the Interactive Exercise at www.harcourtcollege.com/infosys/parker2000/student/ exercise/ to complete this exercise.

ONLINE REVIEW

Go to the Online Review at www.harcourtcollege.com/infosys/parker2000/ student/ to test your understanding of this chapter's concepts.

NET 2

INTRODUCTION TO THE INTERNET AND WORLD WIDE WEB

OUTLINE

LEARNING OBJECTIVES

After completing this chapter, you will be able to:

1. Discuss how the Internet has evolved to become what it is today.

2. Identify the resources available on the Internet and explain the particular prominence of the World Wide Web.

3. Explain how the Internet benefits individuals and businesses.

4. Name a variety of tools available for working on the Internet.

5. List and evaluate the available options for connecting to the Internet.

OVERVIEW

It's hard to believe that before 1990 few people outside of the computer industry and academia had ever heard of the Internet. It's really a small wonder, though. Hardware, software, and communications tools were not available back then to unleash the power of this tool and to make it a viable resource for almost everyone, as it is today.

What a difference a few years make. Today, "Internet" is a household word, and in many ways it has redefined how people think about computers and communications. Not since the early 1980s, when microcomputers swept into homes and businesses, has the general public been so excited about a new technology.

Despite the popularity of the Internet, however, many users cannot answer some important, basic questions about it. What makes up the Internet? Is it the same thing as the World Wide Web? How did the Internet begin, and where is it heading? What types of tools are available to help people make optimum use of the Internet? This chapter and the next address such questions.

Chapter NET 2 begins with a discussion of the evolution of the Internet, from the late 1960s to the present time. Then it looks into the many resources that the Internet offers—such as e-mail and the World Wide Web—and how individuals and businesses are using the Internet in their work and leisure time. Next, so you can appreciate how the Internet's content arrives at your desktop, the chapter covers how Internet addresses work. Then, it's on to the software and hardware resources required for access. The final section of the chapter covers connecting to the Internet. Here you will learn about types of organizations available to assist you with making an Internet link and how to select among them.

EVOLUTION OF THE INTERNET

The **Internet** is a worldwide collection of networks that supports personal and commercial communications and information exchange. It consists of thousands of separate networks that are interconnected and accessed daily by millions of people. Just as the shipping industry has simplified transportation by providing standard containers for carrying all sorts of merchandise via air, rail, highway, and sea, the Internet furnishes a standard way of sending messages across many types of computer platforms and transmission media. While "Internet" has become a household word during the past few years, it has actually operated in one form or another for decades.

FROM THE ARPANET TO THE WORLD WIDE WEB

The Internet began in 1969 as an experimental project. The U.S. Department of Defense (DOD) wanted to develop a network that could withstand outages, such as those caused by nuclear attack. A principal goal was creating a system that could send messages along alternate paths if part of the network was disabled. With this purpose in mind, the DOD enlisted researchers in colleges and universities to assist with the development of protocols and message-packeting systems to standardize routing information.

For a tutorial on what the Internet and World Wide Web are, go to www. harcourtcollege.com/infosys/ parker2000/student/tutor/ and click on Chapter NET 2.

■ **Internet.** A global network linking thousands of networks and millions of individual users, schools, businesses, and government agencies.

ARPANET   At its start and throughout many years of its history, the Internet was called **ARPANET** (pronounced *ar-pan-ette*). ARPANET was named for the group that sponsored its development, the Advanced Research Projects Agency (ARPA) of the DOD. During its first few years, ARPANET enabled researchers at a few dozen academic institutions to communicate with each other and with government agencies on topics of mutual interest.

However, the DOD got much more than it bargained for. With the highly controversial Vietnam War in full swing, ARPANET's e-mail facility began to handle not only legitimate research discussions but also heated debates about U.S. involvement in Southeast Asia. As students began to access ARPANET, computer games such as Space War gradually found their way into the roster of applications along with online messaging methods to share game strategies. Such unintended uses led to the development of bulletin boards and discussion groups devoted to other special interests.

As the experiment grew during the next decade, hundreds of colleges and universities tapped into ARPANET. By the 1980s, advances in communications technology enabled many of these institutions to develop their own local networks as well. These local networks collectively served a mixture of DOS and Windows-based computers, Apple Macintoshes, UNIX-speaking workstations, and so on. Over the years, ARPANET became a connecting thread of protocols that tied together such disparate networks. Throw in the government networks also under development during that time—and add to that the decision to let friendly foreign countries participate—and you can see how ARPANET turned into a massive network of networks.

By the end of the 1980s, the Internet—renamed from ARPANET—could perhaps best be described as a vehicle for thousands of technically oriented people throughout the world to communicate electronically about anything from their work to sports to their love lives.

The 1990s and the World Wide Web   Despite its popularity in academia, the Internet went virtually unnoticed by the general public and the business community for over two decades. Why? For two reasons—it was hard to use and slow. Users had to know cryptic programming commands, since attractive graphical user interfaces (GUIs) were still largely unknown.

As always, however, technology improved and new applications quickly evolved. First, communications hardware improved and computers gained speed and better graphics capabilities. Then, in 1989, a researcher named Tim Berners-Lee, working at a physics laboratory called CERN in Europe, proposed the idea of a *World Wide Web*. The Web concept would organize Internet information into pages linked together through selectable text or images on a display screen.

Matters really got rolling with the arrival of Microsoft Windows 3.0 (and later updates) and its widely used graphical user interface. As sales of Windows soared, graphically-rich *Web browsers* sporting the Windows GUI became available to make surfing the World Wide Web both easy and fun (see Figure NET 2-1). The Web is only part of the Internet, but it is by far one of the most popular and one of the fastest-growing parts today. As interest in the Internet snowballed, scores of companies began looking for ways to make it more accessible to customers, to make the user interface even more dazzling, and to make more services available over it. Today, most companies regard the Internet as an indispensable competitive tool.

To show you how fast the Internet and Web have grown, consider that in the middle of 1993, only about 100 computers—called *Web servers*—distributed Web pages throughout the Internet. Talk about rapid change: Today that count is in the hundreds of thousands!

For links to further information about the history and current status of the Internet and World Wide Web, go to www.harcourtcollege.com/ infosys/parker2000/student/ explore/ and click on Chapter NET 2.

■ **ARPANET.** The forerunner to the Internet, named after the Advanced Research Projects Agency (ARPA), which sponsored its development.

```
ftp>dir
100 port command successful
300 opening ASCII mode data connection for file
list
    2415   readme.txt  Mon Apr 10 19:52:04 1990
   32251   pkzip.exe  Tues Sept 6 03:44:18 1991
  145671   mis.zip   Sun Jan 17 10:33:14 1991
<dir> rfc
420 transfer complete
ftp>cd rfc
200 cwd command successful
ftp>get rfc-contents.txt contents.txt
```

EARLY 1990s
Even at the beginning of the 1990s, using the Internet for most people meant learning how to work with a cryptic sequence of commands. Virtually all information was text-based.

TODAY
Today's Internet features the World Wide Web, which organizes much of the Internet's content into easy-to-read pages and replaces the cryptic command sequences with linkages that you can activate with a mouse click. The Web page shown above, with its famous headline, provides a good example.

 **FIGURE NET 2-1**

Using the Internet: Back in the "old days" versus now.

THE INTERNET COMMUNITY TODAY

The Internet community of today is populated by individuals, companies, and a variety of other organizations located both at home and throughout the world (see Figure NET 2-2). Virtually anyone with a computer that has communications capabilities can be part of the Internet, either as a user or as a supplier of information or services. Most members of the Internet community fall into one or more of the following groups.

Users *Users* are people who avail themselves of the information content of the Internet in their work or play. The user base still shows a decided tilt toward the United States, although Europeans widely use the Internet, and access is available in about 200 countries. While users are both young and old and come from a variety of backgrounds, recent studies have shown that users are typically college educated, white, male, and above average in affluence. This profile is expected to change considerably in the years ahead, as the Internet begins to approach the popularity of the phone and personal computer. Recent surveys have shown that the user base is gravitating toward numbers that are closer in line with population averages—a sure sign that the Internet is achieving the broadcast type of mass-market appeal.

Service Providers **Internet service providers (ISPs)**—often called *service providers* or *access providers* for short—are organizations that supply Internet access to others. They operate very much like a cross between the cable-television and phone companies in that they provide a window for you to see what's out there in the wider world and to interact with it.

ISPs usually charge each subscriber a monthly fee to access the Internet, and some charge setup fees to open accounts. They also furnish e-mail addresses,

---

■ **Internet service provider (ISP).** An organization that sells basic online access to the Internet.

SERVICE PROVIDERS
Service providers connect individual users and user organizations to the Internet.

USERS
These are the people who work on or play with the Internet.

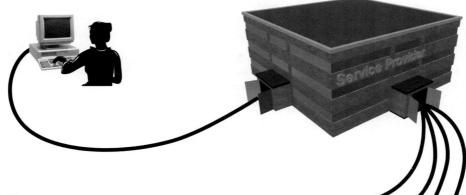

CONTENT PROVIDERS
These consist of the organizations and individuals that create or distribute information on the Internet.

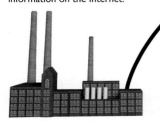
COMPANIES

COLLEGES AND UNIVERSITIES

GOVERNMENT

INDIVIDUALS

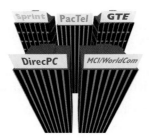

INFRASTUCTURE COMPANIES
These are the enterprises that own or operate the paths along which Internet data travel.

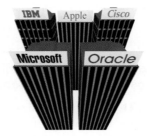

SOFTWARE AND HARDWARE COMPANIES
These companies make Internet-related programs and equipment.

OTHER ORGANIZATIONS
Several groups act as watchdogs on the Internet, make up the rules that govern it, and help manage sections of it.

which are unique like phone numbers and allow users to receive electronic mail. Additionally, many providers offer to post Web pages for subscribers. A later section of the chapter will cover service providers in more detail.

Content Providers **Internet content providers,** or *content providers,* are the parties that furnish the information available on the Internet. If service providers work like the phone companies, content providers resemble the people you talk to when you dial phone numbers. Here are some examples of content providers:

■ A photographer creates electronic copies of some of her best work and places them—along with her e-mail address and phone number—on the Internet.

⬡ **FIGURE NET 2-2**

The Internet community. Today's Internet community is composed of users, service and content providers, government and academia, and several other types of organizations.

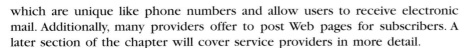
■ **Internet content provider.** An organization or individual providing information for distribution over the Internet.

■ A political-action group sponsors an online forum for discussions between people who share its opinions.

■ A software company maintains an Internet address that users can access to both get product information and download trial copies of software.

■ A television broadcasting company maintains an online site that anyone on the Internet can turn to for late-breaking news and feature stories.

Infrastructure Companies   These are the enterprises that own or operate the paths or "roadways" along which Internet data travel. Included in this group are phone and Internet-backbone companies, cellular operators, satellite and cable-TV companies, and the like.

Software and Hardware Companies   In addition to the types of companies covered thus far, a wide variety of software and hardware companies make and distribute Internet-related products. The firms that supply browser and e-mail software fall into this category. So, too, do the companies that make routers, server computers, server software, and Web-page publishing tools. The customers of software and hardware companies are users, service and content providers, and infrastructure companies.

Other Organizations   Many other organizations influence the Internet and its uses. Governments have among the most visible impact; their local laws limit both information content and access in the Internet community. A voluntary group called the *Internet Society* is another key organization. It proposes guidelines for the direction and technical development of the Internet, and it also decides which protocols to support and how Internet addresses should work. Also playing an important support role is the *Shared Registration System*. A competitive registration system developed by the Department of Commerce, the Internet Corporation for Assigned Names and Numbers (ICANN), and Network Solutions, Inc., registrar companies included as part of the Shared Registration System are charged with registering Internet addresses and ensuring that no two are the same. Last but not least, many colleges and universities support Internet research and manage large blocks of the Internet's resources.

MYTHS ABOUT THE INTERNET

Because the Internet is so unique in the history of the world—and still a relatively new phenomenon—several widespread myths about it have surfaced.

Myth 1: The Internet Is Free   This falsehood has been perpetuated largely by the fact that people can freely engage in long-distance e-mail or chat exchanges without paying extra. It is true that the Internet's design never anticipated distance billing, and it is certainly also a fact that many people, such as students and employees, pay nothing to use the Internet. Yet it should also be obvious that someone, somewhere has to be forking out money to keep the Internet up and running.

Businesses, schools and public libraries, self-employed individuals working from home, and content providers often pay service providers flat monthly fees to link to the Internet. The service providers—along with the phone companies—pay to keep the physical links of the network running smoothly. Providers also pay software and hardware companies for the resources they need to support users. Of course, most of these costs are eventually passed along to ordinary users in the way of higher taxes or higher costs.

Some industry observers feel that, in some not-too-distant day, market forces will determine much about who has access to what on the Internet. As more and more demands for bandwidth clog the Internet—including memory-hungry multimedia Web pages, phone calls, video and videoconferencing applications, and software robots that cruise Web sites for information—customers who need speed and reliability will be forced to pay for it.

Myth 2: Someone Controls the Internet   The popularity of conspiracy theories in recent years has contributed to the spread of this myth. In fact, no one group or organization controls the Internet, although many would undoubtedly like to do so. Governments in each country have the power to regulate content and use of the Internet within their borders. However, legislators often face serious obstacles getting acts passed into law—let alone getting them enforced. Making governmental control even harder is the bombproof design of the Internet itself. If a government tries to block access to or from a specific country, for example, users can establish links between the two countries through a third one.

Guidelines of watchdog groups such as the Internet Society have sometimes even given way before the tidal wave of people and organizations that have flocked to the Internet. For instance, the policy that discouraged commercial use has fallen by the wayside in recent years. In the middle of 1994, only about 14 percent of Web sites were deemed to be commercial; today, that number is close to 90 percent.

Myth 3: The Internet and World Wide Web Are Identical   Since you can use Web browser software to get virtually anywhere on the Internet today, many people think the Internet and the Web are the same thing. They're not, as you will see in the next section, which describes the different parts of the Internet. While the Web is the fastest-growing component of the Internet, it's not even the largest one. More people, in fact, use the Internet's e-mail facility than the Web.

WHAT DOES THE INTERNET HAVE TO OFFER?

Since the Internet evolves so rapidly, the features offered over it also change constantly. This section describes some of the more popular features now in use. Figure NET 2-3 covers many commercial and leisure opportunities that these features have made possible.

E-MAIL

Electronic mail, or **e-mail,** was one of the first applications to appear on the Internet, and it remains the most widely used one—Americans alone send over 2 billion e-mail messages a day. If you are connected to the Internet, you can send an e-mail message to anyone with an Internet e-mail address, just as you can reach anyone with a phone number through the phone system. Figure NET 2-4 illustrates how the Internet distributes e-mail. You may also want to refer back to Figure NET 1-1, which illustrates the components of a typical e-mail message.

You can create an e-mail message either on your word processor or—as most people do—with e-mail software. When you finish composing the message, you then send it via the e-mail program to the electronic mailbox of another person (or the mailboxes of several people). Many e-mail programs enable users to attach documents, voice clips, and graphics to outgoing messages and to receive messages enhanced in this way. Other common features are an address book and message management. An *address-book feature* lets you store the e-mail addresses of friends and associates. A *message-management feature* provides the ability to organize and file incoming messages and to filter out junk e-mail before it reaches your eyes.

For a tutorial on using e-mail, go to www.harcourt college.com/infosys/ parker2000/student/tutor/ and click on Chapter NET 2.

■ **Electronic mail.** The computer-to-computer counterpart for interoffice mail or the postal service. Also called **e-mail.**

Electronic mail. Internet mail service now links people in about 200 countries. Futurists predict a universal electronic mail network similar to the phone system.

Information retrieval. Virtually any type of information can be found on the Internet—tutorials on various subjects, hobby information, legal and medical advice—you name it.

Bulk file transfer. Products such as electronic newspapers and magazines—as well as software and music—are distributed over the Internet, saving the cost of print media, disks, and mailing.

Chats and forums. You can take part in worldwide chats and forums on matters of personal interest— simply browse the network to find topics you wish to discuss.

On-demand movies and television. Someday it will be possible to order virtually any movie and television show by computer, choosing your own viewing times.

Social video gaming. Games in which several people participate are now available over the Internet. As video and communications capabilities improve, expect participation in TV game shows via Internet links.

Shopping and procurement. It is now possible to search through scores of electronic malls for products. "Intelligent agent" programs will help you find what you want.

Customer support. Many companies assist customers over the Internet. The Internet is also widely used to distribute advertising literature about products and to update software.

News and weather. Information about news events and weather happening all over the globe are updated regularly on the Internet. You can even access satellite data.

Education. You can find learning materials on virtually every topic imaginable on the Internet. Eventually, you will be able to access millions of books online instead of having to go to your local library to find them.

Access to remote computing. If your own computer isn't powerful enough to perform certain types of tasks, you can access larger computers located elsewhere—and their software, too.

Conferencing. Futurists predict that a picture phone—a phoning device that enables people to see each other as they speak—will someday be a standard feature on the Internet.

FIGURE NET 2-3

Commercial and leisure opportunities made possible by the Internet.

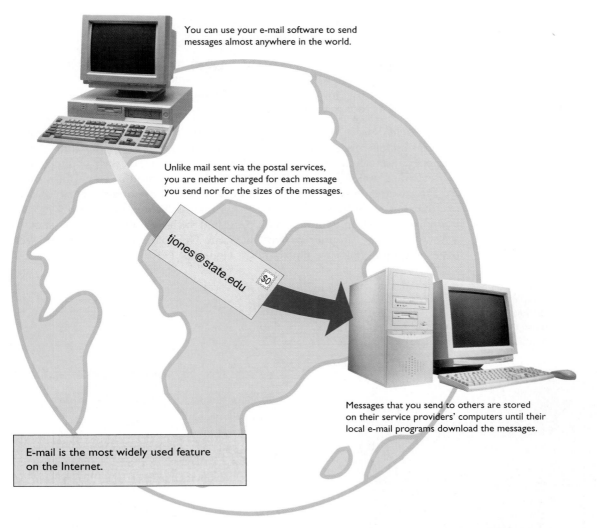

You can use your e-mail software to send messages almost anywhere in the world.

Unlike mail sent via the postal services, you are neither charged for each message you send nor for the sizes of the messages.

tjones@state.edu $0

Messages that you send to others are stored on their service providers' computers until their local e-mail programs download the messages.

E-mail is the most widely used feature on the Internet.

 **FIGURE NET 2-4**

E-mail over the Internet.

Users can send and receive e-mail over private networks, the Internet, or some combination of the two. Corporate local area networks (LANs), which often use network protocols other than TCP/IP (the Internet standard), sometimes use special LAN-based e-mail programs. The growth of the Internet and corporate intranets, and the resulting spread of standards based on TCP/IP, have led to a variety of less-expensive, Internet-based e-mail options, such as Eudora Pro, Netscape Messenger, and Microsoft Outlook Express.

You don't have to spend a dime on an e-mail program, though, if you don't want to. Most browsers today have built-in e-mail routines, and many service providers include the use of an e-mail program in their basic fee. What's more, e-mail is increasingly being offered as a free service on the Web. The services—which include Hotmail and Yahoo! Mail—provide users free mailboxes and software, as long as they have an Internet connection and don't mind a little advertising on their message screens in return. People without an Internet connection can send and receive free e-mail using Juno, a company that offers free e-mail plus free connection time to send and retrieve your e-mail, provided that there is a local access telephone number for your area. Unlike Internet service providers, however, the free Juno service allows you access only to e-mail, not to other Internet resources.

For links to a wide variety of interesting Web sites, go to www.harcourtcollege.com/ infosys/parker2000/student/ explore/ and click on Chapter NET 2.

FIGURE NET 2-5

How hyperlinks work.

INFORMATION RETRIEVAL AND THE WORLD WIDE WEB

One of the most popular uses of the Internet today is information retrieval. While the World Wide Web is by far the most popular way for people to access information on the Internet—and the method to which this and the next chapter will devote a great deal of attention—it is not the only one.

The World Wide Web   The **World Wide Web (WWW),** or *Web,* is a retrieval system based on technology that organizes information into pages. The pages are called *Web pages,* or "documents." Web pages are connected by **hyperlinks,** which are often referred to as **hypermedia.** Hyperlinks often appear onscreen as different colored or underlined text or as selectable icons or other images. When you select a hyperlink by clicking on it with a mouse, the current page on your screen is refreshed with new information—such as a new Web page, another part of the same Web page, or a movie clip. Web pages and hyperlinks are illustrated in Figure NET 2-5.

Hyperlinks commonly appear as boldfaced or underlined text, images, or icons, that—when you click on them—take you to other pages on the Web.

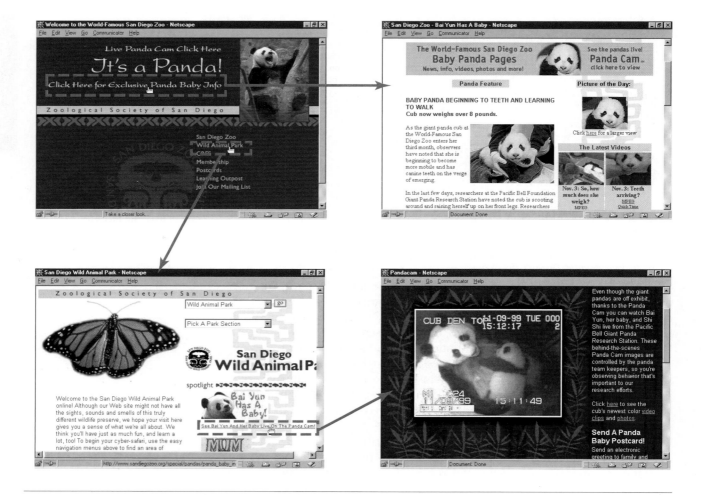

■ **World Wide Web (WWW).** A network within the Internet consisting of data organized as page images with hyperlinks to other data. ■ **Hyperlink.** An icon, image, or specially marked text located on a World Wide Web page that summons new information to the screen when the user selects it. Often also called **hypermedia.**

One or more related Web pages belonging to an individual or organization is called a **Web site.** Today, most medium-sized to large companies in the United States maintain one or more Web sites, and millions of individuals and small firms have them too. A computer that hosts one or more Web sites is called a **Web server.** Servers run specialized software for each type of Internet application, including the Web, e-mail, UseNet news (discussed shortly), and so on.

A Web site can contain anywhere from one to hundreds or thousands of pages. Your visit to a Web site often begins at the site's **home page.** A home page at a large multipage site usually presents a table of contents with hyperlinks to other pages on the site. The Web lets you freely navigate among such pages and others by selecting any of the hyperlinks, in any order you wish.

You need a piece of software called a *Web browser* to see pages on the Web and to navigate between Web sites (called *Web surfing,* when the navigation is done in a casual manner). In client-server terms, desktop browsers are often called *Web clients.* Web clients display Web pages by putting in specific requests for pages stored on Web servers. Often today the processing work on the Web is shared between client and server. With servers bending under ever-larger page-request burdens as the Web grows, clients are taking over a lot more of the computing work—from determining how to display pages to running small interactive elements called "applets" that make pages more exciting.

A later section of the chapter will cover Web browsers in much greater detail. Suffice it to say for now that these programs have been evolving into one-stop solutions for users to link up not only to Web pages but to virtually all other resources of the Internet, including e-mail (discussed earlier), and Gopher and FTP (discussed next).

A guide to several useful sites on the World Wide Web is provided in the Window at the end of this chapter.

Gopher **Gopher,** developed at the University of Minnesota, is another information-retrieval feature within the Internet. Gopher generates hierarchical, text-based menus that allow the user to access resources by making successive menu selections with their mouse or other pointing device.

Gopher is almost as easy to use as the Web. In fact, before the Web came along with its flashy, tantalizing graphics, Gopher was the rave of the Internet. While you will find far fewer Gopher sites than Web sites today, and the growth of Gopher has slowed, thousands of sites still offer valuable content. What's more, a lot of information is available on the Gopher system that has not yet been put on the Web. Many academic institutions, companies, and government agencies maintain Gopher sites in addition to their Web sites.

Gopher is organized similarly to the Web. People who want to distribute information in this way set up Gopher sites on Gopher servers, and people who want to download from such sites must have Gopher "client" software built into their browsers. Web pages often contain links to Gopher sites and vice versa.

File Transfer Protocol (FTP) FTP sites preceded both Web and Gopher sites in the evolution of the Internet, and they remain good places to visit to get copies of programs and files. **FTP** stands for **file transfer protocol,** the communications protocol that facilitates the transfer of files between an FTP server and a user's computer. FTP sites allow you to upload or download files by selecting them from menus that list file and folder names (see Figure NET 2-6).

For a tutorial on downloading files, go to www.harcourtcollege.com/infosys/parker2000/student/tutor/ and click on **Chapter NET 2.**

■ **Web site.** A collection of related Web pages belonging to an individual or organization. ■ **Web server.** A computer that stores and distributes Web pages upon request. ■ **Home page.** The starting page for a Web site. ■ **Gopher.** An information-retrieval tool for the Internet that generates hierarchical, text-intensive menus; successive topic choices narrow a search to a particular resource. ■ **File transfer protocol (FTP).** A communications protocol that facilitates the transfer of files between a host computer and a user's computer.

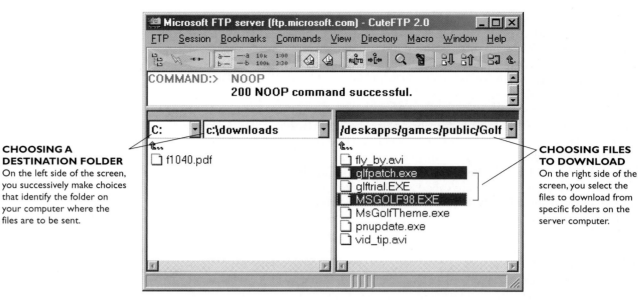

CHOOSING A DESTINATION FOLDER On the left side of the screen, you successively make choices that identify the folder on your computer where the files are to be sent.

CHOOSING FILES TO DOWNLOAD On the right side of the screen, you select the files to download from specific folders on the server computer.

FIGURE NET 2-6

Downloading files with FTP software. The procedures taken to download files is illustrated. Uploading works in a similar way, only on the left side of the screen you choose the files to be uploaded from the local client computer and on the right side you choose the destination folder on the remote server.

Most people who access FTP sites extensively do so through an FTP program. For instance, the development of this textbook was facilitated by FTP software, with the author, editors, and artists uploading and downloading text and graphics files to and from the publisher's FTP site. Most Web browsers also allow you to visit FTP sites and to download files from them.

While such reputable companies as Microsoft and Corel distribute free utility software through secure FTP sites, you cannot always count on bug-free software from less-reliable FTP sources. Consequently, it's a good idea to run a virus scan through any program files downloaded from unknown sources before running the software.

At most FTP sites, you must log on before you can access files. If you don't have an account at the site—and most people won't—you will usually be logged in as an *anonymous* FTP user, or guest. Many FTP sites limit access by anonymous users to certain files, and some do not allow anonymous log-ins at all. Many FTP sites require passwords to access their files.

Telnet In today's networking environment, desktop clients often download software from remote network servers and run it themselves. Powerful desktop personal computers have made this arrangement possible. However, in earlier days, servers—or *hosts,* as they have been traditionally called—had to do virtually all of the processing. The remote workstations hooked up to them were dumb terminals that could do little more than send and receive data. Users typed commands at their terminals, which sent them to the host; the host ran the programs and delivered the results back to the terminals. To accommodate such simple transmissions, Telnet was developed. **Telnet** is a communications protocol that lets a workstation behave like a dumb terminal when interacting with remote servers.

Many applications—even modern ones—still require the host to run the application and treat your fancy desktop computer as a dumb terminal. In a popular application, people often play games over networks with others, and Telnet hosts run the games for all players. Many bulletin-board systems are also set up on Telnet computers throughout the world.

Telnet is another feature built into many Web browsers. You can access Telnet sites using an enabled Web browser just as easily as you can reach Gopher and FTP sites.

■ **Telnet.** A communications protocol that lets workstations serve as terminals to a remote server computer.

MAILING LISTS

In addition to e-mail and information retrieval, people often use the Internet to distribute information through mailing lists. A **mailing list** is a topical discussion group that communicates through shared e-mail messages. Hundreds of mailing lists provide messages about all sorts of topics on the Internet.

Mailing-list participants typically focus their discussions on specific subjects, for instance, the Grateful Dead or classic movies or diabetes. In some cases, anyone can send messages to a mailing list and sometimes they are generated only by the hosting business or organization, but you must subscribe to receive any e-mail from it. To handle mailing-list applications, a server computer must run a mailing-list-manager program. When mailing-list subscribers send e-mail messages to the program, it makes copies and sends one to each of the subscribers on the list. Some mailing lists are completely automated, whereas others involve some human intervention.

The individual or company that controls the mailing list, called the *mailing-list administrator,* may or may not charge subscribers. To subscribe to a mailing list, you must generally send an e-mail request directly to the administrator's mailbox. Mailing lists are sometimes *moderated,* meaning that someone screens messages for appropriateness before distributing them.

Mailing lists often evolve into online communities. Even though subscribers may never physically meet, they often develop close personal relationships.

NEWSGROUPS

Like mailing lists, Internet newsgroups are targeted to specific topics, such as a particular television show or hobby or software program. Participants must first subscribe to the newsgroup and then they will receive newsgroup messages (which usually look similar to e-mail messages) each time they access the newsgroup. To post messages to the newsgroup, participants send e-mail messages to a central site. What's more, newsgroups can be moderated or unmoderated. Unlike mailing lists, however, **newsgroups** function like electronic newspapers. Newsgroup messages are grouped together and organized before users see them.

Newsgroups have their own vernacular and set of tools (see Figure NET 2-7). For instance, messages sent to a newsgroup are called *articles,* and original articles together with their replies are known as *threads.* Most Web browsers interface with a *newsreader*—software that displays articles and threads in an attractive way.

You can often determine the type of information addressed by the newsgroup by the newsgroup's name—for instance, sci.military.moderated or rec.arts.tv. The first three or four letters tell you the category of the topic being discussed, and each of the abbreviations that follow narrow the topic area.

UseNet is the protocol that determines how newsgroup messages are handled between computers. UseNet servers are computers that host newsgroup sites.

A special etiquette—referred to as **netiquette**—has evolved on the Internet to guide communications via newsgroups and other forms of electronic mail (see Figure NET 2-8). Newcomers to a newsgroup—called "newbies"—are advised to read the newsgroup's posted **FAQs, or frequently asked questions.** FAQ files enable you to learn many of the accepted ground rules about

For links to further information about newsgroups, go to www.harcourtcollege.com/ infosys/parker2000/student/ explore/ and click on Chapter NET 2.

■ **Mailing list.** A service through which discussion groups communicate via shared e-mail messages. ■ **Newsgroup.** A service that works like an electronic newspaper, carrying *articles* posted by subscribers and responses to them (together called *threads*). ■ **UseNet.** A protocol that defines how server computers handle newsgroup messages. ■ **Netiquette.** Proper etiquette for exchanges on the Internet. ■ **Frequently asked questions (FAQs).** Typical questions asked by newcomers to Internet newsgroups, mailing lists, and chat rooms, accompanied by the answers to those questions.

NEWSGROUP NAMES

A newsgroup is named by category—the type of topic it discusses. Names consist of two or more words separated by periods.

rec. sport.basketball.college

The first identifier describes the main category area (example: **rec** for recreation).

Each subsequent identifier further narrows the category.

NEWSGROUP CATEGORIES	
alt	alternative
biz	business
comp	computer
k12	education
misc	miscellaneous
rec	recreation
sci	science
soc	social
talk	controversial

EXAMPLES OF NEWSGROUPS	
alt.video.games.reviews	Reviews of video games
alt.yoga	Various aspects of yoga
biz.jobs.offered	Job openings
comp.security.misc	Computer security issues
misc.consumer.house	Home ownership and maintenance
rec.arts.movies.reviews	Movie reviews
rec.pets.dogs	Dogs
soc.women	Issues related to women
talk.environment	Environment-related issues

ARTICLES AND THREADS

E-mail messages sent to newsgroups consist of articles and responses to those articles.

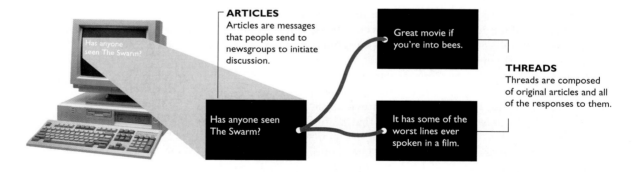

ARTICLES

Articles are messages that people send to newsgroups to initiate discussion.

Has anyone seen The Swarm?

Great movie if you're into bees.

It has some of the worst lines ever spoken in a film.

THREADS

Threads are composed of original articles and all of the responses to them.

FIGURE NET 2-7

All about newsgroups. Each newsgroup is formed around a different category or topic. E-mail sent to a particular newsgroup is organized and grouped together before it is sent on to subscribers.

communicating with the newsgroup and read answers to common questions, so that your interactions with the newsgroup do not disrupt those of more informed members or waste their time.

CHAT

Chat refers to a facility that enables people to engage in interactive conversations over the Internet. The oldest but still most common type of chat is Internet relay chat.

Internet Relay Chat   *Internet relay chat (IRC)* allows people to type messages to others and to get responses in real time (see Figure NET 2-9). Thus, IRC works like a regular phone call, except you're typing instead of talking.

■ **Chat.** An Internet feature that supports interactive discussion groups on selected topics.

A MINIGUIDE TO NETIQUETTE

Read the FAQs

FAQs are frequently asked questions and answers to them. Reading a FAQ list will help you to avoid common mistakes in protocol that could disrupt the group.

Lurk before you leap

Lurking refers to observing the articles and threads of the newsgroup for a period of time, to get the particular spin of the group, before actively participating.

Watch what you say

Chances are, the newsgroup has people from a reasonably wide variety of backgrounds. Things you say could be interpreted as being sexist, racist, ethnocentric, xenophobic, or in just general bad taste. Also check spelling and grammar—nobody likes wading through poorly written materials.

Avoid flame mail

While we're on the subject of being objectionable, try to avoid *flame mail*—caustic or inflammatory remarks directed toward certain people in the group. That includes taking part in *flame wars,* in which several people participate in being jerks.

Don't shout

SHOUTING REFERS TO TYPING YOUR ENTIRE E-MAIL MESSAGE USING CAPITAL LETTERS. THIS IS CONSIDERED GAUCHE AND NEANDERTHAL IN NET CIRCLES; USE CAPITAL LETTERS ONLY FOR EMPHASIZING A FEW WORDS.

Choose good titles

The first thing that people read in your article is what will catch their interest or turn them off. Titling an article by its subject matter (such as "Martians spotted in Marblehead") is much better than a vague choice (such as "Here's my article").

FIGURE NET 2-8

Netiquette.

Two people or several can participate in IRC. Multiperson chats are usually organized around specific topics, and participants often adopt nicknames to maintain anonymity. To participate in IRC, you need a client program that enables you to connect to an IRC server.

IRC takes place in an electronic area called a *chat room.* Chat rooms can be private—that is, reserved only for users who know the proper password to get in—or open to all. A chat room may be run by a service provider like America Online, by a search-engine service such as Yahoo! or Excite, by a community of users with a shared interest, or by virtually anyone else with software and an Internet connection capable of hosting online meetings. While most chat rooms are free, some—such as those where you get to mingle with high-priced business consultants—cost money.

Other Types of Chat   Various other, more sophisticated types of chat exist. Several of these are discussed next.

3-D VIRTUAL CHAT   This type of chat is a graphical extension of IRC. It enables you to take on the persona of a 3-D character who appears on the screen. In the chat, you mingle with other people having their own onscreen personas. The personas of the chat participants can be seen on the display moving about and interacting in a virtual chat room. To use this feature, you need 3-D chat software, a speedy computer, and a fast Internet connection.

INSTANT MESSAGING   Instant messaging is a cross between the IRC chat room and e-mail. It began around 1996, when America Online popularized buddy lists. A *buddy list* contains the names of your friends and associates; a small window pops up on your screen from your ISP telling you when they're online. At that time, you can invoke *instant messaging* by sending any of them a message that immediately appears on their screen. The receiver can respond in kind, sending an instant message back to you. All of the back and forth communications appear in an onscreen window; thus, the feature

IRC Chat

<Knuckles> Do you think that the Cubs will ever win a World Series in our lifetimes?

<Rug Rat> Depends on how many decades you plan to live.

<K-Man> Hey, watch what you say about my team. I'm from Chicago.

<Rosie> At least you got your thrill with the Bulls. It'll be a long time before we have a championship pro team here in Phoenix.

<Rug Rat> I'll take the weather you have in the Southwest over a championship, any day.

<Knuckles> So would I. It's only September 3rd and it's freezing here in my part of the world.

<K-Man> Where are you from, Knuckles?

FIGURE NET 2-9

Internet relay chat (IRC). IRC is like a regular phone call, except you type instead of talk.

works like a two-person chat room. Instant messaging is faster than e-mail because the latter is stored on a server that may not make messages immediately available to recipients.

INTERNET TELEPHONY Sometimes called *voice chat,* this form of chat lets two or more people speak to each other as they would on the phone. The call is routed over the Internet, however, instead of through the regular phone system. There are many varieties of voice chat. At the low end are systems that use half-duplex cards and programs that enable only one person to speak at a time; participants use headsets attached to their computers. At the high end are sophisticated commercial services with fiber-optic lines that enable people to converse over their regular phones.

Like other Internet services, virtually all forms of chat—the exception being high-end Internet telephony—do not involve incurring separate long-distance phone charges. Research has shown that people spend more time at Web sites when they have a chat feature and are more likely to visit again.

ONLINE SHOPPING

In a growing use of the Internet, people have begun to shop online. You can buy products directly from large companies—like L. L. Bean, Dell Computer, Wal-Mart, and Microsoft—at their Web sites, or you can shop at the Web sites of electronic malls (called *e-malls),* where thousands of smaller companies collectively display their wares.

Electronic catalogs on the Web show you color graphics of products. Search tools and *intelligent agents* may help you to locate the product you desire without excessive browsing (see the Tomorrow box). If you want to buy a

Intelligent Agents

Benevolent Servants and Potential Social Problems

Imagine arriving at work each morning to find your PC booting up as soon as you walk in your office building. On the screen, you see today's agenda, a list of phone calls and e-mails that came in since you left your desk last night, and a file of news items culled from the morning paper and neatly organized in a folder. These events show software agents have been busily at work, saving you time and attention that you can devote to more useful tasks.

Software agents are small pieces of program code that carry out specific, repetitive, and useful tasks for a computer user. Put another way, software agents are digital servants. The concept of software agents is not new; it originated in the 1950s with the evolution of the field of artificial intelligence (AI). What's more, you are probably using agent code today without even knowing it. Software agents are often built into communications software, operating systems, e-mail programs, and a variety of other products. Today's use notwithstanding, the golden age of software agents lies in the future—especially programmable agents that can be customized by users, and agents that can search the contents of multiple databases.

Potential uses for agents abound. You could request them to throw out junk e-mail and arrange all other messages in decreasing order of importance; they could also search for stocks that meet certain buying criteria that you specify or browse through scores of online e-malls to find the best price on a Pentium III computer with 128 MB RAM and at least 20 gigabytes of hard-disk space (see image).

Agents perform a variety of useful services for businesses too. Internet search engines like Yahoo! use them to travel across the

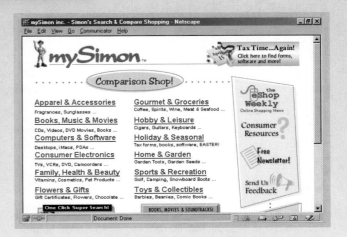

Okay, but where can I find . . . ? Agent sites like www.mysimon.com will search the Web to find the lowest price on items for sale online.

World Wide Web and pick up information about new sites, such as keywords with which to classify those sites. Companies in the telecommunications industry use agents to monitor network transmissions and report traffic problems. Some companies even use agents to spy on their competitors. For instance, a computer dealer can use the agent to search for and collect prices at competitive sites. Then it can scale down its own prices slightly and boast it has the lowest on the Net.

The use of agents leads to some very important social concerns. Will companies regularly rely on software agents to monitor the performance of employees? What types of workers might intelligent agents eventually replace? Should agents be allowed to automatically carry out tasks like supplying intravenous medicine to hospital patients? Can sensitive databases protect their contents from hostile agents? Questions like these are sure to merit serious debate as the twenty-first century unfolds.

computer, you may be able to configure your system online so it precisely meets your needs. If you want software, there's a good chance that you'll be able to download a copy of it.

While many businesses have engaged in electronic commerce for years, online shopping by consumers is a relatively new phenomenon. According to some industry experts, it's also about to take off in a big way. Online shopping benefits both businesses and consumers, since businesses don't need salespeople to sell online and some of the savings in labor costs can be passed on to consumers. Today, the most popular online-shopping categories are PC hardware, travel, entertainment products such as books and music, and flowers and gifts. Shopping over the Web is in a state of rapid evolution, running the gamut from sites that represent conventional stores to online auctions (see Feature NET 2-1).

One of the major obstacles to electronic commerce so far is consumer concern for *security*. Many customers feel uncomfortable paying by credit card over the Internet, where cyberthieves lurk. (The Tomorrow box in the next chapter addresses this topic.) Another concern is *privacy*—consumers would

Online Bidding

Is "One Price Serves All" Going the Way of the Dinosaur?

With each passing day, electronic commerce is changing the way a lot of buying and selling is done.

Almost without exception, the first generation of commercial activity on the Internet has been conducted a lot like it has been offline, in the physical world. A price for each item is posted, and if you want to buy, you pay the suggested price. Even today on the Internet, most selling and buying is done with fixed prices.

The ability of modern communications networks to enable anonymous and virtually instantaneous communication between multiple parties has added a new dimension to this old model—online bidding. Finagling a price by computer is primarily done in one of two ways, as described below.

■ FLEXIBLE PRICING This method, popularized by online Web sites like Priceline.com (located at www.priceline.com), allows users to bid for such items as airline seats, new cars, hotel rooms, and mortgages (see image). Take airline seats. The consumer submits a bid to Priceline.com indicating departure and arrival dates between two cities, a maximum price he or she is willing to pay for the tickets, and a credit card number. Priceline.com will then contact the airlines that service the route, and, within an hour, it will e-mail the acceptability of the offer back to the consumer. If the offer is accepted by an airline, the consumer's credit card is charged accordingly. The arrangement is ideal for economically minded, last-minute fliers who are flexible on the times of day at which they depart and arrive or who are willing to make extra stopovers for a cheaper ticket. It's also great for airlines, who are pressed to sell empty seats before flights take off.

Automobile bidding works pretty much the same way. At Priceline.com, consumers fill out an online form that indicates the make and model of the vehicle desired, including colors and options. They also state the maximum price they are willing to pay, the date the car must be available, and how far they are willing to travel to pick up a vehicle. Then, computers at Priceline.com fax the form to dealers, seeking one that is willing to meet the terms. Dealers have three choices: accept the offer, refuse the deal, or make a counteroffer.

■ CYBERAUCTIONS This approach to online commerce is known as a *cyberauction*—the electronic counterpart to a traditional auction. At such events you can buy toasters, golf clubs, computers, theater tickets—theoretically, anything you can pick up at any other type of auction. The most popular items sold at online auctions include computer hardware and software, consumer electronics such as cameras and VCRs, and houseware items such as coffeemakers, all of which can be described unambiguously with text and pictures. Cattle have just recently hit the cyberauction block too.

Cyberauctions work in various ways. At eBay (located at www.ebay.com), one of the most popular auction sites with over a million auctions daily, first sellers notify eBay that they have items to auction. The items are then listed on the eBay site (see image) with the minimum opening bid and the ending date and time of the auction (usually three to ten days after the auction for that item begins). As the auction progresses, potential buyers (who find items to bid on using eBay's search facilities) place bids and the current bid is immediately updated for each item. When the auction is over, both the seller and the successful bidder are notified by e-mail and the seller is responsible for contacting the buyer and arranging shipment and payment. The seller then pays eBay a nominal listing fee plus a percentage of the sales price. One of the things that gets online shoppers excited about cyberauctions is the community spirit involved. If your price beats all others, it's not like you just bought something—you've won it.

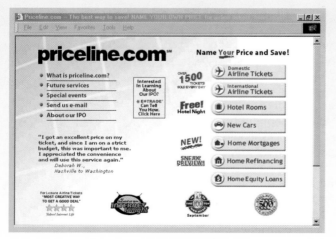

Priceline.com. A cool place for finding travel, car, and home-financing bargains.

eBay. An online auction site that lets you place bids on any of a million items.

rather browse the Web without letting merchants know who they are, but merchants feel that they could do a much better and more pleasant job of selling if they knew the identities and tastes of their customers.

INTERNET ADDRESSES

An **Internet address** performs the same function as a residential or business address in everyday life. It tells where to locate something on the Internet—a particular person, Web site, or Web page. Addresses on the Internet are unique; each one is assigned to one and only one person or resource.

Mailbox Addresses   People are most often located on the Internet through their e-mail addresses. An individual's e-mail address usually consists of a user-name (a set of characters, unique to accounts on that person's mail server, assigned to the individual's mailbox) followed by the @ symbol, followed by the mail server's **domain name.** For instance,

```
mjordan@harcourt.com
tarzan@harcourt.com
```

are the e-mail addresses of two hypothetical mailboxes at Harcourt College Publishers, the publisher of this textbook, respectively assigned to mjordan and tarzan. The characters "harcourt.com" state the name of Harcourt's server computer. People with e-mail addresses can be reached via private networks or over the Internet.

Note that domain names—and the server computers they represent—function like apartment buildings in everyday life. Each apartment building's address is unique to the mail system, but several individuals may have mailboxes at the building address.

The set of three letters that generally appears as the rightmost part of a domain name is called the *root domain.* Root domains—such as *com* (for *commercial*), *edu* (for *education*), *gov* (for *government*), and *mil* (for *military*)—indicate the type of organization that the domain name represents. Two symbols occasionally follow or replace the root domain to indicate the country of origin. For instance, the domain name

```
www.fs.fed.us
```

suggests a government computer in the United States—the one at the USDA Forest Service.

Addresses for World Wide Web Pages   Web pages and links to information at Gopher, FTP, and other sites are most commonly located on the Internet through **uniform resource locators,** or **URLs** (see Figure NET 2-10). Every Web page has its own URL (sometimes pronounced "earl"). If you know a page's URL, type it in the specified area of your Web browser's screen and the page will be displayed.

Web-site URLs often contain the three letters *www* preceded by the *protocol identifier* http:// (for *hypertext transfer protocol*). For instance, the Web home page for Microsoft Corporation, the University of Virginia, and the Yahoo! search site, respectively, have the following URLs:

```
http://www.microsoft.com
http://www.virginia.edu
http://www.yahoo.com
```

For a tutorial on accessing Web pages using Internet addresses and hyperlinks, go to www.harcourtcollege.com/ infosys/parker2000/student/ tutor/ and click on Chapter NET 2.

■ **Internet address.** A unique identifier assigned to a specific location on the Internet, such as a host computer, Web site, or user mailbox. ■ **Domain name.** An ordered group of symbols, separated by periods, that identifies an Internet server. ■ **Uniform resource locator (URL).** A unique identifier representing the location of a specific Web page on the Internet.

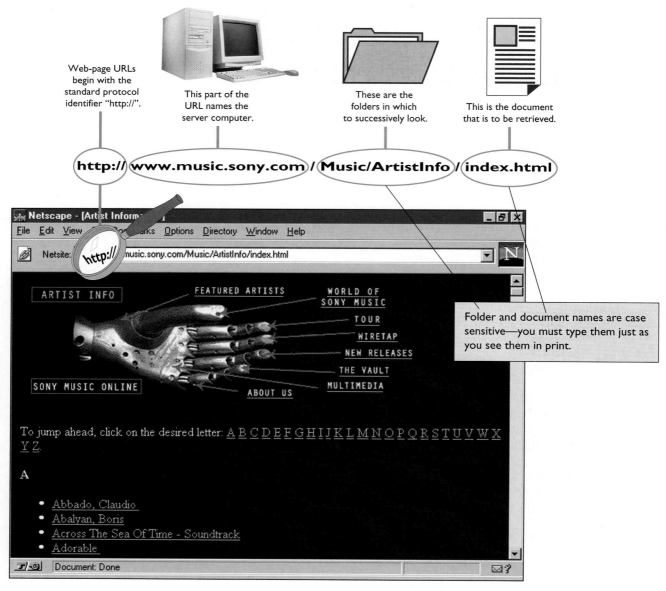

Web-page URLs begin with the standard protocol identifier "http://".

This part of the URL names the server computer.

These are the folders in which to successively look.

This is the document that is to be retrieved.

http:// **www.music.sony.com** / **Music/ArtistInfo** / **index.html**

Folder and document names are case sensitive—you must type them just as you see them in print.

FIGURE NET 2-10

How URLs work.

The set of symbols after the double slashes—for instance, "www.microsoft.com"—identifies a server by its computer name and domain name.

Often, URLs contain more specific types of information. For instance, the URL

`http://www.music.sony.com/Music/ArtistInfo/index.html`

identifies the music section of Sony Corporation's Web site. To the right of the computer and domain name (www.music.sony.com), the URL identifies a sequence of two *folders* (Music and ArtistInfo) that you must open in order to find the specific *document* (index.html). In many contexts, folders are referred to as *directories,* a set of folders is referred to as a *directory path,* and documents are referred to as *files.*

Sometimes the part of the URL that contains the folder names and the document name is called the *request.* In the Sony example, note that the request—Music/ArtistInfo/index.html—contains a mixture of uppercase and lowercase letters. Requests are *case sensitive,* which means that you must type in this part of the URL in uppercase or lowercase letters, just as you see them. The domain name, by contrast, is not case sensitive; capitalization makes no difference.

As you have probably already noticed, URLs can become lengthy and take time to type. Fortunately, you often don't need to type them to reach desired Web pages. If the page you are currently viewing contains a hyperlink to the desired page, you can simply point to and click the appropriate hyperlink.

Addresses for Pages on Other Servers   When you are retrieving information from, say, a Gopher or FTP site through a Web browser, the characters *gopher* or *ftp* will often replace *http* in the URL, depending on the particular interface to be used. For instance,

```
gopher://gopher.micro.umn.edu
    ftp://ftp.microsoft.com
```

are URLs you would type into your browser to access, respectively, the University of Minnesota Gopher site and Microsoft's FTP site.

DESKTOP TOOLS FOR ACCESSING THE INTERNET

This section covers the software and hardware you need to become a user of the Internet. Most people can accomplish what they want with a good Web browser and e-mail package, a few search tools, and reasonably current computer hardware. If you need a capability that your browser doesn't have, you can usually find it in a plug-in or helper package.

BROWSERS AND PLUG-IN PACKAGES

As mentioned earlier, the Internet was not always so easy and so much fun to use. The first text-intensive Web browsers were not much to rave about. It was not until 1993, when a browsing program called NCSA **Mosaic** became available, that the world began to notice the Web. Mosaic presented an easy-to-use graphical user interface, and you could download it for free. Today, most commercial browsers improve upon and extend the interface popularized by the original Mosaic.

What, Exactly, Is a Browser?   A **browser,** or *Web browser,* is a software program that enables you to display Web pages as well as navigate the Web and work with other parts of the Internet. The concept of a browser is evolving rapidly. Originally, most browsers were stand-alone products; today, browser functionality is woven into many other types of software packages, enabling you to tap immediately into the Web from wherever you are on your computer.

A wide variety of browsers compete for attention on the market today. The two most popular browsers by far are **Netscape Navigator** (available as part of the Netscape Communicator software suite) and **Microsoft Internet Explorer** (integrated into the latest versions of the Windows operating system and Microsoft Office). Other familiar products include Spyglass Mosaic and Sun's HotJava, as well as the proprietary browsers offered by such large ISPs as America Online. Some browsers, like NCSA Mosaic, Netscape Navigator, and Microsoft Internet Explorer, are available as freeware over the Internet.

Properties of Browsers   The rapid evolution of browsers brings with it frequent product updates—sometimes as frequently as every few months—with

■ **Mosaic.** A freeware tool that was the first GUI Web browser to gain wide acceptance; most commercial browsers today are enhanced forms of Mosaic. ■ **Browser.** A software tool that makes it easy for users to find and display Web pages. ■ **Netscape Navigator.** A widely used Web browser. ■ **Microsoft Internet Explorer.** A widely used Web browser.

NETSCAPE NAVIGATOR

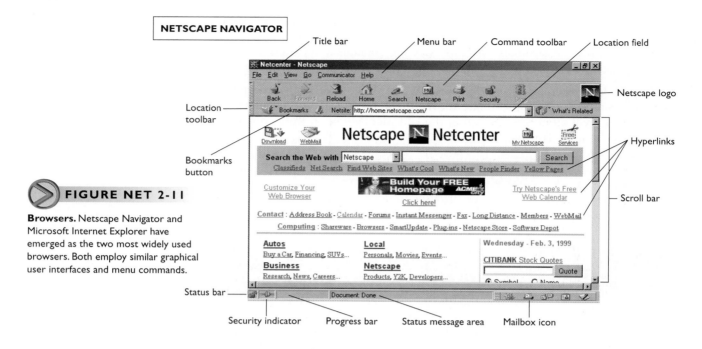

Title bar · Menu bar · Command toolbar · Location field · Netscape logo · Location toolbar · Bookmarks button · Hyperlinks · Scroll bar · Status bar · Security indicator · Progress bar · Status message area · Mailbox icon

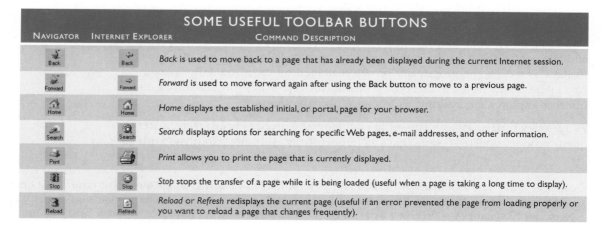

FIGURE NET 2-11

Browsers. Netscape Navigator and Microsoft Internet Explorer have emerged as the two most widely used browsers. Both employ similar graphical user interfaces and menu commands.

MICROSOFT INTERNET EXPLORER

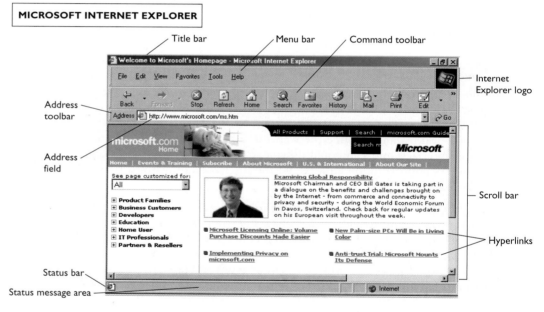

Title bar · Menu bar · Command toolbar · Internet Explorer logo · Address toolbar · Address field · Scroll bar · Hyperlinks · Status bar · Status message area

SOME USEFUL TOOLBAR BUTTONS		
NAVIGATOR	INTERNET EXPLORER	COMMAND DESCRIPTION
Back	Back	*Back* is used to move back to a page that has already been displayed during the current Internet session.
Forward	Forward	*Forward* is used to move forward again after using the Back button to move to a previous page.
Home	Home	*Home* displays the established initial, or portal, page for your browser.
Search	Search	*Search* displays options for searching for specific Web pages, e-mail addresses, and other information.
Print	Print	*Print* allows you to print the page that is currently displayed.
Stop	Stop	*Stop* stops the transfer of a page while it is being loaded (useful when a page is taking a long time to display).
Reload	Refresh	*Reload* or *Refresh* redisplays the current page (useful if an error prevented the page from loading properly or you want to reload a page that changes frequently).

each new version incorporating more and more features. When selecting a particular browser for your own use, you should look for several important properties:

■ FUNCTIONALITY   What basic functions does the browser perform? While many of the earliest browsers were designed mostly to help users navigate the Web, increasingly they are evolving into multipurpose Internet tools that accommodate additional functions like e-mail, chat, Gopher, FTP, Telnet, mailing-list and newsgroup applications, and Web publishing capabilities. Because most users would strongly prefer to learn a single software product rather than mastering several, Web browsers are becoming "one-stop shopping" solutions.

■ NAVIGATIONAL TOOLS   Virtually all browsers offer easy-to-use navigational tools such as a menu bar, toolbars, and special navigation buttons (see Figure NET 2-11). These tools enable you to retrieve, display, find, save, and print Web pages along with a variety of other operations.

For a tutorial on the parts of a browser window, go to www.harcourtcollege.com/ infosys/parker2000/student/ tutor/ and click on Chapter NET 2.

Browsing through Web pages is like reading a book; often you would like to return to earlier pages. To help you locate those pages painlessly, a full-featured browser should incorporate such features as a *history list* (to record pages you've visited during the current session or previous ones), *bookmarks* or *favorites* (to let you save the addresses of your favorite sites in a folder), and *toolbar buttons* (to help you easily access, save, or print chosen Web pages). Figure NET 2-12 illustrates the usefulness of history lists and bookmarks.

Browsers differ in their implementation of navigational tools. For instance, some browsers may let you organize bookmarks into multiple lists and arrange and edit bookmarks in many ways. Others provide less-flexible options.

■ SPEED   Web browsers often incorporate a variety of techniques to speed applications. For instance, a *progressive graphics display* capability (see Figure NET 2-13) lets you see some text and a low-resolution version of images almost immediately while your computer downloads more data and sharpens the images in front of you. Through an interlacing process, the software draws alternate lines of each image on a page, so you get the flavor of the image while waiting for the rest of it to display. If you don't like what you see as the image is displaying, you can abandon the Web page for another.

To display Web pages extremely quickly, most graphical browsers allow you to toggle off their graphics features. While pages with graphics may look more exciting than those composed entirely of text, they take far longer to display and can slow information retrieval down to a crawl on a busy day. Incidentally, while most browsers today support graphics, not all do. Users with older equipment or with text-only workstations rely on text browsers such as Lynx to get their Internet information.

■ CUSTOMIZABILITY   A browser has settings so that you can tweak it to your liking. For instance, you can change your Web **portal**—the page your browser first displays when you turn it on—to any page on the Web. You can also change the way that pages are displayed—altering colors and text size, eliminating graphics, and so on. What's more, have you ever been to a site where your browser seems to know what your preferences are? This is made possible by **cookies,** small files stored on your hard drive by your browser by Web servers you visit. The cookie feature is customizable; you can turn it off if you don't want cookies (see also Feature NET 2-2 on page NET 72).

■ **Portal.** The page your browser first displays when you turn it on. ■ **Cookies.** Small files stored on your hard drive by your browser at the request of the Web servers you visit.

ADDING BOOKMARKS
If you are currently viewing a page for which you want to add a bookmark, select Add Bookmark from the Bookmarks pull-down menu to add the entry to the bottom of your bookmark list, or select File Bookmark to add the bookmark to an existing folder.

BOOKMARKS
A bookmarking feature lets you save the locations of your favorite Web sites so that you can easily return to them.

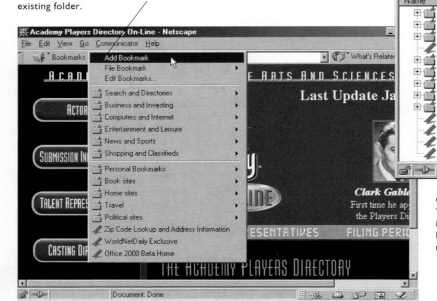

ORGANIZING BOOKMARKS
You can create new folders, move bookmarks into a folder, or delete bookmarks by selecting Edit Bookmarks from the Bookmarks menu.

HISTORY LIST
A history-list feature displays the names and descriptions of sites you've most recently visited.

GOING TO A PAGE OR ADDING A BOOKMARK FROM THE HISTORY LIST
Highlight the page as illustrated here, and then use the appropriate option on the File menu.

FIGURE NET 2-12

Using bookmarks and a history list.
The figure shows how to use the bookmarking and history-list features of Netscape Navigator. In Internet Explorer, bookmarks are called "favorites."

■ FRAMING A *frame* is an independent area, or window, on a screen page. A browser's *framing capability* allows a screen to be partitioned into separate frames, with different Web pages (each with its own set of scroll bars, if necessary) displaying in each of the frames (see Figure NET 2-14). The framing technique is also catching on in the television world, allow-

Some text usually appears onscreen within a few seconds, so you can begin reading parts of the page right away. Low-resolution versions of graphics images also appear so that you can quickly get an idea what's in store.

Depending on the speed of your modem and your Internet connection, you may have to wait from several seconds to a minute or more for the graphics images to show at full resolution.

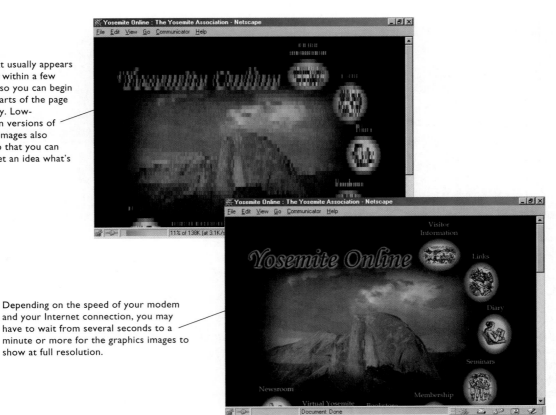

FIGURE NET 2-13

Progressive graphics display. This feature lets you see a low-resolution version of an image while your computer downloads all of the data needed to display the image at full resolution.

ing viewers to divide the viewing screen into several areas and watch a different channel in each one.

■ JAVA AND ACTIVEX SUPPORT   *Java* is a programming language developed by Sun Microsystems. A browser with a built-in Java translator can accept small programs called Java *applets* located on or linked to a Web page and run them. Such a feature has the potential to add tremendously exciting interactive functions to a Web page. A person shopping on the Web for a car or home loan, for instance, can download a calculator applet from a Web page and figure out monthly payments on the spot.

ActiveX is a set of controls developed at Microsoft Corporation. It does for Web pages what OLE (object linking and embedding) does for office applications; that is, it provides a containering method whereby one application can be launched within another. Thus, ActiveX allows you to do things like edit a Word or WordPerfect document while in your browser or, conversely, edit a Web page within your word processor. Likewise, you can use ActiveX controls to embed animations into Web pages—just as you might do with a Java applet.

Java and ActiveX will be discussed in more detail in Chapter NET 3 together with other similar products.

■ WEBCASTING   A *webcasting feature* enables a browser user to see webcasts on a display screen. A webcast works like a television broadcast; once you tune to it, you sit back and passively watch while the screen changes to keep it current. On TV, most channels follow particular themes—history, news, music, sports, and so on. Webcasting works in a similar way. If you visit a news-service Web channel—*channels* are what webcasting sites are called—new news content continually refreshes your screen. Unlike surfing for individual pages, where you must actively pull

NET 2-2

Cookies

They May Not Agree with Every Web-Surfer's Diet

Have you ever noticed that your browser sometimes knows the choices you made on your last visit to a particular Web site? Or that when you visit your favorite newspaper online it always gives you the sports pages first? Or that onscreen ads are targeted to your particular interest areas—say, movies or the stock market?

It's cookies that make all of this possible.

Cookies are small electronic tags installed on your hard drive by your browser at the request of the Web server that's hosting the pages you visit. On subsequent visits, the server uses the cookies on your hard disk to customize information being sent to you.

Web servers neither save cookies nor do they pass them to other servers. They rely on your hard disk to store and then later supply them on demand. They can be useful when you want personalized information, such as news, sports, or TV listings, or to avoid typing a user name and password every time you access a password-protected site from your home computer. Still, many people are concerned about their personal privacy. After all, not everything a person reads or buys is something he or she wants to be public knowledge. That millions use the Internet and that clever people are always finding new ways to penetrate remote systems are often enough to give almost every Web user concerned over cookies cause to worry.

Not all cookies are alike. Some simply record selections you have made at a single Web site. More powerful ones, called *tracking cookies,* follow you virtually everywhere. Tracking cookies let marketers combine multiple-site cookie data on your hard drive with the personal information you volunteer when filling out registration forms. Armed with such facts, cybermarketers may be

Cookie traces. The content and the layout of this personalized Web page were determined by the user and are stored in a cookie file.

able to determine how much you make and your personal interests to help them target appropriate advertisements to you.

Users who want to eliminate cookies from their computers have several options. Most widely used browsers contain cookie files and provide tools for users to disable them at any time. They also give you the choice of refusing cookies—all cookies or possibly just tracking cookies. Still another way is asking the browser to send a warning message every time it attempts to download a cookie. Additionally, software packages are available that will let you name sites from which you will accept cookies.

specific information to your screen, a webcast is designed to push information to it while you sit back and watch.

■ WORKGROUP COMPUTING Most modern browsers incorporate support for workgroup computing—allowing two or more people to collaborate on common projects. This feature is especially beneficial for users on corporate intranets and to users who need to share ideas with people in other organizations.

■ MULTIMEDIA Most browsers support a number of forms of *multimedia*—for instance, several types of compressed sound and video files. Unfortunately, your desktop hardware and the phone line going into your home may not handle data fast enough for you to run high-end multimedia applications. Live digital video is currently the toughest frontier; it requires 100 times the bandwidth of audio. To optimize audio and video applications on client PCs, many software publishers use a *streaming* approach, whereby sounds or video images start outputting

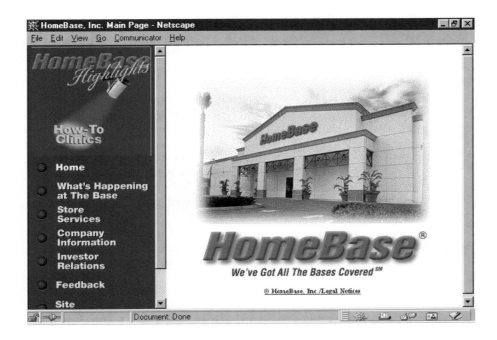

FIGURE NET 2-14

Framing. A framing capability allows users to see screens divided into separate areas, with each area displaying a different Web page and its own set of scroll bars.

on your computer before the associated files are fully downloaded (see Figure NET 2-15).

■ REALTIME PROCESSING   A *realtime processing* capability enables two or more users to interact on projects as if they were working side by side in the same room. Realtime capabilities can run from the simple—such as voice chat—to the complex—such as videoconferencing applications in which people can both see and hear each other. In between are a variety of other applications—such as workgroup software in which changes made to documents on one desktop system are reflected immediately throughout the organization via the Internet. As with multimedia applications, special hardware and transmission facilities—and even special software—may be needed to supplement a browser's capabilities.

■ VIRTUAL REALITY   A *virtual reality* feature allows users to explore three-dimensional environments on the Web, observing them from any number of views. If the interior of a house were modeled in virtual reality, you

FIGURE NET 2-15

Streaming audio and video. Streaming audio and video players are widely available on the Internet—often for free. These players let you hear sound clips and play video clips available on Web sites.

could walk through rooms, observe the objects in it closer or further away or from different angles, and so on. To explore virtual worlds, you need either a 3-D browser program that supports virtual-reality modeling language (VRML) or a plug-in 3-D package that works with your regular browser. Three popular 3-D programs are WebSpace, WebFX, and World-View. The biggest problem today with viewing VRML sites on the Web is that virtual-reality applications require a lot of graphics, which in turn require a lot of bandwidth.

■ WEB-PUBLISHING CAPABILITIES   Increasingly, people are rushing to the Web to post their own home pages. Many browsers have built-in publishing capabilities that will let you create Web pages of your own. In addition, you can test your pages in a simulated Web environment. Web publishing has become a particularly hot area of late because of the popularity of corporate intranets and the arrival of tools that enable office documents to be automatically converted to Web pages. Chapter NET 3 is all about Web publishing, so this subsection won't dwell on it.

■ SECURITY   Browsing software can protect the confidentiality of the data you are sending—such as your credit-card number—and it can tell you about security safeguards at sites to which you send data. Some even come with a *digital signature* feature, which downloads only pages with a special code from sources that you preapprove; at the other end of the line, this feature can identify you to a commercial site. Java's ability to supplement desktop browsers with applets downloaded from remote servers has raised a whole new security issue: Will browsers be able to keep applets from implanting viruses on your computer system?

Plug-In Packages   The rapid evolution of the Internet has created a large market for *browser plug-ins*—programs that update your browser with features that it currently lacks.

One widely used plug-in package, Adobe Acrobat, enables your browser to view pages that have been formatted as Adobe PDF files (see Figure NET 2-16). PDF files display documents more or less exactly the way they appear in print. Precision can be critical in some applications; a misplaced digit in a financial statement or an altered angle in a technical drawing can result in a major legal

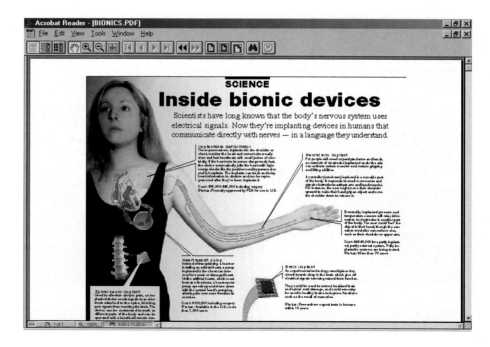

FIGURE NET 2-16

Adobe Acrobat. Acrobat enables your browser to display a document in a format very similar to the way it appears in print.

problem. Acrobat also helps Web-page authors to control the way their pages display on other computer systems that support PDF.

Other popular types of plug-in packages include those that offer full-duplex phoning and videoconferencing capabilities, and those that offer improved support for multimedia and virtual-reality applications. A listing of some widely used browser plug-ins appears in Figure NET 2-17.

A drawback to plug-ins is their sheer number. Close to 200 exist for Netscape Navigator alone. Many users are put off by the effort required to download plug-ins and are afraid that ones they've never heard of may interfere with other, working programs on disk. In response, many designers are building into their Web pages self-loading Java and ActiveX code that doesn't require user intervention and that is not saved to local hard disks. In addition to the large number of plug-ins, *helper packages* are available that work alongside (as opposed to inside) your regular browser to enhance your Internet experience.

If history is a good indicator of the future, expect the next generation of browsers to incorporate many of the best features from the current crop of plug-in and helper programs. What's more, operating systems and software suites are rapidly gaining browser features themselves. The latter trend has led many people to predict that browsers as we know them today may become extinct in a few years, their functions absorbed into other software packages.

SEARCH ENGINES

While casual surfing is a popular Web pastime, people often turn to the Internet to find specific types of information as well. When you know generally what you want but don't know at which URL to find it, one of your best options is a search engine. A **search engine** is a software facility that often

FIGURE NET 2-17

Browser plug-ins.

Package	Vendor	Description
Acrobat	Adobe Systems	Displays documents similar to the way they appear in print
Broadway	Data Translation	Lets you view MPEG videos from your browser
Carbon Copy	Software Publishing	Lets you direct Internet outputs to a computer other than your own
Flash	Macromedia	Used by Web-page authors to create navigational interfaces, animations, and illustrations
Live3D	Netscape	Lets you enjoy virtual-reality worlds
NetMeeting	Microsoft	Adds Internet/intranet telephony, a whiteboard and shared clipboard, a chat area, and the ability to share Microsoft Office applications in a conference
NetShow	Microsoft	Lets you add audio- and video-streaming capabilities to your browser
Pronto96	CommTouch Software	Lets you handle voice messages as e-mail attachments
Quicktime	Apple	Lets you view Quicktime videos from your browser
RealAudio	RealNetworks	Provides realtime audio and FM-quality sound to your browser
RealPlayer	RealNetworks	Lets you add audio- and video-streaming capabilities to your browser
Shockwave	Macromedia	Lets you receive multimedia Web pages
Sizzler	Totally Hip	Enhances your browsing experience with animation
VR Scout	Chaco Communications	Lets you enjoy virtual-reality worlds

■ **Search engine.** A software tool used to look for specific information over the Internet.

How Dave and Jerry's Guide to the Web Became Yahoo!

Yahoo!—the Web's first search engine—started in 1994 as the hobby of a couple of graduate students, Dave Filo and Jerry Yang. According to Yang in a recent interview in *Internet World,* the two were "wasting" a lot of time on the Web in late 1993. They began collecting URLs for sites they found because "David was sick of me asking him where was that link we saw yesterday." As their collection of sites grew, other people wanted access to it, and soon they had the makings of a thriving business.

Filo and Yang thought that the original name of their search engine—Dave and Jerry's Guide to the Web—sounded stupid, so one night they resolved to lock themselves in the office to change it. They decided they wanted an acronym for a name and that the full name should start with the words *Yet Another.* At that point, they consulted a dictionary and found the word *yahoo.* It was catchy, and they liked thinking of themselves as a couple of yahoos.

What does *Yahoo!* stand for? Yet Another Hierarchical Officious Oracle. Good thing they wanted an acronym.

Yahoo! founders. Search engine began as a hobby.

resembles both a table of contents and an index, with the full power of a computer behind it to electronically locate Web pages on specific topics and make it easy for you to retrieve them.

Using a Web-Resident Engine You can use many of the best search engines—such as **Yahoo!** (profiled in the Inside the Industry feature), Excite, Lycos, and Alta Vista—free of charge by accessing their Web sites. Once you locate and enter a site (see Project 6 at the end of this chapter for several addresses), you can perform two types of search operations: (1) selecting successive hyperlinks from categories displayed on the screen or (2) typing in a search string that represents a relevant keyword before you begin selecting hyperlinks (see Figure NET 2-18).

In the first type of search operation—doing a category search—you will first be presented with several categories on the screen. Then, after you select a hyperlink, you will next see a screen showing a finer breakdown of choices. Eventually, after making choice after choice on a sequence of such screens, you should arrive at an appropriate Web page.

To understand the second type of search—inputting a search string—let's say you need to find the text of one of the articles of the U.S. Constitution and you do not see an associated link on the list of categories. You would type *Constitution* into the area of the screen that's specifically provided to enter search strings. Clicking the Search button will retrieve a list of Web pages concerning the Constitution; it may also display some matching categories. By clicking on Web page or category links, you will eventually wind up with a page containing the text of the Constitution.

For a tutorial on searching the Web, go to www. harcourtcollege.com/ infosys/parker2000/student/ tutor/ and click on Chapter NET 2.

■ **Yahoo!.** A widely used search engine.

Specifying strings enables you to do *boolean searches*—that is, searching on multiple keywords using the operators AND, OR, and NOT. For instance, if you wanted a search engine to find all documents that covered *both* the Intel and AMD microprocessor manufacturers, you might specify your request to an engine supporting boolean searches as *Intel AND AMD*. If, instead, you wanted documents that discussed *either* (or both) of these companies, the request *Intel OR AMD* would be your entry. On the other hand, if you wanted documents about microprocessors that are cataloged with no mention of Intel, *microprocessors NOT Intel* is what you would type in the search text box. Every search engine has its own way of letting you do a boolean search, so you should check out the preferred style before conducting one.

If you follow the stock market, you'll notice that the prices of search-engine companies—Yahoo!, Excite, and Lycos, to name three of the fastest risers—have in recent years been bid up well in excess of their current earnings. This is because these companies hold a key strategic niche on the Web: users like them as *portals*—the page their browser first displays when they turn it on (see Feature NET 2-3 on page NET 80).

Search Databases   At the core of a search engine is a database that resembles a huge index. Typically, the database contains millions of pieces of information about Internet sites throughout the world. When you select a hyperlink or type in a search string, the search engine consults its index to find all URLs with descriptions that match up to that word. It then provides results of the search within seconds.

Search engines differ in their comprehensiveness. Some, such as Alta Vista, search deeper than others and will produce matches even to obscure references. This result can be good or bad, depending on how long a list of matches the search returns—it can run into the thousands of documents—and how much time you want to spend manually looking through the list for something interesting enough to pursue further. Once you find a match, generally you can simply point and click to retrieve the underlying information.

Some search engines are *metaengines*—that is, they consult multiple databases, including those of other search engines. Some of the Web-based search engines, for instance, query not only their own databases but also those at other sites. A few of the more sophisticated metaengines can query more than a dozen other sites simultaneously and then provide you with a listing in which duplicate entries are eliminated. To trim the listing further, some will even let you search on a second string.

Many search engines employ intelligent software called *spiders, crawlers,* or *robots* to gather information. These programs visit Web sites daily to collect vital data, such as URLs, descriptive information, and hyperlinks. Spiders can be tremendously fast, visiting in excess of 1 million sites per day. Search engines also collect information by having people who create Web sites submit URLs and keywords to them.

Web Site Search Capabilities   Many companies have search capabilities at their Web sites to allow visitors to locate documents on the site regarding a particular topic, or to locate particular products. Effective Web site search capabilities are becoming increasingly important as more and more buyers are shopping online for products. If visitors can't find a product on a site, they can't buy it.

HARDWARE CONSIDERATIONS

As earlier sections of this chapter and book have hinted, a more powerful computer system is more likely to give you access to the advanced features of the Internet. A 56 kbps modem, an SVGA monitor, and a good sound system will

DOING A CATEGORY SEARCH

As each menu comes up, you make a selection from it. As you do this, the search progressively narrows until, eventually, you access a specific Web site.

FIGURE NET 2-18

Using a search engine. Most search engines—such as Yahoo! and Excite— enable you to search either by selecting from menus of categories (left) or by typing search strings (right).

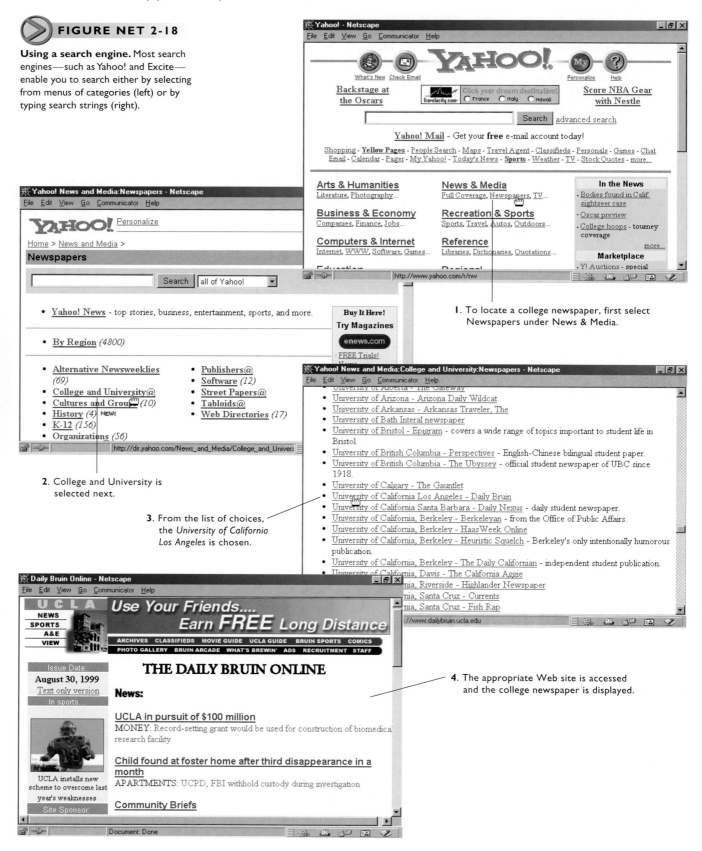

1. To locate a college newspaper, first select Newspapers under News & Media.

2. College and University is selected next.

3. From the list of choices, the *University of California Los Angeles* is chosen.

4. The appropriate Web site is accessed and the college newspaper is displayed.

DOING A STRING SEARCH

A string search lets you type in a keyword or phrase that relates to the topic on which you desire information.

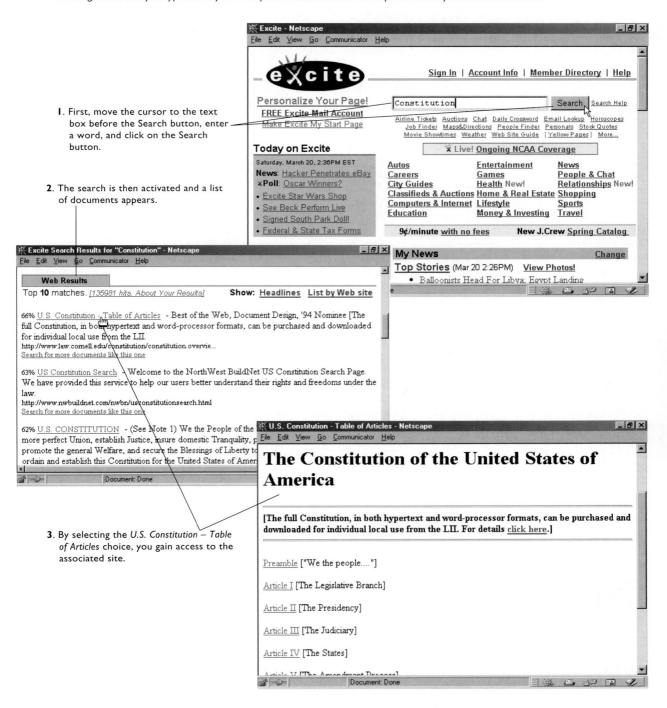

1. First, move the cursor to the text box before the Search button, enter a word, and click on the Search button.

2. The search is then activated and a list of documents appears.

3. By selecting the *U.S. Constitution – Table of Articles* choice, you gain access to the associated site.

equip you pretty well to handle the complexity of most Web pages today. Increasingly, computer systems are being made with the Internet in mind. Multimedia PCs with a modem targeted for family use are available for less than $500 that will get you up and running on the Internet in relatively high style. Remember, however, that the Internet was set up to run on virtually any type of computer platform. Thus, you can access the text portions of it from most any type of computer system.

Portals

The Battle for Online Eyeballs Is Heating Up

Ever wonder why it costs millions of dollars to run a 30-second TV ad on January's Super Bowl broadcast but only a pittance to run the same message on a 3:30 a.m. infomercial showing how to cook pasta? Well, maybe not. Anyway, it's all about eyeballs. The Super Bowl is watched by millions of people; the infomercial by only a small and sleepy handful.

Now envision the same type of phenomenon on the Internet. Portal companies like America Online and Yahoo! are gradually amassing Super Bowl-sized audiences who are eyeballing their pages daily. Sellers are willing to pay big bucks to portal companies to pitch products in prominent places on these pages or to otherwise have their Web sites receive special mention.

Although many sellers have easy-to-find Web sites, research shows that most people seeking information go first through a portal to find it. Did you forget ESPN's Web address? Then go to a Yahoo! search box and type "ESPN." A list of hyperlinks appears with a description of each entry, and you can select the one that will then launch you directly to the ESPN sports site.

As you might have guessed, companies of all types are spending millions of dollars to become a portal of choice to the consumer. America Online has a strategic perch in the battle for eyeballs in that it is an ISP that provides Internet access to many millions of

Portal wars. Advertisers are willing to pay big bucks for visibility on sites that draw crowds.

users, whereas Yahoo! is the site most users turn to when they want to search for something on the Web. Such companies as Amazon.com and Wal-Mart could figure prominently in the portal battle too, as they are sites that a large niche of users—shoppers—often turn to first.

As sites battle to be the portal of choice, they are wooing Web surfers with freebies to keep them coming back. Enticements include free e-mail, free chat, and personalized Web pages that greet you by name and try to meet your most pressing needs. Many sites use complicated software to try to build up personal profiles of each visitor by combining information from cookie files, past purchases, and data supplied on questionnaires.

Which companies will win out in the battle for consumer eyeballs remains to be seen. Connecticut's Gartner Group, which tries to predict the future of high tech and the businesses that swim in its waters, thinks that less than a half dozen sites will emerge as top portals at the beginning of the twenty-first century.

CONNECTING TO THE INTERNET

Connecting to the Internet usually involves two steps. The first is selecting a service provider. The second is using startup software to get the Internet programs supplied by the provider up and running on your system.

ABOUT SERVICE PROVIDERS

Internet service providers (ISPs) are your gateway to the Internet. An ISP works a lot like a phone company. For a monthly fee and, possibly, a one-time setup cost, it supplies you with a user account that gains you access to the Internet. An ISP can also provide a number of other services and software. Often included among the latter offerings are programs to set up your Internet account, a Web browser, e-mail software and an e-mail address, a newsreader, FTP software, Web-authoring software, space on its file server to hold any personal Web pages you create, and advice. You supply only your own PC, modem, and telephone connection.

Most people hunting for an ISP have two choices: going with a large, national provider or with a small, local outfit. Some prominent examples of large providers are America Online (AOL), the Microsoft Network (MSN), Com-

Web Tutor

For a tutorial on connecting to the Internet, go to www. harcourtcollege.com/infosys/ parker2000/student/tutor/ and click on Chapter NET 2.

puServe, Prodigy, and EarthLink. An example of a small provider is the Route 66 service out of Albuquerque, New Mexico, whose users are mostly local residents. Typically, rates are comparable between large and small ISPs—between $15 and $25 per month. Often other considerations play heavily in the ISP selection decision. In the next section, we will cover many of these.

Internet access is also being increasingly provided by many deregulated companies in the telephone and television industries. Telephone companies like AT&T (via WorldNet) and television-service providers like DirecTV (via DirecPC) are current players in the ISP arena. Based on the growing success of firms like AOL, Earthlink, and AT&T's WorldNet, many industry observers are predicting that large national companies will come to dominate the ISP business within the next few years.

Besides the sources already named, you can connect to the Internet in several other ways. For instance, many colleges and universities—and also thousands of companies—are plugged in. Consequently, if you are a student or an employee affiliated with one of these organizations, you may be able to access the Internet through that connection for free. Many libraries also offer their members free access to the Internet. An additional option is a visit to a cybercafé, a coffeehouse with computers for patrons to access the Internet, or a copy store or other business that offers computer access charged by the minute or hour.

Two popular ways of connecting with an ISP are with SLIP and PPP accounts. A **SLIP** connection (for *serial line Internet protocol*) is the oldest and least expensive method. However, SLIP does not check to see that information arrives to you error free. **PPP** service (for *point-to-point protocol*) checks for errors and also provides better security. Both SLIP and PPP are versions of the **TCP/IP** protocol, a collection of communications protocols that allow PCs accessing the Internet to understand each other and exchange data.

SELECTING A PROVIDER

Many people evaluate service providers with respect to a number of criteria—including those listed here—before making their selections.

Offerings One of the most important steps in choosing an ISP is figuring out what you're getting. ISPs typically differ with respect to access, services, and software.

For instance, not all ISPs will give you full view to all parts of the Internet. On the Web, some ISPs may block access to certain Web sites. Also, not all providers will let you upload files to FTP sites. Consequently, it's important to be prepared ahead of time with a lot of specific questions that help you determine how restricted your Internet usage may be. The smaller providers generally will be able to better customize your access to the Internet.

Subscriber services can also vary dramatically among ISPs. For example, not all ISPs support instant messaging, buddy lists, and e-mail filtering. What's more, many of the large ISPs offer proprietary information and host special events to draw subscribers. You may be offered, say, a free subscription to the *New York Times* Web site, which nonsubscribers have to pay to see. You may also get a chance to engage in online chats with celebrities from time to time. Some ISPs also provide booklets and regular newsletters to their subscribers, thus keeping them educated and informed about useful and new features.

Finally, you will need to check on the software being offered by a prospective ISP. Is free software part of the deal? And if so, are certain brands of software mandated for e-mail, newsreading, FTP uploads and downloads, and Web authoring?

■ **SLIP.** A version of TCP/IP that enables individuals and organizations to connect to the Internet over ordinary phone lines. ■ **PPP.** A protocol that resembles SLIP but allows more reliable and secure communications. ■ **TCP/IP.** A collection of communications protocols through which PC's accessing the Internet can understand each other and exchange data.

Not all software is equal. For instance, the e-mail package you are being given may not support attachments. What's more, this e-mail program may not even be widely used and, consequently, may require extra effort on your part if you have questions on its operation. Also be sure to check the size of your mailbox. Will it be large enough to support the types of data you will be receiving?

Access Speeds   An important consideration centers on how fast the service works. While the speed of your Internet application depends in part on the speed of your modem, it also depends on how fast the provider's line moves data to you. A provider offering 56 kbps lines speeds data along to you twice as quickly as a provider offering only 28.8 kbps lines. If you are connecting from a large town or from a business site, you may be able to take advantage of an ISDN or a high-speed T1 line.

Service and Support   One of the most important service-related issues is reaching help when you need it. Try calling at 7 p.m. on a Saturday or at 11 p.m. on a weekday. Does anyone answer? Some understaffed providers have earned unsavory reputations for letting users linger on the line half an hour or more and for not returning phone calls or e-mails promptly. The quality of support help is important too. You want to talk to people who can solve your problems.

Establishing a connection through your provider can also be troublesome at times. Before signing up, ask the provider about the average number of people it has assigned to each modem or line. If that ratio exceeds 15:1 you may wind up too often getting a busy signal when you're trying to connect. A ratio of 10:1 is optimal. On a related note, look into how often and for how long the provider has had to cut users off from its system due to technical difficulties.

Many people connecting to the Internet as users will eventually want to develop Web pages of their own. If you think that you may become a Web author some day, ask providers what types of support they offer in this area and the cost of such support. Many providers will furnish Web-authoring tools and advice. They will also host a home page for you—and possibly several other pages up to a certain total file size—for free or for a nominal cost.

Ease of Use   At the least, the service you select should be easy enough to use so that you aren't spending too much time seeking technical assistance. The browser and other packages the service provides should have friendly interfaces and possess features that make sense for your needs.

Cost   For most people, the bottom line in choosing a provider is what they have to shell out. Today, most Internet users are on flat-rate plans where they get unlimited hours of **connect time.** This is the amount of time their computer has online Internet access through the provider. Most ISPs charge between $15 and $25 per month. In some cases—and this mostly applies to small, local ISPs—you will also be charged a one-time fee to set up your account, say, $25. Many of the large, national providers offer a free month or a set number of free hours of access to get people to sign on with them.

Some ISPs may also offer variable-rate plans, targeted to subscribers whose Internet usage is relatively modest. For example, $10 per month may entitle you to 15 hours of connect time. If you exceed this usage, you may be billed a $1- to $3-per-hour surcharge for every hour above the basic amount.

You must also consider in your cost evaluation the price of calling up an ISP on a regular basis to get connected to the Internet. Virtually all providers have local phone numbers that subscribers can dial into so that they won't be billed for long-distance calls. However, not every provider has every geographical area covered with a local phone number. What's more, even though an ISP has a local access number, it might not be equipped with a particularly fast line. So, for instance, that $14.95 monthly rate you're being offered by an ISP might not look so great if you're regularly calling from Santa Fe, New Mex-

■ **Connect time.** The amount of time you spend online with a service provider's computers.

ico, with a 56 kbps modem and the nearest access point is a 28.8 kbps line operated out of Colorado Springs, Colorado.

SETTING UP YOUR SYSTEM

The specific steps that you must follow to connect to the Internet depend on the service provider you choose. Many will supply you with a *startup kit* with installation software stored on a CD or diskette. All you generally have to do is follow the directions on the disk to begin running the startup program. After the program takes over, it will supply screens that tell you at each step of the way what to do next. In some cases, you won't have to ask for a startup disk at all. Your operating system's opening screens may already display a *setup icon* for your provider. If this is the case, select the icon and follow the instructions on the screen. Smaller, local providers may just require a Web browser and phone dialing software, and will supply you with instructions on how to set them up properly.

Figure NET 2-19 shows how getting set up with a service provider is done, by illustrating some of the steps you would actually take to connect to America Online (AOL). You would follow very similar setup procedures for other

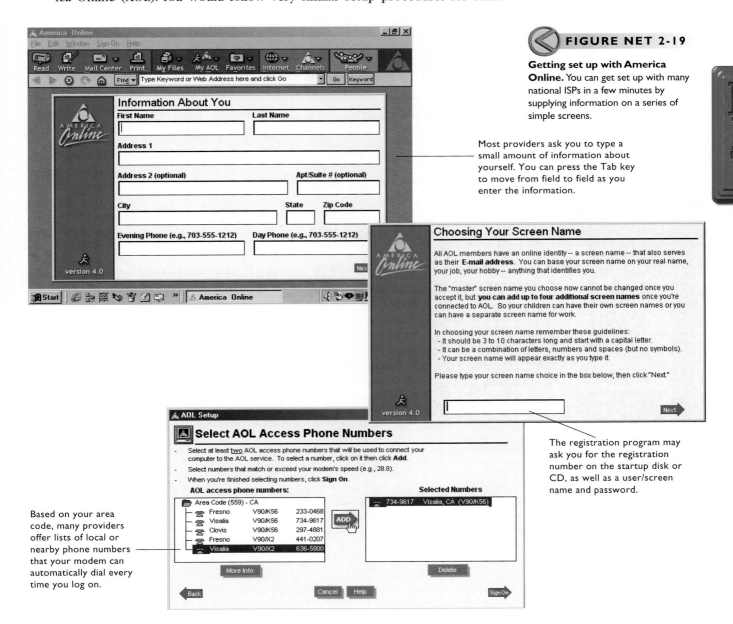

FIGURE NET 2-19

Getting set up with America Online. You can get set up with many national ISPs in a few minutes by supplying information on a series of simple screens.

Most providers ask you to type a small amount of information about yourself. You can press the Tab key to move from field to field as you enter the information.

The registration program may ask you for the registration number on the startup disk or CD, as well as a user/screen name and password.

Based on your area code, many providers offer lists of local or nearby phone numbers that your modem can automatically dial every time you log on.

providers. For any of them, you would need to supply identifying information about yourself, select a plan and choose a method of payment, and provide such connect data as your modem speed and home phone number if your computer system can't figure such information out. Connecting to a small, local provider may involve more steps and complexity, requiring you to select specific protocols and server settings.

After you set up your connection to the provider, you are ready to go. During the setup process, an *access icon* will be placed on one of your operating system's opening screens. Every time you turn on your computer system, you can connect to the provider simply by selecting the access icon and logging on. Then, it's just a matter of following directions on the screen to reach the Internet (see Figure NET 2-20).

FIGURE NET 2-20

Accessing the Web with America Online (AOL).

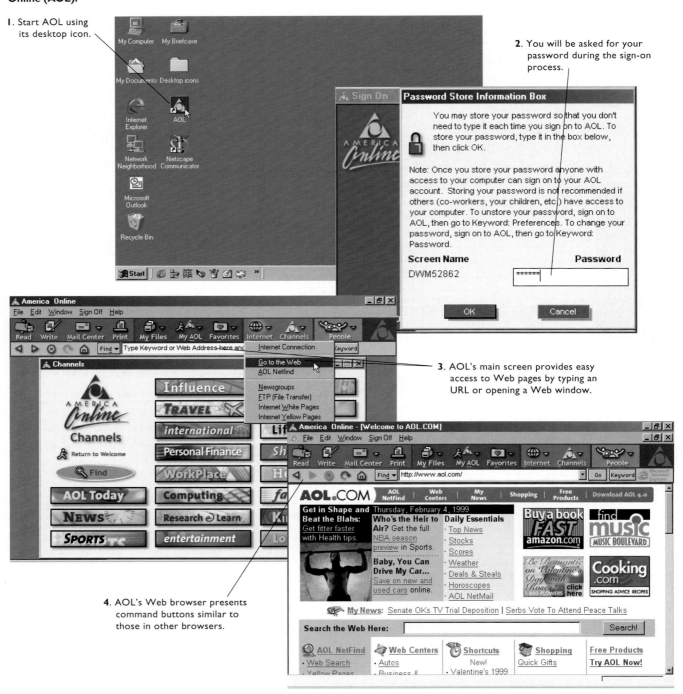

1. Start AOL using its desktop icon.

2. You will be asked for your password during the sign-on process.

3. AOL's main screen provides easy access to Web pages by typing an URL or opening a Web window.

4. AOL's Web browser presents command buttons similar to those in other browsers.

SUMMARY AND KEY TERMS

Go to the Online Glossary at www.harcourtcollege.com/infosys/parker2000/ student/explore/ to review key terms.

Internet has become a household word. In many ways, the Internet has redefined how people think about computers and communications.

Evolution of the Internet The **Internet**—a worldwide phenomenon that consists of thousands of linked networks that are accessed by millions of people daily—dates back to the late 1960s. At its start and throughout many years of its history, the Internet was called the **ARPANET.** It was not until the development of graphical user interfaces and the World Wide Web that public interest in the Internet began to soar.

The Internet community is made up of individuals, companies such as **Internet service providers (ISPs)** and **Internet content providers,** and many other types of organizations. Virtually anyone with a computer that can communicate can be part of the Internet, either as a user or supplier of information or services.

Because the Internet is so unique in the history of the world—and it remains a relatively new phenomenon—several widespread myths about it have surfaced. Three such myths are that the Internet is free, that it is controlled by some central force, and that it is equivalent to the World Wide Web.

What Does the Internet Have to Offer? The Internet is home to many features.

Electronic mail, or **e-mail,** was one of the first applications to appear on the Internet, and it is still the most widely used feature.

The **World Wide Web (WWW),** or *Web,* is one of the features most talked about; it is used for *information retrieval.* Information is organized into chunks called *Web pages,* which are connected by **hyperlinks** (or **hypermedia**)—indicated on-screen by boldfaced and underlined text or by selectable icons or other images. When a content provider creates one or more Web pages that relate to a specific topic or business, the result is called a **Web site.** A Web site contains anywhere from one to hundreds or thousands of pages, with the starting page of the site called the **home page.** Web sites are hosted at computers called **Web servers.**

The Web is one of many information-retrieval tools on the Internet. **Gopher** is another; it generates hierarchical, text-intensive menus that allow users to access resources by making successive selections with an onscreen pointer. FTP sites are good places to visit to get free copies of programs and files. **FTP** stands for **file transfer protocol,** the procedure that facilitates transfers of files between an FTP server and users' computers. **Telnet** is a protocol that lets a desktop workstation behave like a dumb terminal to a remote server.

A **mailing list** is a discussion group that uses e-mail to communicate. Hundreds of mailing lists on the Internet cover a variety of subjects.

Members of **newsgroups** also share e-mail messages, but with a format somewhat like an electronic newspaper. **UseNet** is the protocol that describes how newsgroup messages are handled between computers. A special etiquette—referred to as **netiquette**—has evolved on the Internet for those who communicate via newsgroups and other forms of electronic mail. Newcomers to newsgroups should read through those groups' **FAQs,** or lists of **frequently asked questions.**

Chat refers to a facility that enables people to engage in interactive conversations over the Internet. The most common type of chat is Internet relay chat.

In a growing use of the Internet, many people now shop online.

Internet Addresses An **Internet address** indicates where something on the Internet can be located. Internet addresses are unique; each one is assigned to one and only one resource or person.

People are most commonly reached on the Internet through their *e-mail addresses.* The part of the address before the @ symbol is the person's username; the part following that symbol is the mail server's **domain name.** Web pages and links to information at Gopher, FTP, and other sites are accessed through **uniform resource locators,** or **URLs.**

Desktop Tools for Accessing the Internet A **browser,** or *Web browser,* is a software package that enables you to navigate the World Wide Web as well as other parts of the Internet. The first successful browser was and still is called **Mosaic.** Among a variety of browsers on the market today, the most widely used commercial products are **Netscape Navigator** and **Microsoft Internet Explorer.**

Browser software is constantly evolving. Some properties that you may want to consider in a browser include functionality, navigational tools, speed, customizability (including the ability to change your **portal** and to control **cookie** files), framing capabilities, a workgroup-computing facility, support for multimedia and virtual-reality applications, Java and ActiveX support, publishing capabilities, and security. A large market has developed for *plug-in packages* and *helper packages,* both of which enable you to add features and functions to your current browsing environment.

When you know generally what you want, but you don't know at which URL to find it, one of your best options is a **search engine.** One of the most popular search engines is **Yahoo!,** which can be found on the Web and used for free. You can also purchase auxiliary search software to meet additional searching needs.

A more powerful computer system will more likely give you access to the advanced features of the Internet.

Connecting to the Internet *Internet service providers (ISPs)* furnish Internet connections. Most people hunting for an ISP have two basic choices: going with a large, national provider or with a small, local outfit. Often, you will connect to an ISP through a **SLIP** or **PPP** account, both of which are variations of the **TCP/IP** protocol.

People often select service providers by considering several criteria. Among their priorities are the information a service provides and other features including price, speed, service and support, and ease of use. Fees usually include set monthly amounts and possibly extra charges for **connect time** in excess of the standard amount.

How you connect to the Internet depends on the provider you have chosen, but usually involves installing a program and choosing the appropriate options or settings.

EXERCISES

1. Define the following terms:
   a. Home page
   b. The Internet
   c. Domain name
   d. Content provider

2. Describe the purposes of the following Internet services:
   a. World Wide Web
   b. Chat
   c. Newsgroups
   d. FTP
   e. E-mail
   f. Telnet

3. Match each term with the description that fits best:
   a. History-list feature
   b. Streaming capability
   c. Framing capability
   d. Webcasting capability
   e. Web-publishing capability
   f. Cookie feature

   _____ Designed to push information to the user while he or she passively sits by and watches.

   _____ Enables sound or video images to begin outputting on a client computer before the associated files are fully downloaded.

_____ Permits a Web server to remember selections or preferences you've indicated at an earlier time.

_____ Lets you know what sites you've visited on the Web.

_____ Enables users to see two or more pages on the screen at the same time, each page with its own scroll bars.

_____ Lets users create their own Web pages.

4. Determine whether the followings statements are true or false:
   a. When the Internet was first developed back in 1969, it was called ORACLE.
   b. One of the most prominent browsers available for the Internet is named Yahoo!
   c. On the Internet, an *access provider* and a *content provider* are essentially the same thing.
   d. FAQ files are designed to inform new users about appropriate netiquette.
   e. If the string "mjordan@chicagobulls.com" exists on the Internet, it is most likely the address of a Web page.
   f. The most widely used feature on the Internet is e-mail.
   g. Gopher was originally developed at Microsoft Corporation.
   h. Requests that are part of a URL are case sensitive.
   i. Many browsing environments support multimedia and virtual reality.
   j. Connect time refers to the amount of time your computer is turned on.

5. Fill in the blanks:
   a. Small programs called Java _____ can provide animation to a Web page.
   b. A(n) _____ feature lets you see a low-resolution image on your Web browser before the computer downloads all of the data needed to display the image at full resolution.
   c. _____ is the name of Microsoft's principal browser, whereas _____ is the name of Netscape's principal browser.
   d. The first page you typically encounter on a visit to a Web site is called the site's _____ page.
   e. Newsgroup submissions are called _____ and replies tacked onto the submissions are known as _____.

6. What terms do the following acroynyms represent?
   a. IRC   d. FAQ   g. ISP   j. VRML
   b. FTP   e. URL   h. PPP
   c. WWW   f. HTML i. AOL

7. Newsgroups are organized by topic, as indicated by their names; for instance, *rec* stands for *recreation* and *sci* for *science*. Name as many other newsgroup classifications as you can as well as their associated three- or four-letter abbreviations.

8. Participants in such Internet services as newsgroups and mailing lists should follow proper netiquette. Identify at least five rules of netiquette.

9. For each of the following situations, name the Internet service you would probably be using. Choose from e-mail, newsgroups, mailing lists, the World Wide Web, Gopher, FTP, Telnet, and chat.
   a. You need to find information on virtual reality, in the easiest way possible, for a term paper.
   b. You want to send a letter to a friend at Northern Arizona University.
   c. You would like to visit the Internet Underground Music Archive at http://www.iuma.com.
   d. You want to initiate with other people a series of articles and threads on flying saucers and other extraterrestrial objects.
   e. You want to communicate interactively with a friend in real time, with each of you in turn typing something into your computer.
   f. You want to download free software.
   g. You are communicating with a computer in a foreign country, and it treats your fancy new computer like a dumb terminal.
   h. You want to search through government computers to find the locations of downloadable files on Watergate.

10. You are talking with a friend who has some definite misconceptions about the Internet. What can you tell your friend to set him or her straight on the following misconceptions?
    a. The Internet is free.
    b. The Internet is controlled by the FBI.
    c. The World Wide Web is really the same thing as the Internet; purists just like to say they're different.

11. Describe in your own words the difference between the following terms: *Web client, Web site,* and *Web server.* Into which of those three categories—if any of them—would you place the following?
    a. A computer that stores thousands of Web pages
    b. The home page for television's Discovery Channel
    c. The area on a mainframe computer that stores e-mail going to students
    d. The browser on your PC

12. A large selection of plug-in and helper programs can enhance browsing environments such as those provided with Internet Explorer and Netscape Navigator. Supply at least five examples of such packages and describe what each one does.

13. Name at least three Web-resident search engines. What uses and limitations do such search engines have?

14. Identify several criteria by which people often choose among service providers.

PROJECTS

1. Internet Service Providers Find two local or national ISPs that service your area and compare them with respect to the following criteria:

a. Monthly cost: Assume for sake of comparison that you will need 25 hours of connect time a week.

b. Setup costs, if any.

c. What software products are the providers offering as part of their servicing package?

d. Local lines: Do you have to dial long distance, or are local lines available? How fast are the lines?

e. Browsers available: What browsers are available, and how do they stack up in comparison? Can you use newer versions of Internet Explorer or Navigator once they are available for download?

f. Ease of connecting to the Internet: Compare the procedures involved with both providers.

g. Your "window" to the Internet: To what parts of the Internet do any of the providers deny access?

h. Technical support available: Must you pay any charges for answers to phoned-in questions? During what hours and what days of the week is support available?

2. E-Mail As mentioned in the chapter text, the most widely used feature of the Internet is electronic mail, or e-mail. For this project, research a standalone e-mail package of your own choice and report to the class about it. Two common e-mail programs that run on both the Windows and Macintosh platforms are Qualcomm's Eudora Pro and Pegasus Mail. Windows-only software includes Microsoft Outlook and Microsoft Outlook Express.

Make sure you answer the following questions in your report:

a. What is the name of the program you have chosen? Who is the program's publisher? How much does the program cost?

b. What are the program's main features? Do they include sending and receiving attachments, using an address book and filtering e-mail messages?

3. Online Catalogs Online catalogs have become increasingly popular features of the Web and corporate intranets. Many people have speculated that this trend may bring the end of the printed catalog. Answer the following questions, limiting your comments to two pages or less:

a. What compelling advantages do online catalogs have over their printed counterparts?

b. Do you see any advantages of printed catalogs over their online counterparts? If so, name them.

c. How do you feel about the predicted demise of the printed catalog?

4. Navigating the Web Browsers vary in the way that their *history-list* and *bookmark* features are implemented. For the browser you are using, answer the following questions:

a. How would you return most quickly to the Web page that was on your screen immediately before the one that is there now?

b. How does the history-list feature work?

c. How do you add a bookmark?

d. How do you jump to a bookmark?

e. How can you remove bookmarks when you don't need them anymore?

f. Are all the bookmarks for everyone who uses one particular computer stored together or are they organized by user?

5. Web Browser Features Web browsers come with many exotic features in addition to the standard ones. For the browser you are using in your lab—or, if your lab is not Internet ready, for any browser of your choice (that you can research in a computer journal)—answer the following questions:

a. Is a framing capability available?

b. Are there any workgroup-computing capabilities?

c. Does the browser provide built-in Java support?

d. Can you create your own Web pages with the browser, or do you need some type of plug-in or helper program to do this?

e. What types of security features does the browser provide?

6. Search Engines   You can access several free search engines on the Web, including Yahoo!, Excite, Lycos, and Alta Vista. The URLs of these and other engines can be found in the accompanying table.

For this project, choose any two search engines and compare them with respect to the following items:

a. Quantity of information: Observe the number of links each one provides when you search on specific topics. (Do this by selecting some search topics that interest you. Choose some one-word topics like "motorcycles" as well as some multiword—and therefore more complex—ones like "Arizona wildflowers.")

b. Quality of information: Observe how useful the links are. (Use the same single-word and multiword topics as in part *a* for your searches. Does each search engine locate good links and make them easy for you to access?)

c. Other: Many search sites have added features that go well beyond searching, including e-mail, chat, stock information, and so forth. How do the sites you've chosen compare with respect to such features?

Sites for Web-Resident Search Engines	
AltaVista	www.altavista.com
Excite	www.excite.com
HotBot	www.hotbot.com
Infoseek	infoseek.go.com
Lycos	www.lycos.com
WebCrawler	www.webcrawler.com
Yahoo!	www.yahoo.com

7. Get a Job   In recent years, the Internet has become a great place to look for jobs. As your project, find at least one source that posts job announcements in your career area. Describe the source, telling approximately how many jobs are listed and what types of online tools are available to help with job searches. For instance, some sites offer search tools to help you find particular jobs, information about job and salary trends, and calculators that show how much you will need to make in particular geographic areas to maintain a particular standard of living. Note that the Internet hosts both national and regional job-search sites.

To help you to get started, feel free to check out any of the sites in the "Jobs and Employment" section of the WebGuide window located at the end of this chapter. Also think about using search engines—click on the "Business and the Economy" category—to find more. You may additionally want to look at the "Computer Careers" section that appears in every weekly issue of *Computerworld;* this publication often lists Web sites useful for computer professionals who are hunting for jobs.

8. Cybercafés   Locate a cybercafé reasonably near your home or school and pay a visit. Then answer the following questions:

a. What is the name of the cybercafé? What is its postal address? Its Web or e-mail address?

b. What types of hardware does the cybercafé use—fully equipped PCs with diskette drives or dumb terminals that work through a larger computer?

c. What types of browsers are available? What plug-ins or other helper software is available to enhance your Internet experience?

d. How much do you have to pay per hour to use the computers?

e. Does the cybercafé offer classes or individual instruction? If so, what's the cost?

9. Paying for the Internet   The chapter mentions the expectation of some industry analysts that pay-per-use Internet access is rapidly approaching. Some have suggested that users should pay charges for the Internet just as they would if they used a toll road—say, paying fees that are proportional to the load they create for Internet resources. Others feel that charges for the Internet by usage are both unnecessary and likely to discourage people from learning to use a critical educational resource. They propose that the Internet's cost could be subsidized by advertisers or by a method similar to the way that many states offer residents free roads—by increasing general taxes slightly or by adding taxes to hardware and/or software purchases.

How do you think the Internet should be supported?

10. The Web as a Travel Agent I   People often use the Internet to shop around for places to go on vacation. The Web is populated with thousands of travel-related sites, blanketing the entire world, and covers airlines, hotels, car-rental agencies, cruise companies, travel agencies, and tourist offices. You can even download travel films that feature specific vacation destinations, schmooze with travelers who've been there, and reserve airline seats and tourist packages.

Write a paper (three to five pages) about resources available on the Web that cater to people

who like to travel. Some of the sites listed in the "Travel" section of the WebGuide window located at the end of this chapter will help get you started.

 11. The Web as a Travel Agent II Want to pick up a $1,200 air ticket for less than $200? Try buying it online and at the last minute. In recent years, the Internet has established itself as the place to go for bargain airline tickets.

Unfortunately, you may not have too much advance notice to book a flight and too much flexi-

Air-Ticket Web Sites

Alaska Airlines	www.alaskaair.com
American Airlines	wwwr3.aa.com
Continental Airlines	www.continental.com
Priceline.com	www.priceline.com
Southwest Airlines	www.iflyswa.com
Travelocity.com	www.travelocity.com
United Airlines	www.ual.com

bility with departure and arrival times. The airline companies try to get full price for tickets, but as departure dates get closer and there are still empty seats, they start cutting prices. For a weekend flight, you may be constrained to leave on Saturday and return on Monday or Tuesday. Still, a rock-bottom price can make the flight a deal.

Visit a site that sells discount airline tickets and report on what you found in the way of bargains. Some of the sites listed in the accompanying table will help get you started. Do any of the sites you visited also provide bargains on hotel rooms and rental cars?

 12. Set Up Your Own Chat Room It's getting easier than ever for users to set up, free of charge, their own private chat rooms. An easy way this can be done is through a portal like Yahoo! or Excite. For this project, set up a private chat room and conduct a chat among three or more people. Report to the class the means by which you accomplished this and answer the following questions:
a. How many people participated in the chat room?
b. How did participants gain entry?
c. What types of chat tools were available?

INTERACTIVE EXERCISE

CONNECTING TO AND USING THE INTERNET

 It's time to go online and explore the World Wide Web! Go to the Interactive Exercise at www.harcourtcollege.com/infosys/parker2000/student/exercise/ to complete this exercise.

ONLINE REVIEW

Go to the Online Review at www.harcourtcollege.com/infosys/parker2000/student/ to test your understanding of this chapter's concepts.

WEBGUIDE

A LOOK AT SOME OF THE WEB'S MOST USEFUL SITES

The Web is growing up. Just a few years ago, it was mostly the curious and the cool elements of the Web that drew visitors. Today, Web users are far more practically minded. They want to use the Web to get information, buy products or obtain product support, or get some work done. Although the 11-category list in this window contains several sites with a high entertainment value, all of them have one characteristic in common: Usefulness.

INFORMATION CATEGORIES

Automobiles	Jobs and Employment	Shopping
Business and Finance	News and Weather	Sports
Computers	Portals	Travel
Entertainment	Reference	

For links to all of the Web sites listed in this WebGuide, go to www.harcourtcollege.com/infosys/parker2000/student/explore/ and click on the NET Module WebGuide.

AUTOMOBILES

Autobytel.com	www.autobytel.com	Car-buying site with search tools; covers thousands of dealers
AutoTrader.com	www.autotrader.com	Car-buying site with search tools; covers thousands of dealers
Autoweb.com	www.autoweb.com	Car-buying site with search tools; covers thousands of dealers
Car Talk	cartalk.cars.com	Consumer information and chat on both car buying and repairs
Carfax	www.carfax.com	Accident history available on millions of vehicles
CarFinance.com	www.carfinance.com	Get a car loan online
Cars.com	www.cars.com	Searchable car ads from many of the nation's newspapers
Edmunds.com	www.edmunds.com	Current information and market prices on new and used car models
Microsoft CarPoint	carpoint.msn.com	Car-buying site with search tools; covers thousands of dealers
Priceline.com	www.priceline.com	Online auction for car buyers; make a bid on the car of your choice

Hint: If you need information on a specific make of car, consider going to the manufacturer's Web site, such as www.ford.com for a Ford, or www.bmw.com for a BMW.

BUSINESS AND FINANCE

Business Wire	www.businesswire.com	Current business news
CBS MarketWatch	www.cbsmarketwatch.com	Current news about business and financial markets
CNNfn	www.cnnfn.com	Current news about business and financial markets
Forbes Digital Tool	www.forbes.com	Access to articles and investment information
Fortune Investor	www.fortuneinvestor.com	Access to articles and investment information
Hoover's Online	www.hoovers.com	Company capsules, financial information, stock quotes and charts
Investorama	www.investorama.com	Links to scores of financial Web sites and articles
Fool.com	www.fool.com	Commentary on stocks and other personal finance topics
U.S. Securities & Exchange Commission	www.sec.gov	Government filings made by public companies
USA Today Money	www.usatoday.com/money	Online version of *USA Today's* Money section
Yahoo! Finance	quote.yahoo.com	Free price quotes, news, and portfolio tracker

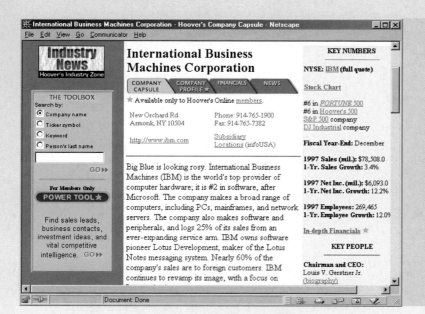

Free Investment Information

Hoover's Online at www.hoovers.com is a comprehensive source for information about companies. The free information found here includes company capsules containing basic information (company's location, top officers, sales, links to stock quotes, news, etc.) for more than 13,000 public and private companies, as well as brief financial data, news, and charts. The fee-based membership to Hoover's Online adds access to more than 3,400 detailed company profiles, as well as in-depth financial information including market data, comparison data, and annual, quarterly, and historical financial statements.

COMPUTERS

Byte Online	www.byte.com	Online version of *Byte* magazine
CNet	home.cnet.com	News and articles about computers
CNN Computing	cnn.com/TECH/computing	News and articles about computers
Computerworld	www.computerworld.com	Online version of *Computerworld* magazine
MacWEEK.com	macweek.zdnet.com	Online version of *MacWEEK* magazine
Macworld Online	macworld.zdnet.com	Online version of *Macworld* magazine
PC Computing Online	www.zdnet.com/pccomp	Online version of *PC Computing* magazine
PC Magazine Online	www.zdnet.com/pcmag	Online version of *PC Magazine*
PC Week Online	www.zdnet.com/pcweek	Online version of *PC Week* magazine
PC World Online	www.pcworld.com	Online version of *PC World* magazine
Presentations.com	www.presentations.com	Online version of *Presentations* magazine
Stroud's CWSApps List	cws.internet.com	Catalog of hundreds of downloadable Windows-based utilities and Internet software
Yahoo! Internet Life	www.zdnet.com/yil	Online version of *Yahoo! Internet Life*
ZDNet	www.zdnet.com	Current computer news and reviews, plus product guides, downloads, and more

Hint: If you need information on a specific computer product, consider going to the maker's site, such as www.microsoft.com for Microsoft products or www.hp.com for Hewlett-Packard products.

ENTERTAINMENT

Blue Mountain Arts	www.bluemountain.com	Send free electronic greeting cards; the recipient is notified by e-mail where to view the card
Broadcast.com	www.broadcast.com	Sports talk, live radio broadcasts, audio books, and more
CDNOW	www.cdnow.com	Download singles to make your own CD-ROMs and purchase videos and DVDs
Classics World	www.bmgclassics.com	Information about classical music
Entertainment Asylum	www.asylum.com	Comprehensive movie, TV, and celebrity site
Internet Movie Database	www.imdb.com	Most comprehensive film resource on the Web
Moviefone.com	www.moviefone.com	Links to film sites; movie tickets also available
NetRadio.com	www.netradio.com	Continuous-music channels
Reel.com	www.reel.com	Movie information; videos and DVDs for sale
Rock & Roll Hall of Fame	www.rockhall.com	Rock & Roll museum
Won.net	www.won.net/gameslist	Play free games, such as *You Don't Know Jack,* online

JOBS AND EMPLOYMENT

CareerBuilder	www.careerbuilder.com	Free job searching and job hunting information
CareerMosaic	www.careermosaic.com	Free job searching, help with résumé writing, and more
CareerPath.com	new.careerpath.com	Free job searching; can also post résumé
JobOptions	www.joboptions.com	A large job-search site, where users can post résumés and look for jobs
Jobtrak.com	www.jobtrak.com	Free job searching; can also post résumé
Monster.com	www.monster.com	The world's largest employment resource, with a half million résumés posted

Computer Magazines Galore

The ZDNet site at www.zdnet.com is home to one of the largest collections of computer magazines on the Web. Here you will find links to the latest online editions of *PC Magazine*, *PC Week*, *MacWEEK*, *MacWorld*, *Yahoo! Internet Life*, and several others. You will also find news and reviews of specific computer products, articles about computing technologies, and comments from leading analysts within the computer industry.

NEWS AND WEATHER

ABC News.com	www.abcnews.go.com	General news; click on a subject for specialized news
AccuWeather	www.accuweather.com	National and international weather forecasts
CNN.com	www.cnn.com	General news; click on a subject for specialized news
Intellicast	www.intellicast.com	National and international weather forecasts
The Internet Public Library	www.ipl.org	Links to over 2,000 magazines and 1,000 newspapers to read online
The Los Angeles Times	www.latimes.com	Online version of this widely read newspaper
MSNBC	www.msnbc.com	General news; click on a subject for specialized news
National Weather Service	www.nws.noaa.gov	National weather forecasts and maps
The New York Times	www.nytimes.com	Online version of this widely read newspaper
NewsDirectory.com	www.newsdirectory.com	Links to hundreds of online periodicals, by subject area or region
USA Today	www.usatoday.com	Online version of this widely read newspaper
The Washington Post	www.washingtonpost.com	Online version of this widely read newspaper
The Weather Channel	www.weather.com	National and international weather forecasts and maps

SPORTS

CNN/SI	www.cnnsi.com	Sports news; joint venture of CNN and *Sports Illustrated*
ESPN.com	espn.go.com	Sports news
Majorleaguebaseball.com	www.majorleaguebaseball.com	Official site of Major League Baseball
NBA.com	www.nba.com	Official site of the National Basketball Association
NFL.com	www.nfl.com	Official site of the National Football League

PORTALS

AltaVista	www.altavista.com	Internet service provider
AOL.com	www.aol.com	Internet service provider
AT&T WorldNet	www.att.net	Internet service provider
CompuServe	www.compuserve.com	Internet service provider
Deja.com	www.deja.com	Locate information on products before you buy them
Earthlink	www.earthlink.com	Internet service provider
Excite	www.excite.com	Search engine
HotBot	www.hotbot.com	Search engine
Infoseek	infoseek.go.com	Search engine
Lycos	www.lycos.com	Search engine
Microsoft Network	www.msn.com	Internet service provider
Snap.com	www.snap.com	Search engine
Yahoo!	www.yahoo.com	Search engine

REFERENCE

Achoo Healthcare Online	www.achoo.com	Access to a wide range of health information
AnyWho's Directories	www.tollfree.att.net/index.html	Look up people, toll-free telephone numbers, maps, etc.
Bartlett's Familiar Quotations	www.bartleby.com/99	Online version of *Bartlett's Familiar Quotations*
FindLaw	www.findlaw.com	Supersite with links to a wide range of legal information
Internet Public Library	www.ipl.org	An online library with online books, exhibits, magazines, etc.
Law.Net	www.law.net	Search for an attorney with specific expertise
The Legal Information Institute	www.law.cornell.edu	Access to a wide range of legal information
The Library of Congress	www.loc.gov	An enormous site, with historic papers, books, films, and much more
Netdictionary	www.netdictionary.com	Online dictionary of Internet terms
NetLingo	www.netlingo.com	Online dictionary of Internet terms
OneLook Dictionaries	www.onelook.com	Online dictionary has access to more than 2 million words in more than 500 other dictionaries
PubMed	www.ncbi.nlm.nih.gov/pubmed	The National Library of Medicine's search service of medical databases
Thesaurus.com	www.thesaurus.com	An online thesaurus and dictionary
RxList	www.rxlist.com	Search online for information about specific drugs
Switchboard	www.switchboard.com	Look up the addresses and phone numbers of people and businesses listed in the telephone book, as well as view a map of a specified address
U.S. Postal Service Post Office	www.usps.gov/postofc	Look up ZIP codes, track packages, buy stamps online, etc.
WWW Virtual Law Library	www.law.indiana.edu/law/v-lib	Access to a wide range of legal information
WWWebster Dictionary	www.m-w.com/netdict.htm	Online version of the long-standing, popular Merriam-Webster dictionary

SHOPPING

Amazon.com	www.amazon.com	World's largest online bookstore boasts more than 2.5 million titles
Barnes & Noble	www.barnesandnoble.com	A large online bookstore
CDNOW	www.cdnow.com	Hundreds of thousands of CDs, videos, and DVDs for sale; reviews and sample clips available too
Classifieds2000	www.classifieds2000.com	Searchable classified ads database
CompUSA.com	www.compusa.com	Computer hardware and software for sale
The Earthlink Mall	www.wizshop.com	A large online mall
eBay	www.ebay.com	A very popular electronic auction house where users can buy or sell goods
Egghead.com	www.egghead.com	Computer hardware and software for sale; also auctions
The Gap	www.gap.com	Popular retail clothing site has a feature that lets you dress mannequins in clothes of your choice
L.L. Bean	www.llbean.com	Online catalog of outdoor clothing and gear
Office Depot Online	www.officedepot.com	Buy office supplies online
OfficeMax.com	www.officemax.com	Buy office supplies and computer products online
Onsale	www.onsale.com	Auction site and products for sale online
Shopping.com	www.shopping.com	A large shopping site with a low price guarantee
ShopNow.com	www.shopnow.com	A huge directory of online stores and auctions
Wal-Mart Online	www.wal-mart.com	Shop for Wal-Mart merchandise online

Hint: If you need information about a specific product or store, consider going to the maker's site or the store's site, such as www.mattel.com for a Mattel toy or www.target.com for Target stores.

TRAVEL

American Wilderness Experience	gorp.com/awe	Adventure travel
Biztravel.com	www.biztravel.com	Travel arrangements for frequent business travelers
Expedia.com	expedia.msn.com	Book plane, hotel, and tour reservations
Golf Travel Online	www.gto.com	Book golfing vacations around the world
Preview Travel	www.previewtravel.com	Book plane, hotel, and tour reservations
Priceline.com	www.priceline.com	Bid prices for airline seats, hotel rooms, and car rentals
Smithsonian Study Tours	www.si.edu/tsa/sst	Educational tours
Travelocity.com	www.travelocity.com	Book plane, hotel, and tour information
TravelWeb	www.travelweb.com	Hotel and flight reservations
TRIP.com	www.thetrip.com	Travel reservations plus maps and flight tracking

Hint: If you need information from a specific airline, hotel, or car-rental service, also consider going to the appropriate company site, such as www.iflyswa.com for Southwest Airlines or www.hertz.com for Hertz rental cars.

DEVELOPING YOUR OWN WEB PAGES

OUTLINE

LEARNING OBJECTIVES

After completing this chapter, you will be able to:

1. Define the many evolving opportunities available in Web publishing.

2. Name the various steps required in developing Web pages for the Internet.

3. Describe the types of tools that authors use to create Web pages.

4. Identify social issues that relate to Web publishing.

OVERVIEW

One of the most compelling attractions to the Web is developing your own Web pages and posting them on the Internet. Look at the alternatives. If you write an article for a magazine—or a book manuscript, movie screenplay, or television script—you have to sell your idea to an agent, publisher, or producer before you can reach an audience. Not so with Web publishing. You can whip up your own Web pages, pay someone with a Web server to host them, and—bingo—you're in business and immediately reaching out to millions of people throughout the world.

One of the main challenges of Web publishing is that it's a relatively new application for computers, one with unbounded potential. In many ways, the state of the art in Web publishing today is like the film industry in the early days of Hollywood or the television industry in the early 1950s. It's a landscape for pioneers, and nobody knows what its killer application—the one that brings mass-market acceptance—will be. The final rule book is still to be written. Anyone can play, and play in his or her own style.

Chapter NET 3 opens with a general discussion of Web publishing. From there, it goes into the steps you will need to follow to create your own Web pages. These steps are pretty much the same ones you would follow in developing any type of computer program or commercial project. The chapter also covers some important side issues that concern Web publishers, such as copyrights, security, and censorship.

THE WEB AS A PUBLISHING MEDIUM

Web Tutor

For a tutorial on the components of a Web page, go to www.harcourtcollege.com/infosys/parker2000/student/tutor/ and click on Chapter NET 3.

The Web is unlike traditional publishing media such as books, newspapers and magazines, and movies and television. In fact, it is quite unlike any publishing medium ever known.

Web publishing is defined as developing pages for the Web; in other words, creating your own **Web site** or *Web presence*. Depending on your needs, the site can range in size and scale from a single page featuring your favorite chili recipe to a multipage electronic catalog from which people can order goods. You can start up your own Web site without owning or operating either server computers or a fleet of modems to distribute your pages to remote users. Most Web authors store the needed files on their service providers' computers.

ADVANTAGES OF WEB PUBLISHING

The Web offers several advantages over traditional publishing media.

Anyone Can Play   One of the big differences from other media that distinguishes Web publishing is that anyone can participate. If you have a great idea, you can immediately get it published and, what's more, published in your preferred style. You don't have to get approval from anyone else. Furthermore, you can often work on your own timetable.

People writing for traditional media regularly feel frustrated when editors say they want submissions that are *different* and then reject works that are

---

■ **Web publishing.** The process of developing pages for the Web. ■ **Web site.** A collection of related Web pages belonging to an individual or organization.

too different and perceived as too risky for one reason or another. As your own Web publisher, you are more or less free to do your own thing. Web *users*—those who read the pages produced by Web publishers—can become bored from look-alike products, so an unusual appearance of a site can be a smart publishing goal. This does not mean that you will never feel any restraints on page design. If you are a company employee developing a Web site, or you are in the business of developing sites for clients, you will probably have to adhere to some guidelines.

The Online Nature of Web Products   Traditional media are distributed through static printed pages, broadcasts, or screenings. These media are essentially *serial* in nature—that is, they are laid out in specific chapter-by-chapter or scene-by-scene order so that their audiences must more or less accept the author's intended method of experiencing the products.

Web pages, by contrast, have hyperlinks that encourage readers to jump around and thereby experience the products in their own personalized ways. In this sense, Web users take on the role of authors; they dynamically determine the content and order of what they read seconds later.

Consider a couple of other, related advantages to online publishing: Web publishers can update pages with fresh materials whenever they want to, and they can include a wide variety of *interactive* elements—such as sound and video clips—that traditional media can't use.

Low Cost   Relative to other media, publishing on the Web is cheap. Take content. As a Web publisher, you don't even have to create all of your content or pay for it. For instance, you can download thousands of free art and audio clips from the Web for use at your own site. Also, you can provide hyperlinks on your home page to any of the millions of Web pages that have been created by others, incorporating other sites as part of your own presentation.

You don't have to spend very much—if anything at all—to publish and distribute your page, either. Many colleges and universities let students, faculty, and staff publish materials on the Internet for free. If you've signed up with a commercial provider, once you pay to get your pages hosted on its server, you face no printing and mailing costs. Many commercial providers let regular users of their services run single home pages for free or for very nominal fees, with modest charges for any additional pages. This fact does not imply that you can expect no hidden costs. Many commercial providers charge you to update pages, and some bill extra if your site creates a lot of traffic.

Keep in mind that, theoretically speaking, all Web pages are equally accessible. Someone can visit your home page about as easily as they can visit the Microsoft or Disney home page. If your pages are interesting and exciting, strong word-of-mouth advertising will inform people about them. Also, other places on the Web will help you to promote your site for free by providing links to it.

DISADVANTAGES OF WEB PUBLISHING

As a prospective Web publisher, be advised that the medium also suffers from certain disadvantages and limitations. For one, developing Web pages takes certain skills. Are you willing to invest the time to pick them up? Also, you have to decide whether you want to commit to keeping your pages constantly updated with fresh material. That process can require a lot of work too, but people generally will not return to your site unless they are constantly rewarded with new, useful information.

Another knotty problem emerges as you try to ensure that your document presents a consistent look over a wide variety of computer platforms. As a later section will discuss, you can count on no absolute guarantee that the beautiful pages you develop on your computer system will look the same on someone else's. Some extra effort on your part, however, will minimize the chances of surprises later on.

WHY PUBLISH ON THE WEB?

The first question every prospective Web publisher needs to answer is both simple and complex: Why am I doing this? It's the same question you should ask before writing a book or a movie script. The answer defines your *goal*, or purpose.

Goals People work toward all types of goals when they create Web pages. Many develop their own Web presence to share knowledge or some burning passion: Making pasta, raising horses, collecting stamps—you name it. If you love, say, raising horses, your home page can contain links to other Web resources in the horse world—online horse publications, Web pages of other horse lovers, Web pages of guest ranches, and so on.

Others establish a Web presence to post their employment résumé or just to announce to the world at large what a great person they are or where they fall in the political spectrum. If you're single, your home page can help you to meet the love of your life. Of course, your Web site can also have profit as a motive. Many businesses set up Web pages to establish organizational presences or images, to generate sales leads by getting visitors to fill out informational forms, and to close sales on the spot by getting purchase commitments. Figure NET 3-1 illustrates several purposes for developing a Web presence.

Knowing precisely why you want to publish on the Web leads to the next critical question: Who is your audience—your target market?

FIGURE NET 3-1

Some goals for developing a Web presence.

CREATING A PERSONAL SITE

People often create a Web presence for personal reasons, such as searching for others who may share their passion for specific types of recreation.

DEVELOPING A TRAILBLAZER SITE

Trailblazer sites are one-stop addresses that provide linkages to a comprehensive list of resources on a given subject—realtors, motorcycles, stamp collecting, or the like.

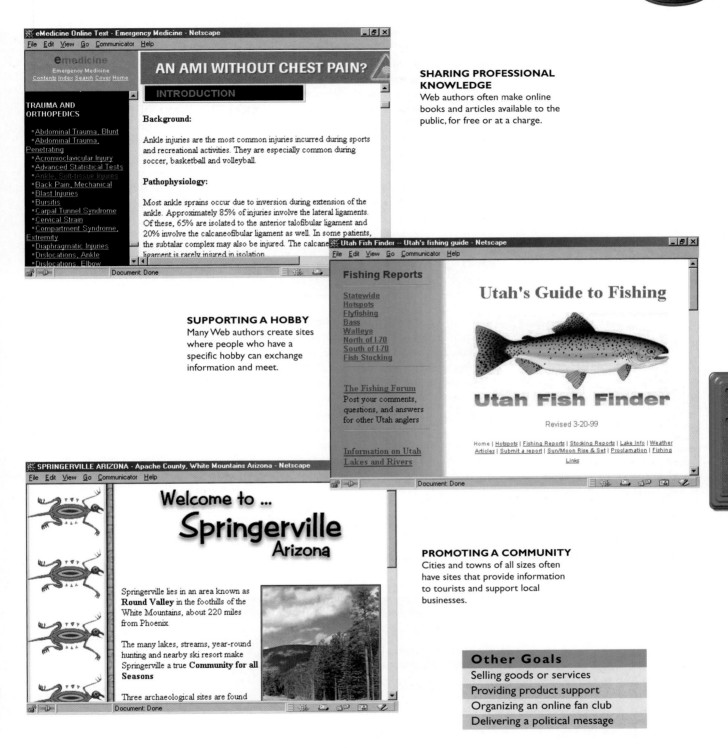

SHARING PROFESSIONAL KNOWLEDGE
Web authors often make online books and articles available to the public, for free or at a charge.

SUPPORTING A HOBBY
Many Web authors create sites where people who have a specific hobby can exchange information and meet.

PROMOTING A COMMUNITY
Cities and towns of all sizes often have sites that provide information to tourists and support local businesses.

Other Goals
Selling goods or services
Providing product support
Organizing an online fan club
Delivering a political message

Audience   Most people who establish their own sites on the Web have something they want to say. The big question is: Do others out there on the Web want to listen? If you feel that an audience wants to see your Web message or product, define who those people are and determine what will turn them on. What is their age range? Is the audience mostly male or female? Who does your audience admire? Would they appreciate an amusing or funky site, or would a more business-like site be more appropriate? You should also ask yourself whether the Web is the best way of reaching these people. Maybe an ad in your local paper would be both easier and far more effective.

Competition   Even if you anticipate finding an audience for your proposed Web site, a competing Web site already on the Internet may duplicate your intentions. You should spend time with search engines like Yahoo! or WebCrawler to see if there are any existing sites that resemble your planned site. Keep in mind that getting a message or product to market first gives you an advantage, but it doesn't guarantee success. The history of personal computers proves this point rather conclusively; such first-to-market companies as Apple (computers), WordStar (word processing), VisiCalc (spreadsheets), and dBASE (databases) have been eclipsed in the marketplace by more nimble competitors.

You can also use competitors' sites to your advantage. By developing links at your site to information at other sites, you might use them to complement what you're doing.

DEVELOPING A PUBLISHING PLAN

You need to spend time thinking about such matters as your purpose, your audience, and the competition as part of developing a *plan* for publishing on the Web. In this planning stage, you size up a prospective Web project before building the site. In other words, you lay out the step-by-step process through which you will develop your own Web pages, as well as the project's benefits and costs. A thoughtful plan will reduce the chance that unexpected events will disrupt your Web-site-development experience.

Figure NET 3-2 shows some of the issues you should resolve during the planning stage of Web-page development. As part of this planning, you should check out prospective **Internet presence providers (IPPs)**—the

FIGURE NET 3-2

Issues to consider during the planning stage.

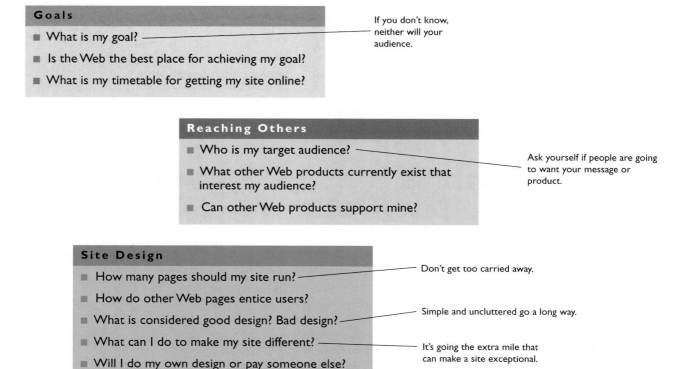

Goals

■ What is my goal? —————————————— If you don't know, neither will your audience.

■ Is the Web the best place for achieving my goal?

■ What is my timetable for getting my site online?

Reaching Others

■ Who is my target audience? —————— Ask yourself if people are going to want your message or product.

■ What other Web products currently exist that interest my audience?

■ Can other Web products support mine?

Site Design

■ How many pages should my site run? —————— Don't get too carried away.

■ How do other Web pages entice users?

■ What is considered good design? Bad design? —————— Simple and uncluttered go a long way.

■ What can I do to make my site different? —————— It's going the extra mile that can make a site exceptional.

■ Will I do my own design or pay someone else?

■ **Internet presence provider (IPP).** An organization whose servers host Web pages.

Internet Presence Providers (IPPs)

- What does it cost to run pages?
- What does it cost to update pages?
- How will my site be named and registered?
- What sort of help will the IPP provide? What's the cost?
- What site-activity statistics are provided?
- What security measures are provided?

Choose a name that's easy for users to remember and not too long to type.

Testing

- How will I test my site *before* going online?
- How will I continue to test my site after going online?

Ask people if your site is exciting and useful.

Coding

- Will I write code or pay someone else to do it?
- What software tools will best get the job done?

There are Web-authoring programs that produce Web pages automatically.

Promotion

- Which sources will I turn to in order to advertise the existence of my site?

Maintenance

- What types of content will keep my site fresh?
- How often must fresh content be supplied?

Don't underestimate the time and trouble this requirement will involve.

Other

- Do I have permission to use materials I don't own?
- Will my site in any way offend others?
- Am I asking for information over the Web that would better be collected by phone or in writing?
- Will the benefits accruing from the site exceed the costs?

This is the ultimate question to ask: What's the "bottom line"?

organizations whose servers host Web pages. Determine how they set their prices, what types of services they offer to help you create pages, how they would name your site, and what types of performance statistics they would provide to help you determine the amount of traffic at your site. Most Internet service providers (ISPs) also act as IPPs.

Beware, when evaluating IPPs, that taking the low-cost route has its drawbacks. Many ISPs who provide Web-authoring privileges for users will only provide them a limited amount of "free" storage for personal pages. Also, you may not be allowed to sell products or services without restraint; CompuServe, for instance, prohibits subscribers from price posting and from directly accepting orders on their personal Web pages. What's more, the Web address that your site is assigned may be long and cryptic looking. If you want a simple uniform resource locator (URL) like www.mybusiness.com, you'll need to go to an IPP that supports personalized domain names.

IPPs that host commercial sites often charge from $10 to $30 per month for about 5 to 20 MB of space and a basic set of services. The services may include assistance with setting up a site, Web-page-authoring tools, and security measures that enable the site to safely interact with customers. Bigger, more complex sites with storage needs in the 50 to 100 MB range often cost anywhere from $50 to a few hundred dollars per month.

As part of your project analysis, you should weigh doing a single home page versus a more substantial presentation of several pages. A single page is easier and less expensive than a larger site to produce—you may even be able to post it for free—but its limited space may not effectively carry out your purpose.

DESIGNING YOUR SITE

For a tutorial on designing a Web site, go to www. harcourtcollege.com/infosys/ parker2000/student/tutor/ and click on Chapter NET 3.

Design refers to the process of planning what your Web site will look like and how it will work. Again, remember the catchphrase "look before you leap." You don't have to be a professional designer to create Web pages that are both attractive and effective. However, you must invest some time to discover the differences that separate good design from bad design.

PRINCIPLES OF WEB DESIGN

Every professional Web-page designer would probably agree with the following two statements: (1) users like interesting, exciting, and intuitive sites; (2) to hold an audience, you must keep refreshing your site content with new information.

A site is *interesting* if it provides information with value to its target audience; visitors find it *exciting* if it rewards them with a stimulating experience. Unfortunately, interest and excitement wear off over time. If visitors see the same old information at your site day after day or week after week, boredom will set in and they will stop coming. *Intuitive* means that pages are easy to use and that the site presents information in a way that makes sense. For instance, users understand more intuitively what to do with a noun-specific hyperlink such as this:

Would you like us to send a brochure?

as opposed to a more ambiguous reference like this:

Click here to get a copy of our brochure.

■ **Design.** The process that defines the look of a product and how it will work.

Web users generally don't have much patience; if they have a hard time figuring out what your message is and how to get useful information from your site, they'll probably just leave it and never return.

One other interesting point affects site design: Web users like freebies. You might not be able to offer much, but if you can point visitors to places where they can get free literature or see other potentially valuable information, or win a coffee cup or a contest that gets their names posted at your next update, your URL is more likely to become a regular destination.

TIPS ON MAKING WEB PAGES SIZZLE

One of the first steps you should take in designing your site is to jump on the Web and surf around it for ideas—page layouts, graphics, backgrounds and colors, navigation buttons, freebies, fill-out forms, and so on. As you learn more about what interests you about certain Web sites, you gain insight for designing your own.

Some of the most creative sites are those maintained by companies in the entertainment and design businesses, so you may wish to begin there. Also, check out the sites of firms with budgets large enough to pay top professional designers. Many places both on and off the Web regularly publish the URLs of cool Web sites; stop there on your tour for ideas. Download onto your hard disk any pages that you wish to study further.

Novice designers may have difficulty identifying certain useful design guidelines just by looking at a few sample pages. One such subtle guideline is the so-called *rule of three*. Professionals who have studied Web users have discovered that most won't look for content if it is buried more than three links away from the starting screen. Pages take time to download, and users who click without any quick reward in sight are soon going to tire.

Be aware that some of your target audience—maybe even most of it—will not be as smart, sophisticated, or energetic as you are. Not all Web users know how to use a scroll bar, for instance, and those who do often won't bother with it. If you have something critical to provide—like your telephone number or e-mail address—it's a good idea to place them where users will see them almost as soon as they arrive at your page. Many designers try to avoid scrolling almost entirely by creating shorter *landscape* pages that fit nicely on most desktop displays rather than *portrait* pages that are longer than their widths, creating a need to scroll.

Keep in mind also that your audience will display your page on any of several different computer platforms. Will most people in your audience have systems that can handle MPEG video clips, or should you limit your design to still images, which far more systems can handle? Consider also the patience factor; studies have shown that users do not like to wait any longer than 30 seconds or so for a page to display. Because of this, omit exotic screens or large images that only a small fraction of your audience can appreciate.

Figure NET 3-3 shows several attractive pages and highlights some of their design qualities.

FLOWCHARTS AND STORYBOARDS

If you are developing a substantial Web presentation rather than just a single home page, tools such as flowcharts and storyboards can assist with the design process.

A Web **flowchart** describes how Web pages relate to one another. The top part of Figure NET 3-4 shows a flowchart for a restaurant's Web presentation.

For links to further information about Web design, go to www.harcourtcollege.com/infosys/parker2000/student/explore/ and click on Chapter NET 3.

■ **Flowchart.** A series of boxes or other symbols, connected by lines, that shows how ideas fit together.

FORMAL
Many businesses like to reflect a conservative image at their Web sites. The site shown here is also particularly well designed in that it is simple, aesthetically appealing, and has clearly labeled navigation buttons.

BUSY
Shopping sites often have a busy appearance, with dozens of links. Designers know that shoppers like to see immediately information about the item they are looking for.

WHIMSICAL
Sites catering to children often have an especially friendly look, sporting cute graphics, splashy colors, and large and fanciful typefaces.

 **FIGURE NET 3-3**

Examples of good page design.
Good design largely depends on the type of audience you are trying to reach. For instance, lots of hyperlinks is usually considered good design if you are luring busy shoppers but bad design if you are trying to appeal to children, who might easily get confused.

Note that each box in the flowchart represents a separate Web page, and the lines between boxes show which pages logically relate to others. Remember that you can hyperlink pages in any way you like; the lines between the flowchart boxes need not represent hyperlinks.

A Web **storyboard** is an ordered series of sketches—done by hand or with the help of software—that show what each page in a Web presentation should look like (see the bottom part of Figure NET 3-4). The storyboard also shows the hyperlinks on each page. If you use a software package to set up a sto-

---

■ **Storyboard.** An ordered series of sketches that show what each page in a presentation should look like.

FLOWCHARTS

A Web flowchart describes how Web pages relate to one another. Each box represents a separate Web page, and the lines between them show which pages logically link.

Flowcharts and storyboards provide useful tools for creating multipage Web sites.

STORYBOARDS

A Web storyboard is an ordered series of sketches—done by hand or with the help of software—that shows what each page in a Web presentation should look like.

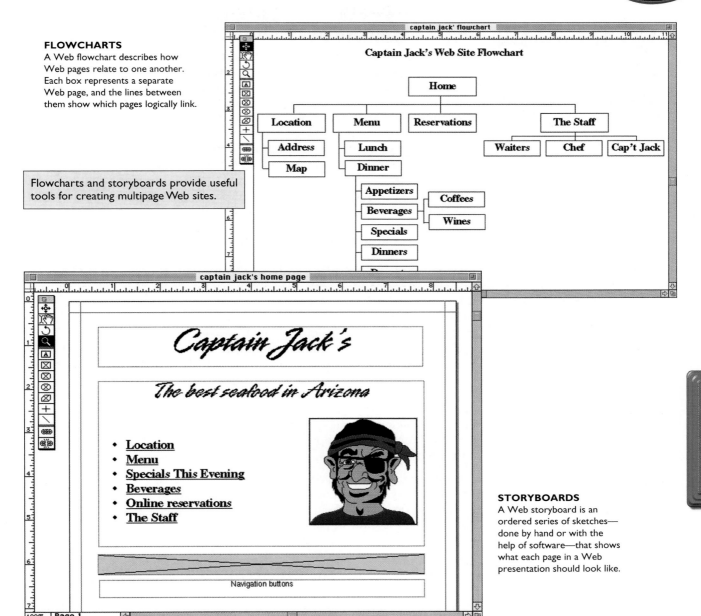

 **FIGURE NET 3-4**

A flowchart and storyboard for a restaurant's prospective Web site.

ryboard, there's a good chance you can load it into a code-generator program that can create much of the Web-page programming you would otherwise later have to produce.

TOOLS FOR CODING WEB PAGES

After you complete the design of your Web presence, the next step is to create the pages in an appropriate computer code. There are several programming languages available for this task, including HTML and Java. This section looks at such coding tools and at page-authoring alternatives that will enable you to develop Web pages without a single peek at programming-language syntax (or with only a quick glance).

Web Tutor

For a tutorial on creating Web pages, go to www.harcourtcollege.com/infosys/parker2000/student/tutor/ and click on Chapter NET 3.

HYPERTEXT MARKUP LANGUAGE (HTML)

Most Web pages today are coded in **hypertext markup language (HTML).** This and other **markup languages** were created to make it possible to rapidly transmit documents over a network using minimal line capacity.

For instance, consider a server computer sending the banner headline "Martians Invade the Earth" in 36-point boldfaced type over the telephone lines to a desktop client computer. Large fonts such as this require lots of storage, and all of those extra bytes take transmission time. Markup languages address this transmission problem by sending the Martian-invasion headline over the wires in regular type *marked* as "very large" and "bolded" text. The client workstation's browser then determines the particular display font, bolds it if possible, and figures out how large "very large" type should be.

The strength of markup languages is also their main weakness. Because they simplify pages to send them rapidly, they also can produce some unexpected surprises. For instance, small type that might just barely be discernible on your screen might look like an unreadable mess on another, because of the browser or computer being used or the size of the display screen. Web authors do have ways, however, to control the look of a screen document. One way they achieve this goal is with plug-in programs such as Adobe Acrobat, as discussed in the previous chapter. Another is with *cascading style sheets,* which allow a Web publisher to set restrictions on the fonts—the typefaces and their sizes—displayed. An upcoming trend is the use of *downloadable fonts,* which are sent by the server with each page.

An example of an HTML document, the Web page it produces, and some sample HTML commands are shown in Figure NET 3-5. Note that HTML command instructions, or **tags,** are contained within angled brackets (<>), while the actual text that will appear on the page lies outside the brackets. Tags perform such tasks as

- Declaring titles for pages
- Identifying the sizes of headings (e.g., first-level head, second-level head, and so on)
- Marking the ends of paragraphs
- Establishing such text styling as underlined, italic, and boldfaced type
- Setting up hyperlinks to other documents
- Identifying complex elements to be inserted into a document, such as pictures and sounds

HTML tags are *not* case sensitive; you can type them in either uppercase or lowercase letters. In addition to formatted text, HTML tags are also used to display images on a Web page. The actual images are located in separate files than the Web page's HTML, and the HTML tags indicate where on the Web page that the image files should be displayed. The two principal file formats used on the Web for still graphics are GIF and JPEG. Images saved in GIF format are used principally for simple spot art like logos and for navigational elements like buttons and imagemaps. The JPEG format, which allows more colors, is often used for photographs. JPEG images may take longer to download to a browser, depending on the amount of file compression used. Audio clips are commonly displayed on Web pages in the form of WAV files; video images, with AVI and MPEG files.

HTML is widely considered a very easy language to learn and use when creating simple Web pages without a lot of advanced features. One of the principal ways that people learn to code in HTML is by identifying Web pages they find

---

■ **Hypertext markup language (HTML).** The most widely used language for developing Web pages. ■ **Markup language.** A language made up of tags or symbols that describe what document elements should look like when displayed. ■ **Tag.** An HTML code that sends a document-formatting instruction to a browser.

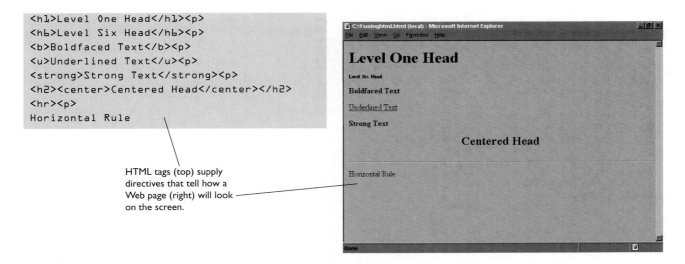

```
<h1>Level One Head</h1><p>
<h6>Level Six Head</h6><p>
<b>Boldfaced Text</b><p>
<u>Underlined Text</u><p>
<strong>Strong Text</strong><p>
<h2><center>Centered Head</center></h2>
<hr><p>
Horizontal Rule
```

HTML tags (top) supply directives that tell how a Web page (right) will look on the screen.

Sample HTML Tags	
HTML tag	**Purpose**
`<html>`	Starts and ends an HTML program
`<title>`	Provides a page title
`<h#>` (where # is a digit from 1 to 6)	Formats a heading in a type size larger or smaller than that used in the main body of text
`<p>`	Marks the end of a paragraph
`<img>`	Designates an imported picture file
`<a>`	Creates a hypertext link
`<b>`	Boldfaces text
`<i>`	Italicizes text
`<u>`	Underlines text
`<strong>`	Makes letters more intense
`<center>`	Centers text and graphics
`<hr>`	Puts a horizontal rule across the page

Some HTML tags begin with backslashes (/) to toggle off certain features. For instance, </b> turns off boldfacing.

FIGURE NET 3-5

HTML tags. People who have learned HTML say it is one of the easiest languages to pick up.

attractive and studying the HTML code that produced the pages. You can usually find the HTML code for any of the Web documents appearing on your browser through a View command on your browser's main menu (see Figure NET 3-6).

The version of HTML that works on your browser supports a specific HTML *standard* (such as HTML Version 4.0). It probably also contains several useful *HTML extensions,* tags that perform operations beyond those of the standard. You should be wary of relying on a browser's extensions; while they may produce stunning pages with that particular browser configuration, other systems without the extensions will consequently ignore them. Web sites often display warnings such as "This site optimized for Netscape Navigator 4.5." This statement means that the site was created using HTML extensions that only a Netscape Navigator 4.5 browser understands.

You can create HTML code using a *text editor* such as Windows' Notepad or a word-processing program such as Word or WordPerfect. Increasingly, productivity software packages of all types are including easy-to-use Web-page-authoring tools, which this chapter covers shortly. These tools enable you to produce HTML pages without coding in HTML.

XML   HTML is a presentation language; its job is to describe how a page will display. One of the latest languages to hit the Web, *XML* (for eXtensible Markup Language), provides a way to describe content sent with each page. For instance, when a Web site visitor makes a request to list all books about Microsoft, XML can tell the server to download not only the list but descriptions of each book

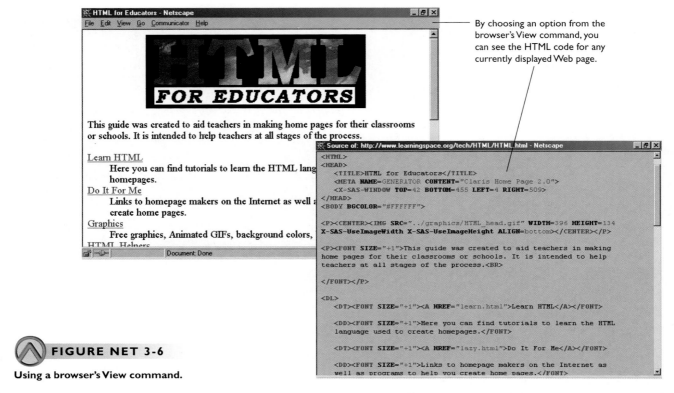

By choosing an option from the browser's View command, you can see the HTML code for any currently displayed Web page.

FIGURE NET 3-6

Using a browser's View command.

and reviews on them as well. That way, if the visitor clicks on a book to get its description or a review, it's right there on the desktop. The client computer doesn't have to make another fetch to the remote server.

JAVA, ACTIVEX, SCRIPTING LANGUAGES, AND DHTML

HTML is principally designed for laying out Web pages that have no moving elements, much as a desktop-publishing program is designed for laying out printed pages. Thus, HTML has minimal tools to create Web pages that change as the user looks at them or to enable users to interact with Web pages on their screens. If you want to develop pages with dynamic instead of static content, you'll have to go to tools such as Java, ActiveX, a scripting language, or dynamic HTML (DHTML).

Java **Java,** a programming language developed at Sun Microsystems, was created to add dynamic content to Web pages. It does this by enabling a Web-page developer to code small programs, called **applets,** that supplement the content of HTML pages. Java applets can be read and executed by any Java-enabled desktop browser (see Feature NET 3-1).

Here's a simple example that shows how a language such as Java can provide dynamic content to a Web page: A user calls up the home-loan Web page of a mortgage company. The page contains a form to fill in various pieces of data about requirements for a mortgage loan. It also comes with an applet that computes for the user monthly payments and other useful loan information based on this input data. When the user finishes filling in the form, he or she selects a Calculate Mortgage Payment button. The button activates the applet, which inputs numbers to a Java-written calculator that figures the payments on the spot.

■ **Java.** A programming language, created at Sun Microsystems, that adds interactive or dynamic features to Web pages.
■ **Applet.** A small program that provides a dynamic or interactive quality to a Web page.

NET 3-1

Java

Will It Fulfill Expectations?

Every few years or so, a hardware or software product comes along that sets the computer world buzzing with excitement. One of the latest such products is Java, a programming language created at Sun Microsystems.

Java was designed to enable programs written in it to run on many different computer platforms, without special accommodation. Such a feat is widely considered to be a big deal in computer programming—generally, programs need modification to port them (translate their code to accommodate system differences) from one computer to another. On the Internet, where countless different equipment configurations mingle, a *machine-independent language* is an especially big plus.

Java is a comprehensive language that can be used to create either Java applets or Java applications. *Java applets* are short programs that are embedded into HTML-coded Web pages to give them interactive features. Applets are designed to be downloaded from a server computer onto a Java-enabled Web browser—such as Netscape Navigator or Microsoft Internet Explorer—running on a PC workstation. Applets reside on servers in a machine-independent "bytecode format." This enables the Java interpreters within the browsers to translate the applets into the machine-language code native to the resident workstation for execution. Typically, a Java-enabled browser identifies a Java applet because its code is preceded by the HTML tag <applet>.

Java applications are more substantial programs that can run in either Internet or non-Internet network environments. For instance, a company's programmers could use the language to write programs that might otherwise be written in a language such as C++ or Visual BASIC. Java is also being applied in so-called *smart appliances*. General Motors is working on a car with a Java-based system for voice-activated e-mail and navigation. Other companies are working on systems that run Java in coffeemakers and toasters, in cell phones, and through room keys used in hotels.

Java's security features remain to be fully worked out to make it 100 percent safe. Ideally, once a Java applet is downloaded to your computer system, it should not be able to perform such po-

Java everywhere? Consumer products from cell phones, to automobiles, to appliances are beginning to use Java.

tentially damaging activities as write to your hard disk, directly address memory, or call your operating system or other programs on its own. When such antipenetration measures become strictly enforceable, they will make it difficult if not impossible for a Java applet to implant a virus on your computer system.

Some people have said that, just as the Web turned the Internet into a giant disk drive, a language such as Java has the potential to turn the Web into a giant computer—one with a never-ending supply of software applications. Others claim that this change will take a long time, because Java applets run much slower on PCs than do native applications. As people begin to create Web documents that contain their own Java or Javalike processors, the difference between applications and applications software may eventually blur.

Java isn't the only alternative for creating applets for the Web. For instance, by using ActiveX controls, users can embed objects from virtually any ActiveX-supported application within an ActiveX-enabled Web page. To date, ActiveX is more machine dependent than Java, working best in a Windows-oriented environment. Also, ActiveX uses a different approach to security than Java, for instance, enabling you to store downloaded code on your hard disk as long as it comes from a certified source.

The applet is originally downloaded from the server along with the Web page, so calculations employ the processing capacity of the user's workstation, eliminating delays for access to a remote computer. Wonder what the monthly payment will be with a different down payment and interest rate? Just enter new figures into the form and recalculate. Later, when the Web page disappears from the user's computer, so does the applet.

Applets provide all sorts of interesting possibilities for Web applications—for instance, a scrolling message that changes every few seconds (see Figure NET 3-7). A real-time news ticker is another example—an applet scrolls the

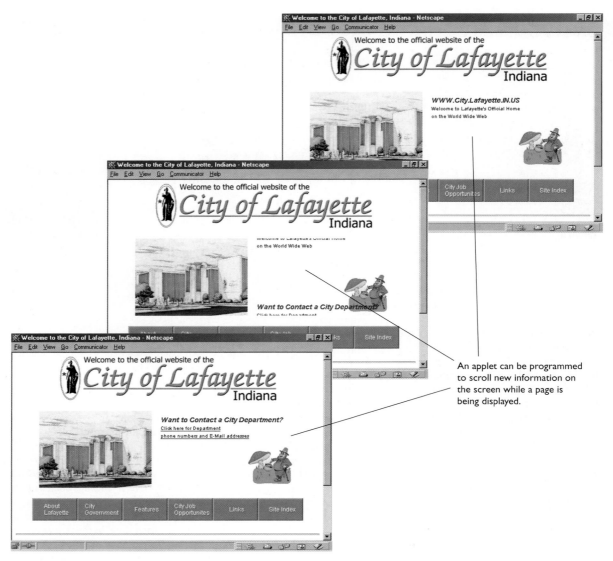

An applet can be programmed to scroll new information on the screen while a page is being displayed.

 **FIGURE NET 3-7**

An applet at work. One of the most common uses of applets today is to scroll messages across an area of the screen while a page is being viewed.

latest headlines, sports scores, and weather forecasts through a small screen window. Applets are also used to animate navigational buttons, changing the color or appearance of the button as the user points to it with the mouse.

You can liven up your own Web pages with applets by choosing among several options. One is learning how to write program code in a language such as Java or one of its main alternatives in the marketplace. Another is downloading free generic applets from the Web. If you do this, make sure you scan the applet code with antivirus software before using it to make sure it doesn't contain anything that will make your system crash. A final option is to use a Web-page-authoring program (discussed in a later section) that automatically configures Java applets for you as animated options are selected.

ActiveX **ActiveX,** developed by Microsoft Corporation, is a set of controls that provides an alternative to Java for creating interactivity on a Web page. In a nutshell, ActiveX extends object linking and embedding (OLE)—also developed by Microsoft and adopted widely as a standard by the software industry—to work on the Web. OLE permits you to take such actions as launching a spreadsheet from your word processor and vice versa. It also lets

■ **ActiveX.** A set of controls that enables programs or content of virtually any type to be embedded within a Web page.

you copy and paste spreadsheet *objects* such as charts and tables into your word-processed document. Put in a more general way, OLE is a containering method that lets you nest any OLE-supported applications inside of each other as you are preparing a document. ActiveX, in extending OLE to the Web, allows you to do such things as launch your word processor or spreadsheet from your Web browser and share objects among applications. It also enables your Web browser to play special content on Web pages; for instance, the Shockwave ActiveX control can play interactive multimedia presentations that are created with Macromedia's popular Shockwave software.

ActiveX content can be virtually any type of object—a Java applet, a C++ program, an animation, a PowerPoint presentation, and so on. Software that supports ActiveX sets up any such object as an interactive component on the Web page; thus, ActiveX forms the "glue" that holds the page elements together. What ActiveX in effect allows Web publishers to do is grab files from their hard disks that are suitable for the Web and drop them directly into HTML documents. Such a capability is especially useful for office intranets, where a lot of potential Web-page content already exists in office documents.

Scripting Languages A third way that Web-page developers can supply interactivity to a page is through a **scripting language.** Such languages enable you to build programs, or *scripts,* directly into HTML page code. Scripts handle actions like checking the accuracy of information a user has entered into the page—such as a name, address, and credit-card number. Also, if your Web pages are going to use freestanding applets that are independent of your HTML pages, scripts can form the threads that connect the pages to the applets.

Two of the major scripting languages in use today are Microsoft's VBScript (which is part of the Visual BASIC development environment) and Netscape's JavaScript (which, oddly enough, bears little resemblance to Java).

Dynamic HTML **Dynamic HTML (DHTML)** combines static HTML programming with some of the capabilities provided by applets and scripting languages. It enables Web-page authors to create pages that change in layout and content without the user having to regenerate any new pages or retrieve any new information from a remote server. This, of course, makes the application look more exciting and run faster on the client browser. Some examples of DHTML applications are scrolling or moving text, text that changes color when pointed to or clicked, and moving objects.

Currently, there is no single standard for DHTML. Netscape Navigator and Microsoft Internet Explorer—the two leading browsers—each use their own versions of DHTML. Thus, DHTML pages created to run dynamically on one of these browsers won't perform as such on the other. Versions of these browsers earlier than release 4.0 do not support DHTML.

WEB-PAGE-AUTHORING SOFTWARE

The coding required in any type of computer language—HTML, Java, VBScript, DHTML, and so on—can create a tedious burden that exceeds the capabilities of many would-be Web-page developers. A variety of **Web-page-authoring software** is available to ease considerably the job of creating Web pages, usually by automatically generating HTML statements to accomplish user-specified tasks.

Web-page-authoring software comes in several forms. For instance, the latest versions of Microsoft Internet Explorer and Netscape Communicator

■ **Scripting language.** A programming language that assists with supplying interactive or dynamic content to HTML documents. ■ **Dynamic HTML (DHTML)** A version of HTML that adds elements enabling the look of Web pages to change. ■ **Web-page-authoring software.** A program that simplifies the creation of Web pages by automatically generating HTML and other types of supporting code.

include web-page-authoring features, as do many office suites today. There are also programs like Microsoft's FrontPage (available standalone or as part of the Microsoft Office 2000 Premium suite), which supply a more comprehensive Web-page-authoring environment. Other software offerings, like America Online's Personal Publisher, are adjunct features built into larger software products; in this case, the America Online Internet-access service. While both FrontPage and Personal Publisher are targeted to general users not interested in writing code, there is also authoring software geared to professional programmers, who are. Some widely used Web-page-authoring programs are listed in Figure NET 3-8 along with features they collectively provide.

Web-page-authoring programs use a variety of strategies to help users create pages. Two principal tools targeted to the most novice class of user are wizards and converters.

FIGURE NET 3-8

Web-page-authoring software.

Wizards An *HTML wizard* is a program that automatically generates an HTML document from screen selections made by the user. A wizard offers one of the

WEB-PAGE-AUTHORING PROGRAMS	
	PUBLISHER
FrontPage	Microsoft
Home Page	Claris
Homestead	Homestead Technologies
HotMetal PRO	SoftQuad International
InContext Spider	InContext
PageMill	Adobe Systems
Personal Publisher	America Online
WebAuthor	Quarterdeck
Web.Designer	Corel

Web-page-authoring software exists in many forms, including standard features of browsers or applications software, plug-ins, and standalone helper programs.

FrontPage, the current market leader, is powerful and flexible but also easy to use.

PageMill provides strong page-design tools, as other Adobe products do.

HotMetal PRO recognizes a wide range of document formats and is popular with advanced users.

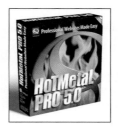

Features of
WEB-PAGE-AUTHORING PROGRAMS*

Wizards and templates that make it easy to create Web pages through onscreen selections

Utilities that convert ordinary text documents into Web pages and vice versa

Libraries of frequently used HTML code and graphics

Clip art, backgrounds, and audio and video clips

Style-sheet features to apply a particular page design to pages

Drag-and-drop tools that let you pull text and graphics stored in other documents on your computer into your HTML documents

Tools for creating such sophisticated Web graphics as imagemaps

Form-filling routines that enable you to create and process interactive forms

Menus for selecting HTML tags, if you want to do HTML coding

Facilities for testing your document

Integration with suite software

Site management capabilities for organizing and maintaining the files on a Web site

*Not all programs include the same features.

easiest ways to create Web pages. Many providers, including America Online with its Personal Publisher, provide wizard software as part of their basic user services (see Figure NET 3-9). Generally, you begin by selecting a template that suggests a basic page design. Then, you successively answer questions about your Web-page text and select from libraries of clip art and backgrounds. Based on your

FIGURE NET 3-9

Using an HTML wizard.

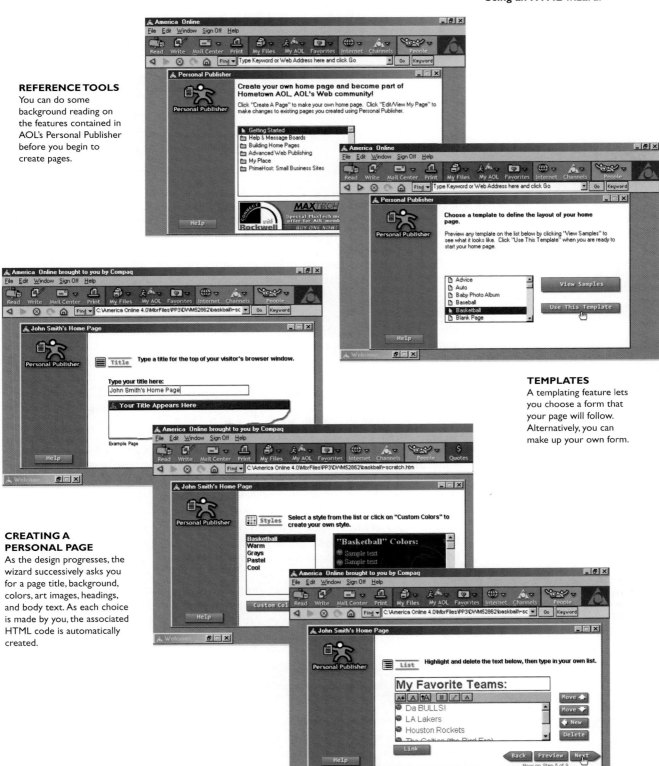

REFERENCE TOOLS
You can do some background reading on the features contained in AOL's Personal Publisher before you begin to create pages.

TEMPLATES
A templating feature lets you choose a form that your page will follow. Alternatively, you can make up your own form.

CREATING A PERSONAL PAGE
As the design progresses, the wizard successively asks you for a page title, background, colors, art images, headings, and body text. As each choice is made by you, the associated HTML code is automatically created.

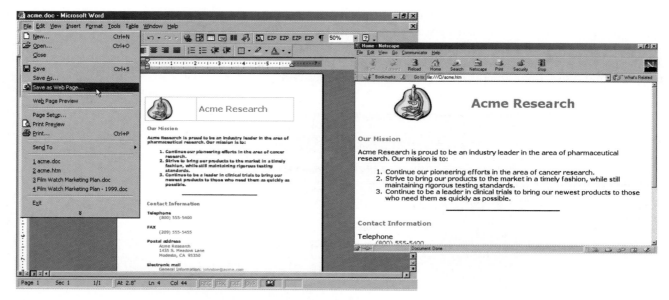

FIGURE NET 3-10

HTML converter. Most of the latest word processors can automatically convert files to and from HTML.

For links to further information about Web-page-authoring software, and free graphics and other Web page development resources, go to www. harcourtcollege.com/ infosys/parker2000/student/ explore/ and click on Chapter NET 3.

selections, the wizard generates HTML code for your Web page. If you don't like what you see on your page, you can edit it either through the wizard or by adding your own HTML directives to the code the wizard has produced.

Be aware that wizard programs can differ dramatically in their capabilities. Free, super-easy-to-use, mass-targeted products such as Personal Publisher often do not support such advanced page features as frames, forms, and animated graphics.

Converters *HTML converters* work differently than wizards. Typically, they are adjunct programs that are designed to produce HTML code from documents already created in other formats. For instance, if your word processor or office suite has an HTML converter built into it—and most of the latest ones do—you can turn virtually any document into an HTML-coded Web page (see Figure NET 3-10). It is becoming increasingly common to find both HTML-wizard and HTML-converter software within the same software packages.

Wizards and converters will spare you a lot of the tedium of writing HTML code, applets, or scripting components—and they will also ensure that your Web pages work within one or more specific browsing environments. Still, these tools do not substitute completely for knowledge of Web-page programming. By becoming proficient enough to write your own code, you gain flexibility to create pages that conform to your precise specifications. For instance, if you don't like the page backgrounds a wizard offers or you want blinking lights on a Christmas tree in the corner of your page, you can do your own thing if you know HTML or Java or know how to modify a Web page using a Web-page-authoring program. Still another important consideration is that many easy-to-use authoring tools generate a lot of unnecessary HTML code. For this reason, they are often avoided by professional developers, who are paid to create pages that both run fast and store efficiently.

TESTING YOUR PAGES

You must perform a certain amount of testing as you create Web pages. The development tools covered in the previous section will enable you to write code for Web pages from scratch or generate the code using a Web-page-authoring program, test the code in a simulated Web environment to ensure that it produces the results you want, and modify it as a result of the tests.

Now, let's say you've finished creating your Web page, and it looks good on your screen. At this point, you should conduct some further tests.

Recall that different browsers implement different versions of HTML. You may also remember reading that people worldwide have access to Web pages over a wide variety of different computer platforms with different configurations. Thus, you will need to check out what happens to your page when it appears on systems other than your own. You can't test every browser in the world, but you can certainly test your page on some of the more common ones—such as Netscape Navigator and Microsoft Internet Explorer. Consider also evaluating your page's support for text-based browsers such as Lynx, if only because a lot of people in the world approach the Web from nongraphical platforms. What's more, some people using graphical browsers turn off the graphics features to speed downloading.

Many Web-page-creation programs let you test a page at a variety of common screen resolutions—such as 480 by 640 pixels, 800 by 600 pixels, and so on. What's more, some programs will indicate how quickly your pages will download over certain types of Internet connections, such as a 56 kbps modem or T1 line. Most importantly, think about your target audience and the computing environments in which they are likely to be working.

In another testing step, you should seek feedback from friends or associates. What do they think of the colors you picked? Did they find any grammatical or spelling errors? The graphics aren't tacky or take too long to download, are they? In addition to getting comments about details, be sure to ask what people think of your site overall. In the end, the most important question may not be how beautiful the screen display looks but whether or not the site works.

Remember that friends often say one thing when their body language suggests another, so observe them working with your site. Do they seem to know what your home page is all about? Are they confused with the navigational buttons or layout?

Testing Web pages is an ongoing activity. One common mistake among page developers results from failure to check from time to time the validity of hyperlinks that reach out from their pages to other parts of the Web. Sites often disappear or change addresses. One of the most frustrating experiences of Web users is pointing and clicking on *dead links* that lead only to error messages.

PROMOTING AND MAINTAINING YOUR WEB SITE

If you've reached this point, you're close to seeing the first results from your efforts. Assuming that you've interacted with your IPP already, getting your Web pages online should be almost as easy as clicking the mouse button a few times. Your IPP will likely offer software that will upload your pages from your desktop computer to its Web server. You will also need to set up a permanent address on your IPP's server so people can reach you on the Web. This process differs from the one for setting up a *user* account, which does not receive a permanent Web address. You should arrange to set up a permanent address through your IPP during the planning stage or at least well before you are ready to go online with your Web site.

Promoting Your Site *Promotion* of your site—that is, advertising its whereabouts—provides a critical connection to people you want to find you. One of the best ways to promote your site is listing it with as many search engines as you can—such as Yahoo!, Excite, Lycos, and so on. Some search-engine

Web Gatekeepers

If you want to have your site listed on a popular search engine like Yahoo!, you have to get past a person known as a gatekeeper. These individuals—there are several dozen working at Yahoo!—inspect your site for suitability, make sure your short listing of it fits within an acceptable format, and help tweak keywords in the listing so that your pages can be flagged by Web surfers who might benefit by them. At Yahoo! gatekeepers are specialized by area—one may cover art, for instance; another, cooking.

A gatekeeper applies several suitability tests to a Web site before it finds its way into Yahoo!'s database. For instance, the site cannot promote illegal activities like bombmaking or child pornography. Controversial topics are acceptable to both Yahoo! and most other major search engines as long as no laws are being broken. Another crucial test: the site must work. Thus, sites that crash, that are more under construction than finished, that have too many dead links, or that put Web surfers in endless loops are rejected. Schlockiness can lose points for a site too, and one can get a thumbs-down simply because the design or appearance is dreadful. A gatekeeper may look at 100 sites in a day and accept only half of them.

The way a site is listed on a search engine is extremely important to any prospective Web publisher—and many go over the line to draw eyeballs. Yahoo! insists on editing listings, to eliminate attention-getting gimmicks like all capital letters as well as tacky marketing hype. After all, the user of a search engine is looking for information and wanting to do it in a pleasant environment. A heavy-handed sales pitch is just going to send users somewhere else to search.

Since getting lots of Web exposure means more business to a commercial Web publisher, many of them have resorted to questionable or unethical tactics to get preferential treatment for their sites. Some have tried to send in bogus listings for competitors, laden with errors designed to frustrate users. Yahoo! now guards against this by requesting that changes be sent in from the same e-mail address that was used in the original filing. Another ploy is trying to register a single site several times in order to get multiple listings for it. Yahoo! has this base covered too. Once caught, you're warned; twice, and you're out of the directory.

companies will allow you to fill out online forms on which you list your site's URL and describe your site to them. There are also sites that allow you to fill out one form and they submit it to several search engines at one time. In your description, you should provide keywords—mostly nouns—that you expect people to enter when looking for a site like yours. If you've developed a Web site for a fishing-tackle-and-outfitter business in Boise, Idaho, for instance, you want to make sure that people can find it through such informative words as fish, fishing, trout, tackle, hobby, outfitter, recreation, Boise, and Idaho. The Inside the Industry box addresses the people who index Web sites for a living.

As another useful form of promotion, you might pursue listings at any *trailblazer sites* that deal with the subject of your site. A trailblazer site, or supersite, is a "metaindex" that provides a comprehensive list of Web resources on a given subject (refer back to Figure NET 3-1). Returning to the fishing-tackle-and-outfitter business example, you would want to locate as many trailblazer sites as you could devoted to fishing, trout, and related subjects. E-mail the administrators of those sites about adding your URL to their sites. The easiest way to locate trailblazer sites is through a Web search engine or by looking for possible matches to your subject area in a comprehensive book like the *Internet Yellow Pages.*

Consider also several other promotional options. You might arrange to rent a storefront in a cybermall, post messages to newsgroups and mailing lists that touch on your subject matter, and print your site URL and e-mail address on your business cards, letterhead, and promotional materials.

Maintaining Your Site   Visitors will come back to your Web site regularly if you constantly refresh it with interesting or exciting information. This is another planning issue that requires careful attention during an early stage of development. What type of information needs refreshing? How often? What will your IPP charge for site updates? Be warned that maintenance can take considerable time. Are you commited enough to provide it?

Your IPP should willingly supply activity statistics showing how much interest your Web site is generating. One such statistic is the number of **hits** your page receives—that is, the number of file accesses each page generates. Judge this potentially misleading statistic with care. A *hit counter,* which records the number of hits, usually will not tell you directly how many visitors came to your site. For example, a visit to a page with four graphics files on it may generate five hits—one for the page and one each for the separate graphics files that the server had to download along with it. A hit counter also cannot tell you how long visitors hung around at your site, whether visitors just passed through on their way elsewhere, or whether visitors represent new or repeat customers. Several new software tools attempt to deduce from hit data more useful statistics, such as the number of visitors per period and the number of times each Web page is visited during a period.

Many IPPs will also provide a summary showing the number of times each *link* at your site was accessed as well as a log that chronicles when each such access was recorded. From such information, you can determine just how far down into your site—and where—users are going. The log showing the precise time each hit took place can help you determine whether those graphics that might take too long to download are working as you had hoped or if users are bypassing them. Also, if your site has several pages, you may be able to calculate the time a visitor lingers on a page or have your IPP tell you the average time spent on each page visit and average number of pages viewed per visit.

Some IPPs will also give you an analysis of accesses by region or by country. Two other useful pieces of information an IPP can provide is the URL of the page a visitor was viewing prior to coming to your site and the type of browser and operating system the visitor was using. When you're trying to attract people, it helps to know how they are finding out about you. Knowing the types of platforms they are most likely to be using is useful because you always have the option of optimizing viewing for certain platforms.

It's a good idea to check with an IPP about the types of statistics it provides for free and which others it offers for a fee well before you begin to design your pages or sign up for service. If you are developing sites for clients, you can turn information on how people are reacting to their Web presence into a valuable marketing tool.

As part of your maintenance routine, you may want to include some type of form that users can fill out to supply vital facts or to voice their opinions (see Figure NET 3-11). Information supplied on such forms can give you an excellent profile of your users. Most people like to be rewarded for extra work, so you may want to consider an offer to entice them to fill out the form—say,

For links to further information about Web site promotion, go to www. harcourtcollege.com/ infosys/parker2000/student/ explore/ and click on Chapter NET 3.

■ **Hit.** One request for access to a page or a graphics file made to a server computer.

Personal Information

First Name: _____   Last Name: _____

Street Address: _____

City: _____   State: [Choose One ▾]

Country: [United States ▾]

Postal Code: ____

Area Code: ____ (US Residents Only)

Highest Level of Education Completed: [Click for options ▾]

Household Income: [Click for options ▾]

Marital Status: [Click for options ▾]

Occupation: [Click for options ▾]

free literature or the ability to win a small prize. Forms are interactive components that require scripting commands; however, many Web-page-authoring programs have this detail covered with built-in routines that will enable you to handle forms without having to do any programming.

PUBLISHING-RELATED ISSUES

As you develop your Web site, you should consider many publishing-related issues. Three of the most important are copyrights, censorship, and security.

COPYRIGHTS

Rights to control intellectual property such as books and movies are protected in the United States by copyright laws. Most of these laws were enacted well before the age of computers. Consequently, confusion prevails in legal circles about how these laws apply to materials on the Internet.

Here's an example: U.S. copyright law forbids anyone from copying books or movies and then selling the copies for a profit without the permission of the owners. Bookstores, for instance, can't print their own copies of this textbook and sell them. They have to pay the publisher of this book for copies; the publisher, in turn, compensates the author. A provision in copyright law does allow *fair use,* in which someone may copy small portions of this book or any other protected work for such noncommercial purposes as teaching, news, parody, or criticism. Fair use has also been successfully extended in recent years to people making videotaped copies of television programs for viewing later at a more convenient time.

Publishers of all types dread the possibility that the Internet will allow people to set up Web sites to distribute books, movies, and music that the publishers own and want to sell elsewhere. Publishers claim that even if such unauthorized sites didn't take money in return for such services, they could have a devastating effect on sales. Historically, copyright laws have supported this viewpoint. You are not permitted to use the creative work of another in a way that impairs the owner's profits.

On the other side of the fence are people who want the Web clear of government interference. They claim that many copyright fears are overexaggerated and that the legal community, with its conflicting priorities, could wind up destroying the very fabric of the Web itself. For instance, the law might interpret even looking at a copy of a copyright-protected work over the Internet as a criminal act. This creates the possibility that even a person who casually surfs onto such a work may be guilty of a crime, since downloading can be construed as copying.

Expect the legal battle regarding copyrights to continue for some time. Members of the online community have proposed solutions to the copyright problem including self-policing and setting up arbitration agencies to deal with disputes. To be on the safe side as a Web publisher, you should ask permission to use any materials that are not your own—except those that are specifically designated in print as royalty-free resources.

One final point: While copyright laws forbid copying the protected work of someone else and selling it for profit, they don't extend to copying an *idea* here and there. This protection has allowed companies to refine product features introduced elsewhere, such as when Microsoft developed its Windows software. Many critics have claimed Windows is a knockoff of the graphical user interface pioneered by the Apple Macintosh—and much earlier by Xerox. Consequently, you can copy ideas from other Web pages. But beware—while copyright laws let you copy ideas here and there, they expressly forbid you to copy a sophisticated sequence of ideas.

For links to further information about copyright laws, security, and other Web publishing related issues, go to www.harcourtcollege.com/ infosys/parker2000/student/ explore/ and click on Chapter **NET 3**.

CENSORSHIP

The First Amendment to the U.S. Constitution guarantees a citizen's right to free speech. This protection allows people to say or show things to others without fear of arrest. People must observe some limits to free speech, of course, such as prohibitions of obscenity over the public airwaves and dealing in child pornography.

But how should the law react to alleged patently offensive or indecent materials on the Internet, where they can be observed by surfing children and the public at large? The courts recently struck down the Communications Decency Act, which proposed making such actions illegal. The courts have so far had difficulty defining just what is "patently offensive" and "indecent." What's more, they have concluded that numerous self-policing mechanisms now available at the *client* level reduce the need for new laws that restrict content made available at the *server* level. For instance, a large selection of **blocking software** on the market allows users to block from view materials on the Internet that are objectionable to them or to family members.

Blocking-software packages work in a variety of ways. Some ISPs automatically censor portions of the Internet with their own software. Some also provide tools that let each user do his or her own blocking. Users can also acquire blocking software on their own, independently of their provider. The software may suggest a list of subjects or keywords that will automatically prevent access to a site; typically, you can trim or add to this list. For instance, parents could block their home computer from displaying information on sex, drugs, bomb making, or hate literature if any of those topics were not already censored by their service provider. Many of the latest browsers also allow users to block access in one way or another (see Figure NET 3-12).

Despite the failure so far of the Communications Decency Act, the censorship battle surrounding the Internet continues to rage. Arguments against

■ **Blocking software.** A program that blocks access to certain parts of the Internet deemed objectionable based on predetermined criteria.

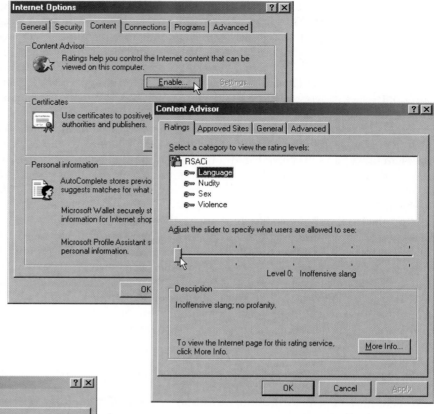

INTERNET OPTIONS
Internet Explorer's censoring options are accessed through the Internet Options dialog box.

CONTENT ADVISOR
When the Content Advisor is enabled, you can specify the maximum allowable level of language, nudity, sex, and violence for rated sites.

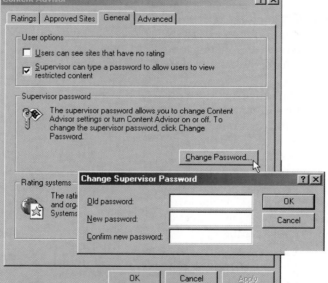

PASSWORD PROTECTION
A supervisor password will prevent the Content Advisor from being changed or disabled by anyone else.

FIGURE NET 3-12

Using a browser to censor content on the Internet.

censorship point out that policing the Internet effectively would require prohibitively expensive and difficult effort. Arguments for censorship claim that blocking software assumes computer-literate parents, and many do not and never will meet this standard. In all likelihood, say many industry experts, the Internet will wind up policing itself, as the movie industry does with its rating system, at least in the short term. (If the situation doesn't improve, harsher measures may follow.)

Momentum is building within the Internet community to create a universal rating system for Web sites. For instance, a site might voluntarily rate its content on a scale of 0 to 4 on each of several dimensions—such as language, nudity, sex, and violence. (Users could automatically assign noncomplying sites

Electronic Commerce

The Quest for Security's Magic Bullet

With the popularity of the Internet and World Wide Web at an all-time high over the past couple of years, businesses are making a push to get consumers—and their money—online. It will probably be some time before most people are comfortable about having their checking or savings account information available online through a public network. However, many consumers are venturing out on the Web to purchase goods as companies lower the risks and increase the incentives of doing business there.

Today, you can buy online using any of several payment plans. The plan you use depends on where you shop. Some of the alternatives now being used are listed here:

- CREDIT CARD You can pay for online purchases with a credit card just as you can over the phone. You simply select the goods you want to buy, type in your credit-card number, and the sale is either approved or rejected on the spot. In recent years, VISA and MasterCard have jointly developed the Secure Electronic Transaction (SET) protocol for encrypting credit-card-transaction data (disguising them with secret codes) for safe passage over networks. A *digital signature* method has also been developed to authenticate the identities of sellers to reassure buyers who they are really sending their information to.

- PAYMENT SERVICES This method is a twist on the credit-card payment system. For it to work, you need a valid credit card, such as VISA or MasterCard, and an e-mail address. At a company called First Virtual, for instance, you set up an account for a small processing fee—such as $2—and get a personal identification number (PIN). When you buy an item from a participating merchant, you supply your encrypted PIN, and the merchant forwards it with the transaction data to First Virtual. First Virtual then e-mails you to confirm the purchase. Upon your approval, your credit card is automatically billed.

- ELECTRONIC WALLETS Various online services set up small accounts for consumers, which are debited for each purchase. One of these, DigiCash's ecash system, loads your PC's memory with virtual money as soon as you sign on. To use the system, you establish an ecash account with any of several participating banks. The ecash is then stored as data on your PC and transferred in secure form to a merchant, who accepts it as

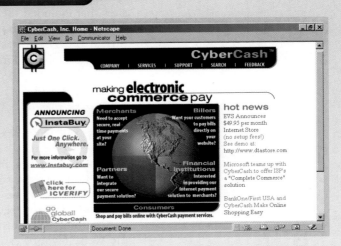

CyberCash. Users employ electronic wallets to pay participating merchants for goods.

payment when you make a purchase. The banks are responsible for certifying the authenticity of the ecash. A similar system is used at CyberCash (see image).

- CONVENTIONAL PAYMENT Many online merchants realize that consumers are wary of conducting business over the Internet. Consequently, they allow buyers to pay by conventional means. As you make selections onscreen, you can check a box to have a person phone you about paying by check or credit card. Alternatively, there may be a toll-free phone number for you to call to make the actual purchase. While merchants usually welcome business of any sort, their costs rise when they have to hire staff to close business in this fashion. As more and more people feel comfortable using all-electronic commerce, you can expect merchants to provide incentives for consumers to transact business that way.

A high-stakes race is taking place to develop systems that make consumers both want to shop online and feel comfortable about paying. How can stores that require human workers to transact business ever compete on a cost basis with staffless electronic stores? Can online shopping catalogs become so alluring that they threaten the survival of hard-copy catalogs? What changes will the age of 3-D, virtual-reality shopping bring? Nobody knows for sure the answers to such questions, but fortunes are expected to be made and lost by companies as they scramble to court the online consumer.

Fasten your seat belts for a wild and interesting ride.

ratings of 4 on all dimensions.) Enabled desktop software, such as a browser, would let users establish the maximum number on each dimension that they would tolerate, placing these controls in password-protected files, out of the reach of children. When anyone navigated the Internet from the user's account, the software would read a site's rating and block access if the rating exceeded the allowable rating.

As a prospective Web publisher, you should be aware that—law or no law—what you say on the Internet is subject to scrutiny and may come back to haunt you. Even if your site inadvertently uses a word that has an offbeat connotation, you could get blocked from a portion of your target audience. Not too long ago, for instance, a well-known service provider blocked access to sites that included the keyword "breast," unintentionally severing earnest users from information about breast cancer. Remember also that many people are turned off by bad taste, so even though you reach them, you may not hold their attention for long. Worse yet, they may complain to your IPP, who may curtly inform you to change or leave.

SECURITY

One of your concerns as a prospective Web publisher should center on securing your Web pages—and any transactions that occur over those pages—from transmission errors and unauthorized uses. You can secure pages in several ways; if you have a sensitive application, you should check with your IPP to determine what types of protections are available. The Tomorrow box on page NET 123 discusses several security methods now in use.

The topic of security requires lengthy discussion that extends well beyond the Web. If your version of this textbook contains the LIV module, refer to Chapter LIV 2 for an in-depth discussion.

SUMMARY AND KEY TERMS

Go to the Online Glossary at www.harcourtcollege.com/infosys/parker2000/student/ to review key terms.

Among the most interesting aspects to Web publishing is its unique contribution to the history of mass communications.

The Web as a Publishing Medium **Web publishing** is defined as developing pages for the Web; in other words, creating a **Web site** or Web presence. Web publishing brings certain advantages: Anyone can do it, people can create their own looks for messages and products, and costs are relatively low. It also creates disadvantages: Most people doing it are required to develop new types of skills, and Web sites often need constantly refreshed content.

Why Publish on the Web? One of the first issues faced by a prospective Web publisher is his or her reasons, or *goals,* for creating a presence on the Web. Sites serve many types of goals—from having a personal home page to selling and advertising products. Prospective Web publishers are well-advised to carefully define their target audiences and competitors before starting site development in earnest.

Developing a Publishing Plan The first step in evaluating a prospective Web-site project is to thoroughly size up its requirements before taking the plunge. Consider both the step-by-step site-development process you will need to complete as well as benefits and costs. During this latter step, check out possible **Internet presence providers (IPPs)**—the organizations whose servers host Web pages.

Designing Your Site **Design** refers to the process of figuring out what your Web site will look like and how it will work. You don't have to be a professional designer to create attractive, effective Web pages, but you should invest some time to discover differences that separate good design from bad design. Two tools that can assist in the design process are Web **flowcharts** and **storyboards**.

Tools for Coding Web Pages Computer code for most Web pages today is written in **hypertext markup language (HTML). Markup languages** reduce the bandwidth requirements for transmitting documents over a network. HTML instructions called **tags** contained within angled brackets (<>) provide formatting instructions, while the actual text of the displayed Web page lies outside those brackets.

Java, a language developed at Sun Microsystems, allows you to add dynamic or interactive content to your Web pages. It does this by creating small programs or objects, called **applets,** which can be placed within the code for the page. An alternative to Java, **ActiveX** controls, can embed within a Web page objects that are applications created in virtually any supported software package. You can also supply interactivity to a page through a **scripting language** or through **Dynamic HTML (DHTML).**

Because writing programming code can be tedious, a variety of software alternatives help to simplify the job of creating Web pages. **Web-page-authoring software** refers to programs that automatically generate Web-page code and thus spare you from some or all of the programming involved. Such software uses a number of tools, two of which are wizards and converters. An *HTML wizard* is a program that creates an HTML document from your onscreen selections. An *HTML converter* produces HTML code from an existing document in another format.

Testing Your Pages Web authors test pages at many levels. You will carry out a certain amount of testing as you create Web pages. After you finish your pages, you will need to check out what they look like on browsers and computer systems other than yours. Also, you should solicit feedback from friends or associates. Testing Web pages is an ongoing activity.

Promoting and Maintaining Your Web Site *Promotion* of your site—that is, advertising its whereabouts—provides critical guidance for people you want to find you. Be sure to get your site listed in as many places as is feasible. A major part of *maintenance* involves keeping your site updated with fresh information. Carefully evaluate the site statistics provided by your IPP, such as the number of **hits** generated by elements at your site.

Publishing-Related Issues You may encounter several publishing-related issues in developing a Web site. Three of the most important concern copyrights, censorship (including **blocking software**), and security.

EXERCISES

1. How is Web publishing different from publishing in a hard-copy magazine or book?

2. Name at least eight different reasons—or goals— for creating a Web presence.

3. For each of the Web-publishing tasks listed in the following table, state whether it forms part of the planning, design, coding, testing, promotion, or maintenance phases of Web-site creation. In other words, fill in each blank with one of those six choices.

ACTIVITY	PHASE
Making a Web flowchart	_____
Choosing a presentation goal	_____
Estimating the cost and time required for site development	_____
Having friends evaluate your site and suggest improvements	_____
Using an HTML wizard to create pages	_____
Developing a Java applet	_____
Getting a search engine to list your site	_____
Adding fresh content weekly to a site	_____
Developing a storyboard	_____
Sizing up your competitors	_____

4. Someone at school offers the following suggestions for designing a Web presence for a small mail-order business selling a single line of sports equipment. Identify whether each suggestion is a good or bad idea:

SUGGESTION	GOOD OR BAD?
Include at least 75 hyperlinks per page	_____
Use the most sophisticated graphics possible	_____
Insert navigation buttons into the site	_____
List the business's e-mail address on the home page	_____
Run hyperlinks at least five levels deep	_____

5. Define the following terms:
   a. Applet
   b. Trailblazer page
   c. Internet presence provider
   d. Blocking software
   e. Java
   f. ActiveX
   g. DHTML

6. What is the purpose of each of the following HTML tags?

TAG	PURPOSE
<b>	_____
<p>	_____
<html>	_____
<h2>	_____
<img>	_____

7. Answer the following questions about markup languages:
   a. Why is the concept of a markup language so important to Web publishing?
   b. What is the main limitation of a markup language?
   c. What is the difference between HTML and Java?
   d. What is the difference between HTML and DHTML?

8. The text described a rating system for blocking certain content on the Internet from view.
   a. Explain briefly how such a system might work.
   b. What part of the system has been proposed to work on a voluntary basis?
   c. What part of the system is controlled by the user?
   d. How can parents keep their children from seeing materials the parents' deem objectionable?

9. Answer the following questions about Web-site performance:
   a. What is a *hit* to a Web site?
   b. How can a hit counter provide misleading results?
   c. What types of statistics can an IPP provide that show how a Web site is being used?

10. Explain, in your own words, how the Internet has posed dangers to companies and individuals who own copyrighted materials.

PROJECTS

1. **Goals** For at least three of the goals listed in the first column of the table that follows, visit a Web site that conforms to the goal. In the Site URL column, provide the Web address of the site. In the Description column, describe the site—for instance, "maintains a list of Web sites for stamp collectors" or "tells the world what a great governor _____ will make." In the Comments column, list what you feel the site did right or wrong to communicate the stated goal.

GOAL	SITE URL	DESCRIPTION	COMMENTS
Sharing professional knowledge	_____	_____	_____
Creating a personal site	_____	_____	_____
Selling goods or services	_____	_____	_____
Supporting a hobby	_____	_____	_____
Creating a trailblazer site	_____	_____	_____

2. **The Good, the Bad, and the Ugly** Find two or three examples each of well-designed and poorly designed Web pages. If you have access to the Internet, print the pages or download them to a diskette. If you don't have Internet access, photocopy them from a book or magazine. In any case, bring your pages into class and be prepared to defend your selections by saying why each one succeeds or fails in implementing standards of good design.

3. **Developing a Polished Web Presence** If you want to see Web pages that really sizzle before you start designing yours, among the best places to go are sites maintained by some of the world's leading corporations. These organizations hire professionals to design their pages, so you can expect a polished look that reflects state-of-the-art design ideas. As your project, check at least five such sites and report your findings to the class. You can find home-page URLs in magazine advertisements, on television, or through a search engine—just type in the name of the company. The accom-

panying figure provides 20 home-page URLs to help get you started.

Which was your favorite site of the five you checked out? What feature did you like the most at this site? Of the sites you looked at, what was the goal of each one—to establish a corporate image, to sell online, to gather sales leads, to provide product support, or something else?

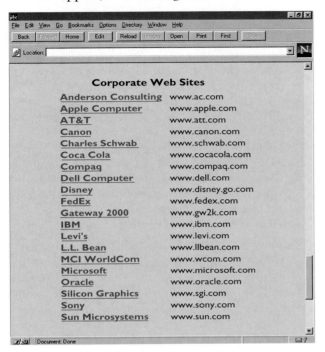

4. Have Résumé, Will Travel: A Design Exercise
Many students will look for jobs after they graduate by posting home pages containing their résumés on the Web. Use your word processor to design a single-page résumé, setting the words you intend as textual hyperlinks in boldfaced and underlined type. Feel free to hand sketch any graphical hyperlinks on the page. Also, describe on a separate piece of paper any graphical information to which each of the hyperlinks will lead—such as, a scanned-in picture of yourself.

Before designing your presentation, you might want to check out a few other professional résumés on the Web to see how others have approached this task. The two sites listed below include résumés that you can inspect:

■ www.resumenet.com
■ tbrnet.com

Scores of résumés can also be found through using a search engine. In Yahoo!, for instance, you can do a category search on the menu selection "Business and the Economy," and successively choose "Employment and Work," "Résumés," and "Individual Résumés" to get links to hundreds of résumés of individuals. You might additionally consult some articles on finding jobs on the Web.

5. Web Flowcharts   Think of a small business you might be interested in starting, other than a conventional restaurant, an example of which appears in the chapter. Develop a Web flowchart of a Web site you might create for this business. Each box on the flowchart should represent a single Web page. Show with lines how lower-level boxes relate logically to higher-level ones, and be sure that the flowchart extends no deeper than three levels (counting the home page). If you don't have any ideas for a small business of your own, here are a few suggestions on which to base your flowchart:

■ Health-food store
■ Bookstore
■ Videotape rental store
■ Music store
■ Travel agency
■ Automobile dealership

6. HTML Resources   Both the Internet and your local bookstore are good places to look for information about HTML programming.

a. Several HTML works are published on the Web. Locate two sites containing tutorials on HTML and write a few sentences about each one that describe what's there. Use a search engine such as Yahoo!, WebCrawler, or Lycos to locate the sites, or follow any of the URLs in the figure below to locate materials. In Yahoo!, use the search string "HTML tutorials" to get links to promising sites.

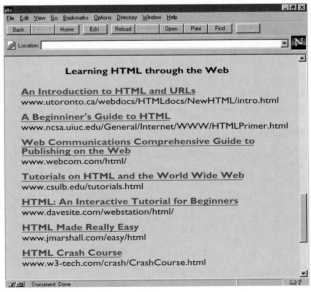

b. Shop for HTML books on the Web. Two Web bookstores you should check out are the Amazon Bookstore (www.amazon.com) and Fatbrain.com (www.fatbrain.com). Use the tools available at these sites to complete title searches on the string *HTML*. How many HTML book titles did you find at each site?

c. At a local bookstore, find a good book on HTML that's on your level. What is its title and who wrote it? Why does the book appeal to you?

7. Freebie Corner Prospective Web authors can find a lot of freebies online. Countless background graphics for Web pages, clip art, and audio files are readily available and cost only the time it takes to download them. Search through the Web and locate at least one free source of downloadable information in each of the categories in the following table. In completing the table, provide the Internet address of the site in the Source URL column; in the Description column, describe what you've found at the site—for instance, "ten audio files of animal sounds."

CATEGORY	SOURCE URL	DESCRIPTION
Web-page backgrounds	_____	_____
Clip art	_____	_____
Audio files	_____	_____

8. Internet Presence Providers Internet presence providers (IPPs) supply resources that help users to develop their own Web sites. Many also act as Internet service providers (ISPs). Find an IPP and answer the following questions about its operations:

a. How does it charge for running a single home page—by the month and/or by the activity it generates? Would the IPP charge less if it were also your ISP?

b. Web pages need to be regularly updated with fresh information to keep users returning. How does the IPP charge for updates?

c. How would the page charges in steps *b* and *c* change if you wanted to post 12 pages instead of just 1? How about 100 pages?

d. What types of Web-page development services does the IPP offer, and how will you pay for them? For instance, will the IPP code your HTML pages and write Java code for you? At what cost? Will the IPP provide you with an HTML editor through which you can develop applications on your own?

e. What types of site-activity statistics will the IPP provide? How often? What statistics does it give for free, and what does it charge for others?

Hint: Yahoo! provides a list of companies that sell Web-site-development services to prospective Web publishers. To see lists of national and regional IPPs and get links to any of the IPPs on the lists, use the search string "Internet presence providers."

9. Blocking Software As mentioned in the chapter text, blocking software can prevent access to objectionable materials. For this project, find a software product that blocks Internet content and write a paper (three to five pages) about it. Your paper should cover the following issues:

a. The name of the product and the company that makes it

b. The cost of the product

c. How the product works with other computer-system resources; in other words, is it a browser plug-in, a stand-alone product that works independently of a browser, or something else?

d. The method by which the product blocks parts of the Internet that the user deems objectionable

10. Free Speech and Censorship Controversy has swirled around the issue of what types of materials are appropriate or inappropriate for display on the Internet. For this project, prepare a paper (three to five pages) stating your views about online censorship. Be sure to cover the following issues:

a. Does the phrase "anything goes" sum up your attitude, or do you feel that some types of materials should never be posted on the Internet?

b. How do you feel about settling the censorship issue at the client-workstation level, where each user can choose for himself or herself whether to view a site or not?

c. How do you feel about the system of voluntary policing discussed in the chapter? Do you feel it can work as is, or do you foresee some implementation problems that will render the entire system useless?

INTERACTIVE EXERCISE

DESIGNING, CREATING, AND PUBLISHING A WEB SITE

You've decided to design and create a Web site. Go to the Interactive Exercise at www.harcourtcollege.com/infosys/parker2000/student/exercise/ to complete this exercise.

ONLINE REVIEW

Go to the Online Review at www.harcourtcollege.com/infosys/parker2000/student/ to test your understanding of this chapter's concepts.

MODULE

PS

PRODUCTIVITY SOFTWARE

Over the past decade or so, computers have completely transformed the workplace. Look at the desktop of a manager, analyst, designer, engineer, secretary, and even company president today, and you will usually see a computer system. At the heart of this workplace transformation is productivity software.

Productivity software refers to applications-software products that help users to perform their jobs. These programs save time, reduce costs, and perform work that people couldn't possibly complete without the aid of a computer system.

This module opens, in Chapter PS 1, with a look at word processors and desktop publishing systems, both of which help people to develop written documents such as letters and reports. Chapter PS 2 covers spreadsheets and presentation graphics. Spreadsheets aid in analysis of numbers, while presentation graphics packages help users to prepare graphs and charts showing information in many pictorial formats. Chapter PS 3 closes the module with a discussion of database management systems, which specialize in providing rapid access to electronically stored banks of facts.

MODULE CONTENTS
Productivity Software

ISBN 0-03-025968-1

PS I

WORD PROCESSING AND DESKTOP PUBLISHING

OUTLINE

LEARNING OBJECTIVES

After completing this chapter, you will be able to:

1. Describe word processing.

2. Identify the operations that you must master to use word processing software effectively.

3. Explain the features common to many word processing programs.

4. Identify the software and hardware components found in many desktop publishing systems.

OVERVIEW

Word processing and desktop publishing are technologies that deal with the manipulation of words. *Word processing* enables a computer system to serve as a powerful writing tool. It summons computer resources that help you quickly create, edit, and print documents and manage them in ways no ordinary typewriter was ever able to match. *Desktop publishing,* available only since high-powered PCs entered the marketplace, carries word processing a step further. With desktop publishing hardware and software, one can more fully create and develop documents that look as though they were prepared by a professional print shop.

In this chapter, we'll first discuss word processing. We'll explore in detail what word processing entails and cover many of the features currently found in programs now in use. Then we'll turn to desktop publishing and the hardware and software found on high-end desktop publishing systems.

WORD PROCESSING SOFTWARE

Web Tutor

For a tutorial on word processing software, go to www.harcourtcollege.com/infosys/parker2000/student/tutor/ and click on Chapter PS 1.

When you use your computer to do the kinds of work that people have performed on typewriters throughout most of this century, you're doing word processing. **Word processing** applies computer technology to create, manipulate, and print text materials such as letters, legal contracts, manuscripts, and other documents. Word processing saves so much time and work and offers so many more capabilities than the ordinary typewriter, in fact, that relatively few people use typewriters any more.

Virtually all formal writing today employs a word processing program. Most such programs are *general purpose;* that is, they are designed to suit the needs of a variety of people—from heavy users such as secretaries and authors to average PC users who may just need to type letters now and then. Among today's best-selling word processing programs are Microsoft's Word, Corel's WordPerfect, and Lotus's WordPro. All three are components of software suites, and many users buy them in these packages rather than as stand-alone products (see the Tomorrow box). Special-purpose word processing programs, such as those designed to serve the needs of scriptwriters for television and movies, are also commercially available.

Most word processing programs offer hundreds of features, but only a handful of them account for 90 percent or more of what most people will do during the course of word processing a typical document. This basic set of word processing operations can be divided into three main groups: *document-handling operations, entering and editing operations,* and *print-formatting operations.*

DOCUMENT-HANDLING OPERATIONS

To use virtually any type of productivity software program—such as a word processor or spreadsheet—you need to know how to carry out a number of general document-handling tasks. Some of these tasks, for example opening a document for use and printing it, are illustrated in Figure PS 1-1. They correspond to such basic activities as starting and braking when driving a car.

■ **Word processing.** The use of computer technology to create, manipulate, and print text materials such as letters, legal contracts, and manuscripts.

Is Bloatware Clogging Your Computer's Arteries?

The End May Not Be in Sight

One of the problems that often frustrates users is that they have too much software on their hard disks, most of which they'll never use. What's more, they're "forced" to pay for this burden, and it often gets in the way of doing work.

One of the main culprits is the software suite. Only a couple of decades ago, for instance, users were ecstatic just to have a word processor that could prepare letters with proportionally spaced typefaces—and maybe a fancy font or two for headings. Today, they have word processors that are virtually fully featured desktop publishing and illustration programs—not to mention complete office systems that can handle spreadsheets, presentation graphics, and databases as well, whether they're needed or not. Oops, did we forget to mention Web surfing?

This enrichment in software capability has led to the term *bloatware*—software that contains "everything but the kitchen sink." While such software can provide some users with useful capabilities that they wouldn't otherwise have, many users actually wind up worse off. Not only does bloatware cost more than software that provides only the basics, but also it gobbles up hard disk space like it's going out of style. Bloatware can get in the way of creating applications too, because screens are clogged with toolbars and icons and rulers and tip wizards and Internet add-ons and . . . oops, did we forget to mention that applications carrying all of this overhead take longer to run?

New network products such as Java and ActiveX are hailed by many as relief for the bloatware burden. These products support programming to create small *applets,* sections of code that wait in network storage for users to download and execute on their own desktops. The applets are built into documents themselves, giving those documents their own native computing capabilities. Thus, when you call for a document over a network, the document can have its own viewer for you to communicate with it, its own audio and video drivers for you to hear sound and see film clips, its own calculator to perform arithmetic, and so on. When you finish your work on the document, all of the software that you used with it return to the network. No need to burden your hard disk. Who even needs a hard disk anyway?

Unfortunately, compelling as the argument may seem for applets taking over chores done by conventional desktop-installed software, it breaks down in a lot of places. For instance, throughout the history of computing, users have shown that they like control over their own environments. Software stored on networks results in having far less control. Phone lines can be hit with power outages or be clogged with traffic, servers can crash, and software can be changed without your approval. Control was one of the big reasons why people switched from mainframe display terminals to PCs in the first place, and it is one of the reasons people like their hard disks packed with software they can trust—with installation CDs tucked safely nearby in case of trouble.

There are other reasons to think that bloatware will not disappear so easily. It costs software publishers very little extra to produce bloatware over a standalone program—that is, if you're a big company like Microsoft, IBM, or Corel. Why not give users extra functionality—at a bargain price—if you have it laying around in other programs that you also produce? Even if users feel they don't need the functionality today, the nagging fear that they may need it tomorrow and that it's available at a giveaway price may be enough to get an edge on a competitive product.

Bloatware is also a strategic weapon for a software publisher in that it raises the barrier to competition and makes user exit-costs higher. For instance, it's harder than ever today for a new company to come out of the blue and develop a superior word processor—unless it has a whole suite of office applications it can peddle with it too. What's more, users who go through torture learning a bloatware program are not quick to abandon it when a new product comes along, no matter how good it appears to be.

So, when you read all of those articles in the press that say bloatware is going away, do so with that proverbial grain of salt.

Bloatware. Byte-hungry software has become the norm on the average PC desktop.

Because almost everyone needs fast access to document-handling commands, these operations are usually located on easy-to-reach menus that are but a mouse click or two away. The norm today in software suites is a document-centered graphical user interface (including a menu bar, pull-down menus, and toolbars) that is similar from program to program. This arrangement makes it easy to learn a new program once you have mastered one or two others.

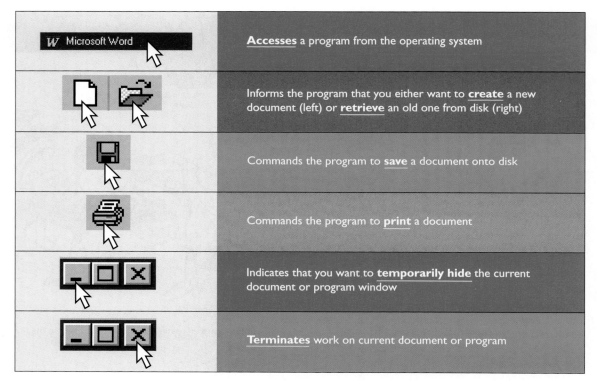

W Microsoft Word	**Accesses** a program from the operating system
	Informs the program that you either want to **create** a new document (left) or **retrieve** an old one from disk (right)
	Commands the program to **save** a document onto disk
	Commands the program to **print** a document
	Indicates that you want to **temporarily hide** the current document or program window
	Terminates work on current document or program

FIGURE PS 1-1

General operations needed for using productivity software.

ENTERING AND EDITING OPERATIONS

Every word processor contains an assortment of entering and editing operations. These capabilities accept both text keyed in by the user and the insertion of graphic images into documents and they allow the user to manipulate both the text and graphics on the screen.

Moving the Insertion Point   Virtually all word processors show a blinking cursor character on the screen called an **insertion point** to designate where a newly entered character will appear (see Figure PS 1-2). The insertion point moves to the right as you type new characters into your document. You can also move the insertion point to other positions within your document by rolling the mouse along a flat surface and then clicking the left mouse button, by tapping any of several cursor-movement keys, or by entering a short directive from a menu or dialog box. As the insertion point changes position, the *status bar* at the bottom of the screen changes correspondingly. The status bar shows where you are in the document by displaying information such as the current page number and the place on the page where the insertion point is positioned.

There are usually dozens of ways to move the insertion point throughout a document. You can move it a character, a word, a line, or a screen at a time, as well as to the beginning or the end of a document. You can also move to a specific page number or to a *bookmark* you've set up to mark a special place.

The insertion point is also used for selecting the place in a document to insert text and computer graphics imported from other programs.

Scrolling   Scrolling lets you move up and down on the screen, changing the segment of the document that is currently being displayed. When you scroll down, for example, lines successively disappear from the top of the screen, and new ones appear at the bottom. Virtually all word processing programs allow you to press the up-arrow and down-arrow keys to scroll a document line by

■ **Insertion point.** A cursor character that shows where the next key pressed will appear onscreen.

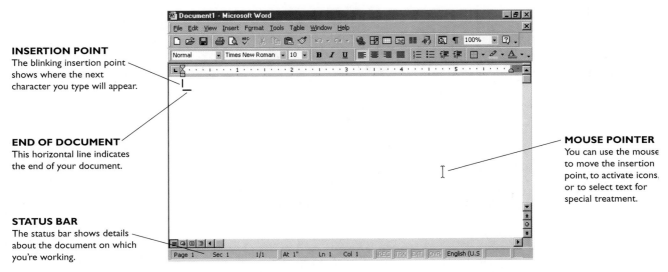

INSERTION POINT
The blinking insertion point shows where the next character you type will appear.

END OF DOCUMENT
This horizontal line indicates the end of your document.

MOUSE POINTER
You can use the mouse to move the insertion point, to activate icons, or to select text for special treatment.

STATUS BAR
The status bar shows details about the document on which you're working.

FIGURE PS 1-2

The insertion point and status bar.

line. By using the PgUp and PgDn keys, you can scroll even faster—page by page instead of line by line. Many people prefer to do most of their scrolling with a mouse and the scroll bars. To move through long documents, you can drag the scroll box with a mouse to achieve maximum scrolling speeds.

Line Returns and Hard Returns   Typing on a conventional typewriter generally requires you to press the Return key to define the end of every line. Not so with a word processor. Word processors provide an automatic line return when the insertion point reaches a certain column position at the right-hand side of the screen. This return is called a **soft return,** and the built-in feature that provides soft returns is called a **wordwrap** feature.

A word processor does also allow you to key in a **hard return**—also called a *paragraph break*—at any point by tapping the Enter key. A hard return automatically moves the insertion point to the beginning of the next line. Normally, you will use hard returns to mark the end of paragraphs or to create space on the page after typing in titles or headings. You should not press the Enter key after you have reached the right margin on each line; it will deny you any chance of reformatting paragraphs later on as you make changes to them.

Inserting and Deleting   Inserting and deleting text are two of the most basic editing operations. Virtually all word processors default to an *insert mode* that lets you insert characters at the insertion-point position on the screen. As each character is added to the screen, all characters to the right of the insertion point slide over to make room for the new character. You can switch out of the insert mode at any time to an *overtype mode* by pressing the Insert key on the keyboard. As new characters are added at the insertion-point position in the overtype mode, they replace characters to the right. Tapping the Insert key while in overtype mode will return you to insert mode.

Word processors generally allow you to delete a character, word, sentence, or block of characters at a time. Deleting one character at a time is normally done using either the Delete or Backspace key, once you have the insertion point properly positioned (the Delete key deletes forward; the Backspace key deletes backward). Deleting one word, a sentence, or a block of text at a time is done by first *selecting* the word, sentence, or block to be deleted and then tapping either the Delete or Backspace key. **Selecting text**—which

---

■ **Soft return.** An automatic line return carried out by word processing software. ■ **Wordwrap.** The feature of a word processor that automatically places soft returns. ■ **Hard return.** A line break inserted when the user presses the Enter key to control line spacing in a document. ■ **Selecting text.** The process of highlighting text on the screen in order to move or copy it, delete it, or apply a special formatting treatment to it.

DELETING TEXT

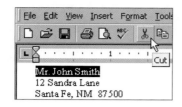

To delete text, select the text and click the Cut button.

MOVING TEXT

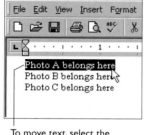

To move text, select the text and then point to it.

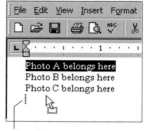

Next, drag the dotted pointer to the new location.

Finally, drop the text into place by releasing the mouse button.

COPYING TEXT

To copy text, hold down Ctrl key as you drag the selected text to its new location.

Then, release both the mouse button and Ctrl key to drop the text into place.

FORMATTING TEXT

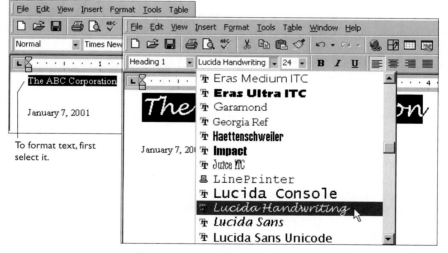

To format text, first select it.

Then, select from the formatting toolbar a desired format, such as 24-point Lucinda Handwriting.

FIGURE PS 1-3

Selecting text.

refers to highlighting the text on the screen—is illustrated in Figure PS 1-3 and is also necessary when you want to move, copy, or format text in a certain manner.

Moving and Copying Moving and copying operations allow you to relocate or replicate text within a document. *Moving* means identifying a specific block of text and physically putting it in a new place in the document. *Copying* is similar to moving except that a copy of the block remains in the original place in addition to being duplicated at the new location.

Moving and copying can often be done through pull-down menu selections, by copy and paste buttons on the word processor's toolbar, with keyboard shortcuts, and by dragging and dropping with the mouse. For instance, to copy a block of text, you can select it and then choose the *Copy* button from the main toolbar. Copying copies the text temporarily into the operating system's clipboard. Then, after you place the insertion point where you want the copy of the text to appear, you use the *Paste* button to insert it. As Figure PS 1-3 suggests, you can also use the mouse to move or copy text by first selecting it and then dragging and dropping the text into its new position. Using the mouse in this way is commonly called *drag-and-drop editing.*

Finding and Replacing   Finding and replacing are extremely useful features of word processing software. The *find operation* lets you search automatically for all occurrences of a particular word or phrase. The *replace operation* gives you the option of changing the word or phrase to something else.

For example, let's say you've typed out a long document that repeatedly refers to a person named Snider. If you've misspelled this name as Schneider, you can instruct the word processor to look up all occurrences of *Schneider* and change them to *Snider.* Some people take dangerous shortcuts when finding and replacing. For example, suppose you ask the word processor to change all occurrences of *chne* to *n.* This will change all *Schneider* occurrences to *Snider,* but it will also change a name such as *Schneymann* to *Snymann,* which you probably did not intend to do.

Figure PS 1-4 shows a document before and after a simple finding and replacing operation.

Spelling- and Grammar-Checking   Virtually every word processing program today includes a routine that searches a document for misspelled words. This routine and its accompanying dictionary are collectively known as a **spelling checker.**

The capabilities of spelling checkers can vary dramatically. Many spelling checkers designed for ordinary word processors have dictionaries that contain more than 100,000 words, whereas professional-level spelling checkers

FIGURE PS 1-4

Finding and replacing.

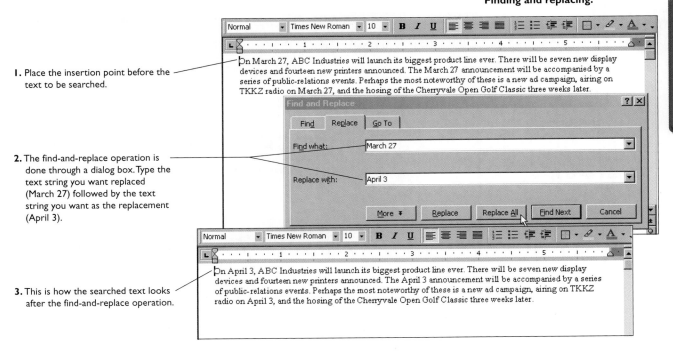

1. Place the insertion point before the text to be searched.

2. The find-and-replace operation is done through a dialog box. Type the text string you want replaced (March 27) followed by the text string you want as the replacement (April 3).

3. This is how the searched text looks after the find-and-replace operation.

■ **Spelling checker.** A program or routine that checks for misspelled words.

used by newspapers and magazines may have a million or more. A particularly important feature is the ability to place additional words into a dictionary. A writer of a computer text or medical article, for example, uses very specialized terms, many of which aren't in the dictionaries of standard spelling checkers. Specialized dictionaries are also available from aftermarket (third-party) vendors.

Spelling checkers allow you to check for misspellings *after* you finish typing text for a document, as well as *while* you type. If you choose the latter option, the word processor monitors input as you type and alerts you whenever you key in a word that doesn't appear in the spelling checker's dictionary, such as by underlining the word with a red wavy line. You can then get a list of suggested correctly spelled words by executing the proper procedure for your particular word processor, such as right-clicking on the word. When you choose to run the spelling checker for the entire document after it has been typed, suggested words will be displayed automatically. A spelling checker is illustrated in Figure PS 1-5.

Spelling checkers cannot catch all spelling errors. For instance, if you misspell the word *their* as *there,* which is also a word in the English language, the spelling checker will not flag it. To root out errors of this sort, you need a grammar checker.

A **grammar checker** is used to check for errors in word usage, such as incomplete sentences, words that are used incorrectly, inappropriate punctuation or capitalization, and the like. When a grammar checker sees something it doesn't like, it highlights it in a noticeable way. Microsoft Word, for instance, uses a wavy green underline. Similar to spelling checkers, grammar checkers display suggested corrections for each potential error.

FIGURE PS 1-5

Using a spelling checker. Many spelling checkers highlight words that they don't recognize.

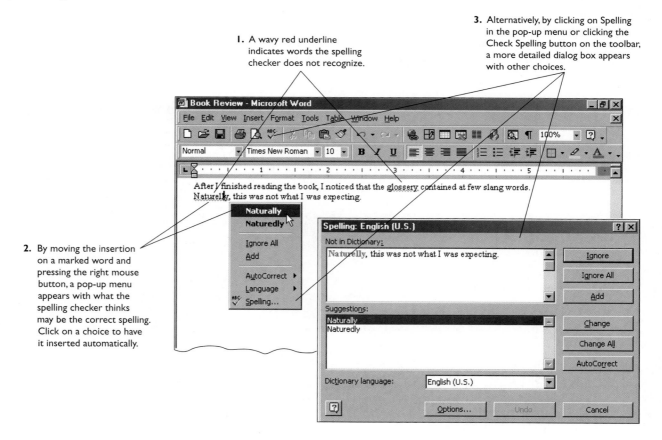

1. A wavy red underline indicates words the spelling checker does not recognize.

3. Alternatively, by clicking on Spelling in the pop-up menu or clicking the Check Spelling button on the toolbar, a more detailed dialog box appears with other choices.

2. By moving the insertion on a marked word and pressing the right mouse button, a pop-up menu appears with what the spelling checker thinks may be the correct spelling. Click on a choice to have it inserted automatically.

■ **Grammar checker.** Software that checks for errors in word usage.

Thesaurus Feature   A **thesaurus feature** allows you to identify possible synonyms for selected words. To use a thesaurus, you first select a word you wish to replace in your document. If the thesaurus feature recognizes the word, it displays suggested replacements in a format resembling that of a hard-copy thesaurus (see Figure PS 1-6). In many programs, when you see a word you like, you can simply click a Replace button to perform the replacement. Many thesaurus routines can provide antonyms as well as synonyms. The thesaurus features that accompany the leading word processors typically contain fewer than 100,000 words. Electronic thesauruses used by companies in the publishing industry have far more.

Displaying Text   Different word processors use a variety of methods for displaying text on the screen. Older products that are built around monitors with minimal graphics capabilities rely exclusively on *embedded formatting codes* to apprise users of what's going on. Boldface, italic, and underlined characters generally do not display as such onscreen even though they print appropriately. So the user of this type of word processing program must place codes for such special formats before and after a word or phrase that is to be output in a special way. A code placed before a word or phrase alerts the printer to turn on a formatting feature; the code following the word or phrase alerts it to turn off the feature. For instance, [BOLD] and [bold] might respectively be used to turn boldfacing on and off.

Now that powerful graphical user interfaces are widely available, most word processors today use a **WYSIWYG** display, in which text shows onscreen more

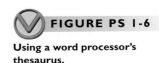

FIGURE PS 1-6

Using a word processor's thesaurus.

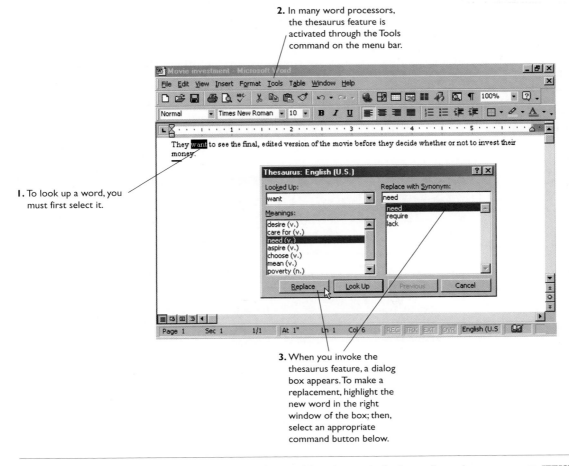

2. In many word processors, the thesaurus feature is activated through the Tools command on the menu bar.

1. To look up a word, you must first select it.

3. When you invoke the thesaurus feature, a dialog box appears. To make a replacement, highlight the new word in the right window of the box; then, select an appropriate command button below.

■ **Thesaurus feature.** A program or routine that enables electronic lookup of word synonyms.   ■ **WYSIWYG.** An acronym for the phrase *what you see is what you get*, indicating a display screen image identical or very close to the look of the eventual printed output.

or less the way it will appear in print. WYSIWYG—which is pronounced "wizzy-wig"—is an acronym for *what you see is what you get*. With WYSIWYG, the user can make toolbar-button choices onscreen to format text in a certain way, leaving it up to the computer to automatically—and transparently—handle any embedded codes.

Typically, users have a choice of WYSIWYG modes in which to enter and edit their documents. A *draft* or *normal mode* reveals the basic look of the document; many users prefer working in this mode. A *page* or *page-layout mode* supplements the document display with elements such as graphics, page numbers, footnotes, and columns that the user has specified. While the latter mode is "more WYSIWYG" than the former, it is slower to work with and better suited to fine-tuning a document that's almost ready to print.

Besides giving you a choice of WYSIWYG modes in which to operate, most word processors have a **zoom feature** that will let you magnify text or graphic elements on a screen page.

PRINT-FORMATTING OPERATIONS

Print-formatting operations tell the printer how to output text onto paper. Several of these operations are discussed next.

Adjusting Line Spacing   Adjusting line spacing is an important word processing operation. Suppose that you've single-spaced a paper, for instance, but your English 101 instructor wants all the essays you hand in to be double spaced. Word processors enable you to adjust the line spacing of the existing text to double-space the paper in just a few keystrokes or mouse clicks. Many programs also permit you to place fractional blank lines between text lines, add additional space before and after paragraphs, and choose several other line-spacing options, as long as those options are supported by the printer that you are using.

The Ruler Line   Most users will occasionally have a need to adjust margins, to set tab stops, and to indent the left, right, or both edges of certain paragraphs or quotes for emphasis. Many word processors have a **ruler line** that enables you to make these types of adjustments as you are typing (see Figure PS 1-7). You can usually also make these changes through pull-down menus and dialog boxes.

FIGURE PS 1-7

Using a ruler line.

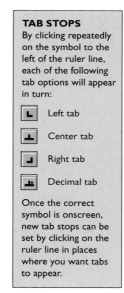

TAB STOPS
By clicking repeatedly on the symbol to the left of the ruler line, each of the following tab options will appear in turn:

Left tab

Center tab

Right tab

Decimal tab

Once the correct symbol is onscreen, new tab stops can be set by clicking on the ruler line in places where you want tabs to appear.

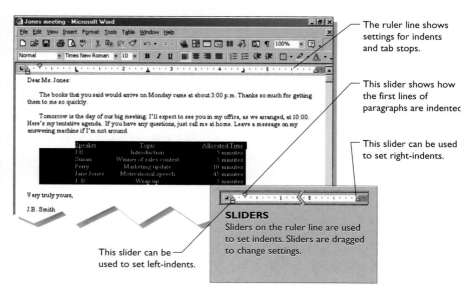

The ruler line shows settings for indents and tab stops.

This slider shows how the first lines of paragraphs are indented

This slider can be used to set right-indents.

This slider can be used to set left-indents.

SLIDERS
Sliders on the ruler line are used to set indents. Sliders are dragged to change settings.

■ **Zoom feature.** A feature that lets you magnify text or graphics images onscreen. ■ **Ruler line.** An onscreen element, resembling a physical ruler, that enables you to set line widths, tab settings, indents, and the like.

Word processors enable you to set several types of tabs—for instance, the popular left tab, where text is left aligned at the tab stop, as well as center, right, and decimal tabs, where text is respectively centered, right aligned, or aligned on a decimal point. The tab-stop positions on the screen are reached through the Tab key. You press Tab to go forward a Tab stop and Shift+Tab to go backward a tab stop. Default tabs are usually preset to left tabs set at every half inch. For more document control, you can use the ruler line to set your own tab stops when necessary.

Justifying   Most documents are formatted with either a ragged or smooth right edge. These style alternatives are respectively referred to as *left justification* (or *left-aligned* text) and *full justification* (or *justified* text). Figure PS 1-8 illustrates both of these styles and two additional ones.

Users who create business documents typically prefer left justification, as the extra blank spaces between words that often result with full justification can sometimes make documents too visually difficult to read. Full justification can look quite attractive, however, if the word processor and printer in use can handle proportional spacing (to be discussed shortly). Many word processing programs also have center- and right-justification options, as the figure shows, but these are used only in special circumstances and not for entire documents.

Centering text is something everyone preparing a document does sooner or later; for instance, when creating a title or a heading. Most word processing programs require you to have the insertion point on the line that will contain the text to be centered when invoking the centering command. Then, as you type, the text is automatically centered. You can also center text that is justified another way—usually by first selecting it and then invoking the centering command.

Establishing a Page Format   Most word processors let you choose overall formatting for the pages in your document. For instance, you can tell the word processor the settings of the left, right, top, and bottom margins, as well as the paper size being used. You can also choose whether to print page numbers on the document. For example, you may want page numbers placed on long reports but not on short letters. Most word processing programs will place page numbers almost anywhere you specify.

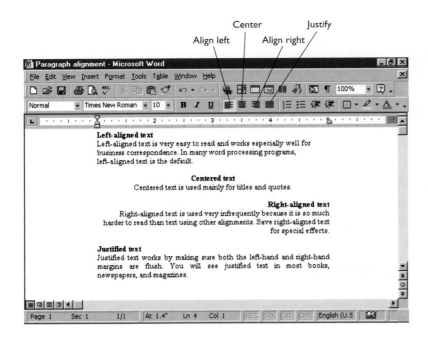

FIGURE PS 1-8

Justifying text.

Reformatting Reformatting places your document in a form suitable for output; for instance, by ensuring that the document is properly fitted within the margins after an insertion or deletion is made. Reformatting normally is necessary when you insert text, delete text, change line spacing, readjust margins, change justification, or change the basic page format. Virtually all programs will reformat your document automatically every time you modify text.

Headers and Footers A *header* is a title that a word processor prints automatically at the top of every page; a *footer* is a title automatically printed at the bottom of every page. Some programs let you specify headers and footers with great flexibility. For instance, you can print both headers and footers on the same page and even alternate the titles placed in a header or a footer on successive pages. Most word processors also allow page numbers to appear within a header or footer. This textbook, like many other books, alternates headers; the chapter number and chapter title appear with the page number on each right-hand page, and the module title and page number appear on each left-hand page.

FIGURE PS 1-9

Typefaces.

Fonts A **typeface** is a collection of text characters that share a common design. Typeface-selection features enable you to output characters in a vari-

Courier

Helvetica

Times

TYPEFACES
A typeface is a collection of visually consistent characters.

SELECTING TYPEFACES
Typefaces are often chosen from a formatting toolbar, using a drop-down list box. Scroll down to the typeface you like and select it.

■ **Typeface.** A collection of text characters that share a common design.

POINT SIZE
Point size refers to the size of type.

This is 10-point Helvetica
This is 12-point Helvetica
This is 18-point Helvetica
This is 24-point Helvetica

SELECTING POINT SIZE
Like typefaces, point sizes are selected from a formatting toolbar.

10 ▼
8
9
10
11
12
14
16
18
20
22
24
26 ▼

FIGURE PS 1-10

Point size.

ety of typefaces and typeface sizes (called **point sizes**). All the characters in a particular typeface and point size are referred to as a **font;** for instance, 12-point Helvetica is a font. Figure PS 1-9 illustrates different typefaces; Figure PS 1-10 illustrates point sizes.

Fonts are either monospaced or proportionally spaced. In documents using the Courier font—a typewriting standard—text is **monospaced.** What this means is that each character takes up the same amount of horizontal space, whether it is an uppercase *W*, a lowercase *i*, or a blank space. This textbook, however, like most others, was typeset on a system capable of **proportional spacing,** which allocates more horizontal space on a line to some characters than to others, depending on their size. For example, a capital *W* would take up more space than a lowercase *i*. **Microspacing** allows further adjustment of spacing within a text line by inserting fractions of a full blank space in inconspicuous places so as to justify the left-hand and right-hand margins without uneven spacing (see Figure PS 1-11).

For you to use proportional spacing and microspacing, both your word processor and your printer must support them. Often, proportional spacing and microspacing are done automatically for you when you select certain typefaces, but many word processors will let you make further microspacing

How tight is tight?
How tight is tight?
How tight is tight?
How tight is tight?

FIGURE PS 1-11

Proportionally spaced characters with microspacing.

■ **Point size.** A measurement for scaling typefaces. ■ **Font.** A typeface in a particular point size—for instance, 12-point Helvetica. ■ **Monospacing.** A printing feature that allocates the same amount of space on a line to each character.
■ **Proportional spacing.** A printing feature that allocates more horizontal space on a line to some characters than to others.
■ **Microspacing.** A technique used by many printers and software products to insert fractional spaces between characters.

adjustments if the situation requires it. Virtually all word processors will also let you create italic, boldface, underline, subscript, and superscript characters in your document—as well as a number of special characters, such as long dashes and square bullets.

Previewing Documents Sometimes, you discover problems with a document after you finish preparing it and printing it. The margins may look too wide, a graphic element on one page may not balance with an element on a facing page, and so on. To save the time and cost of printing documents over and over again until they look right, virtually all word processors have a *preview feature* that enables you to inspect an onscreen version of what the document will actually look like when printed.

Once the preview feature is turned on, there is often a special preview toolbar that will let you magnify documents to see parts of them up close, a feature to put multiple pages on the same screen, and so on. Many word processors will also let you edit documents in the preview mode.

Multiple Columns Multiple-column formatting lets you print text in a columnar format similar to that used in newspapers and magazines. You can print text in double or triple columns, and you can usually specify the width of each column individually. Multiple-column formatting is especially useful when you are printing your own brochures or newsletters (see Figure PS 1-12).

Footnoting A footnoting feature allows you to create, edit, and delete footnotes in a document. Typically, the routine that manages the footnoting is designed to remember footnote references and automatically renumber footnotes if you insert or delete any, as well as move the footnotes from page to page, as necessary, as the document is edited.

FIGURE PS 1-12

Arranging documents in multiple columns.

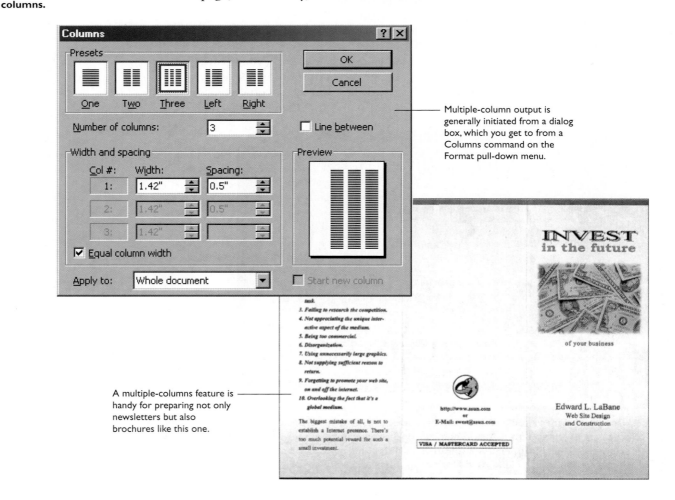

Multiple-column output is generally initiated from a dialog box, which you get to from a Columns command on the Format pull-down menu.

A multiple-columns feature is handy for preparing not only newsletters but also brochures like this one.

Preparing Web Documents The most recent versions of office suites include features that bring document preparation and the Web closer together. With a single click of a mouse, a document can instantly become Web-page content or, conversely, a Web page can become a document capable of being word processed. There are other Web-friendly features, too. In Lotus SmartSuite, an intranet publishing tool called FastSite lets you collect a batch of documents, select a common style for them, and automatically send them to a server computer as HTML pages. The high-end version of Microsoft Office 2000 includes Microsoft's popular FrontPage software, a widely used Web-page-authoring program that lets users build complete Web sites from scratch or from Office or other existing documents.

ADVANCED OPERATIONS

In addition to the basic operations we've just covered, the many word processors enable you to do a number of other useful tasks. Some of these may be especially valuable if you are a professional typist or an author or publisher, or if your business requires a lot of correspondence.

Customizing Your Word Processor As you work with your word processor, you will not only find many ways to speed up your work but also discover ways to alter defaults in order to match your working habits and preferences. You can customize a word processor in a variety of ways, including creating automatic backup copies of documents, changing the location where files are saved, tailoring the spelling checker to more closely meet your individual needs, creating new toolbar buttons and even new toolbars, squelching the potentially annoying beep feature that accompanies some message boxes, and so on. In Microsoft Word, for instance, many types of customization are done by choosing Tools on the menu bar and then either Customize or Options on the corresponding pull-down menu.

Macros All of the major word processors allow you to create macros. A **macro** is a sequence of keystrokes that is saved in a special file so that you can use it whenever you wish.

Understanding that macro programming is beyond the grasp of most users, most word-processing-program publishers also have easy-to-use built-in macros that you can summon for specific tasks. For instance, virtually every word processor has a Date macro—a menu-activated command that places today's date automatically at the insertion-point position. In addition, many packages often include some type of *autotext feature* that lets you store frequently used words or sentences in a special library to replace other text on demand. For instance, let's say you'll be typing several letters containing the phrase "Yours truly, Mary M. Miller." You could save time by typing this information once and saving it in a special library under a specific name, such as "bye." As you type the letter, type *bye* where the closing words are to appear, press a special function key, and—presto—"Yours truly, Mary M. Miller" appears.

Mass Mailings Anyone who sends lots of mail can benefit from a word processor's merge and mailing-label features (see Figure PS 1-13). Individuals and organizations often need to send the same letter—more or less—to dozens or even thousands of people. A word processor's **merge feature** is designed to automate much of the work of producing form letters of this sort. The feature is so named because it prints letters in volume by merging a file containing a list of names and addresses with a file containing the *boilerplate,* or form-letter text.

Further Exploration

For links to further information about word processing software, go to www.harcourtcollege.com/infosys/parker2000/student/explore/ and click on **Chapter PS 1.**

■ **Macro.** A predetermined series of keystrokes or commands that can be invoked by a single keystroke or command.
■ **Merge feature.** A routine specifically designed to produce form letters.

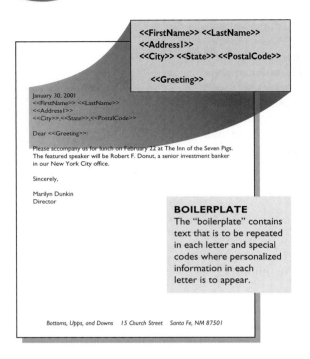

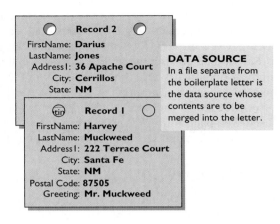

DATA SOURCE
In a file separate from the boilerplate letter is the data source whose contents are to be merged into the letter.

BOILERPLATE
The "boilerplate" contains text that is to be repeated in each letter and special codes where personalized information in each letter is to appear.

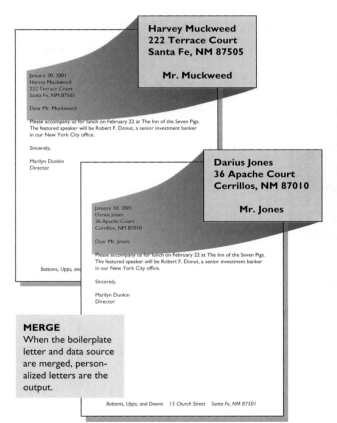

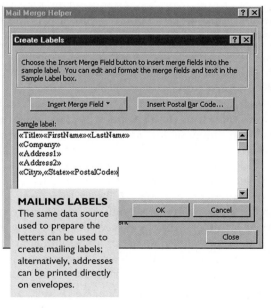

MERGE
When the boilerplate letter and data source are merged, personalized letters are the output.

MAILING LABELS
The same data source used to prepare the letters can be used to create mailing labels; alternatively, addresses can be printed directly on envelopes.

FIGURE PS 1-13

Merging and mailing labels illustrated.

A **mailing label feature** is often used to generate mailing labels. You can usually sort labels by specific fields (such as ZIP code) or extract records having special characteristics (such as all alumni from the class of 1997 living in San Francisco) prior to processing the labels. Virtually all word processors

■ **Mailing label feature.** A routine that generates address labels.

being sold today also have a feature that enables you to print envelopes on demand. All you generally have to do is insert the envelopes into your printer (sometimes using a special feeder) and click on some type of Print Envelopes command. The word processor can then be directed to your document to automatically retrieve the address. If several addresses are involved, it can be directed to a file of names and addresses—such as the same one you use for letter merging.

Redlining   **Redlining,** a popular groupware feature available on most word processors today, enables two or more people to collaborate on written pieces. When making corrections to a hard-copy document such as a magazine article or book, editors have traditionally used a red pen to strike out—or redline—certain words or phrases written by the author and to substitute others. After a document is redlined, the author can see both what he or she originally wrote and the changes made by the editor. Any change can be then approved or vetoed. The redlining feature found in many word processors provides the electronic equivalent of the manual redlining process (see Figure PS 1-14).

Outlining   A word processor's *outlining* feature helps you to organize ideas into a hierarchy. For instance, when organizing topics for a report, you often split them into headings, subheadings, and so on. Most word processors let

ABOUT REDLINING
A redlining feature enables several people to collaborate on a document, so that each is aware what the other is adding or deleting.

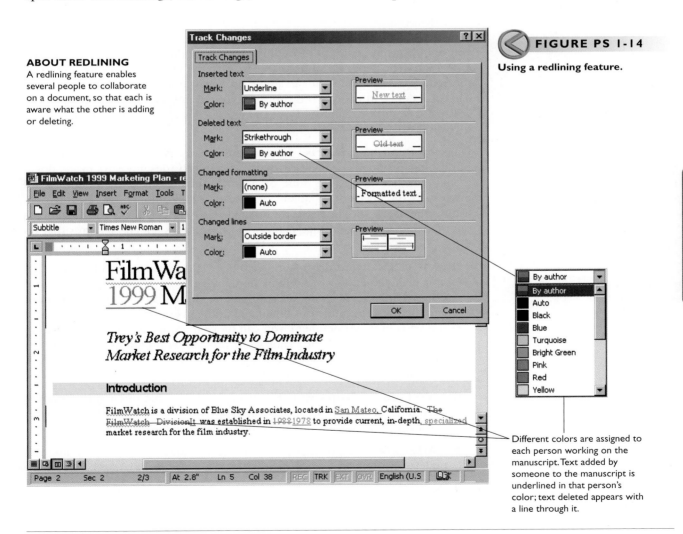

FIGURE PS 1-14

Using a redlining feature.

Different colors are assigned to each person working on the manuscript. Text added by someone to the manuscript is underlined in that person's color; text deleted appears with a line through it.

■ **Redlining.** A word processing feature that provides the electronic equivalent of the editor's red pen.

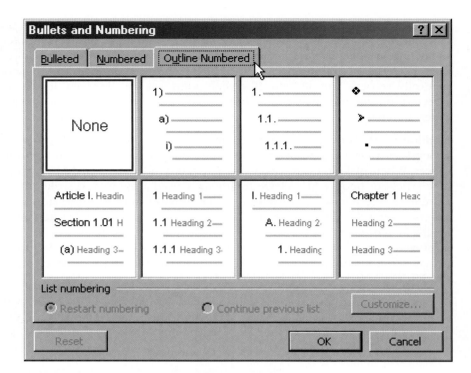

FIGURE PS 1-15

Outlining. Most word processors let you choose from a variety of outline styles, including those shown here.

you choose from a variety of outline styles, including those shown in Figure PS 1-15. As you type the outline, the word processor automatically performs the required formatting—for example, inserting outline numbers and taking care of indents. In many word processing programs, you can also temporarily collapse a long document with several levels of heads into an outline to view its overall structure.

Desktop Publishing Effects Later in the chapter we'll be covering desktop publishing programs—software that's specifically designed to make documents look like they were done by a professional print shop. Modern word processors, however, are capable of a respectable amount of desktop publishing themselves. You've already learned that you can dress up documents with fancy fonts. Beyond that, many word processors contain features that do the following (see also Figure PS 1-16):

- GRAPHICS A word processor's graphics feature enables you to import art into a document—say, a graph or drawing from another program or a **clip-art** image. Generally, all you have to do is find the image you want and then insert it into your document at the insertion-point position. Once the art is in your document, you can move it around at will, resize or crop it, and so forth. All of the major word processing programs, since they are part of an office suite, also have access to a drawing toolbar that lets you do a limited amount of drawing.

- DROP CAPS A **drop cap** is a large capital letter that often appears at the beginning of an article or a book chapter. The drop cap may occupy a vertical distance of several lines, depending on the effect desired.

- WATERMARKS A **watermark** is a lightly shaded image that appears underneath text in a document to impart a professional look. The image

---

- **Clip art.** Prepackaged artwork designed to be imported into text documents or charts, say, by word processing, desktop publishing, or presentation graphics software. ■ **Drop cap.** A large, decorative capital letter that sometimes appears at the beginning of an article or chapter of text. ■ **Watermark.** A lightly shaded image that appears to underlie a document's text.

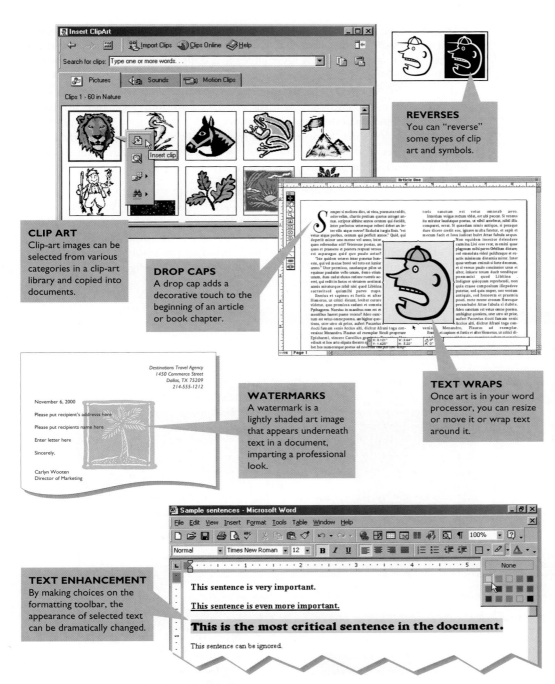

CLIP ART
Clip-art images can be selected from various categories in a clip-art library and copied into documents.

REVERSES
You can "reverse" some types of clip art and symbols.

DROP CAPS
A drop cap adds a decorative touch to the beginning of an article or book chapter.

WATERMARKS
A watermark is a lightly shaded art image that appears underneath text in a document, imparting a professional look.

TEXT WRAPS
Once art is in your word processor, you can resize or move it or wrap text around it.

TEXT ENHANCEMENT
By making choices on the formatting toolbar, the appearance of selected text can be dramatically changed.

FIGURE PS 1-16

Desktop publishing with a word processor.

can be a logo, a decorative graphic, or even a word or phrase—such as *CONFIDENTIAL*—that has the appearance of being stamped on pages. Like any regular piece of art, you can move and resize the watermark to suit your own taste.

■ TEXT ENHANCEMENT   As hinted earlier, you can enhance text in a variety of ways. Once you select text, you can change the font, boldface or italicize it, or change the color of the text; you can also highlight it like you would with a "magic marker" or add a border around the text.

■ TABLES   A word processor's Tables feature lets you organize text or numbers into columns and rows. You can also format the table, adding such embellishments as shading, borders, colors, special fonts, and so on. Alternatively, you can develop the table in your spreadsheet and import it into your word processor.

Style Sheets, Templates, and Wizards A feature that all of the leading word processors have—and that is standard fare in desktop publishing programs—is the **style sheet**. A style sheet is a collection of font and formatting specifications that is saved as a file and later used to prepare documents in a particular way. For instance, if your letters to clients must conform to a certain letterhead style and use a specific typeface and point size, you can declare all of these specifications in one or more style sheets that you apply when preparing such letters. Reports, in contrast, would probably use a different set of style sheets. You can prepare your own style sheets from scratch or use templates and wizards to assist you (see Figure PS 1-17).

■ TEMPLATES A **template** shows the basic style to which documents of a certain type will conform. Templates are frequently used to create a fancy style of letter, a cover-sheet design for sending faxes, or a press release. Once you've selected a template, software will automatically apply the appropriate styling and text, usually including placeholder text for any text that should be customized. The middle screen in the figure illustrates three template choices presented to the user.

FIGURE PS 1-17

Using wizards and templates. Here, a wizard simplifies preparation of a cover sheet to accompany a fax.

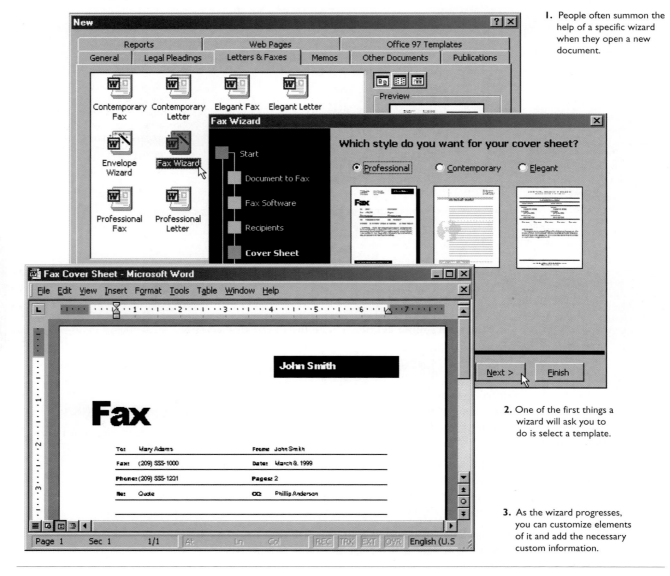

1. People often summon the help of a specific wizard when they open a new document.

2. One of the first things a wizard will ask you to do is select a template.

3. As the wizard progresses, you can customize elements of it and add the necessary custom information.

■ **Style sheet.** A collection of design specifications saved as a file for later use to format documents in a particular way.
■ **Template.** A pattern or style for documents of a certain type.

■ WIZARDS   A **wizard** goes beyond a template in that it consists of a series of screens that tell you, step-by-step, how to create documents of a certain type. Wizards commonly exist for such tasks as creating fax cover sheets, calendars, meeting agendas, newsletters, and résumés. To use the wizard when preparing a document, you merely respond to dialog box, choices and questions, such as those relating to selecting a template and identifying the person to whom you wish to send a fax.

Index and Table-of-Contents Preparation   All of the major word processors allow you to "tag" words or phrases individually so that you can later prepare an index or a table of contents. For instance, if you have tagged a few hundred words in a book for an index, you can later invoke the word processor's *indexing routine,* which will arrange these words in alphabetical order and provide the page numbers on which the words appear. Most indexing routines also let you create index subheadings similar to the ones that appear in the index of this book.

Add-on Programs   When a word processor is missing a potentially useful feature, chances are an aftermarket (third-party) company—or even the company that makes the word processor—will offer such a feature as an **add-on program.** One of the most useful add-on programs for people who write for a living is the reference shelf.

A **reference shelf** provides online access to a number of handy reference tools. The most prominent of these packages, Microsoft Bookshelf (see Figure PS 1-18), packs electronic versions of a dictionary, an encyclopedia, a book of quotations, an atlas, a zip-code directory, a world almanac and book of facts, and an Internet directory onto a single CD-ROM. Bookshelf enables any of its

FIGURE PS 1-18

Microsoft Bookshelf. Users of this CD-ROM-based package can summon information from a variety of reference works—such as an encyclopedia and an atlas—by merely clicking onscreen selections.

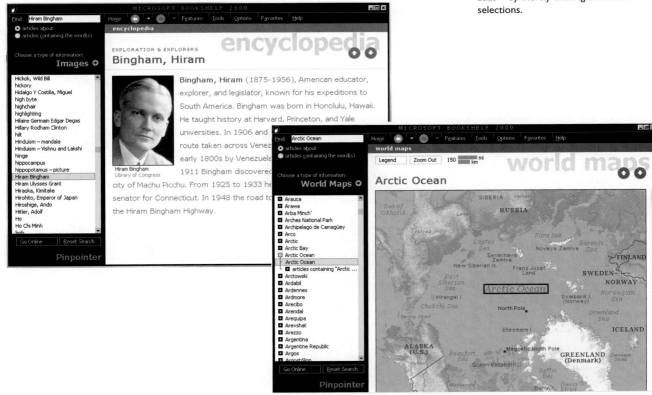

■ **Wizard.** A series of screens that tell you, step-by-step, how to create documents of a certain type. ■ **Add-on program.** Software that supplements the activities of a larger program. ■ **Reference shelf.** A software product that provides a number of handy reference books online.

works to be quickly summoned by a word processor. You can electronically search these works for specific text and, when the text is found, it can be cut and pasted back into the document being word processed.

Large commercial programs such as Word, WordPerfect, and WordPro are regularly revised every couple of years by worker teams at their respective companies. The use of team incentives to get software out the door in time is the subject of the chapter's Inside the Industry box.

DESKTOP PUBLISHING SOFTWARE

In the past decade or so, desktop publishing has rapidly evolved into a major applications area within the field of computers.

WHAT IS DESKTOP PUBLISHING?

Desktop publishing refers to desktop PCs that let you combine and manipulate on a page such elements as text—in any of several typefaces, point sizes, and styles—art, and photos, thus creating attractive documents that look as if they came off a professional printer's press (see Figure PS 1-19). Desktop publishing is designed to replace many of the traditionally manual, labor-intensive tasks associated with cutting, arranging, and pasting elements onto a page. Because desktop publishing makes it possible for publishing to be done in-house, it also enables companies to save money, save time, and have more control over the look of finished documents.

FIGURE PS 1-19

Desktop publishing output. Desktop publishing systems prepare more sophisticated-looking documents than word processors are expected to produce.

■ **Desktop publishing.** A PC-based publishing system that can fit on a desktop.

Team Incentives

Rah rah team! Group T-shirts are a common way to solidify members of a development team.

Hefty salaries and lucrative stock options are the principal ways companies motivate employees. But if you've ever played a sport, you know that there's something beyond both money and individual reward that can get your work ethic up: being part of an exciting team. Humans naturally like to feel part of something bigger than themselves.

High-tech companies are well aware of such tendencies. They know that the ordeal of getting a tight-deadline product out the door can be mentally excruciating and involve a lot of sacrifice. But it can also be a lot of fun if the right types of incentives are offered to employees. Even small prizes can increase the chance of a venture succeeding if there are challenges involved.

Incentives come in all varieties. It has been said, for instance, that programmers will do almost anything for a free meal. Thus, free lunches and dinners to developers who work extra time during ship cycles are a common way to generate excitement on a team. When Lotus was a fledgling company, for instance, developers working late hours were often given unlimited nighttime accounts at a nearby deli and ice-cream parlor. Apple, in its early days, was legendary for its free pizza. On its way to meet one shipping deadline, Microsoft tried a different approach—it offered free massages to developers several times a week to relieve stress.

Another widely used incentive is the team T-shirt (see image). Sometimes everyone on the team gets one; in other cases, team members have to earn them. At Microsoft, Zero Bug T-shirts were once given only to Windows NT members who corrected all of their program glitches. On the completion of another software project—one that had Microsoft programmers working around the clock to meet a tight shipping date—all team members got a Club Mauisoft T-shirt well before the deadline. The garment served as a constant reminder that each team member and a chosen guest were going to get a free, week-long trip to Hawaii at the end of the project if all went well.

You can do desktop publishing with either word processing software, as has been already described, or a desktop publishing program. As you can probably surmise from studying the images in Figure PS 1-19—which were done using a desktop publishing program—the basic difference between embellishing a document with a word processor and a desktop publishing program is in the document's "look." A desktop publishing program provides far more capability as regards typesetting and imagesetting. *Typesetting* implies maximum control over type styles and sizes as well as spacing between words, letters, and lines. *Imagesetting* involves combining and manipulating on a page both type and such artwork elements as sophisticated drawings and full-color photographs.

In addition to publishing traditional hard-copy media, publishing on a PC today is often taken to mean creating Web sites and producing multimedia creations for CD-ROM or DVD. For the purpose of this chapter, we define desktop publishing by its original application—putting type and art on paper. The particularities of publishing on the Web are treated in detail in Chapter NET 3, while creating multimedia presentations is covered in the next chapter.

Naturally, not all desktop publishing software is the same. You can spend about $100 for a program that gives you considerable flexibility over your word processor, but you will pay several times that amount for one that provides the sophisticated look you see in the most high-end books and magazines. Desktop publishing systems targeted for commercial applications often consist of several hardware and software components.

HARDWARE

Hardware for a commercial-level desktop publishing system usually includes a high-end PC, a laser printer, a graphics-oriented monitor, and an image scanner. These devices are covered in depth in the HW module of the text and are therefore addressed only briefly here.

High-End PC   The most important components of a computer for desktop publishing applications are a speedy microprocessor, a respectable amount of RAM, and a hard disk with plenty of storage. Manipulation of graphical fonts, photos, and art is computationally intensive, and each of these elements consumes a lot of storage, as well. Such work requires a system unit like those based on high-end Intel or PowerPC chips. The systems should have at least 128 MB of RAM and several gigabytes of hard-disk storage. Additionally, auxiliary storage devices such as Zip and Jaz drives can be handy if you need to store large volumes of material offline or send large documents or images to others.

Laser Printer   Most laser printers for PC-based desktop publishing applications cost anywhere from about $500 to several thousand dollars, depending on such things as page speed and the ability to produce color. For graphics work, the printer should have at least 4 MB of RAM. Having a lot of RAM allows you to output images of greater complexity. For photographic outputs, a 600 dpi print resolution is satisfactory. If you require higher resolution than this, you can always go to a service bureau (see Feature PS 1-1).

The laser printer in your computer system relies on a specific **page description language (PDL)** to carry out its work. The two most common PDLs are Adobe's *PostScript,* which is widely used in high-end desktop publishing, and Hewlett-Packard's *Printer Command Language (PCL),* which is more popular for the general-purpose work required of most users.

Graphics-Oriented Monitor   Many monitors used with PCs contain a relatively small screen that can comfortably display about a one-third to one-half of a standard printed page at a time. On such screens, the resolution usually is adequate for text and some simple graphics. Users of desktop publishing applications, however, generally prefer at least a 17-inch monitor, both to fine-tune detailed graphics and to see without eye strain either a full-page or a two-page layout on the screen at one time. Some monitors designed for these purposes can also display in portrait (page-length) mode.

Image Scanner   An image scanner allows you to scan photographs, drawings, or text and enter them directly into computer memory or into a file on your hard disk. Later, you can edit the images with illustration software and hardware. Some image scanners also use optical character recognition (OCR) software, which enables them to recognize text characters. Such a feature allows you to later edit any text that you enter with the scanner. Color scanners are widely available, and many cost less than $300. If you don't have a scanner to input photos to your computer system, you may be able to get them scanned at either a service bureau or a Web-resident processing center.

SOFTWARE

A variety of software and software-based products support desktop publishing environments. These include page-makeup software, illustration software, fonts, and image and sound libraries.

■ **Page description language (PDL).** A language for communicating instructions to a laser printer.

PS 1-1

FEATURE

Service Bureaus

How to Extend Your Computer System at a Nominal Cost

You want to create a color brochure on your word processor, but you don't have a color printer. You want to make color 35-mm slides for a meeting coming up in two weeks, but you don't have a film recorder to produce them. Someone sent you some important documents on a Macintosh-formatted disk, but you can't read it—your computer runs only in a Microsoft Windows environment. What do you do? Consider going to a service bureau.

Service bureaus exist in virtually all large and midsized cities throughout North America. A few years ago, many of them were strictly considered copy centers or print shops, because virtually the only thing they did was run off duplicates of hard-copy documents. Although service bureaus still make a lot of their income doing simple duplication tasks, many now also handle more sophisticated chores. With the age of microcomputing in full swing and mainframe power of a few years ago now available on desktops, most service bureaus have expanded their offerings to include any or all of the following:

Color Output Output can be produced for you on any of a variety of print media—paper, slides, transparencies, and the like. Typically, you bring in an electronic disk containing the file you want output, and the service bureau does the rest. Before you prepare your disk, you should make sure it conforms to a file format—such as TIFF, PICT, or EPS—that the service bureau can handle. Hundreds of file formats are in existence, so beware. Some service bureaus are located on the Web; you send images to them online and receive hard-copy outputs in the mail. Or, conversely, you can provide them film and download the images off the Web.

Color Copies Even if you have your own color printer, it's often cheaper and faster to have duplicates made of color output through a service bureau than to print multiple copies at home. The service bureau can also duplicate slides for you and make prints of them. Many will even colorize black-and-white originals, change colors in images, and reduce or enlarge images.

Service Bureau. The place to go if you lack hardware, software, or expertise.

Computer Rental Today, a number of service bureaus rent time on PC-compatible and Macintosh computers by the hour, provided you do your work on site. Staff members may be able to help you get started on a particular computer if you are not familiar with it.

Full-Service Design and Typesetting If you are too busy to do your own desktop publishing or to prepare your own presentation materials, many service bureaus will do this type of work for you. Typical services include creating résumés, custom business stationery, business forms, sales flyers and price lists, newsletters and brochures, promotional materials, and charts and graphs. Some service bureaus will also outsource work that they cannot do in-house.

Videoconferencing Videoconferencing shows images of people on a screen as they talk to one another. Many service bureaus maintain rooms where you can carry on face-to-face meetings with distant clients, business associates, or relatives. Many systems even enable you to share and jointly annotate electronic documents while you confer.

PS

Page-Makeup Software The programs whose principal function is to combine text, photos, and art elements into a finished page are collectively referred to as **page-makeup software** (see Figure PS 1-20). Because page composition is the central function of desktop publishing, page-makeup programs are commonly called *desktop publishing programs.*

The vendors of the leading page-makeup programs have designed their products to accept text prepared with most of the leading word processors. Although page-makeup programs enable you to modify any text that you

■ **Page-makeup software.** A program used to compose page layouts in a desktop publishing system.

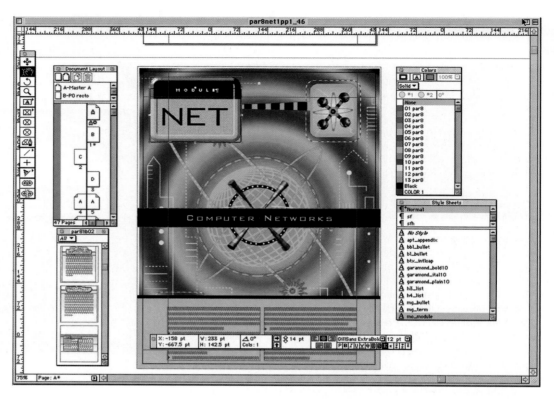

FIGURE PS 1-20

Page-makeup software. Because page makeup is the central function in desktop publishing, page-makeup programs are often called desktop publishing programs.

import to them, it is important to recognize that their primary function is page makeup. Thus, they are not as easy to use for word processing as your average word processor.

Some of the leading page-makeup programs are Adobe Systems' PageMaker, Corel Corporation's Corel Ventura, Quark Inc.'s QuarkXPress, and Microsoft's Publisher. Increasingly, these programs are incorporating Web-publishing tools along with their traditional hard-copy, page-makeup offerings.

Illustration Software **Illustration programs** enable artwork to be created from scratch. Also, they accept existing artwork as input and allow it to be modified using the software's image-manipulation facilities.

Commercial illustration programs are commonly distinguished by whether they are primarily oriented toward painting, drawing, or photography. *Painting programs* enable you to create bit-mapped images and to color them pixel by pixel. Usually, the images you create cannot be resized without loss of resolution. For instance, enlarging them may result in jagged edges, whereas reducing them may result in a blurry mess. In contrast, *drawing programs* enable you to create outlines that can be resized. Once sized, these outlines can be filled in with colors. *Photo programs* are oriented toward getting photographs into storage and being able to do touchup work such as correcting focus, color, and so on. Some illustration programs are multipurpose and will allow you to paint, draw, and handle photos.

The illustration software products on the market collectively enable you to size, rotate, flip, recolor, distort, and edit virtually any digitally stored drawing or photograph to your heart's content. Because these programs handle images at electronically fast speeds, you can try out dozens of possibilities in the time it would normally take to produce only a single image by manual means. Once an image is satisfactory, you can export it to a page-makeup program.

■ **Illustration program.** A program that enables users to paint, draw, or manipulate photographs.

A growing variety of illustration programs is available today. Some of the best-sellers are Adobe's Illustrator, Adobe's Photoshop, Corel's CorelDraw!, Microsoft's PhotoDraw, Fractal Design's Expression, Fractal Design's Painter, Micrografx's Designer, and Macromedia's FreeHand. Some of the programs named here (such as Illustrator and CorelDraw!) are more oriented toward the development of drawings, while others (such as Photoshop)—sometimes called *image-editing programs*—are geared more to such finishing work as making color corrections, retouching images, applying filters, and creating dazzling special effects. The lines defining illustration programs are hazy at best and constantly changing. Anyone considering buying such a program should check carefully the duties the program performs.

Type A variety of fonts and styling features are available for desktop publishing applications. The choices typically go well beyond those that accompany word processors.

Fonts are of two types: bit mapped and outline (see Figure PS 1-21). The distinction between the two is similar to the one between painting and drawing programs. *Bit-mapped fonts* are described by fixed configurations of dots. Although they are the least-expensive kind of font, you cannot scale them to different sizes. *Outline fonts* consist of mathematical curves that describe how characters are shaped. They are more expensive than bit-mapped fonts, but you can scale them to virtually any size you want and also create your own fonts. Two widely used outline fonts are *TrueType* fonts, often bundled with Microsoft and Apple software, and *PostScript Type 1* fonts, which are commonly found in high-end desktop publishing applications.

Even though many word processing and desktop publishing programs come with a variety of fonts, you can add others by acquiring a font library. A *font library* is a collection of fonts that supplements those packaged into your word processor or desktop publishing program. Adobe Systems, for instance, has a library of more than 2,000 typefaces that's available on CD-ROM. To use any particular typeface, you buy the special code that unlocks it. The trend today is selling fonts over the Internet, either by making the fonts downloadable over phone lines or by making it possible to unlock the CD-ROM and charge a user account at the same time.

Image, Video, and Sound Libraries An *image library* is a digital collection of prepared art images—drawings, paintings, photos, and the like. Typically, potential users look through a printed or online catalog showing the images and make their selections. Terms and charges vary; you can buy individual images as well as entire libraries containing hundreds or thousands of images. Also, some vendors charge for images on a per-usage basis, whereas others give you virtually unlimited usage of an image once a flat fee is paid. Since computer systems are able to handle digital video, *video libraries* are now commonplace as well.

Sound libraries contain collections of sounds. Now that desktop publishing of a sort is making its presence felt through Web pages, sounds—including video, voice, and music clips—are yet another way to express oneself through a document.

For links to further information about desktop publishing software, go to www. harcourtcollege.com/infosys/ parker2000/student/explore/ and click on Chapter PS 1.

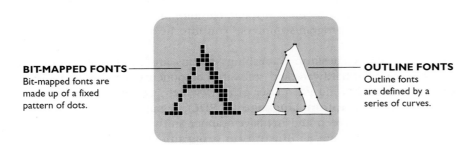

BIT-MAPPED FONTS
Bit-mapped fonts are made up of a fixed pattern of dots.

OUTLINE FONTS
Outline fonts are defined by a series of curves.

FIGURE PS 1-21

Bit-mapped versus outline fonts.

SUMMARY AND KEY TERMS

Go to the Online Glossary at www.harcourtcollege.com/infosys/parker2000/ student/ to review key terms.

Both word processing and desktop publishing technologies deal with the manipulation of words.

Word Processing Software **Word processing** is the use of computer technology to create, manipulate, and print text materials such as letters, legal contracts, manuscripts, and other documents. By far, most people today use *general-purpose* word processing packages, such as Microsoft Word and Word-Perfect.

Using a word processor, or for that matter any type of productivity software program, requires learning several general operations. These operations include accessing the program, creating new documents and retrieving old ones, saving and printing documents, and terminating work on the document or applications program.

Learning to use a word processor at a minimal level involves mastering a number of elementary entering-and-editing and print-formatting commands. Entering and editing operations include moving the **insertion point,** scrolling, making line returns through either a **soft return** (the **wordwrap** feature) or a **hard return,** inserting and deleting, **selecting text,** moving and copying, finding and replacing, using a **spelling checker** and **grammar checker,** using a **thesaurus feature,** working in a **WYSIWYG** display mode, and using the **zoom feature** to adjust text magnification appropriately.

Among the print-formatting operations that one must learn are adjusting line spacing; indenting; using a **ruler line;** justifying text; setting tabs, margins, and page formats; reformatting text; centering; setting up headers and footers; selecting **typefaces, point sizes,** and **fonts;** multiple-column formatting; previewing documents; and footnoting. Many word processors provide **proportional spacing** and **microspacing** capabilities. Without these features, text will be **monospaced.**

Advanced users often make use of customizing options within their word processors. Also, such users are likely to take advantage of many of the following types of activities: using **macros,** working with a **merge feature** and a **mailing label feature, redlining,** and outlining. Today's word processors offer many desktop publishing features—such as **clip-art** libraries, **watermarks, drop caps,** shading and borders, and tables. **Style sheets** automate formatting choices, possibly in combination with **templates** and **wizards.** Several advanced capabilities help users produce more complex documents: index- and table-of-contents-preparation routines, and working with **add-on programs** such as **reference shelves.**

Desktop Publishing Software **Desktop publishing** refers to desktop PCs that let you combine on a page such elements as text (in a variety of fonts), art, and photos, thus creating attractive documents that look as if they came off a professional printer's press. Whereas word processing programs will enable you to do a respectable amount of desktop publishing, desktop publishing programs immerse you into heavy-duty *typesetting* and *imagesetting.*

Professional-level desktop publishing systems are commonly configured with the following hardware and software components at a minimum. Hardware includes a high-end PC, a laser printer (which is used in concert with a specific **page-description language** or **PDL),** a graphics-oriented monitor with an extra-large screen, and an image scanner. Software components include **page-makeup software,** an **illustration program**—such as *painting, drawing,* and *photo* programs—font libraries, and image, video, and sound libraries.

EXERCISES

1. Fill in the blanks:
   a. A word processor's _____ feature automatically places a soft return at the end of each screen line.
   b. _____ is a word processing feature that allocates more horizontal space on a line to some characters than to others.
   c. WYSIWYG is an acronym for _____.
   d. A document with margins aligned at both right and left conforms to _____ justification.
   e. Stored art images used in a desktop publishing environment are referred to as _____.

2. Match each term with the description that fits best:
   a. zoom feature   d. spelling checker
   b. redlining   e. macro
   c. drop cap   f. reference shelf

   _____ A predetermined series of keystrokes or commands that can be invoked by a single keystroke or command

   _____ A feature that highlights changes when one person edits another's written work

   _____ A capability that magnifies onscreen elements

   _____ An example of an add-on program

   _____ A feature that helps to give text a typeset-quality look

   _____ An operation you would use in a word processing program to quickly change the string *MISSIPPI* to *MISSISSIPPI*

3. What differences distinguish the following pairs of terms?
   a. Monospacing and proportional spacing
   b. Insert mode and overstrike mode
   c. Template and wizard
   d. Typeface and font
   e. Copying and moving

4. Define, in your own words, the following terms:
   a. WYSIWYG
   b. Ruler line
   c. Insertion point
   d. Preview feature
   e. Merge feature

5. What is a reference shelf? Name at least three types of resources that you would expect to find in a reference-shelf package.

6. Make the following distinctions between software for word processing and desktop publishing:
   a. Why is it sometimes difficult to distinguish word processing from desktop publishing?
   b. What can you do with a desktop publishing program that you can't do with a word processing program?
   c. Name at least three word processing programs and the companies that make each one.
   d. Name at least three desktop publishing programs and the companies that make each one.

7. Which word processing feature would you use to accomplish each of the following tasks?
   a. Increase the size of text on the screen
   b. Make the first letter of an article very large, wrapping ensuing text around the letter
   c. Import small pieces of art—like the French flag or a globe icon—into a document
   d. Prepare a mass mailing of 1,000 copies of a letter from a list of names and addresses
   e. Edit a document that someone else wrote, with your comments, insertions, and deletions appearing onscreen in a different color than that of the author's work
   f. Place a lightly shaded picture of a flower under the text of a letter you are sending to someone special
   g. Consult an online dictionary or atlas while writing a letter in a word processing program
   h. Create a calendar with your word processor by answering questions in a series of dialog boxes

8. Match the terms with the pictured elements:
   _____ Watermark   _____ Bit-mapped font
   _____ Outline font   _____ Clip art
   _____ Drop cap

   a.

   b.

   c.

   d.

   e.

PROJECTS

1. **What Is Your Opinion?** The following statements call for an opinion. Please provide your ideas, confining your comments on each statement to a single page.
   a. Spelling checkers provide their greatest benefits to people who can spell reasonably well.
   b. Now that people can do relatively sophisticated desktop publishing with ordinary word processing programs, the professional typesetting and print shop has very little commercial future.
   c. Word processing technology causes as many problems in companies as it provides benefits.
   d. Word processing has resulted in people writing better.

2. **Using a Wizard to Create a Job Résumé** Many word processing programs—such as Microsoft Word, Corel WordPerfect, and Lotus Word-Pro—contain wizard software that enables people to create attractive-looking résumés for seeking jobs.
   a. Using the word processing software available at your school, create a résumé that includes your name, address, and phone number, as well as your job objective, work experience, and education.
   b. Create an attractive cover letter to send with the résumé. Many wizards that produce résumés also have a routine for preparing cover letters.

Résumé and cover letter

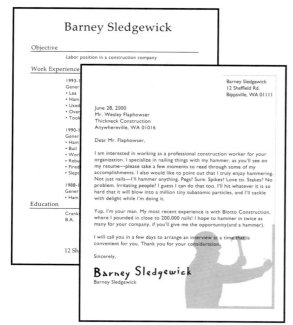

3. **The Word Processing Software at Your School** For the word processing program on your own computer or that available on the computers in your school's PC lab, describe how to do the following tasks:
   a. Change from single-spacing to double-spacing
   b. Summon the thesaurus feature
   c. Preview a document before printing it
   d. Change from full to left justification
   e. Change the typeface and point size on a printed document
   f. Create a two-column text page
   g. Insert a watermark behind a text page
   h. Insert a piece of clip art into a text page
   i. Change a printed-page orientation from portrait ($8\frac{1}{2}$ by 11 inches) to landscape (11 by $8\frac{1}{2}$ inches)
   j. Create a style sheet
   k. Mark your place in a document with a bookmark
   l. Direct the software to automatically insert the current date

4. **Electronic Design and Publishing** Many electronic design and publishing companies maintain Web sites that tell about their products, provide evaluation versions of programs, give hints for using the products, and so on. Visit the site of a company that makes desktop publishing software, illustration software, fonts, clip art, or digital photography software and answer the following questions:
   a. What are the names of the products made by the company whose site you visited?
   b. Can you download for evaluation any of the products you found in part a? If so, what are the evaluation period and the purchase cost of the software?
   c. What other types of information—other than that on specific products—did you find at the site?

   Hint: Here are some Web addresses to get you started.

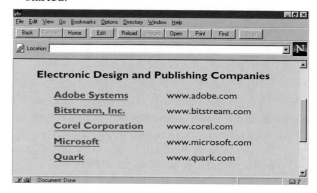

5. The Good, the Bad, and the Ugly The popularity of desktop publishing in recent years has made it possible for people of all types to create documents with a particular flair. In many cases, people who are not professional designers have a good eye for arranging text and art elements on a page; in other cases, they don't. For this project, look through periodicals or journals for at least two examples of advertisements that are well designed and at least two examples of advertisements that are poorly designed. List your reasons why each ad is well or poorly designed.

Note: You should have no trouble finding examples. Look especially to style-conscious, mass-market magazines for exceptionally designed ads and to local publications with small circulations for cheesy-looking ads. Alternatively, if the Internet is available to your class, your instructor may choose to have you do this exercise by evaluating well-designed and poorly designed Web pages.

6. New Key Terms A textbook of this sort cannot cover every importat technology or term regarding word processing and desktop publishing. Several important terms are listed below that are not covered in the chapter. Consult either library journals or Internet resources to determine what any three of these terms or pairs mean, and write out an explanation one-to-three-sentences long describing each one in your own words.

  a. Orphans and widows
  b. Hard page break and soft page break
  c. Footnotes and endnotes
  d. Dingbats
  e. Pantone colors

7. Researching a Word Processor You can find out a great deal of information about any particular word processing program by finding a book about it or by cruising the Internet. For the word processing program of your choice, complete the following project tasks:

  a. Visit a local bookstore and find up to three books about the word processing program you have chosen. Write down the name of each book, the name of the author and publisher, and the copyright date. If you can't find a bookstore with appropriate titles, consider visiting one online. Two large online bookstores are the Amazon Bookstore

        www.amazon.com

  and Fatbrain.com

        www.fatbrain.com

  b. For any of the books you have chosen in part a, write a short (one-to-two-page) reprt detailing the book's level of presentation (i.e., beginning or advanced), the topics it covers, and the features that appeal or don't appeal to you.

 8. Extending a Word Processor through the Web Software publishers regularly enhance their mainstream office products. Often, whenever they develop a new feature that may be useful to current users, they immediately make it available for free on the Web. For this project, visit the Web site of a word processing program—such as Word, WordPerfect, or WordPro—and compile a list of free features at the site that enhance the program's use.

9. Researching a Desktop Publishing Program The chapter text mentions several desktop publishing programs. Choose a particular version of one such program and answer the following questions about it. You may find some answers from information available on the Internet.

  a. What is the name of the program and who is its publisher?
  b. Does the version work on a PC-compatible platform or on the Macintosh platform (or both)? What is the most current version number of the program?
  c. How much RAM and hard-disk storage does the program require? How much does it recommend, if different?
  d. What is the suggested list price or street price of the program?
  e. Name at least two things the program you have chosen can do that your word processor cannot.

10. Researching an Illustration Program The chapter text mentions several illustration software packages. Choose a particular version of one such program and answer the following questions about it. You may find some answers from information available on the Internet.

  a. What is the name of the program, and who is its publisher?
  b. Does the version work on a PC-compatible platform or on the Macintosh platform (or both)? What is the most current version number of the program?
  c. How much RAM and hard-disk storage does the program require? How much does it recommend, if different?
  d. What is the suggested list price or street price of the program?
  e. Identify the types of duties—say, drawing, painting, photo editing, or creating special effects—that the program performs.

11. Styling a Document with Fonts Using the word processor available to your class, create the document shown in the accompanying figure as closely as possible.

Finch Investors Monthly Newsletter

Finch Investments • 330 High Rollers Plaza • Colorado Springs, CO 80903
Phone (719) 888-0000 • Fax (719) 888-0001

<u>March, 2000</u>

Hidey-ho, sports fans. My newsletter to you this month has only two items:

Market Analysis
The continuing demand for mutual funds continues to grow at a good clip, with new customers pouring in every month. Our analyses shows that this trend should continue for *at least* the next nine months.

Economic Report
According to information that our affiliate bureau has gathered, we believe that the following trends will continue:

1. The interest rate will remain steady. We see 2001 offering no surprises. But the year 2002 could be an entirely different story altogether. Due to the aging of baby boomers and an increasing need to import certain types of goods from overseas, inflation could roar again.

2. The budget deficit will continue to be reduced. Again, this is not much of a surprise from the earlier forecasts we made.

3. Capital gains taxes are not likely to be reduced next year, despite what you hear in the news.

That's it for now. Bye, bye.

Chauncey Haverhill Finch III, Esq.
President and CEO

---

12. Digital Images Many people who desktop publish, who prepare multimedia CDs, or who make electronic presentations are regularly on the prowl for good digital images to feature in their work. Some of them turn to professional stock agencies to find what they need in the way of images—and to get it fast. Many such agencies exist on the Web; the accompanying table lists several. You can also find agencies by typing "stock photography" into the search box of a Web-based search engine.

For this project, visit the Web site of a digital-media-stock company and report the following to your classmates.

a. What types of photographic or video materials are available? How large are the collections of images?

b. What does the company charge for its offerings?

c. How easy is it to examine images on the Web versus looking at them in a hard-cover book or on a CD-ROM?

Sites for Acquiring Digital Images	
Fine West Photography	www.finewest.com
FoodPix	www.foodpix.com
The Free Graphics Store Archives	www.ausmall.com.au/ freegraf/freegrfa.htm
PhotoDisc	www.photodisc.com
The Time Machine	www.timelapse.com

ONLINE REVIEW

Go to the Online Review at www.harcourtcollege.com/infosys/parker2000/ student/ to test your understanding of this chapter's concepts.

PS 2

SPREADSHEETS AND PRESENTATION GRAPHICS

OUTLINE

LEARNING OBJECTIVES

After completing this chapter, you will be able to:

1. Describe what spreadsheet packages do and how they work.

2. Identify the basic operations you must master to use spreadsheet software effectively.

3. Explain the use of several intermediate and advanced spreadsheet features.

4. Describe what presentation graphics are and how they are created.

OVERVIEW

Today, one of the most important programs that *any* businessperson should learn—whether he or she is a manager, an analyst, a secretary, or a sales representative—is *electronic spreadsheets.* Spreadsheet software is to the current generation of businesspeople what the pocket calculator was to previous generations—a convenient means of performing calculations. But while most pocket calculators can compute and display only one result each time new data are entered, electronic spreadsheets can present you with hundreds or even thousands of results each time you enter a single new value or command. What spreadsheets can do and how they work are two of the primary subjects of this chapter.

From our discussion of spreadsheets we'll move on to presentation graphics software and hardware, which are designed to present business data, or the results of business analysis or computations, in a visually oriented, easily understood way. This class of business products is easy to learn and use. Most spreadsheets are equipped with built-in presentation graphics features and tools. Also, many dedicated presentation graphics programs, which enable you to produce even more types of presentations than those possible with spreadsheets, are commercially available.

Web Tutor

For a tutorial on spreadsheet software, go to www. harcourtcollege.com/infosys/ parker2000/student/tutor/ and click on Chapter PS 2.

SPREADSHEETS

An electronic **spreadsheet** program produces computerized counterparts to the ruled ledger-style worksheets commonly associated with accountants (see Figure PS 2-1). Electronic spreadsheets first came to public notice in the late 1970s when a Harvard Business School student named Dan Bricklin and a programmer friend produced a microcomputer package called *VisiCalc* (short for "*Visi*ble *Calc*ulator"). Bricklin conceived the idea while watching his accounting professor erase large chunks of blackboard computations every time a single number changed in an interdependent series of calculations. Awed by the amount of repetitive labor involved in such basic updating, Bricklin quickly saw the vast potential benefit of computerized worksheets.

Today, VisiCalc is gone from the scene, having been eclipsed by newer, better products. The leading spreadsheets currently available for PCs include Microsoft's Excel (see the Inside the Industry box on page PS 38), Lotus Development's 1-2-3, and Corel's Quattro Pro. All of these products are components of office-software suites, and users work with graphical user interfaces that are remarkably similar to those of the word processor components of those suites.

HOW SPREADSHEETS WORK

Here we discuss how spreadsheets organize information as well as some of the principles by which spreadsheets work.

The Anatomy of a Worksheet In electronic spreadsheets, the display screen is viewed as a *window* looking in on a big grid, called a **worksheet.** Most major spreadsheet programs allow worksheets that consist of thousands of *rows* and a couple of hundred *columns*. Microsoft Excel 2000 worksheets, for instance, can encompass a maximum of 65,536 rows and 256 columns.

■ **Spreadsheet.** A productivity software program that supports quick creation and manipulation of tables and financial schedules. ■ **Worksheet.** The computerized counterpart to the ruled paper ledgers commonly associated with accountants.

Each of the 16,777,216 (65,536 × 256) **cells** formed by the intersection of a row and a column may contain text, a number, or a formula. Each cell can be accessed through a **cell address,** such as B4 or E223.

In most commercial spreadsheet programs, columns are identified by letters, rows by numbers, and each cell by a letter-and-number pair. For example, Cell B4—highlighted with a pointer in Figure PS 2-1—is found at the intersection of Column B and Row 4. Of course, the display screen is too small to permit the viewing of more than a few rows and columns at any give time. However, users can press certain cursor-movement keys on the keyboard or use the horizontal and vertical scroll bars to move the worksheet window around, letting them view other portions of the worksheet through it.

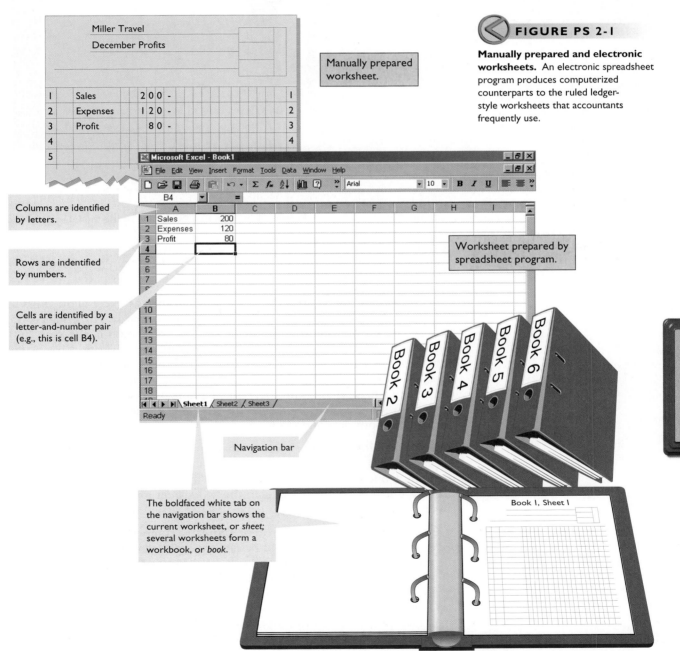

Manually prepared worksheet.

FIGURE PS 2-1

Manually prepared and electronic worksheets. An electronic spreadsheet program produces computerized counterparts to the ruled ledger-style worksheets that accountants frequently use.

Columns are identified by letters.

Rows are indentified by numbers.

Cells are identified by a letter-and-number pair (e.g., this is cell B4).

Worksheet prepared by spreadsheet program.

Navigation bar

The boldfaced white tab on the navigation bar shows the current worksheet, or *sheet;* several worksheets form a workbook, or *book.*

■ **Cell.** The part of the worksheet that can hold a single value or formula; defined by the intersection of a row and a column. ■ **Cell address.** The column/row combination that uniquely identifies a spreadsheet cell.

Easter Eggs

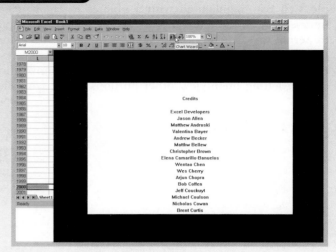

Programmers who develop some of the world's most popular software often place their stamps on those products by implanting "Easter eggs" in the program's code. Easter eggs display splashy screens, animations, and even multimedia productions, more often than not to credit the developers for the long hours they spent bringing the programs to market. To find an Easter egg, you need to press a secret sequence of keys—usually a cryptic chain that an unwitting user of the software is not likely to stumble on when using the program.

One fairly recent Easter egg is contained in Microsoft's Excel 2000 spreadsheet program. To find it, you need to complete the following sequence:

1. Open Excel with a fresh, blank worksheet.
2. Press function key F5 (Go To), type the range X2000:L2000, and press Enter (you should now be on row 2000).
3. Press the Tab key, which will put you in cell M2000.
4. Hold down the Shift and Ctrl keys while clicking on the Chart Wizard button on the toolbar at the top of the screen.

Within a few moments, the list of Excel 2000 developers will scroll by. Exit by tapping the Esc key.

Project 11 on page PS 64 tells how to use the Internet to find other Easter eggs.

Worksheets and Workbooks Many programs, such as Excel, allow users to store related worksheets in a single file called a *workbook.* For instance, the 12 worksheets containing profit statements for each month in the year 2001 can form one workbook. You can use the tabs on the navigation bar at the bottom of the screen (see Figure PS 2-1) to select worksheets within a workbook. From left to right on the bar are several tabs labeled *Sheet 1, Sheet 2,* and so on ("Sheet" is for "Worksheet"), and a horizontal scroll bar that lets you move across the current worksheet to see other columns. Worksheet pages can contain both data and graphs.

The Worksheet Screen Each worksheet screen, as you can see from Figure PS 2-2, is divided into two main areas: a *control panel* and a *worksheet area.* In a nutshell, the control panel is where you select commands and prepare entries for the worksheet; the worksheet area contains the worksheet itself.

THE CONTROL PANEL The **control panel** is comprised of four principal areas, three of which you should be familiar with from previous chapters. At the top of the screen, the *title bar* displays the name of the workbook—"Book 1" in the figure. Below the title bar are the *menu bar* and *toolbars.* The commands on the menu bar and toolbars are like the ones you will see in a word processor that is part of the same office suite; they let you do such things as open files, preview and print files, save files, check spelling, apply fonts, zoom in or out, and so on.

■ **Control panel.** The portion of the screen display used for issuing commands and observing what is being typed into the computer system.

The contents of the current cell display in the contents box.

The formula bar lets you enter worksheet data.

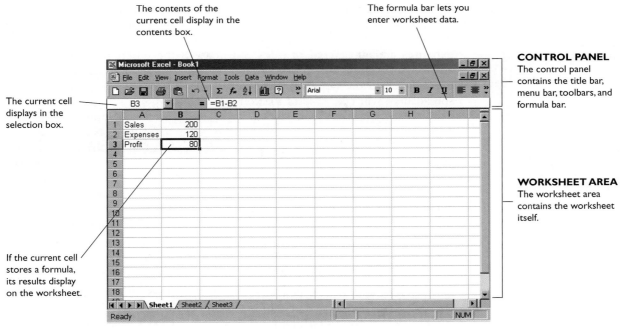

The current cell displays in the selection box.

If the current cell stores a formula, its results display on the worksheet.

CONTROL PANEL
The control panel contains the title bar, menu bar, toolbars, and formula bar.

WORKSHEET AREA
The worksheet area contains the worksheet itself.

FIGURE PS 2-2

An electronic spreadsheet at work.

The final element of the control panel is the *formula bar,* or *edit line.* The formula bar serves several functions, but most important are the two white areas on it. One is the *selection box* that displays the address of the current cell, and the other is the *contents box,* where you can enter what you want placed into the current cell, as well as edit those contents at a later time. The **current cell** is the worksheet cell that can be edited or data can be entered into. There can only be one current cell at any one time; you can always tell which cell is current by looking at the selection box.

THE WORKSHEET AREA   The worksheet itself is displayed in the part of the screen called the **worksheet area,** or **window area.** One important element in the worksheet area is the **cell pointer,** sometimes called the **highlight** or simply the *pointer.* The cell pointer highlights the current cell. As you can see in Figure PS 2-2, the current cell (as indicated in the selection box in the control panel and the highlight in the worksheet area) is Cell B3.

In many spreadsheets, as you are entering data into a worksheet cell, the data you are typing in appear both in the cell and in the contents box. When you finish entering the data in that cell, the cell will contain either the original data you entered or—if you had entered a formula—the formula result. In the figure, the formula =B1−B2 (subtract the contents of Cell B2 from the contents of Cell B1) was typed into the contents box, yielding a result of 80 in the current cell, Cell B3. As you move to the next empty cell, the cell's coordinates appear in the selection box and the contents box clears.

Remember, the worksheet area may not be large enough to show the whole worksheet at a single glance, but you can scroll the window to see other parts of the worksheet if you desire. *Scrolling* is similar to moving a magnifying glass over a large map; the movable glass acts like the window, while the underlying map acts like the worksheet. You can scroll the worksheet a row or column at a time when the highlight is at the right or bottom edge of the screen and you tap one of the arrow keys. Keys such as Tab, Page Up, and Page Down let you scroll the worksheet in window-sized blocks, and you can use the scroll bars to scroll even faster.

■ **Current cell.** The worksheet cell at which the highlight is currently positioned. ■ **Worksheet area.** The portion of the screen that contains the window onto the worksheet. Also called the **window area.** ■ **Cell pointer.** A cursorlike mechanism used in the worksheet area to point to cells, thereby making them active. Also called the **highlight.**

Creating a Worksheet   Now that you are familiar with a few of the mechanics of spreadsheets, let's learn how to create a worksheet. In the worksheet shown in Figure PS 2-2, we are computing a business profit statement in which expenses are 60 percent of sales and profit is the difference between sales and expenses. Here we will show how to enter the text and numbers used in the figure into the computer. We'll also look at some of the details that the spreadsheet will take care of for you.

Into each worksheet cell, you can type either a constant value or a formula. A **constant value** is a cell entry that consists of a text label (such as *Sales* or *James P. Jones*) or a numeric value (such as 200 or 215.1). A **formula,** in contrast, is an entry that performs a mathematical operation on the contents of other cells—such as =B1–B2 or =COUNT(B1:B6). COUNT is a special type of predefined formula called a *function*. We will be covering functions in more detail in a later section.

In the figure, we have entered—one at a time—the following six items into the appropriate cells:

> Cell A1: Sales (a constant value)
> Cell A2: Expenses (a constant value)
> Cell A3: Profit (a constant value)
> Cell B1: 200 (a constant value)
> Cell B2: =.6*B1 (a formula)
> Cell B3: =B12–B2 (a formula)

Since spreadsheet programs automatically assume that each entry beginning with a letter is a constant value, we had to type the formula in Cell B3 with an "=" in front of it.

As you input each cell entry, the spreadsheet software processes it and automatically displays the results on the worksheet. For Cells A1, A2, A3, and B1 in Figure PS 2-2, exactly what was typed is displayed. For Cells B2 and B3, the computer first makes the computations indicated by the formulas and then displays the results in the corresponding worksheet cells.

The Recalculation Feature   Electronic spreadsheets are particularly useful for **what-if analysis.** For example, suppose that you wish to know *what* profit will result in Figure PS 2-2 *if* sales change to $500. You can simply enter the new value, 500, into Cell B1, and the spreadsheet program will automatically recompute all the figures in the worksheet according to the prestored formulas. Thus, the computer responds as follows:

Sales	500
Expenses	300
Profit	200

In seconds, electronic spreadsheets can perform recalculations that would require several hours to do manually or by writing a program in a regular programming language. In fact, it's this easy-to-use **recalculation feature** that makes spreadsheets so popular. You can learn to prepare budgets and financial schedules with them after only a few hours of training. Another type of what-if analysis that is commonly found in modern spreadsheet packages today is *goal seeking,* in which the spreadsheet calculates how much of a cost or resource is needed at one or more points in time to produce a certain result.

■ **Constant value.** A cell entry that contains text or a numeric value. ■ **Formula.** A cell entry that is used to change the contents of other cells. ■ **What-if analysis.** An approach to problem solving in which the decision maker commands the computer system to recalculate a set of numbers based on alternative assumptions. ■ **Recalculation feature.** The ability of spreadsheet software to quickly and automatically recalculate the contents of several cells, based on new operator inputs.

Blocks of Cells: The Range Concept

Often, users need to be able to manipulate data in a set of contiguous cells, such as a row or column of several cells or any other rectangular-shaped block of cells. To do this in a spreadsheet program, you define a **range** of cells. Figure PS 2-3 shows four examples of valid ranges. You will generally have to declare ranges of cells when you want to print, move, copy, insert, delete, format, sort, or graph parts of the worksheet.

For instance, telling the spreadsheet program to print the range B4 through C6 (B4:C6) will result in the output of the three-by-two block of cells identified in Figure PS 2-3. Generally, a range can be declared by explicitly typing it into the control panel—for instance, you would type in all five characters in the string "B4:C6" to declare it as a range—or by selecting (highlighting) the range in the worksheet area using either the mouse or the Shift and arrow keys on the keyboard. In Excel, the colon character (:) is used to specify a range of cells; Lotus 1-2-3 and Quattro Pro, in contrast, use the period character (.).

Most spreadsheet programs contain some type of *autocomplete* feature that makes it easy to enter data into a range when the data conforms to a pattern (see Figure PS 2-4).

	A	B	C	D
1		42	13	21
2	25	A2:A4		
3	10			B1:D1
4	3	5	20	
5		10	25	
6	50	15	30	B4:C6
7		A6:A6		

ABOUT RANGES
A range can be as small as a single cell or as large as a grid with a couple of hundred cells on each side.

FIGURE PS 2-3

The range concept. A range is defined as any rectangular block of cells.

FIGURE PS 2-4

Using an autocomplete feature to fill a range automatically.

PROFIT STATEMENT						
	January	February	March	April	May	June
SALES	$10,570	$12,740	$14,010			
EXPENSES						
Payroll	$4,700	$4,950	$5,220			
Materials	$3,000	$3,120	$3,375			
Rent	$1,500	$1,500	$1,500			
Total	$9,200	$9,570	$10,095			
PROFIT	$1,370	$3,170	$3,915			

ABOUT AUTOCOMPLETE
If you have text labels or numbers that conform to a certain pattern, you can have your spreadsheet package fill in all but the first one or two automatically.

TEXT LABELS
A series of text labels can be generated by entering the first label, selecting it, and using the mouse to drag into cells that need to be filled.

January	February	March	April
Product 1	Product 2	Product 3	Product 4
1st Quarter	2nd Quarter	3rd Quarter	4th Quarter

NUMBER SERIES
A series of numbers can be generated by entering the first two numbers, selecting the two cells containing the numbers, and using the mouse to drag into cells that need to be filled.

2000	2001	2002	2003
1	2	3	4
10	20	30	40

■ **Range.** A set of contiguous cells arranged in a rectangle.

Formatting Cell Entries Many people wish to format the data in a worksheet in some manner. Virtually all spreadsheet programs automatically left-justify text labels in a worksheet cell and right-justify numbers. However, buttons on a formatting toolbar or some such mechanism make it possible for you to change this default alignment for a single cell or for any range of cells. Figure PS 2-5 shows how such buttons work.

Immediately to the right of the alignment buttons in the figure are buttons for applying special formats to numbers. Because spreadsheets are particularly useful for preparing financial schedules, it follows that many of the worksheet cells will contain values that represent monetary amounts. Buttons enable you to quickly put dollar signs, commas, and decimal points into these values. (For example, a single click might change "90000" to "$90,000.00".) Generally, all you have to do is identify the range of cells that you want edited and select the options that automatically insert the proper symbols in the proper places. You can usually add percent signs (%) through an equally straightforward process.

In addition to the basic types of formatting described here, there are several other methods you can use to give your worksheets an exciting look. Font styling, borders, and colors are briefly described in the figure. In a later subsection we will look at other, more advanced formatting methods.

Functions Spreadsheet programs typically contain a couple of hundred or so built-in functions that enable you to create formulas for a wide range of applications, including those in the fields of business, science, and engineering. A **function** invokes a prestored formula (such as that for calculating net present value) or a preset value (such as today's date). Figure PS 2-6 describes some useful functions and shows how a few of them are used. You can learn

FIGURE PS 2-5

Formatting cell entries. Shown here are the uses of command buttons on the formatting toolbar.

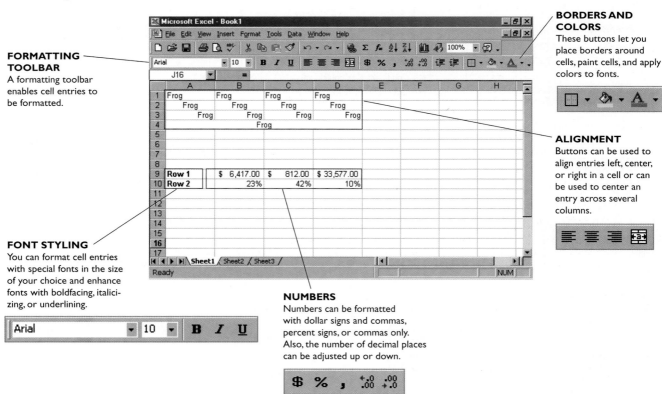

BORDERS AND COLORS
These buttons let you place borders around cells, paint cells, and apply colors to fonts.

FORMATTING TOOLBAR
A formatting toolbar enables cell entries to be formatted.

ALIGNMENT
Buttons can be used to align entries left, center, or right in a cell or can be used to center an entry across several columns.

FONT STYLING
You can format cell entries with special fonts in the size of your choice and enhance fonts with boldfacing, italicizing, or underlining.

NUMBERS
Numbers can be formatted with dollar signs and commas, percent signs, or commas only. Also, the number of decimal places can be adjusted up or down.

■ **Function.** A prestored formula for a standard calculation.

EXAMPLES OF FUNCTIONS

SUM (range)	Calculates the sum of all values in a range
MAX (range)	Finds the highest value in a range
MIN (range)	Finds the lowest value in a range
COUNT (range)	Counts the number of nonempty cells in a range
AVERAGE (range)	Calculates the average of values in a range
ABS (cell or expression)	Calculates the absolute value of the argument
PV (period payment, rate, number of payments)	Calculates the present value of an annuity at a specified interest rate
IF (conditional expression, value if true, value if false)	Supplies to a cell a value that depends on whether the conditional expression is true or false

ABOUT FUNCTIONS

A function is a prestored formula. Major spreadsheets have a couple of hundred or more functions.

EXAMPLES OF USING FUNCTIONS

	A	B	C	D
1	10	5	15	20
2	6	7	3	4
3	8	2	9	4
4	−1	0	3	15

SUM (A1:D1) = 50
MIN (A1:D4) = −1
MAX (A1:D4) = 20
AVERAGE (A1:D1) = 12.5
ABS (A4) = 1
COUNT (A1:D4) = 16
IF (A4 < 0, 10, 20) = 10

FIGURE PS 2-6

Spreadsheet functions.

more about functions either by summoning the online help feature in your spreadsheet software or by using an online function wizard. The function wizard, which can be accessed from the toolbar, or from the formula bar in many spreadsheet programs when you activate a special command, gives you step-by-step instructions on how to enter data for any function.

BASIC OPERATIONS

Spreadsheets offer numerous command options that help users to enter and edit data. The following paragraphs review a sampling of the most important features (see also Figure PS 2-7).

Inserting and Deleting Virtually all spreadsheet programs allow you to insert a new column or row in a worksheet. Also, you can delete a column or row that you no longer need. Generally, inserting or deleting involves moving the cell pointer to the appropriate position on the worksheet and issuing the proper command from the menu bar. Figure PS 2-7a illustrates inserting a blank row.

Copying Virtually all spreadsheets include commands that enable you to copy the contents of one cell (or several cells) into another cell (or several others). Such commands usually require that you first specify the *source range* that contains the data you want to copy and then the *destination range* that will receive the copied data.

If you are going to copy cells that contain formulas, you generally will need to specify when you type in the formulas whether you want the cell references in each formula to be relative, absolute, or mixed. Copying with each of these three types of cell references is illustrated in Figures PS 2-7b, PS 2-7c, and PS 2-7d, respectively.

(a) **Inserting a row.** Both inserting and deleting involve moving the cell pointer to the appropriate position in the worksheet and issuing the proper command.

	A	B	C	D
1		Jan	Feb	
2	Revenue	300	500	
3	Expenses	200	450	
4	Profit	100	50	
5				
6				
7				

Before insertion

	A	B	C	D
1		Jan	Feb	
2					← New row
3	Revenue	300	500	
4	Expenses	200	450	
5	Profit	100	50	
6				
7				

After insertion

(b) **Copying with relative cell references.** In most formulas, cell addresses are relative unless otherwise specified.

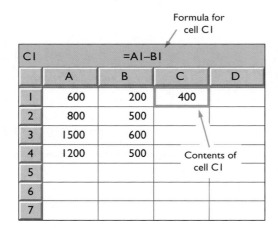

Formula for cell C1

C1			=A1−B1	
	A	B	C	D
1	600	200	400	
2	800	500		
3	1500	600		
4	1200	500	Contents of cell C1	
5				
6				
7				

Before copy operation

Copy from: C1:C1		Copy to: C2:C4		
	A	B	C	D
1	600	200	400	
2	800	500	300	
3	1500	600	900	
4	1200	500	700	
5				
6				
7				

Results when C1 formula is copied into cells C2, C3, and C4

After copy operation

(continued on next page)

FIGURE PS 2-7

Entering and editing operations.

RELATIVE CELL REFERENCES When **relative cell references** are used, the cell references in each copied formula are adjusted relative to the row and column coordinates of the destination range. For example, in Figure PS 2-7b, say that you want the value of each cell in Column C to equal the corresponding Column A entry minus the corresponding Column B entry. In other words, you want

$$C1 = A1−B1$$
$$C2 = A2−B2$$
$$C3 = A3−B3$$
$$C4 = A4−B4$$

Generally you can do this in a typical spreadsheet program by placing the cell pointer at C1 and typing

$$=A1−B1$$

or something very similar. You then copy this formula into Cells C2:C4. Many formulas in a spreadsheet need only relative cell references.

■ **Relative cell referencing.** Copying formulas in a source range of cells into a target range of cells relative to the row and column coordinates of the cells in the target range.

(c) **Copying with absolute cell references.** Using absolute cell references involves marking each column and row reference in the cell address with a dollar ($) sign. All absolute references will be copied exactly as they appear in the source cell.

Formula for
cell C1

C1		=A1−B1		
	A	B	C	D
1	600	200	400	
2	800	500		
3	1500	600		
4	1200	500		
5				
6				
7				

Contents of
cell C1

Before copy operation

Copy from:C1:C1		Copy to:C2:C4		
	A	B	C	D
1	600	200	400	
2	800	500	400	
3	1500	600	400	
4	1200	500	400	
5				
6				
7				

Results when C1
formula is copied
into cells C2, C3,
and C4

After copy operation

(d) **Copying with mixed cell references.** Using mixed cell references involves putting a dollar ($) sign in front of each column or row you wish to fix in place.

Formula for
cell B4

B4		(1+B$3)^$A4			
	A	B	C	D	E
1		Future sum computations			
2					
3	Years	10.0%	10.5%	11.0%	11.5%
4	1	1.100			
5	2				
6	3				
7	4				
8	5				

Before copy operation

Results when B4
formula is copied
into range B4:E8

Copy from:B4:B4		Copy to:B4:E8			
	A	B	C	D	E
1		Future sum computations			
2					
3	Years	10.0%	10.5%	11.0%	11.5%
4	1	1.100	1.105	1.110	1.115
5	2	1.210	1.221	1.232	1.243
6	3	1.331	1.349	1.368	1.386
7	4	1.464	1.491	1.518	1.546
8	5	1.611	1.647	1.685	1.723

After copy operation

(continued on next page)

ABSOLUTE CELL REFERENCES   In the previous example, had you used **absolute cell references** in the formula instead, the spreadsheet package would have copied the formula verbatim into all four cells, leaving the expression

$$=A1−B1$$

with a result of 400 in each one (see Figure PS 2-7c). Absolute referencing provides an ideal tool when a computation yields a constant result that you want to repeat in a range of cells. Any or all cell references in a formula may be made absolute.

To make a cell reference in a formula absolute, dollar signs must be placed before each row number and column letter. For example, to change both of the cell references to absolute references, the formula in the source cell in Figure PS 2-7b would be rewritten in the form

$$=\$A\$1−\$B\$1$$

■ **Absolute cell referencing.** Copying verbatim the contents in one range of cells into another range of cells.

(e) **Moving a row.** When the contents of a block (range) of cells are moved, they are "cut" out of one area of the worksheet and "pasted" into another of identical size.

	A	B	C	D
1	Name	Hours	Rate	Pay
2	Jones	10	$6.00	$60.00
3	Smith	40	$7.00	$280.00
4	Zimmer	20	$4.00	$80.00
5	Able	30	$3.00	$90.00
6				
7	Total			$510.00

Before move operation

	A	B	C	D
1	Name	Hours	Rate	Pay
2	Able	30	$3.00	$90.00
3	Jones	10	$6.00	$60.00
4	Smith	40	$7.00	$280.00
5	Zimmer	20	$4.00	$80.00
6				
7	Total			$510.00

After move operation

(f) **Freezing titles.** Freezing titles allows you to keep certain columns or rows of the worksheet in place while you are scrolling to other parts of it.

	A	B	C
1	Class: CIS 210, COBOL 1		
2	Student name	Exam	Exam
3		1	2
4	- - - - - - - - - - - - -	- - - - -	- - - - -
5	Alice Adams	60	55
6	Bob Andrew	85	92
7	Greg Andujar	88	82

Original window

	A	B	C
1	Class: CIS 210, COBOL 1		
2	Student name	Exam	Exam
3		1	2
4	- - - - - - - - - - - - -	- - - - -	- - - - -
69	Ed James	61	75
70	Jim Jones	80	97
71	Mary Jones	98	85

Scrolled worksheet with frozen titles

Title rows ↔

(g) **Using templates.** The worksheet at the left contains both the blank template and the formulas to calculate the table amounts at the right (once the user supplies the interest rate, principal, and the number of years).

	A	B	C	D
1	Interest rate			
2	Principal			
3	Number of years			
4	- - - - - -	- -		
5	Year	Begin Bal.	Interest	Total
6	1		$0.00	$0.00
7	2		$0.00	$0.00

Blank template

	A	B	C	D
1	Interest rate		10%	
2	Principal		$100	
3	Number of years		10	
4	- - - - - -	- -		
5	Year	Begin Bal.	Interest	Total
6	1	$100.00	$10.00	$110.00
7	2	$110.00	$11.00	$121.00

Filled-in template

FIGURE PS 2-7

continued

MIXED CELL REFERENCES Most spreadsheet programs also allow **mixed cell references**—a combination of absolute and relative references—in which a

■ **Mixed cell referencing.** Copying formulas in one range of cells into another range while varying some cell references and leaving others constant.

row value can be kept constant while a column value is allowed to vary (or vice versa). Mixed cell referencing provides an especially useful tool for handling formulas in which two parameters change. As the first parameter varies across columns (while the second stays constant), the second parameter varies across rows (while the first stays constant).

Figure PS 2-7d shows using mixed cell references when computing interest at varying interest rates. Note that interest rate and years are the two parameters in Cell B4. For each column, we want to keep the interest rate (in Row 3) fixed as we vary the year from one to five. For each row, we want to keep the year (in Column A) fixed as we vary the interest rate from 10 to 11.5 percent. To allow us to do this by copying the formula in Cell B4 (instead of retyping the formula in each cell on the worksheet), we put a dollar sign ($) in front of the coordinate that we want to fix; thus, the formula in the source cell must be written as

$$(1+B\$3)^{\wedge}\$A4$$

Moving   Virtually all spreadsheet programs enable you to move any row or column into another row or column position on the worksheet. As with the Copy command, you will need to specify a source range (the range you're moving from) and a destination range (the range you're moving to).

For example, suppose you decide to move Row 5 into the Row 2 position, as in Figure PS 2-7e. When moving, the software automatically makes all cell references point to the new worksheet locations. If your spreadsheet program also lets you move or copy larger areas, as most do, you will be able to move, say, a contiguous 20-by-40 block of cells from one part of the worksheet to another.

Freezing Titles   A spreadsheet program typically provides a Titles feature that allows you to freeze a portion of the worksheet in place on the screen as you scroll the rest. For example, if the Titles feature were to freeze the first four rows of Figure PS 2-7f, you could use the down arrow key or Page Down key to scroll through data cells while the titles remained in place on the screen. When you freeze rows, you work with a horizontally split screen. You can also freeze columns, resulting in a vertically split screen. Most programs allow you to freeze certain rows and certain columns at the same time.

Using Templates   In the world of spreadsheets, a **template** is a worksheet in which rows and columns are prelabeled and many cells already contain formulas. Only the data are missing. Thus, much of the work involved in setting up the worksheet has already been done, leaving you more time to enter and analyze data. A template is shown in Figure PS 2-7g. In many spreadsheet programs, it is also possible to protect cells on a template or other spreadsheet, such as those that contain the template's text labels and formulas.

Changing Column Widths and Row Heights   Most spreadsheet programs allow you to adjust the widths of columns and the heights of rows in a worksheet (see Figure PS 2-8). You can often assign a width to each column individually, or you can select a single global width that applies to all columns. In many programs, you can specify that long text labels should either spill over into adjacent columns to the right, provided those cells are empty, or wrap within the cell. Individual columns and rows can often be resized by placing the mouse pointer on the border between two column or row identifiers (e.g., between A and B on the bar that contains the column letters) and, when the pointer changes to a sizing arrow, dragging with a mouse in the desired direction.

Dressing Up Worksheets   As has been mentioned already, through the formatting toolbar you can change the typeface or point size of any cell or cell

---

■ **Template.** An onscreen form that requires only that the operator fill in a limited number of input values.

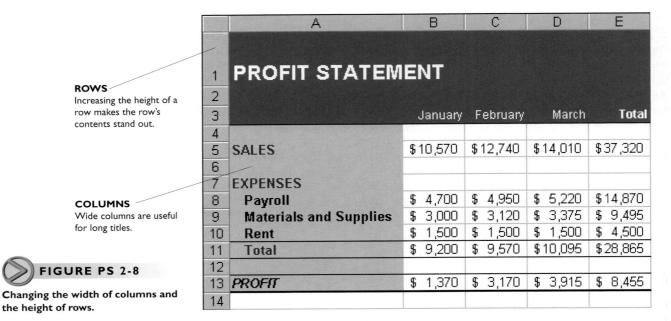

ROWS
Increasing the height of a row makes the row's contents stand out.

COLUMNS
Wide columns are useful for long titles.

FIGURE PS 2-8

Changing the width of columns and the height of rows.

range in your worksheet. You can also apply colors and borders through the same toolbar. As if these styling choices weren't enough, most spreadsheets contain a variety of other styling tools to make your worksheets even more attractive.

For instance, you can format your worksheet automatically by choosing among several different *autoformatting* styles. With autoformatting, the spreadsheet program analyzes your worksheet and automatically applies the format you select based on the position of headings, breaks, and data (see Figure PS 2-9). Other spreadsheet tools let you annotate cells with text or voice explanations, apply text boxes and pointers to circled values in cells, add logos and other graphics, and perform a variety of other styling touches.

Printing Worksheets   You print a worksheet in a way very similar to the way you print a word processed document—that is, you select the Print toolbar button or the Print subcommand from the File command on the menu bar, and you're in business. What's more, you can also preview your worksheets

FIGURE PS 2-9

Dressing up worksheets.

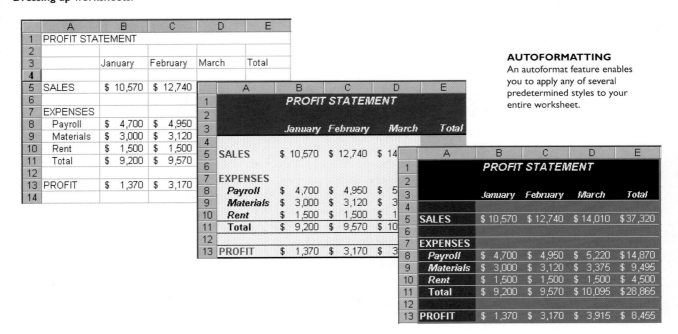

AUTOFORMATTING
An autoformat feature enables you to apply any of several predetermined styles to your entire worksheet.

before printing them out, using a zoom feature just like the one with your word processor. In addition, you can choose to print in portrait or landscape modes, print only certain ranges of cells, and have color screen outputs translated to suitable grayscales—a handy feature if you're going to be outputting graphs or maps on a standard laser printer.

INTERMEDIATE AND ADVANCED FEATURES

In addition to the basic operations covered so far, many leading spreadsheet programs offer rich selections of intermediate and advanced features. Four such features often help spreadsheet users with their work: a facility for sorting records, a facility for filtering records, a pivot-table feature, and a presentation-graphics feature. The following paragraphs discuss the first three features. The last section of the chapter then covers presentation graphics.

Sorting Records   A *sort feature* provides handy benefits in almost any type of business software. With a spreadsheet, a person might use such a tool for preparing phone directories and ordering listings of overdue accounts, student grade books, and reports identifying fast-moving or high-selling products. Virtually all spreadsheet programs allow you to sort on more than one field. Many people who sort also like to perform *control breaks,* showing a subtotal each time the value of the sort (control) field changes (breaks). When the report is finished, a grand total is taken on the control field. Figure PS 2-10 illustrates sorting records, as well as the use of control breaks.

Filtering Records   Each row in a worksheet often represents some type of record—for instance, an employee record that contains the name, hours worked, and pay rate of an employee (see Figure PS 2-7e). If the worksheet has hundreds or thousands of records, it's nice to have a *filtering feature* that will extract records based on criteria that you specify. For instance, you may wish to get the names of all students in a class that receive an *A* grade or a list of employees who are making more than $250 per week.

Pivot Tables   Many spreadsheet programs today contain a *pivot-table feature* that enables table data to be rearranged and viewed from other perspectives. For instance, the president of a company might want to see data broken down by region, while the sales manager might want to see totals on each product. Data views can be changed in seconds in many spreadsheet programs by summoning a pivot-table wizard and then selecting the row and column titles that are to form the new table. Figure PS 2-11 illustrates pivoting data in a table to provide a summary of some of the hidden information it contains.

For links to further information about spreadsheet software, go to www. harcourtcollege.com/infosys/ parker2000/student/explore/ and click on Chapter PS 2.

FIGURE PS 2-10

Sorting worksheet records.

1. ORIGINAL WORKSHEET
The records are in random order.

	A	B	C
1	Store	Region	Sales
2	25	North	$ 7,000
3	11	South	$ 4,000
4	23	South	$ 5,500
5	44	South	$ 3,850
6	15	North	$ 8,200
7	3	North	$ 4,690
8	18	South	$ 5,590
9	36	South	$ 3,700
10			
11			
12			

2. SIMPLE SORT
Records in the original file are sorted alphabetically on the Region column.

	A	B	C
1	Store	Region	Sales
2	25	North	$ 7,000
3	15	North	$ 8,200
4	3	North	$ 4,690
5	11	South	$ 4,000
6	23	South	$ 5,500
7	44	South	$ 3,850
8	18	South	$ 5,590
9	36	South	$ 3,700
10			
11			
12			

3. SUBTOTALED SORT
With the records properly sorted by Region, the Region column is selected for subtotaling. Subtotals are taken as each region breaks for a new one; also, a grand total is provided.

	A	B	C
1	Store	Region	Sales
2	25	North	$ 7,000
3	15	North	$ 8,200
4	3	North	$ 4,690
5		North Total	$ 19,890
6	11	South	$ 4,000
7	23	South	$ 5,500
8	44	South	$ 3,850
9	18	South	$ 5,590
10	36	South	$ 3,700
11		South Total	$ 22,640
12		Grand Total	$ 42,530

1. ORIGINAL WORKSHEET
The original worksheet contains too much data detail to spot useful information.

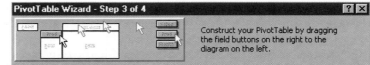

PivotTable Wizard - Step 3 of 4

Construct your PivotTable by dragging the field buttons on the right to the diagram on the left.

	A	B	C	D
1	**Salesperson**	**Order Amount**	**Order Date**	**Product**
2	Mitch Karnes	$ 236.40	2-Jan-98	Widgets
3	Lonnie Burns	$ 1,366.21	2-Jan-98	Widgets
4	Carlos Cora	$ 463.22	2-Jan-98	Sky Hooks
5	Mary Munster	$ 588.44	3-Jan-98	Thigamajigs
6	Carlos Cora	$ 744.33	3-Jan-98	Thigamajigs
7	Lonnie Burns	$ 82.44	3-Jan-98	Sky Hooks
8	Mary Munster	$ 555.89	3-Jan-98	Widgets
9	Carlos Cora	$ 145.90	3-Jan-98	Thigamajigs
10	Mitch Karnes	$ 487.33	3-Jan-98	Sky Hooks
11	Mary Munster	$ 668.32	3-Jan-98	Widgets
12	Lonnie Burns	$ 159.55	4-Jan-98	Sky Hooks
13	Mitch Karnes	$ 472.55	4-Jan-98	Widgets
14	Carlos Cora	$ 1,002.02	4-Jan-98	Thigamajigs
15				

2. PIVOT TABLE
A Pivot Table Wizard is used to summarize data. To tell the wizard how to prepare a summary, the field buttons at the right are dragged with a mouse to the table mockup at the left.

3. OUTPUT
The pivot table created in Step 2 shows how much of each product salespeople are selling and, also, provides column and row totals.

	G	H	I	J	K
16	Sum of Order Amount	Product			
17	Salesperson	Sky Hooks	Thingamajigs	Widgets	Grand Total
18	Carlos Cora	$ 463.22	$ 1,892.25		$ 2,355.47
19	Lonnie Burns	$ 241.99		$ 1,366.21	$ 1,608.20
20	Mary Munster		$ 588.44	$ 1,224.21	$ 1,812.65
21	Mitch Karnes	$ 487.33		$ 708.95	$ 1,196.28
22	Grand Total	$ 1,192.54	$ 2,480.69	$ 3,299.37	$ 6,972.60
23					

FIGURE PS 2-11

Creating a pivot table. Pivot tables are used to rearrange or combine worksheet data into a more useful form.

PRESENTATION GRAPHICS

If you try to explain to others what you look like, it may take several minutes. Show them a color photograph, on the other hand, and you can convey the same or better information about yourself within seconds. The saying "a picture is worth a thousand words" is the cornerstone of presentation graphics.

In this section we first look at the most traditional and still most common types of presentation graphics—text and still images presented in hard- or soft-copy slide form. From there we cover the increasingly popular multimedia presentation, in which voice and video components may be added to the mix of electronic materials. Web-based presentations are also addressed.

For a tutorial on presentation software, go to www. harcourtcollege.com/infosys/ parker2000/student/tutor/ and click on Chapter PS 2.

WHAT IS A PRESENTATION GRAPHIC?

A **presentation graphic**—sometimes called a *presentation visual* or *chart*—is an image that visually enhances the impact of information communicated to other people. Presentation graphics can take many different forms, a number of which are illustrated in Figure PS 2-12. With the right types of software and hardware, the creation of presentation graphics is limited only by one's imagination.

■ **Presentation graphic.** A visual image, such as a bar chart or pie chart, that is used to present data in a highly meaningful form.

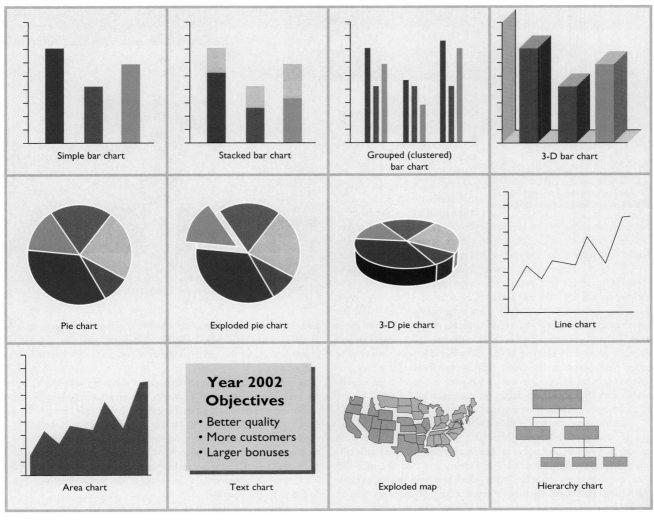

**FIGURE PS 2-12**

Sample presentation graphics.
Presentation graphics include various types of bar, pie, and line charts, as well as more complicated images.

There are several compelling reasons to use presentation graphics in business. A person can often spot trends or make comparisons much more quickly by looking at a visual image than by reading text-only or number-only output containing the same information. Furthermore, a point can often be made far more dramatically and effectively by using pictures. Recent studies have found that presentation graphics also make the presenter look more professional in the eyes of others.

Here, we'll discuss in detail four of the most widely used presentation graphics: bar charts, pie charts, line charts, and text charts. We'll also examine when each is most appropriate. The best graphic in any given situation ultimately depends on the point you are trying to make. Feature PS 2-1 describes the use of psychology in creating presentation visuals. Feature PS 2-2, on page PS 58, additionally explores the area of mapping graphics.

Bar Charts   **Bar charts,** or *column charts,* are useful for comparing relative magnitudes of items and for showing the frequency with which events occur. They can also illustrate changes in a single item over time. Several types of bar charts are available, including the simple bar chart, stacked bar chart, grouped bar chart, range chart, pictograph, and 3-D bar chart (refer again to Figure PS 2-12).

■ **Bar chart.** A presentation graphic that uses side-by-side columns as the principal charting element.

PS 2-1 FEATURE

Presentation Visuals and Psychology

Color, Simplicity, and Other Tricks of the Trade

Probably everyone watching a computer-prepared presentation has at one time or another been subjected to one that fails to do a good job. In some cases, the problem is complicated slides whose low quality is compounded by a speaker who is moving along too quickly. In others, it's a Web site whose colors inappropriately scream out and cause people to see double.

Choice of color is often a major culprit. Take background and foreground coloring. Some color combinations work well together; others do not. For instance, yellow or white text on a black background or dark text on a light background make for easy reading, while red and green together tend to bother most eyes. Red and green are also difficult for color-blind people to distinguish between. Blue on a black background is also a no-no; the retina has fewer blue receptors than receptors for the other primary colors, and these are located out of the focal area. In general, colors opposite each other on the color wheel work better as a combination than ones close together.

Cultural expectations should also play a role in choosing colors. In the United States, green and gold are associated with money and wealth, and red is said to link subliminally with risk taking. Financial services firms such as Fidelity and Merrill Lynch—it should come as no surprise—use green and gold heavily in their marketing literature, on their client-account statements, and at their Web sites. Gambling casinos, you may have noticed if you've ever gone inside one, strongly prefer reds.

The amount of information contained in a visual and the way it is organized are also extremely important. Too many facts and the

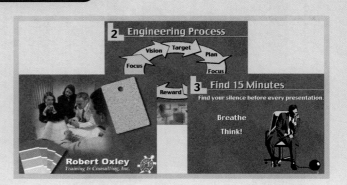

Think before you start. A soothing background color, common style and font, and simplicity make these slides effective.

audience can't absorb all of them. Many people will begin to lose interest, and some may even fall asleep or leave. What's more, making an audience move along at a fast pace can create stress and fatigue.

Timing is another factor that can make a big difference in the success of a presentation. With live presentations, audiences seem to better understand a pitch if they are given a few seconds to absorb each visual before the presenter addresses it. Research has shown that the information in a slide should be absorbed within 5 to 8 seconds. If not enough time is provided between the appearance of the slide and the speaker cutting in, the audience is forced into trying to comprehend the visual at the same time it is trying to listen to the speaker.

Designing and delivering a presentation are more of an art than a science. The best presenters take great pains to make their visuals as simple as possible and to learn as much as they can about their target audience before preparing the presentation.

As shown in Figure PS 2-13, each type of bar chart has strengths and weaknesses relative to prospective applications. A *range chart,* for instance, would be most useful for showing daily highs and lows of a particular stock in the stock market. A *grouped (clustered) bar chart,* on the other hand, would be more useful for showing something such as overall income comparisons for this year and last year by quarter. Grouped bar charts are especially effective when you want to emphasize a difference between two items over time. When one set of bars is consistently bigger than another set of bars, as is the case in the figure, a *stacked bar chart* can also effectively show the differences between the two sets of bars. A *Gantt chart* is particularly handy for showing when events in schedules begin and end.

In a typical bar chart, one axis represents a categorical or *qualitative* phenomenon; the other represents a numeric or *quantitative* one. Such features as grid lines, titles and legends, and attractive fonts can be effectively used to dress up a chart. Figure PS 2-14 illustrates some common elements of bar charts.

When designing bar charts, it's a good idea to keep the total number of categories on the x-axis to a half dozen or less. Any more than this may be too much information to cram into a single visual.

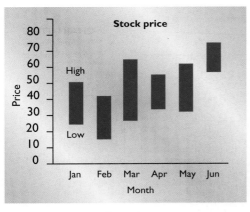

Range chart

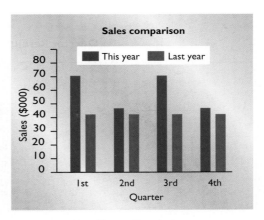

Grouped bar chart

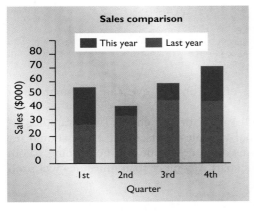

Stacked bar chart

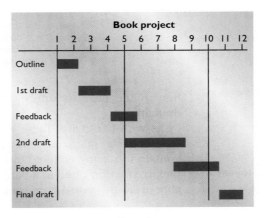

Gantt chart

Pie Charts   **Pie charts** are commonly used to show how parts of something relate to a whole (see Figure PS 2-15). Each slice of the "pie," or circle, represents its percentage share of the total. One of the major advantages of the pie chart is that it is extremely easy to understand.

Most presentation graphics packages enable you to "explode" a pie chart to emphasize one or more of the slices, as shown in the figure. The way a pie slice can be exploded varies from one software package to another. Some packages pull the slice out a fixed predefined distance. Others enable you to specify how far you would like to pull the slice out by using a mouse to select the slice on the screen and drag it to the place where you want it. Virtually all packages allow you to color or texture each of the pie slices as well, as is illustrated in the figure.

Pie charts should not have more than a half dozen or so slices. The more slices there are, the harder it is to recognize relative sizes of the shares they represent. When the number of slices in a pie chart becomes large, the smallest slices should be combined.

Line Charts   **Line charts** (see Figure PS 2-16) are somewhat similar to bar charts. One major difference, however, is that line charts are used in cases where *both* axes represent quantitative phenomena; often line charts illustrate trends over time. A second major difference is that, because the

FIGURE PS 2-13

Four bar charts. Bar charts are especially useful for comparing the relative magnitudes of items and for showing the frequency with which events occur.

■ **Pie chart.** A presentation graphic in which the principal charting element is a pie-shaped image that is divided into slices, each of which represents a share of the whole. ■ **Line chart.** A presentation graphic in which the principal charting element is an unbroken line.

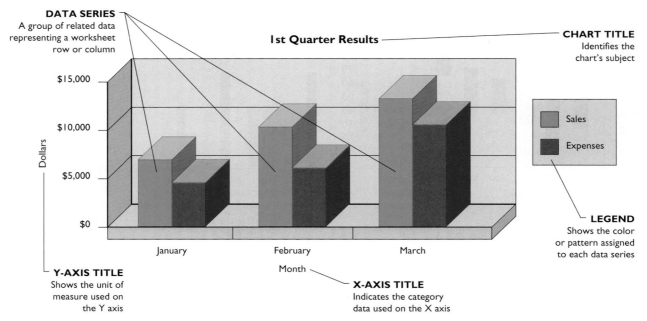

DATA SERIES
A group of related data representing a worksheet row or column

CHART TITLE
Identifies the chart's subject

LEGEND
Shows the color or pattern assigned to each data series

Y-AXIS TITLE
Shows the unit of measure used on the Y axis

X-AXIS TITLE
Indicates the category data used on the X axis

FIGURE PS 2-14

Elements of a bar chart.

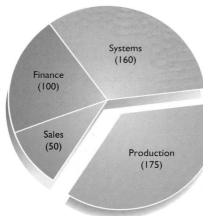

Number of employees (January)

FIGURE PS 2-15

Exploded pie chart. In an exploded pie chart, a single pie slice is moved out slightly from the rest of the pie to call attention to it.

line in the chart is unbroken, the effect on the eye can be much more dramatic.

As with bar charts, there is a rich variety of line charts. Two examples are shown in the figure. Also, as with bar and pie charts, a line chart should not contain too many graphed lines. Lines often cross one another, adding a complexity you don't find in a bar or pie chart. Any more than four lines will probably make the visual confusing.

Text Charts   Some researchers estimate that approximately 70 to 80 percent of the information presented at meetings is text based. Thus, it is not surprising that **text charts** are a widely used form of presentation graphic. Text charts often use a technique called a *build*. As shown in Figure PS 2-17, text is presented as a bulleted list that is built bullet by bullet in a series of visuals. Animation and sound are often used to accompany each new bulleted item, which is often set in a different color to distinguish it from earlier list items. The build technique is more effective than presenting the entire list as a single visual, which may be too much for an audience to absorb at once. In a build, audience attention is always focused on the latest bullet.

HARDWARE AND SOFTWARE

A variety of hardware devices and programs exists for people who prepare and show presentation graphics.

Hardware   Hardware used in the preparation of presentation visuals includes many of the same types of devices used in desktop publishing environments.

- HIGH-END PC Because graphical images generally require lots of computation and storage space, the system should include a fairly high-end PC with plenty of RAM and hard-disk storage.

- COLOR HARD-COPY DEVICES Color output is an essential capability, because most types of presentation graphics need different colors to highlight elements in the most attractive way. A color plotter or color printer is ideal for preparing handouts for meetings that people can take home.

■ **Text chart.** A presentation graphic in which the principal element is text.

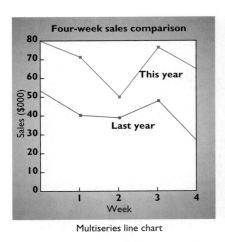
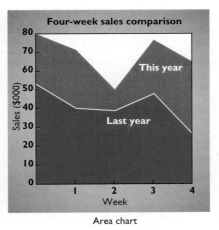

Multiseries line chart　　　　　　　　　　Area chart

FIGURE PS 2-16

Line charts. Because the line in a line chart is unbroken, the effect on the eye can be dramatic.

A film recorder is especially useful if the presentation visuals are to be in hard-copy slide format.

■ OTHER EQUIPMENT Presentation visuals are often shown to audiences on special equipment, such as a 35-millimeter slide projector, an over-head projector that handles transparencies, or a computer projection sys-tem (see Figure PS 2-18). Slides and overheads can be in the traditional hard-copy format or in soft-copy (electronic) format. Soft-copy slides make it possible to run the presentation from a computer, customizing it "on the fly" to the needs of the audience. Navigational buttons similar to those found on Web pages can be used to go from slide to slide and dazzling special sound and visual effects can accompany slides. Digital cameras and image scanners can be used to import photographs into the presentation.

For a tutorial on multimedia hardware, go to www. harcourtcollege.com/infosys/ parker2000/student/tutor/ and click on Chapter PS 2.

Software **Presentation graphics software** provides tools for drawing bar charts, text charts, and similar graphics. Most of this software falls into one of two classes: presentation graphics routines that are part of spreadsheet soft-ware and dedicated presentation graphics programs. Both types of software are included in the major office suites; for instance, Office 2000 contains the Excel spreadsheet program and PowerPoint presentation software.

■ SPREADSHEET PROGRAMS Spreadsheet programs integrate both spread-sheeting and graphics functions into a single product. Such products are ideal for users who require a strong data manipulation capability and whose presentation graphics needs are relatively modest—say, an occasional bar- or pie-chart representation of worksheet data. Using a chart wizard in a spreadsheet program to prepare a presentation

FIGURE PS 2-17

Building a list through text charts. Each text chart shown in the sequence adds a new bulleted item to the list being presented.

Slide 1　　　　　　Slide 2　　　　　　Slide 3

■ **Presentation graphics software.** A program used to prepare bar charts, pie charts—and other information-intensive images—and present them to an audience.

 FIGURE PS 2-18

Presentation hardware.
The use of a computer projection system allows a large display of a computerized presentation, which can include sound effects, video clips, and transition effects between slides.

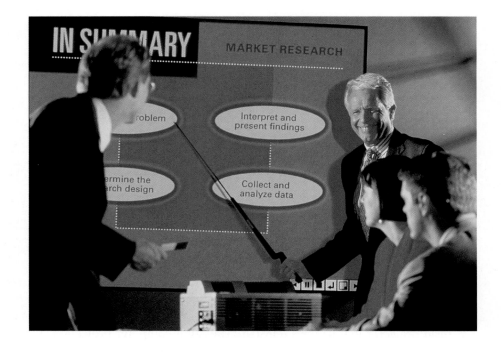

FIGURE PS 2-19

Using a spreadsheet chart wizard to create presentation graphics.

Creating presentation graphics with a spreadsheet package involves selecting worksheet data to be graphed, choosing a chart type, and selecting such elements as legends, titles, and fonts.

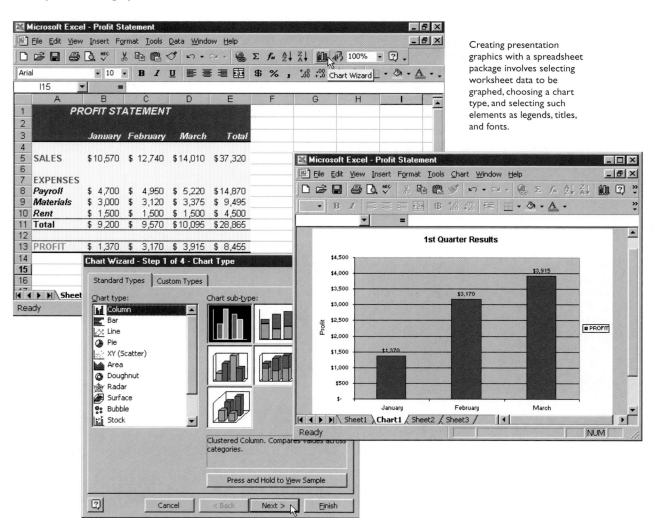

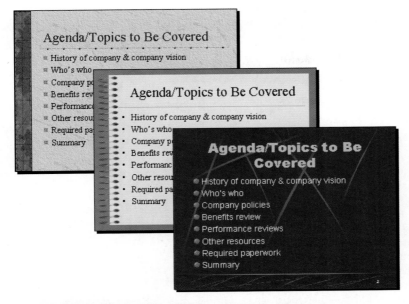

STYLE SELECTION
A mouse click lets you choose any of several styles for your presentation. Preparing each slide is almost just as easy; you type text onto a form or template, refreshing it each time you begin a new slide.

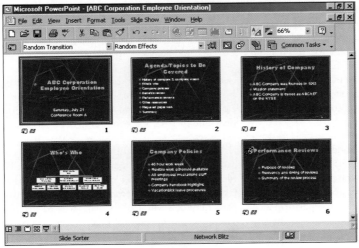

VIEWING SLIDES
Once slides are finished, you can view thumbnails—small pictures—of them in sorted order. If you want to change the sequence of the slides, drag and drop them into a new order with your mouse.

FIGURE PS 2-20

Creating a text-chart presentation with PowerPoint.

For links to further information about presentation software, go to www. harcourtcollege.com/infosys/ parker2000/student/explore/ and click on **Chapter PS 2.**

graphic is illustrated in Figure PS 2-19. Most spreadsheets automatically update graphs when the data in the worksheets upon which the graphs are based are changed.

■ DEDICATED PROGRAMS Dedicated presentation graphics programs provide more powerful features than spreadsheets offer. For instance, you can call on a wider selection of drawing and sound capabilities, many more options for customizing graphics on charts, and a variety of devices such as timers and animation tools that can really make a text-chart presentation sizzle (see Figure PS 2-20). Four of the most widely used dedicated programs are Microsoft's PowerPoint, Computer Associates' Harvard Graphics, Lotus's Freelance Graphics, and Corel's Presentation.

■ OTHER PROGRAMS In addition to spreadsheet programs and dedicated presentation graphics programs, other software exists to enhance presentation visuals. For instance, *image-editing software* is often employed to bring sophisticated art and photorealistic images to visuals. *Clip-art programs* are commonly used to import prepackaged spot art. These and other types of illustration software are covered in Chapter PS 1.

Geographic Information Systems (GISs)

Making Presentations with Maps

For hundreds of years, when information had to be recorded on a map, it was drawn right on the map surface. Transparency overlays, introduced later, were a more sophisticated development, allowing different types of data to be layered on a single map. Sometimes the overlays were used jointly, but using two or more overlays could make the maps confusing. Then, in the late 1980s, GISs were created.

Geographic information systems (GISs) display computer-generated maps that are backed by electronic data—the type that you might find in worksheets or an electronic database. Advances in spreadsheet and database technology, large-capacity storage devices, and improved computer graphics techniques have made GISs possible. Stored in the data repository are map images and useful geographic data such as demographic breakdowns, sales data, store and warehouse locations, trends, and market research data. Anything you can put on a map—including data on animal populations, land use, foliage growth, traffic patterns, mineral deposits, or pollution—is fair game for a GIS database.

Oil companies such as Texaco, Shell, and Amoco use GISs to store exploration maps and related data such as land-leasing arrangements, oil strikes, and terrain features. The systems have reduced the time needed to find promising places in the world to drill and have made the process of locating drilling sites more accurate.

Such franchisers as Arby's use GISs to assess the performance of their outlets and to select new restaurant sites. One of the key types of data Arby's uses for site selection is traffic patterns. An Arby's spokesperson reports that GISs have dramatically reduced the number of bad decisions.

The Satellite Music Network uses GIS tools to produce maps for thousands of its affiliated stations. The maps reveal where potential listeners to various radio formats—say, golden oldies and

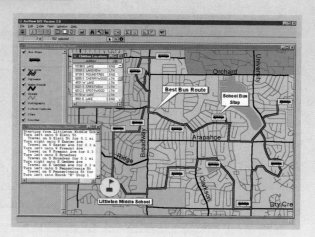

GIS and routing. GISs can be used to find the best route between two points, such as this GIS used to create efficient school bus routes based on school locations and where students live.

country—are likely to be located. The company provides a toll-free number for listener requests, and when listeners call in, their zip codes are recorded—providing data for mapping. Audience distribution data are commonly used to help sell airtime to advertisers.

Gateway Outdoor Advertising, which sells ad space on thousands of billboards, is a strong advocate of GISs. The firm added McDonald's to its roster of clients when it was able to provide the fast-food giant with computer-generated maps that revealed the proximity of several of its billboards to McDonald's restaurants. The maps convinced McDonald's management that the billboards would reach their customers.

In the Pacific Northwest, the city of Tacoma, Washington, is a leader in using GISs. The police use a GIS to track crimes, the fire department uses a GIS to cut response time in getting to a fire, city planners use a GIS to keep track of properties for tax assessment, and the water company uses a GIS to locate meters and valves.

For a tutorial on planning and creating a multimedia presentation, go to www. harcourtcollege.com/infosys/ parker2000/student/tutor/ and click on Chapter PS 2.

MULTIMEDIA PRESENTATIONS

While most presentations consist of simple visuals shown in slide or overhead form—along with supplemental handouts—computer technology has made it possible for presentations to become ever more sophisticated. Increasingly, sound and video components are being added alongside text and graphics to create fully featured multimedia presentations. Two common types of multimedia presentations are CD-based presentations and Web-based presentations. The end-of-chapter Window features several examples of multimedia presentations and the tools used to create them.

CD-Based Presentations At many companies, CDs are created at the request of the marketing department and made available to field salespeople. The CDs contain a variety of presentation materials, such as electronic slides, audio tracks, and videos—for instance, a small speech from the company pres-

Making a Point, circa 2005

Will Creating Web-Based Presentations Become as Commonplace as Writing Reports?

One wonders—with the Internet becoming such a visible presence within the lives of virtually every computer user and with private intranets and extranets springing up left and right—whether someday we'll all be creating presentations for the Web. This, of course, is instead of the current convention of converting disk files to paper or film through laser printers and slide-making machines.

Sound far-fetched? It shouldn't, when you think of how much effort is being put into making the Internet as easy to use as a television set and the power that an electronic report can have over a hard-copy one. Someday in the foreseeable future it will be possible to have all the tools available on your desktop to reliably deliver and receive stunning Web presentations.

Writing presentation materials to be read online requires a much different preparation strategy than that applied by most people to the reports they write today. First, there's the size of the reading hardware to consider. Most display screens are designed to be operated in landscape mode. This is opposite the orientation of most 8½-inch-by-11-inch printed pages, which are output in a portrait mode. If you can't squeeze your information into screen-sized chunks, it better be catchy enough for the reader to scroll to see it. A lot of people won't bother.

Another important thing to consider is that, with a Web page, readers will want to hyperlink. This requires a different way of organizing information than the serial fashion used in most printed documents, where the reader is more or less forced into taking pages in the order in which the table of contents suggests. Web page readers have far more freedom to wander around a document—and many may want to assimilate your presentation in an order different from the one you may have had in mind.

Then, there's the capability to search online and to reference massive volumes of material that you couldn't ever be able to fit into a written presentation. If the user wants to see support material, you could have it waiting in the wings, ready to be accessed by the click of a mouse button. It is also possible to update a Web report frequently, thereby enabling the reader to see the freshest possible facts.

Presentations of the future. Will the Web be the medium of choice?

With an online presentation you can also add video and sound—two elements you can't possibly convert into printed form. Thus, if you have a message or a mood that you want to impart to the reader, you can build in a hyperlink that fetches your voice. An audio clip of you speaking can bestow a sense of concern or comfort that the written word might be hard pressed to convey. Or if you want to show the reader the place that you're referencing, you can embed a small "travel" video in your presentation, literally being able to whisk your reader away to a setting that can have an impact.

The aforementioned is not to imply that the venerable laser printer and overhead projector are dead. Despite the fact that more people will find themselves writing online than ever before, many if not most of us will also require use of the printed document or the need to make presentations by conventional means. When it comes to reading for enjoyment or reading complex material that requires a lot of thinking, nothing beats a good easy chair, hard copy, and a highlighting pen to underline and scribble remarks. And when it comes to making a critical point, it's hard to top showing up in person, using showmanship tools that don't give the audience any wiggle room and that don't deliver annoying error messages at the time when you least need them.

ident attesting to the quality of the product being sold. Navigational controls are included on the CD-ROM so that the presenter can jump at will to different parts of the disk. Also, the presenter can often insert additional materials into the sales pitch, such as supplementary PowerPoint slides stored on a local hard disk or the Web. Two advantages to CDs are that they don't require a remote connection to run and copies of them can be left with the audience after a meeting.

Web-Based Presentations   The recent popularity of the Internet's World Wide Web has enabled thousands of individuals and organizations to make presentations through that medium. At many companies, field salespeople have access to graphics and even fully packaged presentations over the Web in order to make pitches at a client site. Web-based presentations may involve any combination of text, simple graphics, computer animation, digital audio and video, realtime tools, and virtual-reality and 3-D graphics techniques. An advantage to using the Web as a presentation-delivery system is that it's easy to make updates. A disadvantage is that a presenter has no control over such unforeseen events as Web-site and server-computer troubles—either of which can completely derail a presentation. The Web as a presentation medium is treated at greater length in versions of this textbook that contain the NET module. The Tomorrow box (see page PS 59) makes some observations on the future of Web-based presentations.

SUMMARY AND KEY TERMS

Go to the Online Glossary at www.harcourtcollege.com/infosys/parker2000/ student/ to review key terms.

Two useful types of program packages for reporting and arranging data are spreadsheets and presentation graphics software.

Spreadsheets   An *electronic spreadsheet package,* or **spreadsheet,** produces computerized counterparts to the ruled ledger-style worksheets that accountants frequently use. Spreadsheets first came to public notice in the late 1970s when a product named *VisiCalc* was developed.

In electronic spreadsheets, the display screen is viewed as a *window* looking in on a big grid, called a **worksheet.** The worksheet consists of *rows* and *columns* that intersect to form **cells,** each of which can be accessed through a **cell address.** Columns are labeled by letters, and rows are labeled by numbers, so, for instance, Cell B3 is located at the intersection of the second column and third row.

Spreadsheet software often divides the screen into two principal areas. The worksheet itself is displayed in the **worksheet area,** or **window area.** The **control panel** is the area of the screen where users perform tasks such as issuing commands from menus and toolbars and developing entries for cells. Cell entries are one of two types: a **constant value** consists of text and numeric values, whereas a **formula** is a cell entry that performs a mathematical operation on other cells. The control panel also shows you the cell to which you are currently pointing, called the **current cell.** It is also the area used to display commands. The **cell pointer** (or **highlight**) is associated with the worksheet area and points to the current cell.

Spreadsheet packages are particularly valuable because they possess a **recalculation feature**—that is, they can perform recalculations in seconds that would require several hours to do manually or by writing a program in a regular programming language. It's this recalculation feature, and the **what-if analysis** it makes possible, that makes spreadsheets so popular.

A contiguous rectangular block of cells is called a **range.** A range can be typed in explicitly or selected on the screen by pointing and clicking.

In virtually all spreadsheet packages, cell entries can be formatted—say, by changing their alignment or by putting in such special characters as dollar signs and commas.

Most spreadsheet packages contain a couple of hundred or so built-in functions that enable you to create formulas for a wide range of applications. A

function is a reference to a prestored formula (such as that for calculating net present value) or a preset value (such as today's date).

Spreadsheet packages have numerous features to aid in developing worksheet data. Some of the basic operations include inserting and deleting rows or columns, moving or copying the contents of cells from one part of the worksheet to another (using formulas with **relative cell references, absolute cell references,** or **mixed cell references**, as needed), selecting column widths and row heights, freezing titles, printing worksheets, and a variety of features for dressing up worksheets. Also, many packages have a **template** feature that permits the creation, saving, and protection of worksheets that have all of their rows and columns prelabeled, and prewritten formulas, so that only the data need to be filled in.

Most spreadsheet programs today provide users with a variety of data-handling capabilities, including the ability to *sort* records on one or more fields and to *filter* records with specific characteristics. Many programs also have a *pivot-table* feature that makes it possible to rearrange data in a table so as to see new types of relationships among them.

Presentation Graphics   A **presentation graphic**—sometimes called a *presentation visual* or *chart*—is an image that visually enhances in some way the impact of information communicated to other people. A presentation graphic can take any one of a large number of forms.

Probably the four most common types of presentation visuals are bar charts, pie charts, line charts, and text charts. **Bar charts** are especially useful for comparing relative magnitudes of items and for showing the frequency with which events occur. **Pie charts** are commonly used to show how parts of something relate to a whole. **Line charts** are used to represent graph data in which both axes are used to represent quantitative phenomena. **Text charts** are most appropriate for producing lists of items.

Hardware used in the preparation of presentation visuals includes many of the same types of devices used in desktop publishing environments. Also useful are such special equipment as film recorders and projectors.

Presentation graphics software lets you draw bar charts, pie charts, and the like. Presentation graphics packages are either dedicated or integrated into a spreadsheet package. *Dedicated packages* provide the most sophisticated types of presentation capabilities, whereas *spreadsheet packages* consist of modest features.

CD-based presentations and *Web-based presentations* are two relatively new types of multimedia presentation techniques.

EXERCISES

1. Fill in the blanks:
   a. The principle behind an electronic spreadsheet involves viewing the display screen as a(n) _____ looking at a section of a big grid called a(n) _____.
   b. Three types of cell references available for use in formulas in most spreadsheet programs are _____, _____, and _____ cell references.
   c. A worksheet in which all rows and columns are prelabeled and formulas are supplied is called a(n) _____.
   d. The spreadsheet feature that allows users to combine or rearrange data in a table to see new information is called a(n) _____ feature.
   e. Most presentation graphics packages fall into one of two categories: _____ packages and _____ packages.

2. Match each term with the description that fits best:
   a. =SUM(A1:A2)   c. John Smith
   b. D4   d. F18:F28
   _____ A constant value   _____ A function
   _____ A range   _____ A cell address

3. Which type of chart covered in the book—bar, pie, line, or text—is best described by each of the following phrases:
   a. Both axes measure quantitative data.
   b. One axis measures quantitative data; the other measures qualitative data.
   c. There are no axes, but all of the pieces represented combine to make a whole.
   d. The Gantt chart is a type.
   e. It often has an exploded element.
   f. A build is used to present data.
   g. An area chart is a type.

4. Describe each of the following in your own words:
   a. VisiCalc
   b. Control panel
   c. Formula bar
   d. Filtering capability
   e. Worksheet area
   f. What-if analysis
   g. Autocomplete feature
   h. Control break

5. Rank the following from largest to smallest:
   a. Range   c. Workbook
   b. Cell   d. Worksheet

6. Explain the differences among the following:
   a. Moving cell contents
   b. Copying cells using mixed cell references
   c. Copying cells using relative cell references
   d. Copying cells using absolute cell references

7. Name at least eight different types of charts that you can create with a presentation graphics program, and draw a small picture of each that shows what it represents.

8. What is the difference between a dedicated presentation graphics program and a spreadsheet program with graphics capabilities?

9. Given the worksheet in the figure at the top of the next column, what is the value of each of the following?

a. =SUM(C1:C4)   d. =IF(A4<5,10,20)
b. =MIN(A1:D4)   e. =AVERAGE(A1:C2)
c. =COUNT(A3:B4)

	A	B	C	D
1	20	11	8	4
2	18	5	1	12
3	17	13	0	9
4	7	16	15	3

10. Use the accompanying figure to answer the following questions:
    a. How many numbers should automatically be calculated by the spreadsheet program through the use of formulas?
    b. If January payroll is adjusted from $4,700 to $4,750, how many other numbers in the worksheet will be changed when the worksheet is recalculated?
    c. What cell columns or rows can be partially filled in using the autocomplete feature?
    d. What is the current cell?

PROJECTS

1. **Courtroom Presentations** Computer animation technology is being used by courtroom lawyers as a presentation tool. Many people object to the use of such technology in presenting information to trial juries. Others say it represents the wave of the future. Provide as many reasons as you can for and against the use of computer animation in the courtroom. What do you think—is the courtroom an appropriate place for computer animations?

2. **The Spreadsheet Program at Your School** For the spreadsheet program that comes with your own computer or the computers in your school's PC lab, describe how to do the following tasks:

a. Insert columns and rows.

b. Adjust the widths of columns and the heights of rows.

c. Delete columns and rows.

d. Change the alignment of data in Cell A8 from left-justified to centered.

e. Change the typeface and point size on the top row of your worksheet data.

f. Hide columns and rows.

g. Use the pivot-table feature.

h. Autoformat a range—say, by having the spreadsheet program automatically supply month names.

i. Place borders around cells in the worksheet.

j. Sort raw data.

3. **Researching a Spreadsheet Program**   You can find out much more about a particular spreadsheet program by finding a book about it or by cruising the Internet for information. For the spreadsheet program of your choice, complete the following activities:

a. Visit a local bookstore and find as many books as you can—up to a limit of three—about the spreadsheet program you have chosen. Write down the name of each book, the name of the author and publisher, and the copyright date. If there is no bookstore in your area or you are having problems finding titles, consider visiting one online. Two large online bookstores are the Amazon Bookstore (www.amazon.com) and Fatbrain.com (www.fatbrain. com).

b. For any one of the books you chose in part *a*, write a short (one-to-two-page) report telling whether the book serves an audience of beginners or advanced users, listing what it covers, and identifying the features that appeal or don't appeal to you.

c. *Optional: Do this part of the project only if you have Internet access.* Software publishers are regularly enhancing their mainstream products. Often, when they develop a feature that may be useful to current users, they make it available for free on the Web. For this project, visit the Web site of the spreadsheet you have chosen and compile a list of free features offered at the site that enhance the program's use.

4. **Researching a Dedicated Presentation Graphics Program**   Several dedicated presentation graphics programs were mentioned in the chapter. Choose a particular version of one such program and answer the following questions about it. If you have Internet access, you may find some of the answers from information that is available on the Internet.

a. What is the name of the program and who is its publisher?

b. Does the version work on a PC-compatible platform or on the Macintosh platform (or both)? What is the most current version number of the program?

c. How much RAM and hard-disk space does the program require?

d. What is the suggested list price of the program? What is the current selling price at one store or vendor?

e. Name at least two things the program you have chosen can do that your spreadsheet program cannot.

5. **Spreadsheet Functions**   Pick any of the leading spreadsheet programs and tell—for any three of the following—the name of the function that should be used. Also, demonstrate how the function works by trying it on your computer.

a. Compute the standard deviation of a list of numbers.

b. Compute depreciation for an asset by the double-declining balance method.

c. Find the cosine of an angle.

d. Return the value of TRUE if a cell is blank.

e. Round a number down to the nearest integer.

6. **Dressing Up a Worksheet**   Refer to the worksheets in the accompanying figure, and complete the activities on the following page.

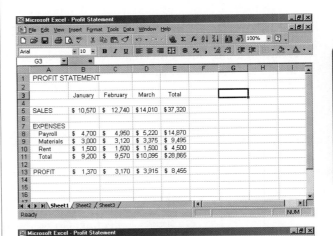

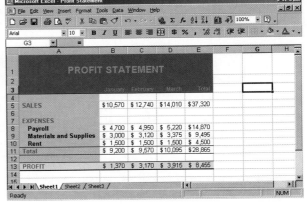

a. Using the spreadsheet program available to your class, prepare the worksheet in the top part of the figure.

b. Dress up the worksheet you just prepared so that it resembles the worksheet at the bottom. Note that you can use lots of tools to make the transition, including applying an autoformat, bolding and increasing point size, widening columns and rows (notice that you will have to add text to Cell A9), centering text, and applying color fills and color fonts to selected cells.

 7. Preparing a Bar Chart Using either the spreadsheet or presentation graphics program available to your class, produce either the grouped bar chart or the stacked bar chart shown in Figure PS 2-13.

8. Preparing a Pie Chart Using either the spreadsheet or presentation graphics program available to your class, produce the pie chart shown in Figure PS 2-15.

9. Preparing a Line Chart Using either the spreadsheet or presentation graphics program available to your class, produce the multiseries line chart shown in Figure PS 2-16.

10. Electronic Slide Presentation Using the presentation graphics program available to your class, do the following:

a. Produce a series of text-oriented electronic slides—at least a half dozen.

b. Add a clip art image to one or two of the slides.

c. Arrange the slides into an automated presentation that can be shown to the class. Use the automatic timer to display each slide, and add transition effects—both a visual effect and sound—between each slide.

d. Prepare a hard-copy script, to read in front of the class, which is coordinated with the automatic slide timer.

11. Easter Eggs Revisited The Inside the Industry box covers Easter eggs—hidden blocks of code in a program that display splashy screens, animations, credits to developers, and the like, all of which have nothing to do with the operation of the program. For this project, find an Easter egg other than the one discussed in the box and report to the class how it works and what it produces. Articles on Easter eggs are frequently found in computer journals like *PC Magazine,* but probably the easiest way to find eggs is using a Web-based search engine such as Yahoo! or WebCrawler. To see what is currently available, type "Easter eggs" into the space that offers the keyword search.

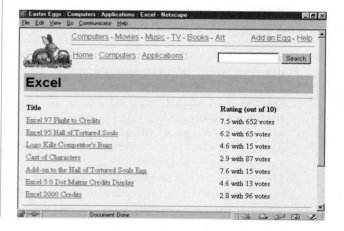

INTERACTIVE EXERCISE

PREPARING A MULTIMEDIA PRESENTATION

 You've been asked to prepare a PowerPoint presentation for the company sales meeting. Go to the Interactive Exercise at www.harcourtcollege.com/infosys/parker2000/student/exercise/ to complete this exercise.

ONLINE REVIEW

Go to the Online Review at www.harcourtcollege.com/infosys/parker2000/student/ to test your understanding of this chapter's concepts.

WINDOW

MULTIMEDIA COMPUTING

A PICTURE ESSAY OF APPLICATIONS

Multimedia computing—in which text, graphics, audio, and video data intermingle—is becoming commonplace in computer applications. Most CDs provide multimedia presentations as do an increasing number of Web sites. Multimedia applications abound and their number is growing each year. On this and the next three pages, a sample of uses is provided that includes multimedia in education and training, in sales and legal presentations, and in reference and entertainment products.

1. If you want to see audio or video presentations over the Web you need a program called a *player* on your PC. The two most widely used players are RealNetworks' RealPlayer Plus (pictured here) and Microsoft NetShow. To experience multimedia at any particular Web site you need to have a player the site recognizes.

2

3

2–3. A test cockpit and video simulator help train commercial and military pilots on the ground. The simulator's databases contain 3-D computer models of terrain and major airports as well as weather patterns such as fog.

4

4. Multimedia computing is frequently applied to help teach people how to drive and to test them on driving rules.

5–6. Increasingly, field salespeople—such as those at Reebok International, the sportswear company—are using state-of-the-art multimedia CDs and notebook computers to make presentations to clients. When updates in Reebok CD's product database occur, such as changes in price or style, salespeople can downloaded the changes onto their PCs via the Internet.

7–8. Lawyers frequently turn to multimedia animations as a courtroom-presentation tool, to enable jurors to better visualize how an accident or crime may have taken place.

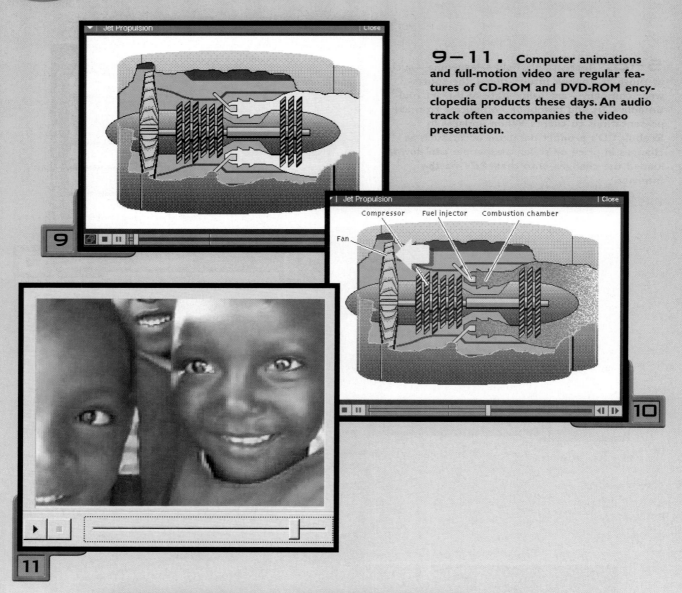

9—11. Computer animations and full-motion video are regular features of **CD-ROM** and **DVD-ROM** encyclopedia products these days. An audio track often accompanies the video presentation.

12. At many Web sites you can view clips of movies and sometimes watch entire films. Multimedia is also frequently used on the Web by merchants selling products and by schools offering telecourses.

PS 3

DATABASE MANAGEMENT

LEARNING OBJECTIVES

After completing this chapter, you will be able to:

1. Explain what database management systems are and how they work.

2. Identify some of the strategies used for database management on both large and small computer systems.

3. Identify the advantages and disadvantages of database management.

OVERVIEW

People often need to summon large amounts of data rapidly. An airline agent on the phone to a client or a busy person on the Web may need to search through mounds of data quickly to find the lowest-cost flight path from Tucson to Toronto two weeks hence. The registrar of a university may have to scan student records swiftly to find the grade-point averages of all students who will graduate in June. An engineer may need to test several structural design alternatives against volumes of complicated safety and feasibility criteria before proceeding with a design strategy.

In this chapter, we'll cover database management systems, the type of software used specifically for such tasks. Computerized database management systems are rapidly making extinct the thick hard-copy manuals that people have had to wade through to find the information their jobs require.

WHAT IS A DATABASE MANAGEMENT SYSTEM?

A **database management system (DBMS)** is a software system that integrates data in storage and provides easy access to them. The data themselves are placed on disk in a **database,** which can be thought of as an integrated collection of related files. The three files shown in Figure PS 3-1, for instance, which we will discuss in detail in the next subsection, collectively form a database.

Although not all databases are organized identically, many of them are composed of files, records, and fields, as shown in the figure. There are three *files* in Figure PS 3-1—one for product, another for inventory, and another for orders. Each file consists of several *records.* For instance, the Product file contains five records—one each for skis, boots, poles, bindings, and wax. Finally, each record consists of distinct types of data called *fields.* The Product file stores four fields for each record—product name, product number, supplier, and price.

The example shown in Figure PS 3-1 is a simplified one. Real-world databases often consist of scores of files, each containing thousands of records (see Feature PS 3-1 on page PS 72). Database management software enables queries and reports to be prepared by extracting information from one file at a time, and, as we will shortly see, from several interrelated files concurrently.

For a tutorial on database software, go to www.harcourtcollege.com/infosys/parker2000/student/tutor/ and click on Chapter PS 3.

DATABASE MANAGEMENT ON PCS

Many different database management systems are commercially available. Not all of them work the same way nor are they all equally easy to comprehend. The best way to understand how a database management system works is by example. The one in this section looks at **relational database management systems**—the type found on most PCs and the easiest to understand. The list of general-purpose commercial products for desktop systems includes

■ **Database management system (DBMS).** A software product designed to integrate data and provide easy access to them. ■ **Database.** An integrated collection of related data files. ■ **Relational database management system.** A computer program for database management that links data in related files through common fields.

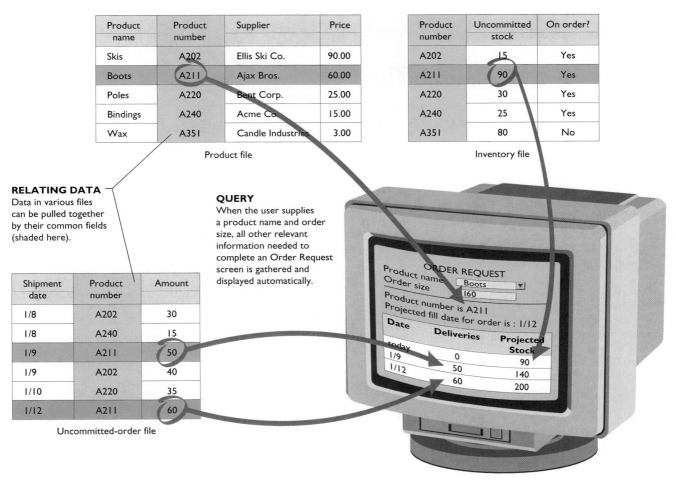

RELATING DATA
Data in various files
can be pulled together
by their common fields
(shaded here).

QUERY
When the user supplies
a product name and order
size, all other relevant
information needed to
complete an Order Request
screen is gathered and
displayed automatically.

Product name	Product number	Supplier	Price
Skis	A202	Ellis Ski Co.	90.00
Boots	A211	Ajax Bros.	60.00
Poles	A220	Bent Corp.	25.00
Bindings	A240	Acme Co.	15.00
Wax	A351	Candle Industries	3.00

Product file

Product number	Uncommitted stock	On order?
A202	15	Yes
A211	90	Yes
A220	30	Yes
A240	25	Yes
A351	80	No

Inventory file

Shipment date	Product number	Amount
1/8	A202	30
1/8	A240	15
1/9	A211	50
1/9	A202	40
1/10	A220	35
1/12	A211	60

Uncommitted-order file

ORDER REQUEST
Product name   Boots
Order size   160
Product number is A211
Projected fill date for order is : 1/12

Date	Deliveries	Projected Stock
today		
1/9	0	90
1/12	50	140
	60	200

FIGURE PS 3-1

Using a relational database management system.

Microsoft's Access, Borland's Paradox (which is sold by both Borland and Corel), and Lotus Development's Approach. Of these, Access is the front-runner in terms of sales. Borland, which once had the lion's share of the desktop database market, was once deemed "the next Microsoft" by some people on Wall Street (see the Inside the Industry box on page PS 73).

A SIMPLE EXAMPLE

Imagine that you're a sales manager at a ski-equipment warehouse, and an order comes in for 160 pairs of ski boots. You first need to find out if the order can be filled from stock in inventory. If it can't, you next need to know how long it will be before enough stock is available. You have an impatient client on the phone who wants an immediate response.

This type of task is especially suited to a DBMS. In Figure PS 3-1, an *inventory file* is used to store current stock levels, an *uncommitted-order file* is used to keep track of future shipments of stock that have not yet been promised to customers, and a *product file* is used to store the product descriptions. The very notion of files is often transparent to the user, who knows only that the information is "somewhere in the database system" and usually has no idea from where the system is extracting it.

The following scenario would be ideal for you. At the PC workstation on your desk, you execute the appropriate command to display an Order Request screen and enter the product description, "Boots," and the order size, 160. The computer system responds with a screen that shows the current level of uncommitted stock in inventory as well as information about stock arriving

PS 3-1

Entrepreneurs on Campus

Students with Computer Skills Cash In

For many students, working one's way through college means taking a job at the campus library or dining hall and being paid a scale wage. That was not what Luis Arellano and Esteban Morales, two students at Stanford University, quite had in mind. Instead, the pair decided to put their computer skills to good use and start their own company.

Called Innetvations (www.innetvations.com), the firm formed by the young entrepreneurs provides online registration services for organizations holding conferences. Preconference and on-site registration of conference attendees can be a logistical headache. Entering and managing data covering hundreds or thousands of people is a time-consuming if not overwhelming task for organizations. Often, such work is outsourced to firms specializing in this area—like Innetvations.

Along with completing their degree work, the two students started out by designing a registration system to meet the needs of a local group. After tasting success and seeing the commercial potential in their work, they refined the system and formed their own company.

At the time of this writing, Innetvations has been using SQL Server as the principal database platform for its Web-based system. According to Morales, the program has worked well for col-

Arellano and Morales. Two students formed a Web database company that provides online conference registration.

lecting information from between 500 and 5,000 conference participants. Recently Innetvations has been contacted by several larger organizations, and it is considering moving up to Oracle, a larger database program.

Innetvations is but one example showing there are plenty of opportunities for hard-working students with computer know-how. According to the U.S. Department of Commerce, only a quarter of the high-tech workers required by industry are entering the job market each year—a shortfall expected to continue at least through 2005.

this week from suppliers that has not been committed to other customers. It also provides its guess as to when the order can be filled: January 12. Thus, within seconds, right in front of you, you have the information you need to respond to the client's request and to be able to close the order.

Data from several files are combined quickly by a relational database management system through the fields (columns) that the files have in common. The name *relational database management system* implies that the software relates data in different files by common fields in those files. In the example we just covered, data from the three files were pulled together through a common product-number field (the shaded column in Figure PS 3-1).

Interrelated Tables   A system that interrelates the files is critical for the type of information-retrieval task just described. Without a program that could interrelate files, you'd have to carry out several successive steps yourself:

1. Access the product file to get the product number.
2. Check the inventory file for that product number to see if the company can fill the order from current stock.
3. If current stock is inadequate, check the uncommitted-order file to see when enough stock will be available to fill the order.

What's more, the date on which the order could be filled would have to be hand calculated. Because this serial file-conscious process would be slower

...And Hold the Fries

McDonald's. The first Borland press conference was a fast-food affair.

The computer industry is full of interesting characters, and a few were also the visionaries who created some of its most successful corporations. One such person is Phillipe Kahn, a multitalented individual who founded Borland International, which at one time was one of the largest software companies in the world. With its Paradox and dBASE product lines—the former now licensed to Corel Corporation—Borland was once the undisputed leader in desktop database software.

When Kahn came to the United States from France he had very little money—but he had a lot of imagination. In 1983, he attended Las Vegas's Comdex convention, the largest computer trade show in the United States. At Comdex, he hoped to get his fledgling company, Borland, a room for a press conference on credit. When he talked to the convention's manager, however, he was curtly told to go to McDonald's to entertain the press if he couldn't afford Comdex's rates. That's exactly what Kahn did. Six journalists showed up, and Kahn received reviews from all but one of them, thrusting Borland into the public's eye.

than having the files automatically integrated, in a manner transparent to the user, both service to clients and efficiency would suffer.

DBMS-like packages that do not automatically interrelate files are sometimes called *file managers,* and the files stored by file managers are often referred to as **flat files.** Flat files can be useful for finding information, but you can see from the example we've just covered how much better it is to have files that can be interrelated. In the context of relational database systems, files are commonly referred to as **tables.** Relational database programs allow more than one table to be stored in a single database, just as more than one worksheet can be stored in one workbook file in most spreadsheet programs. Not all DBMS users choose to interrelate tables or have more than one table in each database, incidentally, even though they have the capability to do so. When a database consists of a single table, the terms *file, table,* and *database* are commonly used interchangeably. In the rest of this chapter, the term *file* will be used instead of *table* because of its wider usage.

INTERACTING WITH A DBMS

Users interact with the database management system through either an easy-to-use retrieval/update facility that accompanies the database package or an applications program written in a programming language.

A typical database program's *retrieval/update facility* presents a graphical user interface that lets users frame queries (questions) onscreen and interact with database applications. The graphical user interface is designed primarily to satisfy the needs of ordinary users. Among the most critical of these needs are creating databases, updating database data from time to time, and retrieving information from a database—either by making simple queries or by requesting to have reports prepared.

■ **Flat file.** A file that is not interrelated with others. ■ **Table.** In a relational DBMS, an entity with columns and rows that is capable of being interrelated with other database data.

A database program's *programming-language facility* allows relatively sophisticated users to develop complex database applications. This feature often is targeted to users and programmers who want to design custom menus or screens or to create applications that go well beyond the standard ones offered with the database package. Most PC-oriented DBMSs come equipped with their own proprietary programming language—such as Microsoft's Visual Basic for Applications. Some also support applications developed in such public-domain programming languages as C++ and COBOL.

A database processing environment for a typical PC is illustrated in Figure PS 3-2. The DBMS serves as an interface between the user at one end and data and programs at the other. As users develop applications and input data at their workstations, DBMS *utility programs,* such as the data dictionary (to be discussed shortly), ensure that the applications and data are properly prepared before storing them on disk. Other utility programs, such as a rich assortment of applications wizards and templates and a help facility, can be summoned when the user needs assistance with a form or report or with executing a command.

DATA DEFINITION

The first step in creating a database is **data definition.** Data definition involves telling the DBMS the properties of the data that are to go into the database—how big the records are, what type of data each of the fields of the records contain, and so on. During the data definition process, a screen form, or **template,** is created for each file in the database. When the template is finished, it is used for entering data.

Each database file that needs to be created will have its own distinctive template. Templates for the database shown in Figure PS 3-1 are given in Figure PS 3-3. As you are creating the data definition for each file, the DBMS will ask for the following types of information:

- The name of each field
- The maximum length of each field
- The type of data (text, numeric, date, etc.) that each field will store

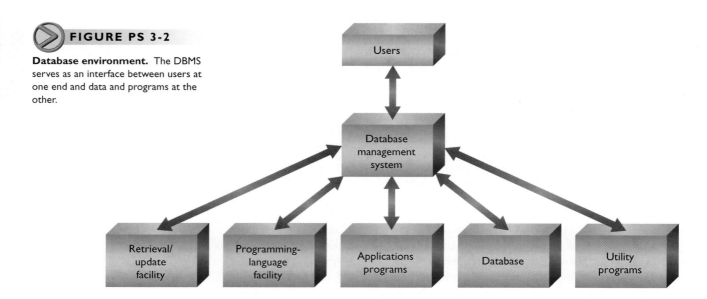

FIGURE PS 3-2

Database environment. The DBMS serves as an interface between users at one end and data and programs at the other.

Users

Database management system

Retrieval/ update facility

Programming-language facility

Applications programs

Database

Utility programs

■ **Data definition.** The process of describing the characteristics of data that are to be handled by a database management system. ■ **Template.** A screen form that requires the operator fill in a limited number of entries.

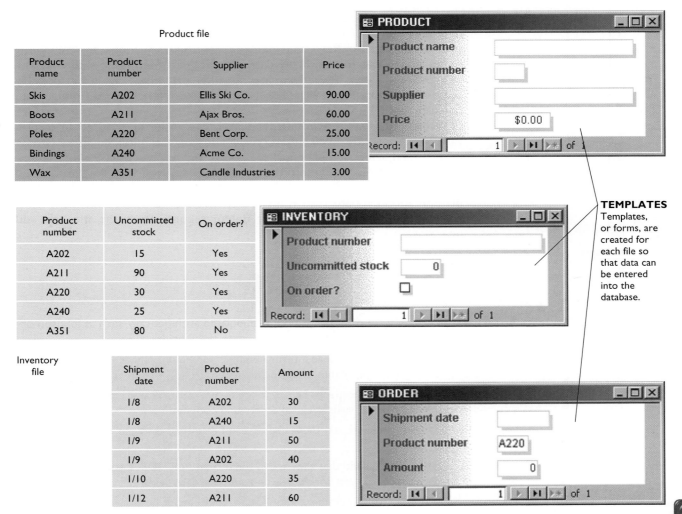

Product file

Product name	Product number	Supplier	Price
Skis	A202	Ellis Ski Co.	90.00
Boots	A211	Ajax Bros.	60.00
Poles	A220	Bent Corp.	25.00
Bindings	A240	Acme Co.	15.00
Wax	A351	Candle Industries	3.00

Product number	Uncommitted stock	On order?
A202	15	Yes
A211	90	Yes
A220	30	Yes
A240	25	Yes
A351	80	No

Inventory file

Shipment date	Product number	Amount
1/8	A202	30
1/8	A240	15
1/9	A211	50
1/9	A202	40
1/10	A220	35
1/12	A211	60

Uncommitted-order file

TEMPLATES
Templates, or forms, are created for each file so that data can be entered into the database.

The finished template is commonly referred to as a **file structure.** For example, suppose you've informed your PC's relational database program that you want to create a file called *Inventory* (see the middle part of Figure PS 3-3). The program will ask you to describe each data field of the records that will go into the file. You might respond as follows:

FIELD NAME	FIELD TYPE	WIDTH	DECIMALS
Product number	Text	4	N/A
Uncommitted stock	Numeric	10	0
On order?	Logical	1	N/A

Roughly translated, this structure declares that three fields will be present in the Inventory file: *Product number, Uncommitted stock,* and *On order?.* The Product number field will store *text,* or character, data. The width of 4 means that product numbers will be four or fewer characters. Uncommitted stock will consist of number, or *numeric,* data that will have a maximum width of ten characters. Because stock is counted in units of product, there will be no decimal places. On order? will be a *Yes/No,* or *logical,* field. A logical field often contains either the value *T,* for true (or *Y,* for yes), or *F,* for false (or *N,* for no). For instance, a product that was on order might be given the value *Y;* a product not on order, the value *N.*

FIGURE PS 3-3

Data definition.

P S

■ **File structure.** A collection of information about the records of a file, including the names, lengths, and types of the fields.

In most DBMSs, arithmetic computations can be performed on data that have been declared as numeric but not on data declared as text or logical. The *text, numeric (number),* and *logical (yes/no)* designations are commonly called **field descriptors.** Many database packages have these three descriptors as well as ones for *currency, date/time,* and *memo* fields and possibly others (see Figure PS 3-4). Field descriptors can often be chosen from a menu when preparing a file structure.

In many database environments, templates can be customized to meet a variety of data-entry needs. In Access, for instance, wizards let users choose from several screen-template styles. Paradox and Approach have similar tools.

As you later place data into the records of a file, you start with an unfilled template for each record to be keyed in. Then you repeatedly fill in the template at the keyboard (see Figure PS 3-5) and save the records onto disk. Subsequently, you can modify or delete records from the file and add new ones.

FIGURE PS 3-4

Field descriptors.

FIELD DESCRIPTORS	
Text	Text (character) fields store data that are not manipulated arithmetically, such as Johnson or 182-45-7782. You can, however, sort, index, or compare these fields.
Numeric	Numeric (Number) fields, which store integer numbers and numbers that contain decimal points, are those that must be arithmetically manipulated.
Currency	Many database packages have a special field type for numeric data that are to be output in a currency format, with dollar signs, decimal points, and commas.
Logical	Logical (Yes/No) fields often store a single character of data—for instance, a "Y" (for "yes") and an "N" (for "no").
Date	Date fields store dates, provided that they are in the format MM/DD/YY (such as 12/13/99) or something very similar. You can sort, index, and subtract date fields.
Memo	Memo fields are used to store comment information. They cannot be arithmetically manipulated or compared, but they can be edited and output.

DBMSs provide a screen that enables you to give each field a name, a field descriptor, a size, and a variety of other properties.

PRODUCT : Table

Field Name	Data Type	Description
Product name	Text	Name of the product
Product number	Text	Company-assigned product number
Supplier	Text	Supplier name
Price	Currency	Current wholesale price

Field Properties

General | Lookup

Field Size	25
Format	
Input Mask	
Caption	
Default Value	
Validation Rule	
Validation Text	
Required	Yes
Allow Zero Length	No
Indexed	Yes (Duplicates OK)
Unicode Compression	Yes

A field name can be up to 64 characters long, including spaces. Press F1 for help on field names.

■ **Field descriptor.** A code used to describe the type of data—say, numeric, text, logical—that occupy a given field in a data record.

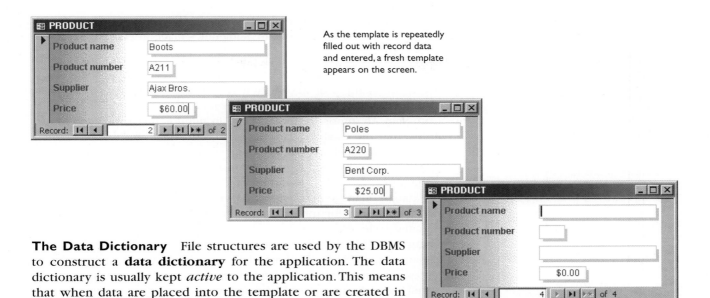

As the template is repeatedly filled out with record data and entered, a fresh template appears on the screen.

The Data Dictionary File structures are used by the DBMS to construct a **data dictionary** for the application. The data dictionary is usually kept *active* to the application. This means that when data are placed into the template or are created in any way by users of the application, the data dictionary is monitoring the applications environment and will not permit data to be entered or used in any conflicting way. For instance, you couldn't enter a seven-character product number if the dictionary expected all product numbers to be a maximum of four characters long. Nor would the dictionary let you type text data into a numeric field.

In many database environments, the data dictionary is also used to protect certain data from unauthorized use or alteration. Sensitive data such as salaries can be hidden so that only certain users of the database, furnished with the proper password, are authorized to retrieve them. Typically, only privileged users with access to a different, special password would be allowed to update the same data.

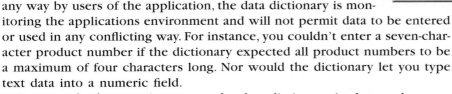

FIGURE PS 3-5

Filling out a template on the screen.

DATA MANIPULATION

The process of creating data for the database or using the database in some hands-on fashion is called **data manipulation.** Users generally can manipulate data in a PC-based DBMS in two ways: through the retrieval/update or the reporting facility within the DBMS, and through applications programs they develop with the DBMS's programming-language facility.

Data manipulation encompasses a variety of activities. The following paragraphs briefly cover some of the most important of them.

Creation of Database Data This task consists of entering record data into the database. As each fresh template is successively summoned to the screen, it is filled with record data. Continuing with the example introduced in Figure PS 3-5, you might begin the record-entry process by summoning the template for the Product file. You would then type in the first record in that file and enter it. After you did this, a fresh copy of the template would appear on the screen. Type in the second record, then the third, and so forth. After entering all the records for the Product file, you would do the same thing for the next file—say, the Inventory file—and so on.

File Maintenance File maintenance consists primarily of updating records. This involves adding new records from time to time, deleting records that are no longer needed, and modifying existing records. Modifications are necessary

---

■ **Data dictionary.** A facility that manages characteristics of data and programs in a database environment. ■ **Data manipulation.** The process of using program commands to add, delete, modify, or retrieve data in a file or database.

For links to further information about database software, go to www. harcourtcollege.com/infosys/ parker2000/student/explore/ and click on Chapter PS 3.

because data such as prices and delivery schedules, like those in Figure PS 3-1, can change and also because errors are sometimes made in entering data.

Information Retrieval (Query) The information on the screen in Figure PS 3-1, where we needed to find out amounts and delivery dates of uncommitted stock, is an example of information retrieval, or query. A *query* feature refers to the ability to extract information from a database without having to write a program. An important fact to keep in mind is that if you can *manually* pull together the database data you need, you should be able to design a query to get your database management system to pull these same data together *automatically*—and a lot faster too. Database queries can be simple or very complex.

Every database management system provides its own tools through which users query databases for information. One such tool is a query language. The command style shown in Figure PS 3-6 is based largely on **structured query language (SQL),** which is recognized as today's de facto standard for information retrieval in relational databases. A number of graphical-user-interface tools are available from database vendors to make it easy for users to construct database queries without having to remember a language syntax like SQL. One of the most widely used of such tools is **query by example (QBE).**

Rather than type a complicated command, users of QBE can simply illustrate their information needs by filling in requirements on a QBE screen offered by the DBMS. Two examples are provided. The first, in Figure PS 3-7, illustrates filling in a QBE screen at a Web site to search for a movie video to purchase. Buyers type their search criteria into a form, and a search program at the site looks through its database of video products to find matches. The second example, in Figure PS 3-8 on page PS 80, features a QBE search with Microsoft Access. As you can see from Figure PS 3-8, you can choose specific fields of records in the database to be output, sort records by any of the fields, and filter records according to specific criteria. Most desktop DBMSs—such as Access, Paradox, and Approach—include QBE in their roster of features.

Reporting Reporting is the process of arranging the information you need in a formal report. Most database management systems require that you define a *report form* for each type of report you need. The form specifies what the report will look like when it is output—how the report title and column head-

FIGURE PS 3-6

Examples of database queries. The two queries given here can be directed to the database data described in Figures PS 3-1 and PS 3-3. Both of the queries conform to SQL, the de facto standard for information retrieval from databases.

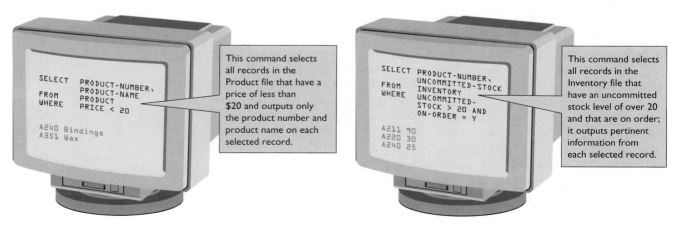

■ **Structured query language (SQL).** A popular language standard for information retrieval in relational databases.
■ **Query by example (QBE).** An onscreen query form in which users can simply illustrate what information they want by filling in filtering criteria.

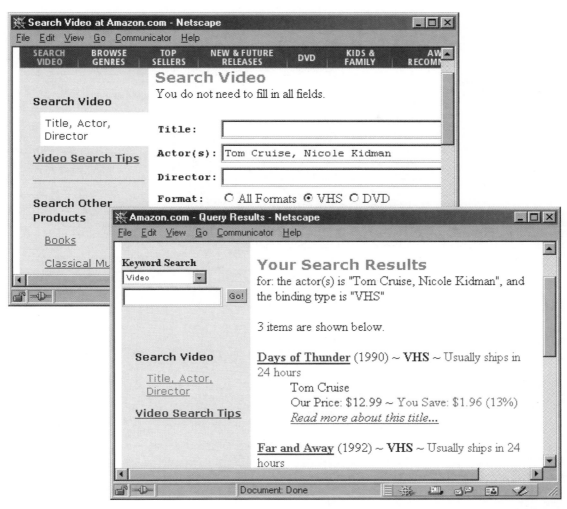

FIGURE PS 3-7

Using query by example (QBE) on the Web. At Amazon.com's video site, you can hunt for videos by filling information into a form. Here, a search is made for a VHS video starring both Tom Cruise and Nicole Kidman.

ings will look, which fields will be placed into which columns, the criteria used to select records for the report, how records are to be arranged in the report, if and when subtotals will be taken, and the like.

Typically, a *wizard* program that comes with the DBMS presents a series of easy-to-use menus to guide users through report preparation (see Figure PS 3-9). The wizard enables you to select from several report types. Also, it provides you with a variety of styling options and lets you tweak the completed report form by, say, widening columns, changing the font used for the column headings, or centering titles.

Sorting and Indexing Sorting is the process of arranging records in a specific order. As already hinted, most database management systems are equipped with the necessary tools to help you do this. You can sort ascending (from *A* to *Z*, or from low to high) or descending (from *Z* to *A*, or from high to low) on virtually any key field, and also do sorts within sorts.

Most DBMSs do not actually physically sort a file every time the user asks for a report but instead use a method called **indexing.** With indexing, you name fields on which you want to arrange data, and the computer automatically sets up an index table on that field that tells which records to put where. It is possible to create multiple indexes for the same file (with each index applied on a different sort of the file) as well as to index a file on multiple

---

■ **Indexing.** A procedure that creates a table, or index, that specifies how data records are to be arranged on output.

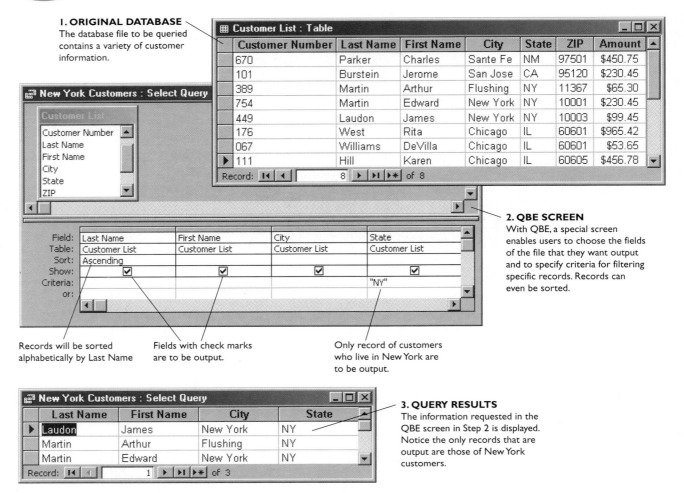

1. ORIGINAL DATABASE
The database file to be queried contains a variety of customer information.

2. QBE SCREEN
With QBE, a special screen enables users to choose the fields of the file that they want output and to specify criteria for filtering specific records. Records can even be sorted.

Records will be sorted alphabetically by Last Name

Fields with check marks are to be output.

Only record of customers who live in New York are to be output.

3. QUERY RESULTS
The information requested in the QBE screen in Step 2 is displayed. Notice the only records that are output are those of New York customers.

FIGURE PS 3-8

Using query by example (QBE) in Microsoft Access.

key fields. When indexing on multiple key fields, the term *primary key* is often used for the field on which the file is first sorted, and the term *secondary key* is used to describe any subordinate key(s). So, for instance, if the State field was declared a primary key in the original database in Figure PS 3-8 and the Last Name field a secondary key—with both keys ascending—records would be arranged first by state (CA to NY), and then, within states, records would be sorted alphabetically by the customer's last name.

Other Features   Often it is necessary to compute sums for columns, take averages, count records, and so forth. Although spreadsheet software is especially suited to these particular mathematical applications, database management systems have access to such features too. Most software suites with database programs include graphing software in their task libraries for you to create such presentation visuals as bar charts and pie charts.

DATABASE MANAGEMENT ON LARGE COMPUTER SYSTEMS

On large computer systems—say, a mainframe or a large network of PCs—DBMSs perform exactly the same sorts of roles as they do on standalone PC systems. However, they are necessarily more sophisticated, for several reasons. One is that data are often more complex—consisting not only of record-oriented text data but also multipage documents and picture information as

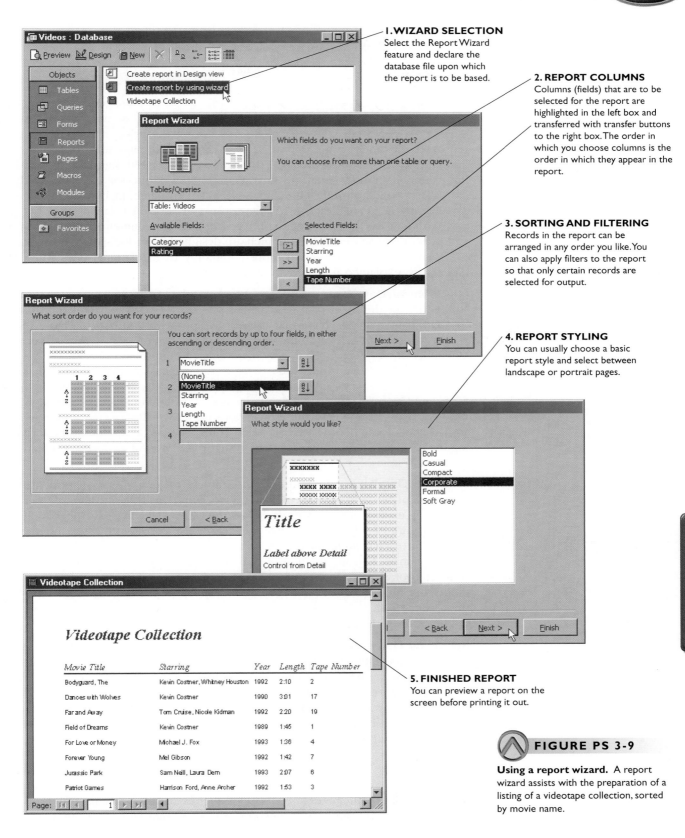

1. WIZARD SELECTION
Select the Report Wizard feature and declare the database file upon which the report is to be based.

2. REPORT COLUMNS
Columns (fields) that are to be selected for the report are highlighted in the left box and transferred with transfer buttons to the right box. The order in which you choose columns is the order in which they appear in the report.

3. SORTING AND FILTERING
Records in the report can be arranged in any order you like. You can also apply filters to the report so that only certain records are selected for output.

4. REPORT STYLING
You can usually choose a basic report style and select between landscape or portrait pages.

5. FINISHED REPORT
You can preview a report on the screen before printing it out.

FIGURE PS 3-9

Using a report wizard. A report wizard assists with the preparation of a listing of a videotape collection, sorted by movie name.

well. Furthermore, because large computer systems contain far more data than those found in personal databases, these data are often organized in a more complex way to provide faster access. DBMSs on large systems must also deal with the problem of several users trying to access the database, perhaps simultaneously.

HIERARCHICAL AND NETWORK DATA MODELS

The relational database model is particularly useful in managerial (decision-support) retrieval situations in which users are free to pose almost any sort of query to the database. A user might first ask for the price of an item, then request a sales total on a group of items, then see how many units of another item are in stock, and so on. Thus, the database must be designed with flexibility in mind. In other situations, however, the types of queries that users need to make are highly predictable and limited. For instance, in banking, tellers usually only need such facts as current customer account balances, deposits, and withdrawals. In such transaction processing environments, hierarchical and network database models—which are designed more for speed and security than flexibility—are found more commonly than relational ones. These models are explained next and shown in Figure PS 3-10.

Hierarchical Databases   A **hierarchical database management system** stores data in the form of a tree, which sets up a one-to-many relationship between data elements. Note that each professor in the top part of Figure PS 3-10 is assigned to one and only one department. If Professor Schwartz were a member of two departments—say, marketing and information systems (IS)—she would have to be represented twice in the database to maintain the hierarchical structure, once under marketing and once under IS. The database system would then treat Professor Schwartz as two distinct individuals. She might even get two separate graduation invitations from the school's computer. Such an inefficiency can be tolerated, however, if it's relatively rare. One of the leading hierarchical database management systems is IBM's IMS (Information Management System).

Network Databases   In a **network database management system,** the relationship between data elements can be either many-to-one (*simple* networks) or many-to-many *(complex* networks). The solid lines in the middle part of Figure PS 3-10 depict many-to-one relationships; one professor and one grader can each handle many courses. The dotted lines, on the other hand, represent many-to-many relationships, where classes can be cotaught by two or more professors or have multiple graders. Complex networks are harder to model, but they can always be decomposed into simple networks. Sometimes this is done when, as in the earlier case of Professor Schwartz, some minor duplication can be tolerated.

Relational Databases   Recall that *relational database management systems* organize data in tables (see the bottom part of Figure PS 3-10). Because the tables are independent, they can be dynamically linked through common fields by the user at program-execution time. This is in contrast to hierarchical and network databases, where data relationships are predefined, data are prelinked, and only linked data can be accessed. Having to link while a query is taking place, of course, eats up time, which is why relational databases are relatively slow.

Although further explanation of how hierarchical and network models work goes beyond the scope of this book, suffice it to say that these models make access faster for predefined types of queries. In large systems with thousands of requests a minute, the speed of processing requests can be all important. Hierarchical and network databases have been around longer too, so the

■ **Hierarchical database management system.** A DBMS that stores data in the form of a tree, where the relationship between data elements is one-to-many. ■ **Network database management system.** A DBMS in which the relationship between data elements can be either many-to-one or many-to-many.

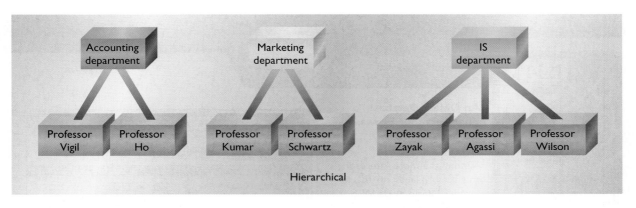

Hierarchical

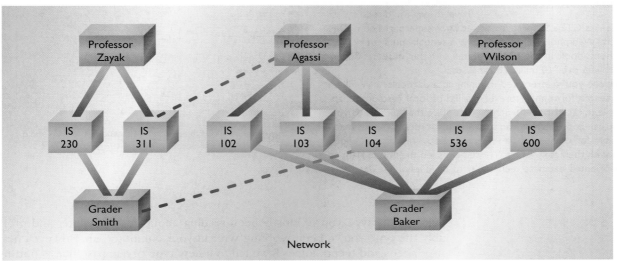

Network

Course	Professor
IS 230	Zayak
IS 311	Zayak
IS 311	Agassi
IS 102	Agassi
IS 103	Agassi
IS 104	Agassi
IS 536	Wilson
IS 600	Wilson

Course	Grader
IS 230	Smith
IS 311	Smith
IS 102	Baker
IS 103	Baker
IS 104	Baker
IS 104	Smith
IS 536	Baker
IS 600	Baker

Professor	Department
Zayak	IS
Agassi	IS
Wilson	IS

Relational

security on these types of database systems is better than security on relational systems. Because hierarchical and network databases are harder to set up and use, professionals known as *database administrators (DBAs)* are commonly hired to assist.

OBJECT-ORIENTED DATABASES

Traditionally, data management software has dealt with *structured* types of data, that is, those that fall neatly into rows and columns of text. Structured

FIGURE PS 3-10

Database models. Many commercial databases are of the hierarchical, network, or relational type.

GTE SuperPages

An Object Database That Lets Your Browser Do the Walking

Among the more interesting and useful places on the Internet's World Wide Web—and one where you don't have to pay for directory assistance—is GTE's Superpages site at www.superpages.com. One of several Web phone directories that essentially puts every business phone book in the United States on your desktop, Super-Pages covers over 10 million businesses.

Suppose you're interested in dining in a particular city. Fill an online search form and—presto—a list of local restaurants appears. Next, click on the hyperlink of a place that appeals to you, and you can zoom in on a map showing its location. GTE has made it possible for companies to integrate audio, graphics, and video data in with their text listings. Those needs led the phone giant to object-oriented database technology to build its online database.

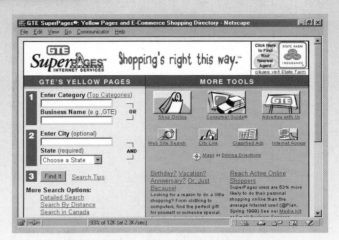

GTE Superpages site. Object-oriented technology enables audio, graphics, and video data to accompany text listings.

data are the type you've mostly been reading about in this chapter and probably the type you've been working with in your computer lab. However, new user needs and technologies have led to a new type of database that is putting an entirely different face on the data management function. The growing interest in other data types and the need to combine them into a multimedia format for applications have given rise to **object-oriented database management systems.**

In addition to handling conventional record data, computers are now being widely used to store documents, diagrams, still photographs, moving images, and sound. The Internet's World Wide Web has certainly been a big factor in pushing database developers to cater to these new data types (see Feature PS 3-2). So also has been the rising number of computer users who clamor for data to be presented in a natural-looking way that resembles experiences from real life. The stakes in the object-oriented-technology-development race are huge, since it will eventually be critical that companies establish friendly and exciting interactive environments in which to conduct electronic commerce over the Web.

Here's how object-oriented databases work. In everyday life, various types of data naturally intermingle. A speech, for instance, consists of two types of data: a voice and a moving image of someone talking. Thus, the entire speech can form an **object** made up of voice, moving-image data, and a set of *methods* or procedures describing how to combine the two. An object can be made from virtually anything—a moving image with people talking, a photograph with a narrative, text with music, and so on.

You can also combine other objects with the aforementioned speech. If the speech is on the environment, for example, data such as pollution statistics

---

■ **Object-oriented database management system.** A database in which two or more types of data—text, graphics, sound, or video—are combined with methods that specify their properties or use. ■ **Object.** A storable entity composed of data elements and instructions that apply to the elements.

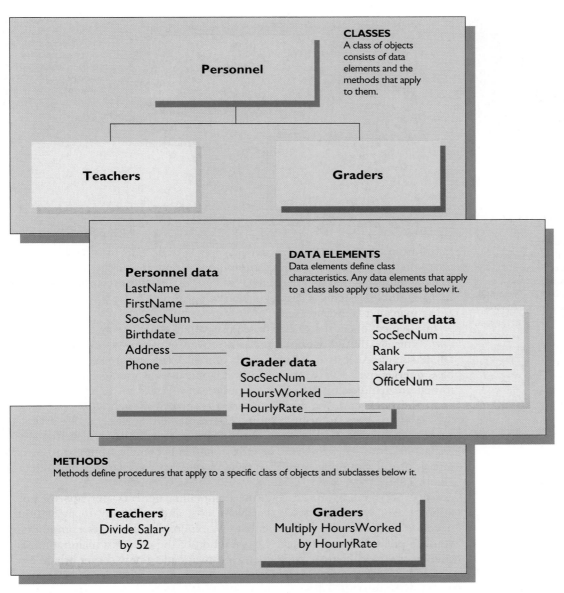

CLASSES
A class of objects consists of data elements and the methods that apply to them.

Personnel

Teachers

Graders

DATA ELEMENTS
Data elements define class characteristics. Any data elements that apply to a class also apply to subclasses below it.

Personnel data
LastName _____
FirstName _____
SocSecNum_____
Birthdate _____
Address_____
Phone_____

Teacher data
SocSecNum_____
Rank _____
Salary_____
OfficeNum _____

Grader data
SocSecNum_____
HoursWorked _____
HourlyRate_____

METHODS
Methods define procedures that apply to a specific class of objects and subclasses below it.

Teachers
Divide Salary by 52

Graders
Multiply HoursWorked by HourlyRate

FIGURE PS 3-11

Object-oriented databases.
Objects are composed of data as well as methods (procedures) that apply to the data.

and photographs of defoliated areas may be useful to tack onto it. These, too, would exist as objects in the database, each with their own set of methods. For instance, the pollution statistics would be accompanied by program instructions telling how the data display onscreen. Unlike a text-only database in which each record has a similar format, little similarity may exist among the data elements that form the objects.

An object-oriented database management system makes it possible to store objects in an object-oriented database and to copy and paste them into applications, where people can manipulate them in any further way they need. Because any stored object is *reusable,* new applications can be developed in a fraction of the time it took before electronic objects existed. Object technology is a broad concept that applies not only to databases but also to programming languages and program-development tools.

Object-oriented databases are illustrated in Figure PS 3-11. Recently, *object-relational database management systems,* DBMSs that combine both object and relational technology, have come into the marketplace. One such example is Oracle, Version 8. Many industry observers speculate that object-relational databases will eventually supplant relational databases as the standard for ad hoc queries on desktop PCs.

FRONT END
Client PCs run a desktop DBMS (such as Access or Paradox) with a graphical user interface.

Transaction

Confirmation

BACK END
The server computer contains the database, running under a network DBMS package (such as Oracle Server or Microsoft SQL Server).

Server computer

Client PCs

FIGURE PS 3-12

Client-server transaction processing. A typical client-server arrangement consists of "front-end" clients that input transactions and a "back-end" server computer—with the database—that processes transactions.

CLIENT-SERVER SYSTEMS

Recall from Chapter NET 1 that *client-server systems* consist of computer networks in which powerful server computers supply resources to PC workstations, which function as client devices. One of the biggest application areas of client-server systems is database processing, in which the principal resource being managed is a database.

In a typical client-server database application, the client is called the *front end.* Typically, the PC workstation at the front end runs a desktop relational DBMS such as Access or Paradox, both of which can handle SQL or QBE database queries over a network. Both the graphical user interface and the query format are handled by the client computer in its own native way.

At the *back end,* the server program—a package such as Oracle Server, Sybase SQL Server, Informix Online, Microsoft SQL Server, or IBM's DB2—runs on a powerful server computer. The back end manages the database itself, and it translates any SQL or QBE commands coming from the front end into a form it can understand. A typical client-server scenario is illustrated in Figure PS 3-12.

Client-server networks have many compelling benefits, perhaps the most important of which are lower hardware cost and scalability to meet future needs. PCs are easier to use and much less expensive than larger computers—you can put a network in place for a fraction of the cost of a mainframe. Also, anytime you need extra capacity, you can always add a new server or add more power to an existing one—again, at a fraction of the cost of a mainframe.

On the downside, client-server networks do not have nearly the successful track record of centralized mainframe systems, which have been around much longer. Hardware costs may not prove especially significant, either, since they often represent only a small fraction of the total cost of a system. Software for centralized mainframe sites is still much easier to develop and support, and data are also more secure on mainframe systems. The cost to an organization if its data get corrupted or its computers go down for a day can easily dwarf the entire purchase cost of a new system.

Drawbacks notwithstanding, client-server networks are a growing trend. Many industry experts feel that—once some of the implementation problems are worked out—the client-server approach will be the main way that database data are delivered over computer networks.

DISTRIBUTED DATABASE SYSTEMS

In many large computer systems, DBMSs are distributed. A **distributed database** simply divides data among several small computers connected

■ **Distributed database.** A database whose contents are split up over several locations.

through a network instead of consolidating them in a single database on a large centralized mainframe—still the most widespread practice for storing massive databases in large companies. For instance, customer-addresses information may be stored at a corporate-office site, while credit histories may be stored in the credit department, which is located in another building across town.

In a distributed DBMS, data are divided so as to optimize performance measures such as communications cost, response time, storage cost, and security. Moreover, data can be placed at the sites at which they are most needed and best managed. A user calling into the database generally will have no idea where the data are coming from; they could be stored in a computer system in the same building, in a different state, or even in a different country.

When the user makes a request to a distributed DBMS, it is up to the DBMS to determine how to best get the data; how it will do this is transparent to the user. Ideally, a common seamless interface exists among member systems. Thus, users should be able to work under the illusion that all the data are stored locally. Consequently, the user at any client workstation need learn only one set of rules to get information from any server hooked into the network, resulting in minimal delays.

A distributed database system differs somewhat from a *replicated database system,* which stores separate copies of the entire database in multiple locations. Replicated systems are feasible where a high-bandwidth link to a centralized database is impossible or impractical. They are also useful in situations where an extra level of protection is needed, so that processing can still take place when, at one location, the database becomes corrupted or the computer crashes. Replicated databases can be problematic in situations where updates to the same data are made in more than a single location and a clear-cut rule for resolving any conflicts that may result does not exist.

DATA WAREHOUSING AND MINING

Two concepts in the database area that have become hot topics in the past few years are data warehousing and data mining. A **data warehouse** is a comprehensive collection of data that describes the operations of a company. In a typical data warehouse, data from transaction processing and other operations are reorganized and put into a form that is optimized for queries. **Data mining** makes use of the data warehouse by applying intelligent software to scan its contents for subtle patterns that may not be evident to management (see Figure PS 3-13). Put another way, data mining finds answers to questions that managers may never have thought to ask.

As you may have already guessed, the amount of data in a data warehouse can be enormous. One estimate of the amount of data in Wal-Mart's customer data warehouse—which contains facts about who buys what at Wal-Mart—is that it contains at least 43 terabytes of data. If that data was printed out on regular $8\frac{1}{2}'' \times 11''$ sheets of paper and laid end to end, it would reach to the moon and back six times.

Here are a couple of examples of data warehousing and data mining in action. An analysis of supermarket shopping carts might show that when nacho chips are purchased, 60 percent of the time soft drinks are also purchased—unless the chips are on sale, in which case soft-drink purchases jump to 70 percent. This example illustrates how data mining reveals

---

■ **Data warehouse.** A comprehensive collection of data that describes the operations of a company. ■ **Data mining.** Intelligent software that can analyze data warehouses for patterns that management may not even realize exist, and to infer rules from these patterns.

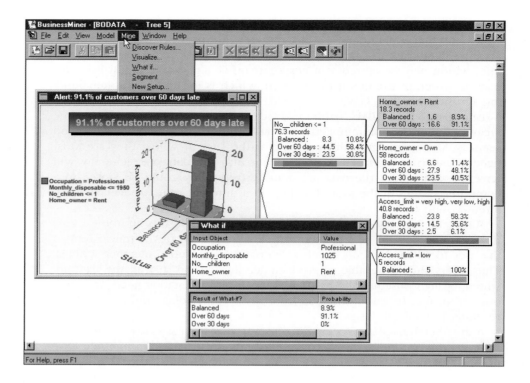

 FIGURE PS 3-13

Data warehousing and mining. The goal of these tools is to find patterns in data that management never imagined existed.

important facts about data *associations.* Other data in another warehouse may suggest that when a new home is purchased, 50 percent of the time a new refrigerator will be bought within a month. In this case, information about *sequences* of transactions is extracted. In both cases, data mining software may provide insight into which types of product promotions pay off and which ones don't.

Prudential Insurance Company of America is one organization using data-mining techniques to figure out how to cross sell to customers. Prudential is made up of about a half dozen business units, each handling a specific product—insurance, securities, healthcare services, and the like. Most of Prudential's customers currently buy from only one of these units. Thus, a goal in the company's data-mining effort is predicting which customers of any given unit would be most likely to buy from another. Prudential's products are more complex than TVs and toasters, and selling them requires more of a personal touch—something that the World Wide Web is increasingly being able to deliver (see the Tomorrow box on page PS 90).

Smaller, specialized versions of data warehouses—called *data marts*—are also quite often seen in practice. Whereas a data warehouse may tackle something as complex as a complete university database, a data mart might take on a small part of that—say, a database of student records.

DATA DEFINITION

DBMS packages targeted to large computer systems usually include a special language component dedicated to the data definition function. Such languages have generically come to be known as **data definition languages (DDLs).** Besides simply defining data, a major function of the DDL in these large packages is security—protecting the database from unauthorized use.

■ **Data definition language (DDL).** A language used to create, store, and manage data in a database environment.

Because a large database management system in a firm is used by numerous people, its databases are particularly vulnerable to security problems. For example, unscrupulous employees may attempt to alter payroll data, access privileged salary or financial account data, or even steal or erase data. To circumvent such possibilities, the DDL may assign passwords when setting up the data dictionary to limit which users access which data. This practice gives users only restricted views of the full database.

Here's an example that shows how restrictions might work: In an airline's passenger reservation database, a regular clerk or agent is not allowed to rebook a special-rate passenger on an alternate flight, but a high-level supervisor, who knows the password, is able to do so.

DATA MANIPULATION

DBMSs targeted to large computer systems often face problems the typical PC-based DBMS user never encounters. For example, on large computer systems (or PCs linked by a network), users often need to access the same data at more or less the same time. This can cause several difficulties. For example:

- Only one seat is available on a flight. Two agents seize it at the same moment and sell it to different customers.

- A program is tallying a series of customer balances in a database. When it is halfway finished, another program controlled by someone else transfers $5,000 from Account 001 (which the first program already has updated) to Account 999 (which it hasn't). Thus, the first program will double-count the $5,000 and obtain erroneous results.

To prevent such problems, most database systems allow access users to place temporary locks on certain blocks of data to ensure that no other modifications to these data will be made during their processing.

Making the COBOL Connection   Another problem unique to DBMSs on large computer systems relates to the need of these DBMSs to tie into programs coded in widely used programming languages. Millions of dollars have been invested in such programs, and many of the programs have been in use well before DBMS technology became a fixture in organizations during the last couple of decades.

An interfacing feature known as a **data manipulation language (DML)** is generally used to handle this problem. The DML is simply a set of commands that enables the language the programmer normally works with to function in a database environment. For example, if the programmer writes programs in COBOL—the most widely used language in business transaction-processing systems—a COBOL DML must be used. The DML may consist of several dozen commands, which the programmer uses to interact with data in the database.

Thus a COBOL program in a database environment consists of a mixture of standard COBOL statements and COBOL DML statements. The program containing this mixture of statements is then fed to the DBMS's COBOL **precompiler,** which translates this program into a standard COBOL program. This program then can be executed with the regular COBOL compiler available on the computer system.

■ **Data manipulation language (DML).** A language used by programmers to supplement a high-level language supported in a database environment. ■ **Precompiler.** A computer program that translates an extended set of programming language commands into standard commands of the language.

Customer Information Systems

How Data Mining and the Web May Change the Balance of Power in Some Industries

With the public becoming ever more comfortable with the World Wide Web as a place to buy—and to get some pretty good deals—many companies are designing strategies to strengthen online ties with consumers. Several types of plans are in the works, and some are ambitious enough to change the very way many products are now being sold.

By and large for companies today, customer service on the Web is still experimental and a cost burden. Many consumers do not use computers and even those that do often find toll-free phone numbers more convenient—especially if there's a complaint or a credit card number to convey. Thus, sellers must maintain both a Web site and a toll-free phone line for customers. It gets expensive. No wonder you hear so much these days about how so few are making money on the Internet.

For some companies, the coming generation of customer information systems (CISs) may change the Web from a cost sink into a gold mine. CISs are computer systems that collect information about buyers. While CISs have existed for years, the latest ones go a step further than their predecessors—they interface with buyers' PCs. Using cookie files, conversation from chat rooms, filled-out questionnaires and registration forms, and other useful information that can be mined from a home PC, a company selling over the Web can build a profile for each visitor. Then, carefully tailored information designed to induce purchases can be downloaded to the PC in the form of a personalized Web site (see image).

Several companies, including Internet bookseller Amazon.com, are currently using data-mining techniques to profile customers and customize sales pitches to them over the Web. Buy a couple of books about French cooking, and you may get a personalized e-mail message or Web page announcing newly published French cookbooks in stock or news that chef Julia Child is hosting an on-line chat at the bookseller's site. A delivery service in Boston that carries groceries and videotapes for people who don't have time to shop goes one step further—it will send its customers a personalized electronic message when it's likely they are running low on key items.

The strategic advantages to studying the behavior of one's customers and treating them in a special way recently hit home in a

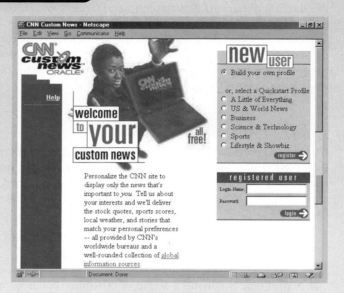

Custom Web site. Technology has made it possible for companies to tailor a marketing strategy to each individual customer.

big way when Amazon.com began also selling CDs and videos at its Web site. Such cross selling has the potential to turn an already big company into a gorilla. Amazon.com, some people feel, has the stuff it takes to become the Wal-Mart of the Internet—that is, the type of place buyers turn to first when they want to buy any type of entertainment product online.

Let's generalize on this phenomenon to see how cross selling online might work miracles for companies in other industries and spell doom for competitors. Suppose that companies such as Dell Computer decide to leverage their famous brand names in the technology area by starting to sell all types of electronics products—not just computers—at their Web sites. Only a limited number of sites have the potential to become major selling portals on the Web, and the victors in the portal battle could rake in the lion's share of the spoils.

Wooing customers isn't easy or cheap, so the gorillas will have an edge here too. Large players can better support the ever-escalating cost of a popular Web site, which includes such freebies as e-mail and personalized chat rooms and Web pages. This has led many futurists to wonder if Web technology—which many people initially thought would level the playing field—will wind up favoring a handful of big, diversified companies as electronic commerce takes off.

High-level languages supported by their own DMLs are called **host languages.** Several host languages may be available on any particular system. Languages that a DBMS commonly employs as hosts are COBOL, C, PL/1, and BASIC.

■ **Host language.** A programming language used to code database applications.

ADVANTAGES AND DISADVANTAGES OF DATABASE MANAGEMENT

A DBMS offers several advantages over filing systems in which data appearing in separate files are not interrelated and centrally managed:

■ BETTER INFORMATION   Because data are integrated in a database environment, information that otherwise might be difficult or impossible to pull together can be collected.

■ FASTER RESPONSE TIME   Because data are integrated into a single database, complex requests can be handled much more quickly.

■ LOWER OPERATING COSTS   Because response time is faster, users can do more work in less time.

■ LOWER STORAGE REQUIREMENTS   In a database system, integration often means that the same data need not appear over and over again in separate files, thereby saving valuable disk space.

■ IMPROVED DATA INTEGRITY   In a database system, integration often means that a data update need be made in only one place to be reflected throughout the system automatically—thereby avoiding the error that is often introduced when the same update has to be made manually in several independent files.

■ BETTER DATA MANAGEMENT   Central storage in a single database gives a DBMS better control over the data dictionary, security, and standards.

However, database processing also has a downside that a company or an individual should consider. The major problem is cost. Significant expenses are normally incurred in the following areas:

■ DATABASE SOFTWARE   Relative to other types of file-management software, a DBMS is expensive. On large computer systems, database packages can cost several thousand dollars.

■ NEW HARDWARE   A DBMS often requires a great deal of memory and secondary storage, and accessing records can be time consuming. Thus, some users find it necessary to upgrade to a bigger, more powerful computer system—with tape or removable-disk backup—after acquiring a DBMS.

■ TRAINING   PC-based database management systems are often considerably more difficult to master than file managers, spreadsheets, and word processors. Relating data in different files can be tricky at times. Also, users who want to custom-design their own applications with the programming-language facility must prepare for a substantial investment in learning time.

Cost is not the only problem. Database processing can increase a system's vulnerability to failure. Because the data in the database are highly integrated, a problem with a key element might render the whole system inactive. Despite the disadvantages, however, DBMSs have become immensely popular with both organizations and individuals.

SUMMARY AND KEY TERMS

Go to the Online Glossary at www.harcourtcollege.com/infosys/parker2000/ student/ to review key terms.

Database management software is widely used to manage large banks of data.

What Is a Database Management System?   A **database management system (DBMS)** is a software system that integrates data in storage and provides easy access to them. DBMSs enable concurrent access to data that could conceivably span several files. The data in a DBMS are placed on disk in a **database,** which is an integrated collection of data.

Database Management on PCs   Database management systems come in several types. **Relational database management systems** are the most common type found on PCs. These systems are so named because they relate data in various database files by common fields in those files. Less-powerful types of packages called *file managers* work with **flat files** that cannot be interrelated. Files in relational DBMSs are commonly called **tables.**

Users gain access to the data they need through an easy-to-use *retrieval/update facility* within their DBMS programs or through applications programs written with a *programming language facility.* DBMSs also contain *utility programs* such as a data dictionary, a large collection of wizards and templates, and a help facility.

One task performed by anyone setting up a database is **data definition**— the process of describing data to the DBMS prior to entering them. The descriptions of these data are used to create a **file structure,** with a screen form or **template** for entering the data, and a **data dictionary** for the application. Both the file structure and data dictionary contain a **field descriptor** for each field of data in the database.

The process of using the database in some hands-on fashion is called **data manipulation.** Data manipulation encompasses a variety of activities, including the creation of database data, file maintenance, information retrieval (query), reporting, sorting, and calculating. **Structured query language (SQL)** is today's de facto standard for information retrieval in relational databases. A tool called **query by example (QBE)** within most PC-based DBMSs allows users to easily frame database queries without knowing how to write SQL commands. A DBMS usually comes with an **indexing** feature that tells how database output is to be rearranged.

Database Management on Large Computer Systems   Traditionally, database systems have conformed to one of three common types: relational, hierarchical, and network. A **hierarchical database management system** stores data in the form of a tree, where the relationship between data elements is one-to-many. In a **network database management system** the relationship between data elements can be either many-to-one or many-to-many. The growing interest in other data types and the need to combine them into multimedia formats for applications have given rise to **object-oriented database management systems.** These databases combine disparate data types into storable entities called **objects.**

One of the largest applications of *client-server systems* is in the database area, in which the principal resource being managed is a database. Typically, the client computers and their desktop DBMSs are called the *front end,* and the server computer that is managing the DBMS is called the *back end.*

Many applications set up **distributed databases.** Instead of a single database existing on a large centralized mainframe—still the most widespread practice for storing database data in large companies—the database is divided among several smaller computers that are hooked up in a network.

Two concepts in the database area that have become hot topics in the past few years are data warehousing and data mining. A **data warehouse** is a comprehensive collection of data that describes the operations of the company. **Data mining** consists of intelligent software that can analyze data warehouses for patterns that management may not even realize exist.

Many PC-based DBMSs come with only a single proprietary language that has commands for data definition, retrieval/update, reporting, and programming functions. Large computer systems that use sophisticated DBMSs usually have a special language dedicated to each of these tasks. For example, a **data definition language (DDL)** handles data definition chores, placing key uses for applications development and security purposes into a data dictionary. A **data manipulation language (DML)** extends the language the programmer normally works with into a database environment. Languages supported by their own DMLs are called **host languages.** A program called a **precompiler** translates DML commands into host-language commands, which in turn can be executed on the regular compilers available at the computer site.

On a large computer system, a DBMS package must deal with the problem of several users trying to access the database at the same time. To prevent problems associated with conflicting uses, most database systems allow users to place a temporary lock on certain blocks of data to ensure that no other modifications to these data will be made during processing.

Advantages and Disadvantages of Database Management   A DBMS can offer several advantages over filing systems in which data appearing in independent files cannot be centrally managed and concurrently accessed. Among these advantages are better information, faster response time, lower operating costs, fewer data storage requirements, improved data integrity, and better data management. The biggest disadvantage is cost. Costs are normally incurred in the areas of new hardware and software, training, and conversion. Still another disadvantage is greater vulnerability to failure.

EXERCISES

1. Fill in the blanks:
   a. Each database record consists of distinct types of data called _____ .
   b. _____ database management systems are the type of DBMSs typically found on PCs.
   c. On corporate database management systems, a knowledgeable professional known as a(n) _____ often sets up database applications for users.
   d. The facility that manages characteristics of data and programs in a database environment is called a data _____ .
   e. SQL is an acronym for _____ .

2. Match each term with the description that fits best:
   a. data mining   d. QBE
   b. front end   e. host language
   c. DDL   f. data definition

   _____ A language used to describe database data
   _____ The language that is extended by a DML (data manipulation language)
   _____ Intelligent software used to analyze data in a data warehouse
   _____ A screen that lets users easily frame database queries
   _____ Organizing data in the database so that programmers and users have access to them, data are stored as efficiently as possible, and the database's security is maintained
   _____ A client PC running Access or Paradox, for example

3. Define the following terms in your own words:
   a. Flat file   d. Object-oriented database
   b. Field descriptor e. File structure
   c. SQL

4. Describe the differences between these pairs of terms:
   a. A file and a database
   b. Data warehousing and data mining
   c. A front end and a back end in a client-server network
   d. Data definition and data manipulation
   e. A distributed database and a replicated database

5. For each of the following types of database management systems, describe how data relate to one another:
   a. Relational DBMS
   b. Hierarchical DBMS
   c. Network DBMS

6. How do large database management systems solve the problem of one user trying to use data that are in the process of being updated by someone else?

7. Describe, using both your own words and an example, how a relational database works.

8. Name at least five advantages and four disadvantages of database management systems.

9. Refer to the two relational database tables at the top of the next column and answer the following questions:
   a. What is the average salary of an employee in the Sales department?
   b. Which employees does Jonas supervise?
   c. What is the average salary under Hurt's supervision?

Employee Table

Name	Location	Department	Salary
Doney	Phoenix	Accounting	$58,000
Black	Denver	Sales	$71,000
James	Cleveland	Sales	$44,000
Giles	San Diego	Accounting	$62,000
Smith	Miami	Accounting	$73,000
Fink	San Diego	Sales	$54,000
...	...	...	...

Office Table

Location	Manager
San Diego	Hurt
Cleveland	Holmes
Miami	Jonas
Phoenix	Alexis
...	...

   d. In which of the preceding questions did you have to relate data in both tables to get an answer? Through what fields did you relate tables?

10. Referring to the table below, answer the following questions:
   a. How many records are there? How many fields?
   b. Are there any logical fields? If so, name them.
   c. How many file structures would have to be created to enter the data in this table into a database?

Customer number	Name	Street	City	State	ZIP	Charge account?
810	John T. Smith	31 Cedarcrest	Boulder	CO	80302	Yes
775	Sally Jones	725 Agua Fria	Santa Fe	NM	87501	Yes
690	William Holmes	3269 Fast Lane	Santa Fe	NM	87501	No
840	Artis Smith	2332 Alameda	Lakewood	CO	80215	Yes
574	Nellie Deutsch	23 E. Spruce	Olathe	KS	66061	No
447	Vernon Pressy	5541 Canyon	Boulder	CO	80302	Yes
480	Benton Fink	440 Arapahoe	Boulder	CO	80302	No
401	Wayne Montoya	600 Tara Lane	Englewood	CO	80155	No
640	C. Foster Kane	P.O. Box 6000	Santa Fe	NM	87501	Yes
505	Alice Evans	5702 North St.	Boise	ID	83704	Yes
102	Maya Ellis	603 Oakwood	Aurora	CO	80011	Yes
754	Shane Williams	275 East Kiowa	Flagstaff	AZ	86001	No
801	Del Lopez	80 Williston	Austin	TX	78755	No
908	Duke Miller	CM Ranch	Stanley	NM	87056	No
665	Bette White	Box 20	Rowe	NM	87562	Yes
760	Kim Lundy	44 West St.	Missoula	MT	59802	No

PROJECTS

1. **You Be the Judge**   The owner of a 40-employee advertising agency is about to purchase a well-known PC database program to manage a growing client list on a desktop computer system. One of her most trusted employees is a computer whiz who has suggested providing her with a free copy of a database management system he has written himself—one he claims will better fit the agency's needs. What would you advise the owner to do in this situation—say yes, say no, or gather more information?

 2. **Large Databases**   Most colleges and universities have large database systems for their student and faculty records, as do companies for their client and employee records. Select one such database for study and write a three-to-five-page paper about it that answers most if not all of the following questions:

   ■ Describe the database briefly. What is its name and purpose?
   ■ What types of data are contained in the database?

- On what type of computer system(s) does the database exist?
- How large is the database?
- Who uses the database? What types of information does the database supply to these users?
- What types of database software products are used with the database?
- Who manages the database?

3. PC-based DBMSs Three of the leading PC-based DBMS programs are Microsoft's Access, Borland's Paradox (sold by both Borland and Corel), and Lotus's Approach. For each of these packages, answer the following questions:

a. Are the programs sold separately? Can you buy any of them as part of a suite?

b. What is the list and street price of each program? Provide the price of both the full standalone program, for users who don't have an earlier version, and the update. Also provide suite pricing.

You can do this exercise through journal-article or book research, by looking at the programs in stores and asking questions, or by seeing what you can find on the Internet. The companies producing these DBMSs can be located at the following Web sites:

COMPANY	WEB ADDRESS
Borland	www.borland.com
Lotus	www.lotus.com
Microsoft	www.microsoft.com

4. Report Wizards Because database management systems are harder to use than word processors or spreadsheets, you are likely to find more wizards available. For a PC database program of your choice, find out what type of wizards it contains, and prepare a list that names each wizard and its purpose. Note that *wizards*—principally, a Microsoft Office term—are called *experts* in Paradox and *assistants* in Access.

5. Creating Your Own Database and Report The finished report in Figure PS 3-9 is part of the first page of a multipage alphabetized report of a videotape collection. The report was prepared on Microsoft Access with a report wizard. The fields in the report show the movie title, the stars, the year the movie was made, the length of the movie, and the videotape on which the movie is located. For this project do the following:

a. Enter your own videotape, CD, stamp, or coin collection—or any other collection of your choice—into the database system available on your own computer system or in your school's computer lab. If you wish, limit the number of records to 15. You should have at least three fields in your database table.

b. Use a wizard to produce a report similar to one in the figure, which is sorted on Movie name. Sort the report on any one key field, and then produce another copy of the report that sorts on another key field.

c. After your final sort, select some criterion to filter records—for instance, in a movie file, selecting only Alfred Hitchcock movies—and have the database manager automatically extract the records for you.

6. Internet Yellow Pages Revisited Feature PS 3-2 explores the usefulness of Web phone directories for looking up information about businesses. For this project, choose any of the directories in the accompanying figure and observe how it works. Report to the class your experiences, being sure to cover such information as how comprehensive the directory is, what types of listings the directory contains, and the search tools available with the directory. More directories can be found by summoning a search engine such as Yahoo! or Excite. At the Yahoo! site, for instance, select Yellow Pages to get you started.

7. Internet White Pages Need to get in touch with a long lost friend or relative, but you don't know their phone number or their e-mail address or where they're currently living? A few sites on the Internet may help; they let you search for people. Three such locations are Yahoo!'s People Search site (people.yahoo.com) shown in the image on the following page, Switchboard's Internet Directory (www.switchboard.com), and Lycos' WhoWhere? site (www.whowhere.lycos.com).

Visit any of these sites—or another, similar one of your own choosing—and report to your class about it. Be sure to tell what types of searching you can do at the site (some will also let you search through Yellow Pages) and how the searching works. Also use the site to try to find a lost friend or relative, and report the results.

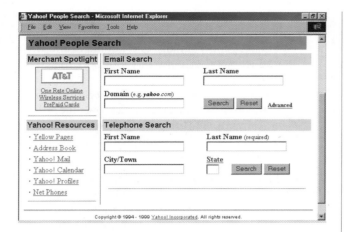

The fields are:
Employee
Telephone
Gender
Employed
Salary
Department

The employees are:

Pratt, John	Smoller, Ellen	Johnson, Frank	Smith, Paul
225-1234	225-3212	223-7928	223-8251
Male	Female	Male	Male
06/22/88	09/15/88	03/20/86	11/01/85
1949	1650	1500	1800
MIS	MIS	MIS	Accounting
Jones, David	Martins, Mary	Sill, Sally	Terrific, Tom
292-3832	222-2132	224-4321	222-1900
Male	Female	Female	Male
06/15/88	11/01/85	02/15/87	10/30/97
1500	1850	1800	1400
Accounting	Accounting	Personnel	MIS
	Beam, Sandy	Knat, Michael	
	225-6912	221-1235	
	Female	Male	
	02/15/86	09/15/95	
	1450	1700	
	MIS	Personnel	

 8. **Creating a Database and Performing Database Operations** Using the database management system available on your own computer system or in your school's computer lab, create a table for the records in the figure at the top of the next column. Count the maximum number of characters in each field and decide on the maximum width of each of the fields. Define monthly Salary as a numeric field, Employed as a date field, and all other fields as text. Then complete the following tasks:
  a. Display the names of all persons in the Personnel department.
  b. Display the names of all persons earning more than $1,600 per month.
  c. Display the names of all persons who are either working in the MIS department or making more than $1,700 a month.
  d. Arrange the file alphabetically by department and, within department, by last name.
  e. Arrange the file from highest-to-lowest-salaried employee. If there is a tie for salary, list tied employees in alphabetical order. On the screen, have only the name of the employee and the salary show, with all other information hidden.

9. **Library DBMSs** Do this project only if your school library has a computerized catalog of book titles. Answer the following questions:

a. What is the name of the software package(s) used to keep track of titles on shelves, book checkins and checkouts, information queries, and so on?
b. Does the library's software use a fully-fledged DBMS or just a file manager? How do you know? If a DBMS is in use, which type of model does it follow—hierarchical, relational, or some other type?
c. What type of reporting system does the library's software include to help librarians better perform their jobs?

 10. **QBE Interfaces** Figure PS 3-7 features a Web-based QBE interface. Find at least two other Web sites that use QBE screens to query users for information and report to your class about them. Each screen should ask users for at least two conditions by which to search.

ONLINE REVIEW

Go to the Online Review at www.harcourtcollege.com/infosys/parker2000/ student/ to test your understanding of this chapter's concepts.

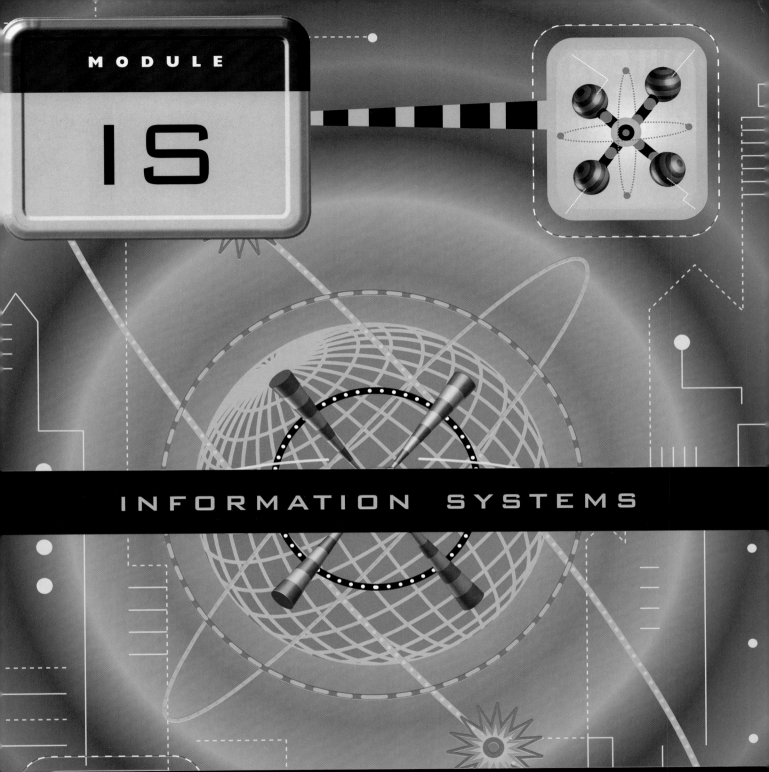

MODULE

IS

INFORMATION SYSTEMS

This module integrates several concepts from earlier chapters. It ties together the basic elements that form computer systems—hardware, software, data, people, and procedures.

Chapter IS 1 looks at computer systems in organizations. In the first part of the chapter you will learn about the principal types of systems used and the roles these systems play. The balance of the chapter is about the sorts of activities performed in system building and the kinds of people involved in this effort.

Chapter IS 2 covers applications software development. Here you'll learn about some of the tools computer professionals use to design and code programs, as well as gain an understanding of what various programming languages do.

MODULE CONTENTS
Information Systems

ISBN 0-03-025968-1

DEVELOPING ORGANIZATIONAL SYSTEMS

OUTLINE

LEARNING OBJECTIVES

After completing this chapter, you will be able to:

1. Explain what a system is.

2. Describe several types of computer systems commonly found in organizations.

3. Define the roles of various people and information systems areas in the systems development process.

4. Identify and describe the components of the systems development life cycle (SDLC).

5. Describe several approaches used to develop systems.

OVERVIEW

In previous modules of this textbook we considered primarily hardware and software. Here we turn to the process of putting these elements together into complete computer systems.

All organizations have various sorts of systems—for example, systems that attend to accounting activities such as sending out bills and processing payrolls, systems that provide information to help managers make decisions, systems that help run factories efficiently, and so on. Such systems require considerable effort to design, build, and maintain. The process that includes the planning, building, and maintenance of systems is called *systems development.*

Unfortunately, since no two situations are exactly alike, there is no surefire formula for successful systems development. A procedure that works well in one situation may fail in another. These facts notwithstanding, there is a set of general principles, that, if understood, will enhance the likelihood of a system's success. Those principles are the subject of this chapter.

The chapter opens with a discussion of systems and systems development. Then we cover the types of systems commonly found in organizations. From there we turn to the computer professionals who are hired to develop systems in organizations and consider some of their primary responsibilities. Then we look at the systems development life cycle—the set of activities that are at the heart of every serious systems-building effort. Chapter IS 1 concludes with a discussion of the major approaches to systems development.

Systems chapters in introductory textbooks often leave readers with the impression that practices within companies usually conform to a predictable, button-down approach. The collection of short stories within the Inside the Industry box may dispel such thoughts.

ON SYSTEMS

A **system** is a collection of elements and procedures that interact to accomplish a goal. A football game, for example, is played according to a system. It consists of a collection of elements (two teams, a playing field, referees) and procedures (the rules of the game) that interact to determine which team is the winner. A transit system is a collection of people, machines, work rules, fares, and schedules that get people from one place to another. Similarly, a computer system is a collection of people, hardware, software, data, and procedures that interact to perform information processing tasks.

The function of many systems, whether manual or computerized, is to keep an organization well managed and running smoothly. Systems are created and altered in response to changing needs within an organization and shifting conditions in its surrounding environment. When problems arise in an existing system or a new system is needed, systems development comes into play. **Systems development** is the process of analyzing a work environment, designing a new system for it or making modifications to the current one, acquiring needed hardware and software, training users, and getting the new or modified system to work.

Systems development may be required for many reasons. New laws may call for the collection of data never before assembled. The government may require new data on personnel, for example. The introduction of new technology, especially new computer technology, may prompt the wholesale revision of a system.

■ **System.** A collection of elements and procedures that interact to accomplish a goal. ■ **Systems development.** The ongoing process of improving ways of doing work.

Did You Know?

- Steve Jobs, Apple Computer founder and current leader, is an ardent Beatles fan. He named his company after Apple Records, the recording label of the famous British rock group.

- Microsoft's campus of more than two dozen structures has no Building 7. When a site was originally chosen, employees objected that too many trees would have to be cut down. Management agreed and went on to Building 8.

- There is a long history at Sun Microsystems of jokes played on founders on April Fools' Day. In 1988, CEO Scott McNealy's office was turned into a golf course; in 1994, it was rearranged into a day-care center. In other years, one founder had a Volkswagen Bug reassembled inside his office and another had his Ferrari put in the middle of a pond at Sun headquarters.

- In 1992, college student Marc Andreessen began a $6-an-hour programming job at a national supercomputing lab, where he worked on the development of a Web browser called Mosaic. About two years later, he started a company called Netscape, whose main product is Navigator, a Mosaic look-alike. Before the end of 1995, Andreessen's share in Netscape was worth over $170 million.

- When Microsoft created PC-DOS in the early 1980s for the IBM PC, IBM insisted on tight security. DOS was developed in a small, secret, windowless room, where temperatures sometimes reached 100 degrees. Talk about programmers sweating it out.

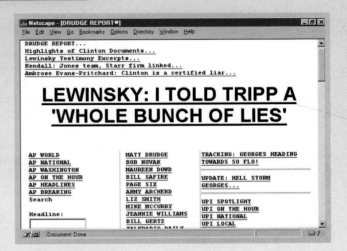

www.drudgereport.com. Word of the Clinton presidential scandal first broke at this site and became a seminal event on the Web, proving the power of the latter as a grassroots communications medium.

- The Monica Lewinsky scandal first broke on the Web, at a controversial and gossipy news site called the Drudge Report (see image). Matt Drudge, founder of the site and quite a character in his own right, became an instant celebrity for beating all of the major news organizations to the punch. He now hosts his own TV show.

- When one famous PC software company first began to ship 5¼-inch diskettes to its customers back in the 1980s, the installation instructions asked users to take the disk out of its sleeve and insert it in the computer. Some naive customers mistook the disk cover as the paper sleeve it came in, cut it open, and put a bare disk into the drive.

Or, as is the trend today, a company may decide to convert certain applications into a global networked environment or, possibly, expand some of its systems so that not only employees but also customers and suppliers can tap into it on the Internet. These and other kinds of new requirements often bring about major changes in the systems by which work is done in an organization.

ORGANIZATIONAL SYSTEMS

Undoubtedly, you've already encountered many types of systems in organizations. When you go into the supermarket, you generally see in use electronic cash registers and various handheld or laser scanning devices that are obviously a part of some supermarket system. Or when you've registered for classes, perhaps you've observed someone at a display workstation checking to see whether a certain class you want to take is still open and whether you've paid all your bills—apparently as part of a registration system.

While hundreds of "types" of computer systems are in existence today, many fall into one or more of four categories: transaction processing systems, information systems, office systems, and design and manufacturing systems. Here we'll look more closely at each of these. We will also explore enterprise resource planning, which ties together several business activities, and artificial intelligence, which can impart to a system certain characteristics that one would normally attribute to humans.

TRANSACTION PROCESSING SYSTEMS

Virtually every company carries out a number of routine accounting operations, most of which involve some form of tedious record keeping. These operations, such as payroll and accounts receivable, inspired some of the earliest commercial applications of computers in organizations and are still among the most important. Because these systems heavily involve processing business transactions—such as paying employees, recording customer purchases and payments, and recording vendor receipts and payments—they are called **transaction processing systems** (see Figure IS 1-1).

Some of the functions commonly performed by transaction processing systems are discussed in the following paragraphs.

FIGURE IS 1-1

Transaction processing systems. Two of the core routines in transaction-processing programs are accounts receivable—which keeps track of money coming in to a company—and accounts payable—which keeps track of money going out.

ACCOUNTS RECEIVABLE
Accounts receivable systems produce customer billings, send reminder notices, and record subsequent payments.

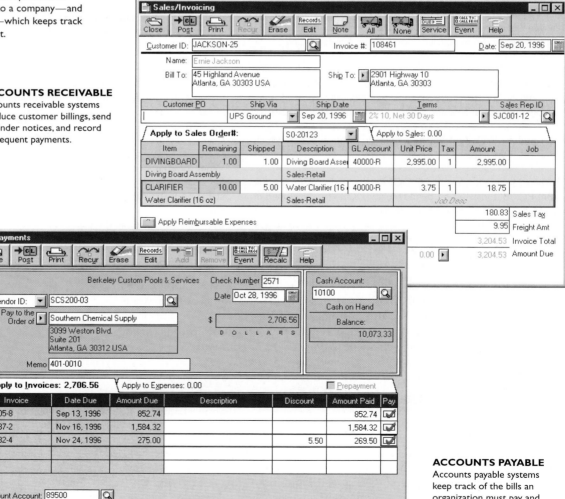

ACCOUNTS PAYABLE
Accounts payable systems keep track of the bills an organization must pay and generate checks to pay them.

■ **Transaction processing system.** A system that handles data created by an organization's business transactions.

Payroll   *Payroll systems* compute deductions, subtract them from gross earnings, and write paychecks to employees for the remainder. These systems also contain programs that prepare reports for management and for taxing agencies of federal, state, and local governments.

Order Entry   Many organizations handle some type of order processing on a daily basis. Customers call in orders by phone, send in written orders by ordinary mail or by computer, or place orders in person. The systems that record and help staff members manage such transactions are called *order-entry systems.*

Inventory Control   The units of product that a company holds in stock to use or sell at a given moment make up its inventory. An *inventory control system* keeps track of the number of units of each product in inventory and ensures that reasonable quantities of products are maintained.

Accounts Receivable   The term *accounts receivable* refers to the amounts owed by customers who have made purchases on credit. Accounts receivable systems are charged with keeping track of customers' purchases, payments, and account balances. They also produce invoices and monthly account statements and provide information to management. Other output includes sales analyses, which describe changing patterns of products and sales, as well as detailed or summary reports on current and past-due accounts.

Accounts Payable   The term *accounts payable* refers to the money a company owes to other companies for the goods and services it has received. An accounts payable system keeps track of bills and often generates checks to pay them. It records who gets paid and when, handles cash disbursements, and advises managers about whether they should accept discounts offered by vendors in return for early payment.

General Ledger   A *general ledger (G/L) system* keeps track of all financial summaries, including those originating from payroll, accounts receivable, accounts payable, and other sources (see Figure IS 1-2). It also ensures that a company's books balance properly. A typical G/L system may also produce accounting reports such as income statements, balance sheets, and general ledger balances.

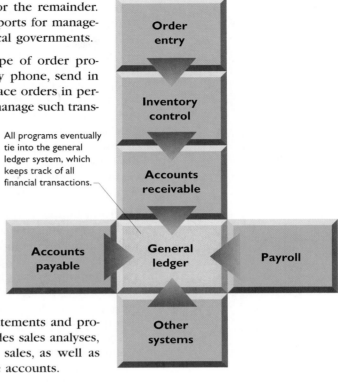

All programs eventually tie into the general ledger system, which keeps track of all financial transactions.

FIGURE IS 1-2

Transaction-processing system.
Transaction-processing systems are comprised of several interdependent programs.

INFORMATION SYSTEMS

In the early days of commercial computing, businesses purchased computers almost exclusively to perform routine transaction processing tasks. Used in this way, the computers cut clerical expenses considerably. As time passed, however, it became apparent that the computer could do much more than replace clerks. It could also provide information to assist managers in their decision-making role.

A system that generates information for use by decision makers is called an **information system.** With an information system, for instance, management can incorporate many more facts into decisions and spend less time gathering them. As a result, managers have more time to do the things they do best—think creatively and interact with people. Although most information systems within organizations serve employees, increasingly information systems are expanding to support the needs of customers and suppliers.

Two major types of information systems are information reporting systems and decision support systems.

■ **Information system.** A system designed to provide information to help people make decisions.

Information Reporting Systems **Information reporting systems** evolved from transaction processing systems and became the first type of information system. They provide decision makers with preselected types of information, generally in the form of computer-generated reports. The types of information that people receive are often preplanned, just like the information you see on your monthly checking account statements. The individual *values* on your statements, such as check numbers and amounts, may change from month to month, but the *types* of information you receive generally remain the same. Also, you and every other person mailed checking account statements by your bank receive virtually the same type of information.

Many information reporting systems provide decision makers with information that is a by-product of the data generated through transaction processing. For instance, a manager in the receivables department will regularly be issued a report listing overdue accounts.

Decision Support Systems A **decision support system (DSS)** helps people organize and analyze their own decision-making information. It is useful to anyone whose requirements for information are unpredictable and unstructured. Each DSS is tailored around the needs of an individual or group. Thus, a sales support system is the name typically given to a DSS aimed at the special decision-making needs of salespeople or marketing personnel. Likewise, a fire-suppression support system might be a DSS targeted to helping a forest supervisor develop specific strategies for fighting wildfires.

Let's put DSSs into perspective with an example. To assist with making product pricing decisions, a sales manager uses a DSS that has been set up on a PC. From menus, the manager first accesses the price of an item. Then he or she asks for the average price of several other items, and then for the inventory turnover of yet a different item. Next, a financial model may be used to predict the sales volumes for specific items five years into the future. As the example suggests, the manager can pose questions as the need evolves and receive answers at once. At the end of the interactive session, the manager uses the DSS to prepare a summary of important findings and some charts for a meeting. The next time the manager uses the DSS, other types of information may be collected and analyzed.

Figure IS 1-3 shows decision support systems at work. One specialized type of decision support system we will cover next is targeted to worker groups, while another is aimed at executives.

GROUP DECISION SUPPORT SYSTEMS A **group decision support system (GDSS)** is a decision support system in which several people routinely interact through a computer network in order to solve common problems. GDSSs fall under the general heading of *workgroup computing* tools, or *groupware,* which includes not only decision-making applications but also other uses involving groups of people, such as scheduling meetings and appointments and engaging in ordinary e-mail.

The insurance field provides a good example of a GDSS. Several photos and forms are often needed to process an accident claim. An adjuster may take a picture of a damaged car and prepare an adjustment form. An estimate and a claim form will also be prepared. Gradually, a dossier on the accident will be developed. All of these documents would be read into the computer system with an image scanner and put into a form that can be annotated, processed, and shared electronically by people working over a network in the claims department. The claims-department employees can each in turn call up the file, sign off on certain documents, and add other documents. They

---

■ **Information reporting system.** A type of information system whose principal outputs are preformatted reports.
■ **Decision support system (DSS).** A type of information system that provides people with tools and capabilities to help them satisfy their own information needs. ■ **Group decision support system (GDSS).** A decision support system that helps several people to routinely interact through a computer network to solve common problems.

A sales-support database helps a field representative from a pharmaceutical firm and a physician inspect clinical results on a blood-pressure medicine.

Some DSSs come with routines that overlay decision-making information on maps. In the application shown here, disaster-relief planners can pull up and analyze flood data, to help minimize property damage. Flood insurance companies also use this data to set premium rates.

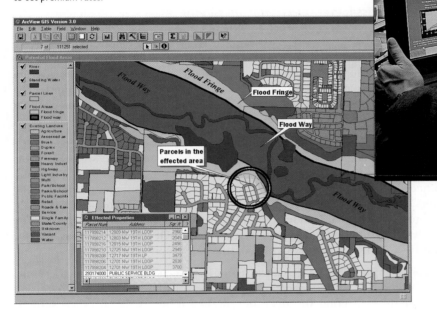

FIGURE IS 1-3

Decision support systems.

can also "meet," using their workstations, to make joint decisions on particular cases.

Software is often used both to run the system and to measure how well it is working. **Workflow software** does the latter chore, automatically keeping track of documents, recording how long documents take to process at each workstation, and spotting any processing bottlenecks that occur. Processing claims with a GDSS and workflow software can be done faster and more cost effectively than with traditional processing methods. There is minimal chance of documents being lost and better service to the policyholder too.

EXECUTIVE INFORMATION SYSTEMS **Executive information systems (EISs)** are DSSs customized to meet the special needs of the people who run organizations. As many executives see it, the business world today is so competitive and fast paced that they need instant access to the freshest information. Among executives' favorite applications are database management systems that access corporate and financial data, networking applications that provide information that is external to the organization, electronic mail systems that streamline contact with subordinates, and customized spreadsheets that let important ratios and trends be displayed in a graphical format. Because many executives don't type, they require easy-to-learn, easy-to-use graphical user interfaces that involve making selections with a pointing device.

■ **Workflow software.** A program that tracks the progress of documents in a system and measures the performance of people processing the documents. ■ **Executive information system (EIS).** A decision support system tailored to the needs of a specific top-level individual in an organization.

OFFICE SYSTEMS

In recent years, computer technology has been used widely to increase productivity in the office. The term **office automation (OA)** describes this phenomenon. Office automation can be achieved through a wide variety of technologies and processing techniques, as described in this section.

Document Processing   The staple of most organizations is the document—memos, letters, reports, manuals, forms, and the like. Consequently, a major focus of office automation relates to the creation, distribution, and storage of documents. Sometimes the catchall phrase *document processing* is used to collectively refer to such office technologies as word processing, desktop publishing, and the types of electronic document handling found in GDSSs.

Electronic Messaging   *Electronic messaging* makes it possible to send memos, letters, manuscripts, legal documents, and the like from one computer system or terminal to another. Two familiar examples of electronic messaging are **electronic mail (e-mail)** and **facsimile (fax).** E-mail is the computer-to-computer equivalent of interoffice mail or the postal service, whereas *fax* refers to an alternative method for the transmission of text documents, pictures, maps, diagrams, and the like over the phone lines. Both e-mail and fax are extensively discussed in detail in the NET module of this textbook.

Desk Accessories   *Desk accessories*—which are sometimes called *desktop organizers* or *personal information managers (PIMs)*—are software packages that provide the electronic equivalents of features commonly found on an office desktop (see Figure IS 1-4). Desk accessory software varies among vendors. Many offer such features as a calendar for scheduling appointments, a daily to-do list, and a Rolodex-type file for storing names and addresses. The latest desk accessories enable some features—such as the calendar—to be shared by a group of workers collaborating on a common product.

Decision Support Tools   Because many key decisions are made by white-collar workers, it's understandable that offices maintain a variety of decision support systems. Among the decision support tools useful in office settings are spreadsheets, presentation graphics, plotters and laser printers, color monitors, and relational database management systems. All of these software and hardware tools have contributed to streamlining life at the office and were discussed in earlier modules of the book.

Teleconferencing   **Teleconferencing** makes it possible for a group of people to meet electronically, thereby avoiding the time and expense they would incur if they were to get together physically in one spot. Applications include business conferences, medical assistance for rural areas, and distance learning. About a decade ago, teleconferencing required specially equipped rooms as well as hardware and software costing several thousands of dollars. Today, just about anyone can add an Internet-based teleconferencing component to their own computer system for a few hundred dollars (see Figure IS 1-5).

Teleconferencing often involves a combination of audio, video, and computer components. Systems vary widely. Many operate over ISDN or regular-telephone lines, or over LANs with dedicated cables. To get the best audio and video quality, you still have to go to a specially equipped room. Tools have also recently become available that enable teleconferencing participants to create images and annotate them in real time, either on the screen or on *whiteboards*

For links to further information about teleconferencing and telecommuting, go to www.harcourtcollege.com/ infosys/parker2000/student/ explore/ and click on Chapter IS 1.

■ **Office automation (OA).** Computer-based office-oriented technologies such as word processing, desktop publishing, electronic mail, teleconferencing, and the like. ■ **Electronic mail.** The computer-to-computer equivalent of interoffice mail or the postal service. Also called **e-mail.** ■ **Facsimile.** A method for the transmission of text documents, pictures, maps, diagrams, and the like over the phone lines. Abbreviated as **fax.** ■ **Teleconferencing.** Using the computer and communications technology to carry on a meeting between people in different locations.

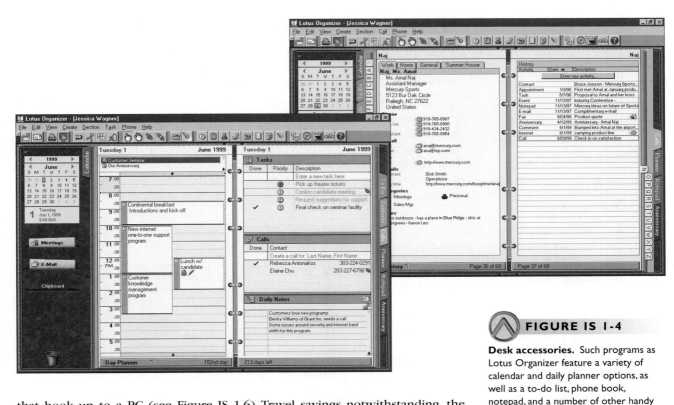

FIGURE IS 1-4

Desk accessories. Such programs as Lotus Organizer feature a variety of calendar and daily planner options, as well as a to-do list, phone book, notepad, and a number of other handy features.

FIGURE IS 1-5

Video teleconferencing. Video teleconferencing hardware and software can be installed on a PC for less than $500 today.

that hook up to a PC (see Figure IS 1-6). Travel savings notwithstanding, the biggest benefit to teleconferencing is something most technology experts may never have anticipated—the ability to bring together company experts quickly in order to solve problems. Teleconferencing may someday enable even larger numbers of office personnel to work out of their homes, a subject to which we now turn.

Telecommuting **Telecommuting** is the term used to describe people working at home and linking up to their employers through a desktop workstation, laptop computer, fax machine, or some other type of computer-age tool. Many computer programmers, for example, telecommute either entirely or in part, because they prefer to do so, because they are more productive at home, or because they don't need supervision.

Telecommuting can save workers both the time and expense involved in traveling to work. It can also save businesses the expense of maintaining office and parking space (see Feature IS 1-1 on page IS 13). On the negative side, telecommuting limits the face-to-face interpersonal contact that people get from working in an office. Also, telecommuting requires a major cultural adjustment for both individuals and organizations accustomed to onsite supervision. Many critics of telecommuting have also pointed out that a person not seen around the office, where interpersonal bonding most effectively takes place, is less likely to be promoted. Yet telecommuting seems to be an unstoppable trend and a computer-age phenomenon that will impact growing numbers of office workers as we go further into the twenty-first century.

■ **Telecommuting.** Working through one's home and being connected by means of electronic devices to other coworkers at remote locations.

DESIGN AND MANUFACTURING SYSTEMS

Computers are widely used in organizational settings to improve productivity both at the design stage—through *computer-aided design (CAD)*—and at the manufacturing stage through *computer-aided manufacturing (CAM)*.

Computer-Aided Design (CAD) By using **computer-aided design (CAD),** designers can dramatically reduce the time they spend developing products. For example, by using light pens and specialized graphics workstations, engineers or architects can sketch ideas directly into the computer system and then instruct it to analyze the proposed design in terms of how well it meets a number of design criteria. Using the subsequent computer output, designers can modify their drawings until they achieve the desired results.

FIGURE IS 1-6

Whiteboards. Electronic whiteboards are designed to let people share visually complex ideas over networks.

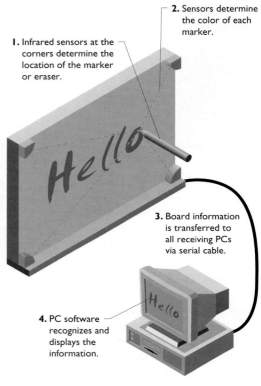

2. Sensors determine the color of each marker.

1. Infrared sensors at the corners determine the location of the marker or eraser.

3. Board information is transferred to all receiving PCs via serial cable.

4. PC software recognizes and displays the information.

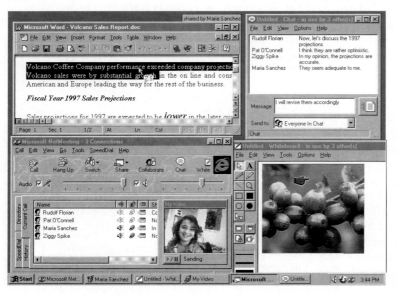

Microsoft's NetMeeting provides both images of conference participants and onscreen whiteboarding at the same time.

■ **Computer-aided design (CAD).** A general term applied to the use of computer technology to automate design functions.

Virtual Offices

Are the Days of the Physical Office Numbered?

For many people, working at home and going to the office only when they choose is the ideal situation. Think of the benefits. You don't have to get dressed up. You avert the bumper-to-bumper commute that can raise your stress level. You're not likely to waste time in idle office chitchat. You save gas money. On and on and on go the advantages. In many organizations, the *virtual office*—working anywhere you are most productive—has become not only a reality but also a growing trend.

At Compaq Computer, many salespeople work from their homes. In the morning, a salesperson might connect to the computer system at headquarters and download on his or her laptop computer all e-mail messages and pertinent account data needed for the day's meetings. On the road, workers can plug their laptops into corporate databases from a phone jack or, if no jack is available, from a cellular modem. If, for example, a client requests a price sheet or a brochure, the salesperson does not need to go to the office to pick one up—it can be downloaded and printed on a local printer.

Some of the nation's largest accounting and consulting firms have also been moving toward a virtual-office scenario for several years. At Ernst & Young's Chicago office, for instance, most of the 1,000 or so accountants and consultants have to book space when they want to work at the office. The process—called *hoteling*—works almost like reserving hotel rooms. Years ago, the company realized that although it was paying for costly office space for all of its employees, a large percentage of them were on the road at any given time.

Virtual offices do not come without their problems. Many people, for instance, prefer to work at the office. Some make the compelling case that a worker not seen is a worker not pro-

A day at the (virtual) office. Work is something you do, not a place to which you go.

moted. Also, when some people are separated from coworkers, they begin to wonder what holds the company together. Additionally, many people have worked years to get nice offices and have come to look at them as status symbols. When these are taken away, the workers may believe they're being demoted. Problems often also result from trying to manage an office complex in a smaller physical space. People who are supposed to come in often do not show up, and sometimes people who are supposed to leave discover they need to stay longer to get their work done.

Will almost every office worker someday be working where he or she pleases? That's a possibility, although the conversion will take time. Today, workers by the tens of millions are operating at least part-time out of their homes, and that number is likely to increase. As Internet videoconferencing becomes more of a reality, the ranks of telecommuters could surge. To get the most knowledgeable workers, more companies will have to abandon old attitudes about the workplace and be willing to make concessions. After all, the virtual-office advocates remind us, work is something you do, not a place to which you go.

CAD is especially helpful in designing automobiles, aircraft, ships, buildings, electrical circuits (including computer chips), and even clothing and the manufacturing process (see Figure IS 1-7). Besides playing an important role in the design of durable goods, CAD is useful in fields such as art, advertising, law, architecture, and movie production.

Computer-Aided Manufacturing (CAM)   Computers have been used on the factory floor for more than 40 years, long before engineers used them interactively for design. **Computer-aided manufacturing (CAM)** refers to the use of computers to help manage manufacturing operations and control machinery used in those processes. One example is a system that observes production in an oil refinery, performs calculations, and opens and shuts

---

■ **Computer-aided manufacturing (CAM).** A general term applied to the use of computer technology to automate manufacturing functions.

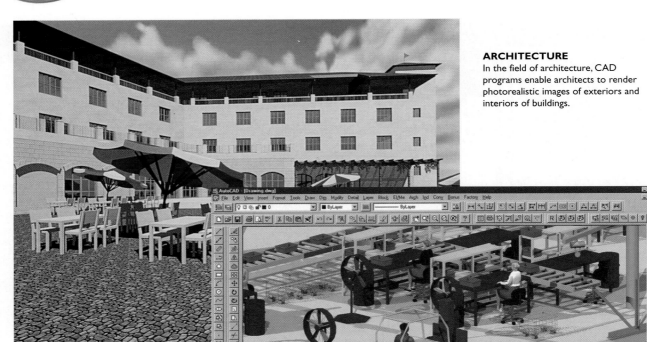

ARCHITECTURE
In the field of architecture, CAD programs enable architects to render photorealistic images of exteriors and interiors of buildings.

MANUFACTURING
Both machinery and manufacturing processes are commonly designed by engineers creating CAD models.

FIGURE IS 1-7

Computer-aided design (CAD).

appropriate valves when necessary. Another system, commonly used in the steel industry, works from preprogrammed specifications to shape and assemble steel parts automatically. Increasingly, robots are used to carry out processes once solely in the human domain (see Figure IS 1-8). CAM is also widely used to build cars and ships, monitor power plants, manufacture food and chemicals, and perform a number of other functions.

ENTERPRISE RESOURCE PLANNING (ERP)

Enterprise resource planning (ERP) ties together CAD, CAM, and other business activities. Here's how enterprise resource planning might work: A large auto distributorship calls an auto manufacturer to check out the feasibility of changing a styling detail on 500 cars that are to be produced next month. The CAD part of the integrated system checks out the design change to see if it can be done and to determine what types of assembly-line changes are necessary. CAM systems on the factory floor determine if the assembly line can make the shift and if new parts can be made available on time. The CAM computers call up the computers of parts suppliers, which are also integrated into the system, to check on parts availability. Finally, all of the information is

---

■ **Enterprise resource planning (ERP).** The use of technology to integrate many of the key operations of an organization into a single, networked system.

A robotic arm at work building a notebook computer.

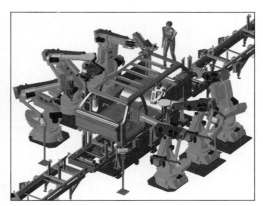

Simulating robot operations by computer can eliminate shutting down a factory for days during product changeovers.

FIGURE IS 1-8

Robots at work.

forwarded to accounting department computers, which calculate the cost impact of the change. Without a system that reaches across operations, such decision making would have to occur by a seat-of-the-pants style.

ERP still has yet to tap its ideal of tying together through a single network all of the major systems within an organization. Such a network would conceivably span all of the processes that impact a company. For an automaker, for example, this could mean starting from the mining of iron ore in Pennsylvania, to making steel in Indiana, to producing cars in Detroit and Mexico, to selling to customers over the Web, to feeding back sales results.

Today's most successful example of ERP software is SAP's R/3. Among SAP's biggest competitors in ERP software are Oracle, Peoplesoft, and Baan. ERP software can be used also by nonmanufacturing organizations.

ARTIFICIAL INTELLIGENCE

A computer is a device that, given some instructions, can perform work at extremely fast speeds, drawing on a large memory. It can also be programmed with a set of rules or guidelines, thereby enabling it to draw certain types of conclusions based on the input it receives. A good deal of mental activity involves these very processes. For this reason, the ability of a computer system to perform in ways that would be considered intelligent if observed in humans is commonly referred to as **artificial intelligence (AI).**

The four main areas of AI are expert systems, natural languages, vision systems, and robotics.

Expert Systems **Expert systems** are programs that provide the type of advice that would be expected from a human expert. In medicine, for instance, expert systems are often used to incorporate the thinking patterns of some of the world's best physicians. For example, an expert system might be given the symptoms exhibited by a patient. If these symptoms point to a disease the program is familiar with, the program may ask the attending physician questions about specific details. Ultimately, through questioning and checking the responses against a large database of successfully diagnosed cases, the program might draw conclusions that the attending physician might never have reached otherwise—and much more quickly as well. A list of several applications for expert systems is provided in Figure IS 1-9.

■ **Artificial intelligence (AI).** The ability of a machine to perform actions that are characteristic of human intelligence, such as reasoning and learning. ■ **Expert system.** A program or computer system that provides the type of advice that would be expected from a human expert.

Applications area	Example application
Credit authorization	Deciding whether to grant credit to individuals and companies based on both their past histories and other similar credit cases
Insurance sales	Helping an insurance agent tailor an insurance package to a client, given the client's insurance, investment, financial planning, and tax needs
Internet commerce	Figuring out how to personalize the Web pages sent to consumers visiting commercial sites
Manufacturing	Finding the best way to design, produce, stock, and ship a product
Portfolio planning	Determining the best securities portfolio for a client, given the client's growth and equity objectives
Repair	Assisting machine repairpeople by providing expert diagnosis of malfunction
Tax accounting	Assisting tax accountants by providing advice on the best tax treatment for an individual or corporation
Training	Putting newly hired employees into computer-simulated situations in which their performance is aided by or compared with experts

FIGURE IS 1-9

Some applications for expert systems.

Most expert systems consist of two parts: a data part and a software part (see Figure IS 1-10). The data part is commonly called a **knowledge base**, and it contains specific facts about the expert area and any rules that the expert system will use to make decisions based on those facts. For instance, an expert system used to authorize credit for credit-card customers would have in its knowledge base facts about customers as well as a set of *rules,* such as "Do not automatically authorize credit if the customer has already made five transactions today." Generally, the knowledge base is jointly developed by a human expert and a specialized systems analyst called a *knowledge engineer.*

The software part often consists of a variety of different programs. For instance, a program called an **inference engine** is used to apply rules to the knowledge base to reach decisions. Other programs commonly enable users to communicate with the expert system in a natural language such as

FIGURE IS 1-10

An expert system at work.

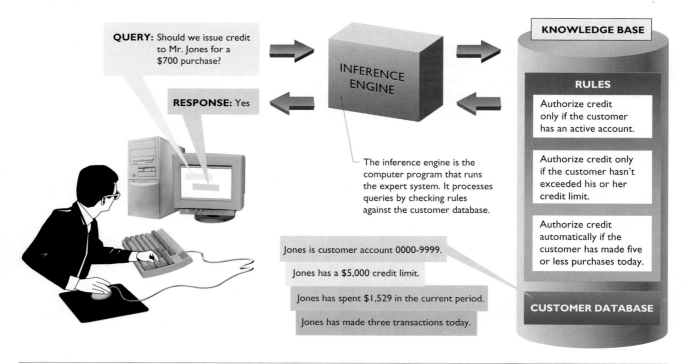

QUERY: Should we issue credit to Mr. Jones for a $700 purchase?

RESPONSE: Yes

INFERENCE ENGINE

The inference engine is the computer program that runs the expert system. It processes queries by checking rules against the customer database.

Jones is customer account 0000-9999.

Jones has a $5,000 credit limit.

Jones has spent $1,529 in the current period.

Jones has made three transactions today.

KNOWLEDGE BASE

RULES

Authorize credit only if the customer has an active account.

Authorize credit only if the customer hasn't exceeded his or her credit limit.

Authorize credit automatically if the customer has made five or less purchases today.

CUSTOMER DATABASE

■ **Knowledge base.** The part of an expert system that contains specific facts about the expert area and any rules the expert system will use to make decisions based on those facts. ■ **Inference engine.** A program used to apply rules to the knowledge base in order to reach decisions.

English or Spanish, provide explanations to users about how the expert system reached a particular conclusion, and allow computer professionals to set up and maintain the expert system.

Expert systems can be built from scratch or acquired as packages that have all the software components in place but lack a knowledge base. This latter type of package is called an **expert system shell.** Shells represent the most common and inexpensive way to create an expert system.

Today, many expert systems use **neural-net computing,** a technology in which the human brain's pattern-recognition process is emulated by a computer. Neural-net systems aren't preprogrammed to provide predictable responses like conventional programs. Instead, they are designed to learn by observation and by trial and error—the way people largely learn. Neural nets are most commonly used to recognize patterns in data. They are employed in such areas as handwriting, speech, and image recognition; credit-risk assessment; stock-market analysis; and crime analysis (see Figure IS 1-11).

Natural Languages   One of the greatest challenges that scientists in the field of AI currently face is providing computer systems with the ability to communicate in *natural languages*—English, Spanish, French, Japanese, and so forth. Unfortunately, this challenge has not been easy to meet. People have personalized ways of communicating, and the meaning of words vary according to the contexts in which they are used. Nonetheless, researchers have made some major strides toward getting computers to listen to and respond in natural languages.

Vision Systems   *Vision systems* enable computer-controlled devices to "see." A vision system might work as follows. Parts produced in a manufacturing process are sent along an assembly line for inspection. A vision system located at a station along the line takes a digital snapshot of each part as it passes by. The picture is decomposed into vital data that are compared to data showing how the part would look if it were produced correctly. An accompanying expert system applies rules to judge whether the part has been made correctly or is flawed. If flawed, the system determines the nature of the flaw and the necessary corrective action.

Robotics   Robotics—the field devoted to the study of robot technology— plays an integral role in computer-aided manufacturing (CAM) systems. Robots are machines that, with the help of a computer, can mimic a number of human motor activities to perform jobs that are too monotonous or dangerous for their flesh-and-blood counterparts—welding and painting cars, mining coal, defusing bombs, going to the bottom of the ocean and peeking around, and so on. Many robots can even "see" by means of embedded cameras and "feel" with sensors that permit them to assess the hardness and temperature of objects. Robots can represent substantial savings to a company, because they don't go on strike, don't need vacations, and don't get sick.

 **FIGURE IS 1-11**

Neural nets. Neural nets specialize in analyzing patterns. In fingerprint identification, a computer can be taught to match similarities that human experts look for, and to do so in a matter of minutes or seconds.

■ **Expert system shell.** A prepackaged expert system that lacks only a knowledge base. ■ **Neural-net computing.** An expert-system technology in which the human brain's pattern-recognition process is emulated by a computer system. ■ **Robotics.** The study of robot technology.

RESPONSIBILITY FOR SYSTEMS DEVELOPMENT

Organizations with thousands of employees and thousands of details to keep track of usually utilize thousands of systems, ranging from personal systems to systems that operate at an enterprise-wide level. Deciding which systems best support the direction of the organization, and how much attention to give each one, is where the job of systems development begins.

A company's *chief information officer (CIO)* has primary responsibility for systems development. Often this position is at the level of vice president. One of the CIO's duties is to develop a strategy that defines the role of information technology within the organization. Another duty is to develop a plan that maps out which systems are to be studied and possibly built or revamped now and over the next several years.

Because information technology plays such a pervasive role within most companies, *steering committees* composed of top-level executives normally approve technology plans and set broad guidelines for performing computer-related activities. These committees do not involve themselves with technical details or administer particular projects. Such functions are the responsibility of the organizations' information systems departments.

THE INFORMATION SYSTEMS DEPARTMENT

The **information systems department**—often called the *information technology department* or some other name—varies in structure from one company to another. It often includes people who design and implement enterprise-wide systems, people who provide support services to PC users, and people who build and manage networks and databases. Figure IS 1-12 describes a number of jobs often found within information systems departments.

Data Processing Area   The pillar of most information systems departments is the **data processing area,** whose primary responsibility it is to keep mission-critical transaction-processing-oriented systems within the company running smoothly. It is these systems that by and large control the money coming into and going out of the organization. The data processing area predates all other areas within the information systems department and is still considered by many to be the most important. After all, if their computers stopped processing high volumes of business transactions, most large organizations would have to shut down.

Within the data processing area, the *systems analysis and design group* analyzes, designs, and implements new software and hardware systems. The *programming group* codes computer programs from program design specifications. The *operations group* manages day-to-day processing once a system has become operational.

The person most involved with systems development is the **systems analyst.** Generally speaking, the systems analyst's job in the data processing area is to plan, build, and implement large systems that will use the computers the organization has or will acquire. When such a system is needed, the systems analyst interacts with current and potential users to produce a solution. The analyst generally is involved in all stages of the development process, from beginning to end.

For links to further information about information systems job opportunities, go to www.harcourtcollege.com/infosys/parker2000/student/explore/ and click on Chapter IS 1.

■ **Information systems department.** The area in an organization that consists of computer professionals. ■ **Data processing area.** The group of computer professionals charged with building and operating transaction processing systems. ■ **Systems analyst.** A person who studies systems in an organization in order to determine what work needs to be done and how this work may best be achieved with computer resources.

Applications programmer

A programmer who codes applications software.

Computer operations manager

The person who oversees the computer operations area in an organization.

Computer operator

A person who is responsible for the operation of large computers and their support.

Control clerk

The person who monitors all work coming in and out of a computer center.

Database administrator

The person responsible for setting up and managing large databases within an organization.

Data-entry operator

A member of a computer operations staff responsible for keying in data into a computer system.

Data processing director

The person in charge of developing and/or implementing the overall plan for transaction processing in an organization and for overseeing the activities of programmers, systems analysts, and operations personnel.

Help-desk troubleshooter

A person who, by phone or computer, assists users in solving software and hardware problems.

Knowledge engineer

The person responsible for setting up and maintaining the base of expert knowledge used in expert-system applications.

Network administrator

The person responsible for planning and implementing networks within an organization.

Programmer/analyst

A person, usually found in smaller companies, with job responsibilities that include both applications programming and systems analysis and design.

Scheduler

The operations person hired to utilize system resources to peak efficiency.

Security specialist

The person responsible for seeing that an organization's hardware, software, and data are protected from computer criminals, natural disasters, accidents, and the like.

System librarian

The person in the computer operations area who manages files stored offline on tapes, disks, microfilm, and so on.

Systems analyst

A person who studies systems in an organization to determine what work needs to be done and how this work may best be achieved with computer resources.

Systems programmer

A person who codes systems software, fine-tunes operating-system performance, and performs other system-sofware-related tasks.

Trainer

A person who provides education to users about a particular program, system, or technology.

Vice president of information systems

The person in an organization who oversees routing transaction processing and information systems activities as well as other computer-related areas. Also known as the *chief information officer* (CIO).

Webmaster

The person responsible for establishing and maintaining an organization's Internet presence.

In most large projects, a team of people will be involved. A systems analyst will probably be appointed as a **project manager** to head up the team. Other people on the team might include users, programmers, an outside consultant, a cost accountant, and an auditor. Users are especially vital to any team because they are the people who know the practical side of the application, and, also, they are the people who must work with any new system on a day-to-day basis.

FIGURE IS 1-12

Information-systems jobs.

OUTSOURCING

When an organization lacks the staff to build or operate a system it needs, it often chooses an outsourcing option. **Outsourcing** involves turning over certain information systems functions to an outside vendor. For instance, many smaller banks outsource their check-processing and customer-statement operations to companies that are skilled at high-volume processing of this sort.

Why do companies outsource? A small firm might find it too expensive to keep specialized personnel or equipment on hand, given its current work volume. Or a large company might not have the capacity or capital to

■ **Project manager.** A systems analyst who is put in charge of a team that is building a large system. ■ **Outsourcing.** The practice by which one company hires another company to do some or all of its information-processing activities.

expand its operations in-house, so it may outsource some of them temporarily. Also, many firms have found it easier to outsource operations in areas where it's too hard to find or too expensive to hire new personnel. Firms often turn to an outsourcer when they think that the outsourcer can do the job better or cheaper than they can. An acute shortage of computer skills in recent years, combined with high domestic labor costs and advances in networking technology, have led to explosive growth in global outsourcing. In the United States, such work as program maintenance, data entry, and system conversion, are often sent to such places as India and the Caribbean.

Along with the benefits of outsourcing come some serious drawbacks. Some firms simply hand over their work to an outsourcer and then expect miracles. Leadership needs to come from the client firm, not from the outsourcer. Also, when in-house personnel have to mix with the outsourcer's personnel, conflicts sometimes arise. The in-house personnel may feel that their jobs are threatened by the outsourcer's personnel, or, perhaps, they may disagree about who is in charge. Finally, the matters of control and security need to be considered. Although an outsourcer provides some assistance in these areas, a company achieves the most control over its information processing and the best security when it keeps its own work at its own site with its own people. When work goes outside, anything can happen.

Despite these drawbacks, outsourcing appears to be an unstoppable trend. Companies are eliminating many in-house jobs because of the high overhead involved in maintaining them. Among the leading suppliers of computer outsourcing services are Electronic Data System (EDS), Computer Sciences Corporation, and Andersen Consulting.

THE SYSTEMS DEVELOPMENT LIFE CYCLE

A systems development project often breaks down into five steps or phases:

- Phase 1: Preliminary investigation
- Phase 2: Systems analysis
- Phase 3: System design
- Phase 4: System acquisition
- Phase 5: System implementation

Collectively, these phases make up the **systems development life cycle (SDLC).** The phases describe the development of a system from the time it is first studied until the time it is put into use. When a new business pressure necessitates a change in a system, the steps of the cycle begin anew.

The five steps of the SDLC define in principle the process for building systems for both large multimillion-dollar information systems that run large corporations and for PCs that sit on many desktops in home offices. The role of the systems analyst during each step of the SDLC is illustrated in Figure IS 1-13.

The five steps of the systems development life cycle do not always follow one another in a strict sequence. Frequently, analysis and design are interwoven. Compare this process with an example from everyday life—the development of a vacation plan. People don't always design the whole plan as the first step and execute it, without modification, as the second step. They might design a plan for Day 1 and, when the day is over, analyze their

---

■ **Systems development life cycle (SDLC).** The process consisting of the five phases of system development: preliminary investigation, systems analysis, system design, system acquisition, and system implementation.

Duties of the Systems Analyst

Preliminary investigation During this phase the analyst studies a problem briefly and suggests solutions to management.

Systems analysis If management decides that further development is warranted, the analyst studies the applications area in depth.

System design The analyst develops a model of the new system and prepares a detailed list of benefits and costs.

System acquisition Upon management approval of the design, the analyst decides which vendors to use in order to meet software, hardware, and servicing needs.

System implementation After system components have been acquired, the analyst supervises the lengthy process of training users, converting data, and the like.

experiences as a basis for designing a plan for Day 2. Many systems are designed this way as well.

FIGURE IS 1-13

The role of the systems analyst in the five phases of systems development.

PRELIMINARY INVESTIGATION

One of the first steps toward developing a new system is to conduct a **preliminary investigation,** or *feasibility study.* The purpose of this investigation is to define and evaluate the problem area at hand relatively quickly, to see if it is worthy of further study, and to suggest some possible courses of action. Accordingly, the investigation should examine such issues as the nature of the problem, the scope of the work involved to solve it, possible alternative solutions, and the approximate costs and benefits of the different solutions.

The analyst must take care to distinguish *symptoms* from *problems* at the outset. For example, suppose an analyst is talking to a warehouse manager, who complains that inventories are too high. This may be so, but this fact in itself is not enough to warrant corrective action. It's a symptom, not a problem. There is a problem, however, if these high inventories are forcing the company to build an expensive new warehouse or if it is unnecessarily drawing on funds that could be used for profit opportunities. Note that even if a serious problem is identified, an organization may not be able to do anything about it. For instance, the aforementioned high-inventory problem may be due to a strike somewhere else.

SYSTEMS ANALYSIS

Systems analysis is the phase of systems development in which a problem area is studied in depth and the needs of system users are assessed. The main activities conducted during systems analysis are data collection and data analysis.

Data Collection The objective of data collection is to gather information about the type of work being performed in the application under study and to ascertain what resources users need to better perform their jobs. Later in this phase, the collection of data should suggest some possible solutions. Which data to collect depends largely on the problem being studied. Four sources of information on the applications area and user needs are documents showing how the application is supposed to work, questionnaires sent to users, interviews of users, and the personal observations of the systems analyst.

■ **Preliminary investigation.** A brief study of a problem area to assess whether or not a full-scale project should be undertaken. Also called a *feasibility study.* ■ **Systems analysis.** The phase of the systems development life cycle in which a problem area is thoroughly examined to determine what should be done.

For example, an organization chart covering the functions being studied and the people in charge of those functions is often an especially useful document to anyone studying a system. The chart shows how work responsibilities are organized and the chain of decision making. Also, because people often don't do what they say they do, the only way an analyst can really determine if a system operates the way it is supposed to is by going to where people work and actually observing what they in fact do.

Data Analysis   As information about the application is gathered, it must be analyzed so that conclusions about the requirements for the new system can be drawn. Two useful tools for performing analysis are diagrams and checklists.

Figure IS 1-14 shows a data flow diagram for the order-entry operation of a mail-order firm. **Data flow diagrams** show the relationship between activities that are part of a system as well as the data or information flowing into and out of each of the activities. They provide a visual representation of data movement in an organization.

Checklists are often developed for important matters such as the goals of the system and the information needs of key people in the system. An accounts receivable system, for instance, should have such goals as getting bills out quickly, rapidly informing customers about late payments, and cutting losses due to bad debts. On the other hand, a decision support system that helps teachers advise students should increase the quality of course-related information and decrease the time it takes to develop suitable curricula for students.

FIGURE IS 1-14

A data flow diagram for a mail-order firm. An order triggers the processes of verification and assembly of the goods ordered, and payment is recorded by accounts receivable.

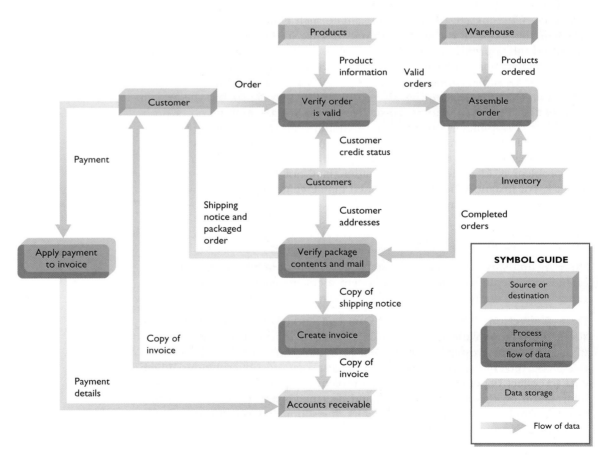

■ **Data flow diagram.** A graphically oriented system development tool that enables a systems analyst to logically represent the flow of data through a system.

Common sense eventually must dictate which type of checklist or diagram is most appropriate for the situation at hand. The principal purpose of these tools is to help the analyst organize his or her thoughts so that he or she may draw conclusions about what the system under study should do.

SYSTEM DESIGN

System design focuses on specifying what the new system will look like. The system design phase primarily consists of developing a model of the new system and performing a detailed analysis of benefits and costs.

Developing a Model of the New System   Once the analyst understands the nature of the design problem, it is usually helpful to draw a number of diagrams of the new system. The data flow diagrams discussed earlier show how data will flow through the new system.

When designing a system, the analyst must take into account output requirements; input requirements; data access, organization, and storage; processing; system controls; and personnel and procedure specifications. Figure IS 1-15 covers some of the issues that the analyst must address in the design specification.

Analyzing Benefits and Costs   Most organizations are acutely sensitive to costs, including computer system costs. Costs of a new computer system include both the initial investment in hardware and software and ongoing expenses such as personnel and maintenance. Some benefits can be computed easily by calculating the amount of labor the new system will save, the reduction in paperwork it will allow, and so on. These gains are called *tangible benefits*, because they represent easily quantifiable dollar amounts.

Other benefits, such as improvements in service to customers or better information supplied to decision makers, are more difficult to convert into dollar amounts. These gains are called *intangible benefits*. Clearly, the existence of intangible benefits complicates management efforts to make decisions. Yet some of the most important systems projects undertaken in a company involve strategic opportunities that are difficult to quantify. On a project with a large number of intangible benefits, management must ask questions such as "Are the new services that we can offer to customers worth the $3 million they will cost us?"

SYSTEM ACQUISITION

Once a system has been designed and the required types of software and hardware have been specified, the analyst must decide from which vendors to buy the necessary components. This decision lies at the heart of the **system acquisition phase.**

RFPs and RFQs   Many organizations formulate their buying or leasing needs by preparing a document called a **request for proposal (RFP).** This document contains a list of technical specifications for equipment, software, and services determined during the system design phase. The RFP is sent to all vendors who might satisfy the organization's needs. In the proposal they send back to the initiating organization, vendors recommend a solution to the problem at hand and specify their price for providing that solution.

In some cases, an organization knows exactly which hardware, software, and service resources it needs from vendors and is interested only in a quote

■ **System design.** The phase of the systems development life cycle in which the parts of a new system and the relationships among them are formally established. ■ **System acquisition phase.** The phase of the systems development life cycle in which equipment, software, or services are acquired from vendors. ■ **Request for proposal (RFP).** A document containing a general description of a system that an organization wishes to acquire.

Output Considerations

■ Who are the system users and what types of information do they need?

■ How often is this information needed? Annually? Monthly? Daily? On demand?

■ What output devices and storage media are necessary to provide the required information?

■ How should output be formatted or arranged so that it can easily be understood by users?

Input Considerations

■ What data need to be gathered and who will gather them?

■ How often do data need to be gathered?

■ What input devices and media are required for data collection and input?

Storage Considerations

■ How will data be accessed and organized?

■ What storage capacity is required?

■ How fast must data be accessed?

■ What storage devices are appropriate?

Processing Considerations

■ What type of functionality is required in the software?

■ What type of processing power is required? A mainframe? A minicomputer? A microcomputer?

■ What special processing environments must be considered? A communications network? A database processing environment?

System Controls

■ What measures must be taken to ensure that data are secure from unauthorized use, theft, and natural disasters?

■ What measures must be taken to ensure the accuracy and integrity of data going in and information going out?

■ What measures must be taken to ensure the privacy of individuals represented by the data?

Personnel and Procedures

■ What personnel are needed to run the system?

■ What procedures should be followed on the job?

FIGURE IS 1-15

Issues to cover during the system design specification. System design ultimately addresses all major elements of a computer system: hardware, software, data, people, and procedures.

on a specific list of items. In this case, it sends vendors a document called a **request for quotation (RFQ),** which names those items and asks only for a quote. Thus, an RFP gives a vendor some leeway in making system suggestions, while an RFQ does not.

Evaluating Bids Once vendors have submitted their bids or quotes in response to an RFP or RFQ, the acquiring organization must decide which bid or quote to accept. Two useful tools for making this choice are vendor rating systems and benchmark tests.

In a **vendor rating system,** such as the one in Figure IS 1-16, important criteria for selecting computer system resources are identified and each is

■ **Request for quotation (RFQ).** A document distributed to potential vendors containing a list of specific hardware, software, and services that an organization wishes to acquire. ■ **Vendor rating system.** A weighted scoring procedure for evaluating competing vendors of computer products or services.

Criterion	Weight (Maximum Score)	Vendor 1 Score	Vendor 2 Score
Hardware	60	50	40
Software	80	70	70
Cost	70	50	65
Ease of use	80	70	50
Modularity	50	30	30
Vendor Support	50	10	50
Documentation	30	30	20
		310	325

1. A list of important purchase criteria is developed.

2. Each criterion is given a weight that reflects its importance. Here, hardware is weighted twice that of documentation.

3. Vendors are awarded scores on each criterion that can range from a zero score up to the maximum allowed.

4. Scores are tallied for each vendor. Here, Vendor 2 winds up with the highest tally.

FIGURE IS 1-16

A point-scoring approach for evaluating vendors' bids.

given a weight. For example, in the figure, the weights of 60 for hardware and 30 for documentation may be loosely interpreted to mean that the organization considers hardware twice as important as documentation. Each vendor that submits an acceptable bid is rated on each criterion, with the sum of the weights representing the maximum possible score. The buyer totals the scores and, all other things being equal, chooses the vendor with the highest total. Although such a rating tool does not guarantee that the best vendor will always have the highest point total, it has the advantage of being simple to apply and relatively objective. If several people are involved in the selection decision, individual biases tend to average out.

After tentatively selecting a vendor, some organizations make their choice conditional on the successful completion of a **benchmark test.** Such a test normally consists of running a pilot version of the new system on the hardware and software of the vendor under consideration. To do this, the acquiring organization usually visits the vendor's benchmark testing center and attempts to determine how well the hardware/software configuration will work if installed. Benchmark tests are expensive and far from foolproof. It's quite possible that the pilot system will perform admirably at the benchmark site but the real system, when eventually installed, will not.

SYSTEM IMPLEMENTATION

Once arrangements for delivery of computer resources have been made with one or more vendors, the **system implementation** phase begins. This phase includes all the remaining tasks necessary to make the system operational and successful. Implementation consists of many activities, including converting programs and data files from the old system to the new one, preparing any equipment to work in the new systems environment, and training personnel.

Converting to a new system can take place using one or more strategies. With a *direct conversion,* the old system is completely deactivated and the new system is immediately implemented—a fast but extremely risky strategy. With a *parallel conversion,* both systems are operated in tandem until it is determined that the new system is working correctly—then the old system is deactivated. With a *phased conversion,* the system is implemented modularly,

■ **Benchmark test.** A test used to measure computer system performance under typical use of conditions prior to purchase. ■ **System implementation.** The phase of systems development that encompasses activities related to making a computer system operational and successful once it is delivered by a vendor.

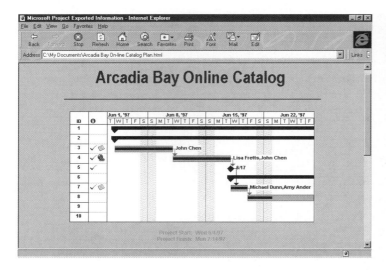

with each module being implemented with either a direct or a parallel conversion. With a *pilot conversion,* the new system is used at only one location within the organization. After it is determined that the new system is working correctly, it is installed at the other locations.

To ensure that the system will be working by a certain date, the analyst must prepare a timetable. One tool for helping with this task is *project management software,* illustrated in Figure IS 1-17, which shows how certain implementation activities are related and when they must start and finish. Once created, schedules prepared by such software can be shared over the Internet and fine-tuned through feedback.

A well-designed system should be flexible enough to accommodate changes over a reasonable period of time with minimal disruption. However, if a major change eventually becomes necessary, the organization must develop another system to replace the current one. At this point, the systems development life cycle—from preliminary investigation to implementation—begins all over again.

 **FIGURE IS 1-17**

Project management software.
Large projects are often managed with the assistance of project management software. Most products, like the one featured here, provide timetables and graphs showing how pieces of a project fit together.

OTHER ACTIVITIES

During and after the five phases of the systems development life cycle, other important activities take place. For instance, as the system is being developed, the systems analyst should be preparing a package of *documentation* containing the data that have been gathered, analyses showing how conclusions were reached, records of meetings, copies of reports, and so on. The documentation is useful for auditors or lawyers who may need to assess that proper procedures were followed as well as for systems analysts who may need to modify the system in the future. Documentation should be done as the system is being developed; when it's left until the end, it's often forgotten.

After the system has been implemented, some type of *postimplementation review* often takes place. This is basically a follow-up evaluation that is intended both to quickly correct any glitches that may have arisen in the system and to provide feedback on the systems development process in general, so that the organization might continue to improve in this area. The postimplementation review checks into such matters as whether or not the system is meeting its intended goals, costs are within expectations, and users are adapting favorably to the new systems environment.

After most systems are implemented, they also require ongoing *maintenance.* For instance, software and hardware often need to be added to a system, either to update what's already in place or to add entirely new features. Maintenance can be costly to an organization, and it's not unusual to spend $8 or $9 in maintenance over time for every dollar that was originally put into building the system.

APPROACHES TO SYSTEMS DEVELOPMENT

In this section, we'll examine the three main approaches to systems development: the traditional approach, prototyping, and end-user development.

THE TRADITIONAL APPROACH

In **traditional systems development,** the phases of systems development are carried out in a preset order: (1) preliminary investigation, (2) systems analysis, (3) system design, (4) system acquisition, and (5) system implementation. Each phase begins only when the one before it is completed. Often, the traditional approach is reserved for the development of large transaction processing systems. Because the traditional approach is usually expensive and extensive, it normally is carried out by knowledgeable professionals—that is, by systems analysts.

Traditional systems development requires system users to consider proposed system plans by looking at detailed diagrams, descriptive reports, and specifications of the proposed new system. The entire system is planned and built before anyone gets to use it or test it. As each phase of development is completed, users "sign off" on the recommendations presented to them by the analyst, indicating their acceptance.

Many organizations have lost faith in the traditional approach to systems development for many types of systems projects. First, by using this approach it often takes too long to analyze, design, and implement new systems. By the time a system finally begins operating, important new needs that were not part of the original plan have surfaced. Second, the system developed often turns out to be the wrong one. Managers almost always have difficulty expressing their information needs, and it is not until they begin to use a system that they discover what they really need.

These problems notwithstanding, traditional development is useful when the system being developed is one with which there is a great deal of experience, where user requirements are easy to determine in advance, and where management wants the system completely spelled out before giving its approval.

PROTOTYPING

To avoid the potentially expensive disaster that could result from completing every phase of systems development before users ever lay their hands on a system, many analysts have advocated **prototyping** as a means of systems development. In prototyping, the focus is on developing a small model, or *prototype,* of the overall system. Users work with the prototype and suggest modifications. The prototype is then enhanced. As soon as the prototype is refined to the point where higher management feels confident that a larger version of the system will succeed, either the prototype can be expanded into the final system or the organization can go full steam ahead with the remaining steps of systems development.

In prototyping, analysis and design generally proceed together in small steps that finally result in a completed system (see Figure IS 1-18). The idea behind the prototyping process is virtually identical to the one described earlier in the chapter for developing vacation plans. Prototyping is highly applicable in situations where user needs are hard to pin down, the system must be developed quickly, and some experimentation is necessary to avoid building the wrong system.

Prototyping and traditional development sometimes are combined in building new systems—for instance, by following the traditional approach but using prototyping during the analysis and design phases to clarify user needs.

FIGURE IS 1-18

Prototyping. Prototyping is an interactive process. After each prototype is built, the user and analyst try it out together and attempt to improve on it.

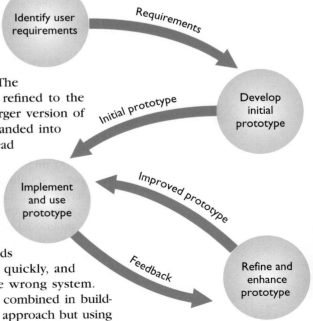

■ **Traditional systems development.** An approach to systems development whereby the five phases of the systems development life cycle are carried out in a predetermined sequence. ■ **Prototyping.** A systems development alternative whereby a small model, or prototype, of the system is built before a full-scale systems development effort is undertaken.

Unauthorized Extranets

Today's Helpful Employee Can Be Tomorrow's Legal Headache

When the Internet became established as a useful tool within many companies, it seemed that the greatest exposure to electronic skullduggery would come from the outside. Companies especially feared hackers and computer thieves stealing or destroying valuable information. While such concerns are still very prevalent and justified today, new ones are surfacing. Odd as it may seem, one such worry involves the average, well-meaning employee who uses the Internet to extend his or her reach to customers.

Imagine this. A big financial-services firm hires a recent college graduate who knows a lot about creating personal Web pages, at least from a technical point of view. At work, where he is a broker, he creates his own passworded site to help his clients. On it he posts his own opinions and forecasts on the stock market, a number of which contradict research reports by analysts of the firm who are trained and paid to make professional judgments of this sort.

Let's take this a step further. Suppose that one of the broker's clients takes his advice, loses a ton of money, and now is suing the company. The client has a copy of the offensive Web pages on a Zip disk, and the brokerage firm—in reviewing the matter—is embarrassed. The pages have a tacky-looking design, the content is replete with both spelling errors and errors in fact, and there is naive overoptimism in the content that glosses over the risks of investing.

It could easily happen. The Internet is putting more and more employees at businesses into direct, online contact with customers. Moreover, the computerized interaction of buyer and seller leaves incriminating recorded evidence behind. When an employee takes an action on the Internet that puts a company at unnecessary risk, who beyond the employee should ultimately take the blame? The information systems department? Company lawyers? The department in which the employee works? Many businesses are still scratching their heads on the matter.

On the one hand, most companies welcome creative, computer-savvy employees who take initiative. Information-systems departments are often swamped with work. And since business is largely about people relationships, anyway, companies like their best frontline workers to forge close ties with customers. What's more, they realize that many of these employees are independent enough to chafe at being on a leash. On the other hand, some type of control clearly needs to be present to avoid expensive mishaps.

At some companies, the solution is requiring all employees who want an extranet to reach their particular customer base to use an existing, official company Web site for such a purpose. At other firms, such an idea is either impossible or unthinkable. Some company Web sites are not set up to let individual employees interact with customers. At other companies, employees are not willing to let one of their most prized possessions—their customers—fall out of their complete control.

END-USER DEVELOPMENT

End-user development is a systems development effort in which the user is primarily responsible for the development of the system. This is in contrast to other types of development discussed here, in which a qualified computer professional, such as a systems analyst, takes charge of the systems development process.

As you might guess, end-user development is feasible only when the system being acquired is relatively inexpensive. A good example is when a user purchases a PC and develops applications on his or her own. In developing the system, the user might follow a prototyping approach or a method similar to traditional development.

Certain dangers exist when users develop their own systems. Among these are users not enforcing proper security measures in their systems, user systems interfering with other systems within the organization, and users building systems that neither they nor the organization can effectively support (see the Tomorrow box). Nonetheless, when computer professionals within an organization are too overloaded to build small important systems to help users, end-user development may be the only alternative.

■ **End-user development.** Systems development carried out by users.

SUMMARY AND KEY TERMS

Go to the Online Glossary at www.harcourtcollege.com/infosys/parker2000/ student/ to review key terms.

Types of systems and how organizations build them are the principal subjects of this chapter.

On Systems   A **system** is a collection of elements and procedures that interact to accomplish a goal. The function of many systems, whether manual or computerized, is to keep an organization well managed and running smoothly.

Systems development is the process that consists of all activities needed to put a new system into place. Systems development may be required for many reasons—for example, changes in government regulations or the availability of new computer technology.

Organizational Systems   Many types of systems are used by businesses and other organizations. **Transaction processing systems** perform tasks that generally involve the tedious record keeping that organizations handle regularly. Among these tasks are payroll, order entry, inventory control, accounts receivable, accounts payable, and general ledger.

Information systems, which fall into two classes—**information reporting systems** and **decision support systems (DSSs)**—give decision makers access to needed information. **Group decision support systems (GDSSs)** refer to DSSs in which several people routinely interact through a computer network in order to solve common problems. **Workflow software** is often used to monitor a GDSS's effectiveness. **Executive information systems (EISs)** are DSSs customized to meet the special needs of individual executives.

The term **office automation (OA)** refers to a wide variety of technologies and processing techniques, including document processing, electronic messaging systems such as **electronic mail (e-mail)** and **facsimile (fax),** desk accessories, decision support tools, **teleconferencing,** and **telecommuting.**

Computers are widely used in industry to improve productivity both at the design stage—through **computer-aided design (CAD)**—and at the manufacturing stage via **computer-aided manufacturing (CAM). Enterprise resource planning (ERP)** refers to the use of technology to tie together all of the important systems in an organization into a single network.

The ability of some computer systems to perform in ways that would be considered intelligent if observed in humans is referred to as **artificial intelligence (AI).** Currently, the four main applications areas of AI techniques are **expert systems,** natural languages, vision systems, and **robotics.**

Most expert systems consist of a **knowledge base** as well as several programs, one of which is called an **inference engine.** Expert systems are commonly built from **expert system shells,** and some rely on a technology known as **neural-net computing.**

Responsibility for Systems Development   The *chief information officer,* or someone with a similar title, holds primary responsibility for the overall direction of systems development. The technical details are the responsibility of individual areas—such as the **data processing area** within the **information systems department. Systems analysts** are the people involved most closely with the development of systems from beginning to end. Often, the systems analyst is the **project manager** on the team assigned to the systems project. When a company lacks the in-house expertise, time, or money to do its own computer processing, it often turns to an **outsourcing** company to provide system services.

The Systems Development Life Cycle   Systems development often proceeds through five phases: preliminary investigation, systems analysis, system design, system acquisition, and system implementation. These phases are often collectively referred to as the **systems development life cycle (SDLC),** because they describe a system from the time it is first studied until the time it is put into use. When a new business pressure necessitates a change in a system, the steps of the cycle begin anew.

The first thing the systems analyst does when confronted with a new project assignment is conduct a **preliminary investigation,** or *feasibility study.* This investigation addresses the nature of the problem under study, the potential scope of the systems development effort, the possible solutions, and the costs and benefits of these solutions.

Next, the **systems analysis** phase begins. During this phase, the main objectives are to study the application in depth (to find out what work is being done), to assess the needs of users, and to prepare a list of specific requirements that the new system must meet. These objectives are accomplished through fact collection and analysis. A number of tools can help with analysis, including **data flow diagrams** and *checklists.*

The **system design** phase of systems development consists of developing a model of the new system and performing a detailed analysis of benefits and costs.

Once a system has been designed and the required types of software and hardware have been specified, the analyst must decide from which vendors to buy the necessary components. This decision lies at the heart of the **system acquisition** phase. Many buying organizations notify vendors of an intention to acquire a system by submitting a **request for proposal (RFP)** or a **request for quotation (RFQ).** Vendors submitting bids are then commonly evaluated through a **vendor rating system** and then, possibly, a **benchmark test.**

Once arrangements have been made with one or more vendors for delivery of computer resources, the **system implementation** phase begins. This phase includes all the remaining tasks that are necessary to make the system successfully operational, including conversion of data, preparing any equipment to work in the new systems environment, and training. System implementation can use *direct conversion, parallel conversion, phased conversion,* or *pilot conversion.*

During and after the five phases of systems development, other important activities will be taking place, including documentation, a postimplementation review, and maintenance.

Approaches to Systems Development   In **traditional systems development** the phases of the SDLC are carried out in a predetermined order: preliminary investigation, analysis, design, acquisition, and implementation. The focus in **prototyping** is on developing small models, or prototypes, of the target system in a series of graduated steps. **End-user development** is a systems development approach in which the user is primarily responsible for building the system. This is in contrast to other types of development, in which a qualified computer professional, such as a systems analyst, takes charge of the systems development process.

EXERCISES

1. Fill in the blanks:
   a. Systems that perform record-keeping and other accounting tasks that many organizations handle regularly are called _____ .
   b. An information system designed to help people at the highest level of an organization is called a(n) _____ .
   c. A(n) _____ holds primary responsibility for systems development in an organization.
   d. A(n) _____ committee composed of executives in key departments and other members of top management normally approves a plan for systems development.
   e. A small model of a new system is often called a(n) _____ .
   f. Developing a model of a new system is part of the _____ phase of the systems development life cycle (SDLC).
   g. Benefits that are easy to quantify in dollars are called _____ benefits.
   h. A(n) _____ test consists of running a pilot version of a new system on the hardware or software of a vendor whose products are being considered for acquisition.

2. State what each of the following abbreviations stands for, and define the underlying term or concept:
   a. CIO
   b. CAM
   c. GDSS
   d. AI
   e. EIS
   f. RFP
   g. ERP
   h. SDLC

3. Match each term with the description that fits best:
   a. design
   b. implementation
   c. preliminary investigation
   d. analysis
   e. acquisition
   _____ The final phase of the SDLC
   _____ The phase of the SDLC that involves studying the system environment in depth
   _____ The phase of the SDLC that involves RFP or RFQ preparation, vendor rating systems, and benchmark tests
   _____ The first phase of the SDLC
   _____ The phase of the SDLC that follows systems analysis

4. Explain the differences between the following pairs of terms:
   a. Systems analysis and system design
   b. Programming group and operations group
   c. Accounts receivable and accounts payable
   d. Request for quotation and request for proposal
   e. Vendor rating system and benchmark test
   f. Workgroup computing and workflow software

5. Define, in your own words, each of the following terms:
   a. Outsourcing
   b. Inference engine
   c. Knowledge base
   d. Enterprise resource planning
   e. Expert system

6. Name the principal function performed by each of the transaction processing subsystems covered in the chapter.

7. What are the similarities and differences among the following types of information systems?
   a. Information reporting system
   b. Decision support system
   c. Group decision support system
   d. Executive information system

8. In the list below are several descriptions of activities performed by computer systems or by people working with computer systems. Put each type of activity into one of the following categories—transaction processing systems, information systems, design and manufacturing systems, systems development.
   a. CAD
   b. Accounts receivable
   c. A manager receiving the same type of report every month
   d. Prototyping
   e. A person buying a software package on the World Wide Web
   f. A group of bank personnel collaborating on the approval of a personal loan on their desktop computers
   g. A person using a computer system to track a package to see if it's been delivered
   h. An architect using a computer system to plan the layout of an office building

9. Answer the questions below and on the next page about telecommuting:
   a. What types of workers are likely to telecommute?

b. What incentives would induce an organization to encourage telecommuting?

c. What are some disadvantages to telecommuting?

10. People in organizations frequently complain that they don't have up-to-date computing equipment. Is this a symptom or a problem? Defend your answer.

PROJECTS

1. **This System Does Not Compute** Frequently reported in the press are examples of computer systems that fail because they were not completely thought out. For instance, a story was recently reported about a ski area that installed a computer system to optionally charge each skier on a per-run basis. Skiers selecting the per-run option got special tickets that were machine-processed at lift sites as they were about to take another run down a slope.

The system failed for many reasons. Skiers had to wait in long lines to get to the machines. What's more, skiers had to physically contort themselves and take their gloves off—often in bitterly cold weather—to get to their tickets. As if these problems weren't enough, at the end of the day some skiers wound up paying far more than they would have for a full-day ticket; the system did not stop charging them even after they had paid a reasonable maximum amount.

For this project, find at least one poorly designed system that is written up in a computer publication and report to your class about it. Be sure to tell why the system failed and to explain what the designers might have done differently to get the system to work.

2. **Research an Information System** Almost all organizations require information systems to run effectively. For an organization with which you are familiar—such as your college or university or the company for which you work—pick a computer-based information system that's currently in place and write a three-to-five-page paper about it. Be sure to cover the following items:

a. Who are the users of the system and what are the particular needs of each user group? How many users of various types are there?

b. What types of useful outputs does the system provide? How are the outputs made available— say, on a screen or in hard-copy reports? How often are the outputs updated?

c. What are the goals of the system? How do the outputs relate to the goals of the system?

d. What types of processing are done from the inputs the system receives?

e. What types of hardware and software does the system use?

f. In your estimation, can the system be improved? If so, how?

3. **Customer DSSs** A growing area within information systems is customer decision support. Customer DSSs enable a company's customers to use their own computers or Touch-Tone phones to call up the company's computer systems to get valuable information. For instance, one Federal Express system allows the shipper's customers to trace package deliveries over the Internet. For this project, identify three additional customer DSSs, describing in a few brief sentences the companies that run them and the benefits they provide to both the companies and its customers.

4. **IS Jobs** Computer jobs in the information systems (IS) area are often listed in computer newspapers—such as *Computerworld*—and over the Internet. Many publications also frequently report the job areas that are in the highest demand. For this project, write a three-to-five-page paper telling which job areas in the computer field appear to be in high demand right now. Also tell what type of facts you are using on which to base your conclusions.

Some job-related Internet sites that you might want to visit are listed in the accompanying figure. Also think about using a search engine to find more. For instance, in Yahoo!, click on the "Business and the Economy" category in the main menu to get you started.

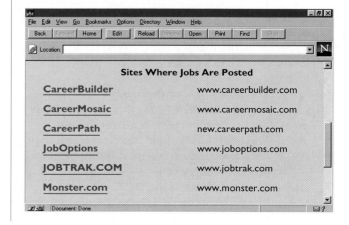

Sites Where Jobs Are Posted	
CareerBuilder	www.careerbuilder.com
CareerMosaic	www.careermosaic.com
CareerPath	new.careerpath.com
JobOptions	www.joboptions.com
JOBTRAK.COM	www.jobtrak.com
Monster.com	www.monster.com

5. **Expert Systems**   Examples of expert systems in organizations are frequently covered in the press. For this project, find an example of an expert system that is being used by an organization and report to the class about it. As part of your report, be sure to cover the knowledge base the system is using and some of the rules that are being used to make decisions. Also, be sure to report what types of benefits the expert system is providing.

6. **Outsourcing**   Examples of companies outsourcing computer work are frequently covered in the press. For this project, find an example of a company that is outsourcing computer work and report to the class about it. As part of your report, be sure to cover the following:
   a. The name of the company having work outsourced and the name of the company that is providing the outsourcing service.
   b. The nature of the work being outsourced.
   c. The types of benefits the company having the work outsourced expects to get out of the arrangement.

   Hint: Journals such as *Computerworld* and *Information Week* are especially good sources of information for this project.

7. **Information Technology and Politics**   Companies everywhere are increasingly outsourcing jobs to foreign countries. Today there is concern in the United States and Canada that manufacturing jobs will be lost to low-wage countries such as Mexico and to countries offshore, such as the Philippines or Taiwan. In nearby Mexico, blue-collar work can often be done for about one-sixth the price of the same work in the United States—perhaps even with better quality. Write a three-to-five-page paper that addresses how information technology has contributed to the trend to move jobs off native soil. Be sure to describe how this trend may have both positive and negative aspects. If you wish, take a position on the matter and defend it.

8. **New Key Terms**   It's impossible for a textbook of this sort to cover every important technology or term regarding systems in organizations. Several important terms that are not covered in the chapter are listed here. Use either library-journal or Internet research to determine what any three of these terms (or pairs of terms) mean, and write out a one-to-three-sentence explanation describing each one in your own words.
   a. Reengineering
   b. Top-down versus bottom-up systems development
   c. Just-in-time inventory (JIT)
   d. Knowledge worker
   e. Structured versus unstructured decisions

9. **Expert System Shells**   Shell programs are especially popular for developing expert systems. For this project, find the name of a company that makes an expert-system shell product and report to the class about it. In your report, be sure to cover the following questions:
   a. What is the name of the product, and how much does it cost? What is the name of the company that makes the product?
   b. For what particular types of expert systems applications is the product designed?
   c. What are the important product features or specifications? List as many as you can—for instance, the amount of RAM or hard disk space required, the maximum number of rules that can be accommodated, and so on.

10. **Computer Careers**   Students seeking a career in computers will often enroll in a computer-oriented degree program. Such programs exist in community colleges and at four-year schools in such departments as business, computer science, computer engineering, and computer operations. For this project, study a computer-oriented degree program at any college of your own choosing and answer the following questions:
    a. What computer courses must you take to get a degree?
    b. Can you get the degree by taking courses online?
    c. What type of degree would you be awarded upon successful completion of the program?
    d. What types of entry-level computer jobs would this degree train you for?

    Consider using the Internet to help you with your research; colleges often have their course listings and degree requirements online.

11. **Trade Associations**   Many college graduates join a trade association after college to keep them regularly informed of happenings in their job area. Such organizations are also a good place to make

professional contacts. For this project, visit the Web site of a trade organization that caters to your work area of interest and report to the class the following:

a. The specific class of professionals the organization services

b. The activities or benefits offered to members

One trade association that you may wish to research if you are studying to be a professional in a computer-related field is the Association for Computing Machinery (www.acm.org). Local chapters

of the Data Processing Management Association also have Web sites.

 12. Running a Dental Office   A dental office needs a transaction processing system and an information system just like other type of organization, and you don't need to be a dentist to figure out what such systems do. What types of duties would a transaction processing system in a dental office carry out? What types of questions should an information system be able to answer?

ONLINE REVIEW

 Go to the Online Review at www.harcourtcollege.com/infosys/parker2000/ student/ to test your understanding of this chapter's concepts.

IS 2

APPLICATIONS SOFTWARE DEVELOPMENT

LEARNING OBJECTIVES

After completing this chapter, you will be able to:

1. Identify and describe the activities involved in applications software development.

2. Recognize why it may be more advantageous to buy software than to develop it in-house.

3. Describe a number of productivity tools used by computer professionals to develop applications.

4. Identify several of the language options available to code programs.

5. Explain some of the activities involved with debugging, maintaining, documenting, and ensuring quality among programs.

6. Explain the role and importance of rapid development.

OVERVIEW

If you wanted to build a house, you'd probably begin with some research and planning. You might speak to various people about home design, draw up some floor plans, estimate the cost of materials, and so on. In other words, you wouldn't start digging a hole and pouring concrete on the very first day. Creating successful applications programs for a computer system also requires considerable planning.

Computer professionals and users need to develop or acquire new applications from time to time. They do this either by using a traditional programming language or an easier-to-use software development tool or, alternatively, by attempting to get what they need by purchasing a finished applications-software product outright. Just as you can acquire a house custom constructed or assembled from prefabricated pieces and do the work yourself or farm it out to others, you can acquire applications in much the same way.

In the previous chapter we spent a great deal of time looking at developing entire computer systems. In this chapter we look specifically at practices for developing the applications programs that make up a system.

The chapter opens by covering the types of activities that need to be considered when new applications programs are required. From there, we turn to the make-or-buy decision, which deals with choosing either to develop applications on your own or to buy them prepackaged. Next we address three of the chapter's most important topics: program design, programming languages, and program coding. Then we turn to program debugging and testing, maintenance, documentation, and quality assurance. The chapter closes with a brief introduction to rapid development.

PROGRAM DEVELOPMENT ACTIVITIES

A professional programmer or a user can acquire applications programs in two principal ways: (1) developing them from scratch and (2) buying them in finished form from an outside source. The method chosen generally depends on factors such as the quality of software available in the marketplace, the nature and importance of the application, the availability and capability of programmers, and time and cost constraints. Some programs, such as word processors, require teams of professionally trained people working years to build. Others, such as the macros used to style reports in a certain way, can be developed in less than an hour by many ordinary users with off-the-shelf, office-software tools. In this chapter, we'll be addressing primarily the types of applications developed by professionals.

The steps associated with creating applications programs are collectively referred to as **applications software development.** Applications software development often begins with the program specifications that are developed during the systems analysis and system design phases of the systems development life cycle (SDLC), which we discussed in detail in Chapter IS 1. Program specifications cover program outputs, the processing to take place, storage requirements, and program inputs. Applications software development primarily consists of the following four activities or steps:

■ **Applications software development.** The process of designing, coding, debugging and testing, maintaining, and documenting applications software.

- **PROGRAM DESIGN**   Planning the specific software solution to meet the program specifications.

- **PROGRAM CODING**   Writing the program.

- **PROGRAM DEBUGGING AND TESTING**   Finding and eliminating errors in the program.

- **PROGRAM MAINTENANCE**   Making changes to the program over time.

While each of these critical development activities is taking place, there should be ongoing documentation. *Documentation* is the process of writing up the details about what the program does and how it works. In a typical organization, the responsibility for successful program development is the job of systems analysts and programmers.

Systems analysts, or simply *analysts,* specify the requirements that the applications software must meet. They work with users to assess applications needs and translate those needs into a plan. Then they determine the specific resources required to implement the plan. For every program, the analysts create a set of technical specifications outlining what the program must do, the timetable for completing the program, which programming language to use, how the program will be tested before being put into use, and what documentation is required.

Programmers then use these specifications to code a software solution— a series of statements in a programming language. *Maintenance programmers* monitor the finished program on an ongoing basis, correcting errors and altering the program as technology or business conditions change. The most massive program-maintenance effort ever has been that associated with the year-2000 changeover, discussed later in this chapter.

THE MAKE-OR-BUY DECISION

Once a set of technical requirements for a software solution to a problem has been established, it must be decided whether the programs should be created in-house or acquired from a software vendor. This consideration is frequently called the *make-or-buy decision.*

The "Make" Alternative   If an organization decides to develop its own applications software, then it can do so in either of two ways. The first option is using a traditional programming language such as COBOL or C. This option usually offers the most control over what the program does, but applications often take longer to develop and maintain. The second option is using the proprietary language that comes with a specific software product—say, the Visual BASIC language that is bundled with some versions of Microsoft Office. This latter option is becoming very popular today, because doing work faster and less expensively are becoming increasingly important priorities.

The "Buy" Alternative   A choice often made by organizations is to select products that require virtually no in-house programming. During the past couple of decades, prewritten applications programs for such tasks as payroll, accounting, financial planning, project management, and scores of others have become more widely available from software publishers. These programs, called **applications packages**, consist of an integrated set of ready-to-run

■ **Systems analyst.** A person who studies systems in an organization in order to determine what actions need to be taken and how these actions may best be achieved with computer resources. ■ **Programmer.** A person whose job is to write, maintain, and test computer programs. ■ **Applications package.** A fourth-generation-language product that when the user sets a few parameters becomes a finished applications program ready to meet specific needs.

programs, documentation, and possibly training modules. Because they provide immediate results at a cost far lower than that of developing similar software from scratch, applications packages are quite popular. It is not always possible to find an applications package that exactly meets an organization's specific needs—in which case, the "make" alternative is preferable.

PROGRAM DESIGN

In the design stage of applications software development, the program specifications developed by the systems analyst are used to spell out as precisely as possible the nature of the required programming solution. The design, or plan, derived from these specifications must address all the tasks that programs must do as well as how to organize or sequence these tasks when coding programs. Only when the design is complete does the next stage—the actual program coding—begin.

PROGRAM DESIGN TOOLS

Program design tools are essentially planning tools. They consist of various kinds of diagrams, charts, and tables that outline either the organization of program tasks or the steps the program will follow. Once a program has been coded and implemented, program design tools serve as excellent documentation. Three widely used program design tools are structure charts, flowcharts, and pseudocode. We will cover each of these next.

STRUCTURE CHARTS

Structure charts depict the overall organization of a program. They show how the individual program segments, or modules, are defined and how they relate to one another. Figure IS 2-1 illustrates a structure chart for a payroll application.

A typical structure chart, with its several rows of boxes connected by lines, looks like a corporate organization chart. Each box represents a program

FIGURE IS 2-1

Structure charts.

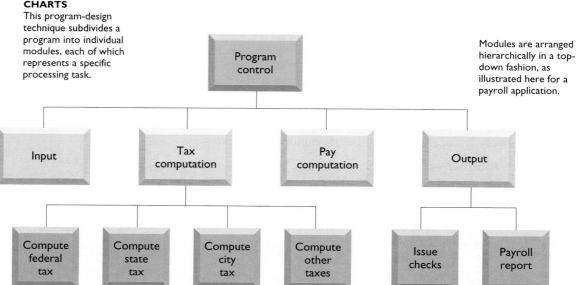

ABOUT STRUCTURE CHARTS
This program-design technique subdivides a program into individual modules, each of which represents a specific processing task.

Modules are arranged hierarchically in a top-down fashion, as illustrated here for a payroll application.

■ **Structure chart.** A program design tool that shows the hierarchical relationship between program modules.

module—that is, a set of logically related operations that perform a well-defined task. The modules in the upper rows serve control functions, directing the program to process modules under them as appropriate. The modules in the lower boxes serve specific processing functions. These latter modules do all the program work. The lines connecting the boxes indicate the relationship between higher-level and lower-level modules.

Structure charts embody a **top-down design** philosophy—that is, modules are conceptualized first at the highest levels of the hierarchy, and then at progressively lower levels. Put another way, the broad functions that are first defined at the highest levels are broken down further, level by level, into well-defined subfunctions. This is similar to what happens in a corporate organization chart—broad functions such as marketing, production, information systems, and the like are defined at the highest levels of the chart, and job areas falling under those functions follow. For instance, under information systems might fall operations, programming, and systems analysis and design; under programming, responsibilities may be further divided into applications programming and systems programming.

Logically speaking, establishing how a program is organized is the first step in program design. Once all functions of the program are carefully laid out in a structure chart or some equivalent tool, the next step of design—showing the step-by-step logic that is to take place in each module—can be started. This is where program flowcharts and pseudocode are useful.

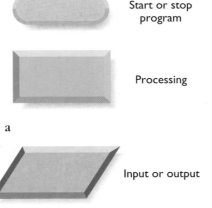

Start or stop program

Processing

Input or output

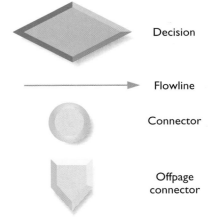

Decision

Flowline

Connector

Offpage connector

FIGURE IS 2-2

Program flowchart symbols.

PROGRAM FLOWCHARTS

Program flowcharts use *geometric symbols,* such as those in Figure IS 2-2, and familiar *relational operators,* such as those in Figure IS 2-3, to graphically portray the sequence of steps involved in a program. The steps in a flowchart occur in the same logical sequence that their corresponding program statements follow in the program. To help you understand what the symbols and operators mean and see how to use them, let's consider an example.

Scanning a File for Employees with Certain Characteristics   A common activity in information processing is scanning an employee file for people with certain characteristics. Suppose, for example, a company's human-resources department wants a printed list of all employees with computer experience and at least five years of company service. A flowchart that shows how to accomplish this task and also totals the number of employees who meet these criteria is shown in Figure IS 2-4.

This particular flowchart uses five symbols: start/stop, processing, decision, connector, and input/output. The lines with arrows that link the symbols are called *flowlines;* they indicate the flow of logic in the flowchart.

FIGURE IS 2-3

Relational operators used in flowcharts.

Operator	Meaning
<	Less than
<= or ≤	Less than or equal to
>	Greater than
>= or ≥	Greater than or equal to
=	Equal to
≠ or <> or ><	Not equal to

■ **Top-down design.** A structured design philosophy whereby a program or system is subdivided into well-defined modules and organized into a hierarchy. ■ **Program flowchart.** A visual design tool showing step by step how a computer program will process data.

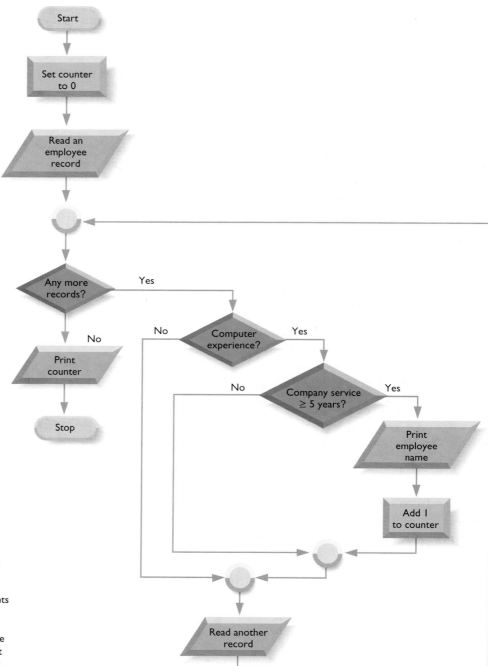

FIGURE IS 2-4

Scanning an employee file. The situation that the flowchart represents is as follows: Print the names of all people in an employee file who have computer experience and at least five years of company service. Also, count the number of such people and print out this count.

Every flowchart begins and ends with an oval-shaped *start/stop symbol.* The first of these symbols in the program contains the word *Start,* and the last contains the word *Stop.* The diamond-shaped *decision symbol* indicates a question, generally with only two possible answers—yes or no (true or false). Decision symbols should always have one flowline entering and two flowlines (representing each the two possible outcomes) exiting.

The rectangular *processing symbol* contains an action to be taken—for example, "Set counter to 0" and "Add 1 to counter." The *connector symbol* provides a meeting point for several flowlines. The *input/output symbol* enables the process depicted in the flowchart to either accept or output data.

The flowchart in Figure IS 2-4 involves a looping operation. We read a record, inspect it, and take an action; then read another record, inspect it, and take another action; and so on until the file is exhausted. When the computer reads a record, as indicated by the input/output symbol, it brings it into its memory and stores its contents (or field values). If a record meets both search criteria, we print the employee's name and increment a counter by 1. After the last record is read and processed, we print the value of the counter and then end the program.

The Three Basic Control Structures Beginning in the 1960s, a number of researchers began to stress program design (planning) and the merits of separating the design process from the actual program coding. Such a division of labor is a natural one, just as you have architects who design buildings and separate construction crews who work from specifications to erect them. Many of the proposed ideas of the researchers caught on, and methods have evolved that have made program design more systematic and the programs themselves easier to understand and maintain. These methods usually are grouped together under the term **structured programming.**

Advocates of structured programming have shown that any program can be constructed out of three fundamental **control structures:** sequence, selection, and looping. Figure IS 2-5 illustrates these structures using flowchart symbols.

A **sequence control structure** is simply a series of procedures that follow one another. A **selection** (or **if-then-else**) **control structure** involves a choice: If a certain condition is true, *then* follow one procedure; *else,* if false, follow another. A *loop* is an operation that repeats until a certain condition is met. As Figure IS 2-5 shows, a **looping** (or **iteration**) **control structure** can take one of two forms: DOWHILE or DOUNTIL.

With **DOWHILE,** a loop is executed as long as a certain condition is true ("do *while* true"). With **DOUNTIL,** a loop continues as long as a certain condition is false ("do *until* true"). With DOUNTIL, the loop procedure will always be executed at least once, because the procedure appears before any test is made about whether or not to exit the loop. With DOWHILE, the procedure may not be executed at all, since the loop-exit test appears before the procedure.

The three basic control structures are the major building blocks for structured program flowcharts and pseudocode.

The Case Structure By nesting two or more if-then-else statements, you can build a fourth structure known as the **case control structure.** For example, in Figure IS 2-4, the two individual choices—"Computer experience?" and "Company service ≥ 5 years?"—result in the following four possibilities, or cases:

- Case I: No computer experience, company service < 5 years
- Case II: No computer experience, company service ≥ 5 years
- Case III: Computer experience, company service < 5 years
- Case IV: Computer experience, company service ≥ 5 years

One Entry Point, One Exit Point An extremely important characteristic of the control structures discussed so far is that each permits only one entry point into and one exit point out of any structure. This property is sometimes called the **one-entry-point/one-exit-point rule.** Observe the marked entry and exit points in Figure IS 2-5. The one-entry-point/one-exit-point convention makes programs more readable and easier to maintain.

■ **Structured programming.** An approach to program design that makes program code more systematic and maintainable. ■ **Control structure.** A pattern for controlling the flow of logic in a computer program. ■ **Sequence control structure.** The control structure used to represent operations that take place sequentially. ■ **Selection (if-then-else) control structure.** The control structure used to represent a decision operation. ■ **Looping (iteration) control structure.** The control structure used to represent a looping operation. ■ **DOWHILE control structure.** A looping control structure in which the looping continues as long as a certain condition is true ("do *while* true"). ■ **DOUNTIL control structure.** A looping control structure in which the looping continues as long as a certain condition is false ("do *until* true"). ■ **Case control structure.** A control structure that can be formed by nesting two or more selection control structures. ■ **One-entry-point/one-exit-point rule.** A rule stating that each program control structure will have only one entry point into it and one exit point out of it.

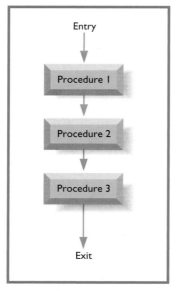

Sequence

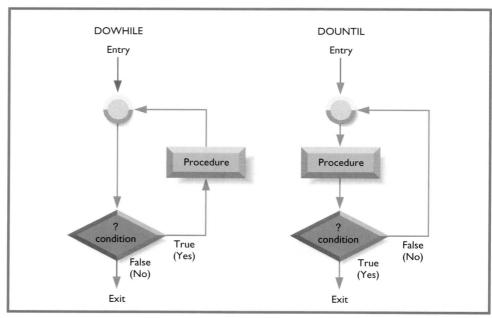

Selection (If-Then-Else)

Looping (Iteration)

 FIGURE IS 2-5

The three fundamental control structures of structured programming. Note that each structure has only one entry point and only one exit point.

PSEUDOCODE

An alternative to the flowchart that has become extremely popular in recent years is **pseudocode.** This structured technique uses English-like statements in place of the flowchart's graphic symbols (see Figure IS 2-6).

Pseudocode looks more like a program than a flowchart. In fact, it's often easier to code a program from pseudocode than from a flowchart, because the former provides a codelike outline of the processing to take place. As a result, the program designer has more control over the end product—the program itself. Also unlike a flowchart, pseudocode is relatively easy to modify and can be embedded into the program as comments. However, flowcharts,

■ **Pseudocode** A technique for structured program design that uses English-like statements to outline the logic of a program.

```
Start
Counter = 0
Read a record
DOWHILE there are more records to process
    IF computer experience
        IF company service ≥ 5 years
            Print employee name
            Increment Counter
        ELSE
            Next staement
        END IF
    ELSE
        Next statement
    END IF
    Read another record
END DO
Print Counter
Stop
```

FIGURE IS 2-6

Pseudocode for solving the employee file problem of Figure IS 2-4. The problem requires printing the names of all people in an employee file with computer experience and at least five years of company service. A count of the number of such people is also included as output.

being visual, are sometimes better than pseudocode for designing logically complex problems and are often faster to create.

No standard rules exist for writing pseudocode, but Figure IS 2-7 describes one set of rules that has a wide following. Note that all words relating to the three control structures of structured programming are capitalized and form a "sandwich" around other processing steps, which are indented. As Figure IS 2-6 shows, indentation is also used for readability. The keywords *Start* and *Stop* are often used to begin and end pseudocode.

Action Diagrams Pseudocode is widely employed in the creation of **action diagrams**—a tool used to develop applications programs rapidly while online

FIGURE IS 2-7

Some rules for pseudocode. In addition to the rules shown here governing program control structures, pseudocode often begins with the keyword *Start* and ends with the keyword *Stop*.

Sequence Control Structure

BEGIN processing task
    Processing steps
END processing task

The keywords BEGIN and END are always capitalized and tiered. Processing tasks and steps are normally written in lowercase letters. The steps should make up a well-defined block of code and be sandwiched between the keywords BEGIN and END.

Selection Control Structure

IF condition
    Processing steps
ELSE
    Processing steps
END IF

The keywords IF, ELSE, and END IF are always capitalized and vertically aligned. The condition and processing steps normally are written in lowercase letters. The processing steps are indented from the keywords in the manner illustrated.

Looping Control Structure

DOWHILE	DOUNTIL

DOWHILE condition
  Processing steps
END DO
	DOUNTIL condition
	  Processing steps
	END DO

The keywords DOWHILE (or DOUNTIL) and END DO are always capitalized and vertically aligned. The condition and processing steps follow the same lowercase convention and indentation rules as the selection control structure.

■ **Action diagram.** A programming tool that helps programmers code structures programs.

For links to further information about program design, go to www.harcourtcollege.com/infosys/parker2000/student/explore/ and click on Chapter IS 2.

to a computer. Action diagrams are composed of brackets into which pseudocode-like statements are written. These statements, from which the computer is automatically able to develop executable code, are usually created with an *action-diagram editor.* Every control structure used in the diagram is encircled by a set of brackets that shows where the structure begins and ends.

When the programmer signals that a particular control structure is to be used, the action-diagram editor creates both the appropriate pseudocode keywords—such as DOWHILE and END DO—and the brackets around them. As programmers provide various conditions or field names at certain places within the brackets, the editor checks to see that the code is both valid and consistent with the existing code for the application. It does the latter by referring to the appropriate entries in the application's active data dictionary. If a problem exists, the editor will issue a warning or error message. Once an action diagram has been completed, it is automatically translated into executable code with a *code generator.*

PROGRAMMING LANGUAGES

An important decision that must be made during the development of a program is the choice of a programming language. A **programming language** is a set of rules used to write computer programs. You can write a program with your word processor or, as is more commonly the case, by acquiring a software package whose principal purpose is to enable you to develop computer programs in a given language. Such a package contains the language translator necessary to convert the program into machine language, and it also includes a variety of tools that make it easy to develop, maintain, and manage computer programs.

Programming languages are commonly divided into three classes: low-level, high-level, and very high-level (fourth-generation) languages.

LOW-LEVEL LANGUAGES

The earliest programming languages—machine and assembly languages—are called **low-level languages.** They are so named because programmers who code in them must write instructions at the finest level of detail—the base level of the computer hardware. In both machine languages and assembly languages, each line of code corresponds to a single action of the computer system. Both types of languages are *machine dependent,* which means that they are usually not transportable between different brands of computers. Machine and assembly languages were respectively developed during the first and second product *generations* that define computer history.

Virtually no one writes machine-language programs, which consist of strings of 0s and 1s, anymore. Nonetheless, all programs must automatically be converted to machine language (by a language translator) before they are executed.

Assembly languages were developed to replace the 0s and 1s of machine language with symbols that are easier to understand and remember. The big advantage of assembly-language programs today is executional efficiency: They're fast and consume little storage compared with their higher-level counterparts. Unfortunately, assembly-language programs take longer to write and maintain than programs written in higher-level languages.

■ **Programming language.** A set of rules used to write computer programs. ■ **Low-level language.** A highly detailed, machine-dependent class of programming languages. ■ **Assembly language.** A low-level programming language that uses mnemonic codes in place of the 0s and 1s of machine language.

HIGH-LEVEL LANGUAGES

High-level languages differ from their low-level predecessors in that they require less coding detail and make programs easier to write. These languages are for the most part machine independent, freeing programmers from knowing the fine details about the hardware on which programs run. Included in this class of languages are what have come to be known as "third-generation" programming languages—BASIC, COBOL, Pascal, C, FORTRAN, PL/1, APL, and many others. A number of high-level languages that one commonly finds in computing environments are briefly discussed next.

BASIC   BASIC (*B*eginner's *A*ll-purpose *S*ymbolic *I*nstruction *C*ode) was designed to meet the need for an easy-to-learn beginner's language that would work in a friendly, nonfrustrating programming environment. Over the years, it has evolved into one of the most popular and widely available programming languages. Because it is easy to learn and use, and because the storage requirements for its language translator are small, BASIC works well on almost all PCs and is one of the most widely used instructional languages for beginners. A sample block of code from a BASIC program is illustrated in Figure IS 2-8.

BASIC is an *event-driven language*. Statements in BASIC enable programmers to write instructions that pause a program so that the user or computer system can take a specific action. When such an instruction is encountered during program execution, the program expects an *event* to take place before it proceeds. A common event is the user making a selection on the display. If the user chooses the print command, the program then branches to the code that involves printing output and changes the screen appropriately. Events can also involve timed phenomena, such as 30 seconds of user inactivity elapsing. When this happens, the program may then default to the routine that turns on the screen saver.

COBOL   COBOL (*CO*mmon *B*usiness-*O*riented *L*anguage) is the principal transaction processing language in use today. Currently, 70 to 80 percent of transaction processing applications on mainframes in large organizations are coded in COBOL. COBOL programs generally take a long time to write and maintain, but with billions of dollars invested in COBOL programs and thousands of programmers versed in COBOL use, the language will likely endure for many more years. Despite the many complaints that COBOL is old-fashioned and cumbersome, if you're interested in making money as a programmer, COBOL is still a good bet.

The infamous year-2000 (*Y2K*) problem—where computers recognized January 1, 2000 as if it were January 1, 1900, unless their software was rewritten to correct the problem—has resulted in a boon of jobs for COBOL programmers in recent years. Many of the programs that needed to be corrected were written

FIGURE IS 2-8

A sample block of code from a BASIC program.

> **BASIC**
> BASIC is widely touted as a beginner's language, with a relaxed set of rules that are designed to not get in the programmer's way.

```
READ Item$, Price, Units
WHILE Item$ < > "Last record"
    Value = Price * Units
    PRINT USING A$; Item$, Price, Units, Value
    READ Item$, Price, Units
WEND
```

■ **High-level language.** The class of programming languages that includes BASIC, COBOL, C, FORTRAN and Pascal. ■ **BASIC.** An easy-to-learn, high-level programming language developed at Dartmouth College in the 1960s. ■ **COBOL.** A high-level programming language developed for transaction processing applications.

```
010-HOUSEKEEPING
        .
        .
        .
    READ DISKFILE
        AT END MOVE 'YES' TO WS-END-OF-FILE.
        .
        .
        .
    PERFORM 030-PROCESSIT
        .
        .
        .
030-PROCESSIT.
    MULTIPLY    UNITS-SOLD-IN
        BY      PRICE-IN
        GIVING SALES-VALUE.
    MOVE PART-DESCRIPTION-IN TO PART-DESCRIPTION-OUT.
    MOVE PRICE-IN            TO PRICE-OUT.
    MOVE UNITS-SOLD-IN       TO UNITS-SOLD-OUT.
    WRITE PRINTLINE FROM DETAIL-LINE
        AFTER ADVANCING 1 LINE.
    READ DISKFILE
        AT END MOVE 'YES' TO WS-END-OF-FILE.
```

> **COBOL**
> Most transaction processing applications on mainframes in large organizations are coded in COBOL.

FIGURE IS 2-9

Sample code from a COBOL program.

in COBOL, some dating back to the 1950s. The Y2K problem originated because, to save space back in the days when computer storage was limited and expensive, years in date fields were handled in a two-digit format. Thus, a date such as October 15, 1964 was often entered as 10-15-64, and the computer then added 1900 to get 1964. Though January 1, 2000 has come and gone, some leftover problems—primarily lawsuits from people damaged by non-compliant Y2K systems—remain. Sample code from a COBOL program is shown in Figure IS 2-9.

Pascal **Pascal,** named after the mathematician Blaise Pascal, was created primarily to fill the need for a teaching vehicle that would encourage structured programming. To say that Pascal is a structured language means that, generally speaking, Pascal programs are made up of smaller subprograms, each of which is itself a structured program. This modular building-block approach makes it easier to develop large programs. In addition, most versions of Pascal contain a rich variety of control structures with which to manipulate program modules in a systematic fashion. Pascal also supports an abundance of data types and even lets you create new ones. A sample block of code from a PASCAL program is shown in Figure IS 2-10.

C **C** combines the best features of a structured high-level language and an assembly language—that is, it's relatively easy to code and uses computer resources efficiently. It is most used by computer professionals to create software products. A sample block of code from a C program is shown in Figure IS 2-11.

A newer version of C called **C++** has been developed to encourage better design and programming practices than C. C++ is a superset of C, making all C programs understandable to C++ compilers. Interest in C++ has made the language even more widely used than C itself. However, in recent years, the excitement in C++ has cooled off somewhat because of its reputation for producing code that is complex and difficult to maintain.

■ **Pascal.** A structured, high-level programming language that is often used to teach programming. ■ **C.** A programming language that has the portability of a high-level language and the executional efficiency of an assembly language. A newer version of the language, **C++,** is more widely used today.

```
BEGIN
FOR INDEX := 1 TO 20 DO
  READ (PART[INDEX]);
  READLN (PRICE, UNITS);
WHILE NOT EOF DO
    BEGIN
    TOTAL := PRICE * UNITS;
    FOR INDEX := 1 TO 20 DO
      WRITE (PART [INDEX]);
      WRITELIN ('      $', PRICE:6:2, UNITS:11,'   $',    TOTAL:9:2);
    FOR INDEX := 1 TO 20 DO
        READ (PART [INDEX]);
        READLN (PRICE, UNITS);
    END;
END.
```

> **PASCAL**
> Pascal is a highly structured language that is often used to teach students how to structure program code.

FIGURE IS 2-10

A sample block of code from a Pascal program.

FORTRAN FORTRAN (*FOR*mula *TRAN*slator), which dates back to 1954, was designed by scientists and is oriented toward manipulating formulas for scientific, mathematical, and engineering problem-solving applications. Because such applications are characterized by numerous computations and frequent looping, execution speed is a primary concern. Most FORTRAN compilers are so effective at producing fast object code for "number crunching" applications that they are even superior in this respect to the compilers of most modern languages. The reasons for this date back to the 1950s. When FORTRAN was first developed, it had to compete with assembly languages for execution efficiency, and this quality has remained an important factor in its development. A sample block of code from a FORTRAN program appears in Figure IS 2-12.

Other High-Level Languages In addition to the languages mentioned here, several other languages are commonly found in programming environments. Several of these are listed and described in Figure IS 2-13. Two of the languages, HTML and Java—the latter a derivative of C—were covered in some depth in Chapter NET 3. HTML and Java have become extremely popular during the past few years as interest in developing Web pages and Web page programming has been soaring.

FOURTH-GENERATION LANGUAGES (4GLS)

Machine language and assembly language characterized the first and second generations of computing, respectively. During the third generation, languages such as FORTRAN, BASIC, and COBOL became dominant. Today, in the so-called

FIGURE IS 2-11

A sample block of code from a C program.

> **C**
> C is widely used to develop commercial software and is not recommended for beginners.

```
while (i<3) {
    value[i] = price[i] * units[i];
    i++;
};
for (i=0;i<3;i++){
  printf("%s\t\t$%5.2f\t\t%4d\t\t$%6.0f\n",
                item[i], price[i], units[i], value[i]);
};
```

■ **FORTRAN.** A high-level programming language used for mathematical, scientific, and engineering applications.

FIGURE IS 2-12

A sample block of code from a FORTRAN program.

```
READ (5, 100) RECORDS
DO 999 COUNT = 1, RECORDS
READ (5, 110) PART, PRICE, UNITS
TOTAL = PRICE * UNITS
WRITE (6, 210) PART, PRICE, UNITS, TOTAL
CONTINUE
```

FORTRAN
FORTRAN's main strength is making it easy to develop programs that require writing formulas.

fourth generation of the computer age, a new breed of languages has arrived. These *very-high-level languages* are appropriately called **fourth-generation languages (4GLs).** In contrast to earlier languages, they are much easier to use and often allow both programmers and users to get by with very little coding, if any. Consequently, they result in increased on-the-job productivity.

The property that makes 4GLs generally easier to use is that they are declarative, rather than procedural, as the third-generation languages are. For instance, to draw a bar chart in a **procedural language,** you must tell the computer pixel-by-pixel how to draw bars and where to place them. In a **declarative language,** you are able to just point to the data you want graphed, select a graph type, and supply some titles to get the same results. Declarative languages are like prefabricated houses to the procedural languages' hand-hewn counterparts; they enable applications to be developed

FIGURE IS 2-13

Other high-level languages.

Ada	A superset of Pascal, Ada is a structured language developed and used by the U.S. Department of Defense.
APL	Stands for A Programming Language; APL is an extremely compact language that uses a special keyboard and facilitates rapid program coding.
HTML	Stands for HyperText Markup Language; HTML is the language of choice for creating World Wide Web pages.
Java	Developed by Sun Microsystems in the mid-1990s, Java is widely used for developing interactive applications for the Internet.
LISP	Stands for LISt Processor; LISP is used to develop applications in the field of artificial intelligence.
Logo	Logo is an easy-to-use language that is primarily used to teach children how to program.
PL/I	Stands for Programming Language /1; PL/I is a structured programming language that combines the capabilities of FORTRAN and COBOL.
Prolog	Stands for PROgramming LOGic; Prolog is used to develop applications in the field of artificial intelligence.
RPG	Stands for Report Program Generator; RPG is a report generator that uses special forms to enable programmers to specify what a report should look like.
Smalltalk	Smalltalk was the first successful object-oriented language commercially available and is still used today.

■ **Fourth-generation language (4GL).** An easy-to-learn, easy-to-use language that enables users or programmers to develop applications much more quickly than they could with third-generation languages. ■ **Procedural language.** A programming language in which the programmer must write code that tells the computer, step-by-step, what to do.
■ **Declarative language.** An applications-development product in which the user or developer can tell the computer that a task needs doing and the computer automatically knows how to do it.

Real Programmers

Just as there are "real men" (who don't eat quiche) and "real cowboys" (who never wash a pair of jeans more than twice), so also are there "real programmers." This latter lot is composed of guys and gals who take their bits and bytes most seriously.

A couple of decades ago, it was relatively easy to spot a real programmer. He or she could code in assembly language and OS/370 JCL, could read "core dumps" (memory-content listings, to us ordinary folks), and knew what such things as "ABEND" and "MVN P+8(1),P+9" meant. Hobbies consisted of such challenges as being the first one in the shop to learn SNOBOL or reverse Polish notation. The rest of the world, by contrast, could only say evasive-sounding things like "computers are way beyond me."

Times have changed. Today, even 12-year-olds can boot up a GW2K E-1000N 233 and tell you what the Win98 registry does. Thus, it's necessary to say something here to put these bright rug rats in their places—to separate them from those who *really* know how to code.

While the definition of a real programmer varies, many people in the computing industry will agree that this class of person possesses some or all of the following characteristics.

■ Real programmers never code in BASIC; most of them grew out of it by the age of 10.
■ Real programmers never work 8 to 5; if any of them are around before noon it's because they were there all night.
■ Real programmers never embed comments into their programs; the code should be obvious, and if you can't understand it you're a pinhead.
■ Real programmers shun documentation; if the program was a torture to write, it should be a torture to understand.

Only a wus seeks help. I dump core.

JCL Spoken Here

■ Real programmers hate Pascal, COBOL, and other self-documenting languages that reward people with weak memories.
■ Real programmers write accounting applications both against their will and in FORTRAN.
■ Real programmers don't write applications programs; they program down to the bare metal.
■ Real programmers ignore specifications; users should consider themselves privileged that they are getting a working program.
■ Real programmers aren't afraid to use GOTO statements— and plenty of them; structured programming is for simps who can't follow a complex train of thought.
■ Real programmers inherently dislike keyboards; gone are the good old days when you could enter a program on toggle switches on the computer's front panel.
■ Real programmers don't cook; they can survive for weeks on Coke, pizza, and Twinkies.
■ Real programmers know the ASCII and EBCDIC code tables better than their significant other's first name.

much faster and less expensively. Coding is reduced to simple commands or mouse clicks that select instructions. However, if you want a highly customized program to do something well beyond the ordinary, you will probably need a procedural language. To provide more flexibility, some software packages have both declarative and procedural components.

One shouldn't jump to the conclusion here that procedural languages are inferior to their declarative counterparts and on their way out. Most of the languages used to create pages for the World Wide Web—HTML, Java, and scripting languages like Perl—are procedural in nature and very popular with both programmers and ordinary users. Procedural programs also result in fewer program statements and more time-efficient object code when they are compiled into binary. Consequently, they conserve storage space and execute faster, and professional programmers are drawn to them for that purpose. There are a number of other reasons—many dubious—that some programmers prefer certain languages over others, however, as the Inside the Industry box looks at in tongue-and-cheek fashion.

The 4GLs found in the market are diverse and serve a wide range of application areas. Some are targeted to users, some to programmers, and some to both. Six types of 4GLs commonly found in commercial software products are described in the following list and summarized in Figure IS 2-14. Many of these language functions overlap in a single product. For instance, Microsoft Excel is a decision support system tool with facilities for report generation, retrieval and update, and graphics and applications generation.

Report Generators A *report generator* enables you to prepare reports quickly and easily. For instance, report generators packaged with database management systems allow you to create reports by declaring which data fields are to be represented as report columns and which report columns are to be used to sort data. The report is then generated automatically.

Retrieval and Update Languages As more and more busy people learned to use computers to search through large files and databases, it became increasingly important to develop *retrieval and update 4GLs* that would make this process as painless as possible. For instance, the query-by-example (QBE) tool included in most relational database packages enables users to interact with a simple dialog box to filter selected database information and then arrange it.

Decision Support System Tools *Decision support system tools* provide computing capabilities that help people make decisions. Perhaps the most familiar of such tools is the spreadsheet. Spreadsheets allow users to easily summarize data into tables and to rearrange these tables to reveal even more information. Other examples are modeling packages (which help create complex mathematical models of organizations), statistical packages (which facilitate statistical analysis), and data-mining software (which enables analysis of databases and data warehouses).

Graphics Generators *Graphics generators* are tools that help you to prepare business graphs. When you invoke a typical graphics generator, it will ask you a number of questions about your graph—what type it is, where the data are to create the graph, what colors and titles you want, and so on. After you satisfactorily respond to all of the questions, the graph is automatically created.

Applications Packages An *applications package* is a "canned" program designed to perform some common business application, such as payroll, accounts receivable, invoicing, or word processing. Like a graphics generator, an applications package usually asks the user a number of questions. The responses are subsequently used to assign values to parameters within the

FIGURE IS 2-14

Fourth-generation languages (4GLs). 4GLs have evolved to make both users and programmers more productive.

Types of 4GLs	
Report generators	Used to generate reports quickly
Retrieval and update languages	Used to retrieve information from files or databases and to add, delete, or modify data
Decision support system tools	Used to create financial schedules, models of decision environments, and the like
Graphics generators	Used to quickly prepare presentation graphics
Applications packages	Prewritten programs for applications such as word processing, payroll, and various accounting tasks
Applications generators	Used to quickly prepare applications programs, without having to resort to programming in a third-generation language

package to customize it to specific needs. For instance, the user of a word processing package can choose fonts, document-styling effects, spell-checking options, and so on.

Applications Generators An *applications generator* is a software product that enables you to code new applications quickly. An example is a wizard program; wizards allow you to create such things as fax cover sheets, database reports, and Web pages. Many applications generators contain both procedural and declarative components. Applications generators work in a variety of ways, several of which are described next.

CODE GENERATORS *Code generators* are programs that allow applications to be created by automatically translating them from one language into another. For instance, code generators are commonly used to translate documents written with a word processing program into HTML-coded Web pages. Also, several code generators exist that translate shortcut declarative instructions into standard COBOL statements. Code-generation routines—such as those that convert documents into Web pages—are often included as adjuncts to more comprehensive packages.

AUTHORING SOFTWARE *Authoring software* is used to quickly develop applications such as those in the Internet, multimedia, and virtual-reality areas, in which text, graphics, audio, and video data are commonly combined to create an interactive training, entertainment, or presentation device (see Figure IS 2-15). A wizard program that enables users to create Web pages by responding to prompts is a common example. Once the user finishes supplying the required information, a code generator on the back end of the wizard produces Web pages from the responses. Several examples of authoring software products are Microsoft's FrontPage (Web pages), Macromedia's Director (multimedia), and Cosmo Software's Cosmo Worlds (virtual reality).

VISUAL BASIC **Visual BASIC** is a 4GL designed to rapidly create sophisticated applications that run under Microsoft Windows (see Figure IS 2-16). Like other similar applications generators, Visual BASIC is also an **object-oriented programming language** (see Feature IS 2-1 on page IS 53). Such languages enable programmers to easily create such *objects* as menus, icons, toolbars, and windows—each with their own set of *properties*—that encapsulate both program code and data. On the front end, Visual BASIC has screen-painting and drag-and-drop tools that enable a programmer to quickly develop screens for graphical user interfaces and, on the back end, code generators to supply the underlying programming code.

Visual BASIC also contains its own procedural language, an object-oriented extension of the regular BASIC language. Visual BASIC has become so widely used in recent years that it has passed C++ in popularity, and there are now nearly as many Visual BASIC programmers as there are COBOL programmers.

FIGURE IS 2-15

Authoring software. Minerva's Impression is a video-authoring product that enables developers to create Hollywood-style DVDs quickly.

■ **Visual BASIC.** A rapid-development product—with both procedural and declarative components—that is used to create Windows applications. ■ **Object-oriented programming language.** A language that works with objects that encapsulate data and instructions rather than with separate instructions and data.

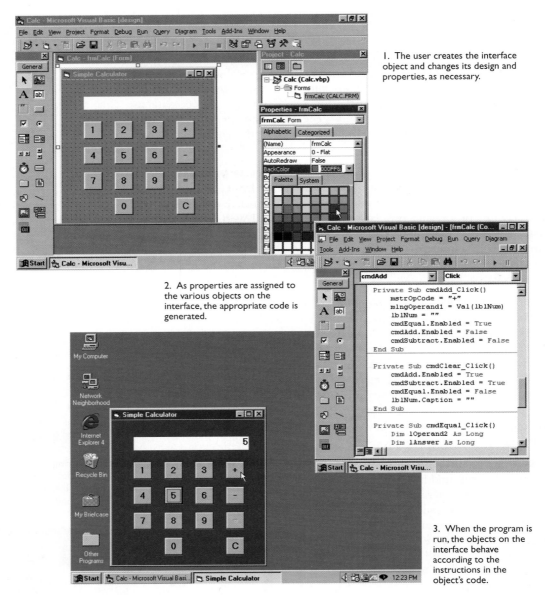

1. The user creates the interface object and changes its design and properties, as necessary.

2. As properties are assigned to the various objects on the interface, the appropriate code is generated.

3. When the program is run, the objects on the interface behave according to the instructions in the object's code.

FIGURE IS 2-16

Visual BASIC. One of the greatest strengths of Visual BASIC is that it simplifies the creation of graphical user interfaces.

NATURAL LANGUAGES

Software that uses a **natural-language interface** enables humans to communicate with the computer system in their native language—whether it be English, Spanish, Japanese, or any other tongue. The user of a natural-language interface does not have to learn the rules, or syntax, of a particular computer language. Instead, the user types out requests at a keyboard or uses voice commands that the computer can understand.

Natural-language processing is still in its infancy. It is most frequently employed as a front end in database or help processing to handle situations in which users need to retrieve information or generate reports. As each request is typed or spoken, the natural-language subsystem determines how it corresponds to a query or command that can be processed by the host program and then hands over the deduced command to the host program for execution. The natural-language subsystem culls key nouns from sentences and then looks for instances in its database where the words it extracts appear.

■ **Natural-language interface.** Software that allows users to communicate with the computer in a conversational language such as English, Spanish, or Japanese.

IS 2-1

Object-Oriented Programming

Multimedia and Easy Revisability Have Made It a Hot Technology

Probably few would argue that one of the most important software trends today is object-oriented programming (OOP). While OOP technology has been around for nearly two decades, only recently have desktop computers become powerful enough to handle it effectively. One of the principal motivations for using OOP is to handle multimedia applications in which such diverse data types as sound and video can be packaged together into executable modules. Another is writing program code that's more intuitive and reusable; in other words, code that shortens program-development time.

Perhaps the key feature of OOP is *encapsulation*—bundling data and program instructions into modules called "objects." Here's an example of how objects work. An icon on a display screen might be called "Triangles." When a user selects the Triangles icon—which is an object composed of the properties of triangles (see figure) and other data and instructions—a menu might appear on the screen offering several choices. The choices may be (1) create a new triangle and (2) fetch a triangle already in storage. The menu, too, is an object, as are the choices on it. Each time the user selects an object, instructions inside the object are executed with whatever properties or data the object holds to get to the next step. For instance, when the user wants to create a triangle, the application might execute a set of instructions that displays several types of triangles—right, equilateral, isosceles, and so on.

Many industry observers feel that the encapsulation feature of OOP is the natural tool for complex applications in which speech and moving images are integrated with text and graphics. With moving images and voice built into the objects themselves, program developers avoid the sticky problem of deciding how each separate type of data is to be integrated and synchronized into a working whole.

A second key feature of OOP is *inheritance*. This allows OOP developers to define one class of objects, say, "Rectangles," and a specific instance of this class, say, "Squares" (a rectangle with *equal* sides). Thus, all properties of rectangles—"Has 4 sides" and "Contains 4 right angles" are the two shown here—are automatically inherited by Squares. Inheritance is a useful property in rapidly processing business data. For instance, consider a business that has a class called "Employees at the Dearborn plant" and a specific instance of this class, "Welders." If employees at the Dearborn plant are eligible for a specific benefits package, welders automatically qualify for the package. If a welder named John Smith is later relocated from Dearborn to Birmingham, Alabama, where a different benefits package is available, revision is simple. An icon representing John Smith—such as John Smith's face—can be selected on the screen and dragged with a mouse to the icon representing the Birmingham plant. He then automatically "inherits" the Birmingham benefit package.

A third principle behind OOP is *polymorphism*. This means that different objects can receive the same instructions but deal with them in different ways. For instance, consider again the triangles example. If the user right clicks the mouse on "Right Triangle," a voice clip might explain the properties of right triangles. However, if the mouse is right clicked on "Equilateral triangle," the voice instead explains properties of equilateral triangles.

The combination of encapsulation, inheritance, and polymorphism leads to code reusability. "Reusable code" means that new programs can easily be copied and pasted together from a library of objects. All one has to do is access them and stitch them into a working whole. This eliminates the need to write code from scratch and then debug it. Code reusability makes both program development and program maintenance faster.

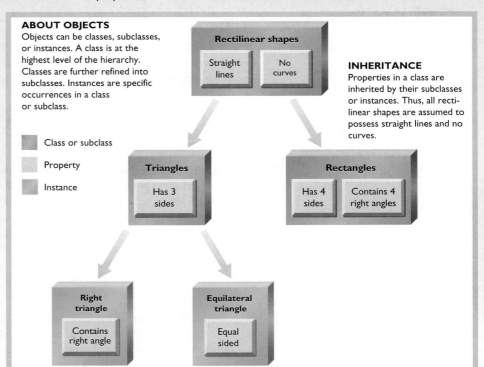

OOP illustrated. OOP technology has been available for nearly two decades, but only recently have computers become powerful enough to handle OOP applications efficiently.

CHOOSING A LANGUAGE

As you can see from reading the preceding subsections, each programming language has its own strengths and weaknesses relative to prospective applications. The choice of a language depends on several factors, such as the following:

■ SUITABILITY   Probably the most important selection criterion is the suitability of the language for the application under consideration. For instance, HTML is the natural choice for creating World Wide Web pages.

■ INTEGRATION   If the application is going to mesh with others that are already coded in a certain programming language, it should probably be coded in the same language. This is largely why COBOL is still a very widely used programming language, even though many people consider it old-fashioned.

■ STANDARDS   Many information systems departments have standards that dictate using a specific language in a given applications environment— say, COBOL for transaction processing or Oracle for server databases.

■ PROGRAMMER AVAILABILITY   Both the availability of in-house programmers fluent in the language and the market for new programmers need to be considered. Choosing a widely used language means programmers can more easily be hired and may not even have to be trained.

■ PORTABILITY   If the application is to run on several computer platforms— say, Windows- and Macintosh-based PCs and Unix-based computers—the ability of those platforms to collectively handle the language becomes a key factor.

■ SPEED   The faster an application is coded, the sooner it can be put into use generating benefits. Applications generators are often ideal because programmers can crank out applications much faster than with high-level languages.

■ COST   Along with speed, cost is often a bottom-line consideration. The initial cost of developing the program as well as ongoing support and maintenance costs are most important.

For links to further information about programming languages, go to www.harcourtcollege.com/infosys/parker2000/student/explore/ and click on Chapter IS 2.

PROGRAM CODING

Once the program design is complete and the development language has been chosen, the next step is to code the program. **Coding** is the actual process of creating the program in a programming language.

During the coding, computer professionals often take advantage of a number of special tools and methods that help make them more productive. The purpose of these techniques is to ensure that programmers produce code rapidly while creating programs that are both easy to maintain and as error-free as possible. Three techniques that are useful in this regard are coding standards, reusable code, and data dictionaries.

Coding Standards   Back in the early days of computers, programmers were largely left to code programs in their own way. The result was often *spaghetti code,* a tangled jumble of statements that, while producing correct results, was difficult for anyone except the original programmer to understand. Those days

---

■ **Coding.** The creation of programming-language instructions.

are long gone. Many organizations today follow a set of *coding standards*—a list of rules designed to standardize programming style. These rules may cover items such as acceptable program structures, field-naming conventions, and comment conventions. Rules such as these help make programs more universally readable and easier to maintain. When programs consistently use the same set of conventions, anyone making changes to the program knows what to expect.

Reusable Code Related programs often use the same blocks of code. For example, a company may have a dozen or more payroll programs—programs that cut checks to employees, report every check issued by the treasurer's office, collect payment for taxing agencies, and so on. Rather than have programmers code each program or program piece from scratch, most organizations keep libraries of reusable code available. **Reusable code,** as you might guess, refers to generic code segments that can be used over and over again by several programs, with minor modifications. Thus, reusable code enables programs to be "copied and pasted" quickly from pretested, error-free code segments.

Data Dictionaries A **data dictionary** is similar to an ordinary dictionary in that it contains rules of usage for an alphabetical list of words. The words are those encountered in the company's information processing environment. Among them would be, for example, the names, descriptions, and rules of usage of fields, records, files, and programs. Most data dictionaries are *active,* meaning they are online to the applications that they support. If, say, a programmer attempts to use a field name improperly or inconsistently, the active data dictionary will immediately warn the programmer, and it will likely prohibit the alleged infraction from being part of the finished application.

DEBUGGING AND TESTING PROGRAMS

Debugging is the process of ensuring that a program is free of errors, or bugs. Debugging is usually a lengthy process, sometimes amounting to more than 50 percent of a program's development time.

Preliminary Debugging The debugging process often begins after the program is initially entered into the computer system. Rarely is any program error-free the first time the programmer attempts to execute it. A very long program may have hundreds or thousands of errors of one sort or another at the outset. Errors rooted out during debugging often are of two types.

A **syntax error** occurs when the programmer has not followed the rules of the language. A computer, for instance, probably won't be able to understand what you're trying to do if you mistyped PRINT as PRNT or if it expected you to enter three arguments for a command when you only entered two. The language's diagnostic software usually provides the programmer with a list of informative error messages indicating the source of syntax errors.

A **logic error,** or *run-time error,* in contrast, is generally much more difficult to detect. Such an error results when the command syntax is correct but the program is producing incorrect results. This may happen if you've

■ **Reusable code.** Program segments that can be reused over and over again in the construction of applications programs. ■ **Data dictionary.** A facility that informs users and programmers about characteristics of data and programs in a database or a computer system. ■ **Debugging.** The process of detecting and correcting errors in computer programs or in the computer system itself. ■ **Syntax error.** An error that occurs when the programmer has not followed the rules of a language. ■ **Logic error.** An error that results when a running program is producing incorrect results.

expressed a procedure or a formula incorrectly, or if you've misdefined the problem entirely. To correct certain types of logic errors, the programmer often uses tracing procedures or dummy output statements that show how a program is branching, the values of key variables as the program progresses, how far the program progressed before it encountered the error, or how it is making computations.

After spotting errors, the programmer makes the necessary corrections and reexecutes the program. This "execute, check, and correct" process will probably be repeated several more times before the program is free of bugs.

Testing   At some point in the debugging process, the program will appear to be correct. At this point, the original programmer—or, preferably, someone else—runs the program with extensive *test data*. Good test data will subject the program to all the conditions it might conceivably encounter when it is finally implemented. The test data should also check for likely sources of coding omissions. For example, will the program issue a check or a bill in the amount of $0.00? Does the program provide for leap years when dating reports? Will it accept a product quantity less than 0? Although rigorous testing significantly decreases the chance of malfunctioning when a program is implemented, there is no foolproof guarantee that the completed program will be bug-free.

Proper debugging is vital, because an error that costs only a few dollars to fix at this stage in the development process may cost many thousands of dollars to correct after the program is implemented.

Beta Testing   Tests done on-site by a company are frequently referred to as *alpha tests*. Programs created for mass distribution—such as new revisions of software made by companies like Microsoft and Lotus—will also undergo several rounds of testing outside the company. With the possible configurations of PC hardware in use so large that it is impossible to fully anticipate many problems that may occur, hundreds or thousands of potential users are sent preliminary versions of a program to evaluate for suitability. In the first of such **beta tests,** only a few hundred copies of the current program version may be sent out for review. Later beta tests often involve thousands of users. For their participation, beta testers are usually given a free copy of the finished program, as well as occasionally a nominal fee or freebie.

PROGRAM MAINTENANCE

Virtually every program, if it is to last a long time, requires ongoing maintenance. Program **maintenance** is the process of updating software so that it continues to be useful. For instance, if new types of data are added to a database and existing programs must be modified to use these data, program maintenance is necessary. Program maintenance is also commonly triggered by software revisions, new equipment announcements, and changes in the way business is conducted.

Program maintenance is costly to organizations. It has been estimated that many organizations spend well over half of their programming time just maintaining existing applications programs. One of the major reasons why such tools as coding standards, fourth-generation languages, object-oriented languages and reusable code, and data dictionaries are so popular today is because these tools can result in lower maintenance costs.

■ **Beta test.** A term that refers to sending a preliminary version or release of a program to users for evaluation purposes.
■ **Maintenance.** The process of making upgrades and minor modifications to systems or software over time.

PROGRAM DOCUMENTATION

Program **documentation** includes hard-copy or electronic manuals that enable users, program developers, and operators to interact successfully with a program. If you've ever had the frustration of trying to get something to work from poorly written instructions, you can appreciate how valuable good documentation can be.

User documentation normally consists of a user's manual. This manual may provide instructions for running the program, a description of software commands, several useful examples of applications, and a troubleshooting guide to help with difficulties. Since many users have difficulty with computers, user documentation must be written to be comprehensible to virtually all. The trend in user documentation is to make it electronic and to bundle it with tutorials and other training resources.

Program developers include people who design, write, test, and maintain programs—that is, anyone contributing to the software-development process. *Developer documentation* usually consists of tools that will simplify any development task. Such tools might include program examples, a description of the design tools incorporated into the product, instructions for debugging and testing, maintenance tips, and so on. Since developers are highly literate about computers, developer documentation is written at a more technical level than documentation targeted at users. Developer documentation is also increasingly becoming electronic.

Operator documentation includes online and hard-copy manuals that assist machine operators in setting up hardware devices, learning the ins and outs of successful hardware operation, and diagnosing machine malfunctions. Operator documentation is machine dependent, and, unless one has a good grounding in hardware specifics, it can be difficult to read through.

QUALITY ASSURANCE

Quality assurance, as it relates to program development, refers to the process of making sure quality programs are written in a quality way. The quality assurance function in many firms is carried out by a staff that's charged with making an independent, unbiased audit of program-development operations.

A major focus in quality assurance is on the outputs produced by programs. Not only are outputs checked for accuracy, but they are also scrutinized for completeness and timeliness. Are all of the outputs required by users present? Is the program going to provide information to users when it's needed? System messages to the user are also evaluated to ensure programs are easy to use.

Program development activities are another major target in the quality-assurance effort. Here, it is important to ascertain that programs have been developed using acceptable design and coding standards and that they have been properly tested and documented. Also considered are steps that could improve the program-development process.

Quality-assurance specialists also look closely at program and system security. It is critical that programs and their data be protected from tampering and unauthorized use and that proper program controls be in place to safeguard against problem situations.

■ **Documentation.** A description of how a program, procedure, or system works. ■ **Quality assurance.** The process of making sure quality programs are written in a quality way.

RAPID DEVELOPMENT

If you ask most managers when they need to get programs delivered to users, you'll get an answer such as "yesterday." The sad truth in business today is that developers are typically under tremendous time pressure to get finished work out the door. In some extreme cases, getting product into the user's hands is not just a priority—it is *the* priority. **Rapid development** refers to a group of program-development methods in which a major goal is meeting an extremely tight timetable.

Some of the tenets of rapid development are focusing on schedule-oriented practices, using people who find working at a grueling pace a challenge and motivating those people properly, applying appropriate development methodologies, managing risks carefully, and avoiding common development mistakes (see Figure IS 2-17).

The need for rapid development techniques is perhaps more acute than ever. There is currently a serious shortage of skilled workers in the information-technology area. Thus, departments developing systems and programs often have to get by with fewer people, all of whom are then under greater pressure to produce. Another solution to alleviating the worker-shortage problem—importing talent from foreign countries—is covered in the Tomorrow box.

FIGURE IS 2-17

Common mistakes made in rapid development.

■ **Rapid development.** A program-development approach in which a principal objective is delivering a finished product quickly.

Are We Running Out of High-Tech Talent?

Meeting Tomorrow's Needs Has Become a Political Football

For the past several years, U.S. firms have been claiming that there's not enough qualified people around with technology skills to hire at home. By some estimates, the number of high-tech jobs in the United States will triple in the next decade. Making the situation worse, there's little unemployment among U.S. college-educated workers, and the number of domestic college graduates is not growing at a rate fast enough to meet future work demands.

The U.S. Department of Commerce has confirmed the shortfall in talent. It reports that colleges are only producing a quarter of the technologically skilled people needed by the U.S. job market each year and that the situation will not turn around until mid-decade.

The solutions being proposed by industry aren't easy ones. Employers of high-tech talent are pointing a finger at the federal government, saying it isn't doing enough to increase visa quotas for skilled workers from overseas. A visa allows a foreign worker to be employed in the United States for up to six years. Many companies in the United States still prefer a worker to come to America rather than shipping work overseas. While some telecommuting is possible over the Internet, there are security risks, and for many types of jobs it's better to have workers onsite.

Many people inside the government are concerned about foreign workers taking away American jobs, which some skeptics say has more to do with politics than reality. Many employers feel that the

Hiring crunch. U.S. firms complain that there are more technology jobs than ever to fill and not enough skilled domestic workers available.

high-tech sector is the engine for the world's future growth; thus, to refuse the best talent in the world the chance to work for the United States pulls down the prosperity of everyone in the country.

Critics of the private sector have their own spin on the matter. They claim that U.S. companies are more interested in foreign workers because they represent cheap labor. They also point out that when visa-permitted workers leave back for their homelands, they're going to take back critical skills that will help foreign companies compete better against the United States. Better to pour money into training programs that will upgrade worker skills at home, many of them say.

The debate is likely to go on for years.

Two classes of tools used in rapid development are CASE and rapid-application-development (RAD) products.

Computer-Aided Software Engineering (CASE) CASE (computer-aided software engineering) tools—or *software engineering workbenches*—refer broadly to products designed to automate one or more stages of applications software development. Like a carpenter's workbench, which consists of a number of carpentry tools—hammers, saws, chisels, drill bits, and the like—software engineering workbenches contain a number of design, programming, and maintenance tools that get software products developed faster.

For instance, such a workbench might consist of programs that produce system and program diagrams, an action-diagram editor, a fourth-generation language, a code generator, a feature that facilitates the development of reusable code libraries, a data dictionary, and tools that help turn unstructured programs into structured ones (see Figure IS 2-18). The specific tools included in the workbench vary from one vendor to another. One of the most widely praised uses of CASE is being able to generate program code directly from the program design.

■ **Computer-aided software engineering (CASE).** Program products that automate systems-development and program-development activities.

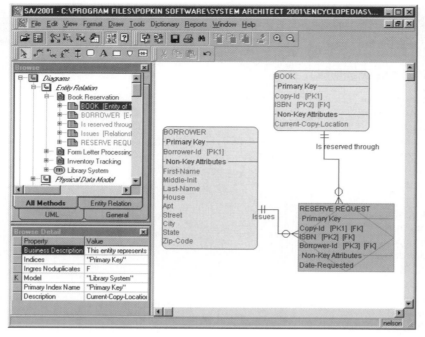

FIGURE IS 2-18

A CASE package. CASE products make it possible to develop applications faster with fewer coding mistakes. Shown here is System Architect, a CASE product that enables information-systems professionals to create a wide variety of diagram types.

One of the principal advantages to CASE tools besides their speed in applications development is their ability to maintain consistency. Thus, if program code is generated from an online diagram, the two will be consistent. Also, if someone later tries to change the program without changing the diagram, a CASE tool can flag the inconsistency. On the downside, there is very little standardization in the CASE area from one vendor to another, and many of the CASE tools currently in the marketplace are targeted only to solving highly specific problems.

Rapid Application Development (RAD) Products In object-oriented programming environments, to provide CASE-like assistance with developing user interfaces and with preparing code for reuse, some vendors provide **rapid applications development (RAD)** tools for analysts and programmers. These tools are targeted to certain widely adopted software platforms—such as Microsoft Windows or Sybase databases. RAD includes wizard software to generate applications quickly, screen painters that provide attractive graphical user interfaces, object-oriented libraries that can be easily stitched together into applications, groupware to manage team development efforts, debugging and prototyping utilities, and so forth. Three widely used RAD products are Microsoft's Visual BASIC, Powersoft's PowerBuilder, and Borland's Delphi.

SUMMARY AND KEY TERMS

Go to the Online Glossary at www.harcourtcollege.com/infosys/parker2000/student/ to review key terms.

Like building a house, creating a successful applications program requires considerable planning.

Program Development Activities The steps associated with creating successful applications programs are called **applications software development.**

In most large organizations, the development of applications software is the job of systems analysts and programmers. **Systems analysts** are the people who work with users to assess needs, translate those needs into a list of technical requirements, and design the necessary software specifications. The design is then handed to a **programmer,** who codes the program from it. Maintenance programmers monitor the software on an ongoing basis, correcting errors and altering the software as applications needs change.

■ **Rapid applications development (RAD).** Refers to program development tools that help with the quick generation of user interfaces and with the stitching of reusable code.

The Make-or-Buy Decision   Many organizations choose to buy their software in the form of prewritten **applications packages** rather than creating it in-house. The consideration to create software or acquire it from a vendor, which often takes place after the analysis and design stages of systems development, is frequently called the *make-or-buy decision.*

Program Design   Many tools are available to help the analyst design programs, including structure charts, program flowcharts, and pseudocode.

Structure charts depict the overall hierarchical organization of program modules. **Top-down design** indicates that modules are defined first at the highest levels of the hierarchy and then at successively lower levels.

Program flowcharts use geometric symbols and familiar relational operators to provide a graphic display of the sequence of steps involved in a program. The steps in a flowchart follow each other in the same logical sequence as their corresponding statements will follow in a program.

A group of techniques has evolved that has made program design more systematic and made the programs themselves easier to understand and maintain. These techniques are often grouped together under the term **structured programming.** Advocates of structured programming have shown that any program can be constructed out of three fundamental **control structures**—sequence, selection, and looping.

A **sequence control structure** is simply a series of procedures that follow one another. The **selection (or if-then-else) control structure** involves a choice: *If* a certain condition is true, *then* follow one procedure; *else*, if false, follow another. A **looping (or iteration) control structure** repeats until a certain condition is met. A loop can take two forms: **DOWHILE** and **DOUNTIL.** By nesting two or more if-then-elses, you can build a fourth control structure, known as a **case control structure.** All of these control structures follow the **one-entry-point/one-exit-point rule**—that is, a structure can have only one way into it and one way out of it.

Pseudocode is a structured technique that uses English-like statements in place of the graphic symbols of the flowchart. Pseudocode is commonly employed in the creation of **action diagrams.**

Programming Languages   An important decision that must be made during the design phase is the selection of a **programming language.** Programming languages are **low-level languages,** such as machine and **assembly languages**; **high-level languages,** such as **BASIC, Pascal, COBOL, C, C++,** or **FORTRAN;** or *very-high-level languages,* which are also called **fourth-generation languages (4GLs).**

The 4GLs are predominantly **declarative languages,** whereas 3GLs are mostly **procedural languages.** Six types of 4GLs commonly used are report generators, retrieval and update languages, decision support system tools, graphics generators, applications packages, and applications generators—such as **Visual BASIC,** an **object-oriented programming language. Natural language interfaces** enable humans to communicate with the computer system in their own native language.

Program Coding   Once analysts have finished the program design for an application, the next stage is to code the program. **Coding,** which is the job of programmers, is the process of writing a program from scratch from a set of design specifications. Among the techniques that have been developed to increase programmer productivity are coding standards, **reusable code,** and **data dictionaries.**

Debugging and Testing Programs   **Debugging** is the process of making sure that a program is free of errors, or "bugs." Debugging is usually a lengthy process, sometimes amounting to more than 50 percent of the total development time for an in-house program. Most bugs can be classified as being either

syntax errors or logic errors. Once preliminary debugging is complete, programs will also have to be *tested*. Good test data will subject the program to all the conditions it might conceivably encounter when finally implemented. Mass-distributed commercial programs are also **beta tested.**

Program Maintenance   Program **maintenance** is the process of updating software so that it continues to be useful. Program maintenance is costly; it has been estimated that some organizations spend well over half of their programming time just maintaining existing applications.

Program Documentation   Program **documentation** includes manuals that enable users, applications developers, and operators to interact successfully with a program. Although noted as the final stage of the program development cycle, documentation is an ongoing process that must be addressed throughout the life of the project.

Quality Assurance   **Quality assurance,** as it regards program development, refers to the process of making sure quality programs are written in a quality way. Closely checked for quality are the outputs produced by programs, the program development process itself, and security.

Rapid Development   **Rapid development** refers to a group of program-development methods in which a major goal is meeting an extremely tight timetable. Two tools used in rapid development are CASE and RAD. **CASE (computer-aided software engineering)** tools—or *software engineering workbenches*—refer broadly to products designed to automate one or more stages of applications software development. To provide CASE-like assistance with such tasks as developing user interfaces and reusable-code libraries, some vendors provide **rapid applications development (RAD)** tools for programmers.

EXERCISES

1. Fill in the blanks:
   a. _____ are the people who define the requirements that applications software must meet to satisfy users' needs.
   b. A(n) _____ interface enables humans to communicate with the computer in their native tongues.
   c. _____ is the principal transaction processing language in use today.
   d. Report generators, retrieval and update languages, applications packages, and applications generators are all examples of _____ languages.
   e. Program pieces designed to be "copied and pasted" into several programs are called _____.

2. Match each term at the top of the next column with the description that fits best:

   a. Visual BASIC   e. flowchart
   b. sequence   f. pseudocode
   c. debugging   g. Pascal
   d. documentation   h. program design tool

   _____ A structure chart, for example.

   _____ The process of ridding a program of errors.

   _____ A graphical design tool with boxes and arrows showing step-by-step how a computer will process data.

   _____ A program control structure.

   _____ A technique for designing programs that uses English-like statements resembling actual program statements to show the step-by-step processing a program will follow.

   _____ A high-level programming language named after a mathematician.

   _____ A written description of a program, such as a manual.

   _____ An applications generator.

3. Name at least two advantages and one disadvantage to buying applications software packages relative to developing them in-house.

4. Supply the following information about control structures:
   a. Name the three fundamental control structures of structured programming and describe each.
   b. Name and describe a fourth control structure that is formed by putting together two or more occurrences of one of the fundamental structures.

5. What is the difference between each of the following?
   a. The DOWHILE and DOUNTIL control structures
   b. A program flowchart and a structure chart
   c. A third-generation language and a fourth-generation language
   d. A high-level and low-level language
   e. Program development and systems development

6. Define, in your own words, each of the following:
   a. One-entry-point/one-exit-point rule
   b. Authoring software
   c. Top-down design
   d. Quality assurance
   e. Object-oriented programming language

7. What particular need is met by each of the programming languages listed at the top of the next column?

   a. BASIC
   b. Visual BASIC
   c. COBOL
   d. FORTRAN
   e. C and C++
   f. Pascal
   g. HTML
   h. Prolog

8. Identify several types of fourth-generation languages. What principal purpose does each one serve?

9. Name and describe several criteria that organizations use to choose among programming languages.

10. What is the difference between each of the following?
    a. A decision symbol and processing symbol in a flowchart
    b. A procedural and declarative language
    c. An action diagram and a code generator
    d. A syntax error and a logic error
    e. An alpha test and a beta test

11. What is an event-driven language designed to do? Provide two examples of program events.

12. Describe the three types of program documentation discussed in the chapter. In what major way do they differ?

PROJECTS

1. **Software Errors** Software errors are frequently covered by the press. For instance, an interesting error made by a Midwestern bank has recently been reported. A program had erroneously spread $924.8 million dollars—several times the bank's total assets—into 826 depositor checking accounts. Just a couple of years before that, incidentally, an eastern bank made a similar error, erasing half of the balances in thousands of checking accounts. A culprit often cited for such errors is the multitude of systems that banks use to process deposits and withdrawals—human tellers, ATM machines, wire transfers, PC-based systems, and so on—all of which have to be coordinated.

   For this project, find an example of a software error covered in the press and report to the class about it. Be sure to cover the nature of the error, the consequences or dollar amount resulting from the error, and the likely cause of the problem.

2. **Flowcharts and Pseudocode** Prepare a flowchart and pseudocode to solve the following problem: A company has several salespeople and needs a computer procedure to figure out the amount to pay them. A salesperson is paid according to a standard commission rate of 12 percent multiplied by total sales dollars generated. Salespeople whose sales exceed $20,000 for the month get a bonus of $500 tacked on to their earnings. As input, assume each employee record contains the name of a salesperson and his or her monthly sales; as output, produce each person's name and the amount he or she is to be paid.

3. **Developing Pages for the World Wide Web** Today, many people are creating their own World Wide Web pages and posting them on the Internet. The process of developing Web pages can be seen as a case study in both systems and program

development. Thus, there are stages that one goes through as regards (1) project analysis, (2) Web-site design, (3) Web-page coding, (4) Web-page debugging and testing, (5) Web-site implementation, and (6) Web-site maintenance. In a few sentences, describe the types of activities that someone developing a commercial Web site might go through in each of these six stages. If you have a version of this textbook that contains Chapter NET 3, you should read this chapter before doing this project.

4. Beta Tests I   While many companies keep the results of beta testing confidential, the press often leaks hints as to how well a particular version of a software product is faring with testers. The hints are often based on feedback the company has gathered from testers or on surveys the press has conducted itself. For this project, find an article in a computer newspaper or journal that tells how a beta test is going and report to the class about it. Based on what the article says, does the product appear to meet expectations or have serious problems?

5. Beta Tests II   At the Web sites of many software publishers, you can apply to be a beta tester. Generally, the site will tell you which software areas are currently seeking beta testers, and you can fill out an online application if you are interested. For this project, visit such a site and report to your classmates which software products are currently being beta tested. Also report any other useful information about the beta tests, such as performance expectations for testers and any compensation or prizes.

6. Programming Languages I   For each of the following questions, write a few sentences in response:

a. With so many programming languages around today, why are new ones constantly being developed?

b. Do any new programming languages really have a chance at wide acceptance, given the large number of languages now in use?

c. Should every student entering college be required to learn a procedural programming language such as BASIC?

7. Programming Languages II   Both the chapter and Figure IS 2-14 cover the properties of several important programming languages. For this project, choose any one of these languages and write a three-to-five-page report about it. Your report should go beyond what the text covers. Be sure to mention in your report what the language is designed to do, uses for the language, and the language's syntax or special features.

8. Error Avoidance   Even error-free programs are not enough to guarantee correct results. If the data being fed to them are inaccurate, most programs can do little to process them and get correct results. To ensure the accuracy of data going into the computer, many software programs have data-checking routines that look for potential problems. For instance, programs often contain a *field check* that will not permit, say, a name to be entered into a field where a number belongs. Also, a *reasonableness check* is used to ensure that a value isn't wildly out of bounds—such as a payroll disbursment to be issued for $924.8 million. For this project, find at least three more checks that might be made to ensure the accuracy of entered data, and describe these checks to the class.

9. Popular Software   Most users and programmers within organizations would prefer to work with a widely used applications package than with a comparable software product developed in-house. Why do you think this is so? What benefits do widely used applications packages also present to the organization?

ONLINE REVIEW

Go to the Online Review at www.harcourtcollege.com/infosys/parker2000/ student/ to test your understanding of this chapter's concepts.

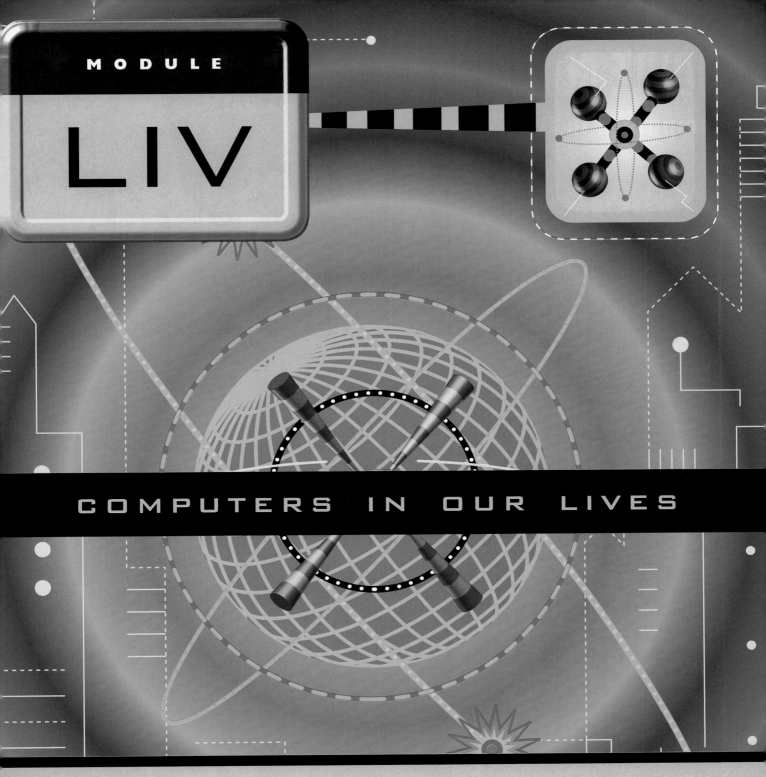

No study of computers is complete without a look at the growing impact of these devices on daily life and the very fabric of society. From home offices to company desktops, more and more people are operating their own computer systems. Children are routinely exposed to computers through school and electronic games. News bureaus regularly report about computer-related issues—hackers breaking into computer systems, the Internet's potential for changing our lives, privacy problems created by computers, and so forth.

Chapter LIV 1 addresses issues that arise in developing one's own personal computer system. It covers many of the facts about PCs that you should understand if you decide to acquire your own system. Today, with unprecedented numbers of people purchasing their own PCs or participating in computer-buying decisions at work, knowledge in this area has become essential for virtually everyone.

Chapter LIV 2 looks at the problems that computers create, including their impact on the physical and mental health of users, computer crime, potential invasions of personal privacy, and new ethical dilemmas.

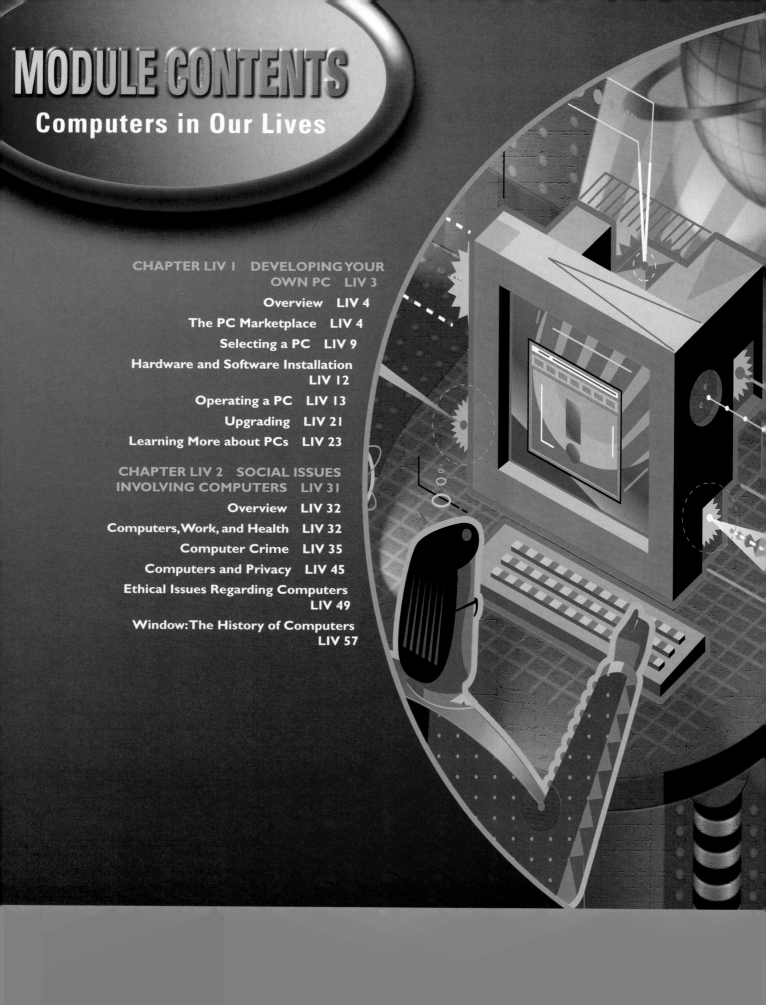

MODULE CONTENTS
Computers in Our Lives

LIV I

DEVELOPING YOUR OWN PC

OUTLINE

LEARNING OBJECTIVES

After completing this chapter, you will be able to:

1. Identify some of the leading companies in critical market segments of the PC industry, as well as the key sales and distribution alternatives for PC products.

2. Explain how to select and install a PC for home or office use.

3. Name some practices designed to protect software, hardware, and data resources from damage.

4. List some important guidelines for troubleshooting problems and seeking assistance.

5. Describe some of the ways to upgrade a PC and explain the conditions that justify an upgrade.

6. Name several sources for learning more about PCs.

OVERVIEW

It is becoming commonplace for a person to own a PC or to use one at work. Consequently, more people than ever before are acquiring their own PC resources, maintaining and upgrading their systems on their own, and so on. The purpose of this chapter is to make you aware of the many ins and outs connected with being a PC owner.

Chapter LIV 1 opens with a discussion of the vendors in the PC marketplace and the distribution channels they use to sell their products at the retail level. Then we look at some of the things you should know when acquiring a PC for home or work. From there we turn to several operation and maintenance issues, including troubleshooting problems and obtaining product support. Next, we cover upgrading a computer system. Finally, we discuss some of the resources that are at your disposal for learning more about PCs.

THE PC MARKETPLACE

The PC marketplace comprises a wide variety of firms that make hardware and software products. Several other companies are in business solely for product support and distribution purposes.

PC PRODUCTS

A quarter of a century or so ago, many of the companies that make today's most familiar PC products didn't even exist. Today, many of them earn more than $1 billion a year in revenues. The PC industry has become both the largest and the fastest-growing segment of the computer industry. A roster of some of the most familiar companies in the PC marketplace appears in Figure LIV 1-1.

FIGURE LIV 1-1

Who's who in the PC marketplace. This list shows the products and product lines for which several leading companies are most famous.

Company	Principal Product(s)
America Online	Internet access and content
Adobe	Assorted desktop publishing software products
Apple	Microcomputer systems
Autodesk	AutoCAD design software
Canon	Printers and related products
Compaq	Microcomputer systems
Computer Associates	A wide variety of software products
Corel	A wide variety of software products
Dell	Microcomputer systems
Gateway	Microcomputer systems
Hewlett-Packard	A wide variety of hardware products
IBM	A wide variety of computing products
Intel	Chips for PC-compatible computers
Intuit	Personal finance software
Lotus Development	A wide variety of software products
Macromedia	Multimedia authoring products
Microsoft	A wide variety of software products
Motorola	Chips for Macintosh-compatible computers; wireless products
NEC/Packard Bell	A wide variety of hardware products
Netscape	Internet-related products
Novell	NetWare operating system
Seagate	Storage products
Symantec	A wide variety of utility-software products
Toshiba	A wide variety of hardware products
Yahoo!	Web-based searching and Internet products

System Units   IBM, Compaq, Hewlett-Packard, Dell, and Apple are among the big names in system units in the PC marketplace. There are other companies—such as NEC/Packard Bell and Gateway—who, like Compaq, Hewlett-Packard, and Dell, have become highly successful largely by producing PC-compatible computers. PC compatibles account for about 90 percent of the systems sold; the remainder are Macintosh systems. Most of the system units sold are of the desktop type, but laptops are gaining fast and some analysts predict that they may eventually overtake desktop systems for business use.

Vendors of system units are often ranked in *tiers*. The top-tier vendors include long-standing industry firms like IBM and Compaq whose equipment commands premium prices. Top-tier companies often are involved in extensive research and development efforts, and their equipment is usually top quality and an all around safe purchasing bet. Second-tier vendors are less well known and often sell at prices of about 10 to 20 percent less than their top-tier counterparts. Second-tier companies often do little research and development, use less-expensive component parts, and farm out service and support to third-party firms. Nonetheless, the equipment coming out of second-tier companies is usually high-quality, service and support are very good, and one's purchase risk is very low.

You might save yet another 10 percent on the purchase price of hardware by going to a third-tier vendor. These companies usually have no name recognition and many have been in business only a very short period of time. Because of the increased risk involved, many organizations have policies forbidding them to do business with any computer vendor below what they consider the second tier.

Software   Many applications programs today are sold as part of *software suites,* which bundle together several full-featured software packages for sale at lower prices than the separate programs would collectively command. Among the largest PC software producers (and their leading products) are Microsoft Corporation (Windows and the Office suite of applications), IBM (OS/2, Lotus Notes, and Lotus SmartSuite), and Corel Corporation (the Word-Perfect suite of applications and CorelDRAW!).

Monitors and Printers   With the exception of a few U.S. companies such as IBM and Hewlett-Packard, these two segments are dominated by Japanese producers. Major players include Epson, Toshiba, Seiko, Brother, Fujitsu, Canon, and Okidata.

Microprocessor Chips   The microprocessor chip market is ruled largely by Intel and Motorola. Intel makes CPU chips for most of the leading PC-compatible system units, whereas Motorola makes chips for Macintosh compatibles. Also, a number of lesser-known manufacturers, such as Cyrix and Advanced Micro Devices (AMD), produce Intel-compatible chips. Cyrix and AMD chips are widely used in lower-cost PCs; however, AMD's recent CPU chips—such as Athlon—are making breakthroughs in the high-end chip area.

SALES AND DISTRIBUTION

Most users buy PC hardware and software products through computer stores, discount and department stores, the Internet, mail-order houses, manufacturers, and value-added resellers (see Figure LIV 1-2).

Computer Stores   When buyers need strong local support in selecting and using PC products, they often turn to *computer stores* such as Computer City and CompUSA (see Figure LIV 1-3). Generally, the salespeople at such places are relatively knowledgeable about computers and many help buyers try out products before making a commitment. Besides hardware, software, and general advice on purchasing a new system, computer stores also often offer consulting, repair, and other support services.

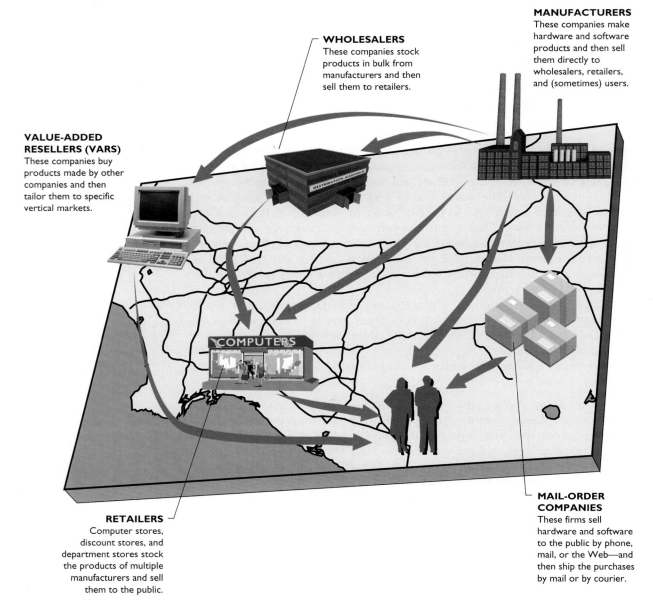

MANUFACTURERS
These companies make hardware and software products and then sell them directly to wholesalers, retailers, and (sometimes) users.

WHOLESALERS
These companies stock products in bulk from manufacturers and then sell them to retailers.

VALUE-ADDED RESELLERS (VARS)
These companies buy products made by other companies and then tailor them to specific vertical markets.

RETAILERS
Computer stores, discount stores, and department stores stock the products of multiple manufacturers and sell them to the public.

MAIL-ORDER COMPANIES
These firms sell hardware and software to the public by phone, mail, or the Web—and then ship the purchases by mail or by courier.

FIGURE LIV 1-2

Distribution channels for PC products.

Computer stores come in many varieties. Most are national or multistate chain stores, but some outfits serve only regional areas such as a single town or a state. Large chains, because they can buy in volume, are likely to have better prices. Many regional stores try to compete by providing superior support. Virtually all computer stores are *resellers*—that is, they sell the hardware and software products made by another company. While many computer stores are as large as the average mall store, massive *computer superstores* have also become popular.

Other Stores During the past several years, PC hardware and software have become so popular that many other types of retail stores have added such items on their showroom floors. Today, you can buy hardware and software at discount stores (such as Wal-Mart), warehouse clubs (such as Price Club and Costco), department stores (such as Sears), office supply stores (such as Office Depot), and bookstores (such as Waldenbooks).

As a general rule, the discount stores and warehouse clubs have the best prices, but there is sometimes less of a selection available and many offer little or no technical support. The smaller selection is often due to deals the store gets on volume purchases and on inventory closeouts—for instance, stock of a printer model the equipment manufacturer wants to get rid of because a replacement model has just come out.

The Internet   In a growing trend, many companies sell hardware and software over the Internet (see Figure LIV 1-4 and the Tomorrow box). To buy a product, you need only go to the seller's Web site and select an item. For software, you can often try out a copy before buying, downloading the program of your choice over the phone lines. If you decide to buy, either the packaged version of the product will be shipped to you immediately, providing you with disks and possibly written documentation, or you will be given a serial or key number that unlocks the program, converting your trial version to a full version of the program. For hardware, you can often make selections to configure the system of your choice online, receiving it by mail, UPS, or Federal Express a few days or weeks later.

Web sites are not only useful for selling products, but they also can economically disseminate to consumers a lot of valuable marketing and support information that is difficult to organize and distribute by any other means. Companies doing business on the Web may or may not make the products they sell; also, many Web sites distribute freeware and shareware. Additionally, the Web provides an ideal place to hold equipment auctions, where buyers submit online bids to acquire computers or peripherals that a seller wants to

FIGURE LIV 1-3

Computer stores. Computer stores are a common sight along highways and in shopping malls. Computer stores are one of the best alternatives for buyers who need strong local support.

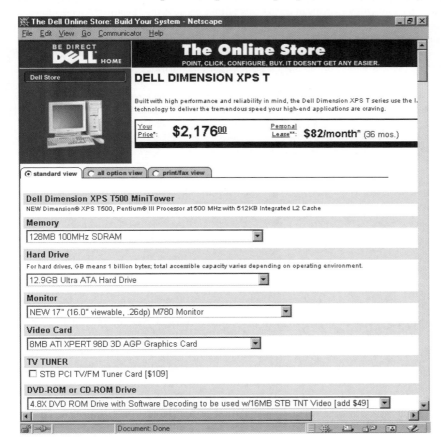

FIGURE LIV 1-4

Configuring a PC on the Web. The Internet's World Wide Web is a good place to shop for PCs. At many Web sites today, you can select how much memory you would like your computer system to have, the size of the hard disk, the size of the monitor, and so on, and immediately see the price of your PC as currently configured.

Are Internet Taxes on the Way?

Buying Online May Soon Cost You More

Increasingly, users are buying their PC hardware and software over the Internet. When the buyer and seller are located in different states—which is most frequently the case—the buyer can often escape without paying sales taxes. State and local governments want that to change.

Currently in the United States there are more than 30,000 jurisdictions—states, counties, and cities—that have the authority to impose sales taxes. And each one that does would like a piece of every purchase transaction made by buyers living within its boundaries, in order to accomplish such worthy tasks as building roads, educating children, and fighting crime. In places that have sales taxes, local merchants back the states in taking a bite out of Internet commerce. Because local merchants are required to levy such taxes on consumers, they worry that untaxed, out-of-state purchases will drive them out of business.

To a great extent, all of the furor over taxing Internet purchases is an online extension of old, offline battles. Examples abound. Consumers in New York City have for decades fled to nearby suburban New Jersey to do their clothes shopping, to avoid the onerous sales taxes on such items where they live. Also for a number of years, consumers in many states have found mail-order-catalog buying especially attractive because they similarly can avoid sales taxes.

Consumer interest in the Internet has grown to a point where many state and local governments are getting alarmed. In 1997, only $8 billion in commerce was conducted online. That figure is expected to mushroom to close to $350 billion by 2002. The Internet merchants are nervous too. They fear that a free-for-all tax-

Online purchases. State and local governments are stepping up the pressure to charge consumers sales tax.

ing environment could produce wild effects and turn consumers off to online commerce.

To ensure that the rush to tax Internet purchases is orderly, the federal government has pushed for a moratorium on Internet taxation until the year 2001. Some taxing proponents are suggesting calling any forthcoming law the *Internet Tax Freedom Act,* a name that many detractors find ironic because they believe the legislation will inevitably cause consumers to be shackled by more taxes.

The issue has sparked a lot of controversy, and not even all consumers agree. Some worry that when a large number of people escape taxes, others wind up paying more. In the end, they feel, governments will get whatever funds they need from taxpayers, any way they can. Robbing Peter to pay Paul, so to speak. One thing is for sure; the battle over whether to tax or not to tax will be a heated one and will likely last some time.

---

unload. *Cyberauctions* are becoming increasingly popular and are covered elsewhere in versions of this textbook that contain a NET module.

Mail-Order Firms   Another common source of computer products is mail-order firms. These companies, which are usually resellers, handle products from scores of hardware or software manufacturers and primarily ship goods to a customer after receiving an order by phone, mail, or over the Internet (see Figure LIV 1-5). These companies usually have access to an enormous selection of goods and can get almost any item to customers quickly via UPS or Federal Express. Mail-order firms regularly publish price lists in PC journals, in their own product catalogs, or on their Web sites.

Because mail-order companies don't have to pay for a showroom and a staff of knowledgeable salespeople, their prices are usually much lower than those of computer stores and are competitive with discount stores and Internet sellers. A disadvantage of mail-order shopping is that buyers need to know exactly what they want, because most mail-order firms don't maintain showrooms or a large technical staff.

For links to further information about PC manufacturers and PC buying sites, go to www.harcourtcollege. com/infosys/parker2000/ student/explore/ and click on Chapter LIV 1.

Software and Hardware Makers Yet another alternative for buying hardware and software is going straight to the product maker. Hardware companies such as IBM and Compaq manufacture many of the components going into their PCs, whereas companies such as Dell and Gateway merely assemble components made by others into finished PCs. Most PC companies today sell directly to the public, either through advertisements in computer journals or through their Web sites. Many of these companies do not maintain finished inventories of computers; they build each system to suit the buyer's tastes as they receive each order. Consumers enjoy the advantage of ordering exactly the computer systems they want from a single source—including free support and service for a limited period of time. Whether or not they make their own component parts, companies that put their own brand names on hardware devices such as computer systems and peripheral devices and sell the hardware directly to the public are called *direct manufacturers*.

Many software manufacturers—or **software publishers**—also sell directly to the public. Buyers generally reach publishers through toll-free numbers that appear in journal advertisements and through the publisher's Web site. Many software publishers will also let you download copies of their products over the Internet for trial purposes.

Value-Added Resellers **Value-added resellers (VARs)** are companies that buy computer hardware and software from others and make their own specialized systems out of them. For instance, many of the computer systems used in the videotape-rental-store business, in medical and dental offices, and in certain other types of *vertical markets* come from VARs. The VAR essentially packages together all of the custom hardware and software needed to run operations in the vertical-market area in which it specializes and often provides full service and support as well. Although going through a VAR is usually more costly than configuring a system on one's own, it is definitely a compelling choice for a small business owner who is not computer savvy or who is too busy with other matters.

Used Equipment When shopping for a computer system, don't overlook used equipment. Ads for used equipment usually appear in the classified sections of local newspapers. If you take this route, ask to try out the equipment before you buy it. If the equipment functions properly during the trial period, it will probably work fine. You should pay considerably less for a used system than you would for a new one. When looking at used equipment, be wary of any computer system originally purchased more than 2 or 3 years ago. Technology changes so quickly that a computer built this long ago may have problems running current software today.

FIGURE LIV 1-5

Mail-order firms. Several mail-order houses regularly print catalogs that showcase products for PC-compatible or Macintosh computers.

SELECTING A PC

Chances are good that at some point in your life, you will need to select a PC to better perform your job. Selecting a PC for home or for business use must begin with the all-important question "What do I want the system to do?" Once you've determined the purposes to which the system will be put, you must

■ **Software publisher.** A company that creates software. ■ **Value-added reseller (VAR).** A company that buys hardware and software from others and makes computer systems out of them that are targeted to particular vertical markets.

choose among the software and hardware alternatives available. Finally, you need a method to evaluate the alternatives and to select a system.

ANALYZING NEEDS

With regard to a computer system, a *need* refers to a functional requirement that the computer system must be capable of meeting. For instance, at a video-tape rental store, a computer system must be able to enter bar codes automatically from tapes being checked in and out, identify customers with over-due tapes, manage tape inventories, and do routine accounting operations. Requiring portability—a computer that you can take with you "on the road"—is another example of a need.

A person owning a computer system will find dozens of ways to use it, but he or she may often justify the acquisition of a PC on the basis of only one or two needs. For example, many writers find word processing so indispensable to their livelihoods that it matters little what else the computer system can do. Sales personnel working out of the office can often justify a notebook computer simply on the basis of its usefulness as a sale-closing tool during presentations at their clients' offices.

If you're not really sure what you want a system to do, you should think twice about buying one. Computer systems that are configured to match the require-ments of certain applications (say, preparing a novel) often perform poorly at others (such as playing power-hungry multimedia games). You can easily make expensive mistakes if you're uncertain about what you want a system to do.

As part of the needs analysis, you should look closely at budgetary con-straints. Every user can easily list many needs, but affordability separates real needs from pipe dreams.

LISTING ALTERNATIVES

After you establish a set of needs, the next step is to list some alternative sys-tems that might satisfy those needs. You should almost always consider appli-cations software first, then look for the hardware and systems-software plat-form that most effectively satisfies your applications-software requirements.

Applications software is selected first because it most directly satisfies needs. For instance, if you want a computer system to do commercial art, it would be wise to first look at the various programs available in this area. It makes no sense to choose hardware first and then find out that it doesn't sup-port the type of art package you prefer. Many artists, for instance, prefer a Mac-intosh platform, so you might completely miss the boat if you buy a PC-com-patible computer and then discover later that the Mac is better suited for the work you want to do. Also, if you skimped on the CPU and storage and later found out that the programs you selected require a lot of power, again you'd be out of luck or would have to already think about *upgrading*, a topic dis-cussed later in this chapter.

You can get a list of leading software and hardware products from the many microcomputer journals available at newsstands and libraries. Many of these jour-nals also periodically describe the best and worst features of products, rate and compare products, and have industry analysts address product trends (see Figure LIV 1-6). Such information can be useful for evaluating buying alternatives.

Leasing versus Buying   When looking for a new computer system, you may want to consider leasing one instead of buying outright. Many direct manu-facturers—among them Compaq, Dell, and Gateway—both sell and lease com-puter systems. Over the long run, leasing is usually more expensive than buy-ing but provides greater flexibility, since you can switch out of your current

PRODUCT REVIEWS
You can get a review of any particular product by searching for it in any of several computer journals—either the online or printed form.

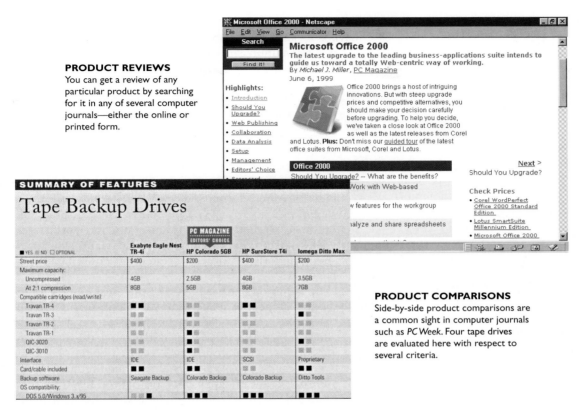

PRODUCT COMPARISONS
Side-by-side product comparisons are a common sight in computer journals such as *PC Week*. Four tape drives are evaluated here with respect to several criteria.

system into a newer model, when necessary, to keep pace with changes in technology. Many leasing plans run for two or three years and provide the lessee the option to buy the system after the lease runs out, at the current market price for used equipment.

FIGURE LIV 1-6

Product evaluations. You can find out about PC products both in print and on the Web.

EVALUATING ALTERNATIVES

Prospective buyers can evaluate alternative products most effectively by "test driving" them. Keep in mind, however, that you observe the performance of a software package only on a given configuration of hardware. A software package that runs smoothly on a Gateway 500 MHz computer system with 128 MB RAM won't necessarily run as well on a Compaq 333 MHz PC with 32 MB RAM, because the varying components used by different manufacturers can affect performance, and because of the different CPU chips and amount of memory in these two systems. Also, the look, feel, and performance of a software package on a computer in the Apple Macintosh line are often noticeably different than they are on a PC-compatible machine. Sometimes it's quite difficult, when selecting a configuration of hardware and software, to see the entire system together, but it's certainly advisable to do this whenever possible.

Selection Criteria As you evaluate software and hardware products, a number of criteria will help you to make your final selection. The most important selection criterion is *functionality*—the type of work the product does. For many people, ease of learning, ease of use, and the availability of phone support follow closely behind. Also, most people prefer widely used products rather than unknown ones, because the large user base with the more popular products ensures that support will be readily available for a long time. In addition, if you are considering using a PC in an office environment dominated by, say, Apple Macintoshes, choosing that type of

System Checklist

- ☑ Product functionality
- ☑ Ease of learning and use
- ☑ Cost
- ☑ Vendor reputation
- ☑ Support
- ☑ Expandability
- ☑ Meets industry standards
- ☑ Performance
- ☑ Favorable reviews
- ☑ Delivery
- ☑ Documentation

FIGURE LIV 1-7

Important selection criteria. Buyers generally select computer systems on the basis of some combination of criteria.

computer would probably be more convenient from the standpoint of having local expertise available for support. Good written documentation showing how to use the hardware or software is also important. When a helping hand isn't readily available, documentation is often the best alternative for answering a tough question. Figure LIV 1-7 lists important criteria for selecting a particular PC.

Shopping for Software and Hardware Before looking over software or hardware products that you might buy, you should make a checklist of features that you want in your eventual system. Also, be sure to watch for these features during the test drive. A rehearsed presentation made by a salesperson is likely to point out only the strengths of a product, not its weaknesses. Some of the items that you should watch for when shopping for a PC are enumerated in Feature LIV 1-1 on page LIV 14.

In acquiring hardware, one of the most common mistakes that people make is not thinking enough about the future. You should buy as much processing speed and storage capacity in your initial purchase as you can afford. New software updates—which come out about every year or two—virtually always require more speed and storage for effective operation. If you buy a bottom-of-the-line system, you might find that the next major upgrade of your favorite software package crawls at a snail's pace. If you buy a system for business use, expect your hardware to last about three years before new software needs force you to buy a new system.

CHOOSING A SYSTEM

After you have considered available alternatives, it's time to choose a system and purchase it. People choose among system alternatives in a number of ways. For instance, some people make a formal list of selection criteria, weigh each criterion with respect to its importance, and quantitatively rate each alternative on each criterion. All other things being equal, they then select the alternative that scores the highest total when the ratings are added.

Others prefer to make their choices less formally. After thinking about their needs and the criteria they apply to evaluate alternatives, they select the first computer system they see that "feels right." Although such an acquisition process could be criticized for lack of thoroughness, many people claim that their busy schedules leave no time to spend researching choices with greater care. Of course, rushing to make a selection has a negative side. Just as a car owner can go through years of torture driving around in the wrong type of car, a computer buyer can also wind up with years of headaches resulting from a poor choice.

HARDWARE AND SOFTWARE INSTALLATION

When you buy a computer system, most of the hardware and software you need will probably already be in place. If it isn't, you can usually buy and install it relatively easily yourself.

Installing Hardware   Historically, users have not always had an easy time installing new equipment on their computers. The cover of the system unit had to be carefully taken off and an add-in board inserted correctly. Then, device drivers had to be correctly installed. From start to finish, the process was time consuming and stressful. Something could easily go wrong—an ultra-thin circuit could get damaged or the add-in board might not work with a component on the motherboard. When a problem cropped up, users could waste hours trying to figure out what was causing it.

Fortunately, the scenario just described is gradually disappearing. To make it easier than ever for PC owners to install hardware on their own, both hardware and software vendors have gravitated toward a *plug-and-play* approach. Consequently, all users of such systems theoretically need to do is plug in any new equipment into the system unit—almost as easily as they would plug a lamp into a wall socket—and they're ready to go. When they start their computers after installing the hardware, the operating system "talks to" the new equipment and automatically configures the proper drivers for it.

Installing Software   Generally, software of any type is relatively easy to install today. When you buy a new program, the package contains one or more *installation disks.* You load the first of the disks into its proper drive and, if instructed to do so on the disk label, enter a command. Then, it's just a matter of following a set of simple instructions on the screen. In most cases, there is very little you have to do beyond entering some identifying information about yourself and deciding what type of installation you would like to do—such as a typical install or a custom install.

A *typical install* places most of the files you will need onto your hard disk. A *custom install* enables you to select such options as the location where the program will be installed, whether or not to keep older versions of the program, which optional components to install, whether to run the program or optional components from the CD-ROM, and so forth. Microsoft Office 2000 Premium, for instance, requires about 250 MB of hard-disk space for a typical install, whereas a custom install can require from 100 to over 500 MB, depending on the programs and options installed.

Also consider new uses for your old computer system. It could, for instance, serve as a backup device.

OPERATING A PC

Once you acquire a PC, you should develop a set of careful practices to protect your software, hardware, and data from damage and costly mistakes. Four important areas in this regard are system backup, proper maintenance of hardware and storage media, security, and problem detection and correction.

BACKUP PROCEDURES

Virtually every computer veteran will warn you that, sooner or later, you will lose some critical files. Maybe lightning will strike nearby, zapping your RAM. Perhaps a small brownout will cause the heads on your hard disk to drop out of orbit and crash onto the disk surface, carving a miniature canyon through the electronic version of a 45-page term paper that's due tomorrow. Or maybe you'll accidentally delete or overwrite the file. Computer veterans will also tell you that file losses always seem to happen at the worst possible times.

PC Shopping Checklist

Some Important Questions to Ask

When buying a new PC, be sure to get answers to the following questions:

Hardware

Should I buy a notebook or desktop PC? If you need portability, you need a notebook computer. Notebook buyers should expect to pay about $500 more than they would for a comparable desktop model, even though the processor and hard disk are usually slightly less capable. A critical decision in the notebook area is battery life; most have to be recharged every two to eight hours. Desktop computer systems are generally easier to upgrade than notebooks, have larger screens and keyboards, and have a mouse instead of a smaller pointing device.

Which platform is best? The two main choices are a PC-compatible computer—most of which run under some version of Microsoft Windows—or a Macintosh. Close to 90 percent of PCs sold today are Windows-based, but the Mac is more popular in the desktop-publishing and graphic arts fields. Because there is less competition in the Macintosh arena, expect to pay slightly higher prices for both hardware and software if you decide to become a Mac owner.

How powerful should the system be? Acquire a system with enough processing power to last for several years. One of the biggest errors made by first-time computer buyers is skimping on price and not acquiring the power they will need in one or two years. When this happens and new software runs too slowly, the buyer is forced prema-

Plan before you buy. The computer equivalent of putting the horse before the cart is making a list of needs for the foreseeable future before buying.

turely to either get another new PC or upgrade the existing PC. This latter task can be time consuming and expensive.

How much memory is necessary? Most people today need at least 64 to 128 MB of RAM or more. The computer you buy should have enough RAM to run your operating system plus your most memory-intensive program and then some—say, enough to accommodate an upgrade to the next version of the program or a switch to a comparable program. A good rule of thumb is to buy twice the memory you initially need.

What types of secondary storage systems should I buy? Most people buying computer systems today will have it configured with

Fortunately, there is a solution to most of these problems—backing up important data and programs. Creating a **backup** means making a duplicate version of any file that you can't afford to lose so that, when the fickle finger of fate causes inadvertent erasure, you're confronted with only a minor irritant rather than an outright catastrophe. Theoretically, you can back up any file on your computer system. The backups you create—through a file-copy, disk-copy, or backup command—can be on diskette, hard disk, tape, or virtually any other secondary storage medium.

One common form of backup that everyone should practice is frequently saving to disk a long file that is being developed in RAM. For instance, suppose you are word processing a paper for a class. About every five minutes or so you should make sure that you save the current version of the document onto disk. After completing the document, it can then be backed up on another medium, if desired. For backup of several files at the same time, many different strategies exist. Some users perform **full backups,** storing all files

■ **Backup.** A procedure that produces a duplicate version of any file that you can't afford to lose. ■ **Full backup.** A procedure that produces a duplicate copy of all files onto a secondary storage medium.

one 1.44 MB standard diskette drive and/or one larger capacity (SuperDisk or Zip) drive, a hard drive with a capacity of a few gigabytes, and a DVD or CD drive. When buying a hard disk, go for as much storage as you can—it usually doesn't cost that much for the additional megabytes and you'll be happy a couple of years down the road that you made the investment.

What about backup? Because hard disks have such great capacities today and there's so much to lose if a hard disk crashes or somehow gets corrupted, many people today are buying tape units or high-capacity removable storage devices to use to backup important software and data. Tape units are generally used only for backup, whereas other devices, such as a Zip or Jaz drive, can be used for other purposes.

Do I need a CD drive? A DVD or CD drive is a standard item on PCs, since many software vendors today require you to use CD installation disks and some software must be run from the CD or DVD disk. Most DVD drives can read both CD and DVD disks, so that is usually the drive of choice—be sure to get a drive at the fastest commercially available speed. You should also equip your computer system with speakers, a sound card, and a good graphics board.

What type of printer is best for my needs? For most people, the choice will be between an ink-jet and laser printer. Ink-jet printers are especially popular at the low end of the market, and most can produce color output. At the higher end of the market, monochrome laser printers dominate because they are faster and produce better output. When selecting a printer, check the speed, output quality, and the cost of consumable items (paper, color or toner cartridges, etc.) Also consider reading evaluations in PC journals.

What do I need to know about modems? Most computer systems today come with an internal modem. Consider an external modem instead only if you need to use the modem with more than one computer. Also, buy the fastest modem speed available. Most modems sold today come with faxing capabilities.

Software

What operating system should I go with? Most people buying a PC-compatible computer will likely be using Windows, whereas those choosing a Macintosh-compatible platform will be using Mac OS. Make sure the vendor from which you are buying your PC is providing you with the current version of an operating system—and for that matter, a current version of all other software.

Should I buy a full-featured software suite or an integrated software package? While some standalone office programs still exist, most people buy office software in the form of suites or integrated software packages. Integrated software packages cost less than suites, yet have most of the features the average user would ever want to utilize. What's more, they require less disk space and memory. Integrated software packages are most suitable for home users. You will probably require a software suite, however, if you work in a business—especially one that uses some of the more sophisticated features of the software and that is trying to standardize applications across a broad spectrum of users. The three most popular software suites are Microsoft Office, Corel WordPerfect Office, and Lotus SmartSuite.

Service and Support

What should I look for in service and support? Service and support are becoming increasingly important factors as system quality and pricing continue to converge among the major PC sellers. What's more, hardware and software prices are falling while your time is becoming more valuable. Be sure your system comes with at least a one-year warranty and find out if repairs are performed on site, or if you have to deliver a defective system to a local vendor or mail it to the manufacturer. Find out if the warranty covers parts and labor or just parts after a period of time. Also check for toll-free technical support—the major PC vendors typically offer some toll-free, 24 hours a day, seven days a week, phone support on both hardware and software.

from their hard disks onto tapes or disk cartridges at the end of a day or a week. The advantage to a full backup is that it is relatively straightforward. On the downside, a full backup takes up more storage space and takes longer than a backup in which only selected files are targeted for copying.

An alternative to the full backup is a **partial backup** in which you copy only the files that you have created or altered since the last backup. Users commonly implement two such types of partial backup procedures. A *differential backup* duplicates all files created or changed since the last full backup. In an *incremental backup*, duplicates are made of all files created or changed since the last backup of any type. Both types of partial backup described here enable you, along with the copy of the full backup, to reconstruct the hard disk if it becomes corrupted. Incremental backups are the faster of the two types of partial backup to perform but result in more work to fully reconstruct the hard disk. Many people who have hard disks will perform a partial backup daily and a full backup weekly. Businesses may perform a full backup every night.

When doing either a full or partial backup, some users back up only

■ **Partial backup.** A procedure that produces a duplicate copy of selected files onto a secondary storage medium.

Why back up?

- A disk sector goes bad, destroying part of a file.
- A file that you thought you no longer had a need for and erased turns out to be important.
- You modify a file in an undesirable way, and the damage done is irreversible.
- You accidentally reformat a disk.
- The disk suffers a head crash.
- A power brownout or failure at the time of saving a file causes "garbage" to be saved.
- You save a file to the wrong subdirectory, overwriting a different file that has the same name.
- While rushing your work, you make a mistake that causes the wrong files to be erased.
- You unwittingly destroy a file while working on it—say, by deleting parts of it erroneously and then saving the file.
- Malfunctioning hardware or software causes files to be erased.
- A computer virus enters your system and destroys files.
- Your disk is physically destroyed—for instance, a diskette is left in the sun or the hard disk is given a jolt. Alternatively, a fire or flood may destroy the disk.
- Someone steals your diskette or hard disk.

FIGURE LIV 1-8

Reasons for file backup.

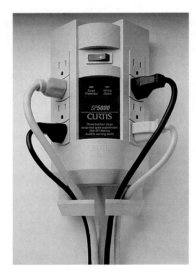

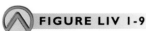

FIGURE LIV 1-9

Surge suppressor. The system unit and its support devices feed into the surge suppressor, which is plugged into a standard wall outlet. All of the equipment can be turned on or off by a single switch.

document files, since program files are already backed up on the program installation disks.

Whenever you back up files on a disk, make sure to place the backup files on a different disk from the originals. In theory, you shouldn't even keep these copies in the same room or building. That way, if a serious accident such as a fire or flood occurs at one location, the files safely stored at the other location will help you to recover. A variety of accidents that can destroy programs and data—all of them good reasons to back up data stored on disk—are listed in Figure LIV 1-8.

EQUIPMENT MAINTENANCE

PCs consist of sensitive electronic devices, so users must treat them with appropriate care. In this section we discuss protecting your computer system with a surge suppressor or UPS unit; caring for disks; protecting your computer system from dust, heat, and static; and protecting monitors.

Surge Suppression One of the best devices to have on your computer system to minimize the chance of unexpected damage is a surge suppressor. A **surge suppressor,** which is installed between your computer system and the electrical outlet providing the power, is a hardware device that prevents random electrical power spikes from impacting your system (see Figure LIV 1-9). Probably the most common problem caused by a spike is loss of data in RAM. Cases have also been reported, however, of loss of data in secondary storage and destruction of equipment. A surge suppressor cannot guarantee complete electrical protection. If lightning strikes your house, a surge suppressor will probably fail to protect your data or equipment. If you are working on your computer system when a storm hits, you should save to disk what you've been working on and turn off your system.

Instead of a plain surge suppressor, some people use an **uninterruptible power supply (UPS)** unit (see Figure LIV 1-10). This device is a surge suppressor with a built-in battery, the latter of which keeps power going to the computer when the main power goes off—say, due to a lightning storm, a

■ **Surge suppressor.** A device that protects a computer system from random electrical power spikes. ■ **Uninterruptible power supply (UPS).** A surge suppressor with a built-in battery, the latter of which keeps power going to the computer when the main power goes off.

brownout, or damage to an outside cable. UPSs designed for the average PC often run for a few minutes without outside power before they have to be recharged; UPSs for larger computers may run for several hours. In either case, it gives the user a chance to save all open documents, transfer files to a removable storage device, if necessary, and properly shut down the system.

Disk Care User precautions with diskettes, hard disks, and CDs help to safeguard any programs and data stored on them. Diskettes may look like inert slabs of plastic, but they are actually extremely sensitive storage media that work well over time only with appropriate care. Never touch the actual diskette surface or bend the diskette. Also, keep the diskette away from magnetic objects, motors, stereo speakers, and extreme temperatures.

The most important precaution for a hard disk is placing it in a location where it is not likely to be bumped or subjected to electrical interference. As far as CDs go, make sure that the nonprinted side remains free of dirt, fingerprints, and scratches, which may impair laser reading.

Dust, Heat, and Static Each of the tiny processor and memory chips in your hardware units are packed tightly with thousands or millions of circuits. Dust particles circulating in the air can settle on a chip, causing a short circuit. Many people use dust covers that fit snugly over each of their hardware devices when the computer is turned off to prevent foreign particles in the air from causing hardware failure.

Desktop and tower system units also generate lots of heat and require cooling fans. When placing your system unit on a desktop or on the floor, make sure it is in a place where the ventilation is good and the outlet from the fan is not blocked.

Static electricity is especially dangerous because it can damage chips, destroy programs and data in storage, or disable your keyboard. So that the electrical discharges from your fingertips don't wreak havoc, you might consider buying an antistatic mat for under your workstation chair or an antistatic pad to put under your keyboard. Static electricity is more likely in dry areas and in the wintertime, when there's less humidity in the air.

Screen Savers CRT-type monitors have a phosphorescent inner surface that is lit up by an electronic gun. If you keep your monitor at a high brightness level and abandon it for several hours with an unchanging image on the screen, the phosphorescent surface may get damaged. Ghosty character images can get permanently etched on the screen, making it harder to read. To prevent this from happening, software packages called **screen savers** are available that either dim your monitor or create constantly changing patterns on the screen when the display remains unchanged for a given number of minutes. Today's monitors are better equipped to prevent screen burn than ones made only a few years ago, so sometimes screen savers are useful only for their entertainment value or to prevent anyone (by using a screen-saver password) from looking at your computer screen when you are away from your desk.

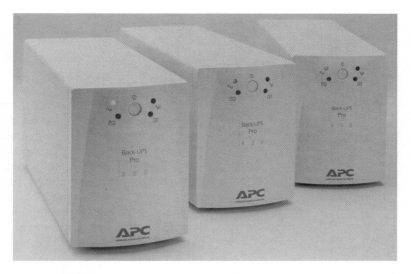

FIGURE LIV 1-10

Uninterruptible power supply (UPS) units.

■ **Screen saver.** A software product designed to protect the phosphor coating on the inside of a display screen from damage when the display is turned on but is not used for an extended period.

SECURITY

Security refers to protecting a computer system's hardware, software, and data from unintentional damage, malicious damage, or any type of tampering. There are many ways to secure a computer system, including locks on doors and lockplates on equipment, protecting files with passwords that only you know, accessories that block people from seeing what's on your screen or hard disk, encryption algorithms that disguise outgoing messages, and programs that prevent computer viruses from infecting storage devices. The topic of securing computer systems is discussed more thoroughly in Chapter LIV 2.

No matter what type of security strategy you decide to go with, it is important to note that no strategy can give you 100 percent protection. Nonetheless, giving a little thought to some of the things that can go wrong and taking a few simple precautions can save you big headaches later on. Studies made on PC users have shown that they tend not to spend a lot of time thinking about security.

TROUBLESHOOTING AND TECHNICAL ASSISTANCE

If you work with computers for any length of time, at some point you will probably have an experience when your hardware or software does not work properly. You may turn on your computer system one day and get no response. Perhaps your monitor screen will begin flickering badly every few seconds. Or maybe you will issue a familiar command in a software package that you work with regularly and the keyboard will lock up or the command will remain unexecuted. When such an event takes place, you will need to troubleshoot to isolate the underlying problem. If the problem is serious enough, assistance from an outside source may be necessary.

Troubleshooting *Troubleshooting* refers to actions taken to diagnose or solve a problem. Unfortunately, many problems are unique to specific types of hardware and software, so no simple troubleshooting remedy will work all of the time. Nonetheless, the following simple steps and guidelines will help you to identify and correct a number of common problems:

- Try again. A surprising number of procedures work when you try a second or third time. You may have pressed the wrong keys the first time, or not pressed the keys hard enough.
- Check to see that all of the equipment is plugged in and turned on and that none of the cables are detached or loose.
- Reboot the system. Many software problems are corrected after the computer is restarted and the program opened again. Some operating systems—such as Windows 98—will also try to reconfigure problem devices when the system is restarted, as well as give you the option of temporarily disabling certain devices if your system crashed, to help you determine the problem device.
- Recall exactly what happened between the time the system was operating properly and the time you began to encounter problems. There might have been an electrical storm outside, and your system was plugged in and damaged by lightning. Or perhaps you installed new systems software during your last session, and it is affecting the way your current application works.
- Be observant. If strange noises came out of the disk drives when you unsuccessfully tried to boot the system up, those noises might be important. Even though solving the problem may be beyond your capa-

---

■ **Security.** A collection of measures for protecting a computer system's hardware, software, and data from damage or tampering.

bilities, you may be able to supply important facts to the people who will assist you in getting your system up and running again.

■ Check the **documentation,** or descriptive instructions, that came with the system. Many products come with a hard-copy manual with a troubleshooting checklist, and many software products have an online help feature that will help you solve many of your own problems.

■ Use diagnostic software. *Diagnostic software* enables you to test your system to see if parts of it are malfunctioning or are just giving you poor performance. Sometimes, when new equipment is added, problems arise with existing equipment or software. Also, hard disks can get fragmented with use over time and may need to be sped up with defragmentation software.

You should weigh the time that it takes to solve a problem yourself against the cost of outside help. It's not a disgrace to give up if the problem is more than you can handle. It is simply an admission that your time is valuable and that you are wise enough to know when to call in a professional for assistance.

Technical Assistance with Hardware and Software One of the most important items in working with hardware or software products is getting technical assistance when you need it. Three such sources of assistance are discussed next.

THE MANUFACTURER One of the best prospects for support is turning to the company that made the hardware or software with which you are working. Probably nobody knows more about correcting problems than the people who may have created them in the first place. It's that very thought that leads people to contact the hardware manufacturer or software publisher first whenever something bad happens.

Many manufacturers provide toll-free phone numbers, fax numbers, e-mail addresses, and Web or newsgroup sites for users to contact to get help with technical problems. To reach others, you will have to make a toll call or, worse yet, dial a 900-area-code number where you get charged by the minute. Some vendors are notorious for keeping users on hold. Check to see if some type of premium service is available where you can get a faster and perhaps higher level of response. Also check if phone support is still covered under your warranty.

With the cost of support escalating, hardware and software makers are increasingly devising more ways to provide assistance over the Web (see Figure LIV 1-11). IBM, for instance, has placed on the Web a vast storehouse of technical-support knowledge that used to be available only to its own support staff. One of its features is a software agent that travels over the phone lines to repair remote computer systems. Intel has a combination Web-and-human-based system called AnswerExpress. The Web part of the system does an online inventory of your computer system's vitals and relays it to a live support technician, who will call you back within minutes.

For links to further information about technical support sites, go to www. harcourtcollege.com/ infosys/parker2000/student/ explore/ and click on Chapter **LIV 1**.

FIGURE LIV 1-11

Web-based technical support. Gateway's Web site provides buyers with information on products as well as customer support.

■ **Documentation.** A description of how a program, procedure, or system works.

THIRD-PARTY SUPPORT Products are often supported through third-party firms that specialize in giving assistance. You can contact one of these firms yourself, or you may be put in touch with them by a hardware or software maker. Many of the latter, incidentally, do not have their own in-house technical support groups but instead farm out customer support to third-party firms.

Third-party firms often have toll-free or 900-area-code phone numbers that you call to get help. In the case of the 900 area codes, many firms will cap charges at a limit—say, $25 or $50—so your bill doesn't become outrageous. When dealing with anyone who charges for support, check to see if any follow-up calls you make once a problem is theoretically corrected will incur an additional charge.

USER SUPPORT If you don't know anyone personally who can give you help, take solace in the fact that many users post problems on the Internet or on public bulletin boards. The message you post might be read by literally hundreds of other users, and there's a good possibility that someone out there has encountered and solved the problem you are now wrestling with. While you may get the answer you are seeking without paying a dime, don't be surprised if you have to wait a week or more to have your plea for help read by the right person.

With the more widely used products, you will also find formal user groups. *User groups* enable you to meet other users in person and to talk about common problems and creative ways to use the hardware or software.

Equipment Repairs In some cases, a problem is so simple that no equipment repair is necessary. However, when a repair is beyond the scope of your capabilities, you will need to seek professional help. Likely sources of such help are the party that sold you the problematic hardware, computer stores in your area, and computer repair technicians listed in the Yellow Pages of your local phone book.

Keep the following questions in mind when asking someone else to diagnose or repair your system:

- Is it better to repair old equipment or to buy new equipment? For instance, if the computer system to be repaired is worth less than $500, it may be cheaper to buy a completely new system.
- Will the repair work be done under **warranty?** Most new equipment is sold with a warranty stating that the manufacturer will pay for certain repairs if the equipment fails within a given number of days or months after purchase. If the warranty hasn't expired, the repair may cost you nothing. Be aware that many manufacturers state in their warranty that the warranty becomes void if you attempt to repair the equipment yourself or if a repair is attempted by an unauthorized person or shop.
- Can you get an estimate before proceeding with the work? In many cases, repair technicians can provide a free estimate of what the repair will cost. If they can't, you might want them to diagnose the problem first and to call you when they are able to provide an estimate. You never, ever want to put yourself in a situation in which you are presented with an unexpected, outrageously expensive repair bill.
- Is priority service available? People who use their computers as part of their jobs often need repairs immediately. Many repair shops realize this and will provide same-day or next-day turnaround for an extra fee. Some will even loan you equipment while repairs are being made.

When you buy a computer system, you can often choose to buy an extended maintenance contract to cover certain types of repairs beyond those stated in the warranty. Figure LIV 1-12 lists a number of the points covered by both warranties and maintenance contracts.

■ **Warranty.** A conditional pledge made by a manufacturer to protect consumers from losses due to defective products.

Warranty and Maintenance

Coverage
The contract should state clearly if both parts and labor are covered.

Contract Period
Many contracts cover a period of one to three years. Some vendors provide a "lifetime" guarantee on certain types of parts or services.

Repair Procedure
A procedure should spell out clearly what steps will be taken when a problem occurs. Often, the vendor will first try to diagnose the problem over the phone. If this fails, either you will have to bring or send the unit to an authorized repair center or a technician will be dispatched to your home or office within a certain number of hours or days. If you can't afford to be without your computer system for an appreciable period, this part of the contract may be the most critical. Some contracts will provide you with a "loaner" system while yours is being repaired.

Support Hotline
Many companies provide a hotline for you to call when you have a question or a problem. Sometimes you can call toll free, and sometimes you won't be billed for the vendor's time. It's a good idea to check out how easy it is to reach the hotline; some of them are so understaffed it takes days for a call to be returned.

Other Clauses
Most contracts will be void if you attempt to repair the equipment yourself or let someone who's not an authorized repairperson do it.

FIGURE LIV 1-12

Contracts. A good warranty or maintenance contract should cover the clauses listed here.

UPGRADING

Hardware and software generally need to be upgraded over time. **Upgrading** a computer system means buying new hardware or software components that will extend the life of your current system. The question you must ask when considering an expensive upgrade is the same one that you would ask when considering costly repairs to a car: Should I spend this money on my current system or start fresh and buy a completely new system?

When you acquire a new PC, it is extremely important to formulate an upgrade strategy. Ideally, you should buy a PC that adheres to a well-supported standard. This and other considerations will give you flexibility to upgrade it to meet reasonable future needs over the course of its lifetime. Of course, you cannot anticipate all of your future needs, but you invite unnecessary and expensive upgrades later on by spending no time thinking about system growth.

UPGRADING HARDWARE

Some common types of hardware upgrades include adding more RAM or a second hard disk to a system, installing a faster modem, adding boards that provide new types of functionality, and adding new peripheral equipment such as an image scanner or DVD drive. Unless your system is powerful enough to handle growth, many upgrades will not be possible. For instance, if you have an Intel 80486-based processor and you want to do a serious upgrade, you should probably just purchase a new PC. You cannot bring a 486 computer up to the level of today's mainstream desktop computers without replacing the motherboard and virtually every other item inside the system unit. With some new PCs selling for $500 or less, it would cost less to buy an entirely new machine.

■ **Upgrading.** The process of buying new hardware or software in order to add capabilities and extend the life of a computer system.

Time Bombs That Produced Unexpected Results

Frequently, when beta programs—prerelease versions of new software—are manufactured, they contain pieces of code called time bombs that forbid the program to work after a certain date. This practice is followed for any or all of a variety of reasons—for example, to force beta testers to upgrade to the fully developed product when it is released, to cut down on software piracy, or to prevent partially developed forms of the program from later creating problems that could cause the company any sort of embarrassment or legal trouble.

When the finished programs are released, these time bombs are supposed to be removed, but occasionally something goes wrong and the code stays in. When this happens, of course, the software that is sold in stores or over the Internet will not work after a certain date, and users get angry. Such an event happened, for instance, when Novell first released PerfectOffice 3.0. The first 100,000 copies contained a time bomb that prevented the program from being installed after December 31, 1995. Adobe Systems ran into a similar problem with PhotoShop 3.0, and it had to recall the product and ship release 3.01 to fix the glitch.

Today, some PCs sold in the marketplace are touted as *upgradable PCs*. These devices are designed with modest and predefined types of replacement in mind, making it possible to swap out components like the CPU chip or the internal hard disk as more powerful ones become available. For instance, many PCs come with special sockets in the system board that make it possible to plug in an Intel *overdrive chip* that takes over the duties of the resident CPU.

UPGRADING SOFTWARE

Many PC software vendors enhance their products in some major way every year or two, prompting users to upgrade. Each of these upgrades—which are called **versions**—is assigned a number, such as 1.0, 2.0, 3.0, and so on. The higher the number, the more recent and more powerful the software. Minor versions, called **releases,** typically increase their numbers in increments of 0.1—say, 1.1, 1.2, and 1.3—or .01, such as release 3.11 following release 3.1. Releases are usually issued in response to bugs or shortcomings in the version. Recently, the versions and releases of many software products began being assigned numbers that correspond exactly or approximately to the year of issue—such as Office 97 (for the 1997 version of Microsoft Office) and Office 2000 (for the 2000 version, which actually came out in 1999). Frequently, when new versions of software are launched, they contain several, reasonably serious bugs that are refined in subsequent releases. It doesn't happen very often, but sometimes these bugs are so profound that the version is barely on the store shelves before a release is on its way (see the Inside the Industry box).

■ **Version.** A major upgrade of a software product. ■ **Release.** A minor upgrade of a software product.

With computer networks now reaching into many homes and offices, any companies are making upgrades available to users with increasing frequency. Thus, between official versions and releases of a product, you may be able to take advantage of free enhancements for only the effort it takes to download them.

Virtually all software products tend to be *upward compatible*. This means that applications developed on earlier versions or releases of the software will also work on later versions or releases. *Downward compatibility* is also commonplace. For example, WordPerfect 9 enables users to save files, say, in either WordPerfect 9 or any of several earlier formats. So, if you are using WordPerfect 9 on your desktop computer but the magazine you are sending an article to requires it in WordPerfect 6.1, no problem.

Cross compatibility is also widely found today. This feature enables you to, say, turn a WordPerfect 9 document into a Microsoft Word 2000 document. When translating documents from one vendor's software package into another, you must be aware that certain details can get lost in the translation. For instance, sometimes boldfacing and italicizing may not be picked up.

Generally, the new software will be offered to current users at a reduced price to make the upgrade more attractive. The potential user has to weigh the benefits of using the new package against its costs. The costs include the sticker price of the software, additional training, setting up new standards for use, and, possibly, equipment upgrades due to the increased sophistication of the software. Each version of a software product is virtually guaranteed to be more sophisticated and complex and to require more RAM and a faster processor than its predecessors.

FUNCTIONAL VERSUS TECHNOLOGICAL OBSOLESCENCE

As suggested in earlier paragraphs, PC products can serve user needs for several years before they must be replaced. A product becomes **functionally obsolete** when it no longer meets the needs of an individual or business. Improvements to hardware and software products are continuous, however, and often a product is replaced in stores with a newer version or release well before it is functionally obsolete. A product in this latter class is said to be **technologically obsolete.**

In upgrading, a common problem is that users believe the product they are using is functionally obsolete when it is merely technologically obsolete. Because of the rapid pace of technology, virtually anyone buying a computer system today will have at least one technologically obsolete component within a matter of months. What's more, it's often smart not to jump into a new version of a product immediately but instead to wait for the initial bugs in it to be fixed.

The term **legacy system** is often used for technologically obsolete products. Most companies have a variety of legacy systems on their hands today, and many of these systems will be capable of years of further use before they have to be replaced.

For links to further information about upgrading a PC, go to www.harcourtcollege. com/infosys/parker2000/ student/explore/ and click on Chapter LIV 1.

LEARNING MORE ABOUT PCS

A wide range of resources fulfill the needs of those who want to learn more about PCs and their uses. Classes, computer clubs, computer shows, magazines, newspapers, newsletters, books, and the World Wide Web are all sources of information.

■ **Functionally obsolete.** A term that refers to a product that no longer meets the needs of an individual or business.
■ **Technologically obsolete.** A term that refers to a product that still meets the needs of an individual or business, although a newer model, version, or release has superseded it in the marketplace. Also commonly called a **legacy system.**

FIGURE LIV 1-13

Computer shows. The weeklong Computer Dealer Expo (COMDEX) in Las Vegas attracts hundreds of thousands of enthusiasts from around the world.

For links to further information about PC magazines and other sites for PC information, go to www. harcourtcollege.com/infosys/ parker2000/student/explore/ and click on Chapter LIV 1.

Classes A good way to learn any subject is to take an appropriate class. Many four-year colleges, universities, and community colleges offer PC-oriented courses for undergraduate, graduate, and continuing-education students. Probably the fastest way to find out about such courses is to phone a local college and speak to the registrar or to someone in a computer-related academic department. Your local computer stores and Internet-enabled coffeehouses (cybercafés) may also organize classes. Some stores provide classroom support as part of system purchases.

Clubs Computer clubs are another effective way to get an informal education in computers. They are also a good place to get a relatively unbiased and knowledgeable viewpoint about a particular product or vendor. Generally clubs are organized by region, product line, or common interests. For instance, Apple computer enthusiasts join clubs such as Apple-Holics (Alaska), Apple Pie (Illinois), or Apple Core (California). Many clubs also function as buying groups, obtaining software or hardware for members at reduced rates. Computer clubs range in size from two or three members to several thousand.

Shows A computer show gives you a firsthand look at leading-edge hardware and software products. Such shows typically feature numerous vendor exhibits as well as seminars on various aspects of computing. Every November, Las Vegas hosts one of the largest trade fairs in the world, the Computer Dealer Expo (COMDEX) show (see Figure LIV 1-13). This weeklong event commonly attracts hundreds of vendors and around 200,000 visitors, many of them from foreign countries. COMDEX is a spectacular event and undoubtedly will remain popular for several years. However, today's trend favors smaller, more specialized exhibitions.

Periodicals Periodicals are another good source of information about PCs. Scores of them fill newsstands, collectively catering to virtually every conceivable interest area. Computer magazines and newspapers can vary tremendously in reading level. You can generally browse through a variety of computer-related publications at your local bookstore or computer store. Evaluate them carefully to determine their appropriateness to your needs. Many PC periodicals also maintain online versions on the World Wide Web. Online periodicals enable users to electronically search for information on specified topics and often give access to back issues.

Books One of the best ways to learn about any aspect of personal computing is to read a book on the subject. A host of softcover and hardcover books is available, covering topics ranging from the simple to the highly sophisticated. Included are how-to books on subjects such as using the more widely known productivity software packages, programming in PC-based languages, and the technical fundamentals of PCs. You can find such books in your local library, computer stores, and bookstores. Many books are also published on the World Wide Web. Always check the copyright date of a book before you use it; computer technology moves along rapidly, and books in the field can go out of date just as fast.

Electronic Media One easy way to learn a subject in our electronic age is to pick up a training disk or view a videotape or television show devoted to the subject. Today many PC-oriented software packages are sold with CDs that

provide screen-oriented tutorials, showing you how to use the program. Other types of professionally prepared *courseware* from a third-party vendor may also be available. Videotapes are plentiful for standard videocassette players, so you can see how something works simply by watching your television. In addition, many television shows—especially on cable and satellite—are oriented toward computer education and knowledge. As if all of these sources weren't enough, the World Wide Web is a veritable treasure trove for all sorts of free information about computers (see Figure LIV 1-14).

FIGURE LIV 1-14

Learning about computers on the Web. Scores of useful Web sites provide news items and articles about computers. Many are either the sites of computer journals (such as www.computerworld.com and www.pcweek.com) or news sites (such as www.cnn.com and www.msnbc.com).

SUMMARY AND KEY TERMS

Go to the Online Glossary at www.harcourtcollege.com/infosys/parker2000/student/ to review key terms.

Chapter LIV 1 covers such related activities as users acquiring their own computer resources, taking care of their own systems, upgrading systems on their own, and educating themselves about PCs.

The PC Marketplace The PC marketplace is composed of a wide variety of firms that make hardware and software products. Most users get their hardware and software PC products from retail stores of various sorts, the Internet, mail-order houses, hardware manufacturers and **software publishers,** and **value-added resellers (VARs).**

Selecting a PC System Steps for selecting a computer system include analyzing needs, listing system alternatives, evaluating alternatives, and choosing a system. Although applications software is normally selected before a computer and systems-software platform, software and hardware choices for PCs are often interrelated, so you must consider them jointly.

Hardware and Software Installation When you buy a computer system today, most of the hardware and software you need will probably already be in place. To make it easier than ever for PC owners to install any new hardware on their own, both hardware and software vendors have moved to a *plug-and-play* approach.

Operating a PC **Backup** refers to procedures for making duplicate copies of valuable files. Two types of backup methods are **full backup** and **partial backup.**

PCs contain sensitive electronic devices, so they need careful treatment and protection from damage. A **surge suppressor** will prevent most random electrical spikes from entering your system and causing damage. A **uninterruptible power supply (UPS)** unit lets you operate your computer when the main power to your home or office fails. Software called **screen savers** can protect your monitor. **Security** measures protect a computer system's hardware, software, and data from unintentional and malicious damage and tampering.

Although no two problems with a computer system are ever totally alike, some useful guidelines can be followed when troubleshooting problems or when seeking outside technical assistance. For instance, just trying a procedure out a second time or checking the **documentation** that comes with a product often solves the problem. Three sources of software assistance are support from the software publisher, third-party support, and user support. When considering an equipment repair, you should check first to see what protection the manufacturer offers under **warranty.**

Upgrading You can **upgrade** your computer system by buying new hardware or software components that add capabilities and extend its useful life. When planning a hardware upgrade, you must consider such things as your current system's storage capacity, the number of expansion slots, and the power of the system unit. Software upgrades are often accomplished by acquiring a new **release** or **version** of the program that you are currently using. You need to ask yourself whether upgrading is better than starting fresh and buying a new computer system. You also must consider whether you are planning to replace a product that's only **technologically obsolete** instead of **functionally obsolete.** Technologically obsolete systems are sometimes called **legacy systems.**

Learning More about PCs A wealth of resources is available to those who want to learn more about PCs and their uses. Classes, computer clubs, computer shows, magazines, newspapers, newsletters, books, and electronic media are all sources of information about PCs.

EXERCISES

1. Fill in the blanks:
   a. A(n) _____ is a program designed to protect your monitor against damaging the phosphorescent coating on its screen.
   b. _____ refers to making, for security purposes, a duplicate copy of a file.
   c. A(n) _____ is a hardware device designed to stop power spikes from damaging a computer system.
   d. A(n) _____ usually states that a product manufacturer will correct defects in software or hardware for a given period of time under certain conditions.
   e. A product that no longer meets the needs of a user is said to be _____ obsolete.

2. Match each company name with the description that fits best:
   a. Compaq
   b. Corel
   c. Intel
   d. Microsoft
   e. Cyrix
   f. Motorola
   g. Seagate
   h. Apple
   _____ Makes CPU chips for the Apple Macintosh line of computers
   _____ A large, U.S.-based maker of PC-compatible computers
   _____ A producer primarily of storage products

_____ The maker of Windows as well as a wide variety of other software products

_____ The maker of most CPU chips for PC-compatible computers

_____ The company that publishes WordPerfect

_____ A producer of Intel-compatible CPU chips

_____ The biggest producer of microcomputers that are not PC-compatible

3. Name as many types of sources as you can for buying PC hardware and software. Which of these sources would you consult in the following situations?

   a. You want to look over a lot of products but don't have time to spend browsing around a store.

   b. You just opened a taco restaurant and need a computer system that specializes in keeping track of fast-food operations.

   c. You want a new microcomputer system but don't want to spend the premium prices the more famous companies charge.

   d. You're nervous about buying a PC system and need a vendor that will hold your hand to help you through any problems.

   e. You want to get a brand-name printer at a low price, and you must have it today. You're willing to accept equipment that just became technologically obsolete when a new model came out last month.

   f. You need a printer and want to see as many printer specifications as you can within the next few hours.

   g. All you need is a 166 MHz Pentium computer that will help you write your novel, and you'll be darned if you'll pay for anything more.

   h. You need a software product immediately, and your local computer store does not stock the product.

4. Define each of the following terms:

   a. Legacy system
   b. UPS
   c. Software publisher
   d. Value-added reseller
   e. Third-tier manufacturer
   f. Incremental backup
   g. Partial backup

5. Name several selection criteria that are important to consider when evaluating alternative computer system purchases.

6. Provide at least eight reasons that illustrate the importance of backing up files.

7. What is the difference between technological obsolescence and functional obsolescence?

8. Name at least five sources from which users can learn more about computers. Also, identify the types of learning resources that are available over the Internet.

9. Each of the following definitions is not strictly true in some regard. In each case, identify how the definition is false and correct the error.

   a. Software publisher: A company that sells the software that other companies create

   b. Legacy system: Technologically obsolescent hardware or software that has been around for awhile in a company, even though its manufacturer continues to update it regularly

   c. Release: A particular version of a software package

   d. Value-added reseller: A company that sells computer systems made by others.

   e. Surge suppressor: A device that keeps a computer system running in the event of a power shortage

10. Why is it sometime better to lease a PC than to buy it outright?

PROJECTS

1. **Buying a Desktop PC** The figure at the top of the next page shows an ad for a desktop PC. To demonstrate your knowledge of computing terms in the figure, most of which have been covered in various chapters of this textbook, respond to the following eleven questions:

   a. What types of storage devices come with the computer system? What is the capacity of each type of storage device?

   b. What type of CPU chip comes with the system? How fast is the CPU chip?

   c. Is the system PC-compatible?

   d. Is this a "multimedia" computer system?

   e. What type of local bus unit does the system contain?

   f. Can the monitor display photographic-quality images? What do _noninterlaced_ and _.25 dp_ mean?

   g. What software comes with this system?

   h. Does a word processing program come with this system? If it does, what's its name?

   i. Does a printer come with this system? If it does, who is its manufacturer?

   j. What options do you have available if the hard disk fails after one year of use?

Z-BYTE™ PLUS

- Intel 500 MHz Pentium III processor
- 128 MB SDRAM expandable to 384 MB
- 512 KB external cache, flash BIOS
- 32-bit PCI bus
- 17.2 GB Ultra ATA hard drive
- 4.8× DVD-ROM drive, 3.5" floppy drive
- 32-bit wavetable sound card with stereo speakers
- 16 MB 3D graphics card
- V.90 PCI modem
- 7-bay minitower
- Two USB ports, one serial port, one parallel port
- Microsoft IntelliMouse, 104-key keyboard
- Microsoft Windows 98
- Microsoft Office 2000 Professional
- 19" (18.0" viewable area, .25dp) noninterlaced monitor
- 5-year/3-year warranty

Z-BYTE POWER™   **Warranty & Support**

- 5-year limited warranty on microprocessor and main memory
- 3-year limited parts-only system warranty
- 1-, 2-, or 3-year optional on-site service agreement
- 30 days of free Z-Byte-supplied software support
- 30-day money-back policy
- 24-hour technical support

All major credit-cards welcome
Call toll free at 1-800-000-000

$1,799

k. What options do you have available if the operating system isn't responding properly after six weeks of use?

2. **Buying a Notebook Computer** The figure at the top of the next page shows an ad for a notebook PC. To demonstrate your knowledge of computing terms, most of which have been covered in various chapters of this textbook, respond to the following questions:

a. What types of storage devices come with the computer? What is the capacity of each type of storage device?

b. Do each of the storage devices offer more or less capacity than the corresponding ones in the computer system detailed in Project 1?

c. Why isn't the system offered with a mouse?

d. Is this a "multimedia" computer system?

e. What does the ad mean by a *Type II PCMCIA slot?*

f. What is the purpose of the infrared port?

g. Would you recommend buying this computer system to gain access to the Internet? Why or why not?

h. What software comes with this system?

i. What's the significance of this computer's Lithium Ion battery feature? How does this technology compare with other types of batteries?

j. Can you hook up a printer directly to this computer system? Why or why not?

k. What options do you have available if the hard disk fails after one year of use?

l. Can you run Windows on this computer? Why or why not?

3. **Buying a Printer** You need a printer for your personal computer system and want to spend no more than $300.

a. Find an ink-jet printer and a laser printer that you can buy for this price. In what important ways do these printers differ?

b. Cut out or copy an ad for a printer from a computer magazine. What does the ad tell you about the features of the printer? Where can you go to get additional information?

c. A call to a local computer store reveals that you can get a product demonstration. What sorts of questions should this demonstration answer?

4. **Buying Hardware over the Internet** Many companies that sell computer hardware maintain sites on the World Wide Web. Such sites often showcase product offerings, offer users the chance to configure hardware and buy it, provide technical support, and so on. Visit two such Web sites—one representing a computer maker and the other an equipment reseller—and report to the class about the sites, making sure that you cover the following points:

a. What are the names of the companies you visited?

b. What types of hardware do they sell?

c. What objectives are served by each of the Web sites—for instance, providing product information, enabling people to buy equipment, offering technical support, and so on?

d. Do the sites offer any types of search or query tools to help you shop online—tools that might lead to better purchase decisions than those you might make after looking at hard-copy advertisements?

Z-BYTE™ 366X

366X Standard Features

- Intel 366 MHz Pentium II processor
- 14.1" Active Matrix TFT display
- 96 MB SDRAM expandable to 384 MB
- 256 KB external cache
- 64-bit graphics accelerator with 4 MB video RAM
- 10 GB Ultra ATA removable hard drive
- Removable combination 2× DVD-ROM and 120 MB SuperDisk 3.5" floppy drive
- 16-bit wavetable sound and stereo speakers
- Internal V.90 modem
- Two 12-cell 60WHr Lithium Ion batteries & AC pack
- One Type II & one Type III PCMCIA slot
- USB, parallel, serial, PS/2, infrared, and game ports
- Touch pad
- 7.1 pounds
- Extendable 1-year limited warranty

Call us toll-free to order your 366X or for information

1-800-000-9999
Monday-Friday, 8am-10pm EST
Saturday, 9am-5pm EST

$2,499

e. Do the sites include any "fun" features that might attract shoppers to make return visits?

f. How do people place orders and pay for the equipment?

Some of the Web sites in the accompanying figure may interest you.

While the sites of computer makers like IBM and Compaq feature their own equipment, Web sites of resellers like BUYCOMP.COM enable you to select from a large variety of products and scores of manufacturers.

5. Buying Software over the Internet Many companies that sell software maintain sites on the World Wide Web. Such sites often showcase product offerings, offer users the chance to try out or buy software, provide technical support, and so on. Visit two such Web sites—one representing a software publisher and the other a software re-

seller—and report to the class about them, making sure that you cover the following points:

a. What are the names of the companies you visited?

b. What types of software are sold at the sites?

c. What objectives are served by each of the Web sites—for instance, providing information about software products, enabling users to buy software, letting users download software on a trial basis, offering technical support, and so on?

d. Do the sites offer any types of search or query tools to help you shop online—tools that might lead to better purchase decisions than those you might make after looking at hard-copy advertisements?

e. How do people place orders and pay for the software?

Some of the Web sites in the accompanying figure may interest you.

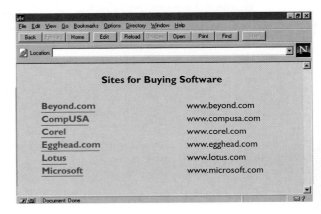

While the sites of software publishers like Microsoft and Corel feature their own programs, sites of

resellers like Egghead.com enable you to select from a large variety of products and scores of publishers.

6. Technology News on the Internet Several Web sites report on news events regarding technology. Three such sources are MSNBC at www.msnbc.com, CNET News.com at news.cnet.com, and the technology news section of CNN at www.cnn.com. Visit any two of these or similar Web sites and report to your class about what you find. What future prospects do you anticipate for interactive news received on your computer system, as opposed to getting news through television or print outlets like newspapers and magazines?

7. Online Magazines You can subscribe to or read for free online versions of many popular computer magazines (see image). For this project, research at least two such magazines published in Web versions and answer the following questions:
a. How much does an online subscription cost, relative to a hard-copy subscription of the same magazine?
b. What types of features do the online versions of these magazines have that you can't get in the hard-copy versions?
c. What do the hard-copy versions of these magazines have that you can't get in the online versions?

8. PC History Many important people have shaped the history of PCs. Several of them are listed here. For this project, choose any three and, for each one, write a sentence or two about his contribution to the history of personal computers.
a. Bill Gates
b. Steve Jobs
c. Scott McNealy
d. Marc Andreesen
e. Gary Kildall
f. Phillipe Kahn
g. Dan Bricklin
h. Brian Bastian
i. Ted Hoff

9. Internet Wars The chapter Tomorrow box hints that companies with physical stores are worried about Internet merchants moving onto their turf. The fretting typically goes far deeper than the issue of taxes. For instance, wine wholesalers are distressed that Web-based wine retailers are hurting their business. Consequently, they have asked the liquor lobby to pressure states into outlawing wine sales on the Internet. In another recent case, more than two dozen car dealerships in the Pacific Northwest banded together to threaten a boycott of a car manufacturer if it continued to sell automobiles to an Internet-based dealership operating in their territory. The Internet merchants counter by claiming that their only "sin" is giving customers exactly what they want: lots of choices and low prices.

How do you feel about the issues described here and in the Tomorrow box? Should the Internet merchants be more closely regulated to give other sellers more of a chance or should market forces largely determine who wins and loses.

ONLINE REVIEW

Go to the Online Review at www.harcourtcollege.com/infosys/parker2000/ student/ to test your understanding of this chapter's concepts.

LIV 2

SOCIAL ISSUES INVOLVING COMPUTERS

OUTLINE

LEARNING OBJECTIVES

After completing this chapter, you will be able to:

1. Describe the health-related concerns that people have regarding computers.

2. Explain what computer crime is, give several examples of it, and describe how computer crime can be prevented.

3. Discuss how computer technology can encroach on people's privacy and describe some of the legislation enacted to prevent such abuses.

4. Explain what is meant by ethics and provide several examples of ethical misbehavior in computer-related matters.

OVERVIEW

Since the era of commercial computing began about 50 years ago, computers have rapidly woven their way into the fabric of modern society. In the process, they've created both opportunities and problems. Consequently, they've been both cursed and applauded—and for good reason.

So far in this text, we've focused on the opportunities more than the problems. We've examined the impact computers have had in organizations and on people. Throughout the text, you've seen how these devices have been used to speed up routine transaction processing tasks, to provide managers with better information for decision making, to design and manufacture better products, and to improve the overall quality of people's lives.

Although the computer revolution has brought undeniable benefits to society, it has also produced some troubling side effects. Like any fast-paced revolution, it has been disruptive in many ways. Some jobs have been created, others lost, and still others threatened. In addition, an increasing variety of health-related concerns have surfaced that affect people who work with computers and related technologies. Computers have also immensely increased access to sensitive information, creating new possibilities for crime and threatening personal privacy. Clearly some controls to limit the dangers that these awesome devices pose will always be needed.

In this chapter, we highlight four key problem areas: computers and health in the workplace, computer crime, computers and privacy, and ethical uses of technology. The computer history window located at the chapter's end provides perspective as to how fast paced the growth of computers has been.

COMPUTERS, WORK, AND HEALTH

Computers have been said to pose a threat to our mental and physical well-being. Although the body of scientific evidence supporting this claim is far from conclusive, and is likely to be that way for many more years, we should all be aware of the major concerns raised about the possible effects of computers on our health.

STRESS-RELATED CONCERNS

Emotional problems such as financial worries, feelings of incompetence, and disorientation often produce emotional *stress*. This stress, in turn, may have been triggered by a computer-related event.

Layoff or Reassignment One of the first criticisms leveled at computers upon their entry into the workplace was that their very presence resulted in job-related stress. When computers were introduced, many people were no longer needed and were subsequently laid off and forced to find new jobs. Workers at the lowest rungs worried most about job security. Many feared the full potential of computers in the office or in the factory and spent much of their time never knowing if machines might replace them. Such fears are still widespread today.

Even people who were not laid off found that their jobs had changed significantly and that they had no choice but to retrain. Airline agents, for example, had to learn how to manipulate a database-retrieval language and to work with computers. Secretaries were pressured into learning word processing and other office-related software to keep in step. Even the pace of work has become faster and far less personal than it was earlier. Many workers never made the transition successfully.

A growing fact of life is that because of computers, fewer people are needed to do many types of work today. Computers also change the way work is done, often in ways that are difficult to predict. For instance, modern computer networks are posing a new threat to workers in that companies no longer have to staff as many physical locations as in the past. Networks also mean that work can be transferred to foreign countries more easily. Also, the Web is threatening to put many small travel agencies, realtors, and booksellers out of business.

Fear of Falling Behind   The microcomputing boom that has taken place since the early 1980s has put computing power of awesome dimensions at almost everyone's fingertips. Many researchers perceive a widespread fear that failure to learn how to use these machines will make one fall behind. One example is the numerous noncomputer-oriented executives, managers, and educators who see themselves being upstaged by their computer-savvy colleagues. There are so many big advances occurring on so many new technology fronts these days that the pace of change is fast enough to make even computer experts feel they are falling behind.

Burnout   Burnout is caused not by fear of computers *(cyberphobia)* but by overuse of them *(cyberphelia)*. The infusion of such technologies as PCs, video CDs, e-mail, pagers and wireless phones, and the Web into the home and office has raised new concerns about emotional health. What will happen to children who withdraw into their computer systems, to computer-bound managers who are being inadvertently swept into the tide of the computer revolution and its relentless pace, or to families whose intimacy is threatened by overuse of computers in their homes? Little research has been done on computer burnout. What makes this area so controversial is the flip-side argument that most victims of computer burnout would burn out on something else if computers didn't exist.

ERGONOMICS-RELATED CONCERNS

Ergonomics is the field that addresses making products and work areas comfortable and safe to use. With respect to technology, ergonomics covers the effects on workers of things such as display devices, keyboards, and workspaces.

Dangers Posed by Display Devices   For more than a decade, large numbers of data-entry operators have reported a variety of physical and mental problems stemming from their interaction with display devices. The complaints have centered on visual, muscular, and emotional disorders resulting from long hours of continuous display device use. These disorders include blurred eyesight, eyestrain, acute fatigue, headaches, and backaches. In response to these problems, several states and cities have passed laws that curb display device abuse. Also, hardware vendors have redesigned their products with features such as screens that tilt and swivel to make them more comfortable to use.

Keep in mind that it is not displays alone that cause physical problems. Humans are often part of the equation too. Operator-induced factors that play a large part include poor posture, not taking frequent breaks, poor exercise habits, bad placement of the display on the desktop, and the like.

Dangers Posed by Keyboards   Years ago, computer keyboards frequently were built into display units, making it difficult for operators to move them about as freely as they could if the keyboards had been detached. Most claims

■ **Ergonomics.** The field that studies the effects of things such as computer hardware, software, and work spaces on people's comfort and health.

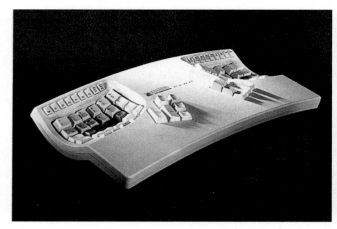

FIGURE LIV 2-1

Stress-reducing keyboards.

that a computer keyboard could result in injury seemed to be put to rest after keyboard manufacturers started making detachable keyboards—that is, until the past few years or so.

Today, some people are experiencing a condition known as *carpal tunnel syndrome,* a painful and crippling complex of symptoms affecting the hand and wrist that has been traced to the repetitive finger movements routinely made when using a keyboard. Carpal tunnel syndrome is an example of a *repetitive stress injury,* in which hand, wrist, shoulder, and neck pains can result from performing the same types of physical movements over and over again. Physicians recommend that to minimize the chance of such injuries you should take breaks every hour or so and relax or stretch your body. Recently, a number of innovatively designed keyboards have come to the fore that claim to reduce stress in the hands and wrists (see Figure LIV 2-1).

Workspace Design   Display devices and keyboards are not the only things that can torture people at workstations. The furniture may be nonadjustable, forcing the user into awkward postures that are guaranteed to produce body kinks. Or the lighting may be so bright that it causes a headache-producing glare on the display screen. Even disconcerting noise levels, present due to poorly designed office equipment or acoustics, may be the culprits. Ergonomics researchers are constantly studying such problems, and the results of their efforts are becoming apparent in the consumer products now being offered to the ergonomics-conscious buyer. Figure LIV 2-2 illustrates some principles of good workspace design.

FIGURE LIV 2-2

Workspace design. Features such as detachable keyboards, tilt capabilities on both keyboards and display devices, and adjustable furniture have contributed to added comfort for display device users.

ENVIRONMENT-RELATED CONCERNS

The surge in personal computer use during the past several years has caused a variety of environmental concerns. Take power use. The U.S. Environmental Protection Agency (EPA) estimates that home and office PC systems now annually consume billions of dollars worth of electricity. This indirectly has resulted in the discharge of tons of pollutants into the atmosphere. The PC industry has responded by adding a variety of energy-saving devices into computer hardware. Among these devices are power-management software that puts the CPU, hard-disk drive, display, and printer into a sleep mode when they are not being used, low-power-consumptive chips and boards, and flat-panel displays.

The environmental threat goes much deeper than just the higher electrical use. For instance, the so-called paperless office that many visionaries predicted for the computer age has become largely a myth. Because computer output is so easy to produce, more paper than ever is now consumed. It is estimated that U.S. businesses generate close to a trillion pages a year—an amount that would stack more than 50,000 miles high!

COMPUTER CRIME

For a tutorial on computer crime, go to www.harcourtcollege.com/infosys/parker2000/student/tutor/ and click on **Chapter LIV 2.**

Computer crime is defined as the use of computers to commit criminal acts. The law is spotty on computer crime. The U.S. government has made it a felony to fraudulently access confidential programs or data in federal-level computers. Most states also have laws that address some aspects of computer crime. But such laws notwithstanding, computer crime is hard to pin down.

One reason is that it is often difficult to decide when a questionable act is really a crime. No one doubts that a bank employee who uses a computer system to embezzle funds from customers' accounts is committing a crime. But what about an employee who steals time on a company computer to balance a personal checkbook for a home or business or someone who uses a company computer to e-mail jokes to friends? Aren't those acts also unauthorized? Where does one draw the line?

Another problem in pinning down computer crime is that judges and juries—not to mention law-enforcement personnel—are often bewildered by the technical issues involved in such cases. Thus, many companies lack confidence that computer crimes will be investigated and prosecuted successfully, and they don't report them. Also, companies that discover computer criminals among their employees frequently are reluctant to press charges because they fear even more adverse publicity. Why get clients worried?

TYPES OF COMPUTER CRIME

Computer crime has many forms. Some cases involve the use of a computer for theft of financial assets, such as money or equipment. Others concern the copying of information-processing resources, such as programs or data, to the owner's detriment. Still other cases involve manipulation of data such as grades for personal advantage. By far, the majority of computer crimes are committed by insiders.

The cost of computer crime to individuals and organizations is estimated at billions of dollars annually. No one knows for sure what the exact figure is, because so many incidents are either undetected or unreported.

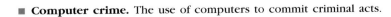

■ **Computer crime.** The use of computers to commit criminal acts.

As in many fields, a specialized jargon has evolved in the area of computer-related crime. Following is a sampling of some of the specific forms computer crime can take.

Data Diddling   *Data diddling* is one of the most common ways to perform a computer crime. It involves altering key operations data on a computer system in some unsanctioned way. Data diddlers often are found changing grades in university files, falsifying input records on bank transactions, and the like.

The Trojan Horse   A **Trojan horse** is a procedure for adding concealed instructions to a computer program so that it will still work, but will also perform prohibited duties. For example, a bank worker can subtly alter a program that contains thousands of lines of code by adding a small patch that instructs the program not to withdraw money from his or her account.

Trojan horses are frequently found today on the Internet to host *computer viruses,* which we'll talk about shortly. They are also being increasingly used for spoofing. A *spoof* is a program buried in a legitimate application that tricks an unsuspecting user into revealing confidential information, such as an access code or credit-card number.

Salami Shaving   *Salami shaving* involves manipulating programs or data so that many small dollar amounts—say, a few cents' worth of interest payments in a bank account—are shaved from a large number of transactions or accounts and accumulated elsewhere. The victims of a salami-shaving scheme generally are unaware that their funds have been tapped, because the amount taken from each individual is trivial. The recipient of the salami shaving, however, benefits from the aggregation of these small amounts, often substantially. Supermarkets have been occasionally accused of salami shaving at the check-out counter by not conscientiously updating computer-stored prices to reflect lower shelf prices (see Feature LIV 2-1).

Trapdoors   *Trapdoors* are diagnostic tools, used in the development of programs, that enable programmers to gain access to various parts of a computer system. Before the programs are marketed, these tools are supposed to be removed. Occasionally, however, some blocks of diagnostic code are over-looked—perhaps even intentionally. Thus, a person using the associated program may be provided unauthorized views of other parts of a computer system. Recently, a trapdoor was discovered in a well-known browser that enabled individuals to remotely view the hard-disk contents of the browser users. In 1998, several trapdoors traced to foreign sources were discovered in computer systems in air force and navy bases in the United States, legitimizing the fear that computer-system break-ins may become a new battlefield between nations in the twenty-first century.

Logic and Time Bombs   *Logic bombs* are programs or short code segments designed to commit a malicious act as soon as the unsuspecting program user performs some specific type of operation. In one documented case, a programmer inserted into a system a logic bomb that would destroy the company's entire personnel file if his name was removed from it. A *time bomb* works just like a logic bomb, except that a date or time triggers the criminal activity.

Computer Viruses   A **computer virus** is a piece of code—often transmitted to a computer system from a diskette or from data or a program downloaded off a network—that is designed to cause damage to the system. Some are like time or logic bombs; they may lay dormant for months and then destroy settings on a hard disk on a specific date or when a certain operator

---

■ **Trojan horse.** Adding concealed instructions to a computer program so that it will still work but will also perform prohibited duties. ■ **Computer virus.** A small block of unauthorized code, concealed and transmitted from computer to computer, that performs destructive acts when executed.

A Computer Crime in Colorado

A Case of Too Many Cooks Spoiling the Broth

It's often been said that if you want to keep a secret, minimize the number of people to whom it's told. That principle was apparently violated by three men who allegedly fleeced a Colorado supermarket chain out of millions of dollars. As a result, the men are now in custody and awaiting trial.

It all started in 1992, when the chain began a serious upgrade of their computer systems. The company at first suspected software bugs were behind the huge number of accounting anomalies it was seeing in its stores in the Colorado Springs area. So the corporate office dispatched a PC manager to the scene. In the end, this manager became a key part of the problem rather than the solution.

After a couple of years investigation, charges were levied at the PC manager and two head clerks. It has been claimed that the three used a variety of methods to defraud the company. One was creating dummy inventory categories for several items. If, say, someone bought milk, the sale might be credited to a phony account. At the end of the day, the account disappeared and the cash accumulated to it was taken from the register and pocketed. A second trick was to void a sale. In this case too, the money collected at the register could be stolen. A third method was tampering with product bar codes so that customers were overcharged.

Certain security procedures within the supermarket chain made it difficult to nail the perpetrators. Log ons to the system weren't being closely monitored. Also, some backup files were overwritten in as few as 60 days—and were eventually lost as evidence.

In the end, however, mistakes made by the suspects mounted. The two clerks had filed for bankruptcy before the crimes started, making them suspicious right off the bat. The men also flashed a lot of cash, took unusually expensive trips, and drove flashy cars—even though none of the three had made more than $33,000 a year. One even had a vanity license plate—BYBYCOP—that appeared to taunt the people who would eventually nail him to the wall. Dumb? You be the judge.

All of the above notwithstanding, the case is expected to be a difficult one to prosecute. If you think that you have a hard time understanding how computers work, consider what judges and juries—many of whom were raised in an era when computers were nonexistent or few and far between—have to go through.

---

action is taken. Other viruses clog memory with garbage as soon as the computer is turned on. Computer viruses often replicate themselves onto new storage media upon contact, infecting programs or data on those media which are then transferred to any other computer those media are inserted into (see Figure LIV 2-3). An upcoming section in the chapter addresses protecting a computer system from viruses.

Eavesdropping Examples abound involving the use of technology to *eavesdrop* on information intended for others. One of the earliest types of eavesdropping, and still one of the most common, was wiretapping. Modern computer systems have made it possible to eavesdrop in new ways—for instance, by simply having access to an identification number, an unauthorized user can peek in on files and even steal from them. Tools such as *sniffer programs* enable criminals to intercept data and access codes on a network, without anyone being any the wiser. Two other examples of eavesdropping are using descrambling systems to intercept satellite transmissions and using scanners to overhear calls made over wireless phones.

Cellular Phone Fraud The goal of *cellular phone fraud,* which takes eavesdropping a step further, is to make calls without paying for them—sticking either the cellular-phone owner or phone company for the charges. The scam works as follows: Each cellular phone uses a unique internal electronic serial number for verification and billing purposes. This number is broadcast when the phone is in use or even just turned on. Criminals using scanners stake out spots along highway overpasses or in airport parking lots, pluck numbers out of the air, and then use black-market software to program other cellular phones with the stolen numbers. Cellular phone fraud collectively costs the public hundreds of millions of dollars a year.

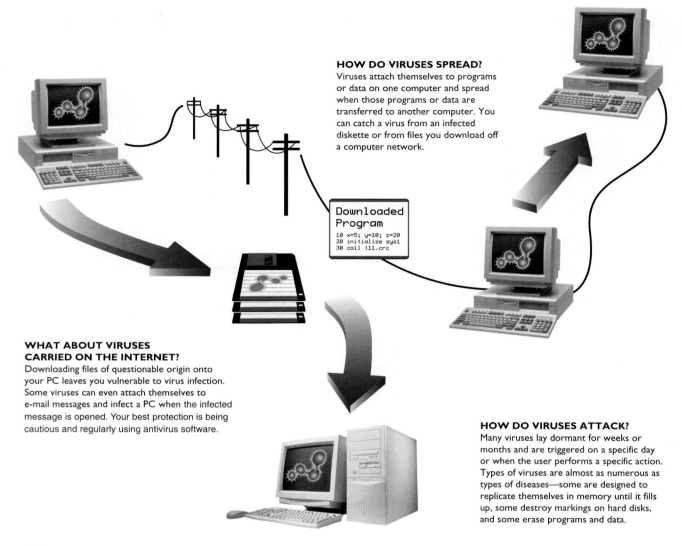

HOW DO VIRUSES SPREAD?
Viruses attach themselves to programs or data on one computer and spread when those programs or data are transferred to another computer. You can catch a virus from an infected diskette or from files you download off a computer network.

```
Downloaded
Program
10 x=5; y=10; z=20
20 initialize sys1
30 call t11.crc
```

WHAT ABOUT VIRUSES CARRIED ON THE INTERNET?
Downloading files of questionable origin onto your PC leaves you vulnerable to virus infection. Some viruses can even attach themselves to e-mail messages and infect a PC when the infected message is opened. Your best protection is being cautious and regularly using antivirus software.

HOW DO VIRUSES ATTACK?
Many viruses lay dormant for weeks or months and are triggered on a specific day or when the user performs a specific action. Types of viruses are almost as numerous as types of diseases—some are designed to replicate themselves in memory until it fills up, some destroy markings on hard disks, and some erase programs and data.

FIGURE LIV 2-3

Computer viruses. A computer virus is harmful computer code that can alter programs or destroy data. Viruses can copy themselves onto legitimate programs and data, thereby spreading damage.

Software Piracy Software piracy, the unauthorized copying or use of a computer program, is often a crime. It is definitely a crime to copy a program and then attempt to sell it for profit. If one just uses an illegitimate copy that was made by someone else, such usage can be a crime as well, although it is rarely prosecuted. Anyone knowingly involved with unauthorized copies of a program can be found guilty of breaking copyright laws. A number of companies have been successfully prosecuted for buying one or a few copies of a software package and distributing many more copies to employees.

Hacking Hacking is a computer term referring to the activities of people who get their kicks out of using computers or terminals to crack the security of remote computer systems. It's a serious problem. For instance, U.S. Department of Defense computers are attacked by hackers hundreds of thousands of times a year, with probably many more times that number of attacks going undetected. Some people engage in hacking purely for the challenge of cracking codes. Others do it to steal computer time, to peek at confidential information, or to cause damage. Intentions aside, hacking often is considered by

---

■ **Software piracy.** The unauthorized copying or use of computer programs. ■ **Hacking.** Using a microcomputer system or terminal to penetrate the security of a remote computer system.

the courts to be a breaking-and-entering crime similar to forced entry into someone's car or home.

In the early days of PCs, the typical profile of a hacker was a propeller-headed teenager who was in it purely for the excitement that came from snooping and bragging about it. Today's hacker is just as likely to be a well-trained professional who aims to steal or destroy computer resources. A favorite target these days is credit-card numbers and other sensitive financial information that travel over the Internet.

Counterfeiting Desktop publishing and color-printing technology are so sophisticated today that they have opened the door to a relatively new type of computer crime—*counterfeiting*. Take desktop publishing. By using a scanner to read in a corporate logo and then a standard desktop publishing program, producing checks that look genuine is something even a novice can do. As far as color technology goes, the total number of phony U.S. currency being produced on color copiers and printers—now estimated in the billions of dollars—rose eightfold in just the first three years of the 1990s. Would-be counterfeiters, beware. Financial instruments are being redesigned with elements that cannot be copied. Also, many color copiers now print invisible codes on outputs, making counterfeit money traceable.

Coverups In recent years, technology has been deployed to cover up criminal activity—which itself is a crime. For instance, many criminals booby-trap PCs containing potential evidence so that data are destroyed if the computer is commandeered by the authorities. For instance, the clicking of a mouse could send a command to erase hard disk data at a rate of 50 megabytes per second. Another trick is rigging the door frame in a computer room with magnetic strips, so that a computer's disk storage is demagnetized (and the disk contents destroyed) as soon as someone tries to cart the computer outside.

Internet-Related Crimes The rise of the Internet has contributed to new varieties of criminal activity that most people scarcely could have imagined only a few years ago. For instance, several individuals have been arrested in recent years for systematically *stalking* children through computer newsgroups. Web sites and e-mail have made possible *cyberporn,* the distribution of pornographic material over computer networks. In another type of case, a university student was indicted for running an Internet bulletin board over which copyrighted software was allegedly distributed for free. Especially worrisome to many individuals is the risk involved to both finances and privacy when using the Internet to engage in electronic commerce.

MINIMIZING COMPUTER CRIME

It's impossible to achieve 100-percent protection from criminal activity; consequently, the emphasis is on minimizing losses. To achieve this end, organizations can combat computer crime in many ways.

Assess Risks The most important way an organization can minimize crime is by having a good plan for security, and the centerpiece of any such plan is an assessment of which operations are most vulnerable to attack. Thus, employers should make a list of disaster-level events that can occur to their businesses and make sure that key areas are protected from the most costly types of mishaps.

Have a Recovery Plan Since no security plan can guarantee 100 percent safety, one should assume the worst can, in fact, happen. Thus, organizations should specifically take steps to have backups ready if or when disruptive events such as fires, floods, or computer outages occur. Backup provisions should include having copies of all important programs and data stored at another site as well as making arrangements for resuming normal day-to-day

For links to further information about computer crime, go to www.harcourtcollege.com/infosys/parker2000/student/explore/ and click on Chapter LIV 2.

operations at a backup site. A plan that spells out what an organization will do to prepare for and recover from disruptive events is called a **disaster-recovery plan.**

Hire Trustworthy People   Employers should carefully investigate the background of anyone being considered for sensitive computer work. Some people falsify résumés to get jobs. Others may have criminal records. Despite the publicity given to groups such as hackers, studies have consistently shown that most computer crimes are committed by insiders.

Beware of Malcontents   The type of employee who is most likely to commit a computer crime is one who has recently been terminated or passed over for a promotion, or one who has some reason to get even with the organization. In cases in which an employee has been terminated and potential for computer crime exists, the former employer should update its records immediately to show that the person involved is no longer employed and terminates that employee's company computer access.

Separate Employee Functions   An employee with many related responsibilities can commit a crime more easily than one with a single responsibility. For example, the person who authorizes adding new vendors to a file should not be the same one who authorizes payments to those vendors. Generally the more people involved in the commission of a crime, the more likely it is that one of them will make a mistake.

Restrict System Use   People who use a computer system should have access only to the things they need to do their jobs. A computer operator, for example, should be told only how to execute a program and not what the program does. Also, users who need only to retrieve information should not also be given updating privileges.

Password Protect Programs and Data   On many systems, users can restrict access to programs and data with **passwords.** For example, a user might specify that anyone wanting access to file AR-148 must first enter the password e5775jummm. To modify the document, a second password may be required. Users are recommended to choose passwords carefully, to change passwords frequently, and to protect particularly sensitive files with several passwords (see Figure LIV 2-4).

Many organizations use measures such as *access cards* and *biometric security devices* in place of or in combination with passwords. **Access cards,** such

FIGURE LIV 2-4

Passwords.

RULES FOR PASSWORDS
■ Make the password as long as you possibly can. A four- or five-character password can be cracked by a computer program in less than a minute. A ten-character password, in contrast, has about 3,700 trillion possible character permutations and could take a computer decades to crack.
■ Choose an unusual sequence of characters for the password—for instance, mix in numbers and special characters with words from other languages or unusual names. The password should be one that you can remember yet one that doesn't conform to a pattern a computer can readily figure out.
■ Keep a written copy of the password in a place where no one but you can find it. Many people place passwords on post-it notes that are affixed to their monitors or taped to their desks—a practice that's almost as bad as having no password at all.
■ Change the password as frequently as you can. Sniffer programs that criminals frequently use can read passwords being entered into unsecured systems.

■ **Disaster-recovery plan.** A plan that maps out what an organization does to prepare for and react to disruptive events. ■ **Password.** A word or number used to permit selected individuals access to a system. ■ **Access card.** A plastic card that, when inserted into a machine and combined with a password, permits access to a system.

as those used in automatic teller machines at banks, activate a transaction when they are used with a password or number. **Biometric security devices** provide access by recognizing some unique physiological characteristic of a person—such as a fingerprint or handprint—or some unique learned characteristic, such as a voice or signature (see Figure LIV 2-5). Because of its reliability and the amount of business beginning to be conducted over the Internet, biometric security is predicated to be a very high-growth area in the near future. According to IrisScan, a firm that uses the human eye's iris to verify people's identity, the chance of two different people's irises matching using their scanner is one in 10^{78}, which makes it more effective than DNA testing.

Passwords, access cards, and biometric security devices are all examples of authentication systems. *Authentication* refers to the process a computer system uses to determine if someone is actually the person they claim to be.

Build Firewalls   To ward off the threat of hackers, more and more organizations are creating firewalls. A **firewall** is a collection of hardware or software intended to protect computer networks from attack. Historically, network attacks originated outside the organization, from hackers. As intranet creation has intensified, however, security experts are advising organizations to build internal firewalls too, to keep nosy employees from browsing through data that they don't need to perform their jobs.

Secure Transmissions with Encryption   Some users and vendors encrypt data and programs to protect them, especially if those resources are going to be traveling over a public network like the Internet. **Encryption**—or *cryptography*—involves scrambling data and program contents through a coding method (see Figure LIV 2-6). The encrypting procedure provides *keys,* or passwords, for both coding and decoding. One key locks the message at the sending end of the transmission to make it unintelligible to a snoop, and only a person who is authorized to see the message can decrypt it with a key at the receiver end. The sender and receiver keys do not have to necessarily be the same. Many software packages today have built-in encryption routines.

Several forms of encryption exist. One of the most common is *public-key encryption,* used to send secure data over such unsecured networks as the Internet. Let's see how this works in electronic banking: Two types of keys are used, one public and one private. *Public keys* are kept in the bank's directory and certain employees will have access to them when an encrypted message needs to be sent to a customer. Each customer has access to a *private key,* known only to him or her, which is used to decrypt the message coming from his or her public key. When a customer sends a message back to the bank, the bank uses its own private key to decrypt the message.

Another popular form of encryption uses *digital certificates* that authenticate a sender as a preapproved or legitimate source. If your browser sends you a warning that the sender has not signed a digital certificate, it should immediately put you on notice that you could be communicating with a thief, a hacker, or a person trying to implant a virus on your system.

For sensitive Internet transactions involving credit card information, banking or other financial information, and the like, Web pages that use encryption

 **FIGURE LIV 2-5**

Biometric security. Biometric security devices enable transactions by recognizing some unique physiological characteristic of a person, such as a fingerprint or handprint, or some unique learned characteristic, such as a voice or signature.

■ **Biometric security device.** A device that, upon recognition of some physiological or learned characteristic that is unique to a person, allows that person to have access to a system. ■ **Firewall.** A collection of hardware or software intended to protect a company's internal computer networks from attack. ■ **Encryption.** A method of protecting data or programs so that they are unrecognizable to unauthorized users.

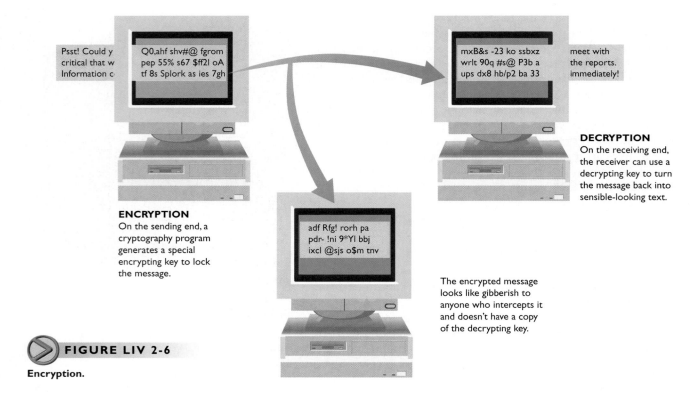

Psst! Could y
critical that w
Information c

Q0,ahf shv#@ fgrom
pep 55% s67 $ff2l oA
tf 8s Splork as ies 7gh

mxB&s -23 ko ssbxz
wrlt 90q #s@ P3b a
ups dx8 hb/p2 ba 33

meet with
the reports.
immediately!

DECRYPTION
On the receiving end,
the receiver can use a
decrypting key to turn
the message back into
sensible-looking text.

ENCRYPTION
On the sending end, a
cryptography program
generates a special
encrypting key to lock
the message.

adf Rfg! rorh pa
pdr- !ni 9*Yl bbj
ixcl @sjs o$m tnv

The encrypted message
looks like gibberish to
anyone who intercepts it
and doesn't have a copy
of the decrypting key.

FIGURE LIV 2-6

Encryption.

or some other approved security method should be used. Most browsers indicate on the toolbar or status bar when a secure Web page is being viewed and often the URL will begin with *https* instead of *http*. When performing a sensitive transaction, if you notice that the page is not secured (some browsers will display a message to warn you), think very carefully before continuing— virtually all companies doing business on a regular basis over the Internet will use secure Web pages.

The chapter Tomorrow box examines encryption in more depth, focusing in on some of the implementation issues that are currently dividing business and government.

Use Crime-Prevention Software A variety of software products are available to help in the fight against computer crime. For instance, **antivirus software** is available to help detect and eliminate the presence of computer viruses (see Figure LIV 2-7). Also, because computers are often used to file false claims, computer programs using artificial intelligence techniques have been deployed by businesses and government agencies to analyze claims for suspicious patterns.

Devise Staff Controls Overtime work should be carefully scrutinized, because computer crimes often occur at times when the criminal thinks he or she is unlikely to be interrupted. Sensitive documents that are no longer needed should be shredded. Access to computer facilities or the program/data library should be strictly limited to authorized personnel. **Callback devices,** which hang up on and call back people phoning in from remote locations, should be used in communications systems to deter hacking and virus implantation.

Monitor Important System Transactions The systems software in use should include a program for maintaining a log of every person gaining or

■ **Antivirus software.** Software used to detect and eliminate computer viruses. ■ **Callback device.** A device on the receiving end of a communications network that verifies the authenticity of the sender by calling the sender back.

The Great Encryption Wars

Will the Impasse Ever Get Resolved?

The federal government wants the capability to access and decode all encrypted messages. It also wants to limit the size of encryption keys on both exported software and applications. Businesses and privacy advocates in the United States are dead set against both ideas.

One of the first major battles in what technology historians may someday call the Great Encryption Wars began in the early 1990s when the U.S. National Security Agency proposed the idea of an encryption device called the Clipper chip. Presumably, this chip would be installed in every computer sold in the United States and would provide government agencies with a key to open messages sent from or received by all Clipper-chip-enabled machines.

The government's concern, many people feel, has a ring of legitimacy—especially with the frightening new dangers posed by communications technology. Terrorists, pornographers, drug dealers, kidnappers, money launderers, Internet thieves, and even hostile governments can use encrypted messages to commit crimes. Unless a method exists to promptly decipher messages, law enforcement and prosecution are made more difficult.

But there's another side of the coin. Business and privacy advocates proclaim that they wouldn't hand over the keys to their offices and homes to the government without any evidence of criminal activity, so why should they hand over the keys to their most private data—their computer transactions? They also feel that the government's doomsday scenario is not backed up by hard facts.

The federal government has backed off somewhat from the Clipper chip idea, but the FBI is pressing hard for easy access to encryption keys. Currently on the negotiating table is an escrow-based proposal in which keys are handed over to a mutually trusted third-party organization. This effectively puts a layer of protection between the public and the government, which cannot gain access to a citizen's computer without a court order. Businesses and privacy advocates are still cool to the idea, and a system that is mutually agreeable is still several years away.

A second battle between businesses and government has been fought over the length of encryption keys that can be exported to foreign countries. The fewer the number of bits in the key, the easier it is to crack. The government, as you might expect, likes shorter, more crackable keys, whereas business wants longer,

Government's need to know. Is your privacy worth stronger safeguards against terrorism, pornography, and other forms of crime?

more secure keys. Keys used domestically are often 128 or 256 bits long, while keys distributed to foreign countries (excluding Canada) have until recently been limited by law to be only 56 bits. A 56-bit key length is short enough for encrypted messages to be cracked with PC software. Keys that are 128-bits or longer, on the other hand, are virtually uncrackable.

U.S. companies complain that a key-length restriction opens the door to the prospect of foreign firms someday dominating international commerce. Today, with more and more business being done online and over the Internet, transaction security is becoming ever more important. Without the ability to secure transactions with a strong code from U.S. suppliers—claim U.S. companies—foreign companies would instead be compelled to buy their software and applications from companies not restricted by U.S. laws. This, in turn, could erode the leadership of the United States as a supplier of software and applications. In late 1999, the U.S. government capitulated, decreeing that software publishers could export long keys to non-terrorist nations. It is still too early to tell, though, if the key-length issue is finally settled.

Since the Cold War era, the U.S. government has classified encryption technology as a munition. This means that U.S. State Department approval is necessary for encryption products to be exported. Back in the 1950s, with computers few and far between, virtually nobody but the government worried about encrypting messages. Hardly anyone dreamed that millions of PCs tapped into a worldwide system such as the Internet would ever exist.

attempting to gain access to the system. The log should contain information on the workstation used, the data files and programs used, and the time at which the work began and ended. Such a log allows management to isolate unauthorized system use.

Conduct Regular Audits Unfortunately, many crimes are discovered by accident. Key elements of the system should be subjected to regular **audits**—inspec-

■ **Audit.** An inspection used to determine if a system or procedure is working as it should or if claimed amounts are correct.

Most antivirus programs will provide you with a list of known viruses.

By clicking on a virus in the list, you can learn about its characteristics.

Antivirus programs will scan memory and any disk drives that you specify. At the end of the scan, they will report their findings.

Antivirus programs should be updated regularly. Every year, hundreds of new viruses are introduced, many of which older programs are not equipped to handle.

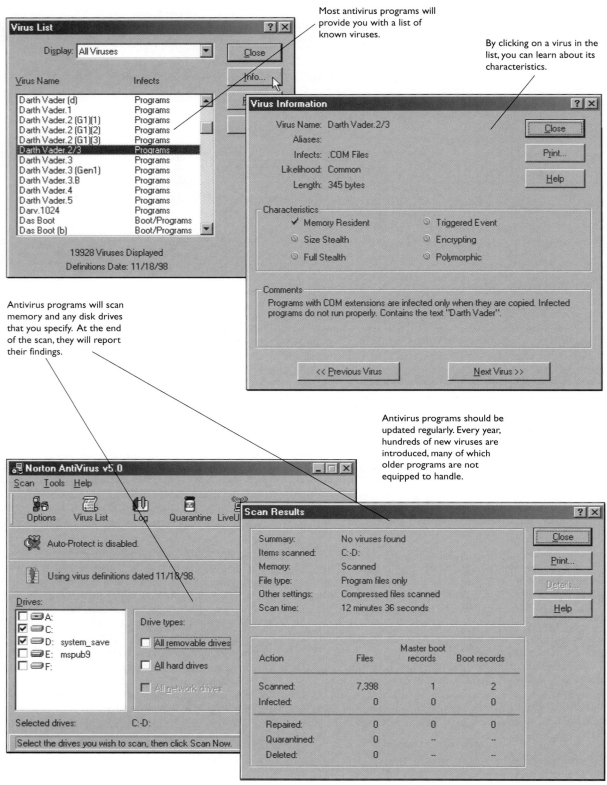

FIGURE LIV 2-7

Antivirus software.

tions that certify that the system is working as expected—to ensure that there is no foul play. Auditing often involves two key components: looking for security loopholes and inspecting system-activity logs to ascertain nothing unusual is taking place.

Educate Employees   One of the best ways to prevent computer crime is to educate employees about security matters. People should be told about various types of computer crime and the conditions that foster them, informed of the seriousness and consequences of computer crime, and instructed on what to do when they suspect a computer crime is taking place or is about to occur.

CRIME LEGISLATION

Federal law has also sought to deter computer crime, with mixed results. The main piece of legislation regarding using computers in criminal ways—the *Computer Fraud and Abuse Act*—has been regularly amended to broaden its scope and to clarify its intent. The law currently outlaws unauthorized access to data stored in computers of the federal government and federally regulated financial institutions. It also outlaws the deliberate implantation of computer viruses in those computers. Actions taken with intent to harm are classified as felonies, while actions performed merely with reckless disregard are considered misdemeanors. Critics say the law doesn't go far enough in that a hacker who is merely curious may not be guilty of a crime at all.

The rapid growth of the Internet has recently pushed the issue of network legislation into the forefront. There have long been laws addressing such offenses as sending indecent material through the mail, libel, harassment, inciting hatred, and the like, but how should those laws apply to computer networks?

One problem is jurisdictional. Because networks can be global, it can be hard to determine where a crime is legally being committed and whose laws apply. A second problem is that many existing laws do not transfer well to networks. Should, say, inflammatory comments over a network be treated like casual chat in a telephone conversation or like carefully crafted words sent through the mail? A third problem deals with responsibility and enforcement issues. Whose job should it be to monitor the massive number of messages sent over computer networks daily? Will the right to personal privacy be compromised? Will the public be willing to pay for the potentially exorbitant cost of having networks policed?

COMPUTERS AND PRIVACY

Almost all of us have some aspects of our lives that we prefer to keep private. These may include a sorry incident from the past, sensitive medical or financial facts, or certain tastes or opinions. Yet we can appreciate that sometimes selected people or organizations have a legitimate need for some of this information. A doctor needs accurate medical histories of patients. Financial information must be disclosed to credit-card companies and college scholarship committees. A company or the government may need to probe into the lives of people applying for unusually sensitive jobs.

No matter how legitimate the need, however, there is always the danger that information will be misused. Stored facts may be wrong. Facts may get to the wrong people. Facts may be taken out of context and used to draw distorted conclusions. Facts may be collected and disseminated without one's knowledge or consent. Victims can be denied access to incorrect or inappropriate data. As it applies to information processing, **privacy** refers to how information about individuals is used and by whom.

For a tutorial on privacy issues, go to www. harcourtcollege.com/ infosys/parker2000/student/ tutor/ and click on Chapter LIV 2.

■ **Privacy.** In a computer processing context, refers to how information about individuals is used and by whom.

The problem of how to protect privacy and ensure that personal information is not misused was with us long before electronic computers existed. But modern computer systems, with their ability to store and manipulate unprecedented quantities of data and to make those data available at many locations, have added several new wrinkles to the privacy issue. The trend for a long time has been for more and more sensitive data to be put online and for such data to be packaged and sold to others. Thus, it is not unusual that more public concern than ever exists regarding privacy rights.

PRIVACY AND ELECTRONIC MAIL

Two issues currently dominate the area that covers privacy and electronic mail: the use of electronic mail within companies and Internet spamming.

Company Electronic Mail   Many people believe that the objective of e-mail within companies is to promote a free-flowing dialogue among workers—that is, to increase the effectiveness of communication. They claim that e-mail should be viewed as the modern-day version of informal chatting around the water cooler, and that e-mail messages should not in any way be confused with official company records. Others claim that any business document created on the premises of an organization is not the property of the individual but of the organization. The issue has largely been resolved in favor of the latter viewpoint; what you say in your e-mail can be legally seized by others and used against you. What's more, you can be prosecuted for destroying e-mail evidence if you deliberately do it to avoid retribution, and your company can get into legal trouble for not taking the proper precautions with employee e-mail.

The issue of employees creating potentially damaging e-mail messages has reached crisis proportions in many companies. In the United States alone, close to 100 million people use e-mail, and the average worker/user sends or receives several electronic messages a day. The growing use of e-mail has made it easier for anyone—clients, employees, disgruntled people, and regulators—to file a lawsuit against a company. Charges already filed have ranged from sexual and racial discrimination to stolen secrets and uncompetitive practices. The latter charge, incidentally, has been one route the Justice Department has chosen to try to nail Microsoft on antitrust charges. The Feds have sorted through years and years of the company's e-mail messages, hoping to find the "smoking gun" that could prove its allegations against Microsoft.

To protect themselves, companies often rely on a formal e-mail policy and software to help enforce it. For instance, at Amazon.com, the online bookseller, a recent policy is that all nonessential documents "should be destroyed when they are no longer current or useful." To help enforce policies, the software industry has responded with products that range from e-shredders (packages that claim to completely obliterate e-mail messages), to snooping software (see Feature LIV 2-2), to "nanny" programs like MailCop. The latter alerts workers with flashing onscreen warnings when the contents of incoming or outgoing e-mail may be in violation of a company's e-mail policy.

Precautions notwithstanding, a large part of the problem is that companies aren't sure what's expected of them. What type of e-mail is appropriate and what's not? What constitutes being prudent and careful in the eyes of the law? How long must e-mail legally be kept?

The matter of whether or not companies should be allowed to eavesdrop on their employees' e-mail messages is a matter of heated debate. Companies are quick to point out that they have to protect themselves from unauthorized use of their e-mail systems. After all, a careless comment in a memo could make the company liable. Privacy-rights advocates often counter that companies don't casually rifle through people's desks or file cabinets so why should

Big-Brother Software

It Blocks, It Snoops, It Snitches

Blocking software that inhibits children from reading online pornography gets most of the attention when it comes to Internet access control. Little is it known that companies often purchase similar software to keep their employees in line—and to snoop on their activities and report on them as well.

With off-the-shelf software, organizations can now determine who's looking at what and for how long on the Internet—and do something about it. Using one highly popular snooping product, for instance, a company can keep track of all Web sites an employee is visiting, ascertain how much time an employee spends online, and get company-wide summary information—say, a report showing the top Web sites being accessed by employees. In addition, the software can block access to tens of thousands of sites in over a dozen different categories, including sex, gambling, hate speech, and sports. Sites falling into such categories, at best, waste employees' time. At worst, they can expose a company to serious liability.

The latest wave of snooping products goes well beyond looking at just Internet use. Programs can also record when you last used your word processor or your e-mail program, how much time you spent on them, and everything you typed at your workstation. Waiting in the wings: electronic badges that can track exactly where you are at any point in time, when you are away from your desk.

Many companies report that they are not interested in busting every employee committing an infraction. The biggest concerns are (1) minimizing liability, (2) catching serious computer abusers,

Snitch central. Companies that monitor computer use are most concerned about minimizing liability and stopping frequent abusers.

and (3) making employees respectful of their online activities through knowledge that someone may be watching what they do.

Privacy advocates, of course, worry about the abuse of such software in the workplace. Anyone reading a snooping program's outputs has the opportunity to use the information in an unauthorized way. Some examples: recreational snooping on people one doesn't particularly care for, spreading potentially embarrassing information about certain users to others, and using information to unfairly gain political advantage.

Many companies have a written computer-use policy in effect, so that employees have clear guidelines as to what does and what does not constitute acceptable activity. Other companies are hesitant to put such a policy in effect, and abuses are dealt with on a case-by-case basis.

they peek at their computer files? Also, the advocates point out, e-mail monitoring can be used for political purposes.

Presently, eavesdropping by companies on their e-mail systems is totally legal, and the law doesn't even require that employees be informed that their messages could be monitored. Nonetheless, it makes good business sense to have a computer-resource-usage policy in effect and to have it read by all employees.

Spamming **Spam** refers to unsolicited, bulk electronic mail sent over the Internet. The electronic equivalent of junk mail, spam most often originates from commercial sources. At best, it is an annoyance to recipients and can clog a mail network so as to slow down the delivery of important messages. At worst, it can disable a mail network completely.

Internet service providers such as America Online often have millions of pieces of spam clogging their networks each day, and the problem is growing worse. Many people use *e-mail-filtering programs* that automatically discard

■ **Spam.** Unsolicited, bulk electronic mail sent over the Internet.

HOW MARKETING DATABASES WORK

When you make an electronic transaction, information about who you are and what you buy is recorded.

The identities of people and what they buy are sold to a micromarketer.

The micromarketer uses its computers to reorganize the data in a way that might be valuable to others.

Companies buy the reorganized data and use it for their own purposes.

 **FIGURE LIV 2-8**

Marketing databases.

incoming messages if they appear to contain spam. Currently, legislation is being drafted at both federal and state levels to curb spam abuse.

One of the principal dangers of spam is that the spammer need not worry about carefully targeting a specific audience, since there is virtually no cost difference between sending 500 e-mails versus 500,000. Every time you register your e-mail address at a Web site, you open yourself up to spam.

PRIVACY AND MARKETING DATABASES

Marketing databases are repositories that contain information about the consuming public. They record where people live, what they are inclined to do, and what they buy. Using such facts, companies attempt to determine the best way to promote specific products to specific types of people. Virtually anytime you leave traceable information about yourself anywhere, there's a good chance that it will eventually find its way into somebody's marketing database and on to a company that wants to sell to you (see Figure LIV 2-8).

When you buy a house, for example, your name, address, and the sales price are recorded in a county courthouse. These records are available to the public, including micromarketers. *Micromarketers* are companies that specialize in creating marketing databases and selling information to companies that sell products or services to others. The micromarketer typically breaks down the neighborhoods in a region into several dozen categories. Consumers are placed into one of these categories according to their address. For instance, a "Blueblood Estates" category might be a neighborhood in which the very wealthy live. A "Shotguns and Pickups" category, by contrast, might refer to a rural area where trailers are the likely abode. There are also categories for urban professionals, the elderly, and so on.

Each category is correlated in the micromarketer's computer system with certain buying preferences, a profiling technique known as *geodemographics.* "Blueblood Estates" types are likely to buy expensive cars and take trips to places such as Aspen and St. Thomas. Those of the "Shotguns and Pickups" sort are more likely to be into country music, chainsaws, and Elvis collectibles. This information helps companies customize a direct-mail campaign to consumers' specific tastes. Consumers, of course, often look at unsolicited direct or electronic mail as junk mail and resent it as an intrusion on privacy.

In addition to geodemographic data, micromarketers also collect data showing consumers' past purchasing behavior. Every time you make a computerized purchase, valuable data can be gathered about your purchasing tastes and entered into a computer system. Records kept by stores, credit-card companies,

For links to further information about privacy, go to www.harcourtcollege.com/ infosys/parker2000/student/ explore/ and click on Chapter LIV 2.

■ **Marketing database.** An electronic repository containing information useful for niche-marketing products to consumers.

banks, the companies whose magazines you subscribe to, and other organizations are sold to the micromarketer. Even the government sells information.

CALLER IDENTIFICATION

Caller identification, or *caller ID,* refers to a technology in which a telephone device contains a tiny display that will output the phone number and name (or organization) of an incoming caller (see Figure LIV 2-9). Thus, the party receiving the call can identify the person at the other end of the line before picking up the phone, regardless of whether the caller is aware of this. Callers can, however, block caller ID by entering a special code number before entering a phone number.

Many people have praised caller identification systems as a good way of screening or cutting down on unwanted calls. Also, businesses such as take-out restaurants are guaranteed a measure of protection against callers who order food and then don't show up. Some people, however, have been less enthusiastic, seeing these systems as a potential invasion of privacy. For instance, a person living in an apartment in a dangerous neighborhood might be afraid to report a crime taking place outside, fearing that his or her identity could be leaked out and cause the criminal to take revenge at some point in the future. Not everyone, of course, is aware that they can block caller ID. Caller identification is not available in every state and country.

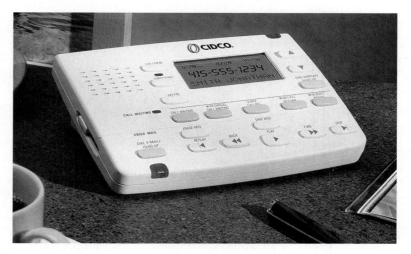

FIGURE LIV 2-9

Caller ID. With a caller ID display, you can tell who's at the other end of the line before answering.

PRIVACY LEGISLATION

Since the early 1970s, the federal government has sought to protect citizens' rights by passing legislation to curb privacy abuses. Some important laws enacted for this purpose are described in Figure LIV 2-10.

Many people inside and outside the computer industry feel that privacy legislation is woefully out of date and due for an overhaul. The major privacy laws were enacted more than two decades ago and largely apply to the conduct of the federal government and the organizations to which it supplies aid. A lot has changed since then. Twenty-five years ago, most information was centralized on mainframes and available only in hard-copy form, whereas today it is much more common for data to travel over networks and never make it into print.

ETHICAL ISSUES REGARDING COMPUTERS

For a tutorial on ethical issues, go to www. harcourtcollege.com/ infosys/parker2000/student/ tutor/ and click on Chapter LIV 2.

Ethics refers to standards of moral conduct. For example, telling the truth is a matter of ethics. An unethical act isn't always illegal, but sometimes it is. For example, purposely lying to a friend is unethical but normally is lawful, but perjuring oneself as a courtroom witness is a crime. Whether or not criminal behavior is involved, ethics play an important role in shaping the law and in determining how well we get along with other people.

■ **Caller identification.** Refers to the use of a telephone or answering device that displays the origin of incoming calls.
■ **Ethics.** A term that refers to standards of moral conduct.

Date	Law and Description
1970	**Freedom of Information Act** Gives individuals the right to inspect data concerning them that are stored by the federal government
1970	**Fair Credit Reporting Act** Prevents private organizations from unfairly denying credit to individuals and provides individuals the right to inspect their credit records for truthfulness
1974	**Education Privacy Act** Stipulates that, in both public and private schools that receive any federal funding, individuals have the right to keep the schools from releasing such information as grades and evaluations of behavior
1974	**Privacy Act** Stipulates that the collection of data by federal agencies must have a legitimate purpose
1978	**Right to Financial Privacy Act** Provides guidelines that federal agencies must follow when inspecting an individual's bank records
1984	**Computer Fraud and Abuse Act of 1984** Makes it a crime to break into computers owned by the federal government
1984	**Cable Communications Policy Act** Limits disclosure of customer records by cable TV companies
1986	**Electronic Communications Privacy Act** Extends traditional privacy protections to include e-mail, cellular phones, and voice mail
1986	**Computer Fraud and Abuse Act of 1986** Amends the 1984 law to include federally regulated financial institutions
1988	**Video Privacy Protection Act** Limits disclosure of customer information by video-rental companies
1988	**Computer Matching and Privacy Act** Limits the use of government data in determining federal-benefit recipients
1991	**Telephone Consumer Protection Act** Requires telemarketing companies to respect the rights of people who do not want to be called and significantly restricts the use of recorded messages
1992	**Cable Act** Extends the Cable Communications Policy Act to include companies that sell wireless services
1994	**Computer Abuse Amendments Act** Extends the Computer Fraud and Abuse Act to include computer viruses
1996	**National Information Infrastructure Protection Act** Punishes information theft crossing state lines and cracks down on network trespassing
1997	**No Electronic Theft (NET) Act** Expands computer piracy laws to include distribution of copyrighted materials over the Internet
1998	**Telephone Anti-Spamming Amendments Act** Applies restrictions to unsolicited, bulk commercial e-mail

FIGURE LIV 2-10

U.S. laws relating to privacy.

SOME EXAMPLES

Today, computers present a number of ethical concerns. Several examples of these are covered in the list that follows:

- Some people regularly use a software package that they aren't licensed to use for personal purposes, claiming they are doing so just to get the feel

The Vaporware Cookbook

When products are not shipped on or shortly after their announced date, they are often labeled as vaporware. Vaporware has for many years been such a common occurrence throughout the computer industry that scholars who observe the practice have cataloged the various forms that it can take.

Form 1: Announce a Similar Product with an Imminent Release Date This strategy is often used when a competitor has a product coming out—or a product that is already out—and users will ignore anything less than a full-blown product announcement. Companies often make such announcements even when they have no product in the works but have to react quickly to a competitive threat.

Form 2: Announce a New Direction Companies that control a market often find this strategy useful when they have no new products on the immediate horizon. For instance, a company may state in a press conference "our upcoming line of holographic storage products will revolutionize . . ." Users will be hesitant to adopt a competitor's product using current technology if they feel it will trap them into an old way of doing work. The market leader can later change its mind and proclaim with false altruism that, so as to not disrupt users, it's not moving in the aforementioned new direction after all.

Form 3: Start Rumors Here, no official announcement is made, but comments are leaked in selected places—to the press, to user groups, and so on—hinting that something big is about to unfold. The advantage to this strategy is that the company cannot be blamed for an outside rumor that doesn't come true.

Form 4: Meet the Release Date, but Do It in a Lame Way There is tremendous pressure to meet release dates, since the company may lose users if it does not deliver the product, its stock price can plummet when it does not meet expectations, and reputations can be on the line. Thus, companies often resort to all sorts of unethical tricks to make it appear as if a date has been met. Some highly questionable methods that companies have been accused of to buy extra time is releasing a bug-laden product that it can inexpensively patch at a later date, shipping limited units of a bug-laden product as a damage-control measure, shipping blank disks, charging a modest fee for an almost finished beta that the general public can use, and providing coupons to the user for promised product features that did not meet the shipping deadline.

of it. Although most vendors encourage limited experimentation with their products, they frown on someone who hasn't bought the software using it regularly, and such use is, at a minimum, ethically questionable.

- A computer professional working for one software company leaves to take a job for a competing company. Almost immediately, the professional divulges product secrets that were entrusted in confidence by the former employer, putting the new employer at an unfair competitive advantage.
- A medical programmer is assigned to code a software routine that is to be part of a system that monitors the heart rate of hospital patients. Before the program can be fully tested, the programmer is ordered to hand it over so that the system can meet its promised deadline. The programmer tells the project supervisor that the code may contain serious bugs. The supervisor responds, "It's not our fault if the program fails because the deadline is too tight."
- A large software company, hearing that a small competitor is coming out with a new product, spreads a rumor that it is working on a similar product. Although the large company never provides a formal release date for its product, it leaves potential users with the mistaken impression that they will be taking a major risk by adopting the small-competitor's product. (Incidentally, as the Inside the Industry box explains, software that's announced long before it is ready for market is referred to as **vaporware.**)

- **Vaporware.** Software that is announced long before it is ready for market.

CODE OF CONDUCT

1. Employees should not copy or use software that belongs to someone else.

2. Employees should not deploy their computers to browse, use, read from, or write to programs of files that are not meant for them.

3. Employees should use computers only to perform job-related tasks.

4. Employees should not use the computers of others, unless authorized or specifically given permission.

5. Employees must not engage in inappropriate electronic communications and are required to read the company's formal e-mail policy.

6. Employees should take reasonable precautions in protecting their computer resources.

7. Employees suspecting inappropriate computer activity within the company should report it immediately to their superiors.

8. Employees must not do anything on their computers that would interfere with larger goals or programs within the company.

9. Employees should not use their computers to engage in activities considered either criminal or in any way harmful to others.

10. Employees must ultimately bear legal and moral responsibility for their actions on the computer.

FIGURE LIV 2-11

Codes of conduct. Here is an example of computer-usage guidelines that an employer may distribute to employees.

WHY STUDY ETHICS?

Why has ethics become such a hot topic? Undoubtedly, ethics has taken on more significance in recent years because the workplace has become increasingly multicultural and diverse. Different cultures have different values, and what might seem ethically problematic to a person in the United States might be a normal way of doing business in other countries—or vice versa. Take bribes, for instance. In the United States, both bribing and taking bribes are generally considered morally off base. They are also illegal. In some other countries, bribing is not only culturally tolerated, but also the salaries of workers are adjusted downward to reflect that bribes are an understood part of the compensation package. Such phenomena as increasing divorce rates and changing family structures have also tended to broaden ethical norms within cultures over time.

Many scholars think that educating people about ethical matters is being pushed aside today in the rush to achieve measurable results. A movement is afoot to change this, however. In recent years, professional computer organizations and some 90 percent of the largest U.S. corporations have established *codes of conduct* covering unauthorized uses of software, hardware, and communications networks (see Figure LIV 2-11). Also, ethics is frequently a topic in computer journals and at professional conferences today.

SUMMARY AND KEY TERMS

Go to the Online Glossary at www.harcourtcollege.com/infosys/parker2000/student/to review key terms.

Since the early 1950s, when the era of commercial computing began, computers have rapidly woven their way into the fabric of modern society. In the process, they have created both opportunities and problems.

Computers, Work, and Health   One of the first criticisms leveled at the entry of computers into the workplace was that their presence resulted in stress. Stress-related concerns triggered by the so-called computer revolution include fear of layoff or reassignment, fear of falling behind, and job burnout. In addition to these problems, other concerns related to **ergonomics** issues, such as display-device usage and workspace design, have surfaced. Many people also worry about environment-related issues such as the energy usage and the paperwork glut.

Computer Crime   **Computer crime** is defined as the use of computers to commit criminal acts. In practice, even though there are laws that deal with computer crime, it is hard to pin down. It is sometimes difficult to decide when a questionable act is really a crime, people are bewildered by the technical issues involved, and companies frequently are reluctant to press charges.

Computer crime may take many forms. Types of computer crime include data diddling, the **Trojan horse** technique, salami-shaving methods, unauthorized use of trapdoor programs, logic bombs and time bombs, **computer viruses,** eavesdropping, cellular-phone fraud, **software piracy, hacking,** counterfeiting, and Internet-related crimes.

Organizations can minimize computer crimes in many ways: assessing risks; having a **disaster-recovery plan;** hiring trustworthy people; taking precautions with malcontents; separating employee functions; restricting system use; limiting access to programs and data with **passwords, access cards, biometric security devices,** and **firewalls;** devising staff controls; concealing the contents of particularly sensitive programs and data through **encryption;** using **callback devices;** monitoring important system transactions; conducting regular **audits;** educating employees; and using **antivirus software** and similar programs.

Computers and Privacy   Most people want some control over the kinds of facts that are collected about them, how those facts are collected and their accuracy, who uses them, and how they are used. Modern computer systems, with their ability to store and manipulate unprecedented quantities of data and make those data available to many locations, have added a new dimension to the personal **privacy** issue. Recently, three relatively new technologies—electronic mail (including intracompany mail and **spam**), **marketing databases,** and **caller identification** phone systems—have created further concerns about invasion of privacy.

Ethical Issues Regarding Computers   **Ethics** refers to standards of moral conduct. Today one of the most important ethical concerns regarding computers is using someone else's property in an improper way. Another is leading people to believe something that's more fiction than fact when it works to one's advantage—such as the case with **vaporware.**

EXERCISES

1. Fill in the blanks:
   a. Fear of computers is known as _____ .
   b. _____ is the field that covers the effects of factors such as equipment and computer workspaces on employees' productivity and health.
   c. _____ refers to a phone-system feature that can display the phone number and name of a caller.
   d. _____ is a crime that involves manipulating programs or data so that many small dollar amounts are trimmed from a large number of transactions or accounts and accumulated elsewhere.
   e. _____ are companies that specialize in creating marketing databases and selling them to companies that sell directly to people.

2. Describe some ways in which computers may adversely affect our health or well-being.

3. Define the following terms:
   a. Vaporware
   b. Firewall
   c. Authentication
   d. Biometric security device
   e. Geodemographics
   f. Encrypting key

4. Match each term with the description that fits best:

a. computer virus   d. hacking
b. data diddling   e. trapdoor
c. spoof   f. sniffing

_____ An example of a Trojan horse.
_____ Refers to software that can glean passwords and other data from a computer system.
_____ Is transmitted through a copy operation.
_____ A diagnostic tool that allows the viewing of computer storage.
_____ The altering of an organization's operations data.
_____ Using a terminal or personal computer system to illegally break into a remote computer system.

5. Answer the following questions about computer viruses:

a. What is a computer virus?
b. Describe, in as many ways as you can, how your computer can become infected by a virus.
c. How do you prevent catching a computer virus?
d. How do you get rid of a computer virus?

6. Computer crime can exist in many forms. In each of the following cases, describe the type of computer crime taking place:

a. A person working for the Motor Vehicle Division deletes a friend's speeding ticket from a database.
b. A brokerage business overcharges by one-tenth of 1 percent on all commissions made on the buying and selling of stocks.
c. A group of people make copies of U.S. software whose rights are owned by others and sell the software overseas for a profit.
d. A disgruntled employee places a program on the company mainframe that instructs key data to be erased on March 15.
e. A person uses a desktop publishing system to create phony checks.
f. A systems programmer implants code into a program that would cause all phone numbers in the company to become inoperative if the company vetos a pay raise.
g. A repairperson implants a device on a company network that enables him to pick up from a remote phone all transmitted account numbers and passwords.

7. What fundamental rights of the individual have computer privacy laws tried to protect?

8. Several situations regarding the use of computers follow. In the space provided, tell whether each act is *unethical,* *criminal,* or *neither* of these. The "neither" category can include both ethical acts and acts that, while not morally wrong, are not commendable either.

a. A company spokesperson tells employees that the company doesn't monitor e-mail messages, knowing full well it does. _____
b. A programmer rigs his company's network so that on April 19 everyone gets a message when they log on telling them that the government was wrong to use force with the Branch Davidians at Waco. _____
c. The executive of a company with no policy as regards e-mail confidentiality randomly snoops through messages to make sure that employees are not goofing off. _____
d. A brokerage house sells a list of clients to a micromarketer, not really caring who the micromarketer deals with. Later, the micromarketer sells the list to a telemarketing company it suspects is involved in shady investing practices.
    Brokerage house _____
    Micromarketer _____
e. A systems analyst is given the job of building a system that will deliver a new computer service to consumers, signing a legally binding agreement to not disclose facts about it to outsiders. She is so fascinated by the service that she immediately quits her job and interests a competitor to hire her on at twice her former salary in order to develop a competitive service. _____
f. A software developer creates an antivirus program. To finance the advertising campaign for this product, the developer calls several computer executives at large firms and gets them to put up $10,000 each. This, the developer believes, will produce the funds needed and make the executives more likely to buy the product.
    Developer _____
    Computer executives _____
g. A fund-raiser for a hospital has access to a continually updated database that reveals the recent deaths of people who were able to afford expensive medical care. The fund-raiser frequently uses the database to target bereaved families for contributions. _____
h. A teenager gets a demon dialer—a program that rapidly generates passwords and tries them out—and uses it to break into the computer of a local business. Once inside the system, the teenager looks around for a few minutes and then leaves, disturbing nothing. When his friends ask him about the incident the next day, he confides, "It was no big deal. I just wanted to see for myself if the demon dialer did what everyone said it could do." _____

9. Determine the differences between the terms listed below and on the following page:

a. Caller identification and a callback device

b. A computer crime and an ethical impropriety regarding computers

c. Encrypting data and password-protecting data

d. Software piracy and hacking

e. A time bomb and a logic bomb

10. Determine whether the following statements are true or false:

a. Carpal tunnel syndrome is a disability that evolves from poor use of display technology.

b. Cellular phone fraud is a prime example of software piracy.

c. A disaster-recovery plan maps out what an organization does to prepare for and react to disruptive events.

d. Access cards are typically used in combination with passwords.

e. The Computer Fraud and Abuse Act is the main piece of legislation governing an individual's right to privacy as regards computer databases.

PROJECTS

1. **Off to the Races**   A clerk in a steel company uses a company-owned, networked computer—on company time—to handicap horses for a local racetrack.

a. Is a crime being committed?

b. Where do you draw the line between a criminal and noncriminal act?

c. From a privacy standpoint, how do you feel about the steel company randomly checking the contents of files on its network, from time to time, to ensure that employees are using its computers for work-related tasks?

2. **Computer Crimes**   Computer crimes are regularly reported in the press. For this project, find an example of a computer crime covered in a newspaper or magazine and report to the class about it. Be sure to cover such details as the nature of the crime, the dollar amount of loss resulting from the crime, how the criminal act was discovered, and the like.

3. **Acceptable Use Policies**   Many schools have a code of conduct governing acceptable uses of their computers. The policies often address such issues as what types of information can and cannot be stored on the computers and what types of uses are considered objectionable. For this project, create what you feel is an ideal acceptable-use policy for your campus. Make sure the policy addresses the following issues:

a. Who the policy covers—students, faculty, administrators, alumni, anyone else?

b. What types of uses are forbidden? Make sure you are specific; a vague use of words creates loopholes and will effectively leave you with no policy at all.

c. What penalties will be levied for first-time and repeat infractions?

If your school already has an acceptable-use policy, compare yours with theirs and comment on the differences.

4. **Antivirus Programs**   Many antivirus programs currently exist on the market. For this project, choose such a program, answering the following questions in the process:

a. What is the name of the product? Who makes it?

b. How much does the product cost?

c. How many types of viruses does the program detect?

d. How are updates received on the product? How much do such updates cost?

e. How should the product be used—at the beginning of a session, continuously throughout a session, or what?

Two Web sites that you might want to visit for product information are listed in the following table:

COMPANY	WEB ADDRESS
MacAfee	www.mcafee.com
Symantec	www.symantec.com

5. **Ergonomics**   One of the problems with diseases like carpal tunnel syndrome and other types of repetitive stress injuries is that the medical profession does not fully understood what causes them. Thus, the vendors of many ergonomic products have no scientific evidence at all to any claim that the products lead to any sort of cure or alleviation of pain. (When a product makes no claims that it can cure illnesses, incidentally, it does not need approval from the Food and Drug Administration.) For this project, find an ad for a product that claims to be ergonomic.

a. What is the product and who makes it?

b. In what way is the product claiming to be ergonomic?

c. Is any sort of research evidence being cited as to the ergonomic effectiveness of the product?

6. **Step Up to the Beef Box**   This chapter and others have touched on a lot of controversial social issues regarding computers. Here's your chance to sound off with your own ideas on one of them. A recent statement made by the American Association of University Professors (AAUP) said of colleges forbidding certain uses of the Internet,

> On a campus that is free and open, no idea can be banned or forbidden. . . . No viewpoint or message may be deemed so hateful or disturbing that it cannot be expressed.

Respond to this statement with your own opinions on the matter. Do you think colleges are crossing any sort of a line when they try to prohibit certain types of speech on their Internet sites or try to block sites accessed by their computers?

7. **Software Piracy**   In a *Computerworld* editorial, a software consultant touched off a flood of fiery protest by remarking that software piracy is overblown as an issue. He argued that

a. Most people who pirate software wouldn't have bought the software in the first place, so the aggregate value of pirated software doesn't necessarily represent lost revenue.

b. Pirates who like a product often legitimately buy future releases of it to access new features, so pirating often has a positive effect on future sales.

c. The value of stolen software—which is estimated to be in the billions of dollars annually—overstates the real drain on profits because it multiplies the number of illegal copies times sales price.

Respond to these comments.

8. **Invoke Your Privacy Rights**   Tired of junk mail, marketing databases, and—perhaps most of all—telemarketers who call you in the middle of your supper? The U.S. Federal Trade Commission (FTC) has a Web site (www.ftc.gov/privacy) to inform people how to put a stop to the marketing of their personal information. Other advice on privacy matters can be found at the nonprofit Privacy Rights Clearinghouse Web site located at www.privacyrights.org. For this project, visit one of these sites and report its contents to your classmates.

9. **Privacy in the News**   Privacy issues regarding computers are regularly reported in the press. For this project, find an example of a privacy issue covered in a journal or newspaper and report to the class about it. Be sure to cover such details as the alleged privacy violation and whose privacy is being compromised.

10. **Online Prescriptions**   The explosion of commerce on the Internet has led to some businesses few people could have imagined only a decade ago. One of these is a new method of health-care delivery: online medical prescriptions. In this high-tech form of health care, doctors with Web sites who have never seen their patients can make prescription drugs available to them through an online questionnaire. For instance, a patient requesting the drug Viagra fills out a form on his home PC and e-mails it back, with a consultation fee, to the doctor. If the request is approved, an electronic prescription can be sent to an online pharmacy, and the cost is often far less than if the prescription had been filled at a conventional, local pharmacy.

a. The American Medical Association has officially frowned on such online prescriptions whereas others see it as the wave of the future. What do you think?

b. Do you see any legal or ethical issues involved in such online health care? Be specific.

INTERACTIVE EXERCISE

SAFEGUARDING YOUR COMPUTER

You'd like to practice some basic security methods, such as checking for viruses and backing up files. Go to the Interactive Exercise at www.harcourtcollege.com/infosys/parker2000/student/ to complete this exercise.

ONLINE REVIEW

Go to the Online Review at www.harcourtcollege.com/infosys/parker2000/student/ to test your understanding of this chapter's concepts.

WINDOW

A PICTURE ESSAY OF THE PEOPLE AND DEVICES THAT PIONEERED THE COMPUTER REVOLUTION

THE HISTORY OF COMPUTERS

Electronic computers as we know them were invented more than 60 years ago. However, the history of computers actually goes back much further than that. Since the beginning of civilization, merchants and government officials have used computing devices to help them with calculations and record keeping.

1. Even long before modern computers came along, many large organizations were beginning to drown in a sea of paperwork. This turn-of-the-century photo, of Prudential's New Jersey headquarters, illustrates the earliest benefit computers provided—replacing armies of clerks with machines that were cheaper, faster, and more accurate.

EARLY HISTORY

Most computers prior to 1900 were predominantly *mechanical* machines that worked with gears and levers. Operation was completely manual. Throughout the 1930s and 1940s, computers came to depend more and more on electricity for power, giving rise to *electromechanical* devices. By 1950, the era of solid-state *electronics* began to mature, ushering in the modern computer age we know today.

2. This crank-driven *difference engine*, built by Charles Babbage in England in the 1830s, was one of the forerunners to today's modern computers. Babbage's attempts to build machines that were more sophisticated were thwarted because the parts he needed could not be produced.

3. A milestone on the way to the modern computer was passed during the 1890 U.S. Census. Herman Hollerith, a federal employee who is pictured here, created an electromechanical device that collapsed the tabulation of the census from a decade to only three years.

4. Throughout the 1930s, IBM was the leader of punched-card tabulating equipment. IBM president and founder, Tom Watson, is shown here greeting some of the stars of his sales force. Watson pioneered the marketing of computer systems—selling business solutions rather than just electronic boxes.

5

5. The age of electromechanical devices reached its zenith in the early 1940s with the development of the Mark I. Despite its sleek, futuristic look, the Mark I was technologically obsolete almost upon completion. The age of electronics was about to dawn.

6

6. The ABC—for Atanasoff-Berry Computer—is today widely acknowledged as the world's first electronic computer. Built by John Atanasoff and Clifford Berry of Iowa State University around 1940, the ABC helped graduate students solve simultaneous linear equations.

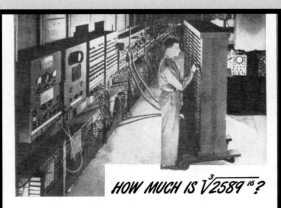

HOW MUCH IS $\sqrt[3]{2589^{16}}$?

The Army's ENIAC can give you the answer in a fraction of a second!

Think that's a stumper? You should see *some* of the ENIAC's problems! Brain twisters that if put to paper would run off this page and feet beyond . . . addition, subtraction, multiplication, division—square root, cube root, any root. Solved by an incredibly complex system of circuits operating 18,000 electronic tubes and tipping the scales at 30 tons!

The ENIAC is symbolic of many amazing Army devices with a brilliant future for you! The new Regular Army needs men with aptitude for scientific work, and as one of the first trained in the post-war era, you stand to get in on the ground floor of important jobs

which have never before existed. You'll find that an Army career pays off.

The most attractive fields are filling quickly. Get into the swim while the getting's good! 1½, 2 and 3 year enlistments are open in the Regular Army to ambitious young men 18 to 34 (17 with parents' consent) who are otherwise qualified. If you enlist for 3 years, you may choose your own branch of the service, of those still open. Get full details at your nearest Army Recruiting Station.

A GOOD JOB FOR YOU
U. S. Army
CHOOSE THIS
FINE PROFESSION NOW!

YOUR REGULAR ARMY SERVES THE NATION AND MANKIND IN WAR AND PEACE

7

7. ENIAC, the world's first large-scale, general-purpose electronic computer, was unveiled in 1946. Built by two former professors at the University of Pennsylvania, ENIAC (for Electronic Numerical Integrator and Calculator) used 18,000 vacuum tubes—like the ones seen in old radios—and was said to dim the lights of Philadelphia when it ran.

THE FIRST GENERATION (1951–1958)

The commercial age of computers is often discussed in terms of its generations. First-generation computers used vacuum tubes (similar to those in **ENIAC**) as their principal logic element. Though the tubes enabled computers to run faster than electromechanical machines, they were large and bulky, generated excessive heat, and were prone to failure.

8. The UNIVAC I, circa 1951, was the first computer to be mass produced for general use. It was also the first computer used to tabulate returns in a U.S. presidential election. In 1952, it declared Dwight Eisenhower the victor over Adlai Stevenson only 45 minutes after the polls closed.

9. Most computers of the first and second generations relied heavily on punched-card input. Each standard punched card held 80 characters of data, with a set of holes in a card column representing a character. Today's high-capacity diskette, which can fit in a shirt pocket, can store the data equivalent of about 20,000 punched cards.

10. An operator at a keypunch machine is shown preparing punched cards for processing. Blank cards were manually stacked in a hopper at the top right of the machine. As each blank card was fetched, it passed through a station that punched holes corresponding to keys struck by the operator. Finished cards were automatically routed to a stacker.

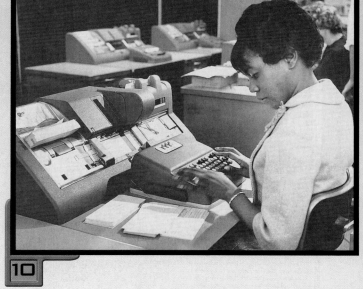

11. Once a keypunch-machine operator finished punching a stack of cards, the cards were manually placed in the input hopper of a card reader—the device used to communicate the contents of the cards to a **CPU**.

THE SECOND GENERATION (1959–1964)

In second-generation computers, transistors replaced vacuum tubes as the main logic element. Other noteworthy innovations of the second generation included more reliance on tape and disk storage, magnetic-core memory, replaceable boards, and high-level programming languages.

12. A second-generation transistor (left) is compared in size to the first-generation vacuum tube it replaced. Transistors performed the same function as tubes but made computers faster, smaller, and more reliable.

13–14. Small doughnut-shaped magnetic cores (left), which were strung on tiered racks (top) within the system unit, became the standard for second-generation computer memory. Each tiny core could hold a computer bit, and data were created by magnetizing each core clockwise or counterclockwise.

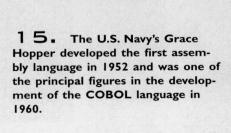

15. The U.S. Navy's Grace Hopper developed the first assembly language in 1952 and was one of the principal figures in the development of the COBOL language in 1960.

THE THIRD GENERATION (1965–1970)

The third generation of computers evolved when small integrated circuits—"computer chips" as we know them today—began replacing conventional transistors. Other noteworthy developments of the third generation were the rise of operating systems, minicomputers, and word processing technology.

16. One of the most important developments of the third generation was the IBM System/360. Unlike previous computers, System/360 constituted a full line of compatible computers, making upgrading much easier. Many of today's mainframes are designed much like the popular 360 line.

17. Digital Equipment Corporation's PDP-8 was the world's first minicomputer. At $20,000, this rugged machine represented a small fraction of the cost of mainframes of its day, and it could be installed almost anywhere.

18–19. Kenneth Olsen and An Wang were two of the early pioneers in the development of minicomputers. Olsen (left) founded Digital Equipment Corporation (DEC) in an old Massachusetts wool mill. Wang (right) founded Wang Corporation, which became an early leader in word processing technology.

THE FOURTH GENERATION
(1971—PRESENT)

The fourth generation of computers is probably best known for the dawning of the age of the microcomputer. Improved manufacturing techniques enabled more and more circuitry to be squeezed onto a chip.

20

20—21. Today, it is possible to manufacture tiny chips that have over a million circuits in an area that can fit through the eye of a needle (left). As electronic components shrunk, smaller computer systems followed and so did computerized consumer devices such as this early spelling toy (below).

21

22. The first computer on a chip was the Intel 4004. On November 15, 1971, *Electronic News* carried the first advertisement for this breakthrough product. With 2,250 transistors—which is less than 1 percent of the circuit elements on most of today's microprocessors—the 4004 was an adequate processor for simple electronic devices such as calculators and cash registers.

22

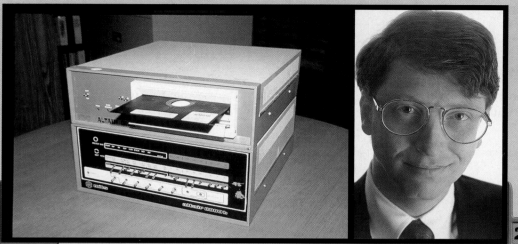

23-24. The first fully assembled microcomputer system unit was the Altair 8800 (left). Although the company that developed the Altair went bankrupt, the BASIC translator for this peripheral-less computer was written by Bill Gates (right), who went on to found Microsoft Corporation and become the world's richest person.

25-26. The first commercially successful microcomputer company was Apple. Pictured here are Steve Wozniak and Steve Jobs, Apple's founders, holding the system board for the Apple I—their first computer (below). Although less powerful than the Altair 8800, the Apple I was cheaper and easier to use.

27. Tim Berners-Lee of CERN—a physics laboratory in Switzerland—created the World Wide Web in 1989. The "Web" and soon-to-follow graphical browsers brought the Internet into the mainstream.

GLOSSARY

The terms shown in boldface are presented in the text as key terms. Numbers in parentheses after the definitions of terms indicate pages on which the terms are boldfaced and defined in the text. The terms shown in boldfaced italic are other commonly used and important words often encountered in computing environments. Numbers in parentheses after the definitions of boldfaced italic terms indicate the pages on which the terms are mentioned.

A

Absolute cell referencing.
Copying verbatim the contents in one range of cells into another range of cells. (PS 45)

Access card.
A plastic card that, when inserted into a machine and combined with a password, permits access to a system. (LIV 40)

Access mechanism.
A mechanical device in a disk drive that positions the read/write heads on the proper tracks. (HW 57)

Action diagram.
A programming tool that helps programmers code structured programs. (IS 43)

Active-matrix.
Refers to a flat-panel display technology that provides very sharp screen images. Contrasts with passive-matrix. (HW 103)

ActiveX.
A set of controls that enables programs or content of virtually any type to be embedded within a Web page. (NET 112)

Ada.
A structured programming language developed by the Department of Defense and named after Ada Augusta Byron, the world's first programmer. (IS 48)

Add-in board.
A circuit board that may be inserted into a slot within a desktop computer's system unit to add one or more functions. (HW 25)

Add-on program.
Software that supplements the activities of a larger program. (PS 23)

Address.
An identifiable location in storage where data are kept. Both memory and disk are addressable. (HW 7)

AI.
See Artificial intelligence. (IS 15)

ALU.
See Arithmetic/logic unit. (HW 6)

American National Standards Institute (ANSI).
An organization that acts as a national clearinghouse for standards in the United States. (HW 12)

Analog.
The transmission of data as continuous-wave patterns. Contrasts with digital. (NET 19)

Analog computer.
A device that measures. Contrasts with digital computer. (HW 4)

Analysis.
In program and systems development, the process of studying a problem area to determine what should be done. (IS 21)

ANSI.
See American National Standards Institute. (HW 12)

Antivirus software.
Software used to detect and eliminate computer viruses. (LIV 42)

APL.
An acronym for A Programming Language. APL is a highly compact programming language popular for problem-solving applications. (IS 48)

Applet.
A small program that provides a dynamic or interactive quality to a Web page. (NET 110)

Applications.
See Applications software. (SW 5)

Applications generator.
A fourth-generation-language product that can be used to quickly create applications software. (IS 50)

Applications package.
A fourth-generation-language product that, when the user sets a few parameters, becomes a finished applications program ready to meet specific needs. (IS 37)

Applications software.
Programs that provide tools for performing the type of work that people acquire computer systems to do; commonly called applications programs or applications. Contrasts with systems software. (INT 11, SW 5)

Applications software development.
The process of designing, coding, debugging and testing, maintaining, and documenting applications software. (IS 36)

Arithmetic/logic unit (ALU).
The part of the CPU that contains circuitry to perform arithmetic and logical operations. (HW 6)

ARPANET.
The forerunner to the Internet, named after the Advanced Research Projects Agency (ARPA), which sponsored its development. (NET 49)

Artificial intelligence (AI).
The ability of a machine to perform actions that are characteristic of human intelligence, such as reasoning and learning. (IS 15)

ASCII.
A fixed-length, binary coding system widely used to represent data for computer processing and communications. (HW 12)

Assembler.
A language translator that converts assembly language instructions into machine language. (SW 59)

Assembly language.
A low-level programming language that uses mnemonic codes in place of the 0s and 1s of machine language. (IS 44)

Note: This glossary shows entries for all 16 chapters of the text. You may have a customized version of the text that may not contain all of the chapters indicated.

Asynchronous transmission.
The transmission of data over a line one character at a time, with variable time intervals between characters. Contrasts with synchronous transmission. (NET 35)

Audit.
An inspection used to determine if a system or procedure is working as it should or if claimed amounts are correct. (LIV 43)

Authentication.
The process of determining that a person is who he or she claims to be. (LIV 41)

Authoring software.
Applications generators designed to help users and programmers more easily create applications in such areas as multimedia, the Internet, and virtual reality. (IS 51)

B

Backbone.
The part of a network that carries the most traffic. (NET 24)

Backup.
A procedure that produces a duplicate version of any file that you can't afford to lose. (LIV 14)

Bandwidth.
The difference between the highest and lowest frequencies that a transmission medium can accommodate. (NET 19)

Bar chart.
A presentation graphic that uses side-by-side columns as the principal charting element. (PS 51)

Bar code.
A machine-readable code that stores data as sets of bars of varying widths. (HW 92)

BASIC.
An easy-to-learn, high-level programming language developed at Dartmouth College in the 1960s. (IS 45)

Batch processing.
Processing transactions or other data in groups, at periodic intervals. Contrasts with transaction processing. (HW 72)

BBS.
See Bulletin board system. (NET 5)

Benchmark test.
A test used to measure computer system performance under typical use conditions prior to purchase. (IS 25)

Beta test.
A term that refers to sending a preliminary version or release of a program to users for evaluation purposes. (IS 56)

Binary.
The numbering system with two possible states. (HW 10, HW 40)

Biometric security device.
A device that, upon recognition of some physiological or learned characteristic that is unique to a person, allows that person to have access to a system. (LIV 41)

Bit.
A binary digit, such as 0 or 1. (HW 10)

Bit mapping.
A graphical output technique in which software individually controls each pixel in a screen image. (HW 104)

Bits per second (bps).
A measure of a transmission medium's speed. (NET 19)

Blocking software.
A program that blocks access to certain parts of the Internet deemed objectionable, based on predetermined criteria. (NET 121)

Board.
A hardware device into which processor and memory chips are fitted, along with related circuitry. (HW 18)

Bookmark.
A place in a program or application that you can immediately go to after selecting the associated menu choice. (NET 69)

Boolean search.
Retrieval of data by using keywords such as AND, OR, and NOT when specifying filtering conditions. (NET 77)

Boot.
The process of loading the operating system into the computer system's RAM. (SW 37)

Bps.
See Bits per second. (NET 19)

Bridge.
An interface that enables two similar networks to communicate. Contrasts with gateway. (NET 33)

Browser.
A software tool that makes it easy for users to find and display Web pages. (NET 67)

Bulletin board system (BBS).
A computer file that is shared by several people, enabling them to post or broadcast messages. (NET 5)

Bug.
An error in a program or system. (IS 55)

Bus.
An electronic path within a computer system along which bits are transmitted. (HW 26)

Bus network.
A telecommunications network consisting of a transmission line with lines dropped off for several devices. (NET 24)

Byte.
A configuration of 8 bits that represents a single character of data. (HW 13)

C

C.
A programming language that has the portability of a high-level language and the executional efficiency of an assembly language. (IS 46)

C++.
A variant of the C language that is more widely used today than C itself. (IS 46)

Cache memory.
A storage area, faster than RAM, where the computer stores data it has most recently accessed. (HW 22)

CAD.
See Computer-aided design. (IS 12)

CAD/CAM.
An acronym for computer-aided design/computer-aided manufacturing. CAD/CAM is a general term applied to the use of computer technology to automate design and manufacturing operations in industry. (IS 12)

Callback device.
A device on the receiving end of a communications network that verifies the authenticity of the sender by calling the sender back. (LIV 42)

Caller identification.
Refers to the use of a telephone or answering device that displays the origin of incoming calls. (LIV 49)

CAM.
See Computer-aided manufacturing. (IS 13)

Cartridge tape.
Magnetic tape in which the supply and take-up reels are contained in a small plastic case. (HW 66)

Cascading.
The overlapping of windows on a display. Contrasts with tiling. (SW 20)

CASE.
See Computer-aided software engineering. (IS 59)

Case control structure.
A control structure that can be formed by nesting two or more selection control structures. (IS 41)

Cathode-ray tube (CRT).
A display device that projects images on a long-necked display tube similar to that in a television set. (HW 102)

CD-ROM.
A low-end optical disk that allows a drive to read data but not write it. (HW 63)

Cell.
The part of the worksheet that can hold a single constant value or formula; defined by the intersection of a row and column. (PS 37)

Cell address.
The column/row combination that uniquely identifies a spreadsheet cell. (PS 37)

Cell pointer.
A cursorlike mechanism used in the worksheet area to point to cells, thereby making them active. Also called the *highlight.* (PS 39)

Cellular phone.
A mobile phone that uses special ground stations called cells to process calls and communicate with the regular phone system. (NET 17)

Central processing unit (CPU).
The piece of equipment, also known as the *computer,* that interprets and executes program instructions and communicates with support devices. (INT 6)

Chat.
An Internet feature that supports interactive discussion groups on selected topics. (NET 60)

Check box.
A screen choice that requires the user to toggle an accompanying check mark on or off, respectively, indicating whether the choice is selected or not. (SW 23)

Client.
A device designed to receive service in a client-server network. Contrasts with server. (NET 28)

Client-server LAN.
A LAN composed of *client* devices, which receive services, and *server* devices, which provide the services. Contrasts with peer-to-peer LAN. (NET 28)

Clip art.
Prepackaged artwork designed to be imported into text documents or charts, say, by word processing, desktop publishing, or presentation graphics software. (PS 20)

Cluster.
An area formed where a fixed number of contiguous sectors intersect a track. (HW 51)

Coaxial cable.
A transmission medium consisting of a center wire inside a grounded, cylindrical shield capable of sending data at high speeds. (NET 14)

COBOL.
A high-level programming language developed for transaction processing applications. (IS 45)

Coding.
The creation of programming-language instructions. (IS 54)

COM.
See Computer output microfilm. (HW 115)

Communications medium.
The intervening link, such as a telephone wire or cable, that connects two physically distant hardware devices. (NET 13)

Communications satellite.
An earth-orbiting microwave-repeater device that relays communications signals over long distances. (NET 16)

Compiler.
A language translator that converts an entire program into machine language before executing it. Contrasts with interpreter. (SW 58)

Computer.
The piece of equipment, also known as the *central processing unit (CPU),* that interprets and executes program instructions and communicates with peripheral devices. (INT 6)

Computer-aided design (CAD).
A general term applied to the use of computer technology to automate design functions. (IS 12)

Computer-aided manufacturing (CAM).
A general term applied to the use of computer technology to automate manufacturing functions. (IS 13)

Computer-aided software engineering (CASE).
Program products that automate systems-development and program-development activities. (IS 59)

Computer crime.
The use of computers to commit criminal acts. (LIV 35)

Computer output microfilm (COM).
A system for reducing computer output to microscopic form and storing it on photosensitive film. (HW 115)

Computer system.
A collection of elements that includes the computer and components that contribute to making it a useful tool. (INT 6)

Computer virus.
A small block of unauthorized code, concealed and transmitted from computer to computer, that performs destructive acts when executed. (LIV 36)

Concentrator.
A communications device that combines control and multiplexing functions. (NET 33)

Connect time.
The amount of time you spend online with a service provider's computers. (NET 82)

Constant value.
A cell entry that contains text or a numeric value. Contrasts with formula. (PS 40)

Context sensitive.
A characteristic of a user interface that adjusts program actions to accommodate the type of operation the user is currently performing. (SW 21)

Control panel.
The portion of the screen display used for issuing commands and observing what is being typed into the computer system. (PS 38)

Control structure.
A pattern for controlling the flow of logic in a computer program. (IS 41)

Control unit.
The part of the CPU that coordinates its operations. (HW 6)

Cookies.
Small files stored on your hard drive by your browser at the request of the Web servers you visit. (NET 69)

Coprocessor.
A dedicated processor chip that is summoned by the CPU to perform specialized types of processing. (HW 21)

CPU.
See Central processing unit. (INT 6)

Cross compatible.
Refers to a software or hardware product that can work with products from other vendors. (LIV 23)

CRT.
See Cathode-ray tube. (HW 102)

Cryptography.
The field that deals with the art and science of encryption. (LIV 41)

Current cell.
In spreadsheet software, the worksheet cell at which the highlight is currently positioned. (PS 39)

Cursor.
A screen character indicating where the next input made by the user is to be entered. (HW 98)

Cyberphobia.
The fear of computers. (LIV 33)

D

DAT.
An acronym for digital audio tape, DAT is a magnetic tape-cartridge standard. (HW 67)

Data.
A collection of raw, unorganized facts. (INT 7)

Data access.
The process of fetching data either sequentially or directly from a storage device. (HW 70)

Database.
An integrated collection of related data files. (INT 14, PS 70)

Database administrator.
The person or group of people in charge of designing, implementing, and managing the ongoing operation of a database. (PS 83)

Database management system (DBMS).
A software product designed to integrate data and provide easy access to them. (PS 70)

Data bus.
The bus that links the CPU to RAM. (HW 27)

Data compression.
A utility function that squeezes data into a smaller storage space than it would normally require. (SW 54)

Data definition.
The process of describing the characteristics of data that are to be handled by a database management system. (PS 74)

Data definition language (DDL).
A language used to create, store, and manage data in a database environment. (PS 88)

Data dictionary.
A facility that informs users and programmers about characteristics of data and programs in a database or a computer system. (PS 77, IS 55)

Data flow diagram.
A graphically oriented systems development tool that enables a systems analyst to logically represent the flow of data through a system. (IS 22)

Data manipulation.
The process of using program commands to add, delete, modify, or retrieve data in a file or database. (PS 77)

Data manipulation language (DML).
A language used by programmers to supplement a high-level language supported in a database environment. (PS 89)

Data mining.
Intelligent software that can analyze data warehouses for patterns that management may not even realize exist and to infer rules from these patterns. (PS 87)

Data organization.
The process of setting up data so that they may subsequently be accessed in some desired way. (HW 70)

Data processing area.
The group of computer professionals charged with building and operating transaction processing systems. (IS 18)

Data warehouse.
A comprehensive collection of data that describes the operations of a company. (PS 87)

DBA.
See Database administrator. (PS 83)

DBMS.
See Database management system. (PS 70)

DDL.
See Data definition language. (PS 88)

Debugging.
The process of detecting and correcting errors in computer programs or in the computer system itself. (IS 55)

Decimal.
The numbering system with ten symbols—0, 1, 2, 3, 4, 5, 6, 7, 8, and 9. (HW 39)

Decision support system (DSS).
A type of information system that provides people with tools and capabilities to help them satisfy their own information needs. (IS 8)

Declarative language.
An applications-development product in which the user or developer can tell the computer that a task needs doing and the computer automatically knows how to do it. Contrasts with procedural language. (IS 48)

Default.
The assumption that a computer program makes when the user indicates no specific choice. (SW 36)

Defragmentation.
The process of rewriting a program that is stored in noncontiguous clusters into contiguous clusters. (SW 55)

Design.
The process that defines the look of a product as well as how it will work. (NET 104)

Desktop computer.
A microcomputer system designed to fit on a desktop. Contrasts with portable computer. (INT 21)

Desktop publishing.
A PC-based publishing system that can fit on a desktop. (PS 24)

Detachable-reel tape.
Magnetic tape wound onto a single reel, which in turn is mounted next to an empty take-up reel onto a tape drive. (HW 68)

Device driver.
A utility program that enables an operating system to communicate with a specific hardware device. (SW 57)

DHTML.
See Dynamic HTML. (NET 113)

Dialog box.
A box that requires the user to supply information to the computer system about the task being performed. (SW 23)

Digital.
The representation and transmission of data as 0 and 1 bits. Contrasts with analog. (NET 19)

Digital camera.
A camera that records pictures as digital data instead of as film images. (HW 94)

Digital computer.
A device that counts. (HW 4)

Direct access.
Reading or writing data in storage so that the access time is independent of the physical location of the data. Also known as *random access.* Contrasts with sequential access. (HW 50)

Direct conversion.
A strategy for converting to a new system that involves completely deactivating the old system and then fully implementing the new system. (IS 25)

Direct manufacturer.
A maker of hardware or software that sells directly to the public. (LIV 9)

Direct organization.
A method of arranging data on a storage device so they can be accessed directly (randomly). (HW 75)

Directory.
A collection of files grouped under a name of its own. Also commonly called a *folder.* (SW 38)

Disaster-recovery plan.
A plan that maps out what an organization does to prepare for and react to disruptive events. (LIV 40)

Disk access time.
The time taken to locate and read (or position and write) data on a disk device. (HW 58)

Disk cache.
A disk-management scheme that directs a drive to read more data than necessary for an immediate processing task during each disk fetch; a part of RAM stores the extra data to minimize the number of disk fetches. (HW 58)

Disk cylinder.
On a disk pack, a collection of tracks that align vertically in the same relative position on different disk surfaces. (HW 57)

Disk drive.
A direct-access secondary storage device that uses a magnetic or optical disk as the principal medium. (HW 54)

Diskette.
A low-capacity, removable disk made of a tough, flexible plastic and coated with a magnetizable substance. (HW 50)

Disk utility.
A program that assists users with such disk-related tasks as backup, data compression, space allocation, and the like. (SW 54)

Display device.
An output device that contains a viewing screen. Also called a *monitor.* (HW 98)

Distributed database.
A database whose contents are split up over several locations. (PS 86)

DML.
See Data manipulation language. (PS 89)

Document.
Any single piece of work that's created with software and then given a name by which it may be accessed. (INT 12)

Documentation.
A description of how a program, procedure, or system works. (IS 57, LIV 18)

Document-centered computing.
A view of computing in which the document itself is more central than the applications program or programs in which it was created. (SW 6)

Domain name.
A ordered group of symbols, separated by periods, that identifies an Internet server. (NET 65)

Dot-matrix character.
A character composed from a rectangular matrix of dots. (HW 105)

Dot pitch.
The distance between display-screen pixels, in millimeters. (HW 99)

DOUNTIL control structure.
A looping control structure in which the looping continues as long as a certain condition is false ("do *until* true"). (IS 41)

DOWHILE control structure.
A looping control structure in which the looping continues as long as a certain condition is true ("do *while* true"). (IS 41)

Downloading.
The process of transferring a file from a remote computer to a requesting computer over a network. Contrasts with uploading. (NET 31)

Downward compatible.
Refers to a software product that enables a user to save files in a form that is acceptable to an earlier version or release of the product. Contrasts with upward compatible. (LIV 23)

Dragging and dropping.
The process of moving an item from one part of the screen to another with a mouse. (HW 86)

DRAM.
An acronym for dynamic random access memory, DRAM refers to a type of memory chip that needs to be regularly recharged as processing is taking place. (HW 21)

Drop cap.
A large, decorative capital letter that sometimes appears at the beginning of an article or chapter of text. (PS 20)

Drop-down menu.
See Pull-down menu. (SW 15)

DSS.
See Decision support system. (IS 8)

Dumb terminal.
A workstation, consisting of a display and keyboard, that can do little more than send and receive data. (NET 24)

DVD.
An optical-disk standard that enables very high capacities. (HW 65)

Dynamic HTML (DHTML).
A version of HTML that adds elements enabling the look of Web pages to change. (NET 113)

E

EBCDIC.
A fixed-length, binary coding system widely used to represent data on IBM mainframes. (HW 12)

E-cycle.
The part of the machine cycle in which the CPU locates data, carries out an instruction, and stores the results. Contrasts with I-cycle. (HW 8)

EDI.
See Electronic data interchange. (NET 11)

EIS.
See Executive information system. (IS 9)

Electronic data interchange (EDI).
A computer procedure that enables firms to electronically exchange standard business documents-such as purchase orders and invoices. (NET 11)

Electronic mail.
The computer-to-computer counterpart for interoffice mail or the postal service. Also called *e-mail.* (NET 4, NET 53, IS 10)

Electronic mailbox.
A storage area on a hard disk used to hold messages, memos, and other documents for the receiver. (NET 5)

E-mail.
See Electronic mail. (NET 4, NET 53, IS 10)

Encryption.
A method of protecting data or programs so that they are unrecognizable to unauthorized users. (LIV 41)

End-user development.
Systems development carried out by users. (IS 28)

Enterprise resource planning (ERP).
The use of technology to integrate many of the key operations of an organization into a single, networked system. (IS 14)

Ergonomics.
The field that studies the effects of things such as computer hardware, software, and workspaces on people's comfort and health. (LIV 33)

ERP.
See Enterprise resource planning. (IS 14).

Ethernet.
A collection of protocols that specify a standard way of setting up a bus-based LAN. (NET 36)

Ethics.
A term that refers to standards of moral conduct. (LIV 49)

Executive information system (EIS).
A decision support system tailored to the needs of a specific, top-level individual in an organization. (IS 9)

Expansion bus.
The path that extends the data bus so that it links with peripheral devices. (HW 27)

Expansion slot.
A socket inside the system unit into which an add-in board is plugged. (HW 25)

Expert system.
A program or computer system that provides the type of advice that would be expected from a human expert. (IS 15)

Expert system shell.
A prepackaged expert system that lacks only a knowledge base. (IS 17)

Extranet.
An extension of an organizational intranet onto the Internet itself. (NET 29)

F

Facsimile.
A method for transmitting text documents, pictures, maps, diagrams, and the like over the phone lines. Abbreviated as *fax.* (NET 5, IS 10)

FAQs.
See Frequently asked questions. (NET 59)

Fault-tolerant computing.
Refers to computer systems that are built with important circuitry duplicated for backup purposes. (SW 43)

Fax.
See Facsimile. (NET 5, IS 10)

Fiber-optic cable.
A transmission medium composed of hundreds of hair-thin, transparent fibers along which lasers carry data as light waves. (NET 14)

Field.
A collection of related characters. (INT 14)

Field descriptor.
A code used to describe the type of data—say, numeric, text, logical—that occupy a given field in a data record. (PS 76)

File.
A collection of related records. (INT 14)

File directory.
A listing on a storage medium that provides such data as name, length, and starting address for each stored file. (HW 54)

File extension.
A group of characters appended to the main part of a filename to qualify it or to identify a specific type of file. (SW 36)

File manager.
A productivity software package used to manage records and files. (PS 73)

File structure.
A collection of information about the records of a file, including the names, lengths, and types of the fields. (PS 75)

File transfer protocol (FTP).
A communications protocol that facilitates the transfer of files between a host computer and a user's computer. (NET 57)

Film recorder.
A device that converts computer output to film. (HW 115)

Firewall.
A collection of hardware or software intended to protect a company's internal computer networks from outside attack. (LIV 41)

Flat file.
A file that is not interrelated with others. (PS 73)

Flat-panel display.
A slim-profile display device. (HW 102)

Floppy disk.
See Diskette. (HW 50)

Flowchart.
A series of boxes or other symbols, connected by lines, that shows how ideas fit together. (NET 105)

Folder.
A container for documents. (INT 13, SW 38)

Font.
A typeface in a particular point size—for instance, 12-point Helvetica. (PS 15)

Formatting.
The process of organizing a disk so that it is usable in a particular operating environment. (HW 51)

Formula.
A cell entry that is used to change the contents of other cells. Contrasts with constant value. (PS 40)

FORTRAN.
A high-level programming language used for mathematical, scientific, and engineering applications. (IS 47)

Fourth-generation language (4GL).
An easy-to-learn, easy-to-use language that enables users or programmers to develop applications much more quickly than they could with third-generation languages. (IS 48)

Fragmented file.
A file on disk that is split up into many noncontiguous areas, making access harder. (SW 55)

Freeware.
Software offered for use without charge. (SW 9)

Frequently asked questions (FAQs).
Typical questions asked by newcomers to Internet newsgroups, mailing lists, and chat rooms, accompanied by the answers to those questions. (NET 59)

FTP.
See File transfer protocol. (NET 57)

Full backup.
A procedure that produces a duplicate copy of all files onto a secondary storage medium. Contrasts with partial backup. (LIV 14)

Full-duplex transmission.
A type of transmission in which messages may be sent in two directions simultaneously along a communications path. (NET 34)

Function.
A prestored formula for a standard calculation. (PS 42)

Functionally obsolete.
A term that refers to a product that no longer meets the needs of an individual or business. (LIV 23)

Function key.
A special keyboard key that executes a preprogrammed routine when depressed. (HW 85)

G

Gateway.
An interface that enables two dissimilar networks to communicate. Contrasts with bridge. (NET 33)

GB.
See Gigabyte. (HW 13)

GDSS.
See Group decision support system. (IS 8)

Ghosted.
Refers to a menu choice that has a faded appearance, indicating that the choice is unavailable in the current context. (SW 16)

Gigabyte (GB).
Approximately 1 billion bytes. (HW 13)

Gopher.
An information-retrieval tool for the Internet that generates hierarchical, text-intensive menus. (NET 57)

Grammar checker.
Software that checks for errors in word usage. (PS 10)

Graphical user interface (GUI).
A term that refers to the graphics screens that make it easier for users to interact with software. (SW 11)

Graphics tablet.
An input device that consists of a flat board and a pointing mechanism that traces over it, storing the traced pattern in computer memory. (HW 88)

Group decision support system (GDSS).
A decision support system that helps several people to routinely interact through a computer network to solve common problems. (IS 8)

Groupware.
Software that enables several people to collaborate in their work. (NET 8)

GUI.
See Graphical user interface. (SW 11)

H

Hacking.
Using a microcomputer system or terminal to penetrate the security of a remote computer system. (LIV 38)

Half-duplex transmission.
Any type of transmission in which messages may be sent in two directions—but only one way at a time—along a communications path. (NET 34)

Handwriting recognition device.
A device that can identify handwritten characters. (HW 96)

Hard copy.
A permanent form of computer system output—for example, information printed on paper or film. Contrasts with soft copy. (HW 85)

Hard disk.
A system consisting of one or more rigid platters and an access mechanism. (HW 55)

Hard return.
A line break inserted when the user presses the Enter key to control line spacing in a document. Contrasts with soft return. (PS 7)

Hardware.
Physical equipment in a computing environment, such as the computer and its peripheral devices. Contrasts with software. (INT 11)

Hashing.
A mathematical transformation in which a record's key field determines where the record is stored. (HW 75)

Helper package.
A program designed to work alongside another program. (NET 74)

Hexadecimal.
The numbering system with 16 symbols—0, 1, 2, 3, 4, 5, 6, 7, 8, 9, A, B, C, D, E, and F. (HW 42)

Hierarchical database management system.
A DBMS that stores data in the form of a tree, where the relationship between data elements is one-to-many. (PS 82)

Hierarchical local network.
A local network in which a relatively powerful host CPU at the top of the hierarchy interacts with workstations at the bottom. (NET 30)

High-level language.
The class of programming languages that includes BASIC, COBOL, C, FORTRAN, and Pascal. (IS 45)

Highlight.
See Cell pointer. (PS 39)

History list.
A browser feature that stores descriptions and addresses of the last several Web sites you visited. (NET 69)

Hit.
One request for access to a page or graphics file made to a server computer. (NET 119)

Home page.
The starting page for a Web site. (NET 57)

Host computer.
The main computer in a network. (NET 24)

Host language.
A programming language used to code database applications. (PS 90)

Hot swappable.
Refers to a hardware device that can be brought online or offline without power to the main computer system being shut off. (HW 28)

HTML.
See Hypertext markup language. (NET 108)

HTML converter.
A program designed to produce Web pages from documents already existing in other formats. (NET 116)

HTML Wizard.
A program that automatically generates Web pages from screen selections made by the user. (NET 114)

Hyperlink.
An icon, image, or specially marked text that represents a link to a new file, application, or Web page. Also called *hyperme-*

dia. (NET 56, SW 19)

Hypermedia.
See Hyperlink. (NET 56)

Hypertext markup language (HTML).
The most widely used language for developing Web pages. (NET 108)

I

Icon.
A graphical image on a display screen that invokes some action when selected. (SW 16)

I-cycle.
The part of the machine cycle in which the control unit fetches a program instruction from memory and prepares it for subsequent processing. Contrasts with E-cycle. (HW 8)

If-then-else control structure.
See Selection control structure. (IS 41)

Illustration program.
A program that enables users to paint, draw, or manipulate photographs. (PS 28)

Imagemap.
A screen image with embedded hyperlinks. (SW 17)

Image scanner.
A device that can read into computer memory a hard-copy image such as a text page, photograph, map, or drawing. (HW 93)

Impact dot-matrix printer.
A device with a print head holding multiple pins, which strike an inked ribbon in various combinations to form characters on paper. (HW 105)

Impact printing.
A technology that forms characters by striking a pin or hammer against an inked ribbon, which presses the desired shape onto paper. Contrasts with nonimpact printing. (HW 105)

Indexed organization.
A method of organizing data on a direct-access storage medium so that they can be accessed directly (through an index) or sequentially. (HW 72)

Indexing.
A procedure that creates a table, or index, that specifies how data records are to be arranged on output. (PS 79)

Inference engine.
A program used to apply rules to the knowledge base in order to reach decisions. (IS 16)

Information.
Data that have been processed into a meaningful form. (INT 8)

Information reporting system.
An information system whose principal outputs are preformatted reports. (IS 8)

Information system.
A system designed to provide information to enable people to make decisions. (IS 7)

Information systems department.
The area in an organization that consists of computer professionals. (IS 18)

Infrared transmission.
Communications in which data are sent as infrared light rays. (NET 18)

Ink-jet printer.
A printer that forms images by spraying droplets of charged ink onto a page. (HW 107)

Input.
What is supplied to a computer process. Contrasts with output. (INT 6)

Input device.
A piece of hardware through which a user supplies data and programs to the computer. Contrasts with output device. (INT 6, HW 85)

Insertion point.
A cursor character that shows where the next key pressed will appear onscreen. (PS 6)

Instruction.
A statement in a computer-programming language that causes the computer to take an action. (HW 17)

Instruction set.
The set of machine-level instructions available to a computer. (HW 17)

Integrated software program.
A collection of abbreviated software products bundled together into a single package and sold at price that is less than the sum of the prices of the individual components. (SW 6)

Internet.
A global network linking thousands of networks and millions of individual users, businesses, schools, and government agencies. (NET 7, NET 48)

Internet address.
A unique identifier assigned to a specific location on the Internet, such as a host computer, Web site, or user mailbox. (NET 65)

Internet content provider.
An organization or individual providing information for distribution over the Internet. (NET 51)

Internet presence provider (IPP).
An organization whose server computers host Web pages. (NET 102)

Internet relay chat (IRC).
An Internet feature that allows people to type messages to others and to get responses in real time. (NET 60)

Internet service provider (ISP).
An organization that provides basic access to the Internet. (NET 50)

Interpreter.
A language translator that converts program statements line by line into machine language, immediately executing each one. Contrasts with compiler. (SW 58)

Intranet.
A private network-often one set up by a company for employees-that implements the infrastructure and standards of the Internet and World Wide Web. (NET 29)

IPP.
See Internet presence provider. (NET 102)

IRC.
See Internet relay chat. (NET 60)

ISA.
A popular PC bus standard; stands for Industry Standard Architecture. (HW 27)

ISDN.
A digital phone service that offers high-speed transmission over ordinary phone lines. Stands for Integrated Services Digital Network. (NET 23)

ISP.
See Internet service provider. (NET 50)

Iteration control structure.
See Looping control structure. (IS 41)

J

Java.
A programming language, created at Sun Microsystems, that is used to add interactive or dynamic features to Web pages. (NET 110)

Joystick.
An input device that resembles a car's gear shift. (HW 87)

K

KB.
See Kilobyte. (HW 13)

Key field.
A field that helps identify a record. (HW 70)

Keyboard.
An input device composed of numerous keys, arranged in a configuration similar to that of a typewriter, that generate letters, numbers, and other symbols when depressed. (HW 85)

Kilobyte (KB).
Approximately 1,000 bytes (1,024, to be exact). (HW 13)

Kiosk.
A computer station—often located in a store, lobby, or exhibit—that provides users information through an easy-to-use input mechanism such as a touch screen. (HW 87)

Knowledge base.
The part of the expert system that contains specific facts about the expert area and any rules the expert system will use to make decisions based on those facts. (IS 16)

L

LAN.
See Local area network. (NET 27)

Landscape.
An output mode with images more wide than high. Contrasts with portrait. (HW 101)

Language translator.
Systems software that converts applications programs into machine language. (SW 58)

Laptop computer.
A portable personal computer weighing about 8 to 15 pounds. (INT 21)

Laser printer.
A printer that works on a principle similar to that of a photocopier. (HW 106)

LCD.
An acronym for liquid-crystal display, LCD refers to flat-panel displays that use charged liquid crystals to provide light and special color filters to paint the screen. (HW 102–103)

Legacy system.
See Technologically obsolete. (LIV 23)

Light pen.
An electrical device, resembling an ordinary pen, used to enter computer input. (HW 86)

Line chart.
A presentation graphic in which the principal charting element is an unbroken line. (PS 53)

Line printer.
A high-speed printer that produces output a line at a time. (HW 111)

LISP.
A language used widely for artificial-intelligence applications. (IS 48)

List box.
A screen-window panel that requires the user to select an item from a predetermined list. (SW 23)

Local area network (LAN).
A local network, without a host computer, usually comprised of microcomputer workstations and shared peripherals. Contrasts with wide-area network. (NET 27)

Local bus.
A bus that connects the CPU directly to peripheral devices that require the most speed. (HW 28)

Local network.
A privately run communications network of several machines located within a few miles or so of one another. (NET 27)

Logic error.
An error that results when a running program is producing incorrect results. Also called a *run-time error.* Contrasts with syntax error. (IS 55)

Logo.
A computer language often used to teach children how to program. (IS 48)

Looping (iteration) control structure.
The control structure used to represent a looping operation. (IS 41)

Low-level language.
A highly detailed, machine-dependent class of programming languages. (IS 44)

M

Machine cycle.
The series of operations involved in the execution of a single machine-level instruction. (HW 8)

Machine language.
A binary-based programming language that the computer can execute directly. (HW 17)

Machine-readable form.
Any form that represents data so that computer equipment can read them. (INT 6)

Mac OS.
The operating system for Apple's Macintosh line of computer systems. (SW 48)

Macro.
A predetermined series of keystrokes or commands that can be invoked by a single keystroke or command. (PS 17)

Magnetic disk.
A secondary storage medium that records data through magnetic spots on platters made of rigid metal or flexible plastic. (HW 50)

Magnetic ink character recognition (MICR).
A banking-industry technology that processes checks by sensing special characters inscribed in magnetic ink. (HW 96)

Magnetic tape.
A plastic ribbon with a magnetizable surface that stores data as a series of magnetic spots. (HW 66)

Mailing label feature.
A routine that generates address labels. (PS 18)

Mailing list.
A service through which discussion groups communicate through shared e-mail messages. (NET 59)

Mainframe computer.
A large computer that performs extensive business transaction processing. (INT 24)

Main memory.
The computer system's principal bank of memory; contrasts with memory products such as ROM and flash memory. (HW 8)

Maintenance.
The process of making upgrades and minor modifications to systems or software over time. (IS 56)

Maintenance programmer.
A programmer involved with keeping an organization's existing programs in working order. (IS 37)

Marketing database.
An electronic repository containing information useful for niche-marketing products to consumers. (LIV 48)

Markup language.
A language made up of tags or symbols that describe what a document should look like when displayed. (NET 108)

Master file.
A file that contains relatively permanent, descriptive data about the subject defined by one of the key fields of the file. Contrasts with transaction file. (HW 72)

Maximize.
Enlarging a window so that it fills the entire screen. Contrasts with minimize. (SW 21)

MB.
See Megabyte (HW 13)

Megabyte (MB).
Approximately 1 million bytes. (HW 13)

Memory.
See Primary storage. (INT 9, HW 7)

Menu.
A set of options from which the user chooses to take a desired action. (SW 14)

Menu bar.
A horizontal list of choices that appears on a highlighted line, usually below the window title. Also called the *main menu.* (SW 14)

Merge feature.
A routine specifically designed to produce form letters. (PS 17)

Message box.
A dialog box that pops up on the screen to warn the user or to provide status information. (SW 24)

MICR.
See Magnetic ink character recognition. (HW 96)

Microcode.
Instructions built into the CPU that control the operation of its circuitry. (HW 8)

Microcomputer.
A computer system driven by a microprocessor chip. Also called a *microcomputer system* or micro. (INT 20)

Microcomputer system.
See microcomputer. (INT 20)

Microfiche.
A sheet of film, often four by six inches, on which computer output images are stored. (HW 115)

Microprocessor.
A CPU on a silicon chip. (INT 20)

Microsecond.
One one-millionth of a second. (HW 9)

Microsoft Internet Explorer.
A widely used Web browser. (NET 67)

Microspacing.
A technique used by many printers and software products to insert fractional spaces between characters. (PS 15)

Microwave.
An electromagnetic wave in the high-frequency range. (NET 16)

Midrange computer.
An intermediate-sized and medium-priced computer. (INT 23)

Millisecond.
One one-thousandth of a second. (HW 9)

Minimize.
Reducing a window to an icon on the taskbar. Contrasts with maximize. (SW 21)

Mixed cell referencing.
Copying formulas in one range of cells into another range, while varying some cell references and leaving others constant. (PS 46)

MMX.
A technology used on recent Intel computer chips to enhance multimedia processing. (HW 18)

Modem.
A communications device that enables digital computers and their support devices to communicate over analog media. (NET 22)

Monitor.
A display device without a keyboard. (HW 98)

Monochrome.
A term used to refer to a device that produces outputs in a single foreground color. (HW 102)

Monospacing.
A printing feature that allocates the same amount of space on a line to each character. Contrasts with proportional spacing. (PS 15)

Mosaic.
A freeware tool that was the first GUI Web browser to gain wide acceptance; most commercial browsers today are enhanced forms of Mosaic. (NET 67)

Motherboard.
See System board. (HW 18)

Mouse.
A common pointing device that you slide along a flat surface to move a pointer around a display screen and make selections. (HW 86)

Mouse pointer.
An onscreen, context-sensitive symbol that corresponds to movements made by a mouse. (HW 86)

MS-DOS.
An operating system widely used on early PC-compatible microcomputer systems. (SW 44)

Multimedia.
A term that refers to computer systems and applications that involve a combination of text, graphics, audio, and video data. (INT 8)

Multiplexer.
A communications device that interleaves the messages of several low-speed devices and sends them along a single high-speed path. (NET 33)

Multiprocessing.
A technique for simultaneous execution of two or more program sequences by multiple processors operating under common control. (SW 43)

Multiprogramming.
Concurrent execution of two or more programs on a single computer. (SW 41)

Multitasking.
A capability of an operating system to execute for a single user two or more programs or program tasks concurrently. (SW 41)

Multithreading.
The capability of a task to be divided into small pieces that provide improved operating-system response. (SW 41)

N

Nanosecond.
One one-billionth of a second. (HW 9)

Natural-language interface.
Software that allows users to communicate with the computer in a conversational language such as English, Spanish, or Japanese. (IS 52)

Netiquette.
Proper etiquette for exchanges on the Internet. (NET 59)

Netscape Navigator.
A widely used Web browser. (NET 67)

NetWare.
The most widely used operating system on local area networks (LANs). (SW 52)

Network.
A system of machines that communicate with one another. (INT 16)

Network computer.
A stripped-down desktop microcomputer that is optimized for the Internet and intracompany communications. (INT 21)

Network database management system.
A DBMS in which the relationship between data elements can be either many-to-one or many-to-many. (PS 82)

Network interface card (NIC).
An add-in board though which a workstation connects to a local network. (NET 21)

Network operating system (NOS).
An operating system that enables the network administrator in an organization to control network tasks. (SW 48)

Neural-net computing.
An expert-system technology in which the human brain's pattern-recognition process is emulated by a computer system. (IS 17)

Newsgroup.
A service that works like an electronic newspaper, carrying *articles* posted by subscribers and responses to them (together called *threads*). (NET 59)

NIC.
See Network interface card. (NET 21)

Nonimpact printing.
A technology that forms characters and other images on a surface by means of heat, lasers, photography, or ink jets. Contrasts with impact printing. (HW 106)

Noninterlaced.
Refers to a monitor that draws every screen line of pixels on each screen refresh. Contrasts with *interlaced* monitors that draw in every other line. (HW 100)

Nonvolatile storage.
Storage that retains its contents when the power is shut off. Contrasts with volatile storage. (HW 49)

NOS.
See Network operating system. (SW 48)

Notebook computer.
A portable personal computer weighing about six to eight pounds. (INT 21)

O

OA.
See Office automation. (IS 10)

Object.
A storable entity composed of data elements and instructions that apply to the elements. (PS 84)

Object module.
A program that is in compiled form. Contrasts with source module. (SW 58)

Object-oriented database management system.
A DBMS in which two or more types of data—text, graphics, sound, or video—are combined with methods that specify their properties or use. (PS 84)

Object-oriented programming language.
A language that works with objects that encapsulate data and instructions rather than with separate instructions and data. (IS 51)

OCR.
See Optical character recognition. (HW 90)

Office automation (OA).
Computer-based, office-oriented technologies such as word processing, desktop publishing, electronic mail, teleconferencing, and the like. (IS 10)

Offline.
A state that *does not* allow a device to send data to or receive data from other devices. Contrasts with online. (INT 18)

OLE.
An acronym for object linking and embedding, OLE refers to programs and applications that can be nested and launched inside each other. (NET 112)

One-entry-point/one-exit-point rule.
A rule stating that each program control structure will have only one entry point into it and one exit point out of it. (IS 41)

Online.
A state that allows a device to send data to or receive data from other devices. Contrasts with offline. (INT 18)

Operating environment.
A term that refers to a user interface or operating system—for instance, DOS, DOS-with-Windows, and Windows. (SW 46)

Operating system.
The main collection of systems software that enables the computer system to manage the resources under its control. (SW 34)

Optical character recognition (OCR).
The use of reflected light to input marks, characters, or codes. (HW 90)

Optical disk.
A disk read by reflecting pulses of laser beams. (HW 63)

Output.
The results of a computer process. Contrasts with input. (INT 6)

Output device.
A piece of hardware that accepts data and programs from the computer. Contrasts with input device. (INT 6, HW 85)

Outsourcing.
The practice by which one company hires another company to do some or all of its information-processing activities. (IS 19)

P

Packet switching.
A transmission technique that breaks messages into smaller units that travel to a destination along possibly different paths. (NET 39)

Page description language (PDL).
A language for communicating instructions to a printer. (PS 26)

Page-makeup software.
A program used to compose page layouts in a desktop publishing system. (PS 27)

Page printer.
A high-speed printer that generates a full page of output at a time. (HW 111)

Palette.
A menu that enables users to choose such attributes as colors and textures. (SW 19)

Palmtop computer.
A portable personal computer that you can hold in your hand. (INT 21)

Parallel conversion.
A strategy for converting to a new system that involves operating both systems in tandem until it is determined that the new system is working correctly. (IS 25)

Parallel processing.
A computing system in which two or more CPUs share work, simultaneously processing separate parts of it. (HW 30)

Parallel transmission.
Data transmission in which each bit in a byte has its own path and all of the bits in a byte are transmitted simultaneously. Contrasts with serial transmission. (NET 20)

Parity bit.
An extra bit added to the byte representation of characters to ensure there is always either an odd or even number of 1 bits transmitted with every character. (HW 14)

Partial backup.
A procedure that produces a duplicate copy of selected files onto a secondary storage medium. Contrasts with full backup. (LIV 15)

Pascal.
A structured, high-level programming language that is often used to teach programming. (IS 46)

Passive-matrix.
Refers to a flat-panel display technology that provides adequate but not outstandingly sharp screen images. Contrasts with active-matrix. (HW 103)

Password.
A word or number used to permit selected individuals access to a system. (LIV 40)

Path.
An ordered list of directories that lead to a particular file or directory. (SW 39)

PBX.
See Private branch exchange. (NET 31)

PC.
See Personal computer. (INT 20)

PC card.
A small card that fits into a slot on the exterior of a portable computer to provide new functions. Also called a PCMCIA card. (HW 26)

PC compatible.
A personal computer based on Intel microprocessors or compatible chips. (INT 22)

PC-DOS.
The operating system designed for and widely used by early IBM microcomputers. (SW 44)

PCI.
A widely adopted local-bus standard; stands for peripheral component interconnect. (HW 28)

PCMCIA.
An acronym for Personal Computer Memory Card International Association. See also PC Card. (HW 26)

PDA.
An acronym for personal digital assistant. See Palmtop computer. (INT 22)

PDL.
See Page description language. (PS 26)

Peer-to-peer LAN.
A LAN in which all of the user workstations and shared peripheral devices operate on the same level. Contrasts with client-server LAN. (NET 28)

Pentium.
A family of Intel microprocessors. (HW 18)

Peripheral equipment.
The devices that work with a computer. (INT 6)

Personal computer (PC).
A microcomputer system designed to be used by one person at a time. (INT 20)

Phased conversion.
A strategy for converting to a new system that involves implementing the new system modularly. (IS 25)

Picosecond.
One one-trillionth of a second. (HW 9)

Pie chart.
A presentation graphic in which the principal charting element is a pie-shaped image that is divided into slices, each of which represents a share of the whole. (PS 53)

Pilot conversion.
A strategy for converting to a new system that involves testing the new system at one location only initially. (IS 26)

Pipelining.
A CPU feature designed to begin processing a new instruction as soon as the previous instruction reaches the next stage of the machine cycle. (HW 29)

Pixel.
A single dot on a display screen. (HW 99)

PL/I.
A structured, high-level language that can be used for scientific, engineering, and business applications. (IS 48)

Platform.
A foundation technology by which a computer operates. (INT 22)

Plotter.
An output device that prints graphs and diagrams. (HW 114)

Plug-and-play.
The ability of a computer to detect and configure new hardware components. (HW 26)

Plug-in program.
A program that enhances another program with features the latter doesn't have. (NET 74)

Pointing device.
A piece of input hardware that moves an onscreen pointer such as an arrow, cursor, or insertion point. (HW 86)

Pointing stick.
A trackball-like device placed between the keys of many portable computers. (HW 88)

Point-of-sale (POS) system.
A computer system, commonly found in department stores and supermarkets, that uses electronic cash register terminals to collect, process, and store data about sales transactions. (HW 93)

Point size.
A measurement for scaling typefaces. (PS 15)

Port.
A socket on the exterior of a computer's system unit into which a peripheral device may be plugged. (HW 23)

Portable computer.
A microcomputer system that is compact and light enough to be carried about easily, for use at different locations. Contrasts with desktop computer. (INT 21)

Portal.
The page your browser first displays when you turn it on. (NET 69)

Portrait.
An output mode with images more high than wide. Contrasts with landscape. (HW 101)

POS.
See Point-of-sale system. (HW 93)

PPP.
A protocol that resembles SLIP but allows more reliable and secure communications. (NET 81)

Precompiler.
A computer program that translates an extended set of programming language commands into standard commands of the language. (PS 89)

Preliminary investigation.
A brief study of a problem area to assess whether or not a full-scale project should be undertaken. Also called a feasibility study. (IS 21)

Presentation graphic.
A visual image, such as a bar chart or pie chart, that is used to present data in a highly meaningful form. (PS 50)

Presentation graphics software.
A program package used to prepare line charts, bar charts, pie charts-and other information—intensive images—and to present them to an audience. (PS 55)

Primary storage.
Also known as *memory,* this section of the computer system temporarily holds data and program instructions awaiting processing, intermediate results, and processed output. Contrasts with secondary storage. (INT 9, HW 7)

Printer.
A device that records computer output on paper. (HW 105)

Privacy.
In a computer processing context, refers to how information about individuals is used and by whom. (LIV 45)

Private branch exchange (PBX).
A call-switching station dedicated to the transmissions of a single organization. (NET 31)

Procedural language.
A programming language in which the programmer must write code that tells the computer, step-by-step, what to do. Contrasts with declarative language. (IS 48)

Processing.
The conversion of input to output. (INT 6)

Productivity software.
Computer programs, such as word processors and spreadsheets, designed to make workers more productive in their jobs. (INT 11)

Program.
A set of instructions that causes the computer system to perform specific actions. (INT 9)

Program flowchart.
A visual design tool showing step by step how a computer program will process data. (IS 39)

Programmer.
A person who writes, maintains, and tests computer programs. (INT 16, IS 37)

Programming language.
A set of rules used to write computer programs. (INT 9, IS 44)

Project manager.
A systems analyst who is put in charge of a team that is building a large system. (IS 19)

Prompt.
Displayed text or symbols indicating the computer system's readiness to receive user input. (SW 10)

Proportional spacing.
A printing feature that allocates more horizontal space on a line to some characters than to others. Contrasts with monospacing. (PS 15)

Proprietary software.
A software product to which someone owns the rights. (SW 7)

Protocol.
A set of conventions by which machines establish communication with one another in a telecommunications environment. (NET 34)

Prototyping.
A systems development alternative whereby a small model, or prototype, of the system is built before a full-scale systems development effort is undertaken. (IS 27)

Pseudocode.
A technique for structured program design that uses English-like statements to outline the logic of a program. (IS 42)

Pull-down menu.
A menu of subcommands that drops down vertically from a horizontal menu bar or appears alongside another pull-down menu. Also called a *drop-down menu.* (SW 15)

Q

QBE.
See Query by example. (PS 78)

Quality assurance.
The process of making sure quality programs are written in a quality way. (IS 57)

Query by example (QBE).
An onscreen query form in which users can simply illustrate what information they want by filling in filtering criteria. (PS 78)

Queue.
A group of items awaiting computer processing. (SW 44)

R

RAD.
See Rapid applications development. (IS 60)

Radio-button box.
A panel of alternative choices—preceded by round, graphical screen elements—in which one and only one choice can be selected by the user. (SW 23)

RAID.
A storage method that hooks up several small disks in parallel to do the job of a larger disk, but with better performance. (HW 61)

RAM.
See Random access memory. (HW 21)

Random access.
See Direct access. (HW 50)

Random access memory (RAM).
The computer system's main memory. (HW 21)

Range.
A set of contiguous cells arranged in a rectangle. (PS 41)

Rapid applications development (RAD).
Refers to program development tools that help with the quick generation of user interfaces and with the stitching together of reusable code. (IS 60)

Rapid development.
A program-development approach in which a principal objective is delivering a finished product quickly. (IS 58)

Read-only memory (ROM).
A software-in-hardware module from which the computer can read data, but to which it cannot write data. (HW 23)

Read/write head.
The component of a disk access mechanism or tape drive that retrieves or inscribes data. (HW 48)

Realtime processing.
Processing that takes place quickly enough so that results can guide current and future actions. (HW 74)

Recalculation feature.
The ability of spreadsheet software to quickly and automatically recalculate the contents of several cells, based on new operator inputs. (PS 40)

Record.
A collection of related fields. (INT 14)

Redlining.
A word processing feature that provides the electronic equivalent of the editor's red pen. (PS 19)

Reduced instruction set computing (RISC).
A processor design architecture that incorporates fewer instructions in CPU circuitry than do conventional computer systems. (HW 29)

Reference shelf.
A software product that provides a number of handy reference books online. (PS 23)

Register.
A high-speed staging area within the CPU that temporarily stores data during processing. (HW 8)

Relational database management system.
A computer program for database management that links data in related files through common fields. (PS 70)

Relative cell referencing.
Copying formulas in a source range of cells into a target range of cells relative to the row and column coordinates of the cells in the target range. (PS 44)

Release.
A minor upgrade of a software product. (LIV 22)

Repeater.
A device that amplifies signals over a network. (NET 32)

Request for proposal (RFP).
A document containing a general description of a system that an organization wishes to acquire. (IS 23)

Request for quotation (RFQ).
A document distributed to potential vendors containing a list of specific hardware, software, and services that an organization wishes to acquire. (IS 24)

Reusable code.
Program segments that can be reused over and over again in the construction of applications programs. (IS 55)

Rewritable CD.
An optical disk that allows users to repeatedly read from and write to its surface. (HW 65)

RFP.
See Request for proposal. (IS 23)

RFQ.
See Request for quotation. (IS 24)

Ring network.
A telecommunications network that connects machines serially in a closed loop. (NET 24)

RISC.
See Reduced instruction set computing. (HW 29)

Robotics.
The study of robot technology. (IS 17)

ROM.
See Read-only memory. (HW 23)

Root directory.
The topmost directory in a directory structure. (SW 38)

Router.
A device used on WANs to decide the paths along which to send messages. (NET 32)

RPG.
A report-generation language used by small businesses. (IS 48)

Ruler line.
An onscreen element, resembling a physical ruler, that enables you to set line widths, tab settings, indents, and the like. (PS 12)

S

Screen saver.
A software product designed to protect the phosphor coating on the inside of a display screen from damage when the display is turned on but is not used for an extended period. (LIV 17)

Scripting language.
A programming language used to create small programs that supply interactive or dynamic content to HTML documents. (NET 113)

Scroll bar.
A horizontal or vertical bar along an edge of a window that allows the user to view information that will not fit within the window. (SW 22)

SDLC.
See Systems development life cycle. (IS 20)

Search engine.
A software tool used to look for specific information over the Internet. (NET 75)

Secondary storage.
Storage on media such as disk and tape that supplements memory. Contrasts with primary storage. (INT 10)

Sector.
A pie-shaped area on a disk surface. (HW 51)

Security.
A collection of measures for protecting a computer system's hardware, software, and data from damage or tampering. (LIV 18)

Selecting text.
The process of highlighting text on the screen in order to move or copy it, delete it, or apply a special treatment to it. (PS 7)

Selection (if-then-else) control structure.
The control structure used to represent a decision operation. (IS 41)

Sequence control structure.
The control structure used to represent operations that take place sequentially. (IS 41)

Sequential access.
Fetching stored records in the same order in which they are physically arranged on the medium. Contrasts with direct access. (HW 50)

Sequential organization.
Arranging data on a physical medium in either ascending or descending order by the contents of some key field. (HW 71)

Serial transmission.
Data transmission in which every bit in a byte must travel down the same path in succession. (NET 20)

Server.
A computer that manages shared devices, such as laser printers or high-capacity hard disks, on a client-server network. (NET 28)

Shareware.
Software that people can copy and use in exchange for a nominal fee. (SW 8)

Shortcut keystrokes.
Keystrokes that make it possible for commands to be entered with minimal keystroking. (SW 11)

SIMM.
An acronym for single in-line memory module, a SIMM is a board on which RAM chips are mounted. (HW 21)

Simplex transmission.
Any type of transmission in which a message can be sent along a path in only a single prespecified direction. (NET 34)

Site license.
An agreement that allows access by several people in an organization to a proprietary software product. (SW 7)

SLIP.
A version of TCP/IP that enables individuals and organizations to connect to the Internet over ordinary phone lines. (NET 81)

Smart card.
A credit-card-sized piece of plastic with storage and microprocessor. (HW 96)

Soft copy.
A nonpermanent form of computer system output—for example, a screen display. Contrasts with hard copy. (HW 85)

Soft return.
An automatic line return carried out by word-processing software. Contrasts with hard return. (PS 7)

Software.
Computer programs. Contrasts with hardware. (INT 11)

Software piracy.
The unauthorized copying or use of computer programs. (LIV 38)

Software publisher.
A company that creates software. (LIV 9)

Software suite.
A collection of software products bundled together into a single package and sold at price that is less than the sum of the prices of the individual components. (SW 5, LIV 5)

Source data automation.
The process of collecting data at their point of origin in digital form. (HW 89)

Source module.
A program before it is compiled. Contrasts with object module. (SW 58)

Spam.
Unsolicited, bulk electronic mail sent over the Internet. (LIV 47)

Speakers.
Output devices that produce sound. (HW 112)

Spelling checker.
A program or routine that checks for misspelled words. (PS 9)

Spooling program.
A program that manages input or output by temporarily holding it in secondary storage to expedite processing. (SW 43)

Spreadsheet.
A productivity-software program that supports quick creation and manipulation of tables and financial schedules. (PS 36)

SQL.
See Structured query language. (PS 78)

Star network.
A telecommunications network consisting of a host device connected directly to several other devices. (NET 24)

Storage.
An area that holds materials going to or coming from the computer. (INT 6)

Storage media.
Objects that store computer-processed materials. (INT 6)

Storyboard.
An ordered series of sketches that shows what each page in a presentation should look like. (NET 106)

Streaming.
A term often used to describe audio or video transmissions that can begin to be played at a client workstation before their associated files have been fully downloaded. (NET 72)

Structure chart.
A program design tool that shows the hierarchical relationship between program modules. (IS 38)

Structured programming.
An approach to program design that makes program code more systematic and maintainable. (IS 41)

Structured query language (SQL).
A popular language standard for information retrieval in relational databases. (PS 78)

Style sheet.
A collection of design specifications saved as a file for later use to format documents in a particular way. (PS 22)

Subdirectory.
Any directory below the root directory. (SW 38)

Subnotebook computer.
A portable personal computer weighing about two to six pounds. (INT 21)

Supercomputer.
The fastest and most expensive type of computer. (INT 25)

Surge suppressor.
A device that protects a computer system from random electrical power spikes. (LIV 16)

SVGA.
A display-device standard widely used on Pentium-class computers. (HW 104)

Synchronous transmission.
The timed transmission of data over a line one block of characters at a time. Contrasts with asynchronous transmission. (NET 35)

Syntax.
The grammatical rules that govern a language. (SW 10)

Syntax error.
An error that occurs when the programmer has not followed the rules of a language. Contrasts with logic error. (IS 55)

System.
A collection of elements and procedures that interact to accomplish a goal. (IS 4)

System acquisition.
The phase of the systems development life cycle in which equipment, software, or services are acquired from vendors. (IS 23)

System board.
The main circuit board of the computer to which all computer-system components connect. Also called a motherboard. (HW 18)

System clock.
The timing mechanism within the computer system that governs the transmission of instructions and data through the circuits. (HW 8)

System design.
The phase of the systems development life cycle in which the parts of a new system and the relationships among them are formally established. (IS 23)

System implementation.
The phase of systems development that encompasses activities related to making the computer system operational and successful once it is delivered by the vendor. (IS 25)

Systems analysis.
The phase of the systems development life cycle in which a problem area is thoroughly examined to determine what should be done. (IS 21)

Systems analyst.
A person who studies systems in an organization in order to determine what actions need to be taken and how these actions may best be achieved with computer resources. (IS 18, IS 37)

Systems development.
The ongoing process of improving ways of doing work. (IS 4)

Systems development life cycle (SDLC).
The process consisting of the five phases of system development: preliminary investigation, systems analysis, system design, system acquisition, and system implementation. (IS 20)

Systems software.
Background programs, such as the operating system, that enable applications programs to run on a computer system's hardware. Contrasts with applications software. (INT 11, SW 4, SW 34)

System unit.
The hardware unit that houses the CPU and memory, as well as a number of other devices. (HW 18)

T

Table.
In a relational DBMS, an entity with columns and rows that is capable of being interrelated with other database data. (PS 73)

Tag.
An HTML code that sends a document-formatting instruction to a browser. (NET 108)

Tape drive.
A secondary storage device that reads from and writes to magnetic tapes. (HW 66)

Task.
A part of a program that performs a well-defined chore. (SW 41)

Taskbar.
In many versions of Windows, a bottom-of-screen area that enables you to launch applications and observe system-status information. (SW 12)

TB.
See Terabyte. (HW 13)

TCP/IP.
A collection of communications protocols through which PCs accessing the Internet can understand each other and exchange data. (NET 81)

Technologically obsolete.
A term that refers to a product that still meets the needs of an individual or business, although a newer version or release has superseded it in the marketplace. Also called a *legacy system.* (LIV 23)

Telecommunications.
Transmission of data over a distance. (NET 4)

Telecommuting.
Working through one's home and being connected by means of electronic devices to coworkers at remote locations. (NET 10, IS 11)

Teleconferencing.
Using the computer and communications technology to carry on a meeting between people in different locations. (NET 10, IS 10)

Telnet.
A communications protocol that lets workstations serve as terminals to a remote server computer. (NET 58)

Template.
An onscreen form that requires only that the operator fill in a limited number of input values. Alternatively, a pattern or style for documents of a certain type. (PS 22, PS 47, PS 74)

Terabyte (TB).
Approximately 1 trillion bytes. (HW 13)

Terrestrial microwave station.
A ground station that receives microwave signals, amplifies them, and passes them on to another station. (NET 16)

Text box.
A space in a dialog box in which the user is expected to type information. (SW 23)

Text chart.
A presentation graphic in which the principal element is text. (PS 54)

Thermal-transfer printer.
A printer that places images on paper by heating ink from a wax-based ribbon or by heating a special dye. (HW 108)

Thesaurus feature.
A program or routine that enables electronic lookup of word synonyms. (PS 11)

Tiling.
Arranging screen windows so that they appear side by side. Contrasts with cascading. (SW 20)

Time-sharing.
An interleaved processing technique for a multiuser environment in which the computer handles users' jobs in repeated cycles. (SW 42)

Token ring.
A ring-based LAN that uses token passing to control transmission of messages. (NET 37)

Toolbar.
An icon menu, comprised of small graphics called buttons, that stretches either horizontally or vertically across the screen. (SW 17)

Top-down design.
A structured design philosophy whereby a program or system is subdivided into well-defined modules and organized into a hierarchy. (IS 39)

Touch-screen display.
A display device that generates input when you touch a finger to the screen. (HW 86-87)

Track.
A path on an input/output medium where data are recorded. (HW 51)

Trackball.
An input device that exposes the top of a sphere, which the user moves to control an onscreen pointer. (HW 87)

Traditional systems development.
An approach to systems development whereby the five phases of the systems development life cycle are carried out in a predetermined sequence. (IS 27)

Trailblazer page.
A Web page that provides links to sites on a given subject. (NET 118)

Transaction file.
A file that contains data resulting from a transaction involving a subject on which data is stored in a master file. (HW 72)

Transaction processing.
Processing transaction data in a random sequence, as the transactions normally occur in real life. Contrasts with batch processing. (HW 73)

Transaction processing system.
A system that handles an organization's business transactions. (IS 6)

Trojan horse.
Adding concealed instructions to a computer program so that it will still work but will also perform prohibited duties. (LIV 36)

Twisted-pair wire.
A communications medium consisting of wires twisted in sets of two and bound into a cable. (NET 14)

Typeface.
A collection of text characters that share a common design. (PS 15)

U

Uniform resource locator (URL).
A unique identifier representing the location of a specific Web page on the Internet. (NET 65)

Uninterruptible power supply (UPS).
A surge suppressor with a built-in battery, the latter of which keeps power going to the computer when the main power goes off. (LIV 16)

Universal product code (UPC).
The bar code that is prominently displayed on the packaging of many retail goods, identifying the product and manufacturer. (HW 93)

Universal serial bus.
A relatively new bus standard that allows enabled devices to hook up to a single, hot-swappable port. (HW 28)

Unix.
A long-standing operating system for midrange computers, microcomputer networks, graphics workstations, and the Internet. (SW 49)

UPC.
See Universal product code. (HW 93)

Upgrading.
The process of buying new hardware or software in order to add capabilities and extend the life of a computer system. (LIV 21)

Uploading.
The process of transferring a file from a local computer to a remote computer over a network. Contrasts with downloading. (NET 31)

UPS.
See Uninterruptable power supply. (LIV 16)

Upward compatible.
The ability of an application to work on a later version or release of the software on which it was created. Contrasts with downward compatible. (LIV 23)

URL.
See Uniform resource locator. (NET 65)

UseNet.
A protocol that defines how newsgroups are handled by server computers. (NET 59)

User.
A person who needs the results that a computer produces. (INT 18)

User interface.
The manner in which a computer product makes its resources available to users. (SW 10)

Utility program.
A general-purpose program that performs some frequently encountered operation in a computer system. (SW 53)

V

Value-added reseller (VAR).
A company that buys hardware and software from others and makes computer systems out of them that are targeted to particular vertical markets. (LIV 9)

Vaporware.
Software that is announced long before it is ready for market. (LIV 51)

VAR.
See Value-added reseller. (LIV 9)

Vendor rating system.
A weighted scoring procedure for evaluating competing vendors of computer products or services. (IS 24)

Version.
A major upgrade of a software product. (LIV 22)

Very-high-level language.
A problem-specific, declarative language that is generally much easier to learn and use than conventional high-level languages such as BASIC, FORTRAN, and COBOL. (IS 48)

VGA.
The display device standard most widely used on 386 and 486 computers. (HW 104)

Virtual memory.
An area on disk where the operating system stores programs divided into manageable pieces for processing. (SW 42)

Virtual reality.
A hardware-and-software technology that allows computer systems to create illusions of real-life experiences. (SW 26)

Visual BASIC.
A rapid-development product—with both procedural and declarative components—that is used to create Windows and Office applications. (IS 51)

Voice chat.
Internet communication that enables you to speak to others. (NET 62)

Voice-input system.
A system that enables a computer to recognize the human voice. (HW 95)

Voice mail.
An electronic mail system that digitally records spoken phone messages and stores them in an electronic mailbox. (NET 5)

Voice-output system.
A system that enables a computer to play back or imitate human speech. (HW 114)

Volatile storage.
Storage that loses its contents when the power is shut off. Contrasts with nonvolatile storage. (HW 49)

W

WAN.
See Wide area network. (NET 31)

Warranty.
A conditional pledge made by a manufacturer to protect consumers from losses due to defective units of a product. (LIV 20)

Watermark.
A lightly shaded image that appears to underlie a document's text. (PS 20)

Web-page-authoring software.
A program that simplifies the creation of Web pages by automatically generating HTML and other types of supporting code. (NET 113)

Web publishing.
The process of developing pages for the Web. (NET 98)

Web server.
A computer that stores and distributes Web pages upon request. (NET 57)

Web site.
A collection of related Web pages belonging to an individual or organization. (NET 57, NET 98)

What-if analysis.
An approach to problem solving in which the decision maker commands the computer system to recalculate a set of numbers based on alternative assumptions. (PS 40)

Wide area network (WAN).
A network that spans a large geographic area. Contrasts with local area network. (NET 31)

Wildcard character.
A character that substitutes for other characters in a filename. (SW 37)

Window.
A box of related information that appears overlaid on a display screen. (SW 20)

Window area.
See Worksheet area. (PS 39)

Windows NT.
An operating system designed by Microsoft Corporation for both workstation and network applications within organizations. Beginning in 1999, Microsoft started naming this operating system Windows 2000. (SW 53)

Windows 3.x.
A graphical operating environment created by Microsoft Corporation to run in conjunction with DOS. Two widely used versions are Windows 3.1 and Windows 3.11. (SW 45)

Windows 95.
The operating system that succeeded the combination of DOS with Windows 3.x. (SW 47)

Windows 98.
The upgrade to Windows 95. (SW 47)

Windows 2000.
Microsoft's high-end operating system, formerly known as Windows NT. (SW 53)

Wizard.
A program feature that assists users in completing tasks, such as creating documents of a certain type. (PS 23, SW 26)

Word.
A group of bits that a computer system treats as a single unit. (HW 20)

Word processing.
The use of computer technology to create, manipulate, and print text materials such as letters, legal contracts, and manuscripts. (PS 4)

Wordwrap.
The feature of a word processor that automatically places soft returns. (PS 7)

Workflow software.
A program that tracks the progress of documents in a system and measures the performance of people processing the documents. (IS 9)

Workgroup computing.
Several people using desktop workstations to collaborate in their job tasks. (NET 8, IS 8)

Worksheet.
The computerized counterpart to the ruled, paper ledgers commonly associated with accountants. (PS 36)

Worksheet area.
The portion of the screen that contains the window onto the worksheet. Also called the *window area.* (PS 39)

World Wide Web (WWW).
A network within the Internet consisting of data organized as page images with hyperlinks to other data. (NET 56)

WORM.
An optical disk that allows the user's drive to write data only once and then read it an unlimited number of times. (HW 63)

WWW.
See World Wide Web. (NET 56)

WYSIWYG.
An acronym for the phrase *what you see is what you get,* indicating a display screen image identical or very close to the look of the eventual printed output. (PS 11)

Y

Yahoo!.
A widely used search engine. (NET 76)

Z

Zip disk.
A removable disk capable of storing 100 or more megabytes of information. (HW 54)

Zoom feature.
A feature that lets you magnify text or graphics images on-screen. (PS 12)

CREDITS

Dedication page photo   Courtesy of Annie Whitney Downey and 4-leggeds.

Throughout the modules   Screen shots of Microsoft® Access®, Excel®, Paint®, PowerPoint®, Publisher®, Virtual Basic®, Word®, and Windows® reprinted with permission from Microsoft Corporation.

Internet Interfaces   Copyright © Netscape Navigator. All rights reserved. Copyright © Microsoft Explorer reprinted with permission from Microsoft Corporation.

INT MODULE

Chapter INT 1

Figure INT 1-1 (top left), (bottom right)   Photograph courtesy of Hewlett-Packard Company.

Figure INT 1-1 (top right)   Photograph provided courtesy of Proxima Corporation.

Figure INT 1-1 (bottom left)   Advertisement for Oldsmobile Aurora, "Caught Their Eye." Director Bob Giraldi, Giraldi Suarez for the Leo Burnett Agency USA. Visual Effects by R/Greenberg Associates, used by permission.

Figure INT 1-2   Copyright © L.L. Bean, Inc. www.llbean.com.

Figure INT 1-3   Photograph courtesy of Hewlett-Packard Company.

Figure INT 1-5 (middle right)   Pegasus Mail System, Copyright © 1990–1999, David Harris.

Figure INT 1-5 (bottom right)   Copyright © Disney Enterprises, Inc.

Figure INT 1-6   Product shot reprinted with permission from Microsoft Corporation.

Tomorrow   Figure by Karl Gude. "Bill of the Future" from Brad Stone and Jennifer Tanaka, "Point, Click and Pay," in FOCUS ON TECHNOLOGY, *Newsweek,* August 17, 1998, page 66. Copyright © 1998 Newsweek, Inc. All rights reserved. Reprinted by permission.

Figure INT 1-9 (all)   Courtesy of International Business Machines Corporation. Unauthorized use not permitted.

Figure INT 1-10   Photograph courtesy of Hewlett-Packard Company

Figure INT 1-11   Courtesy of International Business Machines Corporation. Unauthorized use not permitted.

Figure INT 1-12   Courtesy of Sandia National Labs, Department of Energy, US Government.

Project 5   Copyright © Amazon.com, Inc.

Project 7   Copyright © L.L. Bean, Inc. www.llbean.com

Note: This credits list shows entries for all 16 chapters of the text. You may have a customized version of the text that may not contain all of the chapters indicated.

HW MODULE

Chapter HW 1

Tomorrow   1999 GM Corp. Used with permission of GM Media Archives.

Feature HW 1-1   Courtesy of Intel Corporation.

Feature HW 1-2   "The Other Woman." Copyright © 1998 Corinne Whitaker. Used by permission.

Figure HW 1-10   Courtesy of Intel Corporation.

Figure HW 1-11 (top)   Courtesy of Intel Corporation.

Figure HW 1-11 (bottom)   Courtesy of International Business Machines Corporation. Unauthorized use not permitted.

Figure HW 1-15   Courtesy of Xircom.

Figure HW 1-17   Courtesy of International Business Machines Corporation. Unauthorized use not permitted.

Inside the Industry   Copyright © Sun Microsystems.

Project 1   Courtesy of Intel Corporation.

Project 2   Copyright © Apple Computer, Inc.

Chapter HW 2

Figure HW 2-6 (left)   Courtesy of Iomega Corporation.

Figure HW 2-6 (right)   Courtesy of Imation Corporation. Used with permission.

Figure HW 2-7   Courtesy of International Business Machines Corporation. Unauthorized use not permitted.

Figure HW 2-8   Courtesy of Iomega Corporation.

Feature HW 2-1   Courtesy of International Business Machines Corporation. Unauthorized use not permitted.

Figure HW 2-11 (all)   Courtesy of International Business Machines Corporation. Unauthorized use not permitted.

Figure HW 2-12 (all)   Courtesy of International Business Machines Corporation. Unauthorized use not permitted.

Figure HW 2-13 (bottom left)   Courtesy of Imation Corporation. Used with permission.

Figure HW 2-13 (bottom right)   Courtesy Maxell Corporation.

Figure HW 2-15   Courtesy of Imation Corporation. Used with permission.

Figure HW 2-16 (top)   Courtesy of Imation Corporation. Used with permission.

Figure HW 2-17   Courtesy of International Business Machines Corporation. Unauthorized use not permitted.

Exercise 6 (a)   Courtesy of International Business Machines Corporation. Unauthorized use not permitted.

Exercise 6 (b & d)   Courtesy of Imation Corporation. Used with permission.

Exercise 6 (e)   Courtesy of Iomega Corporation.

Project 3 (right)   Courtesy of Imation Corporation. Used with permission.

Chapter HW 3

Figure HW 3-3   Courtesy of Intermec Technologies Corporation.

Figure HW 3-4 (top)   Photograph courtesy of Hewlett-Packard Company.

Figure HW 3-4 (bottom)   Courtesy of International Business Machines Corporation. Unauthorized use not permitted.

Figure HW 3-5 (top left)   Copyright © Logitech. All rights reserved. Used with permission from Logitech.

Figure HW 3-5 (top right), (bottom left)   Courtesy of International Business Machines Corporation. Unauthorized use not permitted.

Figure HW 3-5 (bottom right)   Courtesy of Wacom.

Figure HW 3-7 (top)   Courtesy of Intermec Technologies Corporation.

Figure HW 3-7 (middle)   Courtesy of United Parcel Service.

Figure HW 3-7 (bottom)   Courtesy of Diebold.

Figure HW 3-8   Photograph courtesy of Hewlett-Packard Company.

Figure HW 3-9   Ricoh Corporation.

Figure HW 3-10 (bottom)   Courtesy of International Business Machines Corporation. Unauthorized use not permitted.

Feature HW 3-1   Copyright © San Diego Padres.

Feature HW 3-1 (bottom)   Courtesy of International Business Machines Corporation. Unauthorized use not permitted.

Feature HW 3-2   Copyright © Unisys Corporation.

Tomorrow   Courtesy of Thompson Multimedia.

Figure HW 3-14   ADI.

Figure HW 3-15 (top left), (top right)   Photographs courtesy of Hewlett-Packard Company.

Figure HW 3-15 (bottom left)   Courtesy of Intermec Technologies Corporation.

Figure HW 3-15 (bottom right)   Courtesy Grid Systems.

Figure HW 3-18   Photograph courtesy of Panasonic Communications & Systems Co.

Figure HW 3-19   Photograph courtesy of Hewlett-Packard Company.

Figure HW 3-20   Photograph courtesy of Hewlett-Packard Company.

Figure HW 3-21 (left)   Copyright © Conde Nast *Bride's Magazine.*

Figure HW 3-21 (right)   Courtesy of Imation Corporation. Used with permission.

Figure HW 3-22   Courtesy of Intermec Technologies Corporation.

Figure HW 3-23   Courtesy Compaq Computer Corporation.

Figure HW 3-24   Courtesy of International Business Machines Corporation. Unauthorized use not permitted.

Figure HW 3-25   Copyright © CalComp Corporation.

Exercise 11   Courtesy Epson America, Inc.

Project 4   Photograph courtesy of Hewlett-Packard Company.

Project 6   Courtesy of UMAX Technologies, Inc.

Project 10   Courtesy of Intermec Technologies Corporation.

Project 11   Photograph courtesy of Hewlett-Packard Company.

Window: The Electronic Canvas

Image 1   Copyright © CalComp Corporation.

Image 2   Corel ArtShow™ 7, January/February Category. Winner, William R. Clegg, Cayey, Puerto Rico, People Plants & Animals, page 30.

Image 3   Corel ArtShow™ 7, June/July Category Winner, Hilario Caballero Sanchez, Madrid, Spain, Technical Drawings and Graphs, page 48.

Image 4   Corel ArtShow™ 7, May Category Winner, Robert Harris, Tacoma, United States, Corporate Identification, page 54.

Image 5   Corel ArtShow™ 7, November/December Category Winner, Montserrat Noguera Muntadas, Barcelona, Spain, Page layout, page 57.

Images 6, 7, 8, 9   Image courtesy of Intergraph Corporation

Image 10   "The New Recruit." Copyright © 1998–1999 Dan Younger/Art Stuff. www.umsl.edu/~dyounger/index.html

Image 11   "Space Shot." Copyright © 1998–1999 Dan Younger/Art Stuff. www.umsl.edu/~dyounger/index.html.

Image 12   "Big Brother." Inkjet Print on 12" x 18" paper. Copyright © 1997–1999 Dan Younger/Art Stuff. www.umsl.edu/~dyounger/index.html.

Image 13   "One Sad Lost Child." Copyright © 1997 Corinne Whitaker. Used by permission.

Image 14   "Reclining Woman." Copyright © Corinne Whitaker. Used by permission.

Image 15   "The Awkward Age." Copyright © 1997 Corinne Whitaker. Used by permission.

Image 16   Photomosaics™ is a trademark of Runaway Technology, Inc. Image. Copyright © Robert Silvers 1999. Reproduced by permission of the artist.

SW MODULE

Chapter SW 1

Figure SW 1-3   Reprinted by permission from Microsoft Corporation.

Figure SW 1-4   Copyright © 5 Star Shareware.

Figure SW 1-7 (left)   IDT Corp. www.NET 2phone.com.

Inside the Industry   Photograph reprinted with permission from Microsoft Corporation.

Feature SW 1-1   Boston Dynamics, Inc. Used with permission.

Chapter SW 2

Feature SW 2-1   Photograph reprinted with permission from Microsoft Corporation.

Tomorrow   Photograph reprinted with permission from Microsoft Corporation.

Figure SW 2-11   Copyright © 1993–1999 VA Linux Systems, Inc.

Project 5   Copyright © Symantec Corporation. All rights reserved.

NET MODULE

Chapter NET 1

Figure NET 1-5   Courtesy of America Online, Inc. www.aol.com.

Figure NET 1-3   Photograph courtesy of Motorola.

Figure NET 1-6 (top), (middle)   Photograph courtesy of Hewlett-Packard Company.

Figure NET 1-6 (bottom)   Courtesy of International Business Machines Corporation. Unauthorized use not permitted.

Feature NET 1-1   Copyright © William Mercer Mcleod.

Project 10   Copyright © MiniStor Peripherals.

Chapter NET 2

Figure NET 2-5 (all)   Screen images courtesy and copyright © Zoological Society of San Diego.

Figure NET 2-10   Copyright © SONY Electronics Inc.

Figure NET 2-11 (top)   Courtesy of Netscape Navigator.

Figure NET 2-11 (bottom)   Microsoft® Internet Explorer. Copyright © 1999 Microsoft Corporation. All rights reserved.

Inside the Industry   Used courtesy of Yahoo! Inc. www.yahoo.com.

Figure NET 2-18   Used courtesy of Yahoo! Inc. www.yahoo.com.

Figure NET 2-19   Courtesy of America Online, Inc. www.aol.com.

Figure NET 2-20   Courtesy of America Online, Inc. www.aol.com.

Chapter NET 3

Feature NET 3-1   Courtesy of Motorola.

Figure NET 3-8 (top)   FrontPage 2000 box shot reprinted by permission from Microsoft Corporation.

Figure NET 3-8 (middle)   Copyright © Adobe Systems, Incorporated. All rights reserved.

Figure NET 3-8 (bottom)   Used with permission from SoftQuad Software Inc. Copyright © 1999 HotMetal Pro at http://www.softquad.com/.

Figure NET 3-9   Courtesy of America Online, Inc. www.aol.com.

Inside the Industry   Used courtesy of Yahoo! Inc. www.yahoo.com.

PS MODULE

Chapter PS 1

Figure PS 1-18 (top)   Bookshelf 2000 screen shot reprinted by permission from Microsoft Corporation. All rights reserved.

Figure PS 1-18 (bottom)   Bookshelf 2000 screen shot reprinted by permission from Microsoft Corporation. *Encarta Desk World Atlas.* Copyright © & patent 1987–1998 Microsoft Corporation. All rights reserved.

Inside the Industry   Photograph reprinted by permission from Microsoft Corporation.

Feature PS 1-1   Copyright © 1995–1999 Kinko's, Inc. All rights reserved.

Chapter PS 2

Feature PS 2-1   Courtesy of Jennifer Rotondo/Creative Minds, Inc.

Figure PS 2-18   Photograph provided courtesy of Proxima Corporation.

Feature PS 2-2   Selected graphic image supplied courtesy of Environmental Systems Research Institute Inc. Copyright © 1998 Environmental Systems Research Institute, Inc.

Window: Multimedia Computing

Image 1   From RealPlayer Plus. Used with permission from RealNetworks, Copyright © 1999. www.real.com.

Images 2, 3, 4   Copyright © 1999. Evans & Sutherland. Used with permission.

Images 5, 6   Copyright © Reebok International, Ltd.

Image 7, 8   Courtesy FTI Consulting.

Image 9, 10, 11   Courtesy Microsoft Encarta.

Chapter PS 3

Feature PS 3-1   Copyright © William Mercer McLeod.

Figure PS 3-13   Compliments of Business Objects. www.businessobjects.

IS MODULE

Chapter IS 1

Figure IS 1-1   Courtesy of Peachtree Software. Peachtree is a registered trademark of Peachtree Software a subsidiary of Automatic Data Processing, Inc. Copyright © 1996 Peachtree Software.

Figure IS 1-3 (top)   Merck & Company.

Figure IS 1-3 (bottom)   Selected graphic image supplied courtesy of Environmental Systems Research Institute Inc. Copyright © 1998 Environmental Systems Research Institute, Inc.

Figure IS 1-4 (both)   From SmartSuite Millennium Edition 9.5. Courtesy of Lotus Development Corporation.

Figure IS 1-5   Courtesy of Intel Corporation.

Figure IS 1-6 (top)   Courtesy of Smart Technologies, Inc. Smart Board 500 Series. www.smarttech.com.

Figure IS 1-6 (bottom)   Screen shot reprinted by permission from Microsoft Corporation.

Figure IS 1-7 (top)   Image courtesy of Intergraph Corporation

Figure IS 1-7 (bottom)   Engineering Animation, Inc.

Figure IS 1-8 (left)   Courtesy of International Business Machines Corporation. Unauthorized use not permitted.

Figure IS 1-8 (right)   Robotic and manual manufacturing operations are designed, simulated, verified and optimized using CAPE systems. Picture courtesy of Technomatix Technologies, Ltd. Used by permission.

Figure IS 1-11   TRW, Inc. Used with permission.

Figure IS 1-12 (underlay)   Courtesy of International Business Machines Corporation. Unauthorized use not permitted.

Figure IS 1-13   Photograph courtesy of Hewlett-Packard Company.

Figure IS 1-17   Screen shot reprinted by permission of Microsoft Corporation.

Chapter IS 2

Figure IS 2-15   Minerva Impression™ Photograph courtesy of Minerva Systems, Inc. All copyrights reserved. (650) 940-1383, www.minervasys.com.

Figure IS 2-18   Popkin Software, Inc. Used with permission.

LIV MODULE

Chapter LIV 1

Figure LIV 1-3   Courtesy of CompUSA Inc.

Figure LIV 1-4   Copyright © Dell Computer Corporation. www.dell.com. Prices and lease quotes may vary with date of sale and models and options available.

Figure LIV 1-5 (left)   Copyright © PC Mall. www.pcmall.com.

Figure LIV 1-5 (right)   Copyright © Mac Zone. Courtesy of www.zones.com.

Figure LIV 1-6 (top)   Copyright © PC Magazine/ZD Net. www.zdnet.com/pcmag.

Figure LIV 1-6 (bottom)   From "First Looks: Summary of Features, Tape Backup Drives," *PC Magazine,* January 6, 1998, page 48. Used by permission from *PC Magazine,* Copyright © 1998 Ziff-Davis.

Figure LIV 1-8 (underlay)   Courtesy of International Business Machines Corporation. Unauthorized use not permitted.

Figure LIV 1-9   Courtesy of Curtis Manufacturing Company, Inc.

Figure LIV 1-10   Courtesy of American Power Conversion.

Figure LIV 1-13   Copyright © ZD Events Comdex/Fall '98, Las Vegas, Nevada.

Chapter LIV 2

Figure LIV 2-1 (left)   Glide Point Wave by Cirque Corp., http://www.glidepoint.com.

Figure LIV 2-1 (right)   Kinesis Keyboard by Kinesis Corp. http://www.kinesis-ergo.com.

Figure LIV 2-5   Recognition Systems, Inc. Used with permission.

Figure LIV 2-7   Norton AntiVirus. Copyright © Symantec Corporation. All rights reserved.

Figure LIV 2-9   Used with permission from CIDCO®. www.cidco.com.

Window: The History of Computers

Image 1   Courtesy of Prudential Insurance Company.

Images 3, 4, 5   Courtesy of International Business Machines Corporation. Unauthorized use not permitted.

Image 6   Courtesy of Iowa State University.

Image 7   Copyright © U.S. Army.

Image 8   Copyright © Unisys Corporation.

Images 10, 11   Courtesy of International Business Machines Corporation. Unauthorized use not permitted.

Image 12   Courtesy of AT&T Archives.

Images 13, 14   Courtesy of International Business Machines Corporation. Unauthorized use not permitted.

Image 15   Copyright © U.S. Navy.

Image 16   Courtesy of International Business Machines Corporation. Unauthorized use not permitted.

Images 17, 18   Photograph courtesy of Digital Equipment Corporation.

Image 19   Photograph courtesy of Wang Labs.

Image 20   Courtesy of International Business Machines Corporation. Unauthorized use not permitted.

Image 21   Photograph courtesy of Texas Instruments.

Image 22   Courtesy of Intel Corporation.

Image 23, 24   Photograph reprinted with permission from Microsoft Corporation.

Images 25–26   Courtesy of Apple Computer Company, Inc.

Image 27   Tim Berners-Lee. Photograph courtesy of World Wide Web Consortium, MIT/laboratory for Computer Science, Cambridge, MA. www.w3.org.

INDEX

Note: This index shows entries for all 16 chapters of the text. You may have a customized version of the text that may not contain all of the chapters indicated.